Mercer Commentary on the Bible

Volume 4

The Prophets

Mercer University Press

Mercer Dictionary of the Bible
July 1990; 4th and corrected printing July 1994

Mercer Dictionary of the Bible Course Syllabi
July 1990

Mercer Commentary on the Bible
November 1994

Cover illustration: Raphael, *The Vision of Ezekiel*. Galleria Palatina, Palazzo Pitti, Florence, Italy. Reproduced by permission of Scala/Art Resource, New York.

Mercer Commentary on the Bible

Volume 4

The Prophets

GENERAL EDITORS
Watson E. Mills, Richard F. Wilson

ASSOCIATE EDITORS
Roger A. Bullard, Walter Harrelson, Edgar V. McKnight

MERCER UNIVERSITY PRESS EDITOR
Edd Rowell

WITH MEMBERS OF THE
National Association of Baptist Professors of Religion

MERCER UNIVERSITY PRESS
September 1996

ISBN 0-86554-509-X   MUP/P136

Mercer Commentary on the Bible: Prophets
Volume 4 of an 8-volume perfect-bound reissue of
the *Mercer Commentary on the Bible* (©1995).
Copyright ©1996
Mercer University Press, Macon GA 31210-3960
All rights reserved; but see acknowledgment on p. ii, above
Printed in the United States of America
First printing, September 1996

Library of Congress Cataloging-in-Publication Data

Mercer commentary on the Bible.
Volume 4. The prophets /
general editors, Watson E. Mills and Richard F. Wilson;
associate editors, Walter Harrelson . . . [et al.].
xxii+360pp. 6x9" (15x23cm.).
1. Bible—commentaries. I. Mills, Watson Early. II. Mercer University Press.
III. National Association of Baptist Professors of Religion.

CIP data available from the Library of Congress.

Contents

Preface

This volume comprises the commentaries on the canonical Prophets (including Daniel) from the *Mercer Commentary on the Bible* (MCB) plus several appropriate articles from the *Mercer Dictionary of the Bible* (MDB) and an article excerpt from MCB. This MCB/MDB portion is for use in the classroom and for any other setting where study focuses on the Prophets and where a convenient introduction text is desired. It is number 4 in the series of MCB/MDB portions or volumes.

That these divisions—and their titles—are arbitrary is obvious. These divisions originate in the classroom as convenient and provisionally appropriate blocks of text for focused study during a semester- or quarter-long course of study. Other divisions are possible, perhaps even desirable (combining Acts with the Gospels, for example, rather than with Paul), but the present divisions seem appropriate for most users.

Regarding the use of this and other MCB/MDB portions, please note the following.

A bracketed, flush-right entry at the head of each MDB article and MCB commentary indicates the original page number(s): for example, "Prophet" [MDB 715-17]; and "Isaiah" [MCB 565-613]. The text of both MDB and MCB is essentially that of the original, differing only in format; that is, it is redesigned to fit a 6x9-inch page (the page size of both MDB and MCB is 7x10 inches).

References to other MDB articles are indicated by small caps: for example, MIRIAM and DEBORAH in the second paragraph of the MDB article on "Prophetess" refer to the articles on Miriam and Deborah in MDB; SEPTUAGINT in the first paragraph of the MCB commentary on Jeremiah refers to the MDB article on the Septuagint. In addition, the "See also" sections at the end of the MDB articles indicate other articles that are appropriate for further study.

(Notice, however, that small caps are used also for B.C.E. and C.E., for certain texts and versions [LXX, KJV, NRSV], and for the tetragrammaton YHWH.)

In addition to the *Mercer Dictionary of the Bible* and the *Mercer Commentary on the Bible*, there is available a booklet of sample course syllabi that includes actual outlines of courses in which a Bible version and MDB are the required texts. (Regarding this booklet, please contact the Mercer University Press marketing department.)

For abbreviations, see the lists in either MDB or MCB. Regarding the editors and contributors, please see both MDB and MCB. The *Course Syllabi* handbook has a complete listing of MDB articles (pp. 73-80). MDB includes a complete listing of articles arranged by contributor (pp. 989-93).

We intend that these texts be available, appropriate, and helpful for Bible students both in and out of the classroom and indeed for anyone seeking guidance in uncovering the abundant wealth of the Scriptures. Your critical response to these and other texts from Mercer University Press is most welcome and encouraged.

September 1996   *Edd Rowell*
Macon, Georgia USA   Mercer University Press

Introduction

Of Prophets and Prophecy

Prophet
[MDB 715-17]

•**Prophet.** [profʹit] In considering the nature of the biblical prophets, six issues must be given consideration. (1) What is the nature of the Israelite prophetic movement; what is its background; and what if anything is unique about Hebrew prophetism? (2) Who are the canonical prophets and by what standards were they limited or defined? (3) What kind of a person became a prophet? (4) What are the common forms of the messages of the prophets and of the contents of the books included in prophetic canon? (5) What brought about the so-called decline in OT prophecy? (6) What is a NT prophet and how do the prophets of the NT relate to the OT prophets?

The Nature of the Israelite Prophet. The OT prophets were not so much predictors as they were proclaimers. Their major interest in the future grew out of their concern with the present. They had been sensitized by the voice and spirit of God and proclaimed God's special word to their specific historical situation. When they spoke of the future, it was not so much in terms of general prediction as in terms of what must happen if their people did not change their lives, repent, and turn to God.

The Hebrew prophets were people who felt deeply. They were devastated by the suffering of oppressed people and by the anger of God over sin and rebellion. Frightened by people with power, they were more afraid of what was going to happen and so proclaimed their message with audacity. The prophets were not philosophers thinking about what was going on in their world. They were activists, concerned with life as it is, with people as they are, with blindness that did not see God at work and with deafness that refused to hear God's warnings.

Perhaps the most amazing feature of the Hebrew prophets was that they were tolerated at all. Their stinging rebukes and scathing denunciations were of such a nature as to be expected to bring violent attacks upon them. The very fact that they survived and that their messages were kept and passed on is a measure of the awareness of the Hebrew people that they did in fact hear the voice of God in the words of the prophets.

The prophets were also intercessors. Even as they brought words from God to Israel, so they took Israel's concerns and their own concerns for Israel to God. They sought to delay judgment, to seize upon God's mercy in order to give their people one more chance. These dual functions kept the prophets under stress. The word of God was stern, stinging and confronting. It demanded decision. Any moment could be the last opportunity for change, for avoiding a coming judgment. There was no time for levity. There was only time for the confrontation of the moment in the hope that the next moment might be better. At the same time, the prophets also had the occasional opportunity of offering comfort, consolation, and hope.

Prophets were a common phenomenon in the ancient Near East. Every nation from which we have religious records had those persons, male and female, who announced the will of their god to people. In general, these were the oracles who gave messages only upon request and upon appropriate payment. They usually served at a specific shrine. Those who sought the will of God went to the shrine, paid the fee, asked their question and received their answer. The answer was usually obtained through an ecstatic trance, the casting of lots, or some other form of divination. This kind of prophet was also present in Israel. SAUL went to the prophet SAMUEL to find his lost donkeys (1 Sam 9:6). He also on occasion joined bands of roving prophets in their ecstasy and trance (1 Sam 10:9-13; 19:19-24). Further, the professional prophets found in Israel's royal courts were also apparently of this type.

At least by the time of the Hebrew monarchy, and perhaps as early as the time of MOSES, prophecy in Israel developed a unique dimension. This was not so much due to something different in Israel as it was to something different about the God of Israel. Hebrew prophets spoke, not to answer Israel's question but to deliver the unsought word of God. Evidence of this transition is found in Saul's visit to Samuel. "Formerly in Israel, when a man wanted to inquire of God, he said, 'Come, let us go to the seer'; for he who is now called *a prophet* was formerly called a *seer*" (1 Sam 9:9; italics added). The earlier prophets had been dreamers of dreams and seers of visions, "seeing" what God willed. The OT development was from the seer to the *nābî'*, a prophet. The word apparently refers to a spokesperson, to one who pours forth God's message unbidden by other human agents. The best description of this function is seen in the relationship between Moses, AARON, and Pharaoh. "See, I make you as God to Pharaoh; and Aaron your brother shall be your prophet. You shall speak all that I command you; and Aaron your brother shall tell Pharaoh . . . " (Exod 7:1-2). As the prophet for Moses, Aaron did not initiate his message, but simply passed on to the chosen recipient the message he was given. It is this that made Hebrew prophetism unique.

In addition to the basic OT term for prophet, *nābî'*, two other descriptive titles of significance add breadth to the Hebrew understanding of the prophetic function. The prophet is also called "the man of God" (1 Sam 9:6; 1 Kgs 12:22; Jer 35:4) and "the servant of Yahweh" (1 Kgs 14:18; 18:36; 2 Kgs 9:7). These clearly indicate the basic relationship between Yahweh and his prophet.

The Identity of the Canonical Prophet. The OT prophetic movement apparently began with Moses. His life and ministry apparently set the pattern for what was best in Hebrew prophetism. DEBORAH, on the other hand, was generally of the nature of ancient Near Eastern prophets. She stayed in one place and was sought out by the people (Judg 4:4-5). However, she also brought forth God's message unbidden. NATHAN and GAD were associated as professional prophets in the court of David. Yet they too at times proclaimed God's word at their own initiative (2 Sam 12:1-12). Other kings had large groups of professional prophets at the royal court (1 Kgs 22:4-6). ELIJAH and ELISHA were clearly different. They proclaimed God's words fearlessly and faithfully.

However, in the eighth century B.C.E., a new development took place in Israel's prophetic movement. With the ministry of AMOS, HOSEA, ISAIAH, and MICAH, books were being written that were largely made up of the messages of a specific prophet. These were usually accompanied by biographical material and historical anecdotes of their times and influence. It is significant that this change did not bring an end to the professional prophets, whether associated with the royal court or with a particular shrine.

No adequate reason has been found or suggested to explain the naming of a book for Amos when there is no such book for Elijah. The content of their messages and the nature of their ministries are not decidedly different. On the other hand, the message and ministry of Elijah is contained in 1 and 2 Kings, which is included in the section of the Hebrew canon known as "the Prophets."

Further, the modern division into major and minor prophets is one of length only. The messages of Amos, Hosea, and Micah, for example, are as significant as that of Isaiah. We merely have less material in those books. In the Hebrew OT, there are actually four books know as "the Latter Prophets." These are Isaiah, Jeremiah, Ezekiel, and the Twelve. This latter book contains what is called the Minor Prophets. It is significant to note that Daniel, although a part of the prophets in our English translations, was not included among the Prophets in the Hebrew canon.

The Individual Prophet. What kind of a person became a prophet? Moses was a shepherd, a fugitive murderer, who had been trained in the court of the king of Egypt. Amos was at the least a wandering shepherd. At the most, he was a sheep-owner or sheepbreeder and a successful businessman. Hosea was a man agonizing over an unfaithful wife, a broken home, and motherless children. Isaiah was an influential citizen of Jerusalem with easy access to king and temple. Micah, in contrast, was a rural, small-town person with an inherent distaste for and suspicion of the city and its people. JEREMIAH began his ministry as an immature, reluctant draftee, possibly descended from an exiled priesthood. EZEKIEL, on the other hand, was of one of the incumbent priestly families. Moses, Isaiah, and Ezekiel were married. Jeremiah was called to a celibate ministry.

Hosea ministered to his own people while Amos was a citizen of Judah called to serve in the foreign territory of Israel. Jeremiah ministered to his own people in Jerusalem and was rebuffed by family, friends, kings, priests, and prophets. Ezekiel ministered to his own people in Exile in pagan Babylon. Haggai was old and ZECHARIAH was young, but both sought to lead the returning exiles in rebuilding the

Temple. HABAKKUK was a poet and the nearest thing to a Hebrew philosopher. JONAH was a rebellious preacher who did not wish to be a missionary.

The point is that each of the prophets was different from the others. Each was unique. They were not copies of one another, but brought their unique personalities into the service of the God of Israel.

One significant feature of the prophetic ministry in the OT was the Israelite attitude toward the uttered word and the symbolic act. To the Hebrew mind, words once uttered had a power of their own. The prophets seemed to believe that their very words released God's power into the situation they addressed. Further, the prophets also included dramatic, symbolic acts in communicating God's truth. Isaiah walked in the garb of a slave for three years in Jerusalem to point up the truth of his message (Isa 20:2-3). Jeremiah wore a wooden yoke to proclaim his message of submission to Babylon. When it was broken by Hananiah, Jeremiah replaced it with an iron yoke, proclaiming an even harsher captivity (Jer 27:1–28:14). And Ezekiel's acts constantly dramatized his message and released God's power into the situation (it is possible that both baptism and the Lord's Supper are similar acts in the NT).

The Common Forms of the Prophetic Books. Form critics of the OT have pointed out that there are a number of common forms found among the prophetic books. These may first be divided between prose and poetical forms.

The prose forms of the prophetic books can be further divided into autobiographical and biographical forms. Autobiographical forms are always in the first person and contain information that only the individual prophet could know. The most common kind of autobiographic form is the call narrative, in which the prophet told how he came to be a prophet. This usually included a report of the divine confrontation, the prophetic commission, a response from the prophet, divine reassurance, and occasionally a sign confirming the call. Beyond the call, autobiographical material also included vision reports. Also in the first person, these recorded either an actual sight, seen with the eyes, or a dream or inner vision, perceived with the mind. Through these visions came divine revelation. Further, the autobiographical forms also included reports of symbolic acts. These included the divine command to perform the act, the report of the act, and a sermon interpreting the act to their people.

Biographical forms are always in the third person, told about the prophet by someone else. The first of these is the prophetic biography, which was usually inserted at the beginning or end of a sermon or a collection of sermons. It is a description of events in the life of the prophet that set the stage or called forth the message or messages. The second category has been identified as the prophetic legend. A legend is defined as an edifying and pious story relating an event or life of a holy man with an emphasis upon the miraculous. It is probably preferable to call both of these simply prophetic biography.

The poetic forms of the prophetic books make up the largest part of the corpus. Most prophetic sermons appear to be in poetic form. The poetry communicated both to the mind and the imagination. In these messages, several major forms have been identified and categorized.

The first major poetic prophetic form is the prophecy of disaster. It usually begins with an introductory word, such as a command to the prophet to speak. Sometimes added to this, at other times standing by itself, is an appeal by the prophet for the attention of his hearers. At this point, the situation calling for the message is described. Here the problem viewed by the prophet is set forth. This is followed by a prediction of judgment, the announcement of a coming disaster. Finally, some concluding characterization of the prophet or of his audience is given. This form was used in addressing either groups or individuals. When aimed at groups, however, the structure is less rigid, though the content is essentially consistent.

The second major poetic form found in the prophets is the prophecy of salvation. This form is essentially identical to the prophecy of disaster, except that there is a prediction of deliverance instead the announcement of disaster. This form was not as common as the foregoing one.

The third major poetic form is the oracle of salvation. This usually appears to be addressed to a person or a group who have been lamenting over a crisis or catastrophe being experienced. The oracle usually begins with a promise of divine intervention on behalf of those in need, accompanied or followed by a statement of the results that will come through God's intervention. Finally, a concluding statement is usually included, giving God's purpose in intervening. Some form critics also identify a separate but related form as the proclamation of salvation. Those who do so claim that the proclamation of salvation looked more to the future than did the prophecy of salvation.

Other forms have been suggested as being present in the poetic material of the prophets. These occur far less frequently and with considerably less uniformity. Among these are the woe oracles, so-called because they begin with "woe" or "alas," and usually conclude with a pronouncement of intense or terrible judgment. Also, two kinds of trial speeches are sometimes found, apparently being drawn from the legal world. The first of these was a simple courtroom scene, beginning with a summons, a trial, and ultimately a verdict. Related to this is the *rîb* or covenant lawsuit. The Hebrew word *rîb* is usually translated as "controversy." It is apparently used either exclusively or primarily in cases of covenant breaking. If this is correct, it lent itself particularly to prophetic attacks on Israel for infidelity or rebellion.

Even more minor forms include the so-called disputation speech. Here the prophet was engaged in a rhetorical disputation with his audience. Still more minor forms are claimed to have been identified; their existence, however, is somewhat problematical. Those forms described here are sufficient for all except the most technical students of the prophets.

The content of the message of the prophets of course varied with the circumstances that they were called to address. All of them, however, were in basic agreement on certain points. God's judgment fell upon the people because of their having

MERCER COMMENTARY ON THE BIBLE: THE PROPHETS

failed to fulfill the demands of the bond that related them to God and to one another. That is, Israel was required to live a life marked by public justice, concern for the oppressed of earth, commitment to just dealings with neighbors and within the family, always remembering that the God of Israel had called the people out of Egyptian bondage and broken the hold of oppression. Just as they had been slaves and had been remembered by a gracious God, so also they were to display graciousness and justice in their dealing with the oppressed of earth.

Israel's life of worship was to grow out of its public commitment to the demands of the God of the covenant. It was intolerable to Israel's prophets to see the community worshiping God with great fervor and generosity and at the same time showing contempt for the poor and the needy, having no concern about dishonest business dealings, and showing no interest in the corrupt legal proceedings. Amos could go so far as to say, with bitter irony: "Come to Bethel, and transgress; to Gilgal, and multiply transgression!" (Amos 4:4). Jeremiah said a similar thing, reminding the people who flocked to the temple in Jerusalem that temple worship would not save them, when their social relations were unjust and perverted. Micah could even go so far as to threaten the complete destruction of Jerusalem and its place of worship (Mic 3:12).

These prophets, however, looked to a coming time when God's promises of blessing and peace and righteousness would find fulfillment. The prophet of the Babylonian Exile (Isa 40–55) in particular spoke of a time near at hand when God would bring to glorious fulfillment the longings of the hearts of the exiles. Israel would become a blessing for the peoples of earth (Isa 49:6), and the whole of nature and history would find transformation (Isa 55).

The Decline of Prophecy. As noted, Hebrew prophecy reached its greatest heights with the advent of the eighth-century prophets: Amos, Hosea, Isaiah, and Micah. This stature was maintained in the ministry of Jeremiah and Ezekiel in the latter part of the seventh and early part of the sixth century B.C.E. These were concerned with the ethics and morality of their people. They preached in two great times of crisis, the periods around the fall of the Northern Kingdom of Israel and around the fall of the Southern Kingdom of Judah. After the Exile, although prophets continued to be on the scene for some time, they never reached the great heights of proclamation and significance that their predecessors did.

With the passage of time, the prophetic ministry and mission appears to have died out. Many reasons have been offered for this decline, but none has been suggested that has been significantly convincing to produce any consensus among scholars. It simply appears that the prophets had filled their place in the arena of God's revelation. With the rise of the influence of the levitical priesthood and with the development of the synagogue, other means were found to communicate God's word to the people. With the rise of the scribes and the development of a written canon, the need for inspired persons speaking for God declined.

New Testament Prophets. Very little is known of the ministry or function of prophets in the NT era. It is obvious that such an office or function was present in the early churches. The church at Antioch had "prophets and teachers: BARNABAS, Simeon called Niger, Lucius of Cyrene, Manaen (who had been brought up with Herod the tetrarch), and Saul" (Acts 13:1). Further, PAUL instructed, or reminded, the church at Corinth that "God has appointed first of all apostles, second prophets, third teachers" (1 Cor 12:28). He later urged the same church, "Therefore, my brothers, be eager to prophesy" (1 Cor 14:39).

We do not know what were the actual functions of these prophetic figures in the NT churches. The very fact that this term is used clearly indicates some relation to the OT prophets. The most we can claim with any assurance is that these persons were communicators of God's message to their people. They were most likely preachers, proclaimers of the divine revelation to the new people of God.

See also FORM/GATTUNG; PROPHECY IN THE NT; PROPHETESS; SERVANT.

Bibliography. A. Heschel, *The Prophets*; E. Marsh, "Prophecy," *Old Testament Form Criticism*; R. L. Cate, *Introduction to the Old Testament and Its Study*.

—ROBERT L. CATE

Prophetess   [MDB 717-18]

•**Prophetess.** [pro'fi-tehs] Feminine form of *nābî'* PROPHET, applied to five women in the OT. No call narratives and very few oracles of these prophetesses have been preserved.

MIRIAM (Exod 15:20) and DEBORAH (Judg 4:4) led the people of Israel in songs celebrating God's victories in battle. Miriam also had a continuing leadership role among the Israelites in the wilderness alongside Moses and Aaron (Num 12; Mic 6:4). Deborah's service as a judge in Israel was interrupted when God gave her a war oracle as a message for BARAK, who then persuaded her to go with him to the battle (Judg 4:4-10). Her ministry parallels that of Samuel, who also judged, prophesied, and summoned Israel to battle.

King Josiah's officials, sent to inquire of the Lord, consulted HULDAH, whose oracle authenticated the book of the Law found in the Temple, announced judgment on Judah, and offered a promise of blessing to Josiah (2 Kgs 22:11-20; 2 Chr 34:19-28). No account of the prophetic ministry of Isaiah's wife has been preserved. She is mentioned only as a wife and the mother of the child with a sign-name (Isa 8:3).

Prophetesses could also be false. Ezekiel prophesied against women who preyed upon God's people by using sorcery and prophesying lies (Ezek 13:17-23). Noadiah was one of several prophets hired by Nehemiah's enemies to frighten him away from his work by prophesying falsely against him (Neh 6:10-14).

Scripture relates that there will be prophetesses in the end times as well, when "your daughters shall prophesy" (Joel 2:28).

See also DEBORAH ; HULDAH; MIRIAM; WOMEN IN THE NT; WOMEN IN THE OT.

—PAMELA J. SCALISE

Vision   [MDB 949]

•**Vision.** A revelation, often at night, in the form of things heard as well as things seen. Visions are akin to dreams, but usually come while the recipient is conscious, and often under great stress. The most common Heb. term translated "vision," *ḥāzôn*, is derived from the verb *ḥāzâ*, to see, though nouns derived from the verb *rā'â* (also meaning to see) are also used. Some interpreters consider the first verb *ḥāzâ* to be an Aramaic loan word with a meaning quite akin to the common Heb. *rā'â*. They claim that two words with the same general meaning would hardly have arisen in Hebrew. An alternative, preferred by many scholars, is that the two terms exist side by side, with *ḥāzâ* and its derivatives being the more technical terms for visions.

While the phenomenon of visionary experiences is widespread in ancient religions, including the biblical religions, visions seem to be particularly prevalent among Israel's prophets. The terms *ḥōzeh*, "visionary," and *rō'eh*, "seer," are common designations for the prophets (Amos 7:12; 1 Sam 9:9), along with the technical term for prophet, *nābî'*. Prophets receive messages from the deity and are charged to speak them faithfully (Jer 23:28). Dreams often lend themselves to allegorical interpretation, while visions focus more upon the message disclosed (e.g., Amos 1:1: "words . . . that he saw"; and Jer 23:28). Later, in apocalyptic texts, the visions get more elaborate and lend themselves to allegorical interpretation as well (e.g., Daniel and 2 Esdras).

In the NT the most common terms for visions are derived from the verb *'oraō*, to see. Visions are most prominent in LUKE-Acts and in the Book of REVELATION. There too, visions seem to lay great stress upon the disclosure of a message from the deity (Acts 9:1-9), rather than upon visual disclosures, though the latter are more common in the Book of Revelation.

Visions often reveal the heavenly world—God's throne-room or assembly hall, where frequently the message for delivery on earth is being spoken, and perhaps discussed (cf. 1 Kgs 22:17-23), or some other locale beyond the ordinary world. The seer is frequently transported and becomes a participant in the heavenly scene (Isa 40:1-11, esp. v. 6; Zech 3:1-4, esp. v. 5). But visions may also concentrate on some particular object or scene on earth (Amos 7:1-9; Jer 1:11-14). Visions may sometimes be induced by MUSIC, DANCING, or the drinking of particular potions, or especially by extended FASTING. That is why it is noteworthy that in the biblical texts the emphasis falls, not on dreams or elaborate scenes disclosed, but on messages that prophets and seers are charged to speak clearly to the people (cf. Num 24:4, 16; Jer 23:28). The truth and authenticity of prophetic visions and their accompanying messages have to be tested.

See also FASTING; MAGIC AND DIVINATION; PROPHET; REVELATION.

Bibliography. A. Jepsen, "חָזָה *chāzāh*," *TDOT*.

—WALTER HARRELSON

Justice/Judgment   [MDB 482-83]

•**Justice/Judgment**. The range of issues addressed by the terms justice and judgment is broad indeed. As an introduction three important perspectives should be considered: (1) justice/judgment as defined essentially by *law*; (2) justice/judgment as *more than legal definition*; and (3) the quest for *divine justice*, particularly as framed in the issue of theodicy.

Justice and Law. The judicial framework of justice/judgment (Hebrew *mišpāṭ*) is most evident in the association with law or commandment. Thus God's *mišpāṭîm* are those laws given through Moses (Exod 24:3) which the people are to hear (*šm'*, e.g., Deut 5:1; 7:12), keep/obey (*šmr*, e.g., Lev 18:5, 26; Deut 7:11; 11:1; 12:1), and do (*'śh*, e.g., Lev 18:4; Deut 11:32; 26:16). These laws are true (*'ĕmet*, Ps 19:10), good (*tôb*, Ps 119:39), right (*yāšār*, Ps 119:137), and righteous (*sedeq*, Ps 119:75) and thus commend themselves to careful observance, for in living according to God's laws people bring themselves into conformity with God's will. The reward for such obedience is the blessing of God (cf. Deut 28:1-14); the consequence for disobedience, God's punishment (cf. Deut 28:15-68).

A judicial nuance is also present in a number of cases where *mišpāṭ* is appropriately rendered "decision," in the sense of a legal ruling by a judge. One may come before the king (e.g., 2 Sam 15:2, 6) or a judge (e.g., Judg 4:5) for such a decision, or one may appeal the case directly to God (e.g., Num 27:5; Job 13:18; 23:4). In all these cases *mišpāṭ* refers to both the process involved in the decision making (cf. Ps 1:5) as well as the content of the decision rendered. The content is described as positive for those who are innocent and therefore have a legitimate claim, or negative for those who are in the wrong, in which case the decision has the character of legal punishment. When God executes justice (*'āśâ mišpāṭ*) in this latter sense, it is the opponents of God who are punished (e.g., Exod 12:12; Num 33:4). The righteous wait expectantly for such judgments on their enemies (e.g., Pss 119:84; 149:9) and indeed count it as their right (cf. 1 Kgs 8:45, 49, 59; Mic 7:9; Pss 9:4; 140:12; 146:7) for maintaining obedience before the God who is proclaimed in faith as the judge of all the earth (Gen 18:25; cf. Judg 11:27; Isa 33:22; Pss 82:8; 96:13; 98:9).

Justice and Righteousness. While justice/judgment is surely to be understood in a judicial sense, it is clearly the case that in the OT neither idea can be limited simply to a question of legal definition. This is especially clear in the frequent collocations of "justice" (*mišpāṭ*) and RIGHTEOUSNESS (*sĕdāqâ*). God is a lover of righteousness and justice (Ps 33:5), characteristics which, when coupled with God's unending love (*hesed*) and compassion (*rahãmîm*), serve as the cornerstones of God's rule (Ps 89:14; cf. Jer 9:23; Hos 2:19 [MT 2:21]; 12:6 [MT 12:7]). The people of Israel are to follow in the way of God by doing righteousness and justice (Gen 18:19), and their leaders, especially their kings, are charged to implement policies that nurture and secure these qualities in the lives of those for whom they are responsible (2 Sam 8:15; Ps 72:1-2; Jer 22:3; cf. 1 Kgs 3:7-9). Such policies are prominently described with reference specifically to social concerns, namely, caring for the poor and the needy (Ps 72:2, 4), securing the welfare of the alien, the orphan, and the widow (Jer 22:3). Faithful attention to these concerns determines God's evaluation of one's true loyalties.

It was primarily the prophets who sounded the charge that Israel's kings (e.g., Jer 22:13-19) and official leaders (e.g., Mic 3:1-12; cf. Jer 2:8; 5:31; 6:13-14; 8:8-12) had failed to live up to this high standard of justice. Certainly the prophetic condemnations focused on the breaking of the Law. This is especially clear in their attacks on such clearly prohibited offenses as bribery, idolatry, and murder (e.g., Jer 7:3-15). But it is also the case that the prophets concerned themselves with behavior which, under the letter of the law, may not have been illegal. They were particularly concerned, for example, with false attitudes that would permit one to observe faithfully the formalities of worship while at the same time plotting to defraud and cheat their neighbors (Amos 8:4-6; cf. 2:6-8; 5:10-12; Mic 3:9-12). Such behavior makes a mockery of justice (Amos 5:7; 6:12), and God will not abide it (cf. Amos 5:21-24; Mic 6:6-8). Gradually the prophets come to look toward the future when the ideal King will at last embody the true justice that is God's (Isa 11:1-4) and toward the new Jerusalem where programs of social reform will assure that justice can be achieved outside the Temple and not only within it (Ezek 45:8-17; 46:16-18).

God's Justice. In a still broader sense, what is at stake in the issue of justice becomes especially clear in those OT texts that raise pointed and probing questions about God's justice. It is evident that there is a standard of justice which is expected of God, in essence that God will faithfully discriminate between the righteous and the wicked (cf. Ps 1), and that God for the most part acts consistently in accordance with this standard, even when external circumstances may raise doubts (e.g., Gen 18:22-25; Ezek 18:1-32). And yet it is also clear that God is in no way bound to human standards of justice. On the one hand this results in magnanimous and undeserved forgiveness from a God whose compassion and mercy override the requirement of justice (e.g., Exod 33:19; Hos 11:8-9; Jonah 4:1-5, 9-11). But on the other hand it leaves many an innocent sufferer groping for answers where none seem available. The OT unashamedly recounts the hard and pressing questions of many of these sufferers, most notably in the significant tradition of lament that runs throughout Israel's encounter with God (e.g., the lament psalms, the confessions of Jeremiah, Job). In their pursuit of relief, or at least understanding, these hurl at God questions and complaints, anger and frustration, even doubt and skepticism, in the hope of finding some clue to the mystery of God's justice. In the end God proclaims, "I am God" (Hos 11:9) and "I am creator" (cf. Job 38–41). Within this proclamation, and within its testimony to God's ultimate sovereignty, the quest for divine justice must find its way.

See also ETHICS IN THE NT; ETHICS IN THE OT; SUFFERING IN THE OT.

Bibliography. R. Adamiak, *Justice and History in the Old Testament: The Evolution of Divine Retribution in the Historiographies of the Wilderness*

Generation; J. Barton, "Natural Law and Poetic Justice in the Old Testament," *JTS* 30 (1979): 1-14; H. J. Boecker, *Law and the Administration of Justice in the Old Testament and in the Ancient Near East*; W. Brueggemann, "Theodicy in a Social Dimension," *JSOT* 33 (1985): 3-25; J. Crenshaw, "Popular Questioning of the Justice of God in Ancient Israel," *ZAW* 82 (1970): 380-95; L. Epsztein, *Social Justice in the Ancient Near East and the People of the Bible*; B. Johnson, "מִשְׁפָּט, *mišpāt*," *TWAT*; J. Mags, "Justice: Perspectives from the Prophetic Tradition," *Int* 37 (1983): 5-17; P. Miller, *Sin and Judgment in the Prophets*.

—SAMUEL E. BALENTINE

The Hebrew Bible [excerpt]   [MCB 16-18]

The Latter Prophets

Much of the treasure of Israelite literature and thought appears in the four prophetic collections called the Latter Prophets. The Book of Isaiah contains material composed over two and one-half centuries, in all probability, all of it bearing Isaiah's name in the manuscripts. Isaiah's own words are found largely in the first thirty-two chapters, although these too have been supplemented by his disciples. But all of the sixty-six chapters claim the ISAIAH heritage and build upon it. If we think, then, of an Isaiah *tradition*, we can with confidence treat Isa 40–55 (a great literary masterpiece from the time shortly before the return of Jews from Babylonian exile, which began in the last half of the sixth century B.C.E.) as an exilic reclaiming of Isaiah's message and heritage. Similarly Isa 33 and 35 and Isa 56–66 are a rich reclaiming of Isaiah's message and heritage by disciples of Isaiah living in Judah (who associated themselves with the Isaiah tradition long after the prophet's death) in the period after the return from exile.

Isaiah of Jerusalem (last third of the eighth century B.C.E.) took with great seriousness both the demands of the covenant and its promises. In chapter after chapter, the Book of Isaiah affirms the divine glory and transcendence, calls on the community of Israel and its leaders to entrust their lives to God's care, even as they amend their ways and begin to practice the faith that they profess, and offers a variety of magnificent word pictures of what it will be like when God does bring the divine purposes and promises to their consummation. Much of the message of the prophet Isaiah and his followers has been captured in the liturgy and hymnody of synagogue and church. Whether the PROPHET is denouncing ISRAEL (Isa 1:2-20) or Israel's enemy ASSYRIA (Isa 10:5-19) or is offering promise to Israel and to the world (Isa 2:2-4; 9:1-7; 11:1-9), his words and images have gained a place in the consciousness of Jews and Christians that transcends the generations.

Jeremiah, too, has such a place in the religious consciousness of succeeding generations. This immensely long book (the longest in the Hebrew Scriptures) also was augmented by later disciples of the prophet, but there is much from the prophet himself and there is much *about* the prophet that can be taken to be historically reliable. Jeremiah's special contribution to Israelite religion is his lyrical account of the love with which God loved and still loves the people Israel. Even as the prophet denounces Israel and its leaders for acts of faithlessness, the prophet's own love for and identification with the people are unmistakable. He affirms with confidence that the exile to Babylon is not the end of God's dealings with Israel. Who can know, humanly speaking, how valuable for Israel's survival this faith of Jeremiah actually was? We have testimony that Jeremiah encouraged the first exiles from Jerusalem (598/7) to build houses, plant vineyards, settle in, and pray for the welfare of the land in which they were living as captives. Jeremiah was convinced that a faithful life could be lived in exile, but he also was fully convinced that God intended that the people of the Covenant return to the land promised to Israel's ancestors.

The prophet EZEKIEL apparently spent his entire career as a prophet among the Babylonian exiles, but his message was addressed to the entire community of Israel, those who were still in Jerusalem and Judah after he had been taken into EXILE, along with many other Israelite leaders, in 598/7 B.C.E., and those who were in exile with him. As the number of exiles swelled following Jerusalem's destruction in 587/6 B.C.E., Ezekiel's message included them as well, and it is remarkable to see how sharply his message changed after the fall of Jerusalem—from threats of divine punishment for sin to promises of restoration and a fresh start.

The message of Ezekiel is couched in rich and often strange symbolism. The prophet also uses strong and often violent language, denouncing the people as no prophet before him had done, while also making grand promises that seem to sweep aside any need for human repentance or amendment of life. The reasons for such sweeping language are not hard to identify. Ezekiel's own personality must surely have been a contributing factor, but in addition, Israel's desperate plight was largely responsible. Ezekiel had to convince those still living in Judah and Jerusalem that their having been spared in 598/7 was no indication that they were favored by God or that they could delay amendment of life.

Especially offensive to the priest Ezekiel were the non-Israelite religious rites being practiced in Jerusalem—in the name of the one God, YHWH. But he had to convince those in exile with him that God had not finished with Israel: the covenant with Israel and with David still held, although Ezekiel, like Isaiah and the other prophets, did much to transform the notion of kingship that was characteristic of ancient Near Eastern views. While God had not abandoned the promise made to David, new conquerors and potentates were not in God's plan and purpose, according to the prophets. A new kind of Davidic ruler was to come to Israel, one whose rule was characterized by justice for all and peace among the nations.

Ezekiel's speech and actions were forceful, graphic, and must often have been found to be offensive. He spoke of Jerusalem's beginnings as a result of a union of two different peoples (chap. 16). The result of the union was the birth of the child Jerusalem, abandoned beside the road, uncared for, left to die. It was God who came to do the duties of a midwife for Jerusalem (Jerusalem clearly includes the whole people Israel), to care for her, and eventually to return and claim Jerusalem as bride. The people's APOSTASY is the more shocking precisely because of these past demonstrations of the divine love.

But the future includes Israel's building up, reconstitution as a people, with God's Spirit breathed in to give life to all (Ezek 37). It includes the reconstitution of the very inner disposition and will of the people, as God removes the stony heart and inserts a heart of flesh (Ezek 36). And above all, it includes the transformation of the entire land, the resettlement of all the tribes, most of them in new locations, with the temple restored and its activities closely regulated, and with blessing and fertility extending throughout the entire land of the Promise (Ezek 40–48).

Many of the treasures of prophetic literature and thought are found in the collection called the Book of the Twelve (Prophets). Chief among these are the Books of Amos (the earliest of the twelve prophets), Hosea, Micah, Habakkuk, and Jonah. As the commentaries below will make clear, each has its distinct emphasis and setting within the life and faith of Israel.

AMOS is known for the rigor of his denunciation of the social and economic evils of Israel in his day and for the power and vitality of his language and imagery. While his message is addressed to North Israel in large part, his words are clearly intended for the whole people of God. As God's messenger, he pronounces divine judgment upon a faithless people, not for religious sins but for socioeconomic and political ones.

HOSEA too follows in that line, as does the prophet MICAH, but for Hosea the great crime is infidelity to God's searching and unrelenting love. God demands faithfulness of the people of the covenant, but God will go to the greatest of lengths to bring an errant people to faithfulness. Especially painful to the prophet was the corruption of the priests, the prophets, and other religious institutions.

HABAKKUK too has a distinctive word of faith to utter. In the period when Judah was about to be destroyed by the Babylonians for their faithlessness to the covenant, the prophet pressed God to show how Israel's destruction can be fair. Is Israel *really* more evil than Assyria or Babylonia? Can God not find some way of bringing divine judgment on faithless Israel that is not itself an act of injustice? The prophet summons hearers to place their utter trust in God, anticipating new things in the near future.

And the Book of JONAH offers a critique of prophetic religion when that religion gets too rigorous and self-righteous, when prophets are bent upon seeing God's judgment fall upon the sinners of earth who deserve punishment. The whole narrative is designed to help hearers and readers feel the oppressive weight of a religious faith that demands that God stick to the divine demands, punishing sinners when they sin. The author's Jonah is a prophet who is never happier than when God brings deserved judgment upon sinners and sticks to the judgment. The problem presented by the Book of Jonah is that God keeps insisting upon finding ways to show mercy, compromising therefore the clean and rigorous judgment that means death to sinners and life to the righteous. The author knows well enough that *all* stand condemned, if God should insist upon exact retribution for human misdeeds (Ps 130).

Isaiah \quad [MCB 565-613]

John D. W. Watts

Introduction

The Vision of Isaiah

Isaiah is the first of the Latter Prophets, as Isaiah, Jeremiah, Ezekiel, and the Book of the Twelve are called in the Jewish Bible. The canonical material identified as "the Prophets" is primarily concerned with portions of the history of Israel, and with the prophets' interpretation in light of the confession that God shapes history. Christian readers often overlook the continuity among the Prophets because the biblical books have been rearranged. The Former Prophets—Joshua, Judges, 1–2 Samuel, and 1–2 Kings—are broken by the insertion of the Book of Ruth, and separated from their companions, the Latter Prophets, by the insertion of the Writings. Remembering the Book of Isaiah in its canonical setting in the Jewish Bible is a helpful point of departure in any attempt to understand this rich and diverse work.

Isaiah and the Other Prophets

Each of the prophetic books in the OT relates in a specific way to the fall of JERUSALEM in 587/6 B.C.E. and the end of the monarchy which that event symbolized. The Former Prophets (Joshua–2 Kings, excluding Ruth which belongs with the Writings) lead up to that event and end with it. Jeremiah and Ezekiel focus narrowly on the decades before the fall and a brief period afterward. Isaiah and the Book of the Twelve take a wider view, surveying the 150 years before and the 150 years after Jerusalem's fall.

In addition, three of the prophetic books focus on the rebuilding of the Temple in Jerusalem as a goal. Ezekiel's vision of the new Temple is told in Ezek 40–48. Isaiah anticipates it in Isa 2 and describes its fulfillment in Isa 66. The Book of the Twelve places the prophecy of a new Temple in the center—Mic 4—and then portrays life in the new Temple in the Book of Malachi.

Parallels. Isaiah 2 and Mic 4 use nearly identical passages to portray the prophecy of the new Temple. Isaiah includes a narrative of SENNACHERIB's siege of Jerusalem in Hezekiah's time at the midpoint of the book, Isa 36:1-39:8, apparently making direct use of 2 Kgs 19–20.

Unique features. Isaiah uses a chronological sequence in its structure that has much more in common with the Former Prophets and Ezekiel than Jeremiah or the Book of the Twelve. God's control of historical events to achieve divine goals with the people is the driving impetus of the narrative. The use of the title *the Holy One of Israel* (1:4, and 24 more times through chap. 60), appears as a distinctive name for God, portraying the sovereign grace of God toward his people in a grander style than is found in any of the other prophets. Only Exodus, in portraying God's use of PHARAOH to accomplish his will with Israel, makes as great a claim to God's use of sovereign power as is found in Isaiah's portrayal of God's use of Assyrian and Persian powers to accomplish the divine will for Israel.

The Book of Isaiah presents a broad interpretation of the history of JUDAH and Jerusalem from the eighth to the fifth centuries B.C.E., guided by God's firm hand.

Authorship

The author, or authors, of the book are unknown. Jewish tradition understood the reference to the PROPHET in the superscriptions (1:1; 2:1 and 13:1) as indications of authorship. Attention to the person ISAIAH certainly suggests that this is a book about the prophet Isaiah, known to us otherwise only through the account in 2 Kgs 19–20. The existence of an apocryphal book, *The Martyrdom and Ascension of Isaiah*, is ample evidence that the figure of Isaiah had an enduring place in Jewish traditions. The superscriptions in 2:1 and 13:1 claim that prophecies of a future temple and the destruction of Babylon also belong to *Isaiah son of Amoz* from 1:1.

Modern critical scholarship has trouble ascribing authorship of the entire book to an eighth-century prophet because the work of chaps. 40–66 so clearly relates to persons and events of the sixth and fifth centuries. The apparent periodization of the material in the Book of Isaiah led to the division of the book into First, Second, and Third Isaiah.

The difficulty of crediting an eighth-century author with so broad an interpretation of history is removed if the phrase *of Isaiah* (1:1) is understood as more than an author's signature (these issues are also treated below in the commentary on the superscriptions). The author or authors remain unknown.

Unity

If the claim for eighth-century authorship is eliminated, no strong reason remains to deny unity to the book. Chapters 1–2 at the beginning and 65–66 at the end form an INCLUSIO around the historical development in the book. The use of the name *the Holy One of Israel* for God continues throughout the book. The plot, which portrays God's decree of destruction in chap. 6, is balanced by his reversal of that fate in chap. 40. Taken together, these three points open the possibility of reading the book as a coherent whole.

Possible Life Settings

The book was intended to confess to its earliest readers the providence of God that had guided Israel through the judgment of EXILE to the rebuilding of the Temple and the new existence of the Jewish people after the Exile. Early Christians read Isaiah to support their messianic interpretation of the life of Jesus. Modern readers rightly see the Book of Isaiah as an important feature in the Bible; they may read the book both as a witness of God's work in Israel's history that led to the beginnings of JUDAISM and as a significant confession of the purpose of God that led to the coming of Jesus his son. This commentary will do some of both, but will primarily try to help the modern reader see what the first readers of Isaiah would have understood from its magnificent vision and verse.

Literary Form

Isaiah, like most prophetic literature, is composed primarily in poetic speeches. They are not speeches by a prophet but are presented like a drama in speeches by God and/or by some beings like angels (1:2 refers to *heavens* and *earth*). The book also has speeches by someone like a prophet (e.g., chap. 6) and choral speeches by groups of people (e.g., 32:9-20). There are also narratives about the prophet and kings (e.g., 7:1-14; 20:1-6; 36:1-39:8). Taking 1:1 as a superscription for the whole literary work encourages the reader to see it as "a Vision." Perhaps the highly dramatic arrangement of speeches for God and other speakers in the book is best characterized by this term. The book is a VISION in the literary sense of a work that includes both audible and visual imagery.

Date

Since the final chapters of the Book of Isaiah do portray the fulfillment of the Vision in the building of the new Temple in Jerusalem, the likely date for completion of the Vision should fall somewhere near the time of EZRA and NEHEMIAH in the fifth century B.C.E. But many parts of the Vision show signs of belonging to a long period of tradition and of prior use, perhaps going back to the time of the prophet himself.

The Prophet Isaiah

The prophet Isaiah is credited with crucial material in the book. The superscription in 2:1 calls attention to the Vision of the future temple as belonging to Isaiah. The narrative of chaps. 7–8 places his intervention at the turning point of AHAZ's reign. Similarly, the superscription in 13:1 credits the prophet with anticipating the failure of Babylon under MERODACH-BALADAN. The narrative in chap. 20 places Isaiah at a crucial point in HEZEKIAH's reign, a claim supported by chaps. 36–39. The Vision of Isaiah is based on these actions and messages from the prophet

Isaiah. The book builds around his work, and a picture of God's work over three centuries in the life of Judah and the exiles.

Historical Background

The Near East forms a land bridge between the great civilizations of Egypt in the south, Mesopotamia in the northeast, and Asia Minor in the northwest. The area is bounded by the Mediterranean Sea to the west. In the ancient world, Egyptian and Aegean shipping brought commerce and occasional invasions to the area. The desert lay on the eastern border. Invaders such as the Midianites or Arabs could enter the land from that side.

Egypt controlled the land during the second millennium B.C.E., repelling invaders such as the Hittites out of Asia Minor, the Amorites out of Mesopotamia, and the Aegean Philistines. But substantial elements from each of these peoples settled in the land. Israel was one of the peoples that settled in the land under the larger controlling influence of Egypt.

In the ninth and eighth centuries B.C.E. Mesopotamian nations became very aggressive and cast aspiring eyes on CANAAN. The dominant nation of that period was ASSYRIA, with its capital at Nineveh on the upper Tigris river. Assyria pushed its campaigns into northern Palestine in the ninth and first half of the eighth centuries B.C.E. About 740 B.C.E. TIGLATH-PILEZER began a series of invasions that eventually won him control of Palestine. Later Assyrian kings would conquer Egypt as well. Assyria continued to be the ascendant power in Palestine until the collapse of Nineveh in 612 B.C.E. and the final defeat of the remnants of its armies in 605 B.C.E.

Babylon under Nebuchadnezzar (or NEBUCHADREZZAR) inherited control of Palestine. Nebuchadnezzar invaded Palestine and threatened Jerusalem in 598 B.C.E. and effectively reduced the nation to a puppet state by installing ZEDEKIAH as king. When Zedekiah began to resist Babylonian control, Nebuchanezzar returned and sacked the city, taking many Judeans into exile.

The PERSIAN EMPIRE succeeded to power in Babylon and Palestine by 540 B.C.E. Under the Persians successive returns of exiles to Palestine were allowed; the returning exiles restored Jerusalem and rebuilt its Temple. They continued to have control of Palestine until the invasions of ALEXANDER the Great in 330 B.C.E.

The Book of Isaiah covers a period that begins with the Assyrian invasions of the Near East in the latter half of the eighth century, and ends with efforts at restoration that continued well into the Persian period. Between those points of beginning and ending the book also offers a significant glimpse of exilic fears and hopes.

For Further Study

In the *Mercer Dictionary of the Bible*: ASSYRIA; BABYLONIAN EMPIRE; CYRUS; EXILE; ISAIAH; ISAIAH, BOOK OF; ORACLE; POETRY; PROPHET; MESSIAH/MESSIANISM; NEBUCHADREZZAR; PERSIAN EMPIRE; TEMPLE/TEMPLES; VISION.

In other sources: P. H. Kelley, "Isaiah," BBC; C. R. North, "Isaiah," IDB; G. L. Robinson and R. K. Harrison, "Isaiah," ISBE; J. M. Ward, "Isaiah," IDBSupp; J. D. W. Watts, *Isaiah 1–33*, *Isaiah 34–66*, WBC, and *Isaiah*, UBT.

Commentary

An Outline

This outline follows traditional breaks in the text except at two points: (1) The death of AHAZ (14:28) suggests a break in a manner similar to the death of UZZIAH (6:1). For that reason the section on Ahaz is extended from the end of chap. 12 to include chaps. 13 and 14.

(2) The sentence *There is no peace, says my God, for the wicked* (57:21) has a parallel at 48:22, and is similar in tone to 66:24. Therefore, they are taken as internal marks that set the divisions of the text in chaps. 40–66.

The Superscription, 1:1

The opening phrase of the Book of Isaiah, *The vision of Isaiah*, suggests that the entire book is written as a VISION. The whole work is clearly related to a man named *Isaiah*, who is identified as a *son of Amoz*, but it need not be narrowly considered as a designation of the author. The issue of authorship involves a number of problems, especially the evidence that the book describes things that happen over a span of centuries. No one person could have recounted all of them.

The *vision* narrates several events from the life of Isaiah of JERUSALEM (chaps. 7–8, 20, 36–39). That prophet's name also is repeated in headings over chaps. 2 and 13. From chap. 40 on, however, it is clear that an era other than the one experienced by *Isaiah son of Amoz* has dawned.

Judah is the tribal district in which the city of Jerusalem is found. After the rebellion of JEROBOAM against the son of SOLOMON the twelve tribes of Israel were divided. Only JUDAH and BENJAMIN remained under a Davidic king in Jerusalem. During the reign of Uzziah—and, of course, before—the northern kingdom of Israel remained intact, with its capital in SAMARIA. But, while Ahaz was king in Judah, Samaria fell to the Assyrians (722/1 B.C.E.) and lost its national identity.

Judah and Jerusalem continued to exist for almost a century and a half under Davidic kings, although they were vassals of the Assyrians or the Babylonians throughout that period. Under the Persians Jerusalem is rebuilt as a temple city, using its own laws, but having no national existence. The people of Judah and Jerusalem were scattered over the empire.

The superscription notes that Isaiah prophesied over Judah and Jerusalem during the reigns of four Judaean kings: UZZIAH, Jotham, AHAZ, and HEZEKIAH. Uzziah had a long reign in the eighth century B.C.E. His death year is noted in 6:1. Jotham apparently overlapped the reigns of his father, Uzziah (they shared a co-regency during Uzziah's last years of rule), and son, Ahaz. Hezekiah succeeded Ahaz. Despite the reference in the superscription, no part of the Book of Isaiah can be placed during the reign of either Uzziah or Jotham. Isaiah of Jerusalem appears to have been prominent in the days of Ahaz and Hezekiah.

Ahaz was already king during the war with Syria and Israel (734 B.C.E.) as told in chap. 7. He survived the Assyrian invasions that followed. His death is noted in 14:28. Hezekiah lived and worked during the last decades of the eighth century and the first decade of the seventh. He was involved in two wars with ASSYRIA. Stories about Hezekiah are found in chaps. 20 and 36–39.

During this period Judah was a tiny kingdom, long separated from the northern tribes that constituted the kingdom of Israel. As the result of Assyrian invasions, the Kingdom of Israel came to an end during the reign of Ahaz, but Judah survived as a semi-independent entity.

The Vision of the Age of Uzziah, 1:2–6:13

The first section of the book contains a series of oracles that establish the relationships between God and Israel, and between God and Judah (and Jerusalem). This section also interprets what God's intentions toward Israel and Judah are in that period, and for the foreseeable future. Israel's (i.e., the Northern Kingdom's) fate is sealed. Although Jerusalem is also charged with many sins, an opening is left for repentance and future restoration. Generations will pass before the hoped for repentance and restoration becomes a reality.

In the Hall of the King of Heaven, 1:2–2:4

God is the principal speaker throughout this section, which has three divisions. God speaks first to Israel, which either may refer to the Northern Kingdom or to the entire elect people. Here *Israel* first has the broader meaning of all of the descendants of ABRAHAM. The second meaning refers to the political unit, the Northern Kingdom.

A second division concentrates on Judah and Jerusalem, while a third looks to the hope of a distant future.

1:2-7. A disappointed father. Heavenly witnesses are called to hear God's complaint against his children, i.e., Israel. Rebellion and lack of knowledge are the charges. The first is a wrong against authority; the second rejects the intimacy of accepting the closeness of family.

The nation is addressed. Its troubles are interpreted as punishment from God intended to lead it to repentance. All in vain. The nation is doomed.

1:8-20 Jerusalem's status. The political and military events of the mid-eighth century swept past Jerusalem, leaving it the isolated exception as other countries lost their sovereignty to become Assyrian provinces. Jerusalem's special circumstance is interpreted as the LORD's work.

Before Jerusalem can claim some special merit that led to this situation, the LORD addresses them. Neither the Temple nor its vain sacrifices, offered without the required concern for justice and right, have protected Jerusalem. The LORD's will, however, offers them a chance to repent and learn how to please God. Nothing else can account for their good fortune. What God wants from them in return is clear:

learn to do good, seek justice, rescue the oppressed, defend the orphan, plead for the widow (v. 17).

Jerusalem's options are made equally clear in the LORD's invitation to dialogue (vv. 18-20). Grace and cleansing are possible. Jerusalem's options turn on the choice between being *willing and obedient* (v. 19) or the city may *refuse and rebel* (v. 20).

1:21-31. Jerusalem's fate. The LORD recognizes how degenerate the city has become (vv. 21-23). This requires God's judgment that will serve to burn out the evil (vv. 24-25) before restoration and regeneration can take place. The theme of redemption, which simultaneously requires elimination of the evil and the rebellious (vv. 27-31), continues throughout the book, with particular application in chaps. 65–66.

2:1-4 God's goal. The Book of Isaiah is oriented toward a future goal, one defined in this paragraph, but only achieved in chap. 66. The goal is not a new nation, but a new temple with its worshiping people who come from all over the world. The vision is attributed directly to *Isaiah son of Amoz* (v. 1), although it also appears in Mic 4.

The goal of a multinational congregation at worship defines more exactly than any other passage of Isaiah the change the LORD intends for Judah and Jerusalem—indeed for all Israel—from being a nation among the nations (cf. 1 Sam 8:4-22) to becoming a people gathered in worship before the LORD. Jerusalem is to become a Temple city, not a political capital.

The *days to come* (v. 2) are pictured in the book in the last two chapters. The *mountain of the LORD's house* is Zion. After many years of humiliation, the Temple and its place will be exalted and attractive, so much so that *the nations will stream to it.* Isaiah 66:18-21 anticipates the fulfillment of this vision.

The purpose of their pilgrimage to the Temple is spelled out in v. 3. They come to be taught God's ways. Then the second great characteristic of postexilic JUDAISM is named. It turns on *instruction* and the *word of the LORD.* It is not the presence of the Davidic king or even of the Aaronic priests, but the opportunity to learn about the word of God and experience his presence that draws the pilgrims.

God's judgment over the nations is asserted, with resultant peace. There is no reference to a restoration of the monarchy. Isaiah does not foresee a future messianic political leader. He does, however, envision God's continued assertion of authority over the nations, as the rest of the book will amply show.

The Day of the LORD, 2:5-22

2:5-9. Israel's rejection. The passage begins with an invitation for Israel to join the pilgrimage. But the rest of the passage gives reasons why they cannot. The usual English translation does not make sense. The explanation is that the first word of v. 6 has been mistranslated. The word in Hebrew can be translated *for* (as in the NRSV), or it may be translated "but." In this context "but" is preferred. Israel is denied access to the pilgrimage and clear reasons for that are given.

The passage looks back to 1:2-7 and repeats the same negative assessment. Israel has permanently forsaken the ways of God and of their ancestors. Apostasy, greed, and militarism, as well as idolatry, have brought them to their current state. The entire people have been *humbled* (v. 9). The LORD is urged not to forgive them.

2:10-22. The LORD's day. This passage is a classic description of the great and terrible Day of the LORD. The Day of the LORD is predominantly judgment against pride and everything haughty and lifted up. These attitudes are the ultimate symbols of rebellion against the authority and lordship of God. In that day the LORD alone will be exalted (v. 17).

The Day, with its expression of God's power, marks the end of IDOLATRY. The idols have proved to be without power to protect or to deflect the LORD's wrath.

The final exhortation is directed to God. The imperative in 2:9 had urged the deity, *Do not forgive them* (meaning the house of Jacob). At the end of this passage (v. 22) God is urged, *Turn away from mortals . . . for of what account are they?* The rest of the Book of Isaiah shows how God ignores this plea. In judgment and in salvation the LORD continues to care for mortals, including those in Israel.

Jerusalem's Travail, 3:1–4:6

Following oracles against Israel, the pendulum of attention swings back to Jerusalem. But the pronouncements are connected to the previous paragraphs by the words *For now* (3:1, RSV "For, behold").

3:1-12. Loss of support. One tends to forget how much of life is dependent upon networks of support. The LORD announces here that Jerusalem's life-support system shall be removed. Leadership and civil government are among the things removed, resulting in chaos.

3:13-15. Leaders at the bar of justice. The LORD stands in judgment over the peoples. The docket includes the elders and princes of his own people. They are accused of *devour[ing] the vineyard* (v. 14). The image is of a steward who had responsibility for a vineyard. Within the image, the vineyard represents the city and its people. Evidence is presented: *the spoil of the poor is in your houses* (v. 14); and the LORD's outrage is expressed: *What do you mean by crushing my people?* (v.15).

3:16–4:1. The women of Jerusalem. The fashions and manners of the capital's women are held up to ridicule; these are then contrasted with the women's situation when the city has fallen to an invader and the men have been lost in battle. The list of cosmetics and jewelry is one of the most complete in ancient literature. Modern readers should recognize the sharp male-female role dichotomy as indicative of the ancient world.

4:2-6. The branch of the LORD. Interpretation of this passage has turned on the phrase, *the branch of the LORD* (v. 2). The Targum gave it a distinctively messianic interpretation, a perspective that has dominated commentary down through the Middle Ages. But early translations like the LXX did not turn on a messianic perspective. In the context of Isaiah, *the branch of the LORD* is parallel to *the fruit of the land* (v. 2) and refers to the LORD's plans and purposes. They will flourish *on that day* (v. 2) and Israel's survivors will take pride and glory in them.

Survivors of the population of Jerusalem will be held in high esteem in the period after the catastrophic events will have purged away Jerusalem's guilt. Mount Zion will stand protected by the special care of the LORD. The prophecy is parallel to 2:2-4 and envisions a glorious future for Jerusalem beyond the judgment.

Israel's Funeral Dirge, 5:1-30

Now the pendulum swings back to attention on Israel. Six times *Ah* (vv. 8, 11, 18, 20, 21, 22; RSV, "woe" in each case) introduces laments over the deceased after a song mourns her death and before an announcement of the coming disaster.

5:1-7. My friend's song for his vineyard. The use of *vineyard* as a symbol for Israel was anticipated in 3:14. The song itself (vv. 1-2) is a love song, perhaps like that sung at a wedding. But it is not a happy song. It is more like a tragedy.

The effort is pictured as the making of a vineyard using the most intensive effort and the best plants. But without success. In vv. 3-6 the owner of the vineyard takes up the song, addressing the people of Jerusalem and Judah. They are invited to join him in deciding what to do about the failed venture. What else could he have done? Now he decides to destroy it.

Only in v. 7 does the real meaning of the song emerge. The owner (or is it the bridegroom?) is the LORD. The vineyard is the house of Israel. The plantings are the people of Judah. The bad fruit is the social injustice evident in the land.

5:8-25. Lamentable acts and their consequences. Six times in this passage the word *Ah* (vv. 8, 11, 18, 20, 21, 22) appears. The *Ah*s mourn the announced death of the Northern Kingdom, of its people, and of men from Judah. Each instance of the word singles out a group who will suffer from the invasion and the exile.

Four speeches begin with *therefore* (vv. 13, 14, 24, 25) and describe the judgments that result. The first such judgment takes the form of an oath that is overheard (vv. 9-10). Verse 13 lists exile and hunger, v. 14 lists the number who die, while v. 13 harks back to 2:9. In contrast to the humiliation of the people, the LORD will be exalted and proved righteous by the events.

Verse 24 sees judgment as a fire sweeping the land because the people have rejected instruction and despised the word of God. He is called *the Holy One of Israel*. This name or title appears often in Isaiah. Verse 25 is the last *therefore*, describing the anger of the LORD as an earthquake. The section ends with the note that God's anger is not finished.

5:26-30. God summons a distant nation. God's punishment of Israel has been pictured in many forms. This passage turns to the historical judgment through invading armies that will hold center stage through Isaiah. God's initiative in the matter is stressed even as the swift and eager response of the armies are pictured. They are awesome in power and skill. The future for the land, meaning Canaan, is dark.

In God's Throne-room, 6:1-13

6:1-8. The vision. Someone, not identified but presumably the prophet, tells of a VISION that came the year King Uzziah died. The vision of the LORD presents the heavenly throne, attended by beings called SERAPHIM who each have six wings (these attendants appear in every picture of the LORD on the throne, but they have different names each time).

The solemnity of the occasion and the awesome character of the place are intoned in the *Holy, Holy, Holy* (v. 3). God is identified as the LORD *of Hosts*. This name is used regularly of God, especially in the prophets. *Hosts* literally means "the armies." It appears to be a military title. *Earth* may also be translated "land." The full range of territory affected by the vision is *full of his glory*. The solemnity is emphasized by the shaking and the smoke.

In this setting the narrator is overcome and fears for his life. But an attendant touches his lips with a live coal and pronounces him fit for attendance on the LORD. The LORD is calling for someone to be his messenger and he volunteers.

6:9-13. The message. Instructions are short and direct. A message is to be delivered to this people. In context this can only be the people of Israel and Judah.

The message is strange. No matter how much they listen, they will never understand. They are commanded not to understand. It is not the LORD's intention that they repent and be healed. The Hebrew text states this as a command. The Greek translation simply states a consequence. Later in Isaiah (43:8) there is reference to these blind, but they have eyes. In the NT Jesus explains the difficulty in understanding his parables by referring to these verses (Mark 4:12 and par.). God's decree of judgment is not reversible for this generation.

The protest, *How long?* (v. 11) evokes the response, not in terms of time, but of effect. Total destruction is decreed. It will be repeated until final. Nothing of the tree will remain. The message concludes with the enigmatic words, *The holy seed is its stump* (v. 13). Despite total destruction, can there be hope? If so, it lies in the stump that remains. This is not interpreted here. In the context of Isaiah, *its stump* must refer to the scattered exiles or the ruins of Jerusalem. In a later era, Christians looking to a horizon beyond those available in the days of Isaiah, have sought here a hint of the coming Messiah, as they have in Gen 3:15 (the so-called "proto-evangelium").

The first section covering the reign of Uzziah ends with a picture of doom on Israel and severe threat to Jerusalem for the foreseeable future.

The Vision of the Age of Ahaz, 7:1–14:32

The age of AHAZ witnesses the precarious survival of Judah and its king at a time when Assyrian invasions subjugate all the kingdoms to the north, including Aram and Israel. According to the Book of Isaiah, Judah is spared when God, through the prophet, orders Ahaz not to resist, but to wait out the events to come.

Sons and Signs, 7:1–9:7 [MT 7:1–9:6]

This section is composed of a series of narratives and speeches in which sons and signs are prominent. It begins by introducing Isaiah and his son, *Shear-jashub* (7:3). The name is significant; readers of English versions (e.g., NRSV, RSV, NIV) must look to the margin for the translation, "a remnant shall return." The narrative continues by introducing the current Davidic ruler of Jerusalem, Ahaz the son of Jotham, for whom the name of Isaiah's son is a meaningful sign (see below, 7:1-9).

Associated with sign of *Shear-jashub* is a comment about *the two smoldering stumps of firebrands* (7:4). Isaiah explains these two images as representing the kings of *Aram* (Syria) and *Ephraim* (Israel), and their kingdoms. The image suggests these last independent rulers and their kingdoms are in their final days.

In the next scene, Ahaz is offered a sign for himself. When he refuses, it is given anyway. A new son will be born whose childhood will mark the time of fulfillment for the previous sign (7:10-16).

The coming Assyrian invasion is announced in figurative language but without signs (7:16-25). But the invasions are confirmed by the name of another of Isaiah's sons, *Maher-shalal-hash-baz* (8:1, again translated in the margin: "The spoil speeds, the prey hastens"). This sign, too, refers to the time in which the previous announcements would take place.

Further figurative language describes the Assyrian invasions and the confusion in Jerusalem related to them. Then Isaiah announces his retirement from public life and commands the conservation of his teachings among his disciples. But he and his sons remain, even in retirement (and later in the publication of the book), to be *signs and portents in Israel from the LORD of hosts* (8:18).

One further passage deals with a son who is a sign (9:1-7 [MT 8:23–9:6]). In the reign of Ahaz, a day with little or no hope or glory, a son is born. Is it the one anticipated in 7:14? Clearly, he is greeted with all the royal pomp and promise that an heir to David's throne deserves.

7:1-9. The sons of Jotham and Isaiah. The various speeches and prose portrayals of the previous chapters are followed by historical narrative for the first time in the book. The narrative describes a confrontation—on divine command—between the prophet Isaiah and the newly crowned King Ahaz. The kingdom faces a critical moment. The kings of Aram and Israel invaded Judah to persuade it to join in revolt against ASSYRIA. They were too much for Judah, had already occupied most of its territory, and now laid siege to Jerusalem to force a change in government to comply with their plans (cf. 2 Chron 28:5-21).

The first son to be named is *Ahaz son of Jotham son of Uzziah, king of Judah* (v. 1). The threat against him is *the son of Tabeel* (v. 6) who is being promoted to be the successor of Ahaz by the enemy kings. The LORD sends Isaiah and his son to meet Ahaz. This son's name carries the LORD's message for Jerusalem and for Ahaz: "A remnant shall return" (NRSV mg.). The child's name is Jerusalem's decreed fate: devastation will leave only a remnant, but that remnant will survive.

Isaiah's name means "the LORD will save." His son's name defines that salvation more precisely.

In light of the message in these names Ahaz is commanded to ignore the threat from the neighboring kings. Their revolt will not succeed. The two kings are themselves symbols of the near end of their kingdoms. Ahaz is challenged: *If you do not stand firm in faith, you shall not stand at all* (v. 9). The verbs are plural. They apply both to the king and to the entire kingdom of Judah.

7:10-16. The LORD's sign—a son. The LORD has the prophet offer Ahaz a sign to strengthen his faith. Ahaz refuses the sign with the excuse that he doesn't want to *test* (v. 12; the Hebrew word also means "to tempt") God. Ahaz has a technical point: according to Deut 6:16 putting "the LORD your God to the test" is forbidden. But there are other OT instances where testing is an approved activity resulting in a sign from God (cf. Judg 6:36-40; 1 Sam 2:34; 10:7). Perhaps the motivation behind the "testing" is also important to consider.

In the case of Ahaz, a sign is offered without his seeking it. A designated, though not identified, *young woman* (v. 14; the LXX uses a specific word for "virgin") conceives and bears a son. She names her son *Immanuel*, which means "God with us" (NRSV mg.). The name of the child would seem to be a good indication that God's presence and providence are obvious when he was born. But the sign goes on to say that by the time the child is old enough to make moral judgments his diet will be of *curds and honey* (v. 15), which would indicate a prosperous period. Finally the purpose of the entire sign is revealed: by the time the child is grown, the countries of Israel and Aram will lie deserted (v. 16).

Christian interpretation of these verses has taken a different turn. The LXX translated the Hebrew *almah* "young woman" of 7:14 with a Greek word, *parthenos*, meaning "a virgin." Matthew 1:22-23 refers to this verse—from the LXX—in the account of the birth of Jesus, thus providing a foundation for the confession of Jesus' "virgin birth." The likelihood that the child foreseen in 7:14 is a royal child, because of a linkage to the Davidic king, makes the subsequent Christian messianic interpretation appropriate.

7:17-25. The Assyrian invasions. The significant historical events during the reign of Ahaz were not the conspiracies of his neighbors, but the serious efforts of Assyria to absorb the Palestinian kingdoms into its own growing empire. The emphasis in the Book of Isaiah, however, is not the Assyrian campaigns. Rather, it is the assertion that the LORD is bringing about this turn of events. The LORD has ordered the invasions and the LORD has decreed the devastation of the land of Canaan. Such assertions fulfill the convictions of 6:11.

The result of the invasions is seen in the destruction of the agricultural economy. Cultivated fields revert to wilderness, forcing survivors to eat a subsistence diet. Food will be available to those who have a goat to give milk and bees to produce honey. The *curds and honey* of 7:15 (associated with prosperity) now is reinterpreted to be the diet of a deprived people—a survival diet (v. 22).

8:1-4. Swift plunder, hastening booty. This entire chapter is a first-person account, following the style of chap. 6, in which the prophet Isaiah is the speaker. The words *Belonging to Maher-shalal-hash-baz* (v. 1; NRSV mg. offers the translation: "The spoil speeds, the prey hastens") are written on a bulletin board (the meaning of the *large tablet*) according to the LORD's command. The words, and the writing of them, are witnessed by *reliable witness* (v. 2). Then the prophet's wife conceives a child. When he is born, he is named *Maher-shalal-hash-baz* (v. 3). This child, then, becomes a walking bulletin board, a testimony to the LORD's word of judgment against Aram and Israel (v. 4). For a second time the coming destruction of Aram (*Damascus*) and Israel (*Samaria*) is indicated.

8:5-10. The waters of Shiloah. The phrase *waters of Shiloah* (v. 6) refers to water used for irrigation, in contrast to a flowing stream or a rushing torrent. It is used here to characterize the peace policies of Ahaz that accept the necessity of Assyrian sovereignty. There was no place for rebellion in that policy. *This people* (v. 6) echoes the covenant identity of 1:3b, the ones who are destined for destruction and exile (6:9-10). They reject Ahaz' policy, which is God's will. *Melt in fear* (v. 6) is a conjecture. A better translation would be "a joy to." Undoubtedly the popular favor that the policies of the kings enjoyed in Israel was a joy to both of them.

The coming Assyrian invasions to quell the rebellious activities of Israel and Aram are described as a rising flood, a contrast to the irrigation *waters of Shiloah*. They will draw Judah into the consequences of their folly.

Immanuel (v. 8) means "God with us." It either can be understood as a prayer, "Oh, God be with us!" or as an affirmation, "God is with us." In v. 8 it appears as a prayer; in vv. 9-10, which stress the immutability of God's decreed fate, it is an affirmation.

8:11-15. The LORD is your fear. The prophet's sense of inspiration is conveyed in the phrase *his hand was strong upon me* (v. 11). Ezekiel uses similar language to express the weight of the spirit's presence. But it is the word of the LORD that is important, not the experience of the spirit. It is a warning not to follow *this people*'s (v. 11; cf. 8:6) way.

This way is further defined as a *conspiracy* or problem, and a *fear* (v. 12). The people have their attention on the situation around them; the prophet is warned to concentrate on the LORD. If he wants to think of God in that way, as *holy* and *a fear*, that is all right. For indeed God will become both to the dynasties of Israel and the Jerusalemites.

Is it possible for God himself to become *a rock one stumbles over* (v. 14; RSV "a stone of offense") to his people? The implication here, with all the ambiguities of language, is that the people understand God's ways as the problem. Through that way of thinking, many will be offended and fall away. Others will be trapped and taken captive.

It is all too true that, when God's ways are clearly and correctly seen, many people find them offensive and intolerable. It was seen as so in 6:9-10. In the NT Jesus offers a beatitude for those who are not offended by his ways (Matt 11:6), and Paul recognizes that the message of the cross was scandalous—"a stumbling block"—to unbelieving Jews.

8:16-18. Binding up the testimony. The words are expressions of despair as well as strong statements of hope. The LORD is hiding his face from the house of Jacob. This is the cause for Isaiah to withdraw. He is sealing his testimony among his followers.

But there is no reason to despair. He will hope in and wait for the LORD. The realism of prophecy that recognizes God's negative judgment upon a generation does not eliminate the strong prophetic sense of God's ultimate good will toward the people. Isaiah's ministry has transformed him and his children into *signs and portents* (v. 18) of the LORD's anger and judgment on Israel. Even after withdrawing, the LORD still dwells in Zion.

8:19-22. Attention to instruction and testimony. This paragraph (although the NRSV does not show a paragraph break, it should) describes the way people in times of crisis tend to turn to various superstitions for guidance. The key phrase is clearly *for* (or *to*) *teaching and instruction* (v. 20). The NRSV ignores the verse division and attaches the phrase to the preceding sentence. But it can also be understood as an answer to the implied question that asks approval of the activity. It says: No! Instead one should turn to Torah and Wisdom.

Persons who turn to such superstitions have no hope and can only end up in disillusioned anger and despair.

9:1-7 [MT 8:23–9:6]. To us a son is born. The tenses of the verbs in translation make it difficult to make sense of this passage. The verbs in translation are not correlated to the Hebrew tenses at all. The passage begins by insisting that present anguish need not indicate future gloom. It suggests a difference between the former times and the latter times. The entire Book of Isaiah deals with the idea of the two eras: the former times of judgment, exile, and distress, the latter times of restoration, rebuilding, of rediscovery of the LORD's presence.

These contrasts move throughout the passage. The distressing condition of the border areas in the north of Canaan will be reversed. Darkness will be replaced by bright daylight. God will increase the people and their joy will know no bounds. Oppression will have been removed. The clothing of warriors will be destroyed because it has no current purpose.

The guarantee of all the preceding statements of reversal is the news that a child has been born to us. Every birth is a sign of hope and future, but this is no ordinary child. He is a royal child with divine promise. His birth anticipates a period of peace, with prosperity to follow.

His names are auspicious: *Wonderful Counselor, Mighty God, Everlasting Father, Prince of Peace* (v. 6). Certainly this is no ordinary child. His authority will expand and carry the promise of *endless peace* (v. 7). He will reign on the *throne of David* (v. 7). So he is clearly a royal heir who brings the promise of peace, prosperity, and longevity. The magnificent picture comes to a close with the assurance that *the* LORD *of Hosts will do this* (v. 7). Perhaps it should be translated as a prayer that the LORD will bring this to pass.

The obvious question is: "Who was this child?" The context would lead the interpreter to look to the promise of 7:14 and ask whether this refers to the next king of Judah. In that case this would be a description of the birth ceremonies of Hezekiah. Ahaz' ability to hold the tiny kingdom together through the crisis of the Assyrian invasions meant that Judah would be able to crown a new king at the right time, a privilege denied to Aram and Israel in the course of events. The passage is not framed as a promise but as a joyous recognition of a current event.

The royal hope that these verses express is a legitimate part of OT messianic theology found in 2 Sam 7:12-14 and royal Psalms like Pss 2, 72, and 89, and elsewhere. But such blatant messianism is not at home in the Book of Isaiah, which has pronounced judgment on the kingdoms, including Judah, and looks beyond them. Isaiah's future, as seen in chaps. 40–66, does not have a place for king or nationhood. But the Book of Isaiah does allow the opposition, with its claim to a royal future, to be heard here and in 10:34–12:6 (see Watts 1985, 135).

Christians have laid hold of the divine elements in the names and their royal setting to find messianic significance in this passage. But Christian messianism has the same difficulty applying these words to Jesus of Nazareth that we do in relating them to the message of the Book of Isaiah. They would identify Jesus as a political messiah who would reestablish the Kingdom of David, which he refused to do. So Christians have applied the vision of the future king to Christ's second coming.

A Word against Jacob, 9:8–10:23 [MT 9:7–10:23]

This section concentrates on an interpretation of God's work through the historical events of that period. It contains three smaller units. The first offers a prophetic interpretation of events in Israel. The second looks at Assyria as God's instrument. The third is an exposition of the name of Isaiah's first son.

9:8–10:4. History from a prophet's viewpoint. The mood and viewpoint change dramatically, returning to that attitude last heard in chap. 5. In these paragraphs there is no resistance to God such as was found in the previous section. The dialogue is more detached, like that of the heavenly observers. The company of mourners that begin "speaking" in 10:1 recalls a similar development in chap. 5. The *Ah* in 10:1 seems to reflect the series of *ah* statements that ended in 5:8-24. Thus, the theme and mood of chap. 5 are revived.

The events are founded on a word sent by God against Israel. All the people knew that it was from the LORD, but they insisted their current plight was only a temporary disaster that they could overcome. They would build a better future (9:8-10).

The LORD met this false hope by raising *adversaries against* the people (v. 11). The political troubles are interpreted as God's way of punishing Israel. The punishment included pressures from the Aramaeans and the Philistines—but that was not the end. God's wrath continues, as shown in the repetition of the phrase *his anger has not turned away*. This refrain first appeared in 5:25, and is used four more times in this passage (9:12, 17, 21; 10:4) to indicate God's attitude. The repetition also serves to explain the tumultuous times (9:11-12).

The people did not heed the LORD, so their leaders were cut off (9:13-17). Wickedness burns in the land, but the wrath of the LORD burns hotter. The people become self-destructive, consuming each other (9:18-21). Through all this, the book asserts, God's punishment works on.

The *Ah* (v. 1; RSV, "woe") turns against those who practice injustice, from the legislators to the perpetrators of oppression who ignore the needs of the poor and of widows. They are asked what they hope to do in the day of *punishment* and *calamity* (v. 3) to come. How will they hope to avoid death or imprisonment? Of course, they have no answer. Their kind of corruption has no appeal to the military conqueror to come who is already gorged with booty. But God's anger still burns (10:1-4).

The passage gives a prophet's view of the events of the 734–721 B.C.E. in the recurrent invasions of the Assyrians, and the attendant political chaos that followed. Modern readers must wonder how a prophet would write the history of our generation?

10:5-19. Assyria, rod of my anger. ASSYRIA became the preeminent world power after the middle of the eighth century B.C.E. This country with its capital, Nineveh, on the upper Tigris river, took control of Mesopotamia to give it a base approximately as large as modern Iraq. With fairly strong neighbors on the east and north, it turned its attention westward toward Palestine, and eventually against Egypt. Assyria's great leaders, TIGLATH-PILESER III (745–727 B.C.E.), SHALMANESER V (727–722 B.C.E.), SARGON II (722–705 B.C.E.), and SENNACHERIB (705–681 B.C.E.), all took part in invasions of Palestine during Isaiah's lifetime. Assyria's dominance of the region continued until near the end of the seventh century.

Significant political units in the region exist at four levels. The big powers who were potential super powers or empires included Egypt, Assyria, Babylonia, Persia, and later the Hellenistic empires and Rome. Secondly, there had been powers whose armies roamed widely, taking booty and sometimes leaving one of their own as king. The Hittites, Mittani, and Midianites fit this category. A third level was that of smaller states, often built on ethnic majorities. Judah, Israel, Aram, Moab, Edom, the Philistines, and Phoenicia belonged to this category. A final significant unit was the city. Cities were often the most durable political unit, preceding the development of states and often surviving their destruction. Babylon, Damascus, Tyre, and Jerusalem belonged to this category.

Assyria was introduced in the vision of 7:17 as the real power to fear because the LORD is bringing them into the land. In 10:5-19 Assyria is personalized and characterized. First the LORD makes clear that the Assyrian is his instrument, *the rod of my anger* (v. 5). Assyria is being sent *against a godless nation* (v. 6, i.e., Israel), a people upon whom the LORD's wrath is being poured. Assyria will utterly destroy and despoil them.

Before anyone can complain, the passage recognizes that the Assyrians are unaware of their divine motivation. They are intent on conquest and empire. Samaria and Jerusalem are just two more cities to add to the list of Assyrian conquests.

Then there is also recognition that criticism of Assyria for its arrogance and boasting (recall 2:10-22!) is justified. The LORD promises to deal with that as soon as Assyria has finished its assigned task in relation to Mount Zion and Jerusalem. The Assyrian's boasts are exemplified in the king's boasts that he has accomplished all his conquests *by the strength of [his] own hand* (v. 13). He has determined new boundaries, stolen national treasures, and destroyed the champions of the peoples. He did all this just as the farmer takes eggs from a sitting hen—without protest of any kind (v. 14).

The discrepancy between the LORD's claim to have sent the Assyrian and the king's boast of self-determination evokes a protest. *Shall the ax vaunt itself over the one who wields it?* (v. 15). Is Assyria an instrument of divine intention, or a self-motivated conqueror? *The LORD of hosts* (v. 16) will settle that issue by *a wasting sickness* among the conquorer's soldiers. Is this dysentery? And does this refer to Sennacherib's sudden lifting of his siege of Jerusalem in 701 B.C.E. (see 37:36)? *His glory* will be undermined as if a fire burned it up. How fleeting and precarious is political glory! The Assyrian Empire did in fact deteriorate and fall from within, not from any military challenge from without, much as the USSR has in our time. *His stout warriors* (v. 16) is literally "his fat ones" and may refer to all who have profited from Assyrian rule.

The light of Israel (v. 17) is a divine title (see Pss 27:1 and 36:10). *His Holy One* means Israel's God as in The Holy One of Israel. God's move to reverse the Assyrian's fortune will be swift and devastating. There will be nothing left. The speed with which a great power's authority, power, and glory can dissipate is always surprising, but it is documented in history again and again.

The effect of this pericope is to emphasize that Assyria is God's chosen instrument for this time, but only for this time and purpose. Assyria will also be judged and found wanting in its time. It is only the authority and power of God that lasts. This is small comfort for Judah when it must face another century of Assyrian power, but it is the basis for continued faith in God and hope for the future. Nonetheless, Assyria's role as God's instrument certainly is the basis for the readers of the book to recognize how God works in history. A sovereign God can use the great powers of the world for the LORD's own purposes, without losing sight of the commitments made to Israel—in the broad sense of the name—and of the deity's future goals.

10:20-23. Only a remnant. When all this happens, there will be a remnant of survivors, but only a remnant. They will not all have been destroyed, even when the invasions have taken their terrible toll. The remnant will include some from Israel and from Judah.

The surviving remnant will no longer depend on the oppressors for their hope and welfare, as eighth century Israel did depend on political saviors by pitting one power against another. Instead they *will lean on the LORD, the Holy One of Israel, in truth* (v. 20).

To an exilic audience hope that *a remnant will return* (v. 21) might, at first glance, promise a return of exiles to Judah, but here the statement clearly means repentance in turning to the LORD. The real goal of God's work in Israel, according to the Book of Isaiah, is the spiritual renewal of the people. That was their sin in chap. 1; it will be their salvation in chap. 66.

The remnant theme is developed in terms of Genesis and the Patriarchs. The word that begins this is the use of *Jacob*. The term *mighty God* (v. 21, an echo of "God Almighty" from Gen 17:1; 35:11?) presents God as a warrior. And the reminder of the promise to Abraham that his seed should be *like the sand of the sea* (v. 22; cf. Gen 32:12) is a reminder of the way Israel had been promised a future of expansion and growth.

Now the promises are contrasted with the current fate: *destruction is decreed* (v. 22) and God is going to make a full end in the land of Canaan to the two king-doms—kindgoms that are the high-water mark of growth and development in terms of the patriarchal promises. Now the future will be based on only a tiny remnant. This paragraph is a concise statement of Isaiah's vision of judgment that permeates chaps. 1–39.

Do Not Fear, You Jerusalemites, 10:24–12:6

In contrast to the decreed destruction of Israel, Jerusalem is called to faith and hope. This section returns to the theme from 10:12 and develops it in a complex lit-erary structure—a CHIASM—that can be understood as an arch that has its center in 11:3b-4:

A—Very soon my anger will turn against the Assyrians, 10:24-25
  B—The LORD will whip them in the way of Egypt, 10:26-27
    C—He marches on Zion and waves at Jerusalem, 10:28-32
      D—The LORD is cutting trees in Lebanon, 10:33-34
        E—The shoot from Jesse's root, 11:1
          F—The Spirit of the LORD rests on him, 11:2
            G—The Fear of the LORD—his delight, 11:3a
Keystone: The LORD's righteousness and justice, 11:3b-4
            G'—Righteousness his belt, 11:5-8
          F'—Knowledge of LORD in all the land, 11:9
        E'—The root of Jesse, a banner to the nations, 11:10

D'—The LORD will recover refugees and restore the kingdom, 11:11-14
    C'—The LORD will dry up the sea, 11:15-16
  B'—You will sing in that day, 12:1-2
A'—And you will drink from the well of salvation, 12:3-6

10:24-27. The LORD's anger against Assyria. Assyria will not destroy Jerusalem. The invasions that would destroy the political structure of Canaan would not destroy the city. It would survive the loss of kingdoms and allies.

The reference is then to Israel's experience in Egypt. The Israelite slaves were not destroyed. Assyria will not be able to do that anymore than Egypt was able to destroy the Israelite slaves. When the time of the LORD's wrath is past, Jerusalem's salvation will be like that when Moses led Israel of old against enemies in the wilderness or raised the LORD's staff over the sea. The power to save, which began Israel's life in Egypt, will still be there. No matter how great the burden of oppression by the Assyrian looks in this moment, Jerusalem's future is held in a greater, more powerful hand.

The use of references to the Torah is interesting here. First, Israel's fate in the destruction of Canaan (10:21-23) is contrasted with the promises to Abraham in Genesis. Then Jerusalem's hope is pictured in terms of the Exodus and the journey through the wilderness in Exodus and Numbers (two obvious examples are the allusions to the water from the rock at Horeb [Exod 17:6], and the crossing of the sea [Exod 14:16]). This prophetic literature is clearly using the Torah to make its point.

10:27d-32. God's march of conquest. The subject of these verses is not clear. *He* (v. 27d) is often thought to be the Assyrians. But the passage has many similarities with 63:1-6 and suits the tradition of the LORD's march on Canaan (cf. Judg 5:4-5 and Ps 68:8-9). The tradition of the LORD's march suggests that this pericope, like the ones before and after it, has the LORD as its subject.

What is the point of the march? The context suggests that it should be positive to Jerusalem. There is terror in the villages, but not in Jerusalem. *He will shake his fist* (v. 32) is literally "he will wave his hand." The words are neutral as to intent. A slight emendation would make it read "he will enlarge Zion" (Watts 1985, 161).

10:33-34. The divine forester. God is pictured in many ways in Isaiah. He was a builder of vineyards in chap. 5. Here he is pictured as a forester whose tasks include trimming trees and choosing those that are to be cut down. The forests of Lebanon were the most beautiful of that part of the world, but those magnificent trees also often represent mighty rulers.

11:1-10. The shoot of Jesse and the LORD's righteousness. This beautiful poem combines two brief statements about Davidic kings (vv. 1-3a and 10) with a longer section that deals with how the LORD judges the poor and helpless with righteousness in a way that produces a city without violence. The entire passage joins the announcement in 10:33 about the work of the LORD.

While the divine forester is going about his business, *a shoot comes out from the stump of Jesse* (v. 1). In other words, a child grows up in the royal palace in Jerusalem. The passage seems to be taking up where 9:7 left off. This child is imbued with every spiritual gift. Apparently the promise inherent in his royal names (see 9:6 for the catalog) is being borne out in his character.

The gifts are fitting for a prince. There is *wisdom and understanding, the spirit of counsel and might, the spirit of knowledge and the fear of the LORD* (v. 2). The last quality is his special delight—he is a pious and religious lad. All of these qualities are thought of as gifts of the divine spirit bestowed on him.

The next paragraph turns to the qualities of the LORD who merits the fear and devotion of the prince. He judges *with righteousness* the poor and the meek of the land. He punishes by *the rod of his mouth* (v. 4), that is, by his words. And these are effective in curbing the wicked. *Righteousness . . . and faithfulness* (v. 5) are the characteristics of his life.

When such a divine ruler is in charge, the quality of life is also perfect. There is no violence or need for fear. All the elements of nature or society work together without friction. His edict is: *they will not hurt or destroy in all my holy mountain.* The concomitant results for the land around the city are stated: *for the land (earth) will be full of the knowledge of the LORD as the waters cover the sea* (v. 9). Recall that Israel's paramount sin in 1:3 was lack of knowledge of God!

Then the passage reintroduces the royal prince. On the day that this reign of God in Jerusalem is accomplished the royal prince will stand as a signal to the peoples. He will be the sign that the LORD does in fact rule there. He will have representatives from those people seeking audience with him as they did with Solomon, his ancestor. And his court will be glorious in every way.

11:11-16. The LORD's second deliverance. *On that day* (v. 11), like the references in 10:20 and 11:10, refers to the LORD's actions that were announced in 10:12 and 33. Note that this section makes no reference to a king who will serve as the LORD's instrument. Instead it is the LORD alone who acts. *A second time* seems to put the anticipated action of deliverance in a parallel relationship to the Exodus. *The LORD will . . . recover the remnant . . . of his people* as he did in bringing up Israel out of Egypt. This time they are brought back from several nations and regions.

Verses 12-14 describe how the LORD goes about the recovering action. A *signal* is raised. Those brought back are *the dispersed of Judah.* The old rivalry between Judah and Ephraim will be overcome. Together they will conquer the neighboring peoples as David had done. Obadiah 17-21 contains a parallel portrayal.

Verses 15-16 describe God's action in broad symbolic terms. *The tongue of the sea of Egypt* is another reminder of the Exodus. It also signals the elimination of the southern boundary of Canaan. *The River* usually refers to the Euphrates, the northern boundary of Davidic Israel, and signals the removal of a fixed northern boundary. With these natural boundaries destroyed, the new nation can expand in both directions. But the passage in v. 16 draws a different implication from these miracles. They remove the barriers to return. Highways from Assyria will be open for the return of God's people *as there was for Israel when they came up from Egypt.* The return, then, is portrayed as a second Exodus.

12:1-6. Hymns for that day. The future held open for Jerusalem requires praise
and thanks. The first hymn (vv. 1-2) gives thanks for the LORD's mercy and comfort
after judgment, and confesses the LORD as Savior.

The second hymn (vv. 4b-6) proclaims the continuation of this state of living
in *salvation* (v. 3). The worship includes thanksgiving, calling on the name of the
LORD, proclaiming his deeds to the nations. Praises are commanded *for he has done
gloriously* (cf. Exod 15:1). Joy is appropriate for Zion *for great in your midst is the
Holy One of Israel.*

This section, including 9:1-7 and 10:24–12:6, presents some of the best
examples of Zion theology and praise. Only the Zion Psalms and the Royal Psalms
are comparable. They present a program of salvation in which Zion—and its
Davidic king—play key roles, in which the restoration of the glories of the UNITED
MONARCHY is the goal. It shouts that the power of the LORD that brought Israel out
of Egypt is adequate to accomplish salvation. The Vision is glorious and is solidly
based on traditions of the Exodus and of Zion.

But the question arises: What does all this have to do with the Vision of Isaiah
(cf. 1:1)? It has some relation to the message of 37:30-35 (= 2 Kgs 19:30-34), but
it does not conform to the message of chap. 6, nor to the overall direction of the
book. It does not fit the picture of 2:1-4. There is nothing in chaps. 40–66 indicating
the conclusion anticipated by the Zion theology as found here. These chapters are
an anomaly in the book. They reflect the kind of ideology of Zion that was put forward by Jeremiah's opponents in the last days of Jerusalem's siege at the hands of
Nebuchadnezzar and Babylon. They probably must be seen as the voice of Isaiah's
opposition who expected Hezekiah to be their Messiah who would accomplish all
these things. The following chapters show how thoroughly wrong they were.

Burden: Babylon, 13:1–14:32

This section brings the period of Ahaz to a close (cf. 14:28), and introduces the
LORD's action against Babylon and the Philistines. Babylon's history during these
days gets little attention, but chap. 39 (= 2 Kgs 20:1-11) provides a clue in the name
of MERODACH-BALADAN, who conquered and held Babylon from 720 until 710, and
again in 703 B.C.E. He sought to organize rebellion among the client states of
Assyria in Mesopotamia and Palestine. Babylon under the rule of Merodach-baladan
is the one against which these passages speak.

These events, Babylon's successful rebellion against Assyria and its attempt to
draw the Philistines and other states into the rebellion, are interpreted as major
threats to the LORD's plan to use Assyria in Palestine. The chapters announce God's
war against Merodach-baladan and against the Philistines. Samaria has recently
fallen to the Assyrians. Ahaz's reign is drawing to a close. Hezekiah's reign will get
caught up in the events related to the destruction of Babylon (cf. 21:1-10; 39:1-8).

13:1-22. The Day of the LORD against Babylon. Chapter 13 has the first superscription since chap. 2. Each of these superscriptions uses the name *Isaiah son of
Amoz.* The final editors of the book thought it important that these two chapters (the

vision of the mountain of the LORD's house and the subjugation of Babylon) be related to Isaiah, the prophet in Jerusalem. Chapter 39 also ties Isaiah to a word about Babylon, but that is the Babylon of the Exile.

The LORD is assembling a huge army *to destroy the whole earth* (v. 5). The destruction is identified as *the day of the LORD* (v. 6), taking up the theme from chap. 2. The same theme appears later in the line *I will put an end to the pride of the arrogant* (v. 11). This poem is one of the most graphic descriptions of the anticipated day of the LORD to be found anywhere.

The poem takes on historical details when it refers to *the Medes* (v. 17) as a major enemy recruited against Babylon. The destruction will be so thorough that Babylon will be like Sodom and Gomorrah. The prediction also claims that Babylon will be so thoroughly destroyed that it will never rise again.

14:1-21 Israel's taunt of the fallen king. This section interrupts the description of the day of the LORD to portray God's compassion and care for Israel. They will again be chosen (elected) and placed in their own land. Nations will help them and serve them. They will rule over those who had oppressed them. Here again is an alternative vision, not centered in Zion but in Israel. But it also is one of conquest and power. The ultimate picture in the Book of Isaiah will confirm the help of nations in return. It will not support the picture of conquest and power.

The passage then looks beyond the *pain and turmoil and the hard service* (v. 3), which are usually code words for the exile, to a day when they will *sing a taunt against the king of Babylon*. Within the narrow context of Isa 1–39 this must refer to Merodach-baladan. Verse 3 also would point exilic and postexilic readers to a double meaning that would include Nebuchadnezzar, the destroyer of Jerusalem. The theme of the world power of this king is more appropriate to Nebuchadnezzar than to Merodach-baladan. The arrogance and pride that are to be brought low are exemplified here. The mighty ruler of the earth is dead and all the world is relieved. He is ushered into the realm of the dead.

In v. 12 the king of Babylon is called *Day Star, Son of Dawn*. The hyperbole of the poem expresses the ambition of emperors to have themselves considered divine. His ambition was limitless. But even emperors must die. The desecrated corpse looks so harmless. One wonders how he could have conquered nations. He is denied a proper burial and tomb. His family is condemned to join him.

Behind the poem there seems to lie an older poem. *Day Star* is *helel* in Hebrew, which is rendered as "Lucifer" in Latin. The Latin rendering explains why the poem has sometimes been taken to depict the fall of Satan from heaven after an unsuccessful revolt against the LORD. Whatever the background and possible applications of the older poem may be, here it has been historicized to portray the death and disgrace of the mighty king of Babylon. Israel is called to join in taunting the mighty oppressor who is now dead and harmless.

14:22-27. Conclusion of the Day of the LORD. These verses conclude the great picture in chap. 13 of the day of the LORD against Babylon. They contain three short but distinct messages. The first asserts that the object of God's wrath is Babylon, not the king. It is a declaration of absolute destruction. The words parallel 13:17-22. The second passage (vv. 24-25) is an oath by the LORD that Assyria will, at the right time, be banished from Palestine. It echoes 10:7 and parallels 13:9-16. The third passage (vv. 26-27) claims that the LORD has a strategy for all his actions. It parallels the verses 13:6-8 and claims that the announcements of destruction over Babylon and the ultimate elimination of Assyria are the LORD's plan for the land (of Canaan) and its nations. It further claims that the LORD's decrees are immutable. No one can deter God. The idea that God's plan determines the course of history is taught in the Book of Isaiah more fully than anywhere else in the Bible.

14:28-32. Burden over the Philistines. The chronology of this period is confused. The year King Ahaz died is probably 718 B.C.E., sixteen years after 735–34 when he assumed the throne (2 Kgs 16:1) or 715 B.C.E., fourteen years before 701 B.C.E. (2 Kgs 18:13) or 728 B.C.E., four years before 724 B.C.E., when Shalmaneser marched on Samaria. The more likely date is 718 B.C.E.

An *oracle* (v. 28) is a prophecy directed against a foreign land. But this is not the kind where kings of the nations are made to bow to Zion's king. Rather it shows how the LORD moves against nations that resist his will. Philistia in rebellion against Assyria has acted against God's plan. The passage is a lesson for Judah and Jerusalem, teaching the futility of resisting God's signals.

The rod that *is broken* (v. 29) may refer to the death of Shalmaneser, the Assyrian emperor. There was a rebellion in Palestine at the time of his death. Ahaz followed his usual policy and continued to be loyal to Assyria. Philistine cities joined the rebellion. *The snake* must also be Shalmaneser. *The adder* and the *flying fiery serpent* would then represent Sargon who put down the rebellion in 718 and 714 B.C.E.

Assyria restores order to the countryside, while the LORD exacts his own punishment from the rebels. The funeral lament is sung over Philistia, which joins Babylon in defeat and destruction.

Verse 32 concludes the section. An embassy from abroad waits for an answer. But what is the question? And what nation wants to know? The context suggests that the occasion for the embassy's presence is the death of Ahaz. The question is whether there will be a smooth succession to the throne. The answer is: The LORD is Zion's foundation. Not SARGON, not alliances, not armed rebellion—but the LORD. It is interesting that Hezekiah's name is not mentioned. *His people* is the term used for Israel (as "the elect ones"). Israel's future rests with Jerusalem. This is the theme of the entire Vision, and this is the message for exilic Israel as well. The city is and will be a secure refuge.

The Vision of the Age of Hezekiah, 15:1–22:25

That HEZEKIAH is the king through this section is conjectured from the listing of the death of *Ahaz* in 14:28, the historical notice of *Sargon*'s invasion of *Ashdod* in 20:1, and the references to *Shebna* and *Eliakim*, in 22:15 and 20, who are ministers in Hezekiah's government. Of particular significance is the fact that Hezekiah's name is never mentioned, although he is listed among the kings in 1:1.

Burden: Moab, 15:1–16:14

This passage appears to react to an attack by some group out of the desert to the east upon Judah's neighbor to the east, Moab. The country is devastated. Refugees push toward Judah and leaders ask for assistance.

A description of the devastation opens the passage (15:1-4), followed by a sympathetic response (15:5), apparently from someone in Judah, and a further description of the devastation (15:6-9). The passage ends (15:9b) with a word, apparently from the LORD, indicating that this is the first of several acts of judgment on Moab.

Moab prepares a delegation to ask Judah to act on its behalf. They ask for advice or direction. They ask for Judah to extend its shadow, that is, to declare that this invasion is a threat that Judah interprets as a threat to its own interests as well. They ask that the border be opened for refugees.

Isaiah 15:4b-5 interprets these events as an opportunity for the Jerusalem monarchy to extend its authority over Moab again. A chorus (15:6-8) exults that Moab's pride has finally caught up with it. Someone expresses grief over the events, but without conviction (vv. 9 and 11). The LORD notes that this is his doing (v. 10). Moab will be worn out with this effort, so that it is actually no longer able to pray. And the LORD declares that within three years Moab's population will be reduced to an insignificant remnant. With the decimation of Moab the circle closes around Judah.

Burdens: Damascus and Egypt, 17:1–20:6

This passage should be interpreted as a self-contained unit. The setting is Jerusalem, which is portrayed as the one entity that has a choice as to the future. Aram and Israel do not have choices. The differences between the choices of Judah compared to those of Aram and Israel are depicted in the outline below; Judah is the subject from D to D'.

These four chapters form one symmetrical whole that climaxes with the bringing of gifts to the LORD in Zion (18:7). The section is characterized by *in that day* passages, with variations *in that time* (18:7) and *in the year* (20:1). The outline is again in the form of a CHIASM (what follows is author's trans.):

A—Behold! Damascus and Ephraim lie ruined!, 17:1-3
  B—On that day Jacob's glory will be leftovers, 17:4-6
    C—On that day one looks to his Maker, 17:7-8
      D—On that day you (fem. sing.) forgot God, your Savior, 17:9-11
        E—Woe! Raging of the nations, 17:12-14
          F—Woe! Go, swift messenger, 18:1-2
            G—Peoples see: The LORD is silent, 18:3-6
Keystone: At that time gifts to the LORD in Zion, 18:7
            G'—Behold! The LORD coming to Egypt, 19:1-15

> F'—In that day Judah will be a terror to Egypt, 19:16-17
> E'—In that day five Egyptian cities speak Canaanite, 19:18
> D'—In that day an altar to the LORD in Egypt, 19:19-22
> C'—In that day a highway:Egypt and Assyria worship together, 19:23
> B'—In that day Israel will be third to Egypt and Assyria, 19:24-25
> A'—In the year Sargon came to Ashdod, the LORD spoke to Isaiah 20:1-6

The letters B, D, G, and G' mark the planting and harvest imagery that is used in key places. The letters G and G' are also speeches from the LORD, the only ones in the passage, aside from the instructions to Isaiah in chap. 20. Because they are from the LORD they have special significance.

17:1-8. Israel's position. Damascus and Ephraim have suffered from the invasions and are no longer viable political units. The passage ends with the call for all to seek *their Maker* (v. 7) and not to seek things *their own fingers have made* (v. 8), such as sanctuaries or idols. Both Aram and Israel are only remnants of their former selves. IDOLATRY is often used to bolster the pride and power of the rich and powerful. When neither riches nor power remain, one must seek divine reality, not just symbols of human ambition.

17:9-14. Focus on Jerusalem. In view of the disasters visited on its neighbors, it appears that Jerusalem has not remembered the God of its salvation (*the Rock of your refuge* [v. 10]). The planting pictured in vv. 10b-11 is probably a pagan rite to an unidentified deity. Verses 12-14 seem to present the terror evoked by the pagan rites, a terror that has no substance.

18:1-7. Messengers from Ethiopia. Egypt is divided into three distinct parts. Its Pharaohs tend to represent one of them. The Ethiopian portion is making a bid to replace the leadership exercised by the princes of the Delta. The messengers are apparently seeking the aid of Assyria and are sent on their way by Jerusalem.

The LORD will not interfere, but simply observe the developments. When the political developments mature, Assyria will send messengers and gifts to Jerusalem, probably as a bribe to secure their loyalty in protecting Assyria's flanks during an invasion of Egypt.

19:1-17. The LORD's invasion of Egypt. God will incite internal turmoil in Egypt and turn the country over to a hard master, a fierce king. This is probably the same Ethiopian referred to in chap. 17. The LORD has decided to determine the matter. God uses internal social unrest, natural disasters, and confused political advice to achieve that end.

The Egyptians are terrified because of the LORD's intervention in their affairs. Because they identify the LORD with Judah, their fear relates to Judah, too. Verse 17 has been a problem for translators. The Hebrew word translated *will become a terror* occurs only here in the Bible. The Greek translation made of it "a terrifying object." The Latin identified it with the word for"festival" and translated "will be in festival mood." NRSV has, with most English translations, followed the Greek. Perhaps both senses play a role.

The internal revolt in Egypt has weakened the country to the extent that even a small country like Judah must be respected. The festival referred to must be PASSOVER. The LORD's involvement in events raises the specter of a repetition of the disasters of the time of the EXODUS. Judah can be a factor here. But only as it cooperates with the LORD's plan involving Ethiopia and Assyria.

19:18-25. The LORD's intervention in Egypt. Four vignettes are developed, beginning with the phrase *on that day* (vv. 18, 19, 23, 24). The first reflects growing Canaanite influence seen in five cities that speak a Canaanite tongue similar to Hebrew and *swear allegiance to the LORD* as all the small nations of Canaan did under David and Solomon. The name of the city is in dispute because of a textual problem caused by two Hebrew letters that look very much alike. The versions differed on them from earliest times. One translation is *City of the Sun*. Another is "the city of destruction."

Then the worship of the LORD in Egypt is pictured (vv. 19- 22). There will be an altar to the LORD and a pillar as a monument to the LORD's saving powers. The LORD will be revealed to the Egyptians so that they worship God with sacrifices and offerings. They will make religious vows and fulfill them, and the relation to the LORD through judgment and repentance will be in effect for them.

A highway will allow full relations between Assyria and Egypt. Presumably the relations will include commerce, but the key binding feature will be common worship. Israel, too, will exist alongside these great powers, serving as *a blessing in the midst of the earth* (v. 24). This great land that stretches from Assyria to Egypt will be a blessing that the LORD has blessed. The key to this whole passage is this blessing from the LORD. A political and religious balance has been achieved that merits the LORD's blessing. The blessing is spoken on all three countries: *Blessed be Egypt my people* (v. 25). The reference to Egypt with a term usually reserved for Israel is significant. *Assyria the work of my hand* reflects the same view of Assyria, as the LORD's instrument, that has been typical of the book. *Israel my heritage* shows the same relation that is usual in the Pentateuch in which Israel is the LORD's portion, the current generation being the direct descendant of the LORD's chosen.

What a beautiful vision of hope and peace! It is presented as the LORD's vision of what could be. Peace did not come in this way, however; the major thrust of the book turns toward another vision that corresponds to the historical developments. This is the second picture of an alternate vision of the future that God could happily support. The first was that of the ideal monarchy in chaps. 11-12. Genesis 2–3 had already shown that God sometimes is forced by human intransigence and sin to change plans. So here the course of events turns back to the previous plan envisioned in chap. 2: the Temple lifted high.

20:1-6. A walking prophetic sign. Instead of performing the mediatorial service of linking Ethiopia with Assyria, apparently Hezekiah chose to join the Philistine cities in an alliance with the princes of lower Egypt against Assyria. Sargon answered the challenge by a campaign in 712 B.C.E. that resulted in the capture of

Ashdod. The LORD registered his disapproval of this course of action on Hezekiah's part through Isaiah the prophet. He was told to take off his clothes and his sandals and to walk about *naked and barefoot for three years as a sign . . . against Egypt and Ethiopia* (v. 4). The LORD's vision of a truce had foundered. In a conflict situation the LORD still backed Assyria, and Hezekiah had chosen the wrong side.

Four Ambiguous Burdens, 21:1–22:14

21:1-10. First burden: a swampland. Babylon is the focus of this ORACLE. Some background to understand Judah's relation to Babylon in the last quarter of the eighth century B.C.E. is needed (see chaps 13-14). Judah seems to have been impressed by MERODACH-BALADAN's ability to hold power in Babylon from 721 to 710 B.C.E. His control also may have influenced Merodach-Baladan to join the Philistine rebellion. When Babylon was finally retaken by SARGON in 710, Merodach-Baladan escaped, fleeing into the marshlands to the south, which was his traditional home. When Sargon died in 705, Merodach-Baladan took Babylon again, only to be ousted again, this time by SENNACHERIB in 703 B.C.E. Either of the occasions when the Assyrians conquered Babylon could fit this chapter, but the latter would fit the connection with chap. 22.

The prophet reports his vision of treachery and violence. *Elam* and *Media* (v. 2) have apparently been summoned to aid Assyria in an attack. The news is emotionally difficult for the prophet. The officers prepare for battle. The visionary is told to post a lookout for messengers; he finally reports someone coming. The message is terse: *Fallen, fallen is Babylon* (v. 9). Babylon's claim to fame and power lay in the favor of its idol god, the very symbol of empire, yet *all the images of her gods lie shattered on the ground.* The picture of Babylon's failure is complete.

This message is taken as a message from the LORD and is devastating to Judah because it had raised its hopes in light of Babylon's example.

21:11-12. Second burden: silence. The Hebrew word is *dumah* means "silence." The Greek translation inserted "Edom," but the term is probably intended to remain ambiguous and mysterious. Also mysterious is the watchman who answers the sensible question, *What of the night?* with a non-answer: *Morning comes, and also the night. If you will inquire, enquire; come back again* (vv. 11-12).

21:13-15. Third burden: in the wasteland. The peoples named here are in Arabia. They are urged to prepare to deal with the persons fleeing from the path of conquest. Within a year the power of Arabian tribes will come to an end.

22:1-14. Fourth burden: the valley of vision. This terrible vision is of the Day of the LORD, and Judah is the victim. Judah has failed to fight and its military leaders have fled. In this ignominious situation many helpless persons are massacred. *Elam* and *Kir* (v. 6) are undoubtedly mercenaries in the service of Assyria. *The covering of Judah* (v. 8) is the circle of fortified cities intended to defend the city of Jerusalem.

Defensive measures for Jerusalem are described in vv. 8b-11. *The House of the Forest* must have been an armory. The issue of a water supply is vital in times of siege. JERUSALEM's water supply was outside its walls and vulnerable to attack, hence the rush to collect water in pools within the city (the SILOAM INSCRIPTION reflects the importance of the water supply in times of battle). But v. 11 makes the LORD's point: *But you did not look to him who did it, or have regard for him who planned it long ago.* In all the feverish military preparation the leaders gave no thought to God's intentions for the attack or to his plans either for Jerusalem or for this historical moment.

So the LORD reveals his intentions. He calls for mourning, but instead they feasted with the happy-go-lucky attitude: *Let us eat and drink, for tomorrow we die* (v. 13). The LORD finds this failure to take seriously the terrible condition of the city to be unforgivable.

Shebna Is Dismissed, 22:15-25

Finally the section moves to naming names of those responsible for the fiasco of Judah's near destruction. Strangely, Hezekiah's name does not occur. Instead, his ministers are the objects of blame and punishment.

Shebna . . . master of the household (v. 15), or prime minister, is arraigned first. He is accused of misusing his office. A specific offense lies in preparing a mausoleum for his own tomb that has all the grandeur of a royal tomb. The LORD is about to dislodge him violently and have him exiled because he is a disgrace to his master's house. Isaiah 22:8-9 should also be seen as accusations against Shebna. His administration had left the little kingdom militarily unprepared.

Eliakim son of Hilkiah (v. 20) will succeed Shebna. The passage describes the duties of the prime minister. He has a special *robe* and *sash.* His authority makes him like *a father to the inhabitants of Jerusalem and to the house of Judah* (v. 21). He holds *the key to the house of David* (v. 22), probably meaning that he serves as steward to the royal house and its estates. Such authority is almost absolute. God promises security and honor for Eliakim and for his entire extended family. But on the Day of the LORD foreseen in this chapter, he too will be cut down and will die.

The elevation of Eliakim brings the passages related to the age of Hezekiah to an end. Whereas the age of Ahaz had briefly brought the hope that the Davidic monarchy might provide the salvation that Israel needed, the age of Hezekiah brought hope that changing political conditions in Egypt and Assyria might make an opening for a new age of peace and blessing. Neither materialized. In the Book of Isaiah the age of Hezekiah is seen as a period of disappointment for things that might have been.

The Vision of the Age of Manasseh, 23:1–27:13

Assyrian power peaked in the half century following SENNACHERIB's siege of Jerusalem. Judah was the abject vassal of ASSYRIA, a spectator of history, rather than a participant. The brunt of Assyria's aggression in this period was borne by EGYPT and especially its Phoenician allies TYRE AND SIDON.

The Vision deals with this period in the bright colors of an end of an age. The clash of the world powers, Assyria and Egypt, is pictured with an appropriate sense of ultimate doom. But the Vision chooses precisely this age to assert the LORD's sovereignty and to deal with the impersonal issues of blessing and curse that determine so much of the course of life.

An outline of the section is again a CHIASM with the center at 25:6 and references to the fate of Tyre providing the outer frame. The whole is introduced by a section on Tyre that has no corresponding element at the end. All of this section contains responses to the fall of Tyre, in the same way the city itself is commanded to respond in the first section. The responses are noted in the chiastic arrangement below.

A—Tyre is ordered to respond, 23:1-7
   B—The LORD planned this against Tyre, 23:8-10 (response of the sailors, 23:10)
      C—The LORD's hand over the sea, 23:11-18
         (responses from sailors and prophets, 23:12b-18)
         D—The LORD is devastating the land, 24:1-20 (responses, 24:4-20)
            E—The LORD judges armies and kings, 24:21-22 (responses, 24:22)
               F—The LORD of Hosts reigns, 24:23-25:5 (individual responses, 25:1-5)
Keystone: The LORD of Hosts's banquet, 25:6
               F'—The LORD destroys death forever, 25:7-9
               (Jerusalem's response, 25:9)
            E'—The LORD judges Moab, 25:10–26:20 (Judah's response, 26:1-20)
         D'—The LORD judges the inhabitants of the land, 26:21
      C'—The LORD judges Leviathan, 27:1-11 (the LORD's response, 27:2-5)
   B'—Israel will take root and the LORD will gather Israel, 27:12-13

On the rising steps of the chiastic ladder, Tyre and the land (of Canaan) are called to respond. On the descending steps JERUSALEM, JUDAH, and ISRAEL respond. We note the frame of *seventy years* provided for the act (23:17). Various primary sections show the LORD's response to the fall of Tyre. In this section the entire land of Canaan, all the cities or city-states, and even the sea, which in this period was becoming the channel of commerce and power, come under the authority of Assyria, "the rod of the LORD's anger."

Tyre Is Ordered to Respond, 23:1-7

The passage is called an *oracle concerning Tyre* (v. 1), the impressive Phoenician city that, with Sidon, had dominated shipping and commerce on the coast of CANAAN during all of Israel's history in Canaan. But now Tyre has been destroyed.

The inhabitants of the city are called to respond. *Ships of Tarshish* (v. 2) were great freighters that were a mark of Tyre's commercial power around the Mediterranean Sea. *Inhabitants of the coast* included Sidon, Philistine cities like ASHDOD to the south, and coastal cities to the north. Sidon is addressed as a type of alter ego to Tyre. All of Tyre's trading partners are called to join the mourning for the destruction of this ancient commercial power.

The LORD Planned This against Tyre, 23:8-10

This passage returns to the theme that plays such a great part in the Vision. *Who planned this?* (v. 8). Tyre had seemed to be untouchable to the currents of history. Its commercial influence and riches had so often put it beyond the destructive tides of history. The answer comes: *The LORD of Hosts has planned it* (v. 9), but why? The answer corresponds to the theme of the day of the LORD in chap. 2: to bring down pride and glory.

Sailors have to respond in a practical way. Tyre is no longer a safe or desirable harbor. They must turn back to their own ports.

The LORD's Hand over the Sea, 23:11-18

The universal authority and dominion of the LORD has been demonstrated. Not only has he *given command concerning Canaan* (v. 11), which led to the destruction of kingdoms and their fortresses. He has also stretched his hand over the sea, which was the element that Tyre ruled with its fleets and commercial influence. So Tyre was no longer exempt from the fate of other Canaanite cities. It had to flee to Cyprus with what was left of its riches.

Verse 13 introduces the Chaldeans (i.e., Babylon), disturbing many interpreters. The NRSV reads as though Babylon destroyed Tyre; however, the Hebrew reads: "See the land of the Chaldeans! This was the people who no longer existed! Assyria assigned them to the wild beasts" (Watts 1985, 301). The destruction of Babylon has played a large role in the Vision. Here it is used as a parallel to that of Tyre.

The ships of Tyre are again called to mourning. But then the passage recognizes that Tyre will rise from its ashes to ply its trade again. *At the end of seventy years* (v. 17), it, like a prostitute who resumes her trade, will lure its trading partners again. It will make profits, as before. But this happens because of the LORD's decision. *Visit* may also mean "decide the fate of." Tyre is restored as profitable again because of the LORD's decision and on the LORD's terms. Its profits will be dedicated to the LORD *and for those who live in the presence of the LORD* (v. 18).

Perhaps the image of the LORD's visit is a foreshadowing of 60:4-16? An earlier king of Tyre provided both expertise and workers to build Solomon's Temple (see 1 Kgs 5:1-10). The profits of Tyre will make possible the restoration of the Temple and its services in proper style.

The LORD Is Devastating the Land, 24:1-20

The same Hebrew word can mean both "the earth" and "the land." "The land" has been the translation consistently used in the Book of Isaiah so far; there is no reason to change now (as the NRSV does in v. 1). Chapter 24 refers to the devastations wrought in the land of Canaan, not on the entire world. The previous chapter had narrowly looked at the effect of the fall of Tyre on the city and its interests. Now the Vision turns to the situation in the hinterlands that reach from the Euphrates through Lebanon, the coastlands and the highlands of Palestine to the border of Egypt in the south. *Twists it surface* (v. 1) could refer to earthquakes. *Scatter its inhabitants* could describe the results of many causes.

The devastation happens to everyone of all layers of society. The LORD's decree calls for the land to *be utterly laid waste* (v. 3). The image continues the decree enunciated in 6:11-12. The fulfillment of the LORD's command is a withered and dried up land.

Verses 5-7 shift the imagery. Instead of the personal commands of God the picture is of violated statutes and a broken covenant that "pollutes" the land. The pollution produces *a curse* that *devours* the land. The *inhabitants suffer for their guilt*. Such an impersonal view of sin, and its consequences, is very different from the personal judgment of God. Both views are evident throughout the OT. The results for the land are the same as for individuals.

The things that make for good living are gone. *The city of chaos* is the theme of vv. 10-12. It can also be translated "a desolate city." References to a city are repeated in 25:2-5, 26:1-6, and 27:10-11, yet the identity of the city remains ambiguous. Certainly the CITY is a counterpoint to the LAND. Both are significantly involved in the destruction. Cities have been prominent in the Vision—Jerusalem, Babylon, and Damascus among them—but the meaning here must go far beyond the destruction of a specific city.

The development of cities and city-states had been a particular phenomenon of the historical period of Israel's presence in Canaan. The Vision is signaling the end of that era (Watts 1985, 318–19). With the rise of the great empires, cities and city states in Palestine would never have the importance and power that they had before. These chapters mark the end of an age. Life would eventually be restored to the area, but things would never return to the previous way of life.

Verse 13 describes the situation in the land and *among the nations* as like that of an olive tree when the harvest is finished. Bare, without leaves or fruit, it can only await another season to restore its beauty, glory, and life.

Verse 14-16 respond to the devastation differently. There is joy and praise of the LORD. The locations of these responses are very exact. *From the west, in the east, in the coastlands of the sea*, from the extremities of the land come sounds of praise. Persons in these areas recognize the hand of the LORD in the turmoil. They see it as just RETRIBUTION. Perhaps they even stand to gain from the Assyrian actions.

But a single voice recognizes the terrors of the situation and the total chaos in the area. The situation appears hopeless. All the natural order is endangered. That is the meaning of the sentence: *for the windows of heaven are opened and the foundations of the earth tremble*. The description of the situation is similar to that of the great flood in Genesis. The utter ruin of the land (*earth* in NRSV) is expressed in vv. 19-20 where the word occurs four times. The fall is related to its sins through the words *its transgressions*. The description is of judgment, not mere happenstance.

The LORD Judges Armies and Kings, 24:21-22

The dominant word in this section is *punish*; it occurs at the beginning and the end. The LORD is the subject. As noted above (see commentary at 23:17) the Hebrew word may also mean "decide the fate of," which fits here. The translation *heaven* goes beyond the usual meanings of this word. Here it means "height." A literal translation would be "the army of the heights in the heights." *Earth* is the word that refers to "tillable land." In contrast to "heights" it would mean "lowlands." So the verse should read: "In that day, the LORD will decide the fate of the army of the highland in the highland, and of the kings of the lowland in the lowland" (author trans.). In Palestine the mountainous highlands and the lowlands together include everything. This is another picture that includes everything in the land.

The response foresees them all gathered as prisoners of war, to be held many days before this judgment takes place. Not only the cities and the kingdoms are to be destroyed completely, but the armies and the kings that used them are to come to an end. The new era will have none of the terror of marauding armies sweeping across the land that had characterized the previous thousand years and more.

The LORD of Hosts Reigns, 24:23–25:5

With this passage the section approaches a climax. The greatness of the moment and the occasion is indicated by the cry concerning the sun and the moon. The stupendous announcement is that "the LORD of hosts reigns on Mount Zion." The present tense fits better than a future (cf. the NRSV *The LORD of hosts will reign on Mount Zion* [24:23]).

The importance of this announcement cannot be exaggerated. All the land lies in ruins. The cities are waste. Tyre's influence and commerce are gone. But the LORD's kingship, instead of being destroyed with all the rest, is actually enhanced. Is this what 24:14-16a had glimpsed?

Since the royal scene is set in Jerusalem the courtiers are called *elders*. The scene in 6:1-8 had called the heavenly courtiers *seraphim*, but both scenes stress the *glory* that surrounds the throne. God's reign and his glory are evident in times of judgment as well as those of victory.

This is the second of three throne-room scenes in the Vision. The one in chap. 6 had declared the edict of a devastated land. That has been fulfilled in chap. 24 after the final loss in the conquest of Tyre. Now it is time for a new edict and a new direction. The Vision takes the reader back into the throne-room of God to hear it. This one, however, is not in heaven; it is in Jerusalem.

A song of praise and thanks adorns the scene. It is sung by individuals, each of whom confesses faith and devotion to the LORD. The first singer confesses faith because the LORD has done *wonderful things* (25:1). Specifically, the song recognizes that God had planned what has been done: the destruction of *the city*. This is the second of the passages that speak of cities and their destruction. Now the destruction is accomplished as previously announced; for that, God has received recognition and glory.

God also is perceived to be *a refuge to the poor* (v. 4). Rather than simply reflecting the power structures of that day, the LORD is seen to have opposed *the ruthless* (v. 5) in the cause of the weak and needy. God has been victorious and that is cause for praise.

Key Verse: The Banquet of the LORD of Hosts, 25:6

The reason for the royal session in Jerusalem is revealed. The LORD has prepared a banquet *for all peoples* who are all to be witnesses to what he has already done and what he is about to do. This is the second element of a royal trilogy. The first (24:23) had portrayed the LORD's appearance on the Jerusalem throne in glory before the elders. This one announces a banquet for all peoples. Note that these are not kings of nations. The kings are now gone, but the *peoples* remain.

The LORD Destroys Death Forever, 25:7-9

Now the third element of the royal trilogy announces a heroic deed. It will bring about an end to the long chain of vengeance and curse that has plagued the land and its peoples in all the military incursions, especially for the previous one to two hundred years. The heroic deed will end the reign of *death* in the land.

A curse was said to "devour the land" in 24:6; now the LORD *will swallow up death forever* (v. 7). Death is *the shroud* or sheet that covers all the peoples and nations. But the banquet has been called to announce that this fearful curse is being destroyed. The LORD alone has the power to destroy the destroyer (cf. Rev 20:13-14).

Two parallels to death are also to be removed. *Tears* are to be wiped from *all faces* (v. 8). The inevitable mourning and grief that accompanies death will be banished. *Disgrace*, or reproach, refers to actions worthy of such blood-guilt. *Disgrace* is a synonym of guilt and contamination (cf. 24:5-6); it, too, will be removed from all the land. The new decree wipes the slate clean and allows for new life and new joy in the land.

The response to such an action reveals the meaning of true faith in times of trouble. The response is a cry of recognition: *This is our God* (v. 9). The confession is a recognition that salvation and deliverance, especially from death, can only come from God. *We have waited for him* (v. 10), the peoples say. Their response is the best reply of faith. Waiting on the LORD is the frequent piety of the Psalmists. Those who wait experience *salvation*.

Such a *salvation* calls for joy and gladness, in sharp contrast to the weeping and mourning throughout the land. Jerusalem's hope in the LORD can be crowned by joy.

The LORD Judges Moab, 25:10–26:20

On the descending ladder of the chiasm, this passage balances the judgment on kings and armies in 24:21-22. *This mountain* (25:10) is Mount Zion. The LORD's hand on the mountain refers to the re-establishment of the LORD's sovereignty there as described in 24:23–25:9. When that happens, Moab must be returned to a place of subservience.

The imagery is drawn from the farm where a manure pit is kept near the barn. Manure is layered with straw. In time all of the mixture will be spread on the fields as fertilizer. So Moab will be trodden down like straw in the manure pit. Their resistance to the defeat and humiliation will be in vain. Fortifications will be leveled.

A song to be sung by Judah gives the response to the judgment of Moab (26:1-20). The song is a pilgrim song to be sung by Judaean pilgrims as they approach Jerusalem. Although the song is a response to the judgment of Moab, it still reflects the period of the fall of Tyre. The song strikes a festive note, but the pall of war still hangs over the land.

A strong city (i.e., Jerusalem, 26:1) stands in contrast to *the city of chaos* of 24:10 (cf. 24:12 and 25:2). *The gates* are those of Jerusalem. *The righteous nation that keeps faith* refers to the pilgrims approaching the city. *Peace* in a time when war is all around is difficult to keep, even if it is only peace of mind. But *steadfast mind* and *trust* can make that possible. So the pilgrims exhort all who will hear: *Trust in the LORD forever* (26:4).

In 26:5-6 the dialogue resumes the theme of the destroyed city. The *lofty city* recalls the earlier words about the high and the mighty (2:11-18) and the great king who would be reduced to SHEOL (14:11). The city is accused of oppressing the poor.

The song of the pilgrims goes on, alternating pious proclamations of faith with cynical observations of an evil time that cannot change. The shifting emphasis is the very sort of thing that one would expect in the period when Judah is helpless, with war swirling all around for well over half a century.

Verses 7-9 are words of faith and piety contrasted with a cynical view of the ways of the wicked in vv. 10-11a. Verses 11b-13 issue a call for God to act with divinely righteous zeal while protesting that the faith of Judah never wavered. Verse 14 disconsolately wails that *the dead do not live*, seeming to deny the efficacy of the LORD's decree in 25:7. Nonetheless, v. 15 insists that what the LORD has done has been for the good of the nation.

The two themes are combined in a confessional stanza in vv. 16-18. Verse 19 returns to the positive view with an affirmation *your dead shall live*, but v. 20 recognizes that the LORD's wrath is still dominant. The people are called to hide themselves for a little while more.

The LORD to Judge the Inhabitants of the Land, 26:21

This verse announces another action on God's part. He is moving out from *his place*, which could be either the heavenly dwelling or the Temple in Jerusalem. *Punish* is again the word that may mean "determine the fate of" (see commentary at 23:17 and 24:21-22). The action is against *the inhabitants of the land*. The reason is explained: *their iniquity*. Midway the verse turns to the other theme of this chapter: the dead. The land will be forced to show where its dead are buried. The earth will no longer hide the bodies of those that died.

The LORD Judges Leviathan, 27:1-11

The announcement of this new act of God is in v. 1. *Punish* repeats the word for "decide the fate of" (see above). And the decision is to *kill* him.

The LORD's sword is described as *cruel . . . great and strong. Leviathan* is called the *fleeing serpent, . . . the twisting serpent, the dragon that is in the sea.* LEVIATHAN is one of the names used in ancient Near Eastern literature for the monster of chaos, but it can also be used as a figure for historical enemies (e.g., Ezek 29:1-16; 32:2-8; Hab 3:1-9). In the same way that *son of Dawn* was used in 14:12 for the King of Babylon, here Leviathan is intended to have an historical reference. It probably is to be understood to stand for Assyria or the Assyrian king. Assyria is having its fate decided; it will be destroyed.

Verses 2-5 give the LORD's response to this turn of events. The prophet returns to the motif of Israel as a *vineyard* (cf. chap. 5) that the LORD guards. This time God is without wrath. God will fight against the *thorns and briers* until Israel comes to *cling to him.* The theme is: *Let it make peace with me.*

Verse 6 is the first of two announcements at the end of this long passage that began at 23:1. It tells of Israel's taking root and prospering in the land. The second announcement, treated below, is found in 27:12-13; both speak of Israel's fate.

Between the two announcements come questions and responses. The first question concerns Israel (v. 7). The questioner recognizes the judgment just made on Assyria and asks whether the same fate befell Israel. The answer (vv. 8-11) rehearses the reasons for judgment that led to *expulsion* and *exile.* It is necessary for *the guilt of Jacob to be expiated* (v. 9). Their sins and idolatries had led to the terrible events of the past century. These in turn had led to abandoned cities and an empty countryside. The Israelites are characterized as a people *without understanding.* The reader is reminded of 1:3. It was this lack that caused God's loss of favor toward them. But now the favor has returned under the new conditions.

The LORD Will Thresh and Gather Israel, 27:12-13

Now the second announcement is offered; it is aware of the existence of a Diaspora of the exiles who are still reckoned as people of Israel. Whether they are in the land of Assyria or in the land of Egypt, they are still recognized as God's people. They will be summoned to come and worship the LORD on the holy mount at Jerusalem. Here again is the theme of *worship on the holy mountain* (cf. 2:2-4).

This section has marked the end of Assyria's usefulness to God as the "rod of his anger." His wrath had achieved its full result. The land was empty and accursed. Hence, with the picture of another scene in God's throne-room a series of events is announced that will bring this dreadful era to an end. Assyria will be destroyed. Israel will be restored in the land and invited to pilgrimage from without.

The Vision of the Age of Josiah, 28:1–33:24

This section assumes an historical background of the reigns of JOSIAH and JEHOIAKIM. The Assyrian Empire is weakening, while Egypt, Babylon and Media jockey for position in the race to succeed Assyria as the world power of that day. Judah is living through the final phase of existence under the judgment pronounced on it more than a century before.

Each of the sub-sections begins with "woe" (as in RSV; NRSV has *ah*) in a kind of funeral litany that denies Judah any real sense of renewal or new chance in that era. The brief surge of new life under Josiah is not the real answer to Judah's fate. The section will continue to depict true hope to be in the LORD's support of Zion as a city of worship, in his promise of grace and the outpouring of his spirit, just as previous sections have done.

The five "woes" here are parallel to the five "woes" for Israel in chaps. 5 and 10. The scenes about Jerusalem are parallel to those in chaps. 2, 4, and 66. But there is a contrast to chap. 11. No Davidic heir appears in this section.

References to Assyria in this section describe its imminent fall (30:31; 31:8). References to Egypt portray the eagerness of some parties in Jerusalem to ally themselves with Egypt against Assyria (30:2; 31:1).

Disaster because of Expansion, 28:1-29

The section is composed of three parts. The first is a doleful review. The second is a reminder of Zion's role in God's plan. The third teaches God's strategy for his people.

28:1-13. Woe, Ephraim's drunkards. The central motif of this passage is the metaphor of drunkenness as applied to Israel. It contrasts the bumbling and repulsive ineptness of *people, priest,* and *prophet* (vv. 1, 3-4, 7-8) with the decisiveness (v. 2), determined compassion (vv. 5-6) and patience (vv. 9-10) of the LORD in working with them.

The passage fits the period when Josiah reoccupied much of the territory of Israel and probably aroused hopes that the days of David's glory might be repeated.

Garland may refer to a city on a hill, such as SAMARIA had been. Pride and glory are contrasted with a *fading flower*, depicting the former and present state of the great city. Drunkenness is the metaphor for the inept bumbling of Israel's leaders a century before. No one now mourns the events that led to their earlier disaster.

One who is mighty and strong (v. 2) refers to the Assyrian emperor, SHALMA-NESER, who besieged Samaria or to SARGON II, who captured the city and took its people into exile. Through these events *the LORD of hosts* received glory and was exalted among the remnant who had suffered under the kings. But then the leaders of the remnant also reeled with wine (vv. 5-8).

The passage scoffs at any attempt by these drunkards to teach or explain anything. They are like children learning the alphabet, repeating the letters. But the passage insists that the LORD could use even those worthless teachers to teach some truth, to accomplish something. They repeated literally precepts and lines (vv. 10, 13), but the result was the breakup, capture and exile of the kingdom and its people. What had begun in v. 10 as mumbling incompetence is changed by the LORD in v. 13 into an authentic word of judgment.

Note the relation of v. 12 with Exod 33:13-14. *Rest* implies dwelling and the security needed for that. This is Israel's rest as paralleled in Deut 12:9; Isa 30:15 and Ps 95:11. The same sovereign LORD acts toward Israel in the time of the Assyrian invasions as he had acted in bringing the people into the land of Canaan under Joshua. The original offer of rest had been conditioned upon Israel's willingness to listen to God and his law. The same condition applied to the eighth century. Israel had failed to meet that condition.

28:14-22. Scoffers in Jerusalem. Attention turns from affairs in old Israel to current events in Jerusalem. Crucial actions by the LORD are about to take place (vv. 16, 21). The leaders posit their *covenant with death* (v. 15) as their reason for holding back. This may refer to their treaty obligation to Assyria in a time of growing Egyptian strength. *The overwhelming scourge* may refer to the Scythian invaders who broke through the Assyrian defenses in the north. *Lies* and *falsehood* apply to a treaty partner, perhaps Egypt. It is hard to believe that anyone in Jerusalem really thought good could come from the confused political situation of the period; the verses display such incredulity.

In v. 16 the LORD answers the argument of political necessity that is put forward as an excuse for this action. He repudiates the idea that the old values can no longer be held. He affirms what he is willing to do in his commitment to Zion. The *cornerstone* or *foundation stone* in Zion may refer either to the Temple or to the Davidic king. What God is doing in Zion is the key to understanding the history of that time. Isaiah 2:1-3 and chap. 66 suggest that the building of the Temple in Zion is the theme of the Vision. The Temple is to continue to be the symbol of the LORD's reign and authority. The believer is encouraged to exercise patience while waiting for the LORD to complete the work.

God commits himself to *justice . . . and righteousness* (v. 17) as the standards by which to measure right and wrong. Policies based on practical politics and personal advancement are not to be trusted.

The message that their self-serving *covenant* (v. 18; see, also, v. 15) is going to be swept away is bound to bring terror to the city. The figure of *the bed* and the *covering* being *too short* and *too narrow* (v. 20) applies to the inadequacies of treaty alignments made with Egypt. These left no room for Judah to accommodate itself to Babylon's rise to power or to the LORD's new moves.

Mount Perazim (v. 21) is not clearly located in the OT, but "Baal-perazim" appears in 2 Sam 5:20 where David defeats the Philistines. The announcement that *the LORD will rise up* implies that God is going to war. Earlier in the OT this meant that the deity would fight for Israel against their enemies, but in Isaiah the LORD's work is that of raising up the Assyrians against Israel. That Jerusalem should cry out, *strange is his deed! . . . alien is his work!* is understandable. They believed that God's proper role lay in saving and supporting Israel. The Vision of Isaiah argues repeatedly that the people were blind, uncomprehending, and unbelieving to this "other work" of God, the work that the prophet announced as God's being responsible for the Assyrian invasions. In the people's eyes their understanding of what God should be doing was contradicted by such a claim.

The last speech urges Jerusalem not to scoff at this word from God. *Your bonds* (v. 22) refers to the political alliances. Prudence and restraint are needed to keep a bad situation from getting worse.

28:23-29. The LORD's strategy: a parable. The prophet employs a parable as a teaching tool, using the experience of farmers. Farmers need to work differently in different seasons and times. They do not confuse the times and seasons, or allow one task to make them overlook another. The scoffers and speechmakers among the people would argue that God's ways are always the same and consistent. The parable defends the prophetic view that God acts in history in ways that fit the times to achieve divine goals.

The story is a parable because it is told as an analogy for another truth. God's strategy for history is wonderful and will succeed. Jerusalem's leaders need to seek instruction from God concerning their plans, just as farmers learn from God when to plant and to reap. And God's strategy is to be trusted, as farmers trust God's instruction about sowing.

God's strategy in the Vision is not pictured as ideal plans fixed in eternity. It refers to the LORD's decisions in specific historical situations. God's success implies prudence that issues finally in success and salvation.

Disaster through Political Relations, 29:1-24

This section consists of three parts. "Woe, Ariel" (29:1-8; NRSV begins *Ah, Ariel, Ariel*) mourns for Jerusalem, which now must be attacked and humbled. "Like a Dream" (29:9-14) describes the fulfillment of the task assigned in 6:11-13 as a terrible nightmare that will be perceived, after it has happened, merely as a dream. "Woe, you schemers" (29:15-24) is directed against the plotters in Jerusalem; it sees new opportunity for Jacob.

29:1-8. Woe, Ariel. This part is a very compact and careful construction relating imagery from a royal Zion festival to the realistic siege of the walls of Jerusalem by the horde of nations. This is developed around three motifs: *Ariel* (vv. 1, 2, 7), the siege or *distress* (vv. 2, 7, 8), and the horde or *multitude* (vv. 5, 7, 8).

The drama of the festival demonstrates the dependence of the city on God. Zion exists by the decree and power of the LORD God. If that is understood in the festival drama, then it is equally true for historical reality. Once the LORD has decided Zion's fate, the oppressing nations will no longer be a factor. Chapters 36–39 are parallel in meaning. The prophetic oracle there serves the same purpose that reference to the festival does here.

Jerusalem was besieged several times in history: In Ahaz's reign (chap. 7, which was 734 B.C.E.), Sennacherib's siege (chaps. 22 and 36–37, which was 701 B.C.E.), and Nebuchadnezzar's sieges (in 598 and 587 B.C.E.). The usual form of a siege account has the LORD defending the city, but here the situation is reversed. The LORD lays siege to the city. This literary inversion portrays a ritual humiliation of the city that is carried to the very point of death.

Ariel may mean "lioness of God," "God's champion or hero," or "the altar-hearth of El." It is certainly applied to Jerusalem. The implication is that although Jerusalem is a city founded by God in ancient Jebusite times, and although David himself claimed the city, the LORD is forced now to fight against it.

Deep from the earth in v. 4 seems to refer to the world of the dead. After being besieged, Ariel will descend into the land of the dead, becoming like a ghost. If the experience humbles Jerusalem to the point of deathly helplessness, the nations around the city are a part of the dust of that deathlike, unreal experience.

The LORD is the only reality. He alone has decisive power. After he has acted, all other threats will be like a dream only partly remembered. This passage, like chap. 7, calls attention away from the immediate historical threat to the underlying reality of God's purpose and action.

By referring to the ancient ritual of humiliation through ordeal, which preceded the "deciding of the fate," this passage interprets Jerusalem's military difficulty as God's humiliation of the city, which must precede his decision about its fate. The LORD's sovereign decisions and his salvation—these are the realities, the only decisive factors that Jerusalem needs to consider.

29:9-14. Like a dream. This passage picks up the theme of the drunken stupor from chap. 28, and from 6:9-10 the theme of blindness caused by God. It also resumes the theme of insincere worship found in the first chapter of the book.

The festival crowds still move through the city, but they walk as though they are asleep. This stupor is from God, as was predicted in 6:9-11. The prophets, leaders and seers are all affected by it.

The *vision of all this*, which has been revealed by the book, of God's strategy, of what God is doing and why, is something the people are unable to see. Having a revelation or a Bible is of no use if the people's lack of faith keeps it *sealed* (v. 11).

The LORD distances himself from *this people* (v. 14). Their religion is only verbal, lacking heart, mind, and will. This affects the character of their worship. *Their worship* (v. 13) means their attitude in worship. It should be inspired by awe, by deep respect for the Holy One. Instead, worship had become a human command that is taught and recited without moving the will.

Because of this, God must intervene with *amazing things* (v. 14) to restore the sense of the holy and awesome presence of the LORD. Because he is intervening directly, ordinary wisdom and teaching can no longer correctly advise what God will do.

29:15-24. Woe, you schemers. This passage has three parts and a conclusion. Woe to planners, who plan without God (vv. 15-16). God's reversal is near (vv. 17-21). The LORD announces a new opportunity for Israel (vv. 22-23). And then even *those who err in spirit* can understand (v. 24).

All who think they can dig deep to escape God's scrutiny are mistaken. In the LORD's plan things will soon be reversed. The *deaf*, the *blind*, the *meek*, and the humble have suffered much in a world that honors power and cunning. But the day will come when God changes the rules to work to their advantage.

God is clearly identified: God of *the house of Jacob, who redeemed Abraham*. The message is about Israel. God expects the sight of surviving *children* among them, after all the terrible things that have happened, to lead them to see these acts as the *work of [God's] hands*, as products of miraculous preservation. This may bring understanding to their leaders again.

Disaster from Self-Help in Rebellion, 30:1-33

This passage brings to a head the struggle between God and the Judean leaders, who are determined to follow their own plans. The first part (vv. 1-18) contrasts God's acts with the policies of Judah's leaders. The second part (vv. 19-26) repeats the doctrine of hope in God, ignoring the terrible plight of their country. The third part (vv. 27-33) presents the religious exercise of cultic prophecy that promises God's salvation no matter what the people are doing.

30:1-18. Woe, rebellious children. God distances himself from Judah and its plans. Pharaoh's promises of protection will prove to be a sham. The historical setting is before the fall of Assyria but after Egypt had begun actively to conspire in Palestinian politics. This would apply to almost any period of Josiah's reign.

The complaint of *rebellious children* picks up a theme from chap. 1. The rebellion takes the form of *a plan* (v. 1). The LORD has a plan for Israel, but the political leaders have another. In Ashurbanipal's late reign and in the reigns of his successors, Assyria became less aggressive and strict. Psamtik I (Psammeticus I), Pharaoh of Egypt, became correspondingly more aggressive and powerful. Jerusalem's leaders were determined to play the game of power politics, pitting one superpower against the one they thought they would take its place.

Their prediction proved to be false. It was a misjudgment. Egypt's power in Palestine was short-lived. Babylon, not Egypt, was destined to succeed Assyria. Babylon's power would last only half a century, so those who depend on Egypt will be shamed.

Rahab (v. 7) is the name of a mythical monster that rules chaos. Here Egypt is called "Rahab" only to be doomed to inactivity. The LORD's word makes it a harmless dragon who breathes fire but is, in fact, innocuous.

The LORD wants his accusation to be written down for a later day. In a sense, this is exactly what the Vision of Isaiah does. It bears witness to Israel's and Jerusalem's unwillingness to heed the LORD's instruction through these twelve generations.

They tried to still the voices of the prophets (v. 10), but the LORD's judgment condemns them for rejecting his word. *Oppression and deceit* (v. 12; Heb. "a perverse tyrant") must refer to Egypt's Pharaoh. The judgment speech uses the metaphor of a masonry wall that bulges in the middle (v. 13). When it falls nothing of any consequence will be left.

God's plan called for retreat and quiet patience, for heroic restraint and waiting. But the activists in the palace could not wait. They saw in the crumbling Assyrian power an unparalleled opportunity. But their plans were short-lived, fixed on the immediate goal of relative autonomy for a brief generation. Josiah's reign lasted from 640 to 609 B.C.E. That slight glory was bought with the price of Jerusalem's destruction by the Babylonians in 598 and 587 B.C.E.

The activists tried to flee, presumably toward Egypt. But their pursuers were faster. So now the LORD's mercy must make way for justice. The phrase *rise up to show mercy* (v. 18) contains an inner tension. "Rise up" usually describes the LORD's rising to do battle with his enemies. Here it is joined to showing mercy. The LORD has to take a violent course of action because Israel refused the quiet course that God had planned, for he is a God of justice. The final line is a sigh over what might have been: *Blessed are all those who wait for him!* Judah under Josiah was not willing to wait.

30:19-26. Hope from the teachers. This little homily on assurance and hope is presented in a style like that of the teaching of the Wise (reflected throughout the WISDOM LITERATURE). It addresses the pilgrims in Jerusalem.

The pilgrims in Zion are called to forget the hard times of the past. They are assured God will hear their prayers and help them. They are reminded of Israel's trials in the wilderness. *Bread of adversity* and *water of affliction* (v. 20) are provisions for prisoners. The bad times are pictured as a prison sentence from God.

Your Teacher is a unique name for God. It could also be translated "your instructor." *Will not hide himself anymore* (v. 20) recognizes periods when God's guiding, instructing presence has not been sensed so clearly. This text promises that this will no longer be true. In 45:15 God is called *a God who hides himself.* The OT understands that God's presence with his people is not simply a fact of existence, presumed to be universal and constant. It is a gracious and deliberate gift offered by God. It is to be recognized and welcomed as such. In JUDAISM, from EZRA on, the Torah was the teacher of the people. In the Vision of Isaiah teaching is done by the instructing, guiding presence of the LORD. Seeing God and hearing his voice as instruction are understood to be the ways of knowing and experiencing his presence.

God's words are like those of a shepherd, spoken from *behind* (v. 21), keeping his flock on the path. The presence of the Teacher makes the getting rid of all traces of idols urgent. The role of idols is to represent a god's presence. The true presence of God among his people removes all reason or excuse for artificial symbols.

Palestinian agriculture is totally dependent on rain. The LORD claims to be able to give or withhold the life-giving rain. *Brooks* on the heights suggests abundance of water. *Great slaughter* (v. 25) and towers falling present a scene of war and destruction. The effect of *the sun* and *the moon* (v. 26) is to be felt on the great day. Moderns would be appalled at the thought of a seven-fold increase of the sun's heat and light. The intention is to represent the participation of the cosmos, which is also a part of the LORD's realm.

The LORD's healing will apply to his people's wounds, even to those that his punishment had caused. The idea of God's punishing and also healing is also found in Deut 32:39, Job 5:18 and Hos 6:1.

30:27-33. A theophany. This passage invites the reader to envision God's approach as in 26:21, 40:10, 66:15 and other OT passages. The use of *the name of the LORD* (v. 27) in such a vision is unique.

We are then called upon to see a list of anatomical features attributed to God:

the name of the LORD	coming from a distance
anger (or nose)	burning
liver	raging
lips	full of indignation
tongue	a devouring fire
breath	like a stream
	to sift the nations
	a bridle for the peoples

A holy festival is the setting. A pilgrimage to Jerusalem is indicated by going *to the mountain of the LORD* (v. 29). The goal of the trip is shown in the *Rock of Israel*. On that festive occasion the LORD will reveal himself in power.

The historical reality that is portrayed is the downfall of Assyria and its king. The funeral pyre for the king has long been ready. *The breath of the LORD . . . kindles it* (v. 33) signals the reversal of the LORD's attitude toward Assyria as portrayed in chaps. 7–10. That nation has performed its assigned task and is now to be turned aside.

The collapse of the Assyrian empire began with its gradual weakening soon after mid-century. Nineveh fell to a combined Babylonian and Median force in 612 B.C.E. and the retreating armies finally fell in Haran in 609 B.C.E. under Babylonian attack, just before an Egyptian column of troops could arrive. A major battle at CARCHEMISH between Egypt and Babylon followed, which put Palestine under Babylonian rule for the following decades.

Disaster because of False Faith in Egypt, 31:1–32:20

The section presents criticism of the parties who called for using help from Egypt to gain independence from Assyria. Such political scheming ignores God's determination of events like those portrayed earlier in the book. The first passage (31:1-9) engages leaders who prefer human dependence on alliances to dependence on an alliance with God. The second passage (32:1-8) teaches a lesson in civic righteousness. The third passage (32:9-20) engages a group of women, contrasting their prosperity with the devastation to come *in little more than a year* (32:10).

31:1-9. Against depending on Egypt. The passage mourns the determination expressed by some of the political leaders to seek military help from Egypt against Assyria. The passage insists that God will be the determinative factor in rescuing Jerusalem and in bringing Assyria down. It calls for Jerusalem to recognize God's control, turn to the LORD, put aside their idols, and wait for the deliverance of God.

32:1-8. A lesson. This is a very different passage, cast in the form of a dialogue between a teacher and students. It begins with a supposition: *See, a king will reign in righteousness.* If one may assume a righteous king, what else will happen? All the wonderful conditions of a righteous reign will result. Especially, it would be true that there would no longer be any confusion about values. No more confusion about who is a fool and who is noble, who is a villain and who is honorable. The ambiguity that surrounds the political process would be put aside. Israelites of that day had the same problem in judging their political leaders that we have today.

32:9-20. Dialogue with women. A group of women are warned that disasters are about to disrupt their pleasant way of life. They cannot conceive of their fields being destroyed. The warning continues, including warnings of the loss of palaces and cities.

The women express their faith (v. 15-16) that an ideal justice will come upon them, even beyond any troubles that come. They feel secure in the belief that *the effect of righteousness will be peace* (v. 17), but the warning is repeated.

God Vows to Punish the Tyrant, 33:1-24.

In this section the Vision approaches a critical point as violence increases and God prepares to intervene. In the first passage (33:1-6) expectation of imminent violence brings reactions from individuals and from a chorus. The second passage (33:7-12) portrays a worsening situation. The last passage (33:13-24) portrays the LORD's intervention. Persons near and far are challenged to assess the event and recognize what the results of God's intervention will be.

33:1-6. Ah, you destroyer. Verse 1 addresses a *destroyer*, announcing his destruction. Assyria is probably the intended figure. The phrase *when you have ceased to destroy* recalls the prediction in 10:12, *When the LORD has finished all his work . . . he will punish the arrogant boasting of the king of Assyria.* Assyria's task as seen from the book itself is to be a destroyer. Now that task is complete and it will itself be destroyed.

A group that says *we wait for you* (v. 2) pleads for mercy. A voice addresses God, recognizing God's approach in the sounds of battle. God is exalted in Zion, and the faith is voiced that God will use these times. The real *stability* (v. 6) for such times is to be found only in God. Then the gifts from God are listed. All of them in Hebrew are related to *the LORD*: saving acts of the LORD, *wisdom* of the LORD, *knowledge* of the LORD, and *the fear of the LORD*.

33:7-12. The LORD rises up. Apparently efforts for peace have failed and the land prepares for the worst. The LORD announces that the time has come for divine intervention. The plans of the human advisors will be nothing more than *chaff* and *stubble* (v. 11); modern readers would say "they were only paper." Because of their wrong judgments, peoples are going to be burnt up.

33:13-24. Who can survive the fire? This passage takes seriously the announcement that the war, with the LORD as its impetus, is about to sweep over them. They ask, Who can survive?

Verses 15-16 provide an answer. A way of life, according to the things that God has taught, gives promise of survival. The rest of the passage portrays the results of the LORD's intervention. The counter and weigher who had collected the tribute due the emperor (v. 18) for so long are gone. The foreign officials, symbols of the tyranny that had oppressed them also are gone.

Zion appears as a very different kind of city: like a tent, but a permanent tent. The LORD will be their king. The contrast to Egypt or Assyria could be implied with *a place . . . no galley with oars can pass* (v. 21), as they might on the Nile or the Tigris rivers. The LORD is confessed as judge and king.

The NRSV has understood v. 23a in nautical terms, but the words can also mean "a measured portion," or "a lot," referring to fields. This would make the verse refer to the fields that are assigned to peasants and to permits to do business in the towns. These had been restricted under the empire. But the fall of Assyria makes land reform and business reform possible. The foreigners can no longer enforce their authority or defend their flag. Hometown people will get their share of things that foreigners had dominated for over a century. Even the lame will get their share.

The sick will participate and there will be a general amnesty for past crimes. The Vision of the Age of Zedekiah, 34:1–39:8

This part differs from the preceding ones. It begins with a long treatment of Edom's curse and Judah's renewal (34:1–35:10). The rest of the section is a series of readings from 2 Kgs 18–20 with an added poem, Hezekiah's Psalm (38:9-20). All this fills the place in the book where one would expect a treatment of the destruction of Jerusalem and the beginning of Judah's exile. Instead, the Vision presents the largest block of prose in the book, narrative borrowed from 2 Kings and specifically dated to a time contemporary with chap. 22. The enigma of the missing details of Judah's fall dominates the interpretation of this section.

Exilic Israel read the HEZEKIAH stories even as their recent experiences, that had turned out so differently, were still fresh in their memories. In 701 B.C.E. the royal house survived in Jerusalem. In 586 B.C.E. the only survivor was JEHOIACHIN, who was a prisoner in Babylon at the time. In 701 the villagers and townsfolk who had fled to Jerusalem were released to return to their homes. In 586 many of them began the long march into EXILE. Near 701 the portent of a Babylonian peril was spoken by Isaiah. In 586 it became grim reality.

The readings present a reverse image of what happened. In this negative image the entire terrible period is brought vividly to mind.

A brief history of the period would have to include the following events. In 605 B.C.E. Nebuchadnezzar, Babylon's king, having defeated Assyria and then Egypt, marched into Palestine to establish his sovereignty over the territory. He gained Jehoiakim's pledge of loyalty, in spite of the Judean king's original loyalty to Egypt.

In 598 B.C.E. Nebuchadnezzar returned to confront JEHOIAKIM, who had been conspiring with Egypt. Rather than face him, Jehoiakim abdicated in favor of his son Jehoiachin who was seized and taken hostage to Babylon along with a number of Jerusalem's leaders and their families. Subsequently ZEDEKIAH was placed on the throne. By 587 he was also in trouble. This time Nebuchadnezzar destroyed the city and killed Zedekiah and his sons. A large proportion of the people were taken into exile.

Edom's Curse—Judah's Renewal, 34:1–35:10

A single theme binds these chapters together: God's vengeance against Edom (34:8 and 35:4), which is seen as an everlasting decision (34:16-17). The form is a "day of the LORD" prophecy. The outline is concentric:

A—The LORD's day of wrath on all nations, 34:1-4
   B—Vengeance and ban on Edom for Zion's sake, 34:5-8
      C—Edom to be burned and deserted, 34:9-15
Keystone: The LORD's decision, recorded and perpetual, 34:16-17
      C'—Wilderness and Arabah—glad and renewed, 35:1-2
   B'—The LORD's action—salvation for Israel, 35:3-4
A'—Festival in Zion again for pilgrims, 35:5-10

Judah's wars with Edom had a long history that reached a peak when Edom supported Babylon in its siege of Jerusalem in 586 B.C.E. Neither the Books of Kings nor the Books of Chronicles recount Edom's alliance with Babylon, but the Book of Obadiah and other passages in the OT clearly indicate it. These chapters imply that Edom impeded the travel of pilgrims through its territory.

Four sentences that begin with *for* claim certain rights for the LORD: the right to anger (34:2), the right to his sword (34:5), the right to a sacrifice (34:6b), and the right to a day of vengeance (34:8).

The LORD's judgment on Edom is interrelated with the salvation of Jerusalem. By pushing Edom back, southern and southeastern Judah regain access to favored lands and to water from which they had been cut off. Pilgrims regain rights of passage to Jerusalem.

The picture of the desolate country contains, among other words, one that requires comment: *Lilith* (34:14). This is the only place in the OT where she is mentioned, unless some suggested emendation to 2:18 and Job 18:15 be accepted. The word is similar to the Hebrew word for "night," but a demon by this name was well known in Mesopotamia. Judaism used the name and Christian demonism picked it up as well. Mention of it here in Isaiah only intends to describe the utter desolation that is to come.

Chapter 35 then turns to a reversal of that sad state when all nature will respond to the approaching glory of the LORD by bursting into life. The weak and sick pilgrims are urged to continue in order to be part of it. The reversal in nature is mirrored by a reversal in personal fortunes (vv. 5-6). A highway for the pilgrims will be opened so that the LORD's ransomed may travel on it to come to Zion with rejoicing that knows no bounds.

The Assyrian's Speech, 36:1-22

This chapter is a reading from 2 Kgs 18:13-37.

36:1-3. Jerusalem 701 B.C.E. The dates of HEZEKIAH's reign are disputed. Biblical evidence is contradictory, but the year of SENNACHERIB's siege of Jerusalem is not, thanks to Assyrian records. The year is 701 B.C.E.; Hezekiah had been in rebellion since the beginning of Sennacherib's reign in 705 B.C.E. He had joined the rebellion of Babylon's MERODACH-BALADAN at that time. But Babylon had been subdued in 703 B.C.E. Now, two years later, it is Jerusalem's turn.

Hezekiah had prepared the outer defenses of Jerusalem as a circle of fortified towns. These fortifications had been overrun. Assyria's main objective was against Egypt. The foray against Jerusalem was a side trip from the headquarters at the Philistine city of Lachish. *Rabshakeh* (v. 2) is apparently a title for a high military official.

Jerusalem's WATER SYSTEMS consisted of springs and pools outside the walls that flowed through conduits into the city. The *Fuller's Field* (v. 2; see 7:3) is the place where people came to wash their clothes. The army was so close to the city that the general could stand this near the city, well within earshot of the people on the walls.

Three officials of Hezekiah's court are sent out to talk to him. The names of two of them are known from chap. 22, but their positions are reversed. There *Shebna* is the higher official, *Eliakim* is his successor.

36:4-10. The general's first speech. This is a very remarkable speech. The hearers of the speech within the narrative itself are the people on the wall in 701 B.C.E. 2 Kings has used the same setting for the context in narrative, but the Book of Isaiah gives it a very different context in the generation of Jews in Jerusalem at, or shortly after, the fall of Jerusalem in 587 B.C.E. They faced—or had faced—a very similar situation. For them the voice might well have been Nebuchadnezzar's.

The speech attacks the confidence of the besieged city that help will be forthcoming. The speaker invites them to negotiate a settlement. The Rabshakeh questions (v. 5) the basis of the residents of Jerusalem's will to resist. He attacks the idea that Egypt will help and offers to arm their troops if they will join his cause. He scorns any ideas that the LORD will help, with the reminder that Hezekiah had destroyed the LORD's altars outside the city in Judah. He closes with the suggestion that the LORD had sent Sennacherib against Jerusalem in the first place.

That the Rabshakeh was using all this as psychological warfare is obvious. But the Book of Isaiah's use of this narrative has another meaning. It has already said the same thing about TIGLATH-PILEZER in 7:17-20. The idea that the LORD was using the Assyrians now places Hezekiah's responses in an entirely different light than they have in 2 Kings.

36:11-12. Protest and response. Hezekiah's officials recognize the negative effect that this speech could have on the listening people; accordingly, they ask the Rabshakeh to speak in Aramaic, the language of the Empire. The request underscores the fact that he had been speaking in Hebrew. Northern Israel had been an Assyrian province for about twenty years, so officials of the occupying power are able to use the language.

The general refuses, insisting that his message is not only for the ears of the king; it should be heard by all. After all, they are the ones risking death by continued resistance.

36:13-20. The general's second speech. The general again speaks for the king and tries to discredit Hezekiah, who had been urging the people to rely on the LORD. Then the general makes his offer. If the people surrender they can all go back to their own villages and eat their own food until arrangements are made for transport to their place of exile in another country.

He discounts any chance for survival otherwise, citing Assyrian victories over many peoples. He claims that none of their gods were able to deliver them from his power and surely the LORD will not be any more able to do so.

36:21-22. No response. The delegation had been given no instructions to answer the general. So they remained silent and went back into the city.

From Hearsay to Knowledge, 37:1-20

37:1-4. Hezekiah's reaction. Hezekiah reacts with extreme grief and anguish. He went into the Temple, but sent his delegation to Isaiah. They ask for a word from God to respond to the mocking blasphemy of the general.

37:5-7. Isaiah's response. Isaiah admonishes them not to be afraid. The prophet then tells them that God promises to rid them of the army by inspiring a rumor that will cause the king to return to Babylon, where he will commit suicide. Other descriptions of the way the LORD will send the king away are found in vv. 28-29 and 36-38.

37:8-13. The general's renewed message. Having had no success in persuading Jerusalem to surrender, the general rejoins the main army. He finds them *fighting against Libnah* (v. 8). An intelligence report lets him know that a major Egyptian force under *King Tirhakah* is marching to meet him.

He is anxious to wrap up the loose ends of his campaign against Jerusalem, so he renews his communication with Hezekiah by letter. His strategy is to shake Hezekiah's faith in God. He again refers to Assyria's victories over other cities and their gods, implying that the LORD can do no better for Jerusalem.

37:14-20. Hezekiah's prayer. When the letter arrives, Hezekiah goes to the Temple and spreads it before the LORD. His prayer is majestic and remarkable.

The address is three-fold. *LORD of Hosts* (v. 16) uses the name for God employed in relation to divine kingship over all the nations; it is a military title. *Hosts* means armies and refers to the heavenly armies. *God of Israel* refers to the LORD's covenant relation to the people through ABRAHAM and MOSES. *Enthroned above the cherubim* places the LORD in the Holy of Holies of the Temple over the Ark of the Covenant.

The prayer begins with a confession that the LORD alone is God. In all the kingdoms of the land there is no other living God. The address closes with the confession that the LORD is creator of heaven and earth.

The prayer begs God to see what is going on and to hear the mocking words of Sennacherib. Hezekiah asks the LORD to recognize the personal challenge to God's own being that is contained in the words of the challenger.

Hezekiah recognizes, and asks God to recognize, the truth in the Assyrian's words. Sennacherib's claim to victories over many nations is no empty boast. His removal of their gods, replacing them with the gods of Assyria, had actually happened. The confession reveals utter helplessness on Hezekiah's part.

The prayer moves to its point: Hezekiah appeals to the LORD to show his unity with Judah and its people, to save them from the Assyrians. This would make all the nations of the land know that he alone is the LORD. The God of Judah bows to no king or emperor.

Isaiah's Response from the LORD, 37:21-38

37:21-29. The LORD's word for Hezekiah. Isaiah brings an answer to the prayer. The first word from the LORD had been a short ORACLE in the usual form of the prophets as we know them in the Books of Kings, but this one belongs to the longer poetic forms that are found in the Book of Isaiah.

The word begins with the messenger formula, *thus says* (v. 21). God is identified by one of the titles Hezekiah used, *the LORD, the God of Israel*. God is responding in his role of the COVENANT God of Israel. The subject of the prayer is acknowledged, then God's word concerning SENNACHERIB is relayed.

First Jerusalem's proud disdain is described; then the point of the general's speech is recognized as a direct insult to God because of the Rabshakeh's claims. This is an act of pride and haughty arrogance toward the LORD (see chap. 2).

God's reply is a reminder that it is he who determines the fate of nations and kings, and that long in advance. God was responsible for the Assyrian successes (as suggested in chaps. 7 and 10). The LORD then reminds Hezekiah that God is well aware of all of Sennacherib's words and thoughts. Nothing is secret from God. So now the LORD will dominate and humiliate him. God will put *a hook in [his] nose*, like a farmer who tames a bull, and put *a bit in [his] mouth* (v. 29). The LORD will turn the Assyrian king around and send him back where he came from.

37:30-32. The LORD's sign for Jerusalem. The words turn to address Hezekiah. He is given a sign, just as Ahaz was offered a sign (cf. chap. 7): *This year eat what grows of itself* (v. 30). It is probably too late for farmers to plant their fields for this year. They will have to eat whatever has come up on its own. The *second year* will not be much better. But, by the *third year*, the normal planting and reaping will occur and the land will be back to normal.

The word turns to the implications of this promise in a broader sense. Judah itself is just a surviving remnant of God's people. Israel has already gone into EXILE. And the group that returns to the villages from the besieged city had certainly suffered its losses, too. But this group will be reestablished on the land and will enjoy its fruits again.

The reestablishment of Judah is accomplished by the direct intervention of *the LORD of Hosts* (v. 32). This is that second title for God that Hezekiah used.

37:33-38. The LORD sends the Assyrians home. The style reverts to prose narrative. A third description of what happened to the Assyrian army is given (cf. 37:7 and 29). The LORD's *angel* (v. 36) annihilated the army, 185,000 of them in a night. Understandably the king withdrew.

He lived in Nineveh, but was assassinated by his sons as he worshiped in his temple. The sons fled. Esar-haddon, another son, ruled in his place. The historical note is correct. Esarhaddon did succeed Sennacherib in 681 B.C.E. after he had been assassinated by two older sons who then had to flee.

Hezekiah's Illness, 38:1-22

38:1-8. Hezekiah becomes ill. The prophet declares Hezekiah's illness to be terminal. The prayer that follows is the second one in the longer narrative.

This prayer is a prayer for remembrance. The king claims to have walked before God *in faithfulness* (v. 3). He speaks of living *with a whole heart*, and *having done what is good in [God's] sight*—a picture of Hezekiah that the dueteronomistic historian of the Books of Kings portrays. Then the king weeps.

Isaiah is then instructed to give God's answer to the prayer. God is identified as *the God of your ancestor David* (v. 5). God is prepared to answer the king in line with his promise in 2 Sam 7:13-16. He is dealing with David's ancestor with a mercy given for David's sake.

God has heard the king's prayer and seen his contrition. The LORD answers by adding fifteen years to his life. Then the LORD renews the promise to deliver him and the city from the king of Assyria. Again the contrast with the events in 587 B.C.E. is evident: on the latter occasion both the city and the king with his family were destroyed.

The LORD offers a sign that a reprieve will happen. He promises to make the shadow cast by the sundial built by Ahaz go back ten steps. The narrative then confirms that the sundial did back up.

38:9-20. Hezekiah's prayer. This Psalm with a superscription identifying it as from Hezekiah on the occasion of his recovery is inserted here. It is not found in Kings. The Psalm is built around a meditation on the king's expected death (vv. 10-14), followed by thoughts after his healing (vv. 15-17). Verses 18-20 form a conclusion.

The mourning over approaching death culminates in a prayer for the LORD to be his security. The Psalm is a liturgical thanksgiving for personal healing like several in the Psalms.

38:21-22. Hezekiah's recovery. The narrative does not actually say that Hezekiah recovered, but that is implied. The story ends with the recognition that Isaiah had ordered a healing poultice for the boil, and that Hezekiah had asked for a *sign*.

Hezekiah's Mistake, 39:1-8

This incident is dated by the reference to *Merodach-baladan . . . of Babylon* (v. 1). This means that it happened prior to Sennacherib's campaign, which is narrated in chaps. 36–37. MERODACH-BALADAN was dislodged from Babylon by 703 B.C.E. An earlier date would also be more plausible for Hezekiah, since he would have had little treasure to show after the 701 siege.

After Hezekiah's illness and recovery, he receives messengers from Babylon. He welcomes them and conducts them on a tour of his armory and *treasure house*. He is obviously proud of his treasure and his armed strength.

The prophet thinks that Hezekiah is less than wise in showing off in front of the Babylonians. Hezekiah was a vassal of the Assyrian king. Babylon was probably in rebellion at this time. This kind of reception could well be seen as encouraging the rebellion, if not actually joining it. Hezekiah's answer seems unbelievably naive.

Isaiah presents the LORD's word that in days to come the entire Davidic family and their wealth will be carried into Babylon. Even some of his sons will become *eunuchs* and servants to the kings of Babylon. A later generation, hearing this read, would identify the fulfillment of this prophecy in what happened to Jehoiakim in 598 B.C.E. (cf. 2 Kgs 24:10-16). The Babylon of that day was a very different Babylon, but the prophecy fit.

Hezekiah's response is remarkably sanguine. He has hoped to win peace and security for his own days, even if that costs his successors the throne and their freedom.

This chapter, although it is exactly like that in 2 Kings, functions in the Book of Isaiah to sketch in the fall of Jerusalem and the exile imposed by the Babylonians. The chapter sets the stage for the following scenes.

The Vision of the Age of Jehoiachin in Exile, 40:1–44:23

The generation of the EXILE still falls under Babylonian rule. Most of the people who once lived in Judah are scattered over the Near East. Only a tiny group survives among the ruins in Jerusalem.

This section announces a pivotal change in God's strategy. It is counterpart to chap. 6. The era in which Israel was fated for destruction has come to an end; a new day of grace and blessing is decreed. The central theme for the section is Israel's new calling, which will be symbolized in the restoration of Jerusalem.

In order to distinguish this section, when chaps. 1–39 were considered to have been written in the eighth century, historical critical scholarship referred to chaps. 40–48 as "Second Isaiah" and claimed that they were written during the Exile. When the entire Book of Isaiah is thought of as having been written in the fifth century—the perspective of this commentary—such a distinction is no longer necessary (see Introduction).

Nonetheless, the recognition that the earlier chapters are understood to fall under the judgment notice of chap. 6 underscores the importance of recognizing the bright new vision of God's grace for Israel that is announced after the fall of Jerusalem.

Prologue: In the Hall of Voices, 40:1-9

The context of this scene is apparently the same throne room described in chap. 6. The announcement of judgment (see commentary at 6:9-13 above) has already been made. Here only the reactions to the announcement are heard.

The announcement is repeated: *Comfort! Comfort my people!* (v. 1). The command comes from God and is directed to Jerusalem as a notice that all the penalty anticipated in chap. 6 has now been paid. The account is completely closed.

Now voices fill the throne room. To fulfill the command to be comforted, preparations must be made for the divine visit. A royal road must be built for the appearance that is expected.

One voice commands *Cry!* But another responds in confusion, *What shall I cry?* And the question is supported by the observation that *all people are grass* (v. 6), implying that they are hardly worth the effort. The first voice responds that the motivation for their message comes from God's command, not an evaluation of the stability of the people because *the word of our God will stand forever* (v. 8).

Like a Shepherd, 40:10-31

God's announced return to his city is described to be like that of a conquering king taking charge of a city. The LORD comes in power, bringing rewards. The royal motif of v. 10 is expanded to include images of a shepherd in v. 11. God's rewards include food and nurture, protection and direction.

The announcement of God's return is met with skepticism, not only in the heavenly council (40:6b), but also in Israel (v. 27). The speeches beginning in v. 12 take on a defensive tone, explaining how God can and will accomplish a return to Jerusalem.

God is great enough to create the worlds and the heavens. The Creator does not rely on someone else for direction and instruction in matters of justice. The LORD moves among the nations as a sovereign God, greater than all of the peoples of the earth.

The challenge continues in v. 18. The skeptics are scorned because they could find nothing or no one to compare with God. No idol is sufficient. They are asked why they do not know. The LORD controls the heavens and history; nothing and no one stands above God. Again the skeptics are challenged to look up at the stars and ask: *Who created these?* (v. 26).

Then Israel is addressed directly (v. 27). Who is Israel at this time? The people of the Northern Kingdom had been scattered over Assyrian territory almost two hundred years before. Judeans were in exile in Babylonia, in Egypt, and a few were still near the ruins of Jerusalem in Palestine. It is no wonder that Israel should be confused about its own identity, not to mention its relation to the LORD.

These people could legitimately wonder what their *way* (v. 27) under God was, or what rights they possessed. This section is addressed to confused Israel, assuring them of God's continued interest in them. It suggests that they may discover their identity as a people in their relation to the LORD. God has not forgotten or abandoned them or the divine hope for them.

Verse 28 reminds the people that the LORD is the Creator whose goals and purposes have persisted from the beginning of time. God's patience and strength are undiminished. The LORD's strength is given to *the faint* and *the powerless*. Lacking these is no excuse for lack of faith. Then the persons who are eligible to be part of the new Israel are identified: *those who wait for the LORD*. This wording will appear several more times in the book.

Those who wait for the LORD (v. 31) can participate in the LORD's renewed activities. This verse is one of the most encouraging confessions found in all of scripture.

Israel Is the LORD's Servant, 41:1-20

The scene continues. The LORD assembles the peoples of Palestine. The *coast-lines* (v. 1) are the habitations of the Philistines and the Phoenicians. *The ends of the earth* (v. 5) should probably be translated "the borders of the land" and refer to the areas that mark the outer border of CANAAN. The groups are summoned to hear the LORD's case: the claim that he is acting faithfully with Israel.

The LORD's evidence is the approach of a new military power in *the east* (v. 2). The historical background for this scene is the status quo that has held firm in the region since the fall of Assyria. Three powers vied to be Assyria's heir. Media agreed with Babylon that it would concentrate on territory to the east and north of Mesopotamia while Babylon could concentrate on Palestine and Egypt. Babylon had used this agreement to consolidate its power in those areas. It defeated Egyptian armies and occupied Palestine, finally destroying Jerusalem and taking Judeans into exile in the process. However, after the death of Nebuchadnezzar, Babylon became complacent and soft.

Meanwhile, Media had expanded its power eastward almost to India and westward into Asia Minor, and after half a century of that arrangement was restless to press on to greater things. There was news of a young prince from a Persian tribe who experienced a spectacular rise and led a combined Median-Persian empire in a series of victories that stripped away Babylon's defenses in the east and the north. These are the historical developments to which vv. 2-3 point.

The LORD asks the rhetorical question: *Who has . . . done this?* Verse 4 provides the answer: *I, the LORD, have done this; I have called the generations from the beginning.* The LORD is not only the creator of heavens and earth, but claims to be the LORD of all history as well.

The coastlands have seen the events that have reshaped the region. They are afraid and prepare for the inevitable as only an idolater can. But from Israel something different is expected. Israel is reminded of who it is, from whom it has come, and what its relation to the LORD is. Israel is the LORD's servant, especially chosen. Israel comes from Abraham, and is the fulfillment of God's promise to God's friend.

Israel is reminded that God has taken it *from the ends of the earth* calling it to be the LORD's *servant* (v. 8). Then comes the most important part: Israel has been *chosen . . . and not cast . . . off* (v. 9). Israel must not interpret the actions that brought an end to the kingdoms, destroyed Jerusalem, and scattered the peoples as abrogating God's special relation to the children of Abraham. The LORD still considers them to be God's people and the heirs of the promises to Abraham.

If Israel is indeed still God's people, and if indeed the LORD is the one bringing the invader *from the east*, they should have nothing to fear. God assures them that *I am with you* and that *I am your God*. Further, the LORD promises to help them with a *victorious right hand* (v. 10). The promise apparently means that the victorious invader will be a benefit to Israel.

Verses 11-13 deal with Israel's problems with groups that hate them and persecute them. Those enemies will disappear when it becomes evident that the LORD protects Israel.

Verses 14-16 contrast the way Israel thinks of itself, as a *worm* or an *insect*, with the power of God. The *Redeemer is the Holy One of Israel*, a title for God that is typical in the Book of Isaiah. It combines the majestic idea of the Holy One with the identification with Israel that makes God so personal and near.

God is going to make Israel an instrument capable of threshing mountains. The role of the nation will be important and great, and the people will rejoice in the LORD.

Verses 17-20 consider the situation Israel faces in terms of being *poor and needy*, with no resources. They face the need of water, a constant worry in Palestine, especially now that the land has been in ruins and uncultivated for so long. Then the passage becomes a reminder of an old theme in the Bible: God is the source of rain and of the life it brings. God promises to provide the water needed to make the land bloom again. The restoration of the land will be a testimony that God has acted again.

The Trial Continues, 41:21–42:12

The coastlands and the borderlands continue to serve as witnesses. The case against Israel continues to identify idolatry as the main cause for its blindness and unwillingness to assume the role for which it has been prepared, and to which it is called.

In vv. 21-24 the LORD's advocate speaks, challenging the idols. The LORD picks up the argument in vv. 25-29, asserting again that God is sovereign.

In 42:1-4 the LORD presents the *servant*, designated to implement justice, the result of the LORD's verdict, first among *the nations* and then in the land (NRSV *the earth*) where the *coastlands wait for* his instructions (the servant role is assigned to CYRUS in chaps. 44 and 45). The servant will avoid ostentation and arrogance; his patient persistence will succeed.

42:5-7 identifies the LORD as creator of heavens and earth and sustainer of the life of all people, before the passage returns to address the servant, defining his role. The servant is to be *a covenant to the people, a light to the nations*. He is to enlighten and to free captive peoples.

42:6-7 appears to address those who stand by. The LORD claims his victory, implies that Cyrus is the fulfillment of his prediction (cf. chaps. 44–45), and now looks ahead to new things. The servants of the LORD have been shown to be Israel and Cyrus. Each of them has a distinct task in separate spheres.

42:10-12 is a hymn calling on the witnesses, coastlands and borderlands, to join in praising the LORD. Under David all these countries had been under the rule of the LORD. Now they are called to worship God, but the relation is religious, not political.

Hear, You Deaf! 42:13–43:21

The passage is a unit with five major parts; once again the form is chiastic (cf. the commentary at 10:24–12:4; 17:1–20:6; 23:1–27:13, above):

A—A presentation concerning Israel and what is happening to her, 42:13-25
 B—A speech promising salvation to Israel, 43:1-7
Keystone: A trial speech against idols, 43:8-13
 B'—A speech promising salvation to Israel, 43:14-15
A'—A closing argument, 43:16-21

Isaiah 42:13-17 introduces the LORD as *a soldier* roused to action without violent results. God the soldier *will lead the blind* (v. 16) in new directions. Perhaps *the blind* represent Israel. The LORD's work will shame all of those people who trust in idols.

Isaiah 42:18-22 appeals to the deaf servants to heed the LORD's servant. This must be an allusion to Cyrus, but Israel is too bruised and broken to respond.

Isaiah 42:23-25 identifies the LORD as the one who turned Israel over to those who preyed on them because of their sins.

Isaiah 43:1-7 identifies the LORD as the one who made Israel in the first place. The passage twice calls on Israel not to fear (vv. 1, 5). First Israel belongs to the LORD who is the savior. Then God is with Israel and will return its sons and daughters from far places because they have been formed for God's glory.

Isaiah 43:8-13 proposes a contest. The people *who are blind, yet have eyes* must refer to Israel. They are summoned to the contest. On one side are the nations. They are challenged to bring witness concerning anyone among them who predicted the coming of Cyrus. Then Israel is summoned to witness that the LORD has predicted the coming of Cyrus and has used him to save the people. The LORD alone is worthy to be God.

Isaiah 43:14-15 claims that the LORD has sent Cyrus to Babylon for Israel's sake. Therefore the LORD deserves to be known as Israel's king.

Isaiah 43:16-21 refers first to the EXODUS and God's victory there, then it calls attention to the *new thing* (v. 19) that the LORD is about to do. This time God will lead the people through the wilderness instead of the sea. They are God's own people, created by the LORD in order that they can declare praise to the Creator.

Remember These, Jacob! 43:22–44:23

Isaiah 43:22-28 is a judgment speech against Israel. The nation has worshiped other gods, but the LORD forgave those sins. God has not abandoned Israel, even though, from its first ancestor (probably Jacob) on, the nation has sinned. Because of these sins God has given Israel over to punishment.

Isaiah 44:1-5 announces a decision in the judgment. It begins with a confirmation that Israel is God's servant—*hear, O Jacob my servant, Israel whom I have chosen.* A decision has been reached in the heavenly council. The LORD will bring new life: water on the parched land, spirit on the new generation. A revival of hope is in store for Israel.

Isaiah 44:6-8 is the third speech by the LORD in this section. It begins with the herald's introduction and ends with the admission of the witnesses. The heart of it is the LORD's claim to be the unique and dominant factor in all that is happening on Israel's behalf. He alone is God.

Isaiah 44:9-20 is a dialogue that makes fun of makers of idols. It breaks the series of speeches by the LORD with an almost comic relief.

Isaiah 44:21-23 reiterates the LORD's announcement that Israel is his servant, that its sins have been removed. God calls Israel to return to him, now that redemption is achieved. Verse 23 closes the section with a call to *heavens* and *earth* to recognize with praise the great event of the LORD's act of redemption with praise.

The Vision of the Age of Cyrus, 44:24–48:22

Cyrus leads a Persian army to Babylon in 739 B.C.E. fulfilling the LORD's words in 41:2-3 and 42:1-4, 6-7. The city is opened to him and he occupies it without a battle, thereby falling heir to the Babylonian empire.

This part of the Vision introduces Cyrus to Israel as the LORD's servant, interprets his role as it relates to Israel's in restoring Jerusalem, rebuilding the Temple and freeing the captives. The LORD urges Israel to accept the plan and insists that Israel is still God's chosen servant.

Babylon's humiliation in having idols moved through the streets is described as a part of the submission to an invader. A final scene describes preparations for an expedition from Babylon to Jerusalem that may be the one described in Ezra 1:8 under the leadership of Sheshbbazzar.

The LORD Introduces Cyrus, 44:24–45:13

The setting is still in the heavenly court, but a new cycle of themes begins with attention on CYRUS. The speeches are in hymnic style, but the tone of disputation is still there. This passage is a bridge between the EXILE and the return to Jerusalem. The themes of redemption, creation, ridicule of idolatry, fulfillment of prophecy, and the rehabilitation of Jerusalem are continued. The role of Cyrus now turns to the subjects that will dominate the rest of the book: the restoration of Jerusalem and the Temple.

44:24-28. To Israel. The LORD introduces himself as Israel's *Redeemer*, and also the creator of all that exists. God is also the one who fulfills valid prophecy, the one who can make prophesied events come to pass. As Creator the LORD is in control of all nature. The point of the introduction is clear: God is the one who has called Cyrus to rebuild Jerusalem.

45:1-7. To Cyrus. The LORD addresses *his anointed* one who has been led to victory after victory. God has chosen him to *subdue nations . . . and kings*. The LORD has gone ahead of Cyrus's armies, smoothing his way and giving his enemies' treasures into his hand. God has done all this so Cyrus may know the LORD and know he is being blessed for Israel's sake.

45:8-13. To Israel. The LORD asserts again his position as Creator and claims the right to determine Israel's way. God threatens anyone who questions the deity's right to shape history. As Creator of the world the LORD claims the right to decide that Cyrus will rebuild Jerusalem.

Righteousness and Strength Are in the LORD, 45:14-25

This passage takes the form of a dialogue between the LORD and Cyrus. The emperor is promised success in his campaign against Egypt. Cyrus is amazed and confesses surprise at Israel's good fortune. He congratulates Israel.

The LORD repeats his claims and his intentions (vv. 18c-19). Cyrus calls refugees of the nations of Palestine to assemble. The LORD tells them to recognize that he has brought this about.

Cyrus calls for the borderlands to recognize him, pay tribute, and avoid military action. The LORD adds his support, legitimatizing Cyrus's right to rule the region. Cyrus proclaims that everyone must submit to him, since the LORD has approved him. Someone observes that Cyrus cannot be stopped and that Israel will be protected.

Bel Bows . . . the LORD's Purpose Stands, 46:1-13

The fall of Babylon to Persia was a most humiliating defeat to its gods, as it was to the rulers. Idols had been moved about to protect them during the war. Their helplessness was obvious.

On the other hand, exilic Israel's fortunes have been enhanced. The LORD claims credit for this turn of events. God has cared for Israel in the time of need.

The LORD calls on Israel to remember the *former things* (v. 9), undoubtedly referring to the centuries that have passed, with their heavy weight of invasion and judgment. The LORD then announces again the decision to put salvation in Zion. Jerusalem is the chosen instrument for these latter times.

Sit in the Dust, Babylon! 47:1-15

The LORD addresses conquered Babylon in a sarcastic and taunting tone, similar to that found in chap. 14. The address begins with a metaphor: the princess has become a slave. A choral section follows, expressing Israel's recognition of God and the judgment that falls over Babylon.

A taunt that notes the reversal of fortunes follows. Babylon is accused here in the same way its king was accused in chap. 14 of having failed to recognize the LORD's hand in all the events.

Babylon had trusted in its oracles and charms. But those in their demonic nature turned back against her and brought about her doom. The last verses mock Babylon's helplessness.

Move out from Babylon! 48:1-22

Israel is summoned to listen to the LORD's speeches. The people are recognized as bearing the name, descending from Judah, and worshiping in the LORD's name. But they have been hypocrites, not worshiping sincerely. They are summoned to hear two speeches of the LORD.

48:3-11. The LORD's first speech. The LORD repeats the previous claims that have foretold the events. But Israel has been deaf, rebellious, and unreliable. The people must still be refined (cf. 1:25).

48:12-20. Dialogue with a chosen leader. The LORD repeats his claims as Creator. A leader picks up the call to Israel in v. 14, calling on Israel to gather, recognize the LORD's fulfillment, and listen.

The LORD repeats that God is the one who has brought Cyrus to power and that it had been announced openly. The leader then claims that the LORD has sent him and granted him the divine spirit. He cites the LORD's presence and promise to accompany them on the way.

The LORD's "if only" speech maintains that none of this exile and return would have been necessary if only Israel had obeyed from the beginning.

The leader calls for the people to move out from Babylon. He calls ahead for Canaan to know: *The LORD has redeemed his servant Jacob!* (v. 20).

The final verses (21-22) signal a distinction between two kinds of Israelites. God's providence watches over those who take up the pilgrimage. But those who are adversaries of God and the group that rally to him shall have *no peace*.

The Vision of the Age of Darius, 49:1–57:21

The Book of Ezra refers to three great Persian emperors who proclaimed or confirmed an order to build the Temple in Jerusalem. CYRUS issued the decree.

DARIUS confirmed the decree for ZERUBABBEL. This commentary suggests that Isa 49–57 should be read against the background of the generation of Darius (522–486 B.C.E.)

The Servant of Rulers, 49:1–50:3

49:1-21. A light to nations. The opening speech, the first part of which (vv. 1-6) is often treated by scholars as the second of the "servant songs," is addressed to *coastlands* and *peoples from far away*. These may well be the nations in Palestine along the coast and in the interior. The speaker identifies himself as *Israel* (v. 3). He recites his testimony to having been called by the LORD before birth. The calling was to be the LORD's servant *in whom he will be glorified* (v. 3). But it had not worked out that way; God knows why not.

A second voice answers with a similar testimony to having been called of the LORD. But his task is *to bring Jacob back to him* (v. 5). In contrast to the first voice, this one testifies that he has been honored in the LORD's sight and received his strength from God. Cyrus received a similar command in 45:13; here the command is renewed to Darius to fulfill what Cyrus had not completed.

The commission is enlarged to include becoming *a light to nations* (v. 6). Darius has become the LORD's instrument to extend his salvation *to the end of the earth. Earth* may also be translated "land"; if so it refers to the farthest extent of the land of Canaan, that is, to all Palestine.

A second ORACLE is recited in v. 7. The speaker of v. 5 is now described. He is one *deeply despised, abhorred by the nations, the slave of rulers*. Darius had been a lowly aide to emperor Cambyses, with no royal status, no position in line for the throne.

The oracle proclaims that recognition and status await him because *of the LORD . . . who has chosen him* (v. 7). Darius's success in establishing his throne and authority over the Empire is attributed to being chosen by the LORD. Darius in fact did gain complete control of the government in all the parts of the existing empire and then proceeded to enlarge it to become the largest empire known to that time.

A second oracle (vv. 8-12) gives the LORD's speech. This is a favorable time, a time of salvation in which God addresses Darius. The LORD has protected Darius and gives him *as a covenant of people*. Darius becomes the way the LORD expresses his faithful relation to the people *to establish the land* of Canaan for them. They will be assigned portions they may cultivate.

Darius's assignment includes freeing the exiled prisoners so that they can return. The LORD will care for them on the way as he did for those that came out of Egypt. Everything will be done to facilitate their return. They will come from far away, and from all directions. The land that is named in v. 12, *Syene*, is unknown. Some have thought it referred to China, others to a city on the Egyptian border.

Verse 13 begins with an address to *heavens and . . . earth*, as in 1:2. They are called to rejoice because the LORD *has comforted his people* (cf. 40:1, 10).

In v. 14 Zion enters the conversation. Zion complains, as Israel had done in v. 4, that *the LORD has forsaken and forgotten me.* The LORD protests that this is not so. He tells of growth and buildings, of increased population and prosperity, all proof that Zion has not been abandoned.

49:22–50:3. Even the captives of a tyrant. The LORD continues with an oracle to the effect that he will use the rulers of nations to rescue Jerusalem. When it happens, Jerusalem will know that the LORD is God. Then the book picks up a theme from 40:31 concerning *those who wait for the LORD.* The theme will appear repeatedly to the end of the book. Those who wait will not be put to shame; they will be vindicated.

Zion is still skeptical. *Can prey be taken from the mighty? Can the captives of a tyrant be rescued?* (v. 24). They have become convinced of the kind of power and absolute authority that the great empires possessed and used. They do not believe anyone, even God, can overcome that. The people of Zion have missed the point of these chapters. The emperors have been made God's servants. The LORD will not act against them, but use them to do his will.

The LORD answers that rescue is possible—and will be done. When it is done, not only Zion, but *all flesh shall know* that God has done it and that Israel and Zion enjoy God's special favor.

In 50:1 the LORD addresses Zion concerning the complaint that it had been abandoned. God asks for proof that Zion had been deserted. God did not do it. Zion was sold as a slave, but its own sinfulness was the cause. It was the people who had abandoned God, and who did not respond when the LORD called.

Then God protests that the divine strength and abilities are as secure as ever. The LORD can deliver or redeem. The language returns to the argument of chaps. 40–41 that God has clothed *the heavens* (v. 3). If the LORD can *clothe the heavens*, surely salvation from tyrants is also possible.

A Student's Tongue, 50:4–51:8

Verses 4-9 are thought to be one of the "servant songs" of Isaiah 40–55, but the passage does not speak of a "servant." Servant language appears outside the unit in v. 10. The first person speech is from a self-described *teacher.* He has been trained and disciplined for the task of *sustaining the weary with a word.*

The teacher is also a pacifist who accepts abuse rather than striking back. He claims the LORD's support and urges his adversaries to confront him. The teacher is confident that the LORD will vindicate him.

Who is this person? Who are his adversaries? This teacher and leader in the age of Darius should be one that represents the LORD's cause in restoring Jerusalem. The Books of Haggai and Zechariah are set in this period. The prophets and and also the priest, Joshua, support the leadership of ZERUBBABEL in efforts to rebuild the Temple. Ezra 3 tells of Zerubbabel's actions in beginning the Temple. Ezra 4:1-4 speaks of adversaries who managed to frustrate the efforts and delay completion for a long time. Perhaps Isaiah's suffering teacher-leader portrays the role of Zerubbabel.

A strong and authoritative voice claiming to represent the servant (Darius) calls for trust in the LORD. He promises to suppress the agitators. He rallies those who *pursue righteousness, [and]* . . . *seek the LORD* (51:1). They are urged to remember what God did for Abraham. They are reminded of God's promise now to *comfort Zion.*

A strong speech closes the section. It is addressed to *my people.* The speech could be understood as spoken by the LORD, yet a number of features, such as *my justice for a light to the peoples* (v. 4), echo the words to the servant in 49:6, a servant whom we identified as Darius. If this is Darius's speech, too, then it is one in which he appeals to the religious traditions and faith of the people in Jerusalem. He claims that his power and authority are being recognized in Palestine and that this established order is to be permanent. He then calls on them to trust his commission to rebuild the city and the Temple.

Awake! Put on Strength! 51:9–52:12

51:9–52:2. Celebrate deliverance. Choral exhortations and the LORD's own words respond to the political challenge uttered in the preceding section. The combination of the words of the chorus and the words of the LORD recognize the events as the LORD's work, comparable to the work in creation when *Rahab,* . . . *the dragon* (v. 9) was destroyed. The returning Judaeans are called the LORD's ransomed ones. They return with joy and singing.

The LORD is identified as the one who *comforts you* (v. 12). Then God addresses the fears of the people; whom they fear is not identified. Perhaps it is the same adversary who persecuted the teacher in 50:4-9. The adversary is certainly *only a human being who fades like grass,* as the voice in 40:6 said. Fear can only come because they have forgotten the LORD under the oppression of that time. But relief is promised for the oppressed, for the LORD who redeems them is the same.

This LORD who stirs up the storms at sea is the same one who has *put my words in your mouth* (v. 16). Israel's and Zion's great treasure is the word of God, which they are to proclaim and confess. This is their calling, as it was for the teacher in 50:4. The LORD has *hidden them in the shadow of his hand.* Israel complained of being hidden in 49:2. But even as he hid them, the LORD had assured Zion: *You are my people.*

The people of Zion are called to rouse themselves from the stupor caused by the events of the past generations when the city was destroyed and left in ruins. Now the LORD promises an end to that. The cup *of staggering* (v. 17) is the fate that caused the destruction of Jerusalem. Now it is being passed on to the oppressors who have walked on them during the time of their humiliation (v. 23).

Jerusalem is called to celebrate its deliverance. The city is no longer a captive, no longer a prey to any alien who chose to enter it.

52:3-12. The messenger who announces peace. The LORD announces his presence in Zion and compares it to the divine appearance in Egypt to deliver the Israelites centuries before. Just as at that time Israel came to recognize who the LORD was both through appearance and action, so this generation will come to know God through the events of the day.

There is a joyous recognition of the approach of messengers who come to proclaim peace. This *peace* is much more than the cessation of war. It announces a coming health and wholeness for the city. This *peace* is nothing less than salvation for the ruined city. The messengers who were ordered sent in 40:1, 9-11 have finally arrived.

The message they bring is found in vv. 9-10. The people in Zion are to rejoice *for the LORD has comforted his people.* The arm God *bares* represents the Persian emperors and their commitment to rebuild the Temple. God's presence in history will become clear to all the surrounding peoples who will see the rebuilding as the salvation of Israel's God.

Verses 11-12 renew the call to *Depart*, first heard in 48:20. The call is for priests and Levites to return, being careful to purify themselves for the travel so that they can be ready to serve on the sacred grounds when they arrive. But they must go with dignity. This is not a backdoor escape. The LORD, the God of Israel, will both lead them and protect their flanks as they travel.

Restoration Pains in Jerusalem, 52:13–54:17b

52:13–53:12. The punishment that made us whole. A number of themes that have been introduced in earlier passages come to a crisis and conclusion in this passage. The LORD's exclamation: *See, my servant prospers, is exalted, is very high* (52:13) opens the section. Two servants were introduced in chap 49. One was Israel; the other we identified as DARIUS, later successor to CYRUS, the servant of chap 45. It seems more likely that this acclamation greets Darius's success in establishing himself as emperor. Verses 14-15 fulfill the announcement in 49:7. The success of the servant is unexpected and the rulers are astonished.

The first verse of chap. 53 presents another incredible report. This is often interpreted as a reference to the servant of the previous verses but that is not necessarily the case. I take it to refer to another person, one who also grew up without promise of great things. He was despised, a man of pains. There is an echo here of the persecuted teacher of 50:4-8, but now a chorus recognizes that the blows he received were their fault. He had carried the burden on their behalf. They had earlier thought this one to be punished by God. Now they recognize that it was their rebellions that caused his suffering. Because he was punished, they were exonerated. Everyone confesses his own part in the guilt but recognizes that for some unexplained reason the LORD had laid on him the iniquity of them all.

In v. 7 the address changes. It is no longer a chorus. Someone speaks of the afflicted person. He is compared to *a lamb that is led to the slaughter.* The persecution led to his death. *He was cut off from the land of the living* by no fault of his own. It happened because of *the rebellion of my people.* Here is that phrase again: *my people.* It occurred in 51:4 where it could have been spoken by the LORD or by Darius. I chose Darius then. If this is Darius speaking here, he is recognizing Zerubbabel's innocence.

But in v. 10 he recognizes the LORD's hand in what has happened. He sees the death *as an offering for sin* through which Zerubbabel will succeed as he never could have in life. *Through him the will of the LORD shall prosper.*

In v. 11 it is difficult to determine to whom the pronouns refer. Suppose we read it as a speech from the LORD: "Out of Zerubbabel's anguish, Darius will see. He will be satisfied. In knowing (about) Zerubbabel, my Servant (Darius) becomes a righteous one for many and will forgive their wrongs."

This passage is ambiguous in many ways and this proposed reconstruction is only one of many ways to view the original meaning of the passage. What is clear is that someone has been killed and the people confess that much of the fault was their own. This person died in their stead. Then this is understood to have been God's will through which a redemption was achieved for the people. The death is perceived as a sort of human sacrifice through which good things came for the people because God accepted it that way.

The NT has used the interpretation of a vicarious sacrifice as a model in explaining the death of Jesus on the cross (Luke 22:37; Matt 27:57-60; Acts 8:32-33). Few modern readers can read these words in Isaiah without hearing the music of Handel's *Messiah* throbbing in the background.

Verse 12 announces the rehabilitation of the name and rights of the one who had died because he had allowed himself to be executed and in so doing he bore the sin of many.

54:1-17b. *Sing, O barren one!* This chapter returns to the call for celebration and joy. Jerusalem is addressed. The barrenness refers to the years of lying in ruins since the destruction of the city over sixty years before. Now the growth of the city will be unbelievably rapid. Jerusalem will have to spread out on all sides to accommodate the increase.

The city must not be afraid. All the changes are due to God's work. The LORD is called both *Maker* and *husband* (v. 5). The God of the whole earth is the redeemer of Jerusalem. What a tremendous thought! Our personal God, who answers our prayers, is the Creator of all things, the LORD of all.

Zion is being called to resume her position after having been *like a wife forsaken* (v. 6), one who has been *cast off.* The LORD recognizes that briefly she has been abandoned; he has hidden his face. But now God moves toward reconciliation, showing compassion and everlasting love. He will gather Zion to himself again.

The LORD swears that this abandonment will not happen again. As in Noah's time, judgment came. But God swore never to send a flood again. The mountains might disappear, but God's *steadfast love shall not* be removed again (v. 10). His compassion is Zion's again.

Zion's restoration is happening. The walls and towers will be built in fine stones. All the children are to be taught by the LORD. The city's future is secure. Anyone striving against Zion cannot claim support from the LORD. God claims to be the creator of power, even the power to destroy, but nothing that is fashioned to be used against Zion will succeed.

A House of Prayer for All Peoples, 54:17c–56:8

This passage announces a great invitation to the LORD's house of prayer. It anticipates the soon completion of the goal announced in 2:4. In 54:17c this hope for completion is announced as *the heritage of the servants of the LORD*. For the first time "servants" occurs in the plural. It refers to the congregation of individual Israelites who choose to worship the LORD. The change is significant, recognizing that not all Israelites want to belong to the Israel of God.

With that in mind the call goes out to assemble all those who choose to serve the LORD. What is offered has no price. It is nothing less than an *everlasting covenant* (v. 3). God's love for David is legendary; now that same love is offered to anyone who will come to God.

David had been called to be *a witness to the peoples* (v. 4). Now the new Israel will understate the task that the Davidic kings used to have. Now the gathered Israel of covenant faith *will call nations that [they] do not know* (v. 5) and they will run to them. They will come because the LORD their God has glorified them. The world of Jewish proselytes comes into view.

The great invitation continues in classic words: *Seek the LORD while he may be found* (v. 6). Even the wicked are called to repent, with the promise of abundant pardon. God declares that divine thoughts are different from human thoughts. His grace is of a sort unknown to human reason. It is higher and greater.

God speaks of the efficacy of his *word* (v. 11). It will accomplish the mission given to it. A symbol of all this will be the evidences that God has led his people back to their land. All nature will be glad. Its flowering will be *a memorial, an everlasting sign* (v. 13).

God has expectations for this new people. *Justice* and right conduct are the order of the day, *for salvation will come; deliverance will be revealed* (56:1). An additional sign of blessing is the keeping of SABBATH. The prophetic emphasis on justice and the priestly emphasis on Sabbath are included and blended.

This is to be an inclusive fellowship. The law normally excluded foreigners. Ezra 10 demanded that all foreign wives be divorced and excluded. Yet there are many signs in the law codes that efforts were made to include foreign bond servants in some of the worship forms. But 56:3 calls on foreigners who have joined themselves to the LORD to have no reason to feel separate or threatened.

Another group that was traditionally excluded were EUNUCHs (see Lev 21:20-21; Deut 23:1). They, too, are urged to feel welcome if they keep sabbath, choose the things that please the LORD, and keep covenant. They have no chance of having children to perpetuate their names. But the LORD will give them both *a monument and a name, better than sons or daughters* (v. 5).

The foreigners who answer the invitation, minister to the LORD, love his name, become his servants, keep sabbath and covenant, will be brought to the holy mountain. The words echo the vision of 2:2-4. They may rejoice in God's house, which is here called his *house of prayer* (v. 7). Burnt offerings and sacrifices will be accepted from them. It will be called *a house of prayer for all peoples.*

The section ends by saying that God's efforts to bring in foreigners and eunuchs will reach out to gather still others to join them. One is reminded of Jesus' parable about the wedding feast (Matt 22).

Rebellion, but Healing, 56:9–57:21

56:9–57:13. The dark side of Jerusalem. The positive and joyful tone of the preceding chapters is interrupted by a very negative and violent section. Not everything is right about Jerusalem.

The watchmen and shepherds are *blind* (56:10) and drunken (56:12). They are unable or unwilling to defend the people from the wild animals. The watchmen are called dogs who are blind and silent. They have great appetites. The shepherds are more concerned with drinking than with shepherding.

This state of affairs puts righteous people at risk. They perish and no one takes note. *Taken away* (57:1) must mean taken to prison. Apparently the innocent are jailed for standing up to the violent ones. God promises that things will be corrected for the righteous when peace comes.

The harsh words that follow are directed to the wicked who obviously have not answered the invitation. Verses 3-5 are addressed to a masculine group. They are called *children of a sorceress, . . . offspring of an adulterer and a whore.* Their mocking ways and lustful behavior, even including the slaughter of children, are castigated.

In v. 6 the address changes to a feminine singular, apparently addressed to pagan Jerusalem. She is both pagan and carnal. And her philandering ways are chronicled.

Verse 11 questions the reasons for such conduct. Who could they have feared so much that they forgot the LORD? God's silence meant that they had no reason to plead that they were terrified of him. God will recognize all their rights and their works, but these do not help. Let their idols help them in their distress. The paragraph ends on a positive note of promise, however, that *whoever takes refuge in [God] . . . shall possess the land* (v. 11). The ancient promise of the land (cf. Gen 12:1-3) echoes here. More importantly, those who flee to the LORD will *inherit [God's] holy mountain.* A place in the assembly in God's presence will be their lot.

57:14-21. I will heal them. The pendulum swings back to a positive word. Verse 14 picks up the practical instructions for the returning group from 48:20 and 52:11-12. The building project is a highway for the pilgrims and returnees as in 40:3-4.

Verse 15 announces that the LORD has taken up his dwelling in the Temple in Jerusalem. God is introduced as *the high and lofty one*, a description fitting for the one who will inhabit *the high and holy place* (v. 15). *Who inhabits eternity* is literally "one who dwells on and on." The language here is similar to that in Pss 33:21, 103:1, and 145:21.

But God is not only to be understood in terms of the Temple's Holy of Holies. The LORD also wants to be known as the spirit who dwells with the contrite and humble in spirit (v. 15), presumably wherever they are. The reason for God's indwelling presence is to revive the spirits and hearts of those who seek him.

Verses 16-18 is a concise apologetic for the way God has acted toward Israel. It begins with the insistence that God will not always be *angry* and accusing, else the spirits and the souls that he has created would grow faint and die. This is an admission that God has been angry and accusing toward the people.

The LORD explains this anger in terms of the *wicked covetousness* of the people. In anger God struck them. This image refers to the historical judgments against Israel through invasions and the judgments through droughts and earthquakes. God says *I hid* from the people, a reference to God's being absent from the Temple when it was destroyed and not answering prayers. The people had complained that God had abandoned them. God says that was true because he was angry with them on account of their sins.

The most disheartening thing to God was that the people kept turning back to their own ways, the conduct that had occasioned divine wrath in the first place. God's frustration in dealing with a people who do not learn from punishment is recounted throughout the book.

In v. 18 the gospel, the good news, comes. God has *seen their ways* of sin and always falling back into rebellion. In spite of that the LORD has determined to *heal them*. The healing process has three stages. God will *lead them* into a way of life fitting for his presence. This may include leading them on the return to Jerusalem.

The second is *repaying them with comfort*. Chap. 40 began with the announcement that God had ordered comfort for his people. This is strengthening of spirit and soul, as v. 15 has said. It includes providing the necessities for their restoration, including the building of the Temple.

The third provision is *creating* for *their mourners* the words that will bring life and hope. "Creating" is the strongest word for God's action that one can use. *The fruit of the lips* is a flowery term for "words." Those words of comfort and restoration are: *Peace, peace, to the far and the near, says the LORD*. What could be better to enunciate the good news that God has determined to *heal them*.

Verses 20-21 give the other side of the hard-earned knowledge that comes from experience. Not all Israel belong to the contrite and the humble, or to those who answer the invitation given in chap. 55 and in many other places. The book has shown repeatedly the dark side of Israel's being. *The wicked* remain. The word can also be translated "the adversaries." They remain stubbornly adverse to everything

God stands for. They are restless and unable to achieve the stillness that characterizes the humble and the contrite. They cannot "wait for the LORD." And their restlessness stirs up the ugly *mire* and *mud* of their inner beings.

The peace God proclaims for the humble and contrite of Israel cannot come to these adversaries. *There is no peace, says my God, for the wicked.* This closing refrain repeats that of 48:22. The final verses of the book will be a variation on this theme.

The Vision of the Age of Artaxerxes, 58:1–66:24

At the end of the reign of Xerxes conditions in Palestine deteriorated. The government had lost control and lawless bands roamed the countryside. When ARTAXERXES took the throne, hope for improvement brought calls for reform in Jerusalem. When stable Persian control was reestablished, the city and the Temple were rebuilt under EZRA and NEHEMIAH.

The LORD's Kind of Fast, 58:1-14

Chapter 58 begins with the LORD's command (vv. 1-2) to announce to his people *their rebellion*. The recipients of this announcement are to be God's people, *the house of Jacob*. The language is reminiscent of chap.1. Although the northern kingdom has long since been destroyed and Judah has also been exiled, God is thinking of the remaining and returning people as the children of Israel, as the LORD's people.

They are religious and want to do right. Yet they must be deemed rebellious and sinful. Things haven't changed much since chap. 1. But this discrepancy between religious intention and perceived rebellion cries out for definition and explanation.

The people in Judah respond with a complaint (v. 3ab). They ask why their religious observances and fasts, particularly, have not gotten a favorable response from God. They think of fasting and prostrating themselves in prayer as things that will elicit the kinds of responses from God that they want.

God's command in v. 2 recognizes that these rebellious people are in fact a religious people. The answers to their questions begin with critiques of their fasts. The motivation for fasting is that they *serve their own interests* (v. 3) or find pleasure in fasting. Another reason, *[you] oppress all your workers*, uses an obscure Hebrew word related to a word meaning "be hurt, or be in pain." The ancient versions and NRSV have understood it to refer to oppression of workers.

A second answer (v. 4) points out that their fasting has led to contention and fighting. Such fasting is clearly not what God wants. Fasting became a common practice in the hard days of EXILE (cf. Lev. 23:26-32; Jer 36:9), but the prophets have frequently objected that God's requirements are not fasting from food, but kindness and justice (Mic 6:6-8; Jas 1:27).

Then the LORD speaks to the issue, defining the kind of fast or religious expression that God would choose (vv. 5-7). The LORD first asks whether self-denigration or groveling is what he wants, implying that it is not.

Verse 6 describes an exercise that promotes freedom that is a worthwhile activity, from God's point of view, or service that responds to the needs of the hungry, the homeless, the naked. That is true service that honors God. *To hide yourself from your own kin* (v. 7) must mean failure to perform the common decencies toward members of one's own family, such as caring for the elderly or ignoring an orphaned cousin, and so forth. One doing service to God doesn't fail to do those things.

That kind of worship and service brings beneficent response from God. When God's people act like that, all kinds of good things can happen (vv. 8-9). Light, healing and vindication will be the characteristics of their time. God's glory will be their protection. Then comes the real answer to the question in v. 2: *Then you shall call, and the LORD will answer* (v. 9).

Verses 9b-12 expand on the type of worship actions that will being God's blessings. They define the kind of community actions that will make the restorations that are being undertaken in Jerusalem a success.

Verses 13-14 relate these to SABBATH observance. The implication is that special fasts are really not necessary. The opportunities to keep Sabbath allow the people to worship in ways that please God. A major objection to the people's actions in this chapter involves *serving their own interests* (vv. 3, 13a, 13c).

Proper service is clearly that which serves God's interests and the needs of others.

Troubled Times in Judah, 59:1-15a

The chapter describes disturbed conditions in Judah. It first speaks from the objective viewpoint of outsiders (vv. 1-8), and then has insiders confessing their relation to the situation. It speaks of the evils:

in general	as *iniquities* (vv. 2, 12b)
	sins (vv. 2b, 12a)
	evil (v. 15a)
specifically as	violent deeds (vv. 3a, 6b, 7)
	lying speech (vv. 3b, 4b, 13b)
	mischief (vv. 4a, 5, 6a, 7b, 13b)
what is lacking	*righteousness* (vv. 4a, 9a, 14a)
	honesty, or truth (vv. 4a, 14a, 15)
	peace, or wholeness (vv. 8a, 8b)
	justice (vv. 8a, 9a, 11b, 14a)
	salvation (vv. 1, 11b)
results	rebellion (vv. 12, 13a)
	oppression (v. 13)
	insurrection (v. 13)

The situation is bad. There is no real government and therefore no peace, justice, or protection from violence. Yet the scene does not blame the outsiders for the troubles. It points its finger at the Judeans themselves. They blame God. But no one of them takes responsibility for action. The scene equates the chaotic conditions with religious sins and turning away from God.

The LORD Decides to Act, 59:15b-21

The first part of this section narrates the LORD's displeasure and response. If vv. 16b-17 are to be understood as we have understood chaps. 44–45 and 49, these must refer to the LORD's raising up a third Persian emperor to restore his people and his city. In this case it would be ARTAXERXES I. The chapter identifies the LORD's intention with Artaxerxes's military intervention in vv. 19-20.

In v. 21 the LORD addresses Artaxerxes, renewing God's covenant with Israel with the promise that his spirit will be on the Persian. His *words* are those spoken first to CYRUS and renewed to DARIUS, as related in the Book of Ezra.

Against this historical background, vv. 15b-20 described the way Artaxerxes enters Palestine as the LORD's instrument to correct the conditions portrayed in the last two chapters. Verses 18-19 indicate the Phoenician and Philistine territories that draw the primary attention of the Persians. V. 20 contrasts the way the invasion will impact Jerusalem, or at least those in Judah who turn away from rebellion.

Zion's Day Dawns, 60:1-22

The chapter builds upon chaps. 40 and 54. Jerusalem's good news is about to become reality. It is a time when light replaces darkness, when people come to Zion from everywhere (vv. 1-5a), and its poverty is to be replaced by riches (vv. 5b-9). Foreigners help to rebuild the city and contribute to sacrificial offerings (v. 10).

The scene is described from another viewpoint in Ezra 7 and Neh 2. The key terms for the city is that it is to be *glorified* (vv. 7b, 9, 13, 19, 21). The riches of the nations are gathered to build the Temple, the walls, and the gates.

The government's authority in the city is reestablished. Peace and order reign. This brings order and safety and the rights of Jews once again to own land (v. 21a). This implies Persian authority to uphold Jerusalem's position (v. 12) and bring relief from oppressive neighbors (v. 14).

The LORD's plan is to use Persian wealth and power to accomplish his purpose. When Artaxerxes re-establishes Persian authority in Jerusalem, the LORD's presence, city, and Temple can flourish. What the Emperor dedicates to the LORD, the LORD gives to Jerusalem. These include:

permission for Jews to travel (vv. 3-4; Ezra 7:13)
support for rebuilding the Temple and the city (vv. 6-7, 11, 17; Ezra 7:15-16, 21; Neh 2:8-9, 13)
support for operating the Temple (vv. 3-4, 9; Ezra 7:23, 26)
threat of imperial reprisal for injury (vv. 12, 14; Ezra 7:23, 26)

rights granted to administer the city under the Torah (Ezra 7:25) and the rights of inheritance (vv. 18, 21).

Light is a major theme in the chapter (vv. 1-3, 5a, 19-20). The idea of beautifying or glorifying the Temple and the city dominates the heart of the chapter (vv. 7b, 8, 9, 13, and 21). The call to rejoice appears in vv. 5a, 15b, 22.

The LORD's Agents Bless Jerusalem, 61:1-11

The Spirit of the LORD God again assumes an important role in the chapters (as in 42:1 and 59:21). Verses 1-3 are like the "servant song" of 50:4-11. Jesus quotes it in Luke 4:16-20; the words pick up the theme of joy from chap. 40.

A solitary person speaks in Jerusalem of the LORD's calling. His task is to *bring good news to the oppressed* (v. 1). The consistent understanding of the prophetic calling relates to the poor and the oppressed. The announcement is of liberty and of release.

The message is all contained in the announcement of *the year of the LORD's favor* (v. 2). This sounds like the Year of Jubilee in Lev. 25. It refers to a time when the land holdings will be reassigned and renewed for all the villagers. *Provide* (v. 3) can be translated "assign" and refer exactly to that.

Judeans, whether returnees or survivors in Jerusalem, fit the description of the oppressed, the captives, the mourners. The time first envisioned in chap. 40 has arrived when all things shall be turned around, with blessing in place of sorrow.

The great reversal in their fortunes is described in v. 3, when they are called *oaks of righteousness* (what a contrast to the stump in 6:13!). Planted by the LORD *to display his glory*. The practical effect is to change the ruined city into a thriving, beautiful city.

Israel's specific calling will be service as *priests of the LORD*. Other peoples can perform the other tasks that are needed. Israel is the servant to worship the LORD. The other roles as rulers can be assigned to the Persian authorities. Supporting roles can well be filled by others. But ministry in the LORD's house must be handled primarily by Israel.

In v. 7 the NRSV's *because* is an unnecessary addition. The verse announces that apportionments of land to till will now be doubled. Joy will now be their permanent lot.

The LORD announces his love of justice and his promise to continue to support the people. God promises to them an *everlasting covenant*. Their very existence will be a testimony among the nations that they are *a people whom God has blessed*. *People* is originally "a seed," reminiscent again of 6:13.

Verses 10-11 have another individual speak, rejoicing in God's gifts of *salvation* and *righteousness*. The speaker could be seen as Israel. But if the second servant, the Persian ruler is also a part of these concluding chapters, it might be he who speaks. In that case *righteousness* might better be understood as legitimacy. By his part in the restoration of Jerusalem he establishes his legitimate place in

Palestine before the nations. And this is a gift from the LORD who called him for this role from the beginning.

A New Name for Jerusalem, 62:1-7

With this chapter the Vision moves toward its completion. The opening verses are a speech that convey an angry determination. The speaker purports to speak for Zion. But who is the speaker? If this were the LORD or the prophet speaking on his behalf, one would expect a continuation of the tone of the previous two chapters.

But the tone and content are different. They are directed against the LORD's silence or inaction. The speaker must be different, perhaps a leader in Jerusalem. He is leading a demonstration in the city against the LORD's announced policy of having an open city that depends on the Persian forces for its defense. The LORD does not speak until v. 8.

The scene creates a tension in the drama. It is opposed to the views of chaps. 60–61, even of the entire Vision to this point. It is true that the speech calls for salvation and righteousness for the city as in other passages. But these are sought for the city in its own right, whereas they had been granted through the Persian emperor who was called to restore, rebuild, and protect the city.

This speech calls for Jerusalem to defend itself (v. 6). The city wants to be closed off from groups around it, in contrast to the Vision's hope for a city open to worshipers and artisans from all nations. The speech pleads for blessings and riches, but it is unrealistic in spurning the aid offered by its neighbors. This policy and plea will also dominate the next two chapters.

An Oath and An Apparition, 62:8–63:6

This scene answers the challenge of 62:1-7 in two ways. First the LORD reviews the situation: the security already provided (vv. 8-9) and the ongoing work on roads that will make travel possible (v. 10). It is known in Palestine that Zion has a powerful patron (vv. 11:a-d); and everyone knows that the restoration is funded and that Jerusalem's functioning sanctuary is a reality.

The LORD does not respond to the speech, but renews the pledge that Jerusalem will not be pillaged again (v. 8). Then the section returns to a summons to go out and begin the work. Announcement should be made to Jerusalem that the author of its salvation is on the way. This returns to the emphasis on the Persian ruler's plans for Jerusalem's restoration. The new city will have wonderful names when it is recognized that the LORD has accomplished this through his chosen vessels.

The second answer is portrayed. A terrible bloodstained figure appears from Edom. *Bozrah* is a major town in that direction. The figure is a soldier who is challenged (63:1-6). He claims to have authority and ample strength to protect the city, put down rebellion, and make the territory safe again. He tells of a battle (vv. 3-6) in which he fought without support from the peoples (i.e., without support from the Persian vassals in the area).

The two answers to the complaints in 62:1-7 demonstrate that the LORD is using Persian military force (63:1-6) to protect and secure the work of restoration (62:8-11). The LORD is in control, even when it takes an application of force to keep things on track.

A Sermon and Prayers (with Interruptions), 63:7–64:12

The passage consists of a recital (63:7-14 and 64:4-9) broken by a series of interruptions (63:15– 64:3, 10-12). The scene is like a preacher who has his sermon or liturgy interrupted by some of his hearers who insist on shouting questions and taunts at God during the service.

The recital is in the form of a sermon like those found in Deut 4–11 and some Psalms. It is unique, however, in using a number of new and different words and themes. It chronicles God's compassionate acts toward Israel in the past ages (vv. 7-9).

But, then it notes that they rebelled (v. 10). God's mercy in the age that follows is in terms of remembering the previous acts and the Israel that was (vv. 11-14). Remembering is a major act of worship and theological reflection. This recital is positive throughout. It recognizes periods of affliction but insists that God shared these with his people and eventually saved them.

The interruptions turn the scene into an occasion for accusations against God and for sectarian complaint. In some of them the perspective changes from portraying God as being at work in history to God who comes down from heaven (63:15a and 64:1-3). The concern for the welfare of all Jerusalem turns into appeals on behalf of segments of the community.

The setting for the entire scene is the same as that of 62:1-7, when there was an appeal for continuous prayer for the safety of Jerusalem. The levitical preacher recites God's saving acts as reminders that can provide a basis for repentance and forgiveness that is acceptable to God. But the crowd is in no mood for such spiritual sermons. It breaks into loud prayers that contain complaints, claims, and demands stating their own sectarian views. They demonstrated how divided the Jerusalem of that day was. There were Zadokite priests, and there were Israelites who were not Judean. There also were militant activists who wanted military respect. These are the evident signs of disunity and rivalry in which each group poses its claim to be God's people.

The preacher is able to resume his sermon in 64:4-9. He proclaims that there has been no God other than the LORD among them throughout this period (vv. 4-5a). Then he appeals to God who despite his justified anger toward them is still their father. He appeals for him to still regard them as his people. The sermon attempts to be inclusive and unifying.

One last protest points to the charred embers of the city (here as in Neh 1:3 much too recent to have been the destruction of 587 B.C.E.) and asks how God can restrain himself from action on their behalf.

The LORD Deals with Opponents, 65:1-16

This passage is composed of a series of speeches by the LORD dealing with enemies, the people within Israel that continue to rebel against God and resist God's course of action. It contains three major speeches and three edicts, with a closing speech interpreting the meaning of separation. The setting is that of the heavenly court.

The LORD's opening speech addresses the court about God's rebellious people (vv. 1-6). God reviews his patience and willingness to receive them, but points out how the LORD received from them provocation through pagan acts and stubborn unwillingness to turn back to God. Now God will have to act.

The first edict is directed to Israel in the second person (NRSV's emendation is wrong). Israel is to be punished for their heathen worship (v. 7). The second edict (v. 8) mitigates the first so that not all of them will be destroyed.

A second speech (vv. 9-10) promises hope for God's *chosen*. They will have descendants who dwell in Canaan, a people *who have sought me*.

A third speech is directed to the sinners who, in contrast, *forsake the LORD* (vv. 11-12). They are destined for slaughter. The reason is clear: they refused to answer God's call.

A third formal edict (vv. 13-15a) defines their fate. In contrast to God's chosen servants who have responded to him, these will be hungry, thirsty, shamed, pained, anguished, and cursed.

A final section (vv. 15b-16) interprets the separation. God's separated people will receive a new name. God will be called *the God of faithfulness*. God and the new people will close the door on the past.

The LORD's Great Day: A New Jerusalem, 65:17–66:24

The outer limits of this section are marked in the beginning by the phrase *For I* in v. 17. The Hebrew is much more dramatic "Behold me creating!" The passage ends in 66:5 after describing the contrast between groups in the new city: one who *trembles at God's word*, and another that hates them for that reason.

The passage is structured around two formal edicts. The first (vv. 24-25) announces: *Before they call I will answer*. The second (66:1-2a) is a question about the kind of house they intend to build for God.

These are framed by speeches from the LORD. Verses 17-23 describe the new creation. The second (66:2b-5) states his rejection of the old priestly ways and his installation of a more directly spiritual form of worship.

The historical background for this scene fits the period after EZRA and NEHEMIAH have returned. The interactions are between Zadokite priests who still wield authority over all sacrifice and the Temple area. The Vision opposes both the view that the sacred area should be limited to the Temple and the view that worship is primarily a matter of sacrifice. It also disputes the views that one priestly family should have exclusive privileges in Jerusalem. This sets the Vision at odds with

Leviticus and with Malachi. The Vision is much more at home with the kind of broad participation in worship pictured in Neh 12:27- 47 through songs, prayers, and processions. It argues that the entire city, not just the Temple, comprises the LORD's sacred mountain.

This debate is understandable in the 5th century. The application of 66:1-3 can be even more clearly defined. Nehemiah was determined to build the city's walls before turning to repairs of the Temple (Neh 2–6). People in Jerusalem as well as their neighbors opposed this (Neh 4 and 6). The policy from the time of Zerubbabel on had been to concentrate only on the Temple. The Vision supports Nehemiah but also goes well beyond him. It sees the entire city as sacred, a place for Jews and other worshipers from all the known world to gather, worship, and be taught God's word.

65:17-25. See the LORD creating. The LORD calls for all to look at what he is doing at Jerusalem as an awesome act of creation. He wants it to be seen in terms like the creation of heavens and earth. But these are new. It is a new order, to be sharply distinguished from the old order.

A series of sharp contrasts is listed in vv. 19b-25:

No more	*but*
cry of distress	*rejoice*
an infant who *lives a few days*	*one who dies at a hundred*
a person dying prematurely	one hundred—an early age to die
build and another live there	build and live there
plant for another to eat	plant and eat their fruit
work for nothing	be like a tree
bear children for terror	wear out their things
receive answers to prayer	before they call, God answers
constant violence	no harm or destruction in all God's mountain

This is to be a place and time of *joy and . . . delight* (v. 18). The temporary relations of life and its arbitrary changes will be gone. Life will be stable and prosperous. God's presence will be clear and constant. It will be a period of peace and there will be no hurt or destruction.

That is God's vision and hope for his new work. It parallels the original vision for creation in Gen 2. But, like that one, it then had to turn to a more realistic experience of life as it is. This comes in chap. 66.

66:1-5. What kind of house? From the vision of new heavens and a new earth, the LORD turns his attention to a proposed building for God in the city. The LORD cannot be concerned about a house separate from the city. God's real attention is devoted *to the humble and contrite who trembles at his word.*

The LORD repudiates sacrificial worship. He describes this as a self-chosen way. The reason is clear. It did not come about in answer to God's call. The people chose what was evil in his sight.

A series of sacrifices recognized in Torah is said to be like some that are prohibited (v. 3):

Acceptable in Torah	Unacceptable
slaughtering an ox (Lev 17:3-4)	striking a person (Lev 24:17-21; Deut 19:6; 27:24-25)
sacrificing a lamb (Lev 14:10-24)	breaking a dog's neck (Exod 34:20 of a donkey)
a cereal offering (Lev 2:1, 13)	swine's blood (Lev. 11:7; Deut 14:8; Isa 65:4; 66:17)
frankincense (Lev 2:2, 16; 6:8) (Lev. 2:2,16;6:8)	an idol

Then the LORD addresses the party to which he is partial, *you who tremble at his word*. He encourages them to believe that those who hate and deride them will be *put to shame*.

66:6-24.The LORD confirms the servants in the new city. The Vision ends as it began with a scene in the heavenly court room of God. But all the speeches relate to the happenings in Jerusalem. The speeches relate to the worship and the attitudes of the worshipers rather than to any historical events.

This scene brings closure for three openings earlier in the book: the city on a mountain to which all the peoples flow (2:1-4) is fulfilled in vv. 18-20, the good news for Jerusalem (40:1-9) is fulfilled in this scene, and the promises of restoration for the city in chaps. 45, 49, 54, and especially chaps. 60–62, are picked up and closed here. It is a grand finale.

66:6. Disturbance noted. Someone takes note of noise offstage, as it were. It is an *uproar* from a city, from a Temple. It is identified as *the voice of the LORD*. Then one can tell from the words and the tone that the LORD is dealing with his enemies. His patience with the adversaries has come to an end.

66:7-14. Like a birth. These verses use birth and child imagery to describe the appearance of the new city. It has come so suddenly! Everyone is surprised. *Yet as soon as Zion was in labor she delivered her children.* EZRA and NEHEMIAH had accomplished more in a few years than everyone before them had accomplished in decades. The destruction of 587 B.C.E. had left scars on the city that were not removed until Nehemiah rebuilt the walls. He completed his work in a short two years. The metaphor picks up the words from 49:20-21.

The children of Zion are the new covenant community there, the faithful servants of the LORD. These might also be the new inhabitants for the city that Neh 11 speaks of.

The LORD describes the stages of birth. God is the midwife. The process must be carried out. In chap. 40 the LORD had initiated the process. Now it has come full term.

Everyone who loves Jerusalem and who has mourned over the city is called to rejoice. Mourning for Jerusalem had been a preoccupation for a long time. Isaiah 60:20, 61:2-3, and the Book of Lamentations witness to the extent of the mourning.

But to mourn now is to indicate a lack of faith in God's plans. Rejoicing with the city is also a theme in the Psalms (26:8; 122:6; 137:6).

The child imagery continues. The people of the dispersion are invited to draw nourishment from Jerusalem's restoration. The city will give them a focus for their faith and hope. They can make pilgrimages to the city. They can take satisfaction and consolation from knowing that Jerusalem is functioning again.

Prosperity renders the Heb. *shalom*, meaning "peace" (and much more). The *wealth of nations* continues the picture in chaps. 60 and 61 of the city's prosperity supported by the contribution from foreigners. Then the child imagery continues. Jerusalem nurtures the faithful as a mother nurtures a baby.

Jerusalem will be comforted by the LORD. When they see they can rejoice. They can know, as the nations know, that the LORD is active on behalf of his city. This is accomplished by separating the fate of *his servants* from that of *his enemies*. The separation described in chap. 65 is now complete.

66:15-18a. The LORD is coming in anger. The verses build on the thought of the LORD's indignation on his enemies. The LORD appears here as the Divine Warrior to execute judgment with the sword. The imagery here is very old in Israel (see also Jer 4:13; Ps 68:17 and Hab 3:8). Fire appears in many others scenes of judgment in the book.

Verse 17 describes pagan rites again. These must be brought to an end. In v. 18 *their* has a clear antecedent in v. 17. The Hebrew lacks a verb, but the two words show God's concern for the sins through their actions and their intentions.

66:18b-21.The LORD will gather. The LORD's coming has another focus more pertinent to the goal of this Vision. God will move to fulfill the rest of the picture in 2:2-4 by gathering people from all nations and tongues to come and see his glory in the new city.

The sign God will establish is the last of a series. In 7:14 the sign was a child to be born. In 19:20 it was a monument on Egypt's border. In 55:13 it was the return and the land's renewal. This sign will be in the nations. The *survivors* are those who remain in the dispersion. They will be sent out to the nations.

These ancient missionaries may include some of those who survive in Jerusalem. The Vision has so far focused on the peoples in Palestine. But now it looks far away. *Tarshish* is a distant port, perhaps as far away as Spain or the Black Sea. *Pul* may be in Africa and *Lud* is in Asia Minor. *Tubal* may be in Asia Minor. *Javan* is Greece. These are ancient names and must be intended symbolically.

They are to go to all those who have not heard or seen. They are to declare the LORD's glory among the nations.

A second task will be for the believers in the diaspora to bring the brothers in faith and covenant to Jerusalem to share in this experience. They will constitute *an offering to the LORD* that is seen as far more acceptable than the ox or the lamb of 66:3. The vision of 2:2-4 is coming true. The effort to transport pilgrims joins the efforts of those who restore the city—and all will be blessed.

The LORD promises that *from them*, the pilgrims from the diaspora, the LORD will choose Levites and priests. The new openness in the city will not reserve the positions of service and leadership for some special group (cf. 56:3-8). The Temple will become *a house of prayer for all nations* (56:7).

66:22-24. Last words. The verse refers back to 65:17 and the new creation in order to promise permanence and security in the LORD. The cycle of worship, both monthly and weekly, for all who will come is permanent. It will continue.

But the dark side is also still apparent. God's judgment on those who stubbornly rebel will be painfully visible to the worshipers as they leave the city.

Works Cited

Watts, John D. W. 1985. *Isaiah 1–33*. WBC; 1987. *Isaiah 34-66*. WBC.

Jeremiah
Leo G. Perdue

Introduction

The Book of Jeremiah is one of the three "major prophets" (major in terms of
length; that is, Isaiah, Jeremiah, and Ezekiel) that, together with the "minor prophets" (Book of the Twelve), comprise the latter prophets (*nĕbî'îm 'ahărōnîm*) in the
OT. The many complex problems present in interpreting this fascinating book
include literary composition and authorship, the differences between the MT, that is,
the Hebrew, and the LXX, that is, the SEPTUAGINT, and identifying the historical
settings in which the various materials may be located.

Literary Composition and Authorship

Like most other prophetic books, the Book of Jeremiah was not written by a
single author, but rather is a collection of various types of materials that were trans-
mitted orally at first, then written down and edited over an extended period of time.
This entire process may have taken some two centuries to complete. These materials
include various types of prophetic sayings, normally in poetry, that may derive from
Jeremiah himself. In the collection and transmission of these sayings, the prophet's
disciples and later editors continued to add to the corpus additional prophetic sayings, prose sermons, narratives about the prophet's life and the people of Judah and
Jerusalem, wisdom texts, and different kinds of psalms (hymns, laments, and thanksgivings). The final composition of Jeremiah, which began at the end of the seventh
century B.C.E., more than likely was not completed until the fifth century B.C.E.

The narrative in chap. 36 may provide some interesting insight into the composition of the book. This chapter refers to two scrolls (vv. 1-31, 32), dictated by the
prophet to Baruch, his disciple and scribe. The first scroll (vv. 1-31) contained the
oracles of Jeremiah from the time of King Josiah (640–609 B.C.E.) to the battle of
CARCHEMISH (605 B.C.E.). The contents of the first scroll are not specified, but they
may have included the call of the prophet (1:3-10), the oracles of judgment, especially those concerning the *evil from the north* (4:6; in this commentary the phrase
"foe from the north" is used—see the outline for chaps. 4–10), and the laments (in-
terspersed throughout 11:18–20:18). When the scroll was read to King Jehoiakim,
he responded by destroying it and ordering the arrest of Jeremiah and Baruch. Later,

Jeremiah dictated a second scroll that included the contents of the first scroll, together with *many similar words* (36:32). This allowed for the inclusion of other materials from the prophet's later life and from disciples and editors over two centuries.

Whatever the precise contents of these two scrolls may have been, it is clear that several collections of materials were edited and then later combined into larger literary sources. These collections, at times identified by an editorial introduction, include the judgment oracles concerning the "foe from the north" (eleven oracles scattered throughout chaps. 4–10), the "laments" (found among the poems in chaps. 11–20), oracles concerning the royal house of Judah (21:11–23:8), oracles concerning the prophets (23:9-40), the so-called "Book of Consolation" (chaps. 30–31), and "oracles against the foreign nations" (chaps. 46–51). Chapter 52 is largely borrowed from 2 Kgs 24:18–25:30.

Jeremiah contains three major literary sources, conveniently designated A, B, and C. Poetic oracles of judgment (Source A) are found primarily in the first twenty-five chapters. Many scholars attribute these oracles to the historical Jeremiah. Prose narratives about the life and times of Jeremiah (Source B) are found primarily in chaps. 26–45. Prose speeches (Source C) that often embellish and elaborate on shorter poetic oracles are embedded throughout the first forty-five chapters. The literary style and theology of the prose materials, including both narratives and sermons, are quite similar to what one finds in the Book of Deuteronomy and the Deuteronomistic History (Joshua, Judges, Samuel, and Kings). Consequently, the prose texts most likely are attributable to deuteronomic scribes who produced two major editions of Jeremiah, the first completed by the sixth century and the second during the fifth century B.C.E. These scribes sought to enable Jeremiah to speak to later exilic and postexilic communities of Jews long after he had died. The first edition is reflected in the LXX that preserves the short text of Jeremiah, and the second is represented by the MT, or long text.

Two major collections of materials in Jeremiah, not usually placed in one of these three sources, are the oracles about the future (the "Book of Consolation," chaps. 30–31) and a collection of oracles against foreign nations (chaps. 46–51). The authorship of these two collections is debated, although it is conceivable that several oracles in each may have been uttered by Jeremiah. The others were added by later prophets who sought to have Jeremiah speak to events of the exilic and early postexilic periods.

The Text of Jeremiah

The MT of Jeremiah contains about 2,700 more words than the text preserved by the LXX. This makes the MT of Jeremiah approximately one-eighth longer than its Greek counterpart. For example, several extensive sections of Jeremiah present in the MT are absent in the LXX: 33:14-26; 39:4-13; 51:44b-49a; and 52:27b-30. Furthermore, the MT and LXX differ in the arrangement of materials, the most notable being the location of the "oracles against the foreign nations" (chaps. 46–51). This collection appears in the LXX in the middle of the book (i.e., 25:13a of the MT). Based on the content of chap. 25, the LXX's location is likely original.

The long (MT) and short (LXX) texts are represented by the manuscript fragments of Jeremiah in Hebrew found at Qumran. This underscores the fluidity of the Jeremiah tradition, prior to the finalization of the canonical text sometime during the transition to the early common era. It is unlikely that the LXX presents an intentionally abbreviated text. Rather, the two texts probably represent two stages of the deuteronomic redaction of Jeremiah. Both versions continued to circulate in different scribal circles until the canonization of the OT in the first century, C.E.

The Historical Setting

Jeremiah, his disciples, and the scribes who shaped his tradition, beginning with BARUCH, lived during a tumultuous period of history that witnessed a significant transformation in the nature and fortunes of the Jewish community. The prose narratives and sermons (1:2, 25:3) trace the call of the prophet (found in 1:3-10) to the *thirteenth year* of King Josiah (627 B.C.E.) and further indicate that he was active during the latter part of this king's reign (640–609 B.C.E.). This date for the call, marking the beginning of his prophetic activity, was an important one in the history of Judah, the southern kingdom. In 627 B.C.E. the last strong king of the Assyrians, Asshurbanapal, died, resulting in revolution throughout the Assyrian empire. The assaults by the Babylonians and Medes led to the overthrow of the Assyrians. Nineveh, the capital, fell in 612 B.C.E. and the surviving remnant of Assyrian forces, located at Harran, was defeated in 610/9 B.C.E. When Nebuchadrezzar, commander of the Babylonian forces, defeated the Egyptians at the battle of Carchemish in 605 B.C.E., Babylon soon became the heir to much of the former Assyrian empire in MESOPOTAMIA and Canaan. When the Babylonian king Nabopolassar died a short time later, NEBUCHADREZZAR became king (605/4–562 B.C.E.). Babylonian suzerainty lasted until 539 B.C.E. when the Persians defeated the Babylonians at Opis and then entered the city of Babylon without resistance. The Persians subsumed the former empire within their expanding domain.

Josiah participated in the general uprising against the Assyrians in 627 B.C.E. and liberated Judah from a tyrannical government that had held the nation in subjugation since 735 B.C.E. During the intervening years between the collapse of Assyrian control and the reconfiguration of power in the ancient Near East, Judah enjoyed a short-lived period of independence (627–609 B.C.E.). Five years later (622 B.C.E.), Josiah led a religious reform inspired by the discovery of "the book of the law" in the Temple. This law was probably an earlier form of what became the Book of Deuteronomy. The reform aimed at the centralization of official religious worship in Jerusalem and the elimination of pagan religions in Judah and the expanding territory under its control. Josiah's political design may have been to re-create the Davidic empire, an ill-fated objective that failed when he led his army into battle against the Egyptian forces under NECHO II (610–595 B.C.E.) at MEGIDDO in 609 B.C.E. Josiah died, and his soldiers were routed by the Egyptians, apparently on their way to aid the Assyrian forces resisting the advance of the Babylonians.

Following the death of Josiah, Judah came under Egyptian control until the battle of Carchemish (605 B.C.E.) that culminated in a Babylonian victory. Jehoiakim, ruling Judah at the time, soon transferred allegiance to the Babylonians. A series of Judahite kings followed Josiah to the throne: Jehoahaz (609 B.C.E.), Jehoiakim (609–598 B.C.E.), Jehoiachin (598–97 B.C.E.), and Zedekiah (597–587 B.C.E.). Jehoiakim rebelled against the Babylonians, leading to the first exile in 597 B.C.E. Zedekiah, succumbing to anti-Babylonian pressures, also rebelled, a decision that led to the destruction of Jerusalem and the Temple, the end of the monarchy, and the second exile in 587 B.C.E. Nebuchadrezzar appointed Gedaliah, a member of the prominent family of Shaphan (Josiah's royal secretary), as governor of Judah, although a group of assassins led by ISHMAEL, a descendant of the royal line, murdered the governor shortly after he had assumed the reigns of government. A third deportation to Babylon may have taken place in 582 B.C.E.

With the former leaders of Judah among the deportees to Babylon, the conditions of those remaining in the land were quite difficult. However, the biblical materials provide little information about life during this period (587–538 B.C.E.). There also is very little information about the Jewish community in Babylon during this same time. It appears that the exiles lived in Jewish communities and attempted to carry out some form of worship of Yahweh. Their captivity ended with the Persian conquest of Babylonia in 539 B.C.E. A year later, the Persian king, Cyrus, issued an edict allowing those Jews who so desired to return to their homeland.

Jeremiah's Life as a Prophet

The life of Jeremiah and indeed the lives of his later disciples and the scribes responsible for shaping his prophetic tradition interfaced with the larger public events in the life of Judah before 587 B.C.E. and the later Jewish community that survived the Babylonian onslaught. The prose materials date his call to 627 B.C.E., that most auspicious time when revolution against the Assyrians was widespread (chap. 1). It may be that the poetic materials probably deriving from Jeremiah himself suggest a later date for the call, perhaps 609 B.C.E. when Josiah died at Megiddo. If so, then 627 B.C.E. could have been the birth date of the prophet. In any event, it is very difficult to associate much of the prophet's own sayings with the events during the lifetime of Josiah. If the prophet were active this early, his ministry would have been largely limited to the area around Anathoth in the tribe of Benjamin in the old territory of the former Northern Kingdom, that is, Israel, for this is where the prophet was born and raised. It is likely that he would have been a supporter of the religious reforms of Josiah, although he probably would have been skeptical about the rising nationalism developing from the king's political ambitions. If the oracles concerning the "foe from the north" (see chaps. 4–10) were uttered during this early period, it is little wonder that his prophecy about an enemy to the north, not identified as the Babylonians until the battle of CARCHEMISH, coming to destroy Judah would have met with either serious opposition or biting ridicule. With the tragedy at Megiddo, however, the prophet soon moved his sphere of activity to Jerusalem where he continued to prophesy doom for the nation, unless there was an abandonment of nationalistic ambitions and a wholesale repentance resulting in returning to Yahweh (see chaps. 2; 3:1–4:4; and 7:1–8:3). During the torrents of national disaster, Jeremiah continued to preach to the people of Jerusalem and the royal house that they should be peaceful servants of the Babylonian king. This message not only led to the official persecution of the prophet on occasion (see chaps. 26 and 36), but eventually fell on deaf ears as first one rebellion and then another met with disaster. Jeremiah's struggles with external persecution and inward doubt in the faithfulness of Yahweh are reflected in the "Laments" found throughout 11:18–20:18. Jeremiah's harsh criticism of both the ruling kings, save for Josiah, and the city of Jerusalem is found in the collection, "Concerning the Royal House of Judah" (21:11–23:8).

Following the sacking of JERUSALEM in 587 B.C.E., Nebuchadrezzar, pleased with Jeremiah's pacifism, offered him the option of going to Babylon or of staying in Mizpah where Gedaliah's government was being set up. The prophet chose to remain behind to help in the rebuilding of the nation. It may have been that Jeremiah then began to speak of hope for the future, envisioning a restoration of Jewish life in Judah and the old territory of Israel at some undetermined time (see chaps. 30–31). However, following the assassination of Gedaliah, a group of Jewish refugees who fled to Egypt forced Jeremiah to accompany them. There he disappears from history.

The tradition of Jeremiah did not die with him. Disciples and editors continued to shape the tradition by adding prose speeches and narratives and a variety of later oracles (e.g., most of the oracles against foreign nations, chaps. 46–51), allowing his prophetic voice to address several groups of survivors of the Babylonian conquest in their own time: those who went into exile in Babylon and Egypt and those who remained in the former territories of Judah and Israel. Indeed, through their activity, they shaped a narrative and preaching tradition that enabled the prophet to address the exiles, those who were left behind, and their successors who faced the challenges of rebuilding national life primarily in and around Jerusalem during the early Persian period.

One of the more intriguing aspects of Jeremiah in the prose tradition is his presentation as the prophet like Moses (cf. Deut 18:15-22). In the passage in Deuteronomy, Moses addresses liberated Israel, assembled in the plains of Moab immediately prior to their entrance into the land of Canaan. He speaks of a future prophet whom the people should heed. In the prose tradition, the deuteronomic scribes make a concerted effort to present Jeremiah as this Mosaic prophet who speaks of new covenant, an inward law, and judgment to a people awaiting and then experiencing liberation from another captivity. Like Moses in Deuteronomy, Jeremiah offers God's redemption to those who are offered the decision for life or death. Life may be chosen by repenting of sins, entering into a new covenant with Yahweh, and living according to the law inscribed on their hearts. Following the Deuteronomic pattern of retributive justice, this Jeremiah blames the destruction of Jerusalem and the Temple, the burning of the palace and the captivity of kings, and the exile on disobedience to the Mosaic covenant, a disobedience that permeated the entire nation, from its political and religious leaders to the people themselves. By returning to the covenant, the nation would be reborn in Judah as the people of God and its institutions, from kingship to temple, would be restored.

The social location of Jeremiah is the tribal, agrarian tradition that was especially nurtured in the towns and villages of the northern state of Israel and, to a lesser extent, the hill country of Judah. In contrast to the monarchic tradition flourishing in the royal cities of Judah, the rural areas tended to favor a tribal society of extended families who cultivated their own farms and practiced a form of social justice that was based on the ideals of kinsmanship, care for the neighbor, and charity towards the poor, including the levite, widow, orphan, and stranger. During the period of the judges (ca. 1200 to 1000 B.C.E.), the political and judicial system inclined towards a system of village elders for local matters and tribal elders for internal and external matters affecting the tribes. A loose-knit federation of tribes was favored as the political system necessary for dealing with tribal disputes and military threats from the outside. Even after the establishment of the monarchy and Solomon's attempt to subvert the tribal tradition by overt pressure, it continued as an active expression of social, political, and religious life. Theologically, the traditions of exodus, wilderness wandering, taking of the land of Canaan, and the covenant were nurtured in these rural enclaves. A strong antipathy developed towards kings and the royal tradition cultivated in Jerusalem and to a lesser extent in other cities and towns in Judah. The royal tradition emphasized dynastic rule (the house of David), established royal boundaries that ignored tribal domains, centralized rule and judicial oversight in the hands of the monarchy, placed national religious institutions including the Temple under the control of the royal house, favored the expansion of aristocratic land holdings, placed economic institutions, including agricultural markets and trade, under monarchial authority, and gave the kings the important powers of control over the military, conscription for both military service and work gangs, and taxation.

Jeremiah was born in Anathoth, a small levitical town less than three mi. north of Jerusalem, but situated in the hill country of Benjamin, once a northern tribe. This village was home to a family of levitical priests who traced their ancestry back to Abiathar, one of David's chief priests who fell into disfavor with Solomon by supporting the royal pretensions of the king's half-brother, Adonijah. After consolidating power in his hands, Solomon took care of his political opponents, including Abiathar whom he exiled to Anathoth. This denied to Abiathar and his descendants any participation in the royal cult in Jerusalem and the Temple eventually constructed by Solomon. More than likely, the deuteronomic traditions were originally nurtured in the northern towns and villages like Anathoth. When the Northern Kingdom fell in 722 B.C.E. to the Assyrians, numerous refugees fled south to Judah, with some establishing a ghetto of northern Israelites on the western hill of Jerusalem. One of the descendants of these northern refugees was Huldah the prophet who perhaps was Jeremiah's aunt (cf. Jer 32:7 and 2 Kgs 22:14). She was the prophet consulted by Josiah when the law book was discovered in the Temple (see 2 Kgs 22:14-20), a text that was likely an earlier form of the Book of Deuteronomy.

A descendant of the levitical, priestly family of Abiathar, Jeremiah was nurtured in the tribal tradition of his ancestors. Subsequently, the social and religious values of the older Mosaic covenant, reformulated by the deuteronomists, played a formative role in shaping his religious and social views. This background also helps to explain Jeremiah's hostile attitude towards the Davidic monarchy, with the exception of Josiah who pursued a vigorous religious reform according to the guidelines of a proto-deuteronomic text, and his virulent attack on the Jerusalem Temple (chaps. 7 and 26). This double edged criticism had deep roots in a tradition strongly opposed to royal pretensions and tyranny. It may have been that Josiah's reform gave the disenfranchised levites the role of priests in the Temple in Jerusalem. This may explain the hostility directed against Jeremiah by his own family and the people of Anathoth when he preached judgment against nation, monarchy, and Temple. Even though he commanded the respect of King Zedekiah, for the most part Jeremiah was a peripheral prophet who lived on the outer edges of power in the Judahite state. Indeed, his association with Baruch may have been developed in part because of the scribe's political connections at court. When Jeremiah spoke of a new social and religious order residing at some distance in the future, he gave no place to kingship and Temple. His deuteronomic editors lessened the severity of this glaring omission by pointing to the reemergence of kingship and the levitical priesthood in the time of restoration.

The Theology of Jeremiah

To understand the theology of Jeremiah, one must begin by recognizing that the different materials collected together to form the book paint different portraits of the man and vary the contents of his message. Consequently, there is not one prophet with a coherent, unified theology, but several prophets with differently nuanced messages.

The first portrait of Jeremiah is found in Source A (see above, "Literary Composition and Authorship") and the "Book of Consolation" (chaps. 30–31). Here Jeremiah is a prophet of judgment who announces the impending doom of Judah and Jerusalem at the hands of a northern enemy because of religious apostasy and the establishment of treaties with foreign nations. Jeremiah does offer the possibility of redemption, but only if the nation abandons foreign gods and treaties with other countries and returns to the Mosaic covenant and a sole dependence on Yahweh. This does not mean political freedom, for Jeremiah preaches that Judah must bow the knee to the newly emerging power that he identifies by 605 B.C.E. as the Babylonians and their king, Nebuchadrezzar. Even though Judah—and especially its leaders—refuse to repent, the disaster promised by the prophet comes, not from an angry God bent on vengeance, but a suffering deity who agonizes over and mourns the destruction of his people.

After the fall of Jerusalem, the destruction of the Temple, the end of the monarchy, and the exile to Babylon, the prophet begins to articulate a theology of hope for the future, grounded in divine compassion that will lead to new acts of divine redemption. Yahweh will reconstitute the people of God by bringing together once again Israel and Judah. The theological traditions on which the prophet draws both for judgment and promise are those of exodus, divine sustenance in the Sinai wilderness, and the Mosaic covenant. These older traditions of faith that Israel before the Babylonian conquest of 587 B.C.E. had violated hold out the promise of divine redemption in the future. The traditions of the promise to David (e.g., 2 Sam 7 and Ps 89) concerning a royal dynasty and Jerusalem (also called Zion) as the city of God, symbolized by the Solomonic Temple, are not expressions of faith for this Jeremiah. Indeed, he is most critical of these traditions, for they embody not the proper expression of religious faith and piety, but rather the corrupt tyranny of many kings and a formal religion more concerned with sacrifice than with justice. Indeed, Jeremiah characterizes dependence on Temple theology and its view of a deity who dwells in its precincts and defends Jerusalem against attack as *a lie* (see esp. chaps. 28–29). In this view of Jeremiah and his message, the "I" of the prophet often merges with the character and being of God. The line between prophet and deity, while not eliminated completely, is often blurred. The personality of Jeremiah, both his rationality and emotions, often blends with that of Yahweh.

A second portrait of Jeremiah emerges in the laments (see 11:18–20:18), which, while different, does have points of connection with Source A and the "Book of Consolation." These confessions, borrowing heavily from the form and content of the laments in the Psalter and the Book of Lamentations, present the inner struggles of the prophet and his conflict with Yahweh. Here the prophet accuses God of injustice and deceit, complains of humiliation and persecution endured because of his prophetic activity, demands vindication for his abused integrity, and cries out for vengeance against his enemies. If read as private prayers, they depict the inward turmoil of prophetic existence that bears the burden of judgment and alienation. At one point the darkness of despair that enshrouds the prophet leads him to curse his birth, negating the tradition of his call that tells of Yahweh's formation of him in the womb for the purpose of becoming a *prophet to the nations* (1:5). If read as a community lament in which Jeremiah voices the grief and pain of Judah, then the prophet utters the people's pain, questioning of divine justice, lack of trust in the faithfulness of God, insistence on vindication, and call for vengeance against their enemies. Jeremiah's role would be, then, more of a prophetic intercessor than an individual struggling with personal questions of faith and existence. In either case, Yahweh responds, at least to the first several laments, promising, not cheap grace, but divine support to endure even more difficulties that lay ahead. Indeed, when Jeremiah (Judah?) abandons God, the promise of acceptance remains intact, but only if repentance occurs. However, the last lament (20:14-18) ends rather shockingly with the prophet cursing his birth and wishing he had never been born. To this God makes no response. The laments emphasize the agony that comes at times to those who seek to embody prophetic existence. It is a life that at times becomes almost unbearable torment.

A third portrait of Jeremiah is present in the prose tradition. In the prose speeches, following the style of paraenetic addresses common to Deuteronomy and the Deuteronomistic History, Jeremiah is a preacher of the law who argues that all history is under the control of Yahweh who administers retributive justice. This means that, because of the violation of the Mosaic covenant, God is bringing disaster upon his own people. The catastrophe of 587 B.C.E. is interpreted as God's punishment of Judah for the sins of its leaders and people. Speaking to a people in exile who hope to return to their homeland, this prophet offers them the alternative of salvation or judgment. The choice belongs to them. Yahweh is powerful, gracious, and ready to save, but they must return to him in trusting faith and ready obedience to the law.

While the prose narratives present the same portrait, they also indicate how the divine word of the prophet is implemented in both his life and the life of the nation. There is a correspondence between word and deed, message and life. The word by which the prophet suffered eventually became the word that brought life to the exiles. This is not yet a doctrine of vicarious or redemptive suffering, but it comes very close. Here one finds biography and history shaped by prophetic preaching. Jeremiah becomes the model of faithful preaching and action to be emulated by those seeking a proper relationship with God.

One other depiction of Jeremiah and his message is found in the "Oracles against the Foreign Nations" (chaps. 46–51). The time for judgment against wicked nations and especially the evil empire of the Babylonians is at hand. This Jeremiah announces divine judgment against the foreign nations who had caused Judah to suffer: Egypt, Philistia, the Transjordanian states, Damascus, the Arab tribes of Kedar and Hazor, Elam, and Babylon all fall beneath the hammer of divine punishment. More than likely, the prophet has in mind both the Medes and Persians as the new instrument of divine judgment. But it is especially Babylon, earlier the instrument of divine judgment, that now is the recipient of the harshest condemnation. Babylon will be utterly destroyed. This harshness towards the foreign nations is ameliorated by the qualification that God will give some of them a future. This Jeremiah preaches judgment and divine vengeance against Judah's enemies that allow for the redemption of the Jewish captives. Indeed, it is out of the destruction of the nations that a new Israel may be built.

For Further Study

In the *Mercer Dictionary of the Bible*: BABYLONIAN EMPIRE; BARUCH; CARCHEMISH; CURSE AND BLESSING; DEUTERONOMIST/DEUTERONOMISTIC HISTORIAN; EXILE; GEDALIAH; JEREMIAH; JEREMIAH, BOOK OF; JERUSALEM; JOSIAH; KINGSHIP; NEBUCHADREZZAR; ORACLE; PROPHET; SOURCES OF THE PENTATEUCH; ZEDEKIAH.

In other sources: J. Bright, *Jeremiah*, AncB; W. Brueggemann, *To Pluck Up, to Tear Down: A Commentary on the Book of Jeremiah 1–25* and *To Build, to Plant: A Commentary on Jeremiah 26–52*, ITC; R. P. Carroll, *Jeremiah*, OTL; S. Herrmann, *Jeremia*, BKAT; W. Holladay, *Jeremiah*, Herm; J. P. Hyatt, "The Book of Jeremiah," *IB*; W. McKane, *Jeremiah*, ICC; E. W. Nicholson, *Preaching to the Exiles*; K. O'Connor, *The Confessions of Jeremiah*, SBLDS; L. G. Perdue and B. W. Kovacs, *A Prophet to the Nations*; P. Trible, *God and the Rhetoric of Sexuality*.

Commentary

An Outline

I. Superscription, 1:1-3
II. The Call and Initial Visions of Jeremiah, 1:4-19
  A. The Call of the Prophet, 1:4-10
  B. Initial Visions, 1:11-14
  C. Interpretation of the Second Vision, 1:15-16
  D. Exhortation to Jeremiah, 1:17-19
III. Israel's Political and Religious Disloyalty, 2:1-37
  A. Israel's Faithfulness as a Young Bride, 2:1-3
  B. Religious Apostasy and the Worship of Baal, 2:4-13
  C. Political Disloyalty—Alliances with Assyria and Egypt, 2:14-19
  D. Religious Apostasy—Baal Worship, 2:20-28
  E. Political Disloyalty—Alliance with Egypt, 2:29-37
IV. Sermon on Repentance, 3:1–4:4
  A. The Adulterous Wife and Disobedient Child, 3:1-5
  B. A Prose Commentary on 3:1-5, 3:6-11
  C. Israel as an Adulterous Wife, 3:12-13
  D. Israel as Faithless Children and an Adulterous Wife, 3:14, 19-20
  E. The New Future, 3:15-18
  F. Israel as Faithless Children, 3:21-23
  G. A Confession of Sin, 3:24-25
  H. Call to Repentance, 4:1-4
V. The Foe from the North (I), 4:5–6:30
  A. The Threat from the North, 4:5-31

  B. In Quest of a Righteous Person, 5:1-9
  C. The Destruction of the Vineyard, 5:10-17
  D. The Destruction Is Not Total, 5:18-19
  E. Judgment against Sinful Israel and Judah, 5:20-31
  F. The Northern Invader Approaches, 6:1-8
  G. Jeremiah's Warnings Are Ignored, 6:9-15
  H. Forsaking the "Ancient Paths," 6:16-30
VI. The Temple Sermon, 7:1–8:3
  A. The Temple Sermon, 7:1-15
  B. Pagan Worship, 7:16-20
  C. Rejection of Sacrifice, 7:21-29
  D. High Place of Topheth, 7:30-34
  E. Disinterment of the Dead, 8:1-3
VII. The Foe from the North (II), 8:4-10:25
  A. Judgment against People and Leaders, 8:4-13
  B. Lamenting the Coming Destruction, 8:14–9:26
  C. An Idol Satire, 10:1-16
  D. The Final Siege, 10:17-25
VIII. The Broken Covenant, 11:1-17
IX. Jeremiah's Laments, 11:18–20:18
  A. The First Lament, 11:18-23
  B. The Second Lament, 12:1-6
  C. Yahweh's Lament, 12:7-13
  D. Judgment against Judah's Neighbors, 12:14-17
  E. The Linen Waistcloth, 13:1-11

Superscription, 1:1-3

The superscription of the book, written by a deuteronomic redactor, follows a typical pattern for prophetic books: the title (*the words of Jeremiah*), personal background (*son of Hilkiah, of the priests who were in the land of Benjamin*), reception of the revelation (*to whom the word of the LORD came*), the subject of the revelation (in Jeremiah's case 1:4-10 identifies the subject as *the nations*), and the date (vv. 2-3). For other examples of prophetic superscriptions, see Isa 1:1; Amos 1:1; Mic 1:1; Zeph 1:1.

Anathoth, located at modern Ras el Kharuba, was a levitical town in the tribal territory of Benjamin, less than three mi. northeast of Jerusalem. The *priests* of v. 1 included the descendants of Abiathar, one of David's chief priests, whom Solomon exiled upon the death of his father. Abiathar had supported Adonijah's claim to the throne over Solomon. Hilkiah is not an uncommon name. While the chief priest of Josiah who figured prominently in the deuteronomic reformation was named Hilkiah (2 Kgs 22:4-14), it is doubtful he is to be identified with the priest who was Jeremiah's father. Except for his profession as a priest, Jeremiah's father is otherwise unknown (see the introduction). The superscription dates Jeremiah's prophetic activity from the thirteenth year of the reign of King Josiah (640–609 B.C.E.), that is, 627 B.C.E., through the reign of King Jehoiakim (609–598 B.C.E.), to the end of the eleventh year of the reign of King Zedekiah (597–587 B.C.E.) *until the captivity of Jerusalem in the fifth month* (v. 3, which would be 587 B.C.E.). Thus, Jeremiah prophesied from 627 to 587 B.C.E. However, the prose tradition presents Jeremiah as active until some time after the assassination of Gedaliah in 586 B.C.E. (see 40:7–44:30).

The Call and Initial Visions of Jeremiah, 1:4-19

1:4-10. The call of the prophet. The opening chapter contains the call of Jeremiah (1:4-10), two initial visions (1:11-14), and two prose additions: the first interprets the second vision in more detail (1:15-16), while the second speaks of Yahweh's concluding exhortation to the prophet (1:17-19). Chapter 1 offers an overture to the entire book by introducing the sounds of important themes, motifs, and words that will be played time and again throughout the subsequent chapters. The date of Jeremiah's call is debated (see introduction). It is clear that the prose tradition dates the prophet's call to the thirteenth year of the reign of King Josiah, that is, 627 B.C.E. (cf. 1:2, 25:3). This early date would make the prophet active during the reign of Josiah and a witness to his political ambitions. Jeremiah would also have been aware of, if not an actual participant in, the comprehensive religious reform of Josiah (see 3:6; 36:2). The major problem with the early dating is the difficulty of locating any of the prophet's poetic sayings in Josiah's reign. One solution to this problem has been to argue that 627 B.C.E. is the birth date of the prophet who believed he had been appointed to be a prophet by Yahweh before he was born (1:5). The poetic tradition may implicitly support this later date. Jeremiah's call, then, would correspond with the death of Josiah in 609 B.C.E., motivating the prophet to move to Jerusalem to begin his prophetic activity.

Jeremiah's call follows the first of two forms of prophetic calls: the encounter with (the word of) Yahweh (cf. Exod 3:1–4:17; Judg 6:11-27; 1 Sam 3); and the vision of Yahweh in the heavenly court (cf. 1 Kgs 22:19-23; Isa 40:1-11; and Ezek 1:1–3:11). The first literary pattern consists of the following parts: the divine confrontation (*Now the word of the LORD came to me*, v. 4), introductory word (*Before I formed you in the womb I knew you, and before your were born I consecrated you*, v. 5a), commission (*I appointed you a prophet to the nations*, v. 5b), objection (*Ah, Lord GOD! Truly I do not know how to speak, for I am only a boy*, v. 6), reassurance (*Do not say, "I am only a boy"; for you shall go to all to whom I send you, and you shall speak whatever I command you. Do not be afraid of them, for I am with you to deliver you, says the LORD* vv. 7-8), and sign (*Then the LORD put out his hand and touched my mouth; and the LORD said to me, "Now I have put my words in your mouth. See, today I appoint you over nations and over kingdoms, to pluck up and to pull down, to destroy and to overthrow, to build and to plant,"* vv. 9-10). The form and content of Jeremiah's call closely parallel those of Moses (Exod 3:1–4.17), indicating that the tradition presents Jeremiah as the "prophet like Moses" (see Deut 18:15-22). It is unlikely that the call of Jeremiah was a personal experience. More probably his call, as well as prophetic calls in general, was set within a liturgical service that commissioned certain individuals for this role.

Yahweh predestined Jeremiah to the prophetic role, "consecrating" (v. 5, literally: "setting aside for divine service") and appointing him to be a *prophet to the nations* (v. 5; see "Oracles Against the Nations," chaps. 46–51). The call picks up the theology of Yahweh's creating of humans in the womb, nourishing them through gestation, assisting in the birthing process, and nurturing them after birth (see Gen 2:4b-25; Job 3; 10; Ps 139:13-16). In his final lament, Jeremiah curses his birth, thus negating his call (20:14-18).

Ah, Lord GOD (v. 6) introduces a complaint or accusation against God (see Josh 7:6-9; Jer 4:10; 14:13; 32:17; Ezek 4:14; 9:8; 11:13; 20:49). *I do not know how to speak* refers to the primary role of the prophet as a spokesperson for God (see Exod 4:10-12). The Hebrew word for "boy" may refer to a child, adolescent, or young man. It normally refers to a male who is unmarried. The presence of this word in Jeremiah's call brings to mind the call of another "prophet like Moses," the lad Samuel (see 1 Sam 3).

Yahweh reassures the prophet of divine presence and redemption: *I am with you to deliver you* (v. 8); but this is a promise that Jeremiah in his laments comes to doubt (see the laments in 11:18–20:18). Yahweh's touching and placing divine words in the mouth of Jeremiah also draws from the imagery of the "prophet like Moses" in Deut 18:15-22 (cf. Jer 15:19). God appoints Jeremiah, not kings, over nations to determine their destiny by the proclamation of the divine word that shapes human history. The word will be both destructive (*to pluck up and to pull down, to destroy and to overthrow* [v. 10]; see the oracles of judgment in chaps. 2–25) and redemptive (*to build and to plant* [v. 10]; see the oracles of salvation in the "Book of Consolation" in chaps. 30–31).

1:11-14. Initial visions. Reports of visions in the prophetic corpus contain an introduction in which the prophet sees something, a description of what is seen, a dialogue between Yahweh and the prophet, and Yahweh's explanation of the meaning of the vision (see Jer 24; Amos 7:1–9:4). These two visions of Jeremiah follow this general pattern. The first vision (vv. 11-12) is built around a word play between *a branch of an almond* (*šāqēd*) and *watching* (*šōqēd*). Yahweh's interpretation, *I am watching over my word to perform it*, emphasizes God's firm intention to enact the content of the prophetic word. The second vision, the *boiling pot* (v. 13), mentions for the first time the imagery of destruction *from the north* (see the "Foe from the North" oracles in chaps. 4–10).

1:15-16. Interpretation of the second vision. The second vision is expanded by a deuteronomic scribe who explains to an exilic or postexilic audience that the Babylonian conquest of Jerusalem and Judah was divine punishment for breaking the Mosaic covenant by worshiping other gods and practicing idolatry.

1:17-19. Exhortation to Jeremiah. A second redactional addition contains the encouragement offered by Yahweh to Jeremiah to persevere in his efforts in spite of strong opposition from his enemies, specified as the leaders of Judah: *kings of Judah, its princes, its priests, and the people of the land* (v. 18; the last phrase is a social term for male land owners who possessed considerable political power). Unlike the city of Jerusalem with walls that were eventually breached, Jeremiah is to be impregnable: *a fortified city, an iron pillar, a bronze wall* (see 15:20), because Yahweh will be present with him (see 1:8).

Israel's Political and Religious Disloyalty, 2:1-37

Chapter 2 is an elaborate poem consisting of several oracles united by the theme of Israel's and Judah's religious apostasy and political disloyalty to Yahweh and the covenant. The elaborate literary structure consists of the following poems: Israel's faithfulness as a young bride (vv. 1-3), religious apostasy—Baal worship (vv. 4-13), political disloyalty—alliances with Assyria and Egypt (vv. 14-19), religious apostasy— Baal worship (vv. 20-28), political disloyalty—alliance with Egypt (vv. 29-37). This literary pattern has the following sequence of poems: A, B, C, B1, C1.

The literary form of the poetic oracles in chap. 2 is the prophetic "law-suit" (*rîb*, see 2:9), consisting of the following parts: heaven and earth are called upon as witnesses, the defendant is summoned to hear the charges, the indictment is presented, rhetorical questions with obvious answers make up part of the diatribe against the defendant, Yahweh's merciful acts on behalf of the accused are remembered, and finally the defendant is judged guilty and sentenced. In the trial, Yahweh serves as both the plaintiff and the judge (see Isa 5:1-7; Hos 9:10-13; 13:4-8; Mic 6:1-8).

If the early date of Jeremiah's call (i.e., 627 B.C.E.) is historically accurate, then one would place these oracles in the first period of Jeremiah's ministry, prior to his move to Jerusalem in 609 B.C.E. Within an environment of a growing nationalism, stimulated by Josiah's early successes, Jeremiah utters oracles of judgment against Israel and Judah that draw upon the theology and language of another prophet from the North, Hosea. Like Hosea, Jeremiah also spoke of Israel as a young bride and the wilderness as a honeymoon period prior to entrance into the land of Canaan (chap. 3). He too condemned Israel for religious and political apostasy in images of a faithless bride and a disobedient child.

2:1-3. Israel's faithfulness as a young bride. The prose introduction (*The word of the Lord . . . Jerusalem*, vv. 1-2) is inserted by deuteronomic redactors who have Jeremiah speak the oracles of the poem *in the hearing of Jerusalem* (v. 2).

Following the imagery of Hosea (chap. 2), Jeremiah describes the beginnings of Yahweh's relationship with Israel in the wilderness of Sinai as a marriage of newly-weds. This depiction of the wilderness experience, which follows the exodus from Egypt, strongly contrasts with the theme of murmuring and rebellion in the Books of Exodus and Numbers (cf. Exod 15:22–Num 36:13). For Jeremiah, Israel was a faithful bride "devoted" (*hesed*, love or loyalty) to her marriage to Yahweh. The metaphor of *a bride* for Israel's relationship to God is a common one (see Hos 2; Isa 49:18; 61:10; 62:5).

The prophet then uses priestly metaphors to characterize Israel's relationship with God. Israel is described as *holy* to Yahweh, meaning "to be set apart or conse-crated for divine service" (cf. Jer 1:5), and as the *first fruits of his harvest*, that is, the initial and best yield of the harvest of crops that also was holy or set apart as an offering to Yahweh (Exod 23:19; 34:26; Deut 26:2, 10). The unauthorized eating of this sacred gift led to defilement and punishment. The prophet indicates, then, that those nations who mistreated Israel met with disaster.

2:4-13. Religious apostasy and the worship of Baal. The mood now changes when Jeremiah issues an indictment of Israel's faithlessness. This relationship of newlyweds deteriorated after Israel's entrance into the land of Canaan. In spite of Yahweh's bringing Israel out of Egyptian slavery, guiding and sustaining her in the Sinai wilderness, and giving her the land of Canaan, Israel became unfaithful by worshiping the Canaanite god Baal (literally "husband") and idols (*worthless things*, v. 5, and *things that do not profit*, v. 8; cf. Deut 32:21; 1 Kgs 16:13; Jer 8:19; 10:8; 14:22). Using priestly language, Jeremiah speaks of Israel's defiling or polluting the land with wicked actions. Those who led Israel's apostasy were priests, rulers, and prophets. This act of changing deities (exchanging its *glory*, v. 11, literally, "divine manifestation or presence") is unparalleled, says the prophet, even among pagan nations. Mentioned specifically are Cyprus, an island and center of trade lying in the eastern Mediterranean that is approximately sixty mi. west of the Phoenician coast, and Kedar, a confederation of Arab tribes that controlled eastern trade routes through Arabia. Jeremiah calls on the heavens as witnesses to Israel's disloyalty to respond in shock.

2:14-19. Political disloyalty—alliances with Assyria and Egypt. Israel's faith-lessness is manifested not only by following after other gods. Jeremiah also indicts Israel for refusing to depend on the power of Yahweh and seeking to make alliances with Egypt and Assyria.

Israel was liberated by Yahweh from Egyptian slavery to experience freedom in a new land. While not a slave to be bought and sold, Israel has become the plun-der of nations. The Assyrians (*lions*, v. 15) and Egyptians (*the people of Memphis and Tahpanhes*, v. 16) both have inflicted terrible destruction on Israel. Even so, instead of turning to God for redemption, Israel goes to the very nations who had ravaged it to seek political alliances that surely will fail. In the hope for political survival and even independence, Judah attempted to strengthen its position by means of military alliances. *Memphis*, a former capital of Egypt, is located on the Nile about fifteen mi. to the south of modern Cairo. *Tahpanhes* is modern Tel Defenneh, near Lake Menzaleh in the northeastern delta region. King Psammetichus of Egypt (664–610 B.C.E.) established a garrison there for Greek mercenaries to defend Egypt's borders against Assyrian attacks. These two cities would have been places where royal diplomats would have gone to attempt to work out political and military alliances. It would be natural then for refugees from Judah to flee to these cities in the aftermath of the Babylonian destruction of the nation (43:7-9; 44:1).

In this oracle, Jeremiah may be alluding to the desires of some advisors within Josiah's government, if not also the king himself, to establish an alliance with the Egyptians and the Assyrians to stop the advance of the Babylonians. If this effort were attempted, it certainly backfired. The Egyptians routed the Israelites at Megiddo, and Josiah was killed.

2:20-28. Religious apostasy—Baal worship. Jeremiah now returns to his indictment of Israel's religious apostasy. He speaks of the former faithful bride becoming a whore who, having broken her marriage vows and throwing off all restraint, offers herself *on every high hill and under every green tree* (v. 20). These are images of fertility religion practiced at a HIGH PLACE or sanctuary located on forested hills. Asherah, an earth mother goddess in Canaanite religion, was represented by a sprouting tree, while Baal's presence was depicted in the form of a free standing stone called a *massebâ*. Jeremiah changes the images in v. 27, perhaps for ironic effect. These gods, whose number Judah has greatly multiplied, do not have the power to redeem in difficult times (see 10:1-16; Isa 40:18-20; 41:5-7, 21-29; 44:6-20; 46; Pss 115; 135).

Images used to depict Israel's faithlessness include those of a whore, an ox that breaks its yoke, a vine that becomes wild, a stain even lye and soap will not wash off, the lust of a young camel, and a wild ass in heat. Again, Judah's leaders are the culprits in this apostasy: kings, officials, priests, prophets (see 1:18).

2:29-37. Political disloyalty—alliance with Egypt. It is ironic, says Jeremiah, that Israel "complains against God" (literally, seeks to indict God), since the people, not their LORD, have been unfaithful. Israel has forsaken her marriage to God and forgotten she was a bride. Although women could not legally divorce their husbands in Israel, Israel has abandoned God, claiming *We are free, we will come to you* (i.e., God) *no more* (v. 31). Even Yahweh's warnings in his causing the death of Israel's disobedient children have not led her to return to him.

Israel's abandonment of Yahweh for other gods and political powers, coupled with her injustice, including the death of the innocent poor, will lead to her shame at the hands of one of the very nations with whom alliances were sought. As Assyria before, so now Egypt will humiliate Israel. Josiah died at Megiddo in 609 B.C.E. at the hand of the Egyptians, led by Necho II, and Judah came for a brief time within the orbit of Egyptian rule, until King Jehoiakim shifted his allegiance to the Babylonians after the battle of CARCHEMISH (see introduction).

Sermon on Repentance, 3:1–4:4

The sermon on repentance is also a collection of oracles, only in this case, they exhort Israel to *return* (v. 1, Heb. *šûb*) to Yahweh (i.e., "repent"). The Hebrew word *šûb* ("return," "repent") occurs sixteen times in this sermon. The collection begins with a law-suit (*rib*) that uses the law concerning marriage and divorce as an analogy for describing Yahweh's relationship to Israel as a faithless wife who has many lovers (3:1-5). The prophetic genre called a "summons to repentance" shapes the three interior poetic oracles: 3:12-13; 14, 19-20; and 21-23 (cf. Amos 5:4-7, 14-15; Hos 14:2). The concluding oracle, 4:1-5, offers the alternative ("either-or") of repentance leading to blessing or persistence in evil and destruction. The conditional formulation of the initial two verses and the emphasis on "return" echo the beginning poem in 3:1-5, thus serving as an INCLUSIO for the whole. The "summonses to repentance" are placed between the first oracle, a law-suit that intends to condemn and punish, and the fifth and final oracle that holds out the condition of blessing for a people who would truly repent. In following Hosea, Jeremiah depicts Yahweh as both father and husband and Israel (as well as Judah) as an adulterous wife and faithless children.

The poetic sections include: vv. 1-5 (the adulterous wife and the faithless child), vv. 12-13 (the adulterous wife), vv. 14, 19-20 (faithless children and adulterous wife), vv. 21-23 (faithless children), and 4:1-4 (faithless Israel exhorted to repent). The poetic call to repentance is addressed to both Israel and Judah. If the early date for the call is historical, this poem consists of oracles most likely issued during the early stage of Jeremiah's activity when Josiah had defeated the Assyrian and Scythian garrisons and moved into the northern territory to reestablish the empire of David. The audience of these sermons would then be both Israelites who continued to live in the former northern kingdom and some who migrated south as well as the people of Judah and Jerusalem.

Deuteronomic editors inserted into this poetic collection three prose speeches: 3:6-11, 15-18, and 24-25. Allowing the prophet to address an exilic or early post-exilic audience, the first prose sermon notes that Israel and Judah are guilty, that Israel (the northern territories) did not return to Yahweh, her husband, and that Israel's *false sister* (v. 7, i.e., "faithless sister") Judah did not learn from Yahweh's divorce of Israel, but also had *played the whore* (v. 6) to become even more guilty than her sister.

The second prose speech addresses the future: Yahweh will raise up faithful *shepherds* (v. 15, i.e., rulers), *the ark of the covenant* (lost or destroyed in the Babylonian destruction of Jerusalem) will not be missed or replaced, Jerusalem will become Yahweh's *throne* (v. 17) to which the foreign nations shall come, and Israel and Judah will be reunited. The last prose speech is a confession of sin uttered by a repenting nation that is the prerequisite for salvation.

3:1-5. The adulterous wife and disobedient child. Israel is characterized as both a faithless wife and rebellious child. Jeremiah uses the same deuteronomic legislation concerning divorce (Deut 24:1-4) that influenced Hosea to speak of Yahweh's return to faithless Israel. In the deuteronomic law, a husband could not remarry his divorced wife, even if her second husband died or divorced her. Jeremiah's two rhetorical questions have rather obvious answers. Yes, the land would be polluted by the violation of this law. And yes, a repentant Israel, having become a prostitute, could return to her divine husband. This second yes is rather shocking, for God would do what the law would not allow a husband to do: take a faithless, divorced wife back. This is Jeremiah's understanding of divine grace: even a faithless Israel could repent and expect God to take her back. The notion that unethical behavior "pollutes" the land, that is, profanes its holiness, is not an uncommon idea in priestly religion (see Lev 19:29; Num 35:33-34). This pollution, caused by Israel's religious harlotry, had led to Yahweh's punishment of withholding rain to water the soil, resulting in crop failure and drought. Jeremiah's reference to Israel's having *the forehead of a whore* (v. 3) may indicate that prostitutes wore a phylactery or cord around their heads.

3:6-11. A prose commentary on 3:1-5. This prose commentary, fashioned in a question and answer style, was written by deuteronomic editors who place at least the opening oracle in 3:1-5, if not the entire collection of 3:1–4:4, in the reign of King Josiah. As is often typical of prose speeches, elements of a poetic speech are picked up, elaborated, and made more specific in terms of time and place. In this prose speech, Yahweh asks Jeremiah if he has seen the harlotry of faithless Israel who has engaged in Canaanite fertility religion. Israel did not return and was divorced by Yahweh, that is, sent into Assyrian exile. Yahweh then notes that *her false sister Judah* (v. 7), failed to learn from Israel's experience and also became a whore, pursuing false gods. Judah also failed to return to Yahweh, who regards Israel as less guilty than Judah, presumably because Judah should have learned from the example of her older sister and did not. This commentary is written primarily to explain that religious apostasy was the occasion for the tragic events that occurred in the time preceding and including the Babylonian exile.

3:12-13. Israel as an adulterous wife. A prose introduction provides the recipient of this oracle: Israel, the territory to the north of Judah. This first summons to repentance is directed to Israel as a faithless, disobedient wife who has committed adultery with multiple partners. Even so, Yahweh exhorts his faithless wife to confess her sins and return, for he is *merciful* (v. 12, Heb. *hasid*), that is, loyal to the marriage (i.e., covenant). It is divine mercy that is the basis for Yahweh's grace and forgiveness.

3:14, 19-20. Israel as faithless children and an adulterous wife. This second summons to repentance may have been addressed to Israelites from the former Northern Kingdom who are invited to return to Zion (Jerusalem) in Judah and become part of the new people of God. If the event is located in the reign of Josiah, then the prophet sees the opportunity to reincorporate remnants of Israelites into the religious community of the greater Israel being fashioned by Josiah. Indeed, Israelite refugees had moved south following the Assyrian destruction of the Northern Kingdom in 722 B.C.E. Jeremiah would not necessarily have in mind, however, physical relocation of refugees or political reunification. He would have in mind the bringing together of Israelites and Judahites in the common worship of Yahweh.

3:15-18. The new future. This is the second prose speech inserted into the collection by deuteronomic editors. More than likely it serves as a commentary on 3:14 that points towards the future return of Israelites in the northern territory, at least spiritually and religiously, to Zion. The prose speech uses this as the occasion to address the future, following the Babylonian conquest and the exile of the leaders of Jerusalem to Babylon. *Shepherds* (v. 15, a metaphor for "kings"; see Jer 10:21; 22:22; 23:1-4; 25:34-38; Ps 78:70-72; Isa 44:28; Ezek 34:1-10; Nah 3:18; Zech 10:3; 11:4-17), obedient to Yahweh, will care for those returning from captivity. After the return from exile, the population, devastated by conquest, will increase. The *ark of the covenant* (v. 16) in the Temple, stolen or destroyed during the taking of Jerusalem and the razing of the Temple, will neither be replaced or missed. First placed in the TENT OF MEETING (2 Sam 6:17), the ark was a chest containing the two tablets of the law (Deut 10:2, 5) and possibly the sacred lots (URIM AND THUMMIM, Judg 20:27; 1 Sam 14:17-18). David's placing of the ark in Jerusalem was done to symbolize the unification of the empire, especially North and South (cf. 2 Sam 6). After the construction of the Temple, Solomon placed the ark in the holy of holies (1 Kgs 8:4-7). Here it was regarded as an empty throne, guarded by two cherubim (2 Kgs 19:15). The primary theological meaning of the ark was the symbolizing of divine presence on an empty throne (cf. Exod 25:10-22; Deut 10:8). In this prose speech, however, Jerusalem in the new age will itself be called the *throne of the LORD* (v. 17).

In expanding the universal character of this eschatological vision, the speech promises that all nations will come to Jerusalem, having rejected their own stubbornness and iniquity. Finally, the remnants of Israel and Judah, having finished their languishing in exile, will be reunited and then will return from the "north country" (cf. Isa 40–55). Jerusalem will then become the center of a world kingdom ruled by God.

3:21-23. Israel as faithless children. The third summons to repentance also was addressed to Israel. *Hills* and *mountains* (v. 23) were important locations for shrines and temples. These sacred sites are sometimes identified as "high places" (*bāmâ*, 1 Kgs 14:23). *Orgies* refer to fertility rites involving sacred prostitution, a central feature of Canaanite religion. Fertility rites were believed to secure the fecundity of flocks and people, as well as bountiful crops.

3:24-25. A confession of sin. This is the third and final prose speech inserted into this collection by deuteronomic redactors. It is shaped in the form of a liturgical confession of sin and placed in the mouth of the exilic or postexilic community. It provides the paradigmatic response that the prophet has urged the community to make. While the earlier generations of Israel, including those addressed by the prophet himself, had failed to repent, now this generation of exilic or postexilic Jews makes the proper confession of sin and does repent. The confession thus serves as the ritual response to the prophet's summons to repentance.

4:1-4. Call to repentance. The final poetic oracle in 3:1–4:4 opens with three conditional clauses that lay out the requirements for Israel to experience blessing. The conditions are as follows: they are to return to Yahweh, remove the trappings of idolatry and fertility worship (*abominations*, v. 1, see Deut 29:17; Jer 7:30; 13:27; 16:18), and *swear "As the LORD lives!" in truth, in justice, and in uprightness* (v. 2). Swearing in the name of Yahweh or by the life of the Almighty is common to oaths in the OT. This means that Yahweh becomes the guarantor of the oath, making sure it is truthful and its conditions fulfilled. Yahweh would punish those who swore falsely. The violation of oaths secured by ritual swearing is one way of taking Yahweh's name in vain (cf. Exod 20:7; Lev 19:12). While there were a variety of oaths in the OT, the type to which Jeremiah is alluding most likely is the oath taken within the context of covenant renewal ceremonies in which the community swears to follow the stipulations of the covenant (cf. Gen 26:28). The conditional clauses echo the initial line of the opening poem in the collection (3:1-5), thus providing an INCLUSIO for the entire unit.

The reference to blessing is also important. A "blessing" is a ritual pronouncement, usually by God through a priest, that secures well-being and enhances life for the recipient. The mentioning of *nations shall be blessed* (v. 2)—alternatively "shall bless themselves"—echoes the promise to Abraham in Gen 12:1-3. The promise of Yahweh to Abraham includes being the ancestor of a great nation, a great name, being blessed, and becoming the conduit of divine blessing to the nations. In the last regard, Yahweh promises to bless any who bless Abraham and curse those who curse him and through him "all the families of the earth shall be blessed" (or "shall bless themselves"). Jeremiah appears to be referring to this significant text and indicates that a faithful Israel will again become the means by which the nations shall be blessed. Swearing and blessing are both examples of language that has the power to effectuate its contents, because Yahweh is associated with them both. In the admonition of v. 4, Jeremiah uses the language of circumcision to refer, not to the ritual removal of the foreskin of the male penis as a covenantal sign of being a descendant of Abraham (cf. Gen 17:9-14; Lev 12:1-5), but rather to the act of repentance and submission to Yahweh's will.

The Foe from the North (I), 4:5–6:30

Oracles of judgment united by the theme of the "Foe from the North" are found throughout chaps. 4–10. Prophetic judgment oracles generally have a common pattern, beginning with a commission or appeal for attention (e.g., 5:20-21), followed by a description of the situation (often introduced by *says the LORD*; e.g.,

5:22-28), and a prediction of disaster (e.g., 5:29), and ending with a concluding characterization (5:30-31).

It is likely that the oracular poems dealing with a "Foe from the North" were compiled as a separate collection before later editors worked the collection into the expanding Jeremiah tradition. The theme figures prominently in eleven different sections: 4:5-31; 5:1-9; 5:10-17; 5:20-31; 6:1-8; 6:9-15; 6:16-30; 8:4-13; 8:14–9:11; 9:17-22; 10:17-25. Deuteronomic redactors added to the collection the following prose speeches and comments: 4:9-12, 27; 5:18-19; 7:1-8:3; 9:12-16; and 9:23-26.

The poetic oracles of judgment about a northern foe most likely would have been delivered by Jeremiah during the reign of Josiah, if the early date for the call is historical. These dire warnings of coming destruction would have directly opposed the rampant nationalism associated with King Josiah's early successes in driving out both the Assyrian garrisons and their Scythian mercenaries and moving into the northern Israelite territories to reclaim them for the Judahite state. Another possibility for their deliverance would have been shortly after the prophet's coming to Jerusalem following the death of Josiah in 609 B.C.E., but before the battle of CARCHEMISH in 605 B.C.E. The oracles would still be powerful warnings in later political efforts at independence that eventually culminated in the destruction of Judah and Jerusalem in 587 B.C.E. and the exile of leaders to Babylonian captivity.

Nowhere in these poetic oracles does the prophet clearly identify the northern foe. The identification of the foe as the Babylonians is made by the deuteronomic redactors in the prose tradition (25:8-14). Jeremiah's strong sense of coming destruction from the North offers a warning to political leaders in Judah who continued to work for an independent state, free of foreign control. After the battle of Carchemish in 605 B.C.E., there is little doubt about the threat the Babylonians posed to the state of Judah. King Jehoiakim's transfer of allegiance to Babylonia from the Egyptians was a move of expediency, but eventually he and then Zedekiah led rebellions that produced disastrous consequences (see introduction).

The prose additions once more redirect Jeremiah's message to exilic and early postexilic audiences who were challenged to come to grips with both the destruction of Judah, Jerusalem, and the Temple and also the exile and the harsh conditions they faced once more in and around Jerusalem following the return to their homeland. These insertions modify the grim announcements of total devastation by allowing for survivors who would become the nucleus to rebuild the future. The speeches and comments also provide the theological explanation that the destruction and exile were divine punishment for disobedience to the covenant of Moses. Finally, the prose speeches promise that the uncircumcised foreign nations and Jews who are not circumcised in the heart will face divine punishment.

4:5-31. The threat from the North. This first section is directed against Judah and Jerusalem. A northern enemy is stirring and threatens destruction. In a macabre poem of striking beauty and sadness, Jeremiah likens this impending destruction to the return of chaos prior to creation. The literary structure of the sections consists of three oracles of judgment and two interludes containing the reactions of the prophet to the terrible destruction: judgment oracle (vv. 5-8), interlude (vv. 9-12), judgment oracle (vv. 13-18), interlude (vv. 19-26), and judgment oracle (vv. 28-31).

The first judgment oracle (vv. 5-8) warns people in the countryside to take refuge in the fortified cities, for Yahweh is *bringing evil from the north, and a great destruction.* The land and cities will be destroyed. The prophet then tells the people to don *sackcloth, lament and wail*, that is, to participate in rites of lamentation that are designed to appease Yahweh's anger, to stop the devastation, and to move him to defend Jerusalem against the invader (cf. Psalms of Lament: Pss 44; 60; 74; 79; 80; 83; 89;123; 125; and 144).

In the initial interlude (vv. 9-12), a prose insertion by the deuteronomic editors, the leaders are *appalled and . . . astounded* over the invasion. Then, like Moses (cf. Exod 32:30-34), Jeremiah begins to intercede on the people's and Jerusalem's behalf, even accusing Yahweh of deceiving them by causing devastation instead of carrying out his promise of well-being (cf. 1 Kgs 22:13-28). *Ah, Lord GOD* (v. 10; see note on 1:6). Then Yahweh speaks that he is bringing judgment, like a fierce desert wind.

In the second judgment oracle (vv. 13-18), Jeremiah describes the next stage of the invasion: their laying siege to the walled cities (vv. 16-17). Jeremiah explains this has happened as a result of the nation's rebellion. He urges Jerusalem once more to repent in the hope that the city might be saved.

The anguish of God is now felt by Jeremiah in the second interlude (vv. 19-26), for he sees the devastation wrought by the invading army. Jeremiah then utters a beautiful although terrifying poem in vv. 23-26 that likens the deadly invasion to a reversal of creation. Drawing on depictions of creation in various biblical texts, but especially Gen 1–2, Jeremiah describes the land after the invasion as *waste and void* (see Gen 1:2), the vanishing of light from heaven (see Gen 1:3-5), the earthquakes that shake the mountains that were considered in ancient cosmology as pillars that support the cosmos, the absence of human population (see Gen 2:5), the flying away of the birds of the air (see Gen 1:20), and the fruitful land becoming a desert (Gen 2:4b-9). The softening of the scene of total devastation is brought about by the insertion of a prose commentary in v. 27 where Yahweh promises *I will not make a full end.*

The final judgment oracle (vv. 28-31) describes the lamentation of *earth* and *the heavens*, the two spheres of creation (see Gen 1:1; 2:1, 4) who were surviving witnesses to the destruction of the nation. Zion (i.e., Jerusalem) is now personified as a woman. Like Jezebel (2 Kgs 9:30-37), Zion dresses and paints herself like a willing prostitute to offer herself to the invaders in the vain hope of escaping destruction, but even this act of desperation does not succeed (see 3:2-3).

5:1-9. In quest of a righteous person. This oracle of judgment also belongs to the collection dealing with the "Foe from the North." Jeremiah tells the audience, most likely the inhabitants of Jerusalem, to search through the city streets and squares to find one righteous person. This compares to Abraham's intercession with Yahweh to save Sodom and Gomorrah for the sake of the righteous (see Gen 18:22-33). Even though the citizens swear an oath, most likely an oath of commitment to the covenant (cf. the discussion concerning 4:2), they are lying. Both the rich and the poor had forgotten the law and their knowledge of Yahweh. Neither divine punishment nor reward has brought about allegiance and faithfulness to God through covenant obedience. The worship of false gods and adultery, both prohibited by the ten commandments (Exod 20:1-17), are mentioned specifically as sins the people have committed against God.

5:10-17. The destruction of the vineyard. This oracle of judgment takes up the metaphor of Israel and Judah as a vineyard that has grown wild and now is to be destroyed. Even *the prophets are nothing but wind* (v. 13), a word play on the Hebrew word *ruah* ("spirit," "wind," "breath") that is a source of divine inspiration (see Num 27:18; 2 Kgs 2:15; Isa 29:10). For Jeremiah these false prophets have prophesied only well-being, believing that Yahweh will not bring punishment (see 5:30-31; 6:14; 23:9-40; 28). By contrast, Jeremiah is to utter words becoming a burning fire in his mouth that will devour the people of Israel and Judah. These words are the words of judgment about the northern enemy who is described as *an ancient nation* (v. 15), speaking a foreign language not known and understood by the people, who will consume their harvest and flocks, kill their children, and destroy their fortified cities.

5:18-19. The destruction is not total. The deuteronomic editors insert a prose speech at this point to make the depiction of destruction less grim. Yahweh promises he will not make a total end of Israel and Judah. Even so, the destruction of the nation followed by exile will occur because of Israel's serving other gods.

5:20-31. Judgment against sinful Israel and Judah. In this oracle of judgment, Jeremiah contrasts the power of Yahweh as the creator who is able to control the great powers of chaos with the stubbornness and rebelliousness of Judah. *The sea* (*yām*) is often personified as the ruler of chaos or of the seas in Canaanite myth. Yam fought with Baal, the god of fertility, for lordship over the earth (also see Job 38:8-11; Ps 74:12-14). Even Yahweh's providential care for creation through the sending of the rains does not evoke in them the "fear of God," that is, the faithful response of religious piety. Their injustice has led to their enrichment, while they abuse the rights and needs of the destitute, including orphans. A concluding observation points to prophets as guilty of false prophecy. Most likely they have spoken only of well-being and prosperity, a message followed by the priests.

6:1-8. The northern invader approaches. The advance of the northern foe is picked up again in this oracle of judgment. Now they are approaching Jerusalem. Jeremiah exhorts his fellow Benjaminites who have sought protection within the walls of Jerusalem to flee the city before it is taken. Watchmen from *Tekoa* (twelve mi. south) and *Beth-haccherem* (Ramet Rahel?, two mi. south) send signals to Jerusalem warning them of the approaching army. Now the attack against the city is launched, not at night to take advantage of stealth aided by darkness, but at noon, during the bright light of day. The military measures of assaulting a city are described. Jeremiah, at the conclusion of the oracle, returns from the terrible vision of future destruction to the present to warn the city to mend its ways or face the prospects of becoming *a desolation, an uninhabited land* (v. 8).

6:9-15. Jeremiah's warnings are ignored. This judgment oracle, a part of the collection dealing with the "Foe from the North," describes the pouring out of Yahweh's wrath upon all groups within the nation: children, young men, married couples, and the old. All will be victims. The injustice of the nation is pervasive, but those especially guilty are the leaders who should be responsible for ethical guidance: the prophets and the priests. However, even these religious leaders have deceived the nation, falsely promising *Peace, peace* (v. 14). They too will be among the victims at the time of disaster.

6:16-30. Forsaking the *ancient paths.* This judgment oracle also speaks of the northern foe and the terrible destruction that they are bringing against Zion (i.e., Jerusalem). Jeremiah exhorts the people to stand at the crossroads to look for the *ancient paths* that should be followed to avoid the coming devastation. These paths are the covenant of Moses and its teaching of life. However, the people are characterized as having rejected this exhortation, choosing instead disobedience. Because Yahweh's teachings and warnings have gone unheeded, he rejects the nation's sacrifices and gifts (cf. Hos 9:4). *Frankincense . . . from Sheba* (v. 20) is a fragrant gum resin from Boswellian trees growing in South Arabia, northeastern Africa, and India for use as perfume (Cant 3:6; 4:6, 14) and incense (Exod 30:34-38). *Sweet cane* was used for anointing oil in priestly ritual (Exod 30:23). *Burnt offerings* and *sacrifices* cover in general the different animal sacrifices offered in worship (see Lev 1–7).

The military power of the foe is once more depicted (vv. 22-23). The people's response in vv. 24-25 is one of helplessness in the face of such a powerful enemy. Jeremiah tells them to initiate rites of lamentation, for the enemy suddenly will appear (v. 26). In vv. 27-30 Jeremiah is likened to a metal-smith, who, having examined the mettle of the people, that is, their religious character, determines them to be *rejected silver,* that is, metal either not containing enough silver or having too many impurities to use for jewelry and decorations (see Job 23.10; Zech 13.9).

The Temple Sermon, 7:1–8:3

Inserted within the larger collection concerning the "Foe from the North" is a prose speech composed by deuteronomic redactors that breaks down into the following components: the Temple sermon (7:1-15), pagan worship (7:16-20), disobedience and rejection of sacrificial ritual (7:21-29), *the high place of Topheth* (7:30-34), and the disinterment of the bodies of the dead (8:1-3). This lengthy speech explains to an exilic or postexilic audience that the destruction of Judah and the exile resulted from pagan worship and disobedience to the stipulations of the Mosaic covenant.

7:1-15. The Temple sermon. Chapter 26 summarizes this sermon and then adds a description of the trial of Jeremiah that follows. According to 26:1-2, this deuteronomic speech occurs in the year of King Jehoiakim's accession to the throne of Judah (609 B.C.E.). Jehoiakim was placed on the throne by Necho II when Judah became a vassal nation to the Egyptians (see introduction), following the death of Josiah at Megiddo and the rout of his army by Egyptian forces. The *people of the land* (male land owners in Judah, cf. 1:18) anointed Jehoahaz, a son of Josiah but younger than his brother Jehoiakim, as the next king. However, Necho II, for unknown reasons, removed Jehoahaz and exiled him to Egypt. Jehoahaz had only sat on the throne of his father, Josiah, for three months before being deposed (see 22:10-12; Shallum is the birth name of Jehoahaz). Subsequently, Jehoiakim did not enjoy either prophetic anointing or the endorsement of the tribal leaders who included the male land owners.

Pilgrims have come to Jerusalem to worship Yahweh. The specific type of worship is not given, although it more than likely would have been one of the pilgrimage festivals, perhaps the Festival of Booths, a seven day festival held in September–October to give thanks for the fall harvest and to remember God's guidance of Israel during the wandering through the Sinai wilderness following the exodus (Lev 23:39-43). According to 1 Kgs 8, Solomon dedicated the Temple during this festival, while Deut 31:10-11 states that the law was to be read every seven years during the occasion of the manumission of slaves.

In the introduction (vv. 1-2), Jeremiah is told to stand in *the gate of the LORD's house* (Jerusalem Temple) and address the pilgrims who are coming to worship. Then follow two exhortations (vv. 3-4 and 5-8). In the first, Jeremiah admonishes the audience to act with moral integrity so that Yahweh either may dwell in their midst or will allow them to dwell in the land, that is, not go into exile. The Hebrew in v. 3b may be read in two ways: "let me dwell with you" (i.e., divine presence in the Temple), or "I will let you dwell" (i.e., not go into exile). If the first translation is followed, then the argument is that a God of justice and holiness may dwell only in the midst of a moral and holy community (cf. Isa 6:5). The second translation emphasizes that a failure to practice justice will result in exile. But in either case, Jeremiah then admonishes the pilgrims not to trust in these *deceptive words* (*šeqer*, "lie, falsehood"), *the temple of the LORD* (v. 4, repeated twice more for emphasis). What Jeremiah denies is not that God dwells in some fashion in the Temple, that is, is present with the community in Jerusalem, or that the Temple belongs to Yahweh. Rather, what he is disputing is the theology of the inviolability of Jerusalem; in other words, God will defend Zion against the attack of its enemies, regardless of obedience to the covenant (see Pss 46; 48; 76; Isa 31:4-5). For Jeremiah, obedience to the covenant, including especially the moral commands of the law, and not the Temple and its theology of an invincible Jerusalem, is the one hope for the city and its inhabitants to avoid devastation. In the second exhortation (vv. 5-8), Jeremiah makes the clear connection between the people's continuing to dwell in the land and obedience to the law. For legislation designed to care for *the alien, the orphan, and the widow* (v. 6), see Deut 10:18-19; 24:17-22; 27:19. The alien is a foreigner residing in Judah (or Israel). In Deuteronomy, the spirit of which is captured in this speech, the care for the destitute who are especially subject to abuse derives theologically from Israel's remembrance of its experience as slaves in Egypt, prior to the Exodus.

In vv. 9-11, Jeremiah then refers to five of the TEN COMMANDMENTS (Exod 20:1-17; Deut 5:6-21) that the nation violates. Jeremiah emphasizes that ethical behavior as defined by the law cannot be separated from religious observance. Indeed, it is ludicrous for worshipers to believe that they can violate the moral stipulations of the law and still expect Yahweh's protection. Having set forth his accusations, Jeremiah then issues in vv. 12-15 his threat. He does so by recalling the destruction of the temple at Shiloh, a town located some eighteen mi. north of Jerusalem (modern Khirbet Seilun). This town served as the seat of the Levitical priesthood and was an important religious center during the period of the Judges (Josh 21:1-2; Judg 21:19; 1 Sam 1:3, 9). However, it was destroyed, probably by the Philistines in the eleventh century B.C.E. (see Jer 26:6-9). In like manner, Yahweh promises he will destroy Jerusalem and its Temple, and he will take the population into exile, just as he did to the northern kingdom (*offspring of Ephraim*, v. 15) at the time of the Assyrian conquest in 722 B.C.E.

7:16-20. Pagan worship. One of the more interesting points is Yahweh's forbidding Jeremiah to intercede to save the people, seeing that intercession on behalf of people to God is a primary task of prophets (see 11:14; 15:1; Exod 32:30-34; Amos 7–9). The reason is the religious apostasy of entire families in Jerusalem and other towns. The *queen of heaven* is the Assyro-Babylonian goddess, Ishtar, an astral goddess of both war and fertility (see 44:15-30). Yahweh's wrath will issue forth in the destruction of the entire land, including both the human population and animals, fruit trees, and crops.

7:21-29. Rejection of sacrifice. The pilgrims gathered in Jerusalem to worship are told to do a thing that was forbidden by law: eat the flesh of burnt offerings. The flesh of this sacrifice was to be consumed by fire, signifying it was reserved for God (see Lev 1). Then Jeremiah makes an astonishing claim: Yahweh did not command Israel to establish the sacrificial cult at the time of the exodus, but rather commanded them to be obedient to the law, that is, the moral imperatives of the covenant. The prophet appears to reject the entire sacrificial system as a human invention. Yahweh has sought to speak to his people through the prophets, but without success. Verses 27-29 warn the prophet that no one would listen to his speech. Verse 29 is a poetic fragment of a judgment oracle, presumably from Jeremiah, that is embedded within the prose. The exhortation, *cut off your hair* (v. 29), refers to part of the ritual of lamentation that the people are to pursue, because they have been rejected by Yahweh (cf. 16:6; Mic 1:16).

7:30-34. High place of Topheth. Jeremiah then condemns the people of Judah for carrying out religious pagan rites even in the Temple (see 2 Kgs 21–23) and for building a pagan high place (sanctuary), Topheth (from an Aramaic word meaning "fireplace"; cf. 2 Kgs 23:10), located in the Valley of the son of Hinnom that was to the west and south of the walls of Jerusalem. The valley was the site of idolatrous practices that included the sacrifice of children (see 19:5; 32:35; 2 Chr 28:3; 33:6). It is possible that the commandment requiring the giving of the first-born to Yahweh (Exod 22:29-30) was at times interpreted to mean child sacrifice, a view Jeremiah counters (see Lev 18:21). However, in the future, this high place and this valley will be known for another horror: the piling up of corpses too numerous to bury.

8:1-3. Disinterment of the dead. The prophet presents a gruesome prediction of the disinterment of the corpses of the population of Jerusalem and its leaders who will perish in the fall of the city. These corpses will be laid out before the astral deities to whom they had looked for life and protection (i.e., the sun, moon, and host of heaven; see Deut 4:19; 17:3; and 2 Kgs 23:5). Jeremiah may be alluding to the Assyrian practice of disinterring the corpses of leaders of a vassal nation that had broken a treaty. Also compare Josiah's desecration of tombs at the sanctuary of Bethel (2 Kgs 23:16).

The Foe from the North (II), 8:4–10:25

Once more the theme of the "Foe from the North" reappears (see 4:5–6:30) in the following poetic oracles of judgment: 8:4-13; 8:14–9:11; 9:17-22; and 10:17-25. Prose speeches are inserted by deuteronomic editors in 9:12-16 and 9:23-26. There is also a poetic diatribe against idol worship (10:1-16) that includes a prose insertion (10:11).

8:4-13. Judgment against people and leaders. In this judgment oracle, Jeremiah indicts the people for refusing to repent and contrasts their lack of knowledge of the revealed law with species of fowl who instinctively know the natural order of the seasons (vv. 4-7). He then announces judgment against the religious leaders for falsely construing the law (scribes, prophets, and priests, vv. 8-13).

Jeremiah's prophetic *word* (v. 9) conflicts with the written law only because the sages (*the wise*) who have the responsibility for interpreting it rightly have made it into a lie, that is, they have offered a false meaning. Sages in Jeremiah's time served the two great national institutions: court and Temple. Royal sages or scribes were members of the monarchic bureaucracy that had the task of governing according to the will of the king, while Temple scribes wrote cultic legislation, interpreted priestly law, and taught the nation God's torah. Sages were often at odds with prophets over discerning and understanding the divine will (see 18:18; Isa 3:1-4; 30:1-5; 31:1-3; Obad 8). The sages understood wisdom to be a divine gift developed through study that gave them the insight into the order of creation, understood as justice, and through this order an understanding of the nature and will of God. By ruling in conformity with the order of the world, kings were believed to govern wisely and well, producing peace and well-being for their nation. Individuals were taught that obedience to wisdom, implemented in life, also led to well being and success. Jeremiah's complaint against the sages is that they have wrongly construed the law to mean there will be peace and well-being for the nation, failing to recognize that judgment is coming.

8:14–9:26. Lamenting the coming destruction. Several prophetic speeches are woven into this long poem: 8:14-17 (the people resigned to their doom); 8:18–9:3 (an interlude describing God's anguish over the suffering of his people); 9:4-9 (the neighbor's deceit); and 9:10-22 (three exhortations to lament over imminent destruction).

In 8:14-17 the people flee into the fortified cities for protection from the invaders, recognizing that the peace they had been promised by their leaders was an illusion. The reference to *Dan* in v. 16 points to the presence of the enemy near this city located on the northern border of Israel. The quaking of the land in v. 16 reflects not only the thunderous sounds of a mighty cavalry but also the chaos tradition that describes the shaking of an unstable cosmos at the approach of divine judgment (see Hab 3). Once more the prophet experiences divine suffering because of the destruction that is soon to engulf his people (8:18–9:3). The false security in the presence of the Temple and the presumed inviolability of Jerusalem because of Yahweh's presence is contrasted with Yahweh's anger seething against his people because of their idolatry (v. 19; cf. 7:1–8:3). The "daughter of my people" (v. 21, RSV; NRSV, *my poor people*, is a metaphor for Jerusalem) has suffered such a grievous wound that even the *balm in Gilead* (v. 22), the resin or gum of the balsam tree used to heal wounds, and their physicians are unable to offer healing.

The deceit of the neighbor and brother is underscored in 9:4-9, a deceit that is so pervasive that it has corrupted the nation with lies and treachery. In 9:10-11, 17-19, 20-22, the prophet issues three exhortations to the inhabitants of Jerusalem, professional mourners, and the women of the city to lament the death of the cosmos and the destruction of Jerusalem occasioned by the invasion. *The mourning women* and *the skilled women* (9:17) are professional mourners paid to weep during a funeral or over destruction of a city (see 22:18-19; Lam). In ancient Near Eastern fertility religions, female mourners engaged in cultic lamentations designed to aid fertility gods in rising from the dead in order to bring new life after a season of languishing in the underworld. Thus, lamentation in these settings was a prelude to life. But not so for Jeremiah, for the invader's destruction is so great the cosmos has been laid waste. There is only death without the promise of life. Verses 21-22 allude to the Canaanite deity Mot ("Death") who in mythology kills his nemesis Baal, the god of fertility, and brings him into the underworld.

Jeremiah 9:12-16 and 9:23-26 are two deuteronomic prose additions interpreting the destruction of the country as due to disobedience to the law, reassuring the exiles of God's covenant love and justice, and promising future punishment of "uncircumcised" pagan nations and Jews who are uncircumcised in their hearts. *Those with shaven temples* (v. 26) are Arabs who engage in the cutting of hair as a religious ritual (see 25:23, 49:32).

10:1-16. An idol satire. Idol satires, like this one, are especially common to Second Isaiah (Isa 40:18-20; 41:6-7; 44:9-20). Jeremiah describes the fashioning of an idol by humans and then lampoons its obvious deficiencies: it cannot speak, walk, breathe, and do good or evil. Only fools worship idols. By contrast, Yahweh is unparalleled in greatness and inspires legitimate fear. He is the creator of the world and providential overseer of cosmos and history.

In v. 9 *Tarshish* is mentioned as the source for silver, although it continues to be an unidentified seaport apparently famous for being a great trading center (see 1 Kgs 10:22; Isa 23:1, 14; 60:9; Ezek 27:25). *Uphaz* has not been identified, although it could be a corruption for Ophir, a place well known for its gold (1 Kgs 9:28). Verse 11 is a prose addition in Aramaic, the only occurrence of this language in Jeremiah. It promises destruction of false gods who did not create the heavens and the earth.

10:17-25. The final siege. This oracle is the last one in the collection dealing with the "Foe from the North." The siege against the cities will not be lifted. The inhabitants of these cities are told to prepare for exile. Once more Zion (i.e., Jerusalem), depicted as a mother who has lost her children, laments her suffering and grievous wound. She castigates *the shepherds* (v. 21, a metaphor for the kings) who, because they did not seek and follow divine guidance (*inquire of the LORD*), have scattered their flocks (see *Rachel . . . weeping for her children* in 31:15-22). In v. 22, there is a warning of the approach of the foe from the north country. Finally, in vv. 23-25 Jeremiah prays for divine mercy towards himself, since he, like all humans, is sinful. It may be that the prophet uses the "I" of the prayer to represent the nation, a not uncommon practice in OT prayers (see laments in the Psalter). In any case, in v. 25 he then offers intercession for Jacob (i.e., Israel) by asking for divine punishment of the foreign nations who do not know God and have destroyed his people. This intercessory prayer, in accordance with the role of the prophet like Moses, comes too late to save Israel from the northern foe (cf. the "Oracles against the Foreign Nations" in chaps. 46–51).

The Broken Covenant, 11:1-17

This prose speech, composed by deuteronomic editors, renders judgment against Judah and the people of Jerusalem for violating the covenant of Moses. The language of the chapter and its theology are strongly reminiscent of Deuteronomy. Examples of deuteronomic language include *cursed be anyone who does not heed the words of this covenant* (v. 3; cf. Deut 27:26); *when I brought them out of the land of Egypt, from the iron-smelter* (v. 3; see Deut 4:20); *that I may perform the oath that I swore to your ancestors* (v. 5; see Deut 7:8; 8:18; 9.5); *a land flowing with milk and honey* (v. 5; see Deut 6:3; 11:9; 26:9, 15; 27:3); *as at this day* (v. 5;

cf. Deut 2:30; 4:20, 38; 6:24; 8:18; 10:15; 29:28). Also following a deuteronomic theological tradition is the explanation that the destruction of Judah and Jerusalem and the Babylonian exile came as a result of the violation of the covenant. Once again the prophet is not allowed to intercede for Judah and Jerusalem in order to divert Yahweh's punishment (v. 14; see 7:16; Exod 32:30-32).

Jeremiah's Laments (Confessions), 11:18–20:18

The poetic and prose materials in 11:18–20:18 are various in nature and include laments, judgment oracles, biographical narratives, and oracles of salvation. However, laments are the major literary form. Jeremiah utters some seven laments (11:18-23; 12:1-6; 15:10-21; 17:14-18; 18:18-23; 20:7-13; and 20:14-18) that follow a typical two part pattern: the prophet's complaint and Yahweh's response. A fragment of a lament describes the conversion of pagan nations in 16:19-21, while sections of two thanksgiving psalms, a genre that serves as a response to laments, are inserted in 17:12-13 and 20:13. Yahweh also utters laments (12:7-13 and 14:17-18), while the people of Jerusalem offer up two of their own (14:1-10 and 14:19-22). Two prose additions speak of Yahweh's prohibiting Jeremiah from offering intercessory prayers on behalf of the people (i.e., laments; 14:11-12 and 16:1-13), while another comments that even if intercessions were offered by the great prophets, Moses and Samuel, the nation's punishment would not be averted (15:1-4).

As a literary form, laments are a common genre in the Psalter (e.g., Pss 3, 4, 5, 6, 7, 9–10, etc.). Yet they are also present in other biblical books, including, e.g., the Book of Job (cf. e.g., chaps. 3 and 29–30). Laments are characterized by a recurring pattern. In full blown examples, one finds the following: invocation, complaint (description of suffering, reproachful questions addressed to God), plea for help, condemnation or cursing of enemies, affirmation of confidence, confession of sins, acknowledgement of divine response, and such hymnic elements as praise of God and blessings. Announcements of salvation by a worship official (priest or cult prophet) or thanksgiving psalms are usually considered the proper response to a lament.

Jeremiah's laments (confessions) are unique in prophetic literature and have received a variety of different interpretations. They may be understood as issuing from the historical prophet's own religious experiences of doubt, persecution, and suffering. Taken in this way they provide a look at the interiority of the prophet. If they are prayers of the historical Jeremiah, these prayers could be placed in any period of his life. However, the laments also may be viewed as expressing corporate experience, and thus are more stereotypical and formal than personal and private. Perhaps Jeremiah is speaking at times as the representative of the nation in both its struggles with God and its reactions to suffering. A combination of these two views stresses that the prophet as intercessor expresses at times his own struggles and at other times those of the community to which he preaches. Finally, there is the question of whether these laments are the words of the historical Jeremiah or prayers that are placed on his lips by later editors who, along with their own religious communities, struggle with important questions of faith, authentic existence, and human suffering.

The laments of Jeremiah are placed in their literary context to interact with various other materials, including especially judgment oracles, both poetic and prose: 13:1-11, 12-14; 13:15-17, 18-19, 20-27; 14:13-16; 15:1-9; 16:16-18, 21; and 17:1-4. The setting presupposed by the judgment oracles appears usually to be the siege of Jerusalem and an imminent exile (thus either 597 or 587 B.C.E.). Biographical narratives are also present for the first time and provide illustrations of both the struggles of the prophet that lead to the laments and the context out of which the oracles of judgment/salvation issue. These narratives include 18:1-12 (the potter and the clay), the broken earthenware jug (19:1-15), and the persecution of Jeremiah by Pashhur (20:1-6).

Finally, two types of prose speeches are present in these chapters: the promise of salvation (12:14-17 and 16:14-15; cf. chaps. 30–31), and an "either-or" sermon on the sabbath that offers the choice between salvation and punishment (17:19-27).

11:18-23. The first lament. Jeremiah's initial lament consists of a poetic complaint to God by the prophet (vv. 18-20) and a prose response by Yahweh (vv. 21-23). Jeremiah complains of being an innocent victim (*gentle lamb*, v. 19) of a plot against his life. He quotes or at least summarizes the words of his opponents who are plotting not only to kill him, but also to destroy even the last traces of his memory: *his name will no longer be remembered*. While belief in life after death did not come to expression in the OT until several centuries after Jeremiah (cf. Dan 12:2-3), there was the hope to continue to exist through one's descendants and through their memory of the deceased (cf. Gen 12:2; Eccl 1:16; 7:1). Looking to God for protection, the prophet asks for divine punishment of his persecutors. This call for vengeance is a common feature of laments (cf. Pss 3:7; 7:6).

In Yahweh's prose response, the enemies of Jeremiah are identified specifically as *the people of Anathoth* (v. 21), that is, his own family and neighbors. This response is likely added by the deuteronomic redactors who typically attempt to make references and events in poetic texts more clear. The reason for persecution of Jeremiah by *the people of Anathoth* is not stated, although Yahweh does issue a promise of judgment against them.

12:1-6. The second lament. In this lament, Jeremiah raises one of the most critical theological questions in the book: the question of the justice of God. Verse 1a may be translated: "Righteous are you, O LORD; nevertheless, I shall bring charges against you." It may be that the prophet begins his complaint with a confession of divine justice but then moves to a lawsuit. Indeed, the standard confession is the legal basis for the suit. Jeremiah makes clear that it must be God who supports the wicked and enables them to prosper. It is interesting to note that when Jeremiah brings this legal charge, God is both defendant and judge.

Once more God responds (vv. 5-6), but not with soothing words of promised salvation or with a reasoned defense of divine justice. Rather, God informs the prophet that his present persecution is only going to intensify and warns him that his own brothers from his father's house are those who seek to do him harm.

12:7-13. Yahweh's lament. Now God utters his own lament in which he grieves over his having given *the beloved of my heart into the hands of her enemies* (v. 7). Judah is destroyed by invaders, but in the last line Yahweh promises to take vengeance against them. This is an interesting display of the inner turmoil of the passion of God who carries out a terrible judgment against Judah, and yet laments for his people; who brings the invaders to effectuate divine judgment, and yet promises they will meet with their own punishment.

12:14-17. Judgment against Judah's neighbors. A prose promise of salvation added by deuteronomic editors comments on the lament in 12:7-13. Judah is promised that as a result of divine compassion God will bring them home after the exile. Judah's neighbors who have been its enemies are also offered salvation, but only if they convert to the worship of Yahweh (see 30:10-11).

13:1-11. The linen waistcloth. This prose narrative tells the story of a symbolic action that illustrates the message of the prophet (see also chaps. 19 and 32). The typical pattern of symbolic actions of prophets has three parts: God commands the prophet to perform a symbolic act, the narrative describes the completion of the act, and then an explanation of the act is provided. In this narrative, the action centers on a linen waistcloth. A waistcloth was an undergarment covering the middle portion of the body. The material from which the waistcloth was made is linen, also used for various types of clothing, sheets, curtains, and burial shrouds. All garments worn by priests were made of linen (Lev 16:4), but there is no suggestion here of some connection with priestly apparel.

The Euphrates and the Tigris were the two major rivers (hence, the word Mesopotamia, a Greek term meaning "in the midst of rivers") in Babylonia. It is doubtful that the prophet made the journey to Mesopotamia twice; this would have been a journey of at least 400 miles one way. Instead of the Euphrates (Heb. *pĕrātâ* or *pĕrāt*), an alternative reading is Parah, modern Khirbet Farah, located about eight km. northeast of Jerusalem. However, it is more likely that the journey, like the larger narrative, is a symbolic action, not to be taken literally. Indeed, the event may have been created by deuteronomic editors seeking to illustrate Jeremiah's judgment against his people. In any event, the spoiled waistcloth illustrates the sinful corruption of Israel and Judah.

13:12-14: The symbolism of the wine-jars. This prose speech, coming from the hands of deuteronomic editors, takes the form of a promise of judgment against both the leaders of Judah (kings, priests, and prophets) and the inhabitants of Jerusalem. Jeremiah apparently quotes a popular proverb, *every wine-jar should be filled with wine* (v. 12), to which the audience responds that they know this saying. Jeremiah then makes the application: the leaders and the inhabitants of Jerusalem will be filled with wine from the wine-jar and become drunk, an image either of stupor that inhibits their making wise decisions or of a "cup of wrath" from which they are made to drink (see 25:15-29).

13:15-27. Exile. Three poetic oracles addressing the exile either of 597 or 587 B.C.E. are shaped into a larger poem that describes the tragedy of captivity. In the first oracle (vv. 15-17), Jeremiah calls the people to repentance. The expression, *give glory to the LORD* (v. 16), refers to a doxology uttered by a person found guilty of a crime. The doxology praises the God of justice, and its utterance indicates that the judgment has been fair, even when the verdict is guilty (see Josh 7:16–21; 2 Chr 30:8). Images of chaos are used to describe the effects of impending judgment: *darkness, twilight, gloom*, and *deep darkness* (cf. Job 3). Since the nation is guilty, it should utter a doxology, repent, and hope for a reprieve. Otherwise the prophet will grieve for the departing captives.

The second oracle is one of judgment and addresses a *king and queen mother* who have been deposed (vv. 18-19). *The king and queen mother* would be Jehoiachin and Nehushta, if 597 B.C.E. is the time in question (2 Kgs 24:8-17). If it is 587 B.C.E., the identities of the two would be Zedekiah and Hamutal (2 Kgs 24:18-20). In Judah, the *queen mother* was the mother of the ruling king and not one of his wives. This position had significant political influence (see 1 Kgs 2:19; 15:13; 2 Kgs 8:26; 11:1-3). The *Negeb* was the southern part of Judah. While a hot and arid region, the Negeb at the time was dotted with villages that were engaged in agriculture and with fortresses to protect both Judah from the south and the several trade routes through the area. For Jeremiah, even Judah's more remote towns will be emptied of its people in the coming invasion and exile.

The third oracle is a law-suit that attributes the ravages of exile to religious apostasy (vv. 20-27). *Those who come from the north* are again mentioned as the ones who bring destruction (see chaps. 4–10). Judah, like a prostitute who has shared her favors with false gods, will be raped by the invaders. Yahweh will lift up her skirts over her face, exposing her nakedness. In v. 23, the prophet asks two rhetorical questions to emphasize that a corrupt nation cannot change its ways. Ethiopian refers to an inhabitant of Cush, a country located south of Egypt.

14:1-10. The lament of the people. The first section provides a poetic description of the devastation of a lengthy drought (vv. 1-6). The people of Judah and Jerusalem engage in a lamentation, but to no apparent avail. The second section (vv. 7-9) contains the lament of the people in which they acknowledge their sins and ask for Yahweh to deliver them. The reproach of God in vv. 8-9 is common in laments of accusation. In v. 10 Yahweh responds, not with an oracle of salvation, but rather with an announcement of his rejection of their plea due to their continuing wickedness.

14:11-12. Jeremiah may not intercede. In a prose speech from deuteronomic editors, Yahweh forbids Jeremiah from engaging in intercessory prayer on the people's behalf (see 7:16; 15:1; 16:5-9). In following up v. 10, the prose speech emphasizes that Yahweh will not accept the people's petition and sacrifices, for he intends to bring judgment against them (6:20; 7:21-29).

14:13-16. Lying prophets. In spite of this commandment against intercession, Jeremiah still voices his protest (*Ah, Lord GOD*, v. 13; see 1:6). The point raised by the prophet is the deceit of those prophets who have prophesied peace and not destruction (see 23:9-40; 28). Jeremiah may be implying that Yahweh has sent them to deceive (cf. 1 Kgs 22). In any case, God denies that he has sent these lying prophets, for they are speaking the illusions of their own invention. The very prophets who deny that Yahweh will send famine and a sword against his people will themselves, along with those who listen to them, be victims of the same judgment. These victims will suffer the onerous curse of not being buried (see 7:29–8:3).

14:17-18. Yahweh's second lament. God again laments over the destruction of his *virgin daughter*, the city of Jerusalem (see 12:7-13). Prophet and priest are once more singled out as the cause of the disaster that is coming.

14:19-22. The people lament again. The people of Judah and Zion (i.e., Jerusalem) once again express an accusatory lament reproaching God for the devastation they are experiencing. They confess their sinfulness and ask God to save them. The throne of Yahweh (v. 21) in this context is either Jerusalem (see 3:17) or the Temple (see 17:12; Ezek 43:7).

15:1-4. Intercession cannot divert destruction. In the language of a deuteronomic prose speech, Yahweh contends that Moses (Exod 32:11-14, 30-34; Num 14:13-19) and Samuel (1 Sam 12:17-18) could not be successful in interceding on Judah's behalf. Yahweh still would not change the decision to bring judgment against the nation (see 7:16; 14:11-12; 16:5-9). In the prose tradition, Jeremiah becomes a deuteronomic prophet, one like Moses (Deut 18:15-22). Manasseh reigned over Judah for forty-five years (687/86–642 B.C.E.) as a loyal Assyrian vassal. The deuteronomic editors of 2 Kings blame him for the eventual destruction of Jerusalem and the exile of Judah, because of his leading the people into religious apostasy (2 Kgs 21:1-18). According to deuteronomic justice, the destruction of Judah and the exile were at least in part the result of the sins of the ancestors.

15:5-9. The announcement of Jerusalem's end. This judgment oracle announces the final destruction of Jerusalem, using the image of winnowing the chaff from the grain (see 51:2; Isa 21:10). Earlier disasters did not cause the people to change their evil ways. The bearing of seven children is a sign of divine blessing of the womb (Ruth 4:15; 1 Sam 2:5). The mother of seven faints, because of the loss of her children.

15:10-21. Jeremiah's third lament. (see note on 11:18-23). This lament follows what has been the usual pattern: complaint by the prophet (vv. 15-18) and Yahweh's response (vv. 19-21). However, deuteronomic scribes added a prose lamentation and response in vv. 10-14. Jeremiah utters a lament to his mother, telling her he wishes he had never been born. The reason: he has become the object of cursing. One should remember that God determined before his birth that he would be a prophet (see 1:5). In the last lament, Jeremiah curses his birth, wishing he had been aborted (20:14-18). A *man of strife and contention* (v. 10) refers to Jeremiah's being both the object of persecution involving at times legal action against him (see chap. 26; 36:20-26; 37:11–38:13) and the mediator of Yahweh's lawsuit against the nation (see 2:1-37). Even his own family sought to destroy him (11:21-23). The Hebrew word for "curse" (*qillēl*) refers to both verbal abuse (Eccl 7:21-22) as well as physical harm (Gen 8:21). Curses were considered to have the potency to harm the person against whom they are directed.

In the response to this prose complaint, Yahweh takes responsibility for Jeremiah's suffering, although he argues that he has intervened in the prophet's life *for good* (v. 11). This probably means Yahweh has protected him from his enemies (cf. 1:8). Even so, persecution builds the prophet's character, making him fit to endure the great sufferings inflicted by the northern invader (see 1:17-19). Yahweh then announces, probably to Judah, that it will be plundered and forced into exile (vv. 13-14).

In this complaint (vv. 15-18), Jeremiah states he has "eaten Yahweh's words," a graphic metaphor for his having received the prophetic message given to him by God (1:9; see Isa 55:1-11; Ezek 2:8–3:3). *I am called by your name* (v. 16): Jeremiah's name means "Yahweh exalts." While he rejoiced in the call and reception of the divine word, his prophetic ministry has led to alienation and an often burdensome life. *Weight of your hand* (v. 17) is a rather common metaphor for prophetic inspiration (see 1 Kgs 18:46; 2 Kgs 3:15; Isa 8:11; Ezek 1:3; 3:14). Jeremiah concludes his lament with a rather harsh indictment of God. The prophet uses two related metaphors for Yahweh: *deceitful brook* and *waters that fail* (v. 18). These metaphors oppose Yahweh's affirmation of being a *fountain of living water* (2:13) and denial of being *a wilderness to Israel* (2:31).

Yahweh's response in vv. 19-21 implies that Jeremiah has relinquished his role as a prophet. Three times Yahweh uses the term *turn back* (v. 19, Heb. *šûb*), recalling the sermon on repentance in 3:1–4:4. "To stand before the Lord" refers either to a messenger who stands before the king, waiting for the royal proclamation, or to one who offers intercession in a ritual setting or a law court. The language of v. 20 echoes that of 1:18-19 (the conclusion of the call), while the promise to redeem the prophet from the wicked reflects 1:8.

16:1-13. The symbolism of Jeremiah's lack of family. In this deuteronomic prose sermon, Yahweh prohibits the prophet from marrying and having a family. This prohibition helps to illustrate Yahweh's coming judgment that will afflict families. Those who die by means of disease, famine, and the sword will not be buried. Rather their corpses will be consumed by birds and wild animals. Once more Jeremiah is commanded by Yahweh not to lament on behalf of the people, for their punishment is inevitable (7:16; 14:11-12; 15:1). Their ancestors and they have committed religious apostasy, and this is the basis for understanding why they have suffered.

The *house of mourning* in v. 5 is a room or hall in a house where a funerary banquet is held (see Amos 6:7). *Gashing* and *shaving* (v. 6) the head were prohibited funerary practices associated with pagan worship (Lev 19:28; 21:5; Deut 14:1). The question and answer form recurs throughout the prose tradition (5:19; 13:12-14; 15:1-4; 22:8-9).

16:14-15. The future return from exile. This prose sermon of salvation promises that in the future a new confession will replace the one centering on the exodus from Egypt. The confession will focus on the new act of God's liberation, this one the return from Babylonian captivity. Confessions like these were central to religious faith and worship. Jeremiah 23:7-8 almost exactly duplicates this passage.

16:16-21. The fishers and hunters of Judah. The prose sermon that left off with v. 13 now continues and speaks of fishermen and hunters who will seek out the people of Judah in every conceivable place. These fishermen and hunters are likely the Egyptians (Isa 19:5-10) and Babylonians (Lam 4:18-19.). Verses 19-20 are a part of a lament that expresses faith in God and a universal recognition by the nations of his lordship (see Ps 2; Isa 2:3 = Mic 4:2). Verse 21 continues v. 18, stating that with this punishment Judah will finally know Yahweh.

17:1-4. Judah's sin. This prose sermon announces judgment against Judah for practicing fertility religion. The reference to *an iron pen; with a diamond point* (v. 1) suggests an engraving instrument used to incise characters on stone. The point more likely was a hard stone, possibly emery, and not diamond. The ten commandments were engraved on tablets of stone (Exod 31:18; 32:16). In this case the sin of Judah is to be incised on the tablet of their heart and the altar's horn (cf. Job 19:24). This text in v. 1 is similar to 31:31-34 that speaks of writing the law on the heart. The image points to the embodiment of either sin or of the commandments (31:31-34). Altars had *horns*, that is, projections from their four corners (Exod 27:2) on which the blood of sacrificial animals was smeared (Lev 4:7). People seeking asylum would grab hold of the altar's horns (1 Kgs 1:50-51; 2:28-34). Tablets were made of stone, metal, or wood.

Sacred poles (v. 2, *'ăshērâ*) were either carved wood (Judg 6:25) or living trees (Deut 16:21) that represented the Canaanite fertility goddess, Asherah (see 1 Kgs 15:13; 18:19; 2 Kgs 21:7; 23:4; Mic 5:13-14).

17:5-11. A collection of wisdom. Inserted at this point is a collection of wisdom sayings, most likely originating with sages like the ones who wrote and collected the wisdom texts of Job, Proverbs, and Ecclesiastes. Jeremiah 17 contains a wisdom poem (vv. 5-8), a rhetorical question (v. 9), a first person proverb (v. 10), and a comparative proverb (v. 11). The editors or compilers of Deuteronomy, the deuteronomistic history (Joshua through Second Kings), and Jeremiah may have been scribes raised in the wisdom tradition passed down in scribal schools.

The poem consists of two strophes (vv. 5-6; 7-8) and is reminiscent of the one that begins the Psalter (Ps 1). While the psalm stresses that the study of the law results in blessing, the poem in Jeremiah emphasizes trusting in Yahweh in contrast to self-reliance or trusting in mere human beings. The imagery of the *tree planted by water* (v. 8) in both texts calls to mind the "tree of life," a common wisdom motif originating in myths of the ancient Near East dealing with paradise (see Gen 2:9; 3:22; Prov 3:13-18). The sages believed that wise behavior led to well-being in life. Rhetorical questions (v. 9) are queries that have obvious answers (see "the voice from the whirlwind" in Job 38–41; and Amos 3:3-8). The mind and the will are associated with the heart in the OT (Prov 14:10; 16:9, 23; 25:3). Yahweh has the ability to discern even the thoughts of people and to requite each person according to his/her deeds (see Pss 7:10; 17:3; 139:14; Jer 20:12). Comparative proverbs (v. 11) are sayings in which two things are compared in order to discover an underlying unity or an element held in common. This saying underscores the theory of retributive justice by an analogy or comparison from nature.

17:12-13. The praise of Yahweh and the ark. This text is a hymnic fragment in praise of Yahweh and the sacred ark (i.e., the *throne*, v. 12). The ark was an empty throne placed in the holy of holies of the Temple to signify divine presence (see note on 3:16).

17:14-18. Jeremiah's fourth lament. (see note on 11:18-23). For the first time in the sequence of Jeremiah's lament, there is no response from Yahweh. Jeremiah turns to the divine physician for healing and salvation, two areas often related in the OT (see Pss 6; 41:4; 147:3). Jeremiah denies he has pressured Yahweh to send disaster, but notes that the delay has led to skepticism that he speaks the truth. He has played the role of earnest intercessor, hoping to delay Yahweh's judgment so that Judah and Jerusalem may finally repent and avert the promised disaster. However, the prophet continues to press Yahweh to destroy his (Jeremiah's) enemies.

17:19-27. Honoring the sabbath. This deuteronomic prose speech assumes the form of "either-or" and exhorts Judah to honor the sabbath day. The decision the people make will be either life or death, blessing or punishment. Recurring seven times in this speech, *the sabbath* was the seventh day of the week and was observed as both a day of rest and of worship (see Exod 16:23; 20:8-11; 23:12; 31:12-17; Lev 23:3; Deut 5:12-15). In priestly theology (cf. Gen 2:1-4a; Exod 20:8-11), the emphasis was placed on the place of the seventh day in the temporal order of creation: by remembering the sabbath and keeping it holy (i.e., separating it from the work days of the week as a day of rest and religious observance), creation would be blessed and life enhanced. In deuteronomic theology (cf. Deut 5:12-15), the day was a time of rest and remembrance of Egyptian slavery and exodus liberation. The observance of the sabbath was an important commandment of the Mosaic covenant (also see Amos 8:5; Neh 13:15-22). The prose speech in Jeremiah on one hand explains that the judgment of disaster against Judah and Jerusalem was due, at least in part, to violating the sabbath commandment. On the other hand, the speech offers hope to the exilic and postexilic communities that the monarchy and the kingdom will be restored, if the sabbath is observed.

Jeremiah stands *in the People's Gate* (v. 19), one of the entryways to the Temple, and delivers the speech. *The Shephelah* (v. 26) refers to the low hills between the coastal plain and the central hill country to the east. Most biblical references are to the "Shephelah of Judah." For *the Negeb* (v. 26), see the note on 13:18-19.

18:1-12. The potter and the clay. This deuteronomic prose narrative combines a symbolic act with a promise of judgment (see 13:1-11). In the story, Yahweh directs Jeremiah to go to a potter's house where he will obtain a divine message. Jeremiah then observes a potter fail in making the first vessel, but later succeed in shaping the clay into another type of vessel. Yahweh then issues a promise of judgment in which he is the divine potter shaping nations for destruction or salvation depending on whether or not they repent. Yahweh announces he is *a potter shaping evil against* Judah and Jerusalem, but will alter this plan if they will repent of their evil ways (v. 11). Thus, the people of Judah and Jerusalem are given a choice to determine their own fate. Verse 12 quotes the people who in defiance declare they will follow their own plans and their own stubborn will.

The pottery industry was a significant one in ancient Israel. Villages and cities normally had their pottery workshops. Pottery-making required important skills that could be significantly enhanced by artistic creativity. Pottery in ancient Israel was shaped by hand according to a variety of methods: attaching clay to the inside of a basket that was then fired to harden the new vessel; shaping clay in the palm of one hand with the other hand; piecing clay strips around a base; and connecting lengths of clay with slip (clay mixed with water). The most advanced procedure was the use of a potter's wheel. One hand or foot turned the wheel, with the free hand or hands used to shape the clay moving on the platform. While some vessels were sun-dried, most were hardened by means of firing. Artistic enhancements included incisions, painting, and burnishing (polishing the slip which coated the dried pottery before firing).

The metaphor of God as the divine potter who created humanity (Gen 2:7) and determined the destinies of people and nations (Isa 29:16; 64:8) is an important one in the OT. However, the image does not convey a strict view of the divine determination of destiny. As is the case in the speech, humans still possess the freedom to be able, within the limitations of their humanity, to participate in creating their futures. In v. 12, it is the stubborn refusal of the people to repent that leads to their punishment.

18:13-17. The folly of idolatry. Jeremiah engages in another lawsuit against Israel, this time for idolatry. Because of this sin, Yahweh convicts Israel of sin and announces judgment. The oracle is quite similar to the lawsuit in chap. 2. One possible historical setting is Josiah's move into the northern territory of the former state of Israel to bring it back under Judahite control. Jeremiah argues that Israel will be scattered like the wind, an image of the devastation to be brought by the northern enemy.

The *snow of Lebanon* and *crags of Sirion* (v. 14) allude to the range of mountains north of Israel that extends northward for another 100 mi. Sirion is also called Mt. Hermon, a mountain with three peaks that rises some 9,230 ft. above sea level (Deut 3:9; 4:48). The charge that *my people have forgotten me* (v. 15) or that they perish for a lack of knowledge is a common one in Jeremiah (cf. 2:32; 13:24-25). *Delusion* refers to idols (see Ps 31:6; Jonah 2:8). Jeremiah picks up again the image of *ancient roads* to refer to the traditional religion of Yahweh worship that Israel has left in order to take other paths, that is, those of pagan idolatry (see 6:16). The *wind from the east* (v. 17, also known as "sirocco") is a strong hot wind that blows in from the desert carrying dust particles (see Exod 10:13; 14:21; Ps 48:7; Jonah 4:8).

18:18-23. Jeremiah's fifth lament. (See note on 11:18-23). The fifth lament of the prophet returns to the theme of his enemies plotting against his life. The prose introduction (v. 18) is added in order to make more explicit the identity of Jeremiah's opponents. His enemies are the religious leaders of Judah who make their case for removing the prophet for laudable reasons. They wish to preserve the priestly instruction (the law), the counsel of *the wise* (or sages), and the prophetic word (see 8:8). These were the three forms of divine revelation that were believed to provide proper knowledge of God and the divine will for the nation. The priests are probably the chief priestly officials of the nation, *the wise* were either royal counsellors to kings or interpreters of the priestly law, and the prophets were so-called court prophets who prophesied peace and prosperity.

In the poetic lament, Jeremiah contends that he had in times past offered intercession even in behalf of his enemies (see 4:10, 19-22; cf. 14:11-12; 15:1; 16:5-9 where Jeremiah was forbidden to intercede). But now it is time, argues the prophet, for Yahweh to cause them to perish. This call for vengeance against his enemies, including even their families, is common in the laments (see 11:18-23; 12:6; 15:15; Pss 3:7; 5:4-10; 7:6). Once more Yahweh does not respond to this lament.

19:1-15. The broken jug. This prose narrative, written by deuteronomic redactors, is another symbolic action connected with a prose judgment speech (see 13:1-11). Yahweh tells the prophet to purchase *an earthenware jug* (v. 1) from a potter (see 18:1-12), *take some of the elders and some of the senior priests . . . to the valley of the son of Hinnom* (see 7:31 and note), and prophesy the destruction of Jerusalem. The judgment speech is to be reinforced by the breaking of the jug. Jeremiah then returns to the Temple and announces that Yahweh will bring evil against Jerusalem and its surrounding towns (v. 15).

The Potsherd Gate (v. 2), perhaps another name for "the Dung Gate" (Neh 2:13; 3:13-14; 12:31), may have been located in the south wall of Jerusalem. The groups and Jeremiah would have exited the gate through which the refuse of Jerusalem was taken for disposal in the garbage dump located in the Hinnom valley. This valley was also the general location of altars to false gods where various idolatrous practices, including child sacrifice, were carried on (see 7:30–8:3 and note).

Eating the flesh of one's children, and of one's neighbors (vv. 6-9; cf. 2 Kgs 6:24-31; Lam 4:10), was a curse for disobedience to the covenant (Lev 26:29; Deut 28:53; Isa 9:20; 49:26; Zech 11:9).

Smashing pottery (vv. 10-13) was a ritual act designed to destroy one's enemies (see Ps 2:9). In Egyptian execration texts, the names of the king's enemies were written on pieces of pottery, and then curses against the enemies were recited while the pottery was smashed.

20:1-6. Pashhur's public punishment of Jeremiah. In this prose narrative, *Pashhur*, a priest and *chief officer* of the Temple, is in charge of the Temple police responsible for order in the Temple precinct. Because Jeremiah was in the court of the Temple (19:14-15) when he preached against the city of Jerusalem, Pashhur arrests him, has him beaten, and then puts him in stocks located in the upper Benjamin Gate that led to the Temple. A day later, when Pashhur releases the prophet, Jeremiah utters a judgment speech against Judah, Jerusalem, and Pashhur (vv. 3-6). The prophet tells Pashhur that his name will be changed to *"Terror-all-around"* (v. 3, cf. 6:25; 20:10). NAMES in the OT often bore a meaning that spoke of peoples' character or destiny. In this case, Pashhur's new name refers to the northern foe who will surround the city in siege (hence, "Terror-all-around"), destroy it, and take its survivors into exile, a fate that Pashhur and his family will share (see chap. 28; and Amos 7:10-17). Jeremiah tells Pashhur that he will die in captivity and be buried there, along with his friends.

20:7-13. Jeremiah's sixth lament. (See note on 11:18-23). Jeremiah's sixth lament is found in vv. 7-12 and is followed by a fragment of a thanksgiving psalm in v. 13. *Enticed*, occurring twice in v. 7, means both to deceive and to seduce. The connotation of deception echoes the motif of Yahweh's sending lying spirits to inspire prophets to "entice" Ahab to wage battle and then fall at Ramoth-gilead (1 Kgs 22:19-23). The same word means "to seduce" a virgin in Exod 22:16-17 (MT 22:15-16). In Hos 2:14 (MT 2:16) Yahweh will "seduce" Israel in bringing her back to the wilderness in order to renew the romance with this faithless wife. *Overpowered* (v. 7) is a term that on occasion refers to rape (e. g., Amnon's rape of Tamar in 2 Sam 13:14). The deuteronomic law sentences to death a man who "overpowers" a betrothed virgin in the open countryside (Deut 22:25-27). The woman is spared, since no one can hear her when she "cries out" (see Jer 20:8).

Jeremiah complains that Yahweh has "seduced" and then "raped" him, and although he cries out no one rescues him. Even when he decides to keep silent (cf. 15:19-21), the compulsion is so great to speak that he must. Jeremiah's enemies also use the language of seduction and rape in their plotting to do him harm (v. 10).

Verse 13 expresses a worshiper's testimony and exhortation to a community to praise Yahweh, affirming that he redeems *the needy* from those who work evil. Thanksgivings are usually given as a response to a lament, either in anticipation of salvation or its experience (see note on 17:12-13).

20:14-18. Jeremiah's seventh lament. (See note on 11:18-23). In this concluding lament, at least in the editorial sequencing, Jeremiah curses the day of his birth (cf. Job 3). For other curses, see 11:1-17; 17:5-8. Curses were designed to harm those against whom they are uttered. They contrast with blessings that are to effectuate well-being and life for their intended subjects. By cursing his birth, Jeremiah wishes to destroy his own life, not just wish that he were dead. The curse is also an assault on creation theology in the OT, in that God is active in conception, cares for the fetus, and helps in the birthing process (see note on 1:5). Jeremiah's curse against his birth (cf. 15:10) is also a rejection of his call. In the OT, birth, and especially the birth of a son, was considered good news to be celebrated (cf. Ruth 4:13-17). The comparison of the one who announced to Jeremiah's father the good news of the birth of a son is cursed by the prophet to be like the two cities Yahweh *overthrew without pity* (i.e., Sodom and Gomorrah; see Gen 19; Isa 1:9-10; 3:9; Jer 23:14; Amos 4:11; Zeph 2:9). The prophet wishes his mother had resorted to ABORTION so that he would never have drawn breath.

Concerning Zedekiah and Jerusalem, 21:1-10

This narrative and the accompanying oracles appear to be an alternative rendition of 37:1-10. Perhaps it was placed in its present location because of the reference to another Pashhur in the preceding narrative (20:1-6) and because the collection of oracles that follow in 21:11–23:8 have the same theme of warning and judgment against the kings and the city of Jerusalem. In any case, the narrative provides the framework for oracles of judgment against King Zedekiah and Jerusalem and for a promise of conditional salvation for the inhabitants of the city.

A prose narrative, originating in the exile or early post-exile, provides the setting for two oracles of the prophet. *King Zedekiah* (597–587 B.C.E.) sends two people to Jeremiah to obtain a word from Yahweh concerning NEBUCHADREZZAR's invasion. This would be perhaps 588 B.C.E., sometime after Zedekiah has rebelled against the Babylonians. In vv. 3-7, Jeremiah utters an oracle indicating that the city will fall into the hands of Nebuchadrezzar and that Zedekiah, his servants, and the people of the city will be struck down by the sword. However, to the inhabitants of Jerusalem Jeremiah offers the alternative of remaining in the city and dying or surrendering to the Babylonians and saving their lives. The city shall be burned with fire (vv. 8-10). Also compare 34:1-7, which contains another warning to Zedekiah.

Nebuchadrezzar replaced Jehoiachin (598–97 B.C.E.) with his uncle, Zedekiah, another son of Josiah, after the first Babylonian conquest of Jerusalem in 597 B.C.E. Jehoiachin had been on the throne only three months, following the death of his father Jehoiakim who, so it seems, died in the siege. Although a faithful vassal to Nebuchadrezzar at first, Zedekiah yielded to anti-Babylonian pressure at court and rebelled. This foolish action led to the destruction of Jerusalem and the second exile in 587 B.C.E. Nebuchadrezzar killed Zedekiah's family, blinded him, and took him captive to Babylon (2 Kgs 24:18–25.7).

This *Pashhur* (v. 1), not to be identified with the person of the same name in 20:1-6, was the *son of Malchiah*, a prince who owned the cistern in which Jeremiah was imprisoned (38:6), and possibly a son of King Zedekiah (38:1). *Zephaniah* was the priestly overseer of the Temple who refused to rebuke Jeremiah for his announcement to the exiles in 597 B.C.E. that their captivity would be a long one. Nebuchadrezzar executed Zephaniah at Riblah after the fall of Jerusalem in 587 B.C.E. (52:24-27).

Zedekiah sent the two emissaries to Jeremiah to persuade him to *inquire of the LORD*, that is, to ask for an oracle (10:21; 37:2). The king hoped for a *wonderful deed* (v. 2, "deeds" in Heb.), that is, mighty acts of redemption, that would defeat Nebuchadrezzar and save the city of Jerusalem (cf. Exod 3:20; Pss 9:1; 26:7; 86:10). "Mighty deeds" in Israelite faith included acts of redemption such as the exodus from Egypt, victory at the Red Sea, guidance in the Sinai wilderness, and the taking of the land of Canaan. Zedekiah hopes that Yahweh will perform a similar act of deliverance.

However, according to Jeremiah (vv. 2-7), Yahweh will not protect the city, in spite of the strong belief in Judahite confession that he defends the city against all enemies (cf. Pss 46; 48; 76; Isa 31:4-5). On the contrary, Yahweh himself is fighting against the city and will destroy it. Even the son of David, in this case Zedekiah, will not enjoy Yahweh's protection. Royal theology in Jerusalem was grounded in the belief that Yahweh entered into a perpetual covenant with the house of David, meaning that he would defend the monarchy against its enemies (see 2 Sam 7; Pss 2; 18; 20; 21; 45; 72; 89; and 110).

In vv. 8-10, Jeremiah addresses an oracle of conditional salvation to the inhabitants of the city of Jerusalem. The prophet uses a covenantal formula found elsewhere only in Deut 30:15, 19: *I am setting before you the way of life and the way of death*. This "either-or" formulation offers life to those who leave the city and surrender *to the Chaldeans* (i.e., Babylonians).

Concerning the Kings of Judah and Jerusalem, 21:11–23:8

This collection of poetic oracles and prose speeches about the *house of David* (21:12) and the city of Jerusalem more than likely represents a later form of a once independent collection. The deuteronomic editors shaped it into its present form, added speeches and comments that made the references more specific, and enabled the poetic Jeremiah to speak to later generations. The recurring motifs are *house* (dynasty and palace) and (cedars of) *Lebanon* (representing the city of Jerusalem, palace, and Temple). The references to Lebanon recall that cedars of Lebanon were used to build both the palace and Temple (1 Kgs 5–7; 9:10-28). The general oracles addressed to the Davidic dynasty (*house of David*) are 21:11-12 (poetry), 22:1-5 (prose), and 22:6-7 (poetry), while the poetic oracles concerning individual kings are 22:10 (Jehoahaz = Shallum), 22:13-19 (Jehoiakim), and 22:28-30 (Jehoiachin =

Coniah). The prose sermons that deal with specific kings are 22:11-12 (Jehoahaz) and 22:24-27 (Jehoiachin).

It is interesting to note that Jeremiah does not address directly two kings: Josiah and Zedekiah. Josiah is indirectly mentioned in 22:10, 11, and 15-16, while an allusion may be made to Zedekiah in word plays on *righteous Branch* and *the LORD is our righteousness* in 23:5-6 (the name "Zedekiah" means "Yahweh is my righteousness"). Jeremiah 23:1-8 also contains prose speeches that broach the future: the promise of *shepherds* (i.e., kings) who will rule faithfully, and a *righteous Branch* who will rule according to wisdom and justice. The oracles and speeches in the rest of the collection pertain to Jerusalem (Lebanon): 21:13-14 (poetry), 22:8-9 (prose), and 22:20-23 (poetry).

In this collection, Jeremiah takes on the twin pillars of royal theology in Jerusalem: the promise to David and Zion (i.e., Jerusalem) as the city of God. The strong criticism of both the kings and Jerusalem (the location of palace and Temple) is in line with Jeremiah's blaming of the leadership as primarily responsible for the religious and political apostasy of the nation. While Jeremiah may not have been opposed in principle to the existence of the dynasty and Temple, these institutions and their theological understandings did not play a decisive role in his own religious views. Later prose speeches written by the deuteronomic editors attributed to the prophet the view that both kingship and Temple would play an important role in the future restoration (23:1-8; 30:9; 33:14-26). However, it is doubtful if this adaptation of the words of the prophet accurately reflects his own views.

21:11-14. General oracles against the house of David and Jerusalem. Two poetic oracles introduce the larger collection: a warning to kings to rule justly (vv. 11-12), and a judgment against Jerusalem (vv. 13-14). Assuming the form of an admonition, Jeremiah issues a warning to kings to practice social justice (see Isa 1:16-17; 56:1; Ezek 45:9; Amos 5:4b, 14-15). The imperative, *execute justice* (v. 12), recurs in 22:3, 15, and 23:5 and provides a major theme for the entire collection. Jeremiah stresses that it is the implementation of justice in social life that guarantees the continuation of the monarchy and the nation. He never refers to God's eternal covenant with the *house of David* (cf. 2 Sam 7 and Ps 89) that guarantees rule to the descendants of David. The deuteronomic formulation of the Davidic covenant (2 Sam 7), does promise punishment of kings who strayed from the Mosaic law, but does not allow for the end of the monarchy. Justice, for which the king is primarily responsible, brings well-being to the nation (Ps 72).

The initial oracle against the *inhabitant of the valley* (v. 13) (better translated: "one enthroned over the valley") includes a threat in v. 13 (see 23:30-32; 50:31; 51:25) and announcement of judgment in v. 14. The *inhabitant of the valley* refers to Jerusalem (cf. 22:23). The word "inhabitant" is a feminine participle and agrees in gender with the Hebrew word for "city," a feminine noun. Jerusalem is not called a *rock of the plain* (v. 13) elsewhere in the OT, although some thirty-three times

God is called the "rock," usually describing divine strength and support (see Deut 32; Isa 17:10; Pss 31:3; 62:7; 71:3).

This image of *rock of the plain* may be a parody of Jerusalem that considers itself impregnable because of its fortifications, Davidic king, and Temple housing the powerful God who will defend the city against forces of chaos and human invaders (Pss 46; 48; 76; Isa 31:4-5). *Forest* (v. 14; "of Lebanon" is understood) may be a term for either the palace (see 22:14; 1 Kgs 7:2-12; 10:17, 21; Isa 22:8) or the Temple (1 Kgs 6:9-36), since Solomon purchased cedar wood from Lebanon to construct both of them. In either case, Jeremiah announces a *fire* will burn down this *forest* of Lebanon (cf. 22:7).

22:1-5. A warning to kings of Judah. The deuteronomic redactors compose and insert into this collection a prose speech that makes the oracle against the kings in 21:11-12 more specific. Jeremiah is told to *go down to the house of the king of Judah* (i.e., to go down from the Temple to the palace) and address the king. Written in the conditional "either-or" style, this speech tells the reigning king that the implementation of justice, not only for the victim who has been robbed but also for the alien, orphan, and the widow (see Deut 16:11, 14; 24:19-21; and the note on 7:6), will enable the monarchy and the nation to endure. But if not, this *house* (either the monarchy or the palace) will become a *desolation*. The term, "desolation" is used to characterize the ruins of cities (Lev 26:31; Isa 44:26; Jer 25:18; 27:17; 44:2, 6).

To underscore the certainty of the warning, Yahweh swears by his own name. Oaths in the OT were often accompanied by swearing in the name of Yahweh to stress that the OATH maker was entering into an agreement with God to perform a certain activity. Consequently, oaths were serious pledges that were expected to be carried out (Ps 15:4; Lev 5:1-4). Curses, whether stated or implied, were usually a part of oath taking (Ruth 1:17; 1 Sam 3:17; 1 Kgs 2:23). In this context (22:5), Yahweh will make the dynasty (or palace) a desolation, if the royal house does not practice justice. This sermon explains that royal injustice was the cause of the destruction of Jerusalem, the end of the monarchy, the fall of the nation of Judah, and the Babylonian captivity (cf. the blame placed on kings in 1 and 2 Kings by deuteronomic editors).

22:6-7. Judgment against the royal palace. The language of this poetic oracle of judgment is similar to the one directed against the *inhabitant of the valley* in 21:13-14 (*cedars* and *fire = fire in its forest*). However, the prose introduction in v. 6 indicates it was addressed to the house of the king of Judah, that is, the dynasty of the Davidic monarchy. And masculine language is primarily used, including male pronouns. Masculine language fits the monarchy rather well. At the end of v. 6, the Hebrew noun "cities" is modified by a feminine participle. This suggests that the plural "cities" originally may have been a singular. If so, the NRSV translation is correct: *an uninhabited city*. While the palace or dynasty may have been addressed by this oracle, the close relationship between the Davidic monarchy and the City of

David (i.e., Jerusalem) even to the point of merging identities is clear in this collection.

The oracle compares the house of the king of Judah to *Gilead* (v. 6), a territory located in the Transjordan between Bashan and Moab, and to the *summit of Lebanon*. Both regions contained thick forests, especially on their mountain ranges. Solomon's palace was called a forest, because it was constructed of cedars from Lebanon (1 Kgs 7:1-12; see note on 21:13-14).

22:8-9. Commentary on Jerusalem's destruction. The deuteronomic editors compose and insert a prose commentary on vv. 6-7 in the form of a question and answer in order to explain why Jerusalem and the palace were destroyed. When foreigners pass by and see the ruined city and wonder why, the answer to be given is that the city has violated the covenant and worshiped other gods (see 5:19; 9:12-16; 13:12-14; 15:1-4; 16:10-13; Deut 29:22-28; and 1 Kgs 9:8-9).

22:10-12. Concerning Josiah and Jehoahaz (Shallum). This part of the collection contains a fragment of a poetic oracle (v. 10) concerning two unidentified males (one dead and the other in exile) and a prose speech (vv. 11-12) by the deuteronomic editors that specifically identifies the person exiled as *Shallum* (i.e., King Jehoahaz).

Verse 10 admonishes an audience, presumably the citizens of Jerusalem, not to continue lamenting *for him who is dead*, presumably King Josiah who perished in 609 B.C.E. during the battle against the Egyptians at Megiddo (2 Kgs 23:28-30). The lament over this popular king would have been even greater, because with his death Judahite independence, enjoyed since 627 B.C.E., came to an abrupt end. The hopes for the restoration of the Davidic empire also died with Josiah.

Instead of lamenting for Josiah, the people are exhorted to grieve for one who has been taken into exile. More than likely this would have been Jehoahaz, a son of Josiah chosen by the *people of the land* (male land owners, cf. 1:18). Rather, the people should lament the exile of Jehoahaz (609 B.C.E.) who was chosen to reign in Josiah's stead. Jehoahaz, condemned by the deuteronomic editors of 2 Kgs as "doing evil in the sight of the LORD," was to reign for only three months. Necho II, King of Egypt, replaced him with another son of Josiah, Jehoiakim (2 Kgs 23:30-34). Jehoahaz was taken to Egypt where the Books of Kings says he died. Consequently, Jeremiah seeks to put an end to any popular speculation that one day this son of Josiah would return and claim the throne.

The deuteronomic editors make clear in their prose speech that follows (vv. 11-12) that the one who has gone into exile and will die there is Shallum, the birth name of King Jehoahaz (see 1 Chron 3:15; Ezek 19:2-4). Kings in Israel had two names: a birth name and then a name given at the time of coronation and installation.

22:13-19. Against King Jehoiakim. Jeremiah's harshest oracle against members of the royal lineage was directed against King Jehoiakim (609–598 B.C.E.). Necho II replaced Jehoahaz (cf. 22:10-12) with his older brother Jehoiakim. Jehoiakim's birth name was Eliakim (2 Kgs 23:34). Jehoiakim came to the throne without the popular support of the *people of the land* (cf. 1:18) and without any stated anointing by priests or prophets. Following the Babylonian victory over the Egyptians at CARCHEMISH in 605 B.C.E., Jehoiakim quickly switched his allegiance to Nebuchadrezzar II. Seeking Judahite independence, Jehoiakim decided after serving the Babylonians for three years to rebel, a foolhardy action that led to a Babylonian invasion culminating in the surrender of Jerusalem and the first exile in 597 B.C.E. Jehoiakim's heavy taxation, mainly necessitated by the demands for tribute by the Egyptians, is singled out for mention in 2 Kings (see 2 Kgs 23:34–24:7). He too is condemned by the deuteronomic editors of the Books of Kings as one who "did what was evil in the sight of the LORD." The death of Jehoiakim occurred in 598 B.C.E. during the Babylonian siege of Jerusalem, although the exact circumstances of his passing remain unclear. Second Kings simply notes that Jehoiakim "slept with his ancestors" and was succeeded by his son Jehoiachin. Second Chronicles 36:6 states that he was placed in chains to be transported to Babylon by Nebuchadrezzar. Jeremiah suggests an ignominious death for the king: he would die without a proper burial and funeral (22:18-19; 36:30).

The speech against Jehoiakim in 22:13-19 is a poetic judgment oracle with a prose insertion by the deuteronomic editors in v. 18a to specify Jehoiakim as the person addressed. The term *alas* (or "woe," "ah") in v. 18 originates in the funeral lament and is used on occasion by the prophets to announce the demise of the audience (see Isa 10:5; 17:12; 28:1; Amos 5:18; 6:1; Hab 2:6, 9, 12, 15, 19). The lengthy indictment of the king centers on Jehoiakim's injustice, particularly the use of unremunerated labor in the building of a palace or a renovation of an old one (vv. 13-17). Solomon also used uncompensated labor in the building of royal projects (see 1 Kgs 5:13-18; 9:15-22). The use of cedar recalls the wood that Solomon had purchased for the building of the palace and Temple. The palace of Jehoiakim was painted *with vermilion* (v. 14), that is, red ocher. Jeremiah contrasts Jehoiakim, described in the images of the great tyrant Solomon (cf. 1 Kgs 3–11), with Josiah who practiced social justice. Jehoiakim also is condemned for stealing (v. 17, *dishonest gain*), most likely heavy taxation and refusing to compensate workers, and *shedding innocent blood* (cf. 2 Kgs 24:4). *Shedding innocent blood* is one of the twelve curses associated with violating the Mosaic covenant. It especially refers to the corruption of the legal process when judges were bribed to condemn innocent people (Deut 27:25).

Jeremiah's judgment (vv. 18-19) speaks of the death of Jehoiakim who will be denied a royal funeral with full honors. The references to *brother*, *sister*, *lord* (father), and *majesty* suggest either the stereotypical language of funeral songs, adapted to the occasion, or the symbolism of the king fulfilling various family roles on behalf of his people. Jehoiakim's burial will be like that of *a donkey* who dies in the city and then is dragged through the city gate to a garbage dump to rot in the open (the Valley of Hinnom? see 36:30). The denial of burial was a horrible fate (see 8:1-3; Deut 28:26).

22:20-23. Judgment of Jerusalem. Once again Jeremiah directs a judgment oracle against the "inhabitant of Lebanon," the city of Jerusalem. The city is personified as a woman, addressed in feminine language (cf. 21:13-14), and told to go to the mountains and lament (see Jephthah's daughter who weeps over her fate in Judg 11:37-38, and Rachel weeping for the children she lost, Jer 31:15-22). Jerusalem has been an adulterous woman with many lovers; an inclination to fornication has accompanied her since her youth (see 2:2; Ezek 16:22, 43, 60; Hos 2.17). She is called upon to lament her approaching humiliation (see 4:8; 9:17-22; 14:1-10). The three mountainous areas where she is to wail over her imminent destruction are *Lebanon, Bashan,* and *Abarim,* respectively north, northeast, and southeast of Israel. Jerusalem's lovers may be either false deities (Hos 2) or allies (Ezek 23:5, 9) who promised her support. These lovers and their kings (*shepherds*), as well as the rulers of Jerusalem, shall go into exile (see 2:8; 3:15; 23:1-4).

22:24-30. Against King Jehoiachin (Coniah). The judgment against the next king, Coniah (i.e., Jehoiachin), comprises two parts. The first part is a prose speech in vv. 24-27, written by deuteronomic editors who wish to give more specific information about Coniah in vv. 28-30. Coniah was the birth name of King Jehoiachin who came to the throne most likely during the last weeks of the siege of Jerusalem in 597 B.C.E., succeeding his father Jehoiakim, who died in mysterious circumstances. Jehoiachin ruled for only three months before Nebuchadrezzar deported him to Babylon (2 Kgs 24:6-17) and replaced him with Zedekiah, his uncle and another son of Josiah. While Jehoiachin died in exile, speculation about his possible return to the throne (cf. 28:4) and the recognition of his continuing authority by some of the people of Judah gave his successor, Zedekiah, added difficulty in ruling. The Jewish community in exile calculated their calendar by reference to Jehoiachin's captivity (e.g., Ezek 1:2), while Babylonian texts continued to call Jehoiachin "King of Judah" after his exile and even indicate he received a pension from Nebuchadrezzar. Inscriptions on jar handles from the period demonstrate that royal property belonged to Jehoiachin, not Zedekiah. Second Kings fuels this speculation by ending with the report that Jehoiachin, in the thirty-seventh year of his captivity (560 B.C.E.), was released from prison by "Evil-merodach of Babylon" (2 Kgs 25:27; "Amel-Marduk" is the Babylonian name), given a place of honor above the other exiled kings, and provided with food from the king's table and a regular allowance.

However, the deuteronomic speech, like Jeremiah's that follows, emphasizes that Jehoiachin will die in exile and will not return home. Indeed, Jeremiah predicted the exiled king would never return home. *As I live* (v. 24) introduces an oath (see notes on 4:2 and 22:5) to underscore that Yahweh will not allow Jehoiachin to return home. The reference to Jehoiachin as the *signet ring* in v. 24 is to the authority of the king as Yahweh's representative. The bearer of the signet ring was authorized to press clay seals on official documents with the king's stamp. Zerubbabel, a descendant of David, is called Yahweh's "signet ring" in Hag 2:20-23, thus stimulating messianic expectations.

The second part of this section about Coniah is Jeremiah's judgment speech (vv. 28-30) which dispels any hope that Jehoiachin will rule again in Judah. He has been taken away into exile, along with his children, and will never return. The same is true of his offspring. It is as though Jehoiachin were childless (actually, he had seven sons, 1 Chr 3:17-18). Neither he nor one of his sons shall come to the throne of David.

23:1-8. Sermons of future hope. The concluding section of the collection concerning the House of Judah and Jerusalem is written by deuteronomic editors who compose three prose speeches that address the future. The first speech (vv. 1-4) uses images of the "woe oracle" (see note on 22:13-19) to place the blame for the disasters that befell Judah and Jerusalem on the kings (*shepherds*), and then promises the future return from exile when the people will have new rulers. The language of being "fruitful and multiplying" echoes Yahweh's promises to Abraham and Jacob whose descendants would be many, inherit a land, and become a mighty nation (Gen 17:1-8, 20; 28:3; 48:4). Thus a judgment speech is followed by one of salvation.

The second speech focuses on the *righteous Branch*, a descendant of David whom Yahweh will raise up to be a just and wise king (vv. 5-6). This speech is repeated in 33:15-16. It is an example of the messianic hope that a future king would rule wisely and righteously and enable Judah and Jerusalem to prosper (cf. Isa 9:1-6; 11:1-9). The word "branch" is a messianic title in Zech 3:8, 4:12, and 6:12 that refers to Zerubbabel, a descendant of David who some thought might reestablish the Davidic monarchy during the early Persian period following the return from captivity (cf. Hag 2:20-23). The deuteronomic editors may be alluding to Zerubbabel in this speech.

The name of the future ruler is in Hebrew *yhwh sidqēnû*, meaning "the LORD (Yahweh) is our righteousness" (or "our legitimate [ruler]"). This is a wordplay on the name of Zedekiah, the last king of Judah. His name means "righteous or legitimate one (ruler) of the LORD (Yahweh)." Nebuchadrezzar gave him the regnal name Zedekiah when appointing him to reign as king in place of Jehoiachin. Zedekiah's birth name was Mattaniah (2 Kgs 24:17). Nebuchadrezzar may have chosen the regnal name to emphasize that Zedekiah, not Jehoiachin or any other pretender to the throne, was the legitimate king (cf. note on 22:24-30). While Jeremiah did not question Zedekiah's right to rule, many looked to Jehoiachin as the legitimate king. The deuteronomic editors may be suggesting that in the future the new king will convey in his name the faith of the community: "Yahweh is our righteousness or legitimate (ruler)." Thus, it is Yahweh who is the true king.

The third and final speech indicates that in the future the return from Babylonian captivity will surpass the exodus from Egypt in importance in religious confession (vv. 7-8). This speech is a promise of salvation that holds out the hope of the return from the north country. The centrality of exodus liberation in Israelite and Jewish faith is seen in its prominence in the ancient confessions found in Deut 26:5-9; Josh 24; Pss 78; 105; 106; 135; 136; and Neh 9. It is especially Second Isaiah who speaks of a "new exodus" from Babylonian captivity that will be even greater and more glorious than the liberation from Egypt (cf., e.g., Isa 43:15-21; 51:9-11).

Concerning the Prophets, 23:9-40

A collection of prophetic oracles and speeches about false prophets follows the one about kings and Jerusalem. For a narrative about a prophet of good fortune, see the one about Hananiah in chap. 28. The collection consists of three parts: a section of poetic oracles (vv. 9-22, except for vv. 16-17), a lengthy prose speech and commentary in vv. 23-32, and a commentary on the meaning of *the burden of the LORD* (vv. 33-40).

The first section divides into the following parts: the wickedness that priest and prophet share (vv. 9-12), an oracle of judgment against the false prophets of both Samaria and Jerusalem (vv. 13-15), a warning in deuteronomic prose not to listen to the false prophets (vv. 16-17), rhetorical questions and a vision report about the failure of the false prophets to see the coming judgment of Yahweh (vv. 18-20), and a rejection of false prophets (vv. 21-22). The second section is a sermon stating Yahweh's opposition to false prophets (vv. 23-32). The third section, as previously noted, presents a commentary on the meaning of the expression *the burden of the LORD* (vv. 33-40).

One of the great difficulties that confronted not just Jeremiah but also ancient Israel and early Judaism throughout their history was the problem posed by false prophets (see Ezek 13). How to distinguish between true and false prophets continued to be a perennial problem (e.g., see 1 Kgs 13; 22; Jer 28). Even the effort represented by Deut 18:15-22 to distinguish true from false prophets was not especially pragmatic and helpful: false prophets prophesied in the name of false gods, falsely represented themselves as speaking in the name of Yahweh, and foretold events that did not transpire. In chap. 23 Jeremiah presents his own tests: false prophets were immoral, speak sometimes in the name of Baal, see visions and dreams of their own mind, prophesy good fortune and not disaster, tell lies, and have not *stood in the council of the LORD* (v. 18). Yet what of false prophets who spoke in the name of Yahweh and at times even predicted disaster? What of those times when "true" prophets spoke of good fortune?

23:9-12. The wickedness of priest and prophet. The first oracle expresses judgment against priest and prophet. Verse 9 uses images of lamentation (see note on 11:18-23) to describe the state of inspiration when a prophet receives a divine revelation (see 4:19-21; 1 Sam 10:1-13; 19:23-24). Jeremiah likens it to trembling and shaking *like a drunkard*. These religious leaders will be punished.

23:13-15. Against the prophets of Samaria and Jerusalem. This oracle announces judgment against the prophets and Jerusalem. While the prophets of Samaria are indicted for deceiving the people and for prophesying in the name of Baal (see 1 Kgs 18:25-29 for a description of the activities of Baal prophets), the prophets of Jerusalem are worse, for they are adulterous liars who support the wicked. The people and country have become *like Sodom* and *Gomorrah*, two cities renowned for their evil (see Gen 18–19; Isa 1:10; and the note on Jer 5:1; also see 20:16; 50:40).

23:16-17. A warning about false prophets. This deuteronomic speech is a warning not to listen to false prophets who speak visions of their own minds and not the word of Yahweh. Especially emphasized is the content of false prophecy that promises well-being.

23:18-22. False prophets cannot see Yahweh's judgment. This oracle distinguishes between the true prophet like Jeremiah *who has stood in the council of the LORD* (vv. 18, 22) to receive the divine message and the false prophet who has not. The "council of Yahweh" is an assembly of divine beings in the royal court of heaven over which Yahweh presides (1 Kgs 22:19-23; Job 1–2; Pss 82; 89:7; Isa 6:1-8). This is the place where Yahweh issues his decrees concerning the fate of nations and people. Had false prophets truly stood in this council, they would have perceived that Yahweh's judgment was one of disaster and not salvation. The *storm of the LORD* in vv. 19-20 (repeated in 30:23-24) describes a theophany in which Yahweh comes to do battle against evil and then, following victory, sentences the wicked to destruction (see 25:32; Job 38:1; 40:6; Hab 3). Prophets ran in the sense that they were messengers of Yahweh who carried his decrees to speak to the audiences he chose.

23:23-32. Yahweh's rejection of false prophets. This prose judgment speech uses a series of rhetorical questions to indicate that the ever-present Yahweh is able to know that the false prophets have preached lies in his name. They dream their own concocted dreams, lie, and deceive. Yahweh denies he has sent them, and instead is "against them," that is, is entering into judgment against them.

23:33-40. The burden of Yahweh. The final section of this collection on false prophets focuses on the enigmatic expression, *the burden of the LORD*. Using a question and answer format (cf. 5:19; 9:12-16; 13:12-14; 15:1-4; 16:10-13; and 22:8-9), Jeremiah identifies the people, their priests, and their prophets as the *burden of the LORD*, and he indicates that they shall be punished. The commentary focuses on the word *burden* (*maśśā'*), that also means "oracle" (see Nah 1:1; Hab 1:1; Mal 1:1). When Jeremiah is asked for a *maśśā'* (i.e., "oracle") from Yahweh, he is to respond: "You are the *maśśā'* (i.e., *burden*) of the LORD." Further, the *maśśā'* ("oracle") is now simply everyone's own word, not a divine revelation. The multiplying of false oracles claiming to be from Yahweh results in corrupting the true word.

The Baskets of Figs, 24:1-10

This prophetic vision report (see 1:11-14, 15-16; Amos 7:1–9:4) has the following structure: introduction (*The LORD showed me* . . . ; v. 1), description (v. 2), dialogue (v. 3), and interpretation (vv. 4-10). The deuteronomic redactors place the narrative in the period after the first exile in 597 B.C.E. According to the deuteronomic editors, the first exiles were the *good figs* (v. 2), that is, the group chosen by Yahweh to build a new future for Judah after the return from Babylonian captivity. Jehoiachin would have been included in this group. The emphasis on Yahweh's giving them a heart to know him describes the transformation of the will and character that will occur among this group (see also 31:33-34; 32:39; Deut 29:4). The covenant language, *they shall be my people and I will be their God* (v. 7), occurs elsewhere in 7:23; 11:4; 30:22; 31:1, 33; and 32:38.

On the other hand, the *bad figs* (v. 2) were those left behind in Jerusalem following the exile, including especially Zedekiah and his officials, and those who were in Egypt. The latter would have included Jehoahaz and his entourage. Because Jeremiah had earlier spoken of Jehoiachin's dying in exile (22:24-30), it is unlikely that this narrative reflects the views of the prophet himself. The narrative would best be seen as religious propaganda used to enhance the claims of the first exiles in 597 B.C.E., including Jehoiachin and his officials, to be those who would be the true remnant around whom a new future would be built (see 28:3-4; 2 Kgs 25:27-30). This view of Yahweh especially favoring the exiles is found also in Ezra and Nehemiah in the fifth and fourth centuries B.C.E. On *return* (v. 7) see notes on 3:1–4:4. This text anticipates the new covenant passage in 31:31-34.

Judgment against the Nations, 25:1-38

25:1-14. The Babylonian captivity. This prose speech is composed by the deuteronomic editors to conclude and summarize the content of Jeremiah's speeches from the beginning of his prophetic activity (627 B.C.E., *the thirteenth year of King Josiah*, v. 3) to *the fourth year of Jehoiakim* (v. 1, which coincides with the date of the battle of CARCHEMISH, 605 B.C.E.; see chap. 36).

The sermon issues a call to repent in vv. 5-6 (see the summons to repentance in 3:1–4:4; 18:11), then quickly moves to an announcement of judgment because of Judah's and Jerusalem's lack of repentance. The refusal to listen to Jeremiah compares to the general lack of receptivity of prophets sent by Yahweh to call his people to repentance. The judgment is the coming of the *tribes of the north* (v. 9; see chaps. 4–10, the "Foe from the North"), now specifically identified as Nebuchadrezzar and the Babylonians. Nebuchadrezzar is called Yahweh's *servant* (v. 9), emphasizing that this foreign king's triumph over Judah is due to his carrying out the will of God (cf. Second Isaiah who calls Cyrus the Persian king the "anointed" of Yahweh, 45:1-7).

However, *after seventy years* (v. 12), Babylon will receive the punishment of God. Even they will become slaves to *many nations and great kings* (v. 14; cf. chaps. 50–51). This period of "seventy years" may be a rounded number for the period of time from 605 B.C.E. (the battle of Carchemish) to 539 B.C.E. (the conquest of Babylonia by the Persians). In Zech 1:12 the period of seventy years begins with the destruction of the Temple (587 B.C.E.) and concludes with its rebuilding (516/15 B.C.E.). Seventy may also suggest the normal life-span (Ps 90:10). *This book* in v. 13 may refer to the first or more likely the second scroll (see chap. 36; and introduction).

25:15-29. The cup of wrath. Serving as the original introduction to the "Oracles against the Nations" in chaps. 46–51, this prose narrative describes a symbolic action in which Jeremiah receives from Yahweh's hand the *cup . . . of wrath* (v. 15) and makes the nations listed drink and become drunk (see 13:1-11, 12-14; 18:1-12; 19:1-15). Drinking from a cup is a frequent image of punishment in the Bible (49:12; 51:7; Pss 11:6; 75:8; Isa 51:17, 22; Lam 4:21; Ezek 23:31-34; Hab 2:15-16; Rev 14:10; 16:19; 17:4; and 18:6). In the LXX, the "Oracles against the Nations" in 46–51 follow 25:13a. Judgment oracles against foreign nations are found in other prophetic texts (see Isa 13–23; Ezek 25–32; and Amos 1:3–2:3).

The nations listed in this passage roughly parallel those in chaps. 46–51. *Mixed people* (v. 20) refers to people of various cultural and ethnic identities who comprise a larger political grouping. Uz is an area in the desert east of Israel, possibly to be found in *Edom. Ashkelon, Gaza, Ekron,* and *Ashdod* are Philistine cities located on the southern Coastal Plain. *Edom, Moab,* and *Ammon* are the countries in the Transjordan, located to the east of Israel. *Coastland across the sea* (v. 22) refers to islands and coastal areas in the Mediterranean settled by the Phoenicians. *Dedan* and *Tema* are tribes in northwest Arabia. The location of *Buz* is unknown. *Elam* and *Media* are located in what is now western Iran. *Zimri*'s location is unknown. Hebrew letters are substituted in reverse alphabetical order to refer to Babylon as *Sheshach* (see 51:41). While all the nations listed are threatened by Babylonia, ultimately it too shall drink from the same cup.

25:30-38. Judgment against the nations. This poetic oracle of judgment continues the theme of the preceding section (25:15-29) by announcing that Yahweh is bringing disaster against the foreign nations. The section breaks down into two parts: an announcement of *judgment* (vv. 30-32) and a call to *shepherds* (i.e., kings and rulers) to lamentation (vv. 34-38; see 4:8; 13:18-19; and Joel 1:13-14). Verse 33 is a prose insertion that describes the cosmic devastation caused by Yahweh's judgment and the lack of funeral laments and burial for those slain (see 8:2; 9:22; 16:4).

The Trial of Jeremiah, 26:1-24

The deuteronomic narratives in chaps. 26–45 point to the actualization of the prophetic word in the life of the prophet. They show the correspondence of word and life. Jeremiah 26:1–29:32 contains three episodes in the life of Jeremiah that illustrate his conflict with the priests and the prophets (see 23:9-40). The first episode involves the trial that followed the Temple sermon (see notes on 7:1-15). The prose sermon is abbreviated in 26:1-6, with the rest of the chapter devoted to narrating Jeremiah's trial for his life.

26:1-6. The Temple sermon summarized. Chapter 7 is the first mention of Jeremiah's Temple sermon. The heading of this chapter dates the sermon and trial that follows to *the beginning* of Jehoiakim's reign (609 B.C.E.). When Josiah died in battle against the Egyptians at Megiddo in 609 B.C.E., his son Jehoahaz succeeded him to the throne. However, the reign of Jehoahaz was short-lived (only three months), for Necho II deposed him and put Jehoiakim on the throne. Jehoahaz was exiled to Egypt (see notes on chap. 22). The *beginning of the reign* probably means the king's "accession year." One possibility for a specific setting for the sermon is Jehoiakim's coronation during the New Year's festivities in early autumn, perhaps in association with the Festival of Tabernacles, when large crowds would be in Jerusalem and coming to the Temple. The sermon is a conditional one, offering the possibility of salvation in return for repentance. Otherwise, Jerusalem will become a curse among the nations and the Temple will suffer the fate of the one at Shiloh (see notes on 7:1-15).

26:7-24. The trial of Jeremiah. Jeremiah's sermon sounded treasonous to the priests, the prophets, and all the people assembled in the Temple court. They tell him that he must die. Hearing the noise because their offices were nearby (see chap. 36), the officials of Judah came from the palace and took the seat of judgment located at the entry of the New Gate of the Temple. The location of this gate is unknown.

In vv. 12-15, Jeremiah defends himself by claiming to be a prophet, mentioning once more the possibility of salvation in return for repentance, and then warning the officials and the crowd that his execution would bring innocent blood upon the city. The officials and the people tell the priests and the prophets that Jeremiah is innocent, for he has spoken in Yahweh's name. Deuteronomy stipulated death for prophets who spoke in the name of a false god or falsely claimed to speak a word in Yahweh's name. In the latter case, the only test for authenticity was whether the prophecy came to pass (18:15-22), but it is clear that the officials and people believed Jeremiah.

Some of the elders of the land, perhaps leaders among the *people of the land* (male land owners, cf. 1:18), defend Jeremiah by referring to earlier precedents of prophets who spoke against Jerusalem. They first mention Micah's prophecy against Jerusalem (Mic 3:12) during Hezekiah's rebellion against Assyrian rule (Hezekiah, 715–687/6 B.C.E.). They indicate that Hezekiah did not bring Micah to trial to punish him. The elders then mention the story of Uriah's execution, although this may have been added to the narrative at a later time. Uriah was executed by the wicked ruler Jehoiakim for speaking similar oracles of judgment against Judah and Jerusalem. Unlike good King Hezekiah, Jehoiakim has Uriah executed. Finally,

Ahikam supported Jeremiah, and he was not handed over for execution. Ahikam was an officer who served Josiah (2 Kgs 22:12, 14). His father, Shaphan, was Josiah's secretary who was involved in reporting the discovery of the law in the Temple to the king. According to the story, this law became the basis for Josiah's reforms. Ahikam also was among the entourage who consulted the prophet Huldah after the discovery of the law (2 Kgs 22). Ahikam was the father of Gedaliah, the governor of Judah after the fall of Jerusalem who was later assassinated (Jer 40–41). The association between Jeremiah and the family of Shaphan was a long and important one.

Submission to Babylon, 27:1–29:32

The second and third episodes in the life of Jeremiah that illustrate his conflict with the priests and the prophets are found in chaps. 27–29. Jeremiah's prophetic word and the actualization of that word in life in the deuteronomic narratives throughout chaps. 26–45 reach a level of heightened tension in the conflict with other religious leaders also claiming divinely given authority for their views. In chaps. 27–28, Jeremiah opposes the efforts at court to persuade King Zedekiah (597–587 B.C.E.) to rebel against the Babylonians. And in chap. 29 Jeremiah confronts by means of correspondence similar revolutionary efforts spurred on by certain religious leaders of the exiles taken to Babylonia in 597 B.C.E. Some of the Jewish exiles in Babylon, incited by nationalistic prophets, were involved in the conspiracy against Babylonia brewing at home in Jerusalem (chap. 29). The date for these confrontations between certain religious leaders and Jeremiah was probably 594/593 B.C.E. (see 28:1) when emissaries from Edom, Moab, Ammon, Tyre, and Sidon met in Jerusalem to plan revolution against the Babylonian empire. Hananiah, a prophet, predicts the breaking of the yoke of the Babylonian king and that within two years Jehoiachin, the other exiles, and the sacred vessels of the Temple, taken away by Nebuchadrezzar in 597 B.C.E., would return to Jerusalem. In the royal court, some of the conspirators looked to Egypt for help, especially with the accession of their new king, Psammetichus II (594–589 B.C.E.). Jeremiah opposed rebellion, arguing that Judah's only hope was to remain a vassal to the Babylonians. For Jeremiah, those prophets and other leaders who promised a successful rebellion were wrong and, if followed, would lead Judah down the path to destruction. Jeremiah advised the exiles in Babylon to settle down and rebuild their lives, for it would be seventy years before the restoration. Zedekiah decided not to rebel, at least on this occasion. However, under increasing pressure he eventually changed his mind and revolted, a disastrous decision that led to the destruction of Jerusalem and the major exile in 587 B.C.E.

27:1-22. The yoke of Babylon. This prose text, written by deuteronomic editors, centers on a symbolic act of Jeremiah: the fashioning and wearing of a yoke that is interpreted to mean that Judah should continue to submit to Babylonian rule (see 13:1-11; 16:1-13; 18:1-12; 19:1-15; and 24:1-10). Jeremiah preaches some three sermons: one is addressed to the envoys of foreign kings (vv. 3-11), another is directed at King Zedekiah (vv. 12-15), and the third has as its audience priests and people (vv. 16-22).

The superscription in v. 1 dates the events in chaps. 27–29 *in the beginning of the reign of Zedekiah* (597 B.C.E.), but this date does not fit the chronology of the period. While most Hebrew manuscripts read, "in the beginning of the reign of King Jehoiakim," it is likely this reading reflects a scribal error. In 28:1, the error is repeated (*the beginning of the reign of King Zedekiah*), although it is corrected in the following phrase: *in the fifth month of the fourth year*. This second date is far more likely, since the events described in chaps. 27–29 would correspond well with the fourth year of Zedekiah (594/93 B.C.E.; see 28:1).

In v. 2 Yahweh tells Jeremiah to make a *yoke of straps and bars, and put them on your neck*. This is the type of yoke that would be placed on two oxen to pull a heavy load. Normally, yokes had a crossbar with nooses made of leather, rope, or wood that would be fitted around the necks of the oxen. Attached to the crossbar would be a wooden shaft for pulling the load (see Deut 21:3; 1 Sam 6:7; 11:5; 1 Kgs 19:19). The yoke is attached to two oxen to pull a heavy load. As is the case here, yokes are at times symbolic of submission to a greater power (cf. 1 Kgs 12:1-11).

Jeremiah is then told to wear the yoke and address the envoys sent by the kings of Edom, Moab, Ammon, Tyre, and Sidon to persuade Zedekiah to join in revolution against the Babylonians. The message contains a warning that Yahweh, who controls the destiny of creation and nations, has given Nebuchadrezzar, his servant (see 25:9), rulership over their nations. The nation that refuses to serve him will face devastation. The religious leaders of the foreign nations who are attempting to persuade their rulers to revolt and promising success are prophesying lies.

The prediction in v. 7 was not fulfilled, at least literally, since the last king of the Babylonian Empire was Nabonidus (556–539 B.C.E.), the fourth king to succeed Nebuchadrezzar. Also, Nabonidus was not a descendant of Nebuchadrezzar. The reference appears to be to Nebuchadrezzar, Nabonidus, and the latter's son Belshazzar (see Dan 5.2). While Belshazzar did not become king of Babylonia, he did serve as a viceroy who filled in for his father when he was absent from Babylon.

In vv. 12-15, Jeremiah delivers to King Zedekiah almost the same warning issued to the foreign rulers through their emissaries in vv. 3-10: do not believe the prophets who are encouraging him to revolt against the Babylonians. They too are prophesying lies. Zedekiah is told to submit to the yoke of Nebuchadrezzar or face destruction. The lying prophets are the subject of the oracles in 23:9-40, and Jeremiah encounters several deceitful prophets in chaps. 28–29 (Hananiah in chap. 28, and Ahab and Zedekiah in chap. 29).

In vv. 16-22, Jeremiah warns the priests and the people not to listen to the prophets who are prophesying that the sacred vessels of the Temple, carried to Babylon in 597 B.C.E. will be returned. Jeremiah calls this prediction a lie and announces that such talk will lead to the devastation of Jerusalem. Indeed, Jeremiah predicts that the sacred objects that remained after 597 B.C.E. also will be taken away to Babylon, there to remain until Yahweh decides to return them. Among the items that Jeremiah lists as destined for eventual removal to Babylon were two bronze, free-standing *pillars* (Jachin and Boaz) at the entrance of the Temple (1 Kgs 7:15-22) and the *sea*, a very large basin standing approximately ten feet in height, made out of bronze, and located perhaps at the entrance to the Temple and before the altar (1 Kgs 7:23-26). The basin may have held approximately 12,000 gallons of liquid. According to 2 Kgs 25:13 and 16, the Babylonians broke the pillars and the basin into pieces and transported them to Babylon in 587 B.C.E. Also destined for Babylon were the *stands*, ornamented bronze wagons that formed the basis for the ten lavers or wash basins in the Temple (see 1 Kgs 7:27-39). These specific items and other Temple vessels would be taken to Babylon (see 2 Kgs 25:13-17). Jeremiah would be willing to concede his prophetic opponents are true prophets, if they are able to intercede with Yahweh to keep these sacred items of the Temple from being taken to Babylon.

28:1-17. Jeremiah's conflict with the prophet Hananiah. The oracles concerning the false prophets stirring up revolution in chap. 27 become more specific in chaps. 28–29 when Jeremiah enters into conflict with several prophets: Hananiah, Ahab, Zedekiah, and Shemaiah. In chap. 28 Jeremiah contends with *Hananiah*. The date provided in the deuteronomic narrative for this controversy poses a problem. The NRSV accurately translates the Hebrew: *at the beginning of the reign of King Zedekiah of Judah, in the fifth month of the fourth year* (v. 1). This is obviously contradictory, for the *beginning* would be 597 B.C.E., while the *fourth year* would be 594/593 B.C.E. The LXX leaves out the reference to the beginning of Zedekiah's reign and reads "in the fourth year of Zedekiah king of Judah, in the fifth month." The LXX must relate the correct date.

Hananiah, whose name means "Yahweh has been gracious," came *from Gibeon*, modern el-Jib, five and a half mi. northwest of Jerusalem. It contained a great high place where Solomon prayed for wisdom (1 Kgs 3:4-15). Hananiah was a revolutionary prophet who uttered an oracle of salvation: the yoke of Babylon has been broken and within two years Yahweh will return to Jerusalem King Jehoiachin, the exiles of 597 B.C.E., and the sacred vessels taken from the Temple. Hananiah, speaking in the name of Yahweh, announces that God has *broken the yoke of the king of Babylon* (v. 2). To counter the prophecy, Jeremiah, wearing the yoke that symbolizes submission to Babylon (see chap. 27), opposes Hananiah and his oracle of salvation. In doing so, Jeremiah refers to earlier prophets whose messages were filled with disaster, contrasting these with the good news of salvation announced by Hananiah. This is one of the criteria used by Jeremiah earlier to distinguish between true and false prophets: false prophets usually prophesied good fortune, while true ones normally announced judgment (23:17). Jeremiah then uses the criterion of fulfillment in Deut. 18:15-22—when a prediction comes true, then the prophet is proven to be a true prophet.

Hananiah performs his own symbolic act by taking Jeremiah's yoke and breaking it, proclaiming at the same time that Yahweh *will break the yoke of King Nebuchadrezzar of Babylon from the neck of all the nations within two years* (v. 11), that is, the Babylonian empire will soon fall. Jeremiah leaves, only to return to face Hananiah at a later time. In this confrontation, Jeremiah announces Yahweh has replaced the wooden yoke broken by Hananiah with an iron one, signifying that all the nations of the Babylonian empire will be forced to wear it. Jeremiah then utters an oracle of judgment against Hananiah, predicting that within the year he will die for speaking rebellion against Yahweh. The narrative concludes with the statement that Hananiah died *in that same year* (v. 17).

29:1-32. Jeremiah's letters to the Babylonian captives. This deuteronomic prose narrative describes the third incident in the life of Jeremiah involving conflict with the priests and prophets. Prophets living among the exiles taken to Babylon in 597 B.C.E. also were predicting a quick return to Judah. Jeremiah attempted to oppose this sedition by sending a letter (vv. 1-23) to the exiles *by the hand of Elasah . . . and Gemariah* (v. 3). Elasah was *the son of Shaphan*, probably the same Shaphan who served as secretary to King Josiah (2 Kgs 22–23), and therefore the brother of Ahikam who intervened on behalf of Jeremiah during his trial following the Temple sermon (26:24). Gemariah was *the son of Hilkiah*, probably the chief priest of Josiah who was involved in the discovery of the book of the law that became the basis of the reform (see 2 Kgs 22–23). This indicates that Jeremiah was supported by two very powerful families involved in the religious reform of Josiah. In the first letter, Jeremiah states his opposition to the false hopes that deceitful prophets are raising in predicting an early return. Two prophets condemned by Jeremiah by name are *Ahab son of Kolaiah and Zedekiah son of Maaseiah* (v. 21). He prophesies they will be executed and their names will become part of a common curse. The Babylonians would have executed them for sedition, although Jeremiah says it is because they have *committed adultery* (v. 23) and prophesied lies in Yahweh's name (see 23:9-22). Jeremiah tells the exiles not to expect an early return, but rather to settle down in the land and even pray on behalf of Babylon.

This was a rather radical exhortation, seeing that it could be misconstrued as treason. Jeremiah adds that God will bring the captives home, but not for *seventy years* (vv. 10-14; see 25:11; 27:7). Indeed, Yahweh will carry out a judgment of disaster and exile against Jerusalem and the reigning king (vv. 16-20). Verses 16-20 are similar to chap. 24, the vision of figs, and do not sound very much like Jeremiah. Absent in the LXX, these verses were a later insertion in the prose tradition, seeking to favor the exiles of 597 B.C.E. over those who had remained behind.

In vv. 24-32, Jeremiah confronts by letter another false prophet, *Shemaiah of Nehelam*. Shemaiah had written a letter to the new overseer of the Temple, the priest Zephaniah (see 21:1; 37:3; 52:24-27), questioning why he had not rebuked Jeremiah and put him in stocks (cf. 20:1-6) for being a *madman who plays the prophet* and for telling the exiles to settle down, seeing that the exile will be a long one. Learning of the contents of Shemaiah's letter, Jeremiah writes the exiles telling them that Yahweh has decreed that neither Shemaiah nor his descendants would witness the future time of release.

The Book of Consolation, 30:1–31:40

The Book of Consolation is a largely self-contained collection that consists of oracles in both poetry and prose that address the future restoration of both Israel and Judah. More than likely, this collection existed as a separate unit before the addition of later oracles by Jeremiah's disciples and the deuteronomic insertions of prose speeches. The deuteronomic editors would have been responsible for inserting the collection into the growing tradition.

These chapters contain the following materials: a general introduction that specifies the nature of the collection and its recipients, Israel and Judah (30:1-4); a poetic oracle that laments the Day of Yahweh (30:5-7); a prose oracle of salvation that promises the removal of the yoke of Babylon and the restoration of the house of David (30:8-9); a poetic oracle concerning the salvation of Jacob (30:10-11); a poetic oracle of salvation describing the restoration of Jerusalem (vv. 12-17); a poetic oracle of salvation that speaks of the restoration of Jacob (i.e., Israel, 30:18-22); a poetic oracle describing a theophany (30:23-24); a prose covenant formula (31:1); a poetic oracle of salvation describing the redemption of Israel and the return to Zion (31:2-6); a poetic oracle celebrating Israel's return (31:7-9); a poetic oracle in which Israel praises Yahweh for salvation (31:10-14); a poem promising a weeping Rachel the future restoration of her children (31:15-22); a prose oracle promising the restoration of fortunes in Judah (31:23-26); a prose oracle promising the repopulation of Israel and Judah (31:27-30); a prose oracle that promises a new covenant (31:31-34); a poetic oracle comparing Israel's future with the continuing order of creation (31:35-37); and a prose oracle promising Jerusalem will be rebuilt and purified (31:38-40).

Which of these oracles may have come from the historical Jeremiah is not easy to determine. It is doubtful that any of the prose oracles were original with the prophet, although it is possible that they at times captured and developed his thinking. In addition, it is difficult to attempt to date these oracles with any real success. The most likely oracles to have come from Jeremiah are those in 30:5-7, 12-15; 31:2-6; and 31:15-22. Two time periods would be possible for these oracles: the early date of Jeremiah's ministry (627–605 B.C.E.) and the period shortly after the fall of Jerusalem in 587 B.C.E. The second possibility is the more likely. This would have been the time between Gedaliah's appointment as governor and his assassination (40:7–41:18; 2 Kgs 25:22-26). The later oracles would come from the exilic and early postexilic periods.

The most frequent literary form in this collection is the "prophecy of salvation" that consists of the following: the appeal for attention and/or the introductory messenger formula (e.g., *Thus says the LORD* [Yahweh]), the description of the present situation, the prediction of salvation, a final characterization either of God or of the message, and the concluding messenger formula (*says the LORD* [Yahweh]).

30:1-4. General introduction. The deuteronomic editors were responsible for writing this introduction to the collection of oracles of salvation in chaps. 30–31. The oracles address at times Israel, at times Judah, and at times both.

30:5-7. The day of the Lord. The "day of the LORD" is a time of Yahweh's judgment, either against the nations or against Israel or Judah (cf. Isa 2:12-21; Amos 5:18-20; and Zeph 1:14-18). Using rhetorical questions that have obvious answers, this poetic oracle makes use of the language of lament when Jeremiah describes the rituals of lamentation that people are pursuing because of the day of Yahweh's judgment (cf. the laments in 11:18–20:18). However, the last line of v. 7 indicates that Jacob (Israel) will be rescued from the terrible day. Thus, what sounds at first like a judgment oracle referring to lamentation is transformed, at least in the editing of the oracle to fit the collection, into a prophecy of salvation.

30:8-9. The removal of the yoke of Babylon and the restoration of the Davidic monarchy. This prose oracle of salvation promises that the yoke of Babylon will be removed and that no longer will he (Nebuchadrezzar) be Yahweh's servant (see chaps. 27–28). In addition, the oracle promises the restoration of the Davidic monarchy (23:5-6; 33:14-26; Ezek 34:24; and Hos 3:5). In the collection of oracles concerning the house of David (21:11–23:8), Jeremiah was especially critical of kings. Indeed, the historical Jeremiah more than likely did not anticipate the restoration of the monarchy. But this was not the case in the deuteronomic tradition that regarded the restoration of the institution as vital to the future (cf. 23:1-6).

30:10-11. The salvation of Israel. This poetic oracle of salvation is repeated with minor variation in 46:27-28. The language and content are patterned after Second Isaiah (see Isa 41:8-14; 43:1-5). Second Isaiah does refer to Israel (Jacob) as the servant of the LORD (cf. 49:3).

30:12-17. The restoration of Jerusalem. In this poetic oracle, the divine physician will heal an incurably wounded Zion (Jerusalem; see 15:18) and will punish her enemies who have devoured her. Zion's distress and lamentation are described in similar terms to 4:31; 8:18-21; and 9:17-19. In her distress, Zion's lovers (here probably her allies) have forsaken her. Perhaps the reference is to the Egyptians who withdrew before the Babylonian advance (37:5).

30:18-22. The restoration of Jacob. This poetic oracle of salvation promises Yahweh's restoration of Israel, the rebuilding of *the city* (Jerusalem most likely), the joyous thanksgiving of those who have returned, their increase in population, and the appearance of their own prince who *shall approach* (v. 21) Yahweh. This ruler shall be an Israelite, not a foreigner (see Deut 17:15). To "approach" Yahweh was normally a priestly prerogative (see Exod 29:4, 8; 40:12, 14; Lev 7:35). Compare Ezekiel's prince in 46:1-18. The oracle concludes with the repetition of the covenant formula (24:7; 31:1).

30:23-24. The storm of Yahweh. This poem describing a theophanic storm is a repetition of 23:19-20. The earlier setting is the collection of oracles dealing with false prophets. Part of a judgment oracle, these verses in this context suggest that Yahweh will destroy the wicked as a part of the restoration of Israel and Judah in the future.

31:1. The covenant formula. This verse repeats the covenant formula found earlier in 24:7 and 30:22.

31:2-6. Yahweh's everlasting love. This poetic oracle of salvation grounds Israel's future redemption in the everlasting love of Yahweh. According to the prose introduction and images in the poem itself, the prophet addresses the Northern Kingdom (*Israel, mountains of Samaria*, and *hill country of Ephraim*). Jeremiah draws on the wilderness tradition once more (2:2-3; Hos 2), this time to indicate that the redemption of Israel experienced in the wilderness following liberation from Egyptian slavery (*found grace in the wilderness*, v. 2) will be experienced in the future because of the everlasting love and faithfulness of Yahweh. In Hosea and Jeremiah, the wilderness was a period of intimacy between Yahweh and Israel. However, both also spoke of the entrance into Canaan as a line of demarcation between Israel's faithfulness and unfaithfulness. In the present context, Jeremiah assures Israel that God's everlasting love has not diminished, but rather is the basis for her future redemption and rebuilding. One day both Israel and Judah will be reunited and will worship Yahweh in Zion (Jerusalem).

31:7-9. Joy over Israel's return. In this oracle of salvation, the call is extended to sing in joyous celebration on Jacob's (Israel's) behalf, asking God to redeem the remnant of Israel. Then Yahweh announces his intention to redeem Israelites from all the countries to which they have gone. The redeemed will include even the blind and the lame, those with child, and those in labor. In v. 9 Yahweh is called *father*, a common metaphor to depict God in the OT (see especially Hos 11:1; Jer 3:19; 31:20). The *firstborn* son was privileged in Israelite society, receiving a double share of the father's estate, the paternal blessing, and the position of familial authority after his demise. Here Israel is Yahweh's *firstborn*, an expression of election (cf. Exod 4:22).

31:10-14. The joy of returning exiles. This poetic oracle of salvation speaks of Yahweh's future redemption of Israel and the exiles coming to Zion to praise him for the gifts of bountiful crops and productive herds. The lamentation of despair in a time of judgment and destitution will turn into an unending period of joyous praise and unlimited bounty. In this oracle, Yahweh is presented as the savior who, like the next of kin, "redeems" (v. 11) Israel from the powerful oppressor (see the redeemer and law of redemption in Lev 25:25; also see Yahweh as redeemer in Exod 15:13).

31:15-22: Rachel's weeping for her children. This poem of five strophes is replete with feminine imagery: Rachel cries for her children (v. 15), Yahweh consoles her (vv. 16-17), Ephraim (Israel) confesses (vv. 18-19), Yahweh has a mother's compassion on Ephraim (v. 20), and Jeremiah exhorts virgin Israel to return (vv. 21-22).

In biblical narratives about Israel's ancestors (cf. Gen 25–35), Rachel was the more favored wife of Jacob (Israel) and the mother of Joseph and Benjamin. Joseph had two sons, Ephraim and Manasseh. Ephraim is the name for the large tribe in the North that became synonymous with Israel. Along with her sister Leah and their handmaidens, Rachel is one of the matriarchs of the nation. According to 1 Sam 10:2, Rachel was buried in the tribal territory of Benjamin, thus to the north of Jerusalem. This poem suggests the specific burial place was Ramah, approximately five mi. north of Jerusalem (modern er-Ram) and a staging area for the deportation of exiles to Babylon (40:1, 4). For an alternative location for Rachel's burial place, see Gen 35:16-20; 48:7; and Matt 2:18. In v. 15 of the poem, the dead Rachel is heard weeping over her dead and exiled children.

The verb in the last line of the poem is subject to many translations and interpretations: "a woman protects a man," "the woman woos the man," "the woman sets out to find her husband again," "the woman must encompass the man with devotion," "a woman is turned into a man," "a woman (Israel?) embraces the man (Yahweh?)," "a woman is pregnant with a male." Two meanings seem likely. One, Virgin Israel is the woman who is pregnant and will bear a son (a posterity). This is in contrast with Rachel whose children are dead or exiled. Two, the man, Ephraim, is "embraced" by the women who are mentioned in the poem (Rachel, the nurturing Yahweh, and Virgin Israel). Phyllis Trible argues for the latter meaning on the basis of the rhetorical structure of the poem: the male Ephraim is surrounded by women or feminine images of the larger poem that support and sustain him. She offers the translation: "female surrounds man."

31:23-26. Judah's restoration. This prose oracle of salvation points to the restoration of worship in the Temple in Jerusalem and the resettlement of the land of Judah and its towns. People again will utter a blessing for Zion. In v. 26, Jeremiah awakens from his dream of the future restoration.

31:27-30. The repopulation of Israel and Judah. In the future time, Yahweh will rebuild the nation (cf. the language of 1:10). In this time of new beginning, no longer will people suffer for the sins of their parents, but rather will receive punishment for their own misdeeds. This doctrine of individual responsibility, probably influenced by the prophet Ezekiel (see esp. chap. 18), replaces the teaching of corporate guilt where later generations inherit the punishment for the crimes and sins of their ancestors (cf. Exod 20:5-6). The land of Israel and Judah will be repopulated with people and herds (Ezek 36:9-11).

31:31-34. The new covenant. This prose oracle of salvation promises a new covenant for the restored community that will not be breached by a sinful people. The old covenant established at Sinai had been violated, but the new covenant will continue because the law will be written on the human heart, and not just on tablets of stone. This metaphor indicates that the character of the people will be transformed by their embodiment of the teachings of the law. They will no longer need a teacher to tell them the content of the law, but rather they will know instinctively the will of God. Further, in this new age, Yahweh will not only forgive their sins but also will forget them. The fact that the teaching of the law will no longer be required is a remarkable assertion for Deuteronomic teachers to affirm.

The language in v. 33, *I will make,* reads literally "I will cut." "Cutting a covenant" reflects the ritual practice of sacrificing animals, cutting the larger carcasses in half, and then walking between the slaughtered animals (34:18; Gen 15:7-21). In the Genesis passage, Yahweh's presence is represented by taking a smoking fire pot and a flaming torch and walking between the sacrifices.

31:35-37. Israel's unlimited future. This is a poetic oracle of salvation that praises God as the creator who orders and sustains the cosmos (cf. Pss 19, 33, and 104). Jeremiah compares the power of God to create and sustain the cosmos with his ability to recreate and then sustain a new Israel. As the cosmos will continue into perpetuity, so then will Israel. This combination of creation and redemption theology is developed especially by Second Isaiah (see Isa 40:12, 26; 42:5; 44:24; 45:7, 18; 54:10).

31:38-40. The rebuilding and purification of Jerusalem. This prose oracle promises the rebuilding of Jerusalem, the expansion of its precincts, and the purification of the areas that have been desecrated by death (see Zech 14:10-11). The passage mentions several boundaries of Jerusalem: *the tower of Hananel* located in the northeast (Neh 3:1), *the Corner Gate* found in the northwest (2 Kgs 14:13), the southern boundary of Hinnom (7:31-32), the eastern boundary of Kidron (2 Kgs 23:4, 6), and the *Horse Gate* situated in the southeast corner (Neh 3:28). *Gareb* and *Goah* are unknown. The *valley of the dead* most likely alludes to the Valley of Hinnom, the location of child sacrifice (see 7:31-32; 19:2, 6; 32:35; 2 Kgs 23:10).

The Field of Anathoth, 32:1-44

Once more Jeremiah is told to engage in a symbolic action that will enhance his prophetic message (see notes on 13:1-11). And as is true for all the prose narratives in chaps. 26–45, there is a correspondence of the life and word of the prophet. The structure of the narrative divides into four parts: Jeremiah's arrest (32:1-5), the purchase of the field at Anathoth (32:6-15), the prayer of Jeremiah (32:16-25), and Yahweh's response (32:26-44). This narrative continues the theme of future restoration in chaps. 30–31.

32:1-5. Jeremiah's imprisonment. This deuteronomic prose narrative is placed in the context of Nebuchadrezzar's siege of Jerusalem, in the tenth year of the reign of King Zedekiah (588 B.C.E.). Jeremiah had been imprisoned in the court of the guard in the royal palace. When the prophet had attempted to go to Anathoth during a temporary lifting of the siege of the city, he was accused of deserting to the enemy and placed under arrest (see 37:11-21). Zedekiah accused Jeremiah of giving aid and comfort to the enemy by prophesying that Yahweh was giving the city of

Jerusalem into the hands of the Babylonians and that the king would be taken captive. For another accusation of prophetic treason, see Amos 7:10-17.

32:6-15. The purchase of the field at Anathoth. Yahweh tells Jeremiah that his cousin would come to the court of the guard and ask him to purchase his field at Anathoth. The *right of redemption* (v. 7) refers to the responsibility that the next of kin had to "redeem" the property of an impoverished relative in order to keep it within the family (see Lev 25:25-28). The purchase price of seventeen shekels of silver (about seven oz.) refers to weight, not coins. Coins were probably not used until the Persian period (beginning in 539 B.C.E.). The original deed of purchase was rolled up and sealed, while the open copy remained unsealed for easy reference. Baruch, Jeremiah's secretary and companion (see chaps. 36 and 45), was given the deed and witnesses signed it. Both copies of the deed were then placed in a jar for preservation. Then Jeremiah prophesied that in the future restoration, property (houses, fields, and vineyards) would once again be bought. This purchase of a field, occurring at the time of siege, emphasizes the prophet's faith in Yahweh's promise of a future restoration.

32:16-25. A prayer of Jeremiah. Jeremiah then offers a prayer of confession that begins by praising Yahweh for being the creator who directs history. Yahweh's great deeds of salvation, the exodus from Egypt and the gift of the land of Canaan, are also the basis for praise. These acts of salvation are contrasted with Israel's disobedience to the law. The prayer explains that disobedience is the reason for the siege and the imminent fall of Jerusalem to the Babylonians. For a similar prayer of confession and intercession on behalf of a sinful people, see Neh 9:6-37. For hymns that recount great acts of salvation see Pss 78, 105, 106, 135, and 136.

32:26-44. Yahweh's response. Yahweh responds to Jeremiah's prayer by outlining the sins of the people as the basis for the fall of Jerusalem. Israel's history has been one of disobedience (see Ezek 20:1-32). Yet, Yahweh also promises that the exiles will return home and the covenant will be renewed (see 31:31-34). Once again fields will be bought in the land, a future reality that is underscored by Jeremiah's purchase of the field in Anathoth.

Promises Concerning the Future Restoration, 33:1-26

Continuing the theme of salvation in chaps. 30–32, this chapter consists of several prose speeches that address future restoration.

33:1-9. Judah and Israel will be rebuilt. Still under arrest in the court of the guard (see 32:1-3), Jeremiah prophesies that the Babylonians will succeed in taking the city of Jerusalem and cause great slaughter. However, the speech then turns to salvation: Judah and Israel will be rebuilt as before, the sins of the people will be forgiven, and the name of Jerusalem will be synonymous with joy and praise.

33:10-13. Promises of salvation. The first prose speech (vv. 10-11) announces the return of joyous song and thanksgiving in the future restoration (contrast 7:34). Thank offerings and thanksgiving psalms were delivered by individuals and communities who were the recipients of divine salvation (see Lev 7:11-18; Ps 107). Verse 11b is taken from Ps 136:1, an antiphonal thanksgiving psalm that praises God for creation and great deeds of salvation on Israel's behalf, including the exodus from Egypt, the defeat of Pharaoh and his army at the Red Sea, guidance through the Sinai wilderness, victory over the kings of Canaan, and the gift of the land of Israel.

The second prose speech (vv. 12-13) promises that the desolate land will once again have pastures, flocks, and shepherds.

33:14-26. Davidic rulers and levitical priests. This prose sermon, absent in the LXX, expands upon the one in 23:5-6. Jeremiah promises the restoration of two institutions: the Davidic monarchy and the Levitical priesthood. Yahweh will raise up a *righteous Branch* who will *execute justice and righteousness* (v. 15; cf. 21:11–23:8; Hag 1:1; 2:23; Zech 4:11-14; 6:9-13). While this sermon may be speaking of an individual who will one day come to the throne, the promise is that the dynasty of David will continue. The covenant of David in 2 Sam 7 that contains Yahweh's promise of a perpetual dynasty is as sure as the divine covenant with day and night that sustains the temporal order of creation (cf. Gen 8:22). The divine covenant with the Levitical priesthood also insures that they will continue to serve, and their role will include the priestly prerogative of offering sacrifices (see the roles given to the Levitical priesthood in Deut 18:1-8). The offspring of the two families that appear to be rejected by Yahweh, Jacob (Israel) and David, are promised divine mercy and the restoration of their fortunes. This promise is as good as God's covenant with creation.

Judgment against Jerusalem and the Broken Covenant, 34:1–35:19

34:1-7. Warning to Zedekiah. This prose sermon, placed in the context of the Babylonian siege of Jerusalem (588 B.C.E.), announces to King Zedekiah that Jerusalem will fall to the Babylonians and he will be taken captive. However, the king is promised that he will die a peaceful death and have a proper funeral (contrast Jehoiakim in 22:18-19). According to other texts, Zedekiah was blinded and exiled to Babylon where he died in prison (39:7; 52:8-11; 2 Kgs 25:5-7). The ritual of burning spices was part of a royal funeral (2 Chr 16:14; 21:19). Verse 7 mentions that at the time of this speech only two fortified cities in addition to Jerusalem had not yet been conquered: LACHISH and Azekah. Lachish is modern Tell ed-Duweir, located thirty mi. southwest of Jerusalem, while Azekah is modern Tell ez-Zahariyeh, situated to the northeast of Lachish. The fourth letter of the Lachish ostraca, composed just before the fall of Jerusalem, mentions that Hoshaiah, an official in an outpost to the north of Lachish, writes Yaosh, the military commander of Lachish: "We are looking for the signals of Lachish, according to all the indications my Lord has given, because we do not see Azekah."

34:8-22. The release of slaves and the broken covenant. This prose narrative relates an incident during the siege of Jerusalem (588 B.C.E.). In the effort to obtain

Yahweh's help against the Babylonians, King Zedekiah enters into covenant with the people of Jerusalem to release their Hebrew slaves. This action would bring them into accord with the requirements of Deut 15 that Hebrew slaves are to be set free in the seventh year, unless the slave does not want to leave. In that case, the slave will be a slave for life. In sending forth the released slave, Deut 15 specifies that released slaves should be given provisions for their sustenance by their former owners. The theological basis for this release is the exodus: Israelites are to remember that they once were slaves in Egypt and Yahweh redeemed them.

However, the people of Jerusalem broke their covenant and took back their slaves when Nebuchadrezzar lifted the siege in order to meet an advancing Egyptian army (37:6-15). Jeremiah then utters a prose speech that refers to Deut 15 and condemns the people for taking back their slaves. Yahweh is going to grant a release to the citizens of Jerusalem (v. 17), a release to destruction. They will be like the calf cut in two in the covenant ceremony (see Gen 15:7-21; Jer 31:33).

35:1-19. The faithfulness of the Rechabites. According to v. 1, this narrative describes an event in the life of Jeremiah that occurred sometime during the reign of King Jehoiakim (609–598 B.C.E.). The location of this narrative in the Book of Jeremiah serves to contrast the faithfulness of the Rechabites with the faithlessness of the people of Jerusalem who broke their covenant and took back their released slaves (34:8-22). The Rechabites were a religious sect founded by Jonadab, the son of Rechab, during the reign of Jehu (842–815 B.C.E.). Jonadab supported Jehu in the slaughter accompanying the revolt against the dynasty of Omri (2 Kgs 10:15-28). This sect was distinguished by the following practices: abstaining from wine, living as nomads in tents, and refusing to settle down to farm the land. They believed that the practice of Yahweh religion was better suited to a nomadic life. Indeed, they considered agricultural life, including the drinking of wine produced from vineyards, to be a corrupting influence in the direction of Canaanite fertility religion. The Rechabites had come to Jerusalem to seek refuge from the Babylonian army.

Jeremiah uses the Rechabites as an example of faithfulness to religious beliefs. In contrast to their devotion to religious principles, the people of Jerusalem and Judah have been disobedient to Yahweh. While disaster will overtake them, Jeremiah promises that Jonadab will continue to have descendants *to stand before* (v. 19) Yahweh. "To stand before Yahweh" is an expression that refers to priestly service. While the Rechabites were not priests, their religious zeal is likened to divine service.

The Scrolls of Baruch, 36:1-32

This narrative provides important insight into the composition of the Book of Jeremiah, at least as seen through the eyes of the deuteronomic editors. The story begins in the *fourth year of King Jehoiakim* (605 B.C.E.), the very same year that Nebuchadrezzar defeated the Egyptians at CARCHEMISH (see introduction). In essence, the narrative tells about the origins of two scrolls written down by Baruch at the dictation of Jeremiah.

36:1-3. Jeremiah commanded to write down his oracles. The contents of the first scroll consisted of the prophecies of Jeremiah from the time of his call (627 B.C.E.) to the fourth year of Jehoiakim's reign (605 B.C.E.). The description of these prophecies suggests they were largely oracles of judgment. Jeremiah's scribe and companion, Baruch son of Neriah, appeared to be a royal scribe with powerful political connections (36:32; see chaps. 32 and 45). He was a member of an important Judahite family. Seraiah, his brother, was a minister to King Zedekiah (51:59). Archaeological excavations in the City of David have yielded scribal seals belonging to these two brothers. Baruch's seal reads: "to/from Baruch // son of Neriah // the scribe."

36:4-10. Baruch's reading of the scroll in the Temple. Jeremiah had been barred from the Temple precinct, perhaps because of the Temple sermon (see chaps. 7 and 26). Following the writing of the first scroll, Baruch read it aloud *in the chamber of Gemariah* (v. 10), the son of Shaphan, in the fifth year of Jehoiakim's reign (604 B.C.E.). The chamber was located in the New Gate entrance into the Temple, thus allowing the people who had assembled in the sacred precincts during a fast day to hear him. Public fasts were observed during times of national difficulty or threat (see 2 Chr 20:3; Ezra 8:21-23; Neh 1:4-11). The threat more than likely was posed by Nebuchadrezzar's army advancing into the Philistine plain and conquering Ashkelon in 604 B.C.E. Shortly thereafter, Jehoiakim decided to shift his allegiance from Egypt to Nebuchadrezzar. A fast would have been a most auspicious occasion for the people to hear Jeremiah's oracles of judgment, especially those dealing with the "Foe from the North." Jeremiah's scroll is to be read in the hope that the people of Judah will repent, be forgiven, and avoid the judgment that Yahweh is planning to bring against them (see 3:1–4:4).

36:11-19. Baruch reads the scroll before the royal officials. When Gemariah's son hears the contents of the scroll, he informs the royal officials sitting in the secretary's chamber in the palace. Baruch was then summoned to the secretary's chamber and directed to read it again.

36:20-26. Jehoiakim burns the scroll. After the officials warned Baruch to go into hiding along with Jeremiah, the king's secretary, Elishama, reported the words of the scroll to King Jehoiakim. When the scroll is brought and read to the king, he responded by cutting the scroll into strips and placing them in the fire burning in the brazier. The king then ordered Baruch's and Jeremiah's arrest, but they were in hiding. This response to Jeremiah's prophecy is in sharp contrast to Josiah's when he hears the Book of the Law read. Josiah lamented, inquired of Huldah the prophet to obtain a word from Yahweh, declared a day of covenant making, swore along with the people to follow the law, and began a major religious reformation (2 Kgs 22–23).

36:27-32. Baruch writes a second scroll. Yahweh later tells Jeremiah to dictate his prophecies to Baruch once again. The contents of the second scroll included those of the first, but the narrative notes at the end that *many similar words were added to them* (v. 32). This allows for the addition of other oracles from Jeremiah as well as from later disciples and redactors. Jeremiah also utters a judgment oracle against Jehoiakim, saying he would have neither a successor to sit on David's throne nor a burial. Rather his dead body would be exposed to the elements (cf. 22:13-19).

As noted in the introduction, these two scrolls are difficult to reconstruct. However, the first scroll probably included at least the call (1:4-10), some of the poetic oracles of judgment, especially those concerning the "Foe from the North" (see chaps. 4–10), and possibly the laments (see 11:18–20:18). The second scroll and the additional words added to it probably refer to the larger book, or at least much of its contents.

Jeremiah's Encounters with Zedekiah, 37:1–38:28

Chapters 37–45 set forth the "passion history" of Jeremiah. Composed by the Deuteronomic editors, this largely continuous story points to the relationship between the prophetic word and the life of the prophet. The prophet's life participates in the suffering occasioned by the word of judgment.

These deuteronomic prose narratives in chaps. 37–38 describe Jeremiah's encounters with King Zedekiah in 588 B.C.E., shortly before the fall of Jerusalem to the Babylonians (cf. 34:1-7). Once more the narrative reflects the confluence of prophetic word and life.

37:1-10. The Egyptian advance and Nebuchadrezzar's lifting of the siege. In order to meet the threat of an advancing Egyptian army, Nebuchadrezzar lifted the siege against Jerusalem (see 34:21). The Egyptian king was Hophra (589–570 B.C.E.) who only a short time before had ascended to the throne (see 44:30). Zedekiah's rebellion against the Babylonians was based in part on his anticipation of Egyptian support (cf. Ezek 17:15) and the hope that other states in Canaan would join in the rebellion (cf. chap. 27). How many states in Canaan actually did rebel is unclear, although apparently not very many. It is the case that Tyre and Ammon revolted along with Judah, but it is doubtful that other states joined in revolt. Edom eventually sided with the Babylonians. The Egyptian army was quickly repelled, and the siege was resumed.

During this interlude, Zedekiah sends his envoys to ask Jeremiah to make intercession for the city to save it from destruction (see 21:1-10). Jeremiah responds that the Babylonians will return and destroy Jerusalem.

37:11-15. Jeremiah arrested for desertion. While the siege was lifted, Jeremiah attempts to leave Jerusalem to go to Benjamin to receive his "portion," that is, his share of his family's property. This is probably not directly connected to the prophet's redemption of his cousin's field in chap. 32. In any event, Jeremiah is arrested and accused of deserting to the Babylonians. He is beaten and put in prison.

37:16-21. Zedekiah's secret audience with Jeremiah. Once again Zedekiah attempts to receive a favorable word of Yahweh from the prophet. Jeremiah tells him that he shall be delivered into the hand of the king of Babylon. Yet the prophet does plead successfully with the king to be transferred from the prison located in the house of Jonathan the secretary to the court of the guard. There the king provides him a ration of bread until the bread is gone as the siege intensifies.

38:1-13. Jeremiah imprisoned in a cistern. Jeremiah's prophecy that those who surrender will save their lives is considered treason by his enemies, including those officials who were pro-Egyptian and supportive of the rebellion. These officials, conspiring to kill Jeremiah, cast him into a muddy, but waterless cistern. The charge of treason against Jeremiah is similar to a charge in letter six of the Lachish letters against some officials in Jerusalem (see note on 34:7).

Ebed-melech the Ethiopian (v. 7), who was either a eunuch or palace official (*sārîs*), intercedes for Jeremiah with King Zedekiah. The king directs him to remove Jeremiah from the cistern. Later, Jeremiah promises Ebed-melech that he would survive the destruction of Jerusalem (39:15-18).

38:14-28. Zedekiah's last consultation with Jeremiah. Zedekiah meets for the last time with Jeremiah in a private conference held at *the third entrance* of the Temple. Jeremiah warns the king to surrender in order to save the city and himself. If not, the city will be burned and Zedekiah will not escape with his life. Zedekiah's fear of the officials at court is clear.

The Fall of Jerusalem, 39:1–40:6

39:1-10. The fall of the city. These verses are a more succinct version of 52:4-16 (see 2 Kgs 25:1-12). The dates for the beginning of the siege and the fall of the city are given in reference to the regnal years of King Zedekiah. The siege commenced in late 589 or early 588 B.C.E. with the city falling in 587 B.C.E. When the city is taken, the Babylonian officials meet in the middle gate. Their names and titles are Nergal-sharezer the Simmagir, Nebushazban the chief court official, and Nergal-sharezer the Rab-mag. Simmagir and Rab-mag are titles of Babylonian offices. Nergal-sharezer the Rabmag (see v. 13) was Nergalsharusur (Neriglissar). He was Nebuchadrezzar's son-in-law who became king of Babylon in 560 B.C.E. and ruled until 556 B.C.E.

Zedekiah attempts to escape the city, but is captured and brought to Nebuchadrezzar at Riblah in Hamath. Riblah was a fortified city in the Beqaa Valley in Lebanon that guarded the highway between Egypt and Mesopotamia. Nebuchadrezzar orders Zedekiah to witness the execution of his sons, blinds the Judahite king, and sends him to Babylon in chains (cf. 52:8-11; 2 Kgs 25:5-7). According to 52:11, Zedekiah died in a Babylonian prison. The city is burned, its walls are broken down, and its inhabitants are exiled.

39:11-14. Nebuchadrezzar's protection of Jeremiah. See 40:1-6. Nebuchadrezzar orders the captain of his guard to treat Jeremiah well and to allow him to determine his own future. This good treatment of Jeremiah was probably due to the prophet's opposition to the rebellion and to his insistence that the officials and people surrender to the Babylonians, once the rebellion had begun.

39:15-18. The salvation of Ebed-melech. Prior to Jerusalem's fall, Jeremiah promises Ebed-melech, the Ethiopian who had saved him from the cistern (38:7-13), that his life will be spared, because he trusted in Yahweh. The people Ebed-melech fears are probably not the Babylonians, but rather the officials who sought Jeremiah's life and had him thrown into the cistern (38:1-6).

40:1-6. Jeremiah chooses to remain with Gedaliah at Mizpah. This is a somewhat different version of Jeremiah's good treatment at the hands of the Babylonians than the one in 39:11-14. In this version, Jeremiah had been taken with the other exiles to Ramah, a staging area for transporting the captives to Babylon. It is interesting to note that Nebuzaradan, the captain of the guard and a Babylonian, speaks an oracle of Yahweh to Jeremiah, explaining that Yahweh made an end of the city because of its evil. The Babylonian official allows Jeremiah to choose his own future. Jeremiah chose to remain behind and to dwell at Mizpah with the newly appointed governor, Gedaliah.

The Governorship of Gedaliah, 40:7–41:18

This section compares to 2 Kgs 25:22-26. Following the Babylonian conquest of 587 B.C.E., the Davidic monarchy and the royal state of Judah came to an end. Judah was incorporated into the provincial system of the Babylonian empire. The devastation of the country, the destruction of the former capital along with the Temple, and the execution or deportation of many of the leaders and officials left those who remained in the Babylonian colony enormous challenges to rebuild the future. Nebuchadrezzar appointed Gedaliah, a member of the prominent family of Shaphan (cf. 26:24 and 2 Kgs 22–23), to be governor. He set up his provincial government in Mizpah, perhaps modern Tell en-Nasbeh, located on the border between Benjamin and Judah and some eight mi. north of Jerusalem. He attempted to convince those who remained behind to rebuild their lives and to submit to Babylonian rule. How long Gedaliah was governor is not known, although he was assassinated by rebels, an action that may have led to a third exile in 582 B.C.E. (52:30). Ishmael, a member of the house of David who conspired with Baalis, king of the Ammonites, to resist Babylonian rule, and his small group of rebels assassinated Gedaliah, killed his Jewish supporters at Mizpah, and wiped out the Babylonian garrison located there. The survivors of Mizpah, including Jeremiah, were taken captive with the intent of going to Ammon. Intercepted by Johanan, a Judahite military commander and ally of Gedaliah, Ishmael escaped with a small band of eight men to Ammon. Fearing Babylonian reprisal for Ishmael's deeds, Johanan and his forces decided to seek refuge in Egypt, taking an unwilling Jeremiah with them.

40:7-12. Gedaliah as governor. Gedaliah's rule as governor was short-lived. He exhorted the survivors of the Babylonian destruction who remained in Judah to settle down, rebuild the country, and serve the Babylonians.

40:13-41:3. Gedaliah's assassination. Although warned by Johanan of the assassination plot of Baalis, king of the Ammonites, and Ishmael, Gedaliah refused to believe the report. Ishmael carries out the plot, murdering Gedaliah, his Jewish supporters at Mizpah, and the Babylonian soldiers stationed there.

41:4-10. Ishmael's slaughter of pilgrims. On the day after the slaughter, a group of pilgrims arrive at Mizpah on their way to participate in a fast at the Temple in Jerusalem. Ishmael and his cohorts slaughter all but ten of them and cast their corpses into a cistern. He then takes the survivors of the slaughter at Mizpah, including Jeremiah (cf. 42:2), with him on his journey towards Ammon.

41:11-18. Johanan's victory over Ishmael. The military commander, Johanan, intercepts Ishmael and his party at the *great pool . . . in Gibeon* (v. 12; cf. 2 Sam 2:13). While the captives are freed, Ishmael makes good his escape to Ammon. Johanan and his party, fearing the Babylonians response to the slaughter at Mizpah, decide to go to Egypt. They stop at Geruth Chimhan (an inn?) near Bethlehem.

The Flight to Egypt, 42:1–43:7

This prose account narrates the details of the decision of Johanan's party to flee to Egypt, in spite of Jeremiah's opposition to the plan. The prophet and Baruch are forced to accompany them to Egypt.

42:1-6. Jeremiah asked to intercede with Yahweh. Unsure of their future, Johanan's group asks Jeremiah to intercede with Yahweh in their behalf and to obtain a divine word to tell them what they should do. Jeremiah agrees, but warns them he will speak forthrightly what Yahweh tells him. The people swear that they will follow the divine directive.

42:7-22. Yahweh's reply. After ten days, Jeremiah receives Yahweh's instructions. The prophet delivers a prose sermon that takes the form of a promise coupled with a warning. They should remain in the land and thereby receive God's blessings, including protection from the king of Babylon. However, should they disobey by going to Egypt, they will suffer many disasters and die in Egypt, without a survivor.

43:1-7. The flight to Egypt. The people deny that Jeremiah has spoken the word of Yahweh, thus categorizing him as a deceitful prophet (cf. 23:9-40; Deut 18:15-22), and contend that he has taken the advice of Baruch whom they charge with plotting to turn them over to the Babylonians. The group decides to reject Jeremiah's word and to flee to Egypt, taking Jeremiah and Baruch with them. They arrive in Tahpanhes in Egypt (see note on 2:16).

Jeremiah in Egypt, 43:8–44:30

This narrative contains Jeremiah's two prose sermons of Jeremiah: the first is an announcement of judgment against Egypt (43:8-13) and the second is directed against the Jewish refugees in Egypt (44:1-30). This negative indictment of the Jewish community in Egypt demonstrates that the deuteronomic editors considered them to be apostate Jews who had no claim to being the people of Yahweh.

43:8-13. Egypt is no safe haven from Nebuchadrezzar. Jeremiah is instructed by Yahweh to engage in a symbolic act (see 13:1-11; 16:1-13; 18:1-12; 19:1-15; 27:1-22; and 32:1-44) and then to deliver an accompanying oracle that indicate Nebuchadrezzar will invade Egypt and cause great devastation, including the taking of Tahpanhes. Jeremiah indicates that even Egypt is not a safe haven for Jewish refugees. Nebuchadrezzar (Yahweh's "servant," cf. 25:9, 27:6) did invade Egypt during the reign of Amasis in 568/67 B.C.E. (cf. 46:13-26). Verse 11 generally repeats 15:2. Jeremiah notes that in this invasion the temples of Egypt will be burned and the Egyptian gods will be carried away. Among the cities and temples that will be devastated, Jeremiah mentions in particular Heliopolis (modern Tell Hisn and Matariyeh) which was the center for the worship of Re, the Egyptian sun god, and noted for its obelisks (four-sided, granite pillars with pyramidal tops).

44:1-14. Condemnation of the Jews in Egypt. Jeremiah's second prose sermon begins with a reminder of Yahweh's devastation of Jerusalem and Judah because of their *wickedness* (v. 3), in particular their serving other gods and refusing to repent. Then the prophet condemns the Jewish refugees, including those who desire to come to Egypt and those already residing there, for abandoning their homeland in Judah and for pagan worship. In addition to the one in Tahpanhes (2:16; 43:7), other Jewish settlements in Egypt include Migdol, Memphis, and the land of Pathros. Migdol may be modern Tell el-Heir, located in northern Egypt (46:14). Memphis was a former capital of Egypt located on the west bank of the Nile River, some fifteen mi. south of Cairo. The land of Pathros is Upper Egypt. They also will experience devastation at Yahweh's hand, and most will not survive or return home to Judah.

44:15-19. The stubborn refusal to listen. The Jewish refugees refuse to listen to Jeremiah, announcing that they will continue their pagan worship of the queen of heaven (see note on 7:18). They argue that when their ancestors in Judah and Jerusalem worshiped her they prospered. The refugees contend that their cessation of worshiping her led to their hardships.

44:20-30. The continuation of Jeremiah's condemnation of the Jews in Egypt. Jeremiah continues his sermon of judgment, indicating that Yahweh will destroy most of the Jewish refugees with only a few to escape to return to Judah. The sign that this judgment will come to pass is Yahweh's deliverance of Pharaoh Hophra (Aphries) *into the hands of his enemies* (v. 30; cf. 37:5). Hophra (589–570 B.C.E.)

was assassinated by Amasis (570–526 B.C.E.), a court official who had ruled as co-regent for three years.

Oracle of Salvation concerning Baruch, 45:1-5

Jeremiah addresses a prose sermon of salvation to his secretary and companion, Baruch (see notes on chaps. 32 and 36). The sermon is situated in 605 B.C.E. when Jeremiah dictated the first scroll to him (see notes on chap. 36). Baruch offered up his own lament to which Yahweh responds through the prophet (cf. the laments in 11:18–20:18). Baruch is promised that in the coming period of destruction his life will be spared. It is not clear what *great things* (v. 5) Baruch desired for himself. He did have important political contacts in the government, perhaps indicating he was an important official himself. For the language of *break down what I have built, and pluck up what I have planted* (v. 4), see 1:10; 18:7-9; 24:6.

Oracles against the Foreign Nations, 46:1–51:64

46:1. Superscription. The last major collection of oracles in Jeremiah is the collection of "Oracles against the Foreign Nations," so named because of the superscription in 46:1 (cf. Isa 13–23 and Ezek 25–32). The LXX places this collection after 25:13a, a more likely original position. Why the oracles were relocated to this part of the book and when this occurred are not known. The authorship of this collection and its individual oracles, most of which are poetic, is a matter of debate, although certain oracles may have come from the historical Jeremiah (e.g., the oracle against Egypt in 46:2-12). However, it is likely that most of these oracles were added by later prophets and editors.

46:2-26. Against Egypt. Two oracles of judgment are uttered against Egypt. The first concerns the Egyptian defeat at CARCHEMISH (vv. 2-12), and the second signals the approach of Nebuchadrezzar (vv. 13-26). The prose superscription, inserted by a later editor, dates the first oracle of judgment to the fourth year of King Jehoiakim's reign, that is, 605 B.C.E. when Nebuchadrezzar defeated Necho II and the Egyptians at the battle of Carchemish. The vivid language describing the battle calls to mind the images of war associated with the "Foe from the North" (cf. chaps. 4–10). Three Egyptian allies are mentioned: Ethiopia, Put (probably a region in Libya), and Ludim (a group of people either in North Africa or Asia Minor).

The prose introduction (v. 13) to the second oracle of judgment against Egypt has Jeremiah predicting Nebuchadrezzar's invasion of Egypt in 568/567 B.C.E. (see note on 43:8-13; and Ezek 29:19-21). Apis was an Egyptian fertility deity worshiped in Memphis as a sacred bull. The prose addition in vv. 25-26 explains that Yahweh's judgment through Nebuchadrezzar was against Egypt, its kings, and its gods. The one deity specified is Amon, an Egyptian sun god whose cultic center was Thebes. The addition concludes by promising that Egypt will once again be inhabited *as in the days of old* (v. 26).

46:27-28. Salvation for Israel. This promise of salvation reduplicates 30:10-11 (see note). Israel in exile is promised a return home after a period of punishment. The foreign nations among whom the exiles are living will come to an end. This reference to the foreign nations is the likely reason this fragment of a salvation oracle is placed here.

47:1-7. Against the Philistines. The prose introduction in v. 1 places the oracle against the Philistines in the period shortly before an unidentified Pharaoh attacked the city of Gaza. One possibility for a specific historical location is offered by the Greek historian Herodotus (2.159) who writes that Necho II conquered Kadytis (Gaza) following his victory at Megiddo (609 B.C.E.). Yet, from the content of the oracle itself (especially the *waters rising out of the north* (v. 2) and the reference to Ashkelon), a better historical location would be Nebuchadrezzar's successful campaign against Philistia in 604 B.C.E., following the battle of Carchemish in 605 B.C.E. Nebuchadrezzar conquered Ashkelon in 604 B.C.E. In any case, Tyre and Sidon, two Phoenician cities, are mentioned in v. 4, suggesting that they were allied with the Philistines as Nebuchadrezzar made his entrance into the Coastal Plain of Israel. Caphtor is the island of Crete, one of the places from which the Philistines came (see Amos 9:7). For the association of the Anakim with the Philistines (v. 4), see Josh 11:21-22. The Anakim were supposed to be a race of giants (Deut 2:10-11).

48:1-47. Against Moab. This chapter contains several judgment oracles against Moab, one of the Transjordan countries to the east of Israel. Throughout the history of Israel and Judah, Moab was usually an enemy, receiving at times prophetic condemnation (Isa 15–16; Zeph 2:8–11). According to 2 Kgs 24:2, Moab raided Judahite territory following Jehoiakim's rebellion against Nebuchadrezzar. While Moab participated in conspiratorial talks against Babylonian rule in 595 or 594 B.C.E. (27:1-22), it is unlikely that the nation joined in the actual rebellion. The oracles indicate significant borrowing from Isa 15–16. These oracles may anticipate a future destruction of Moab by Nebuchadrezzar.

The first oracle (vv. 1-10) is a lament over the destruction caused by Nebuchadrezzar's advance against Moab. Nebo and Kiriathaim are cities in Moab, the former likely modern Khirbet Mekhayyet located five mi. to the southwest of Heshban (Isa 15:2). Kiriathaim probably was located near modern el-Qereiyat, five and a half mi. northwest of Dibon (Ezek 25:9). Heshbon (modern Heshban) was located in the north of Moab. Horonaim was a city in Moab, while Luhith, a Moabite city, was located at the south end of the Dead Sea. Chemosh was the national god of the Moabites (1 Kgs 11:7). Verse 10 offers a double curse that in its context is directed against those who do not carry out the slaughter against Moab.

The second oracle announces judgment against Moab (vv. 11-17) and begins by noting the country's good fortune in not suffering devastation, heretofore. But this soon shall change when an invader comes to destroy the country and bring down its ruling house. The prose announcement of judgment in vv. 12-13 indicates that at the time of Moab's destruction, it will be ashamed of Chemosh, its national deity, even as Israel was ashamed of Bethel. The city of Bethel, the location of a royal sanctuary of the Northern Kingdom, was criticized for the infiltration of pagan worship and political apostasy from the house of David ruling in the south (1 Kgs 12:25-33; Amos 7:10-17).

Verse 18-28 contain a taunt uttered against destroyed Moab. Dibon (modern Dhiban) was a Moabite city on the King's Highway some thirteen mi. east of the Dead Sea (Isa 15:2, 9). Aroer was a fortress (modern Khirbet Ara'ir) on the Arnon River that cuts through Moab from the east and empties into the Dead Sea. The prose insertion in vv. 21-24 contains a list of several towns and cities in Moab that had been the recipients of judgment. Verses 26-27, also in prose, explain that arrogant Moab who had taunted Israel during the latter's time of destruction is now the object of derision from other nations.

Verses 29-39 express a lament over fallen Moab (cf. the laments in 11:18–20:18). Yahweh, the destroyer of Moab, now laments over the country (cf. God's lament in 14:17-18). The capital city of Moab was Kir-heres (modern el-Kerak; see Isa 15:1), located approximately eleven mi. east of the Dead Sea. Sibmah is perhaps modern Qurn el-Kibsh, some five mi. southwest of Heshban. Jazer was another Moabite city located perhaps to the west of Amman. Added to the end of the poetic lament (vv. 29-33) is a prose lament of Yahweh over the destruction of Moab (vv. 34-39).

Verses 40-44 contain a poetic judgment oracle against Moab that depicts the invader in images of an eagle. The reason for Moab's destruction is its arrogance.

Missing in the LXX, vv. 45-47 speak of the reversal of fortunes of destroyed Moab. Yahweh will restore the nation in the future. This stereotypical language of the restoration of a country's fortunes occurs at the end of several units detailing the destruction of the foreign nations (e.g., 49:6, 49:39). Sihon was an Amorite king defeated by Israel during its journey toward Canaan (Num 21:21-30; Deut 2:24-37; and Judg 11:18-22).

49:1-6. Against Ammon. Located in the Transjordan that is east of Israel, Ammon was Israel's perpetual enemy. The Ammonites participated with the Babylonians in the attack on Judah following Jehoiakim's revolt (2 Kgs 24:2). They also were participants in the conspiratorial talks against Babylonia (Jer 27:3) and decided to revolt (Ezek 21:18-23). Ammon continued to struggle against the Babylonians after Jerusalem had fallen in 587 B.C.E. Ammon's king supported Ishmael, the member of the royal house of Judah who assassinated Gedaliah (see chap. 41). Eventually Nebuchadrezzar brought an end to the state.

The poetic judgment oracle in 49:1-6 announces the coming destruction of Ammon. In vv. 3-5, the prophet calls on the cities of Heshbon and Rabbah to begin rituals of lamentation (cf. 6:26; 9:10; 9:17-22). The prose verse, added at the end (v. 6) and promising the restoration of the Ammonites, is absent in the LXX (cf. 48:47).

Ammon had occupied the territory of the Israelite tribe of Gad in the Transjordan (Judg 10:6–12:6; 2 Sam 12:26-31). Milcom was the national deity of

Ammon (see 1 Kgs 11:5, 33). Rabbah (modern Amman) was the capital of Ammon (see Ezek 25:5; Amos 1:14). Heshbon (see comments on 48:1-10) may have fallen into Ammonite hands. The word "Ai" means "ruin" (Tell), and thus may refer to Rabbah mentioned in the next line.

49:7-22. Against Edom. According to the patriarchal traditions, Esau was the twin brother of Jacob (Israel) and the ancestor of the nation of Edom (Esau; see Gen 25:19-28). Located to the south and east of Israel, Edom was a hated enemy of Israel, often the object of condemnation (see Ps 137; Isa 11:14; 34:5-17; Ezek 35; Amos 1:6, 9, 11; 2:1; Obad; Mal 1:2-5). Folded into Nebuchadrezzar's empire not too long after the battle of Carchemish, Edom participated with the Babylonians in the conquest of Jerusalem in 587 B.C.E. and rejoiced over the fall of the city (Ps 137:7; Lam 4:21-22; Obad 10-16). After 587 B.C.E. Edom took control of southern Judah with Hebron as their capital (Lam 4:21-22; Ezek 25:12-14).

This poetic oracle of judgment is largely shaped by Obadiah. Compare vv. 14-16 to Obad 1-4, and vv. 9-10a to Obad 5-6. Edom was especially famous for its wisdom. Teman was an important city located in central Edom, while Bozrah was the major city in northern Edom (see Isa 34:6; Amos 1:12). Dedan was a country located in northwest Arabia (see Ezek 25:13).

Two prose insertions are made in this oracle. Verses 12-13 refer to the cup of wrath first mentioned in 25:15-38. In vv. 17-22 the destruction of Edom is compared to that of Sodom and Gomorrah (see note on 20:16).

49:23-27. Against Damascus. This brief judgment oracle is issued against Damascus, the capital of Syria (see 1 Kgs 11:24; 15:18; 19:15; 20:34; 2 Kgs 8:7, 9; 16:10-12; Isa 7:8). The city was conquered by the Assyrians in 733/32 B.C.E. and made into the center of a region ruled by various foreign empires. Little is known of Damascus after the Assyrian conquest. Damascus is not listed among the foreign nations in 25:18-26, suggesting that the oracle is quite late.

Prior to the taking of Damascus, the Assyrians conquered the cities of Arpad in 740 B.C.E. and Hamath in 738 B.C.E. (see 2 Kgs 18:34; 19:13; Isa 10:9; 36:19; 37:13). Arpad (Tell Erfad), located some twenty-five mi. north of Aleppo, was a city in northern Syria, while Hamath (modern Hama) was a Syrian city located on the Orontes River between Damascus and Aleppo. Verse 27 is borrowed from Amos 1:4.

49:28-33. Against Kedar and Hazor. The Arabian tribes of Kedar and Hazor now receive from Jeremiah a poetic judgment oracle (see 25:23-24). Kedar controlled the trade route from Arabia to the Fertile Crescent (2:10-11; Isa 21:16-17; Ezek 27:21). They were apparently conquered by Nebuchadrezzar. Hazor is an unknown site in the Arabian desert, also possibly conquered by Nebuchadrezzar. For *shaven temples*, see note on 9:26.

49:34-39. Against Elam. This prose oracle, dated to the beginning of the reign of Zedekiah in 597 B.C.E., reflects Nebuchadrezzar's conquest of Elam. Elam was a country located east of the Tigris River and had its capital at Susa. The conquest occurred in 597 B.C.E. Earlier, Elam had been conquered by the Assyrians and became an ally in the Assyrian invasion of Israel (see Isa 11:11; 21:2; 22:6).

50:1–51:58. Against Babylon. The largest number of oracles in the collection of "Oracles Against the Foreign Nations" is directed towards Babylon (see chaps. 24, 25, and 29). The authorship of these oracles, both poetic and prose, is a subject of debate. When the historical Jeremiah mentions Babylon prior to 587 B.C.E., he speaks favorably of them. They are the instrument of Yahweh in bringing judgment against Israel and Judah, and Nebuchadrezzar II is the "servant" of Yahweh. Jeremiah tells the people of Judah and Jerusalem that they should submit to Babylonian rule. In the prose tradition, Jeremiah tells the exiles of 597 B.C.E. who are living in Babylon not to expect an early return, but rather to settle down, build homes, raise families, and pray for the welfare of Babylonia (chap. 29). Nebuchadrezzar sees to it that Jeremiah is treated well after the fall of the city (39:11-14; 40:1-6).

It is possible, of course, that after the fall of Jerusalem in 587 B.C.E. Jeremiah altered his views concerning Babylon, asserting that in the future the empire will face Yahweh's wrath and be destroyed. However, it is more reasonable to think that these oracles against Babylon came from later prophets of the exile (cf. Second Isaiah) who predicted the fall of the evil empire, making it possible for the exiles to return home. The Persians and Medes conquered the Babylonian empire. Cyrus, the Persian king, allowed the Jews in exile to return home in 538 B.C.E. (Ezra 1:1-4).

50:1. Superscription. (see Hag 1:1; Mal 1:1). The superscription notes that the following collection consists of Jeremiah's oracles concerning Babylon.

50:2-3. Judgment from the north. In his poetic oracle of judgment, the prophet tells his audience to announce the fall of Babylon. Bel is one of the names of Marduk, the major god of Babylonia worshiped as creator and determiner of destinies. Merodach is the biblical name for Marduk. The language of the "foe from the north" (see chaps. 4–10) is now used to speak of the enemies of Babylon: the Medes and the Persians.

50:4-5. The return of Israel and Judah. This brief prose sermon portrays the return of Israel and Judah to Zion (Jerusalem) as a pilgrimage. United, they will both enter into an everlasting covenant that shall never be forgotten (cf. chaps. 30–31).

50:6-7. Israel's shepherds. In this prose oracle, Yahweh announces that the shepherds of Judah (i.e., their kings; cf. 23:1-4) have led them astray.

50:8-10. Exhortation to flee Babylon. The prophet warns people, probably the Jewish exiles, to flee Babylon in expectation of the attack of nations from the north (see chaps. 4–10; and 50:3).

50:11-16. The invaders are commanded to attack. In this poetic oracle of judgment, Mother Babylon (cf. Mother Jerusalem in 10:20) shall be shamed, because her children have plundered Judah. Yahweh commands the invaders to attack the city. Historically speaking, Babylon was not taken by force and destroyed. The city surrendered to the armies of Persia, led by Gobryas.

50:17-20. The Restoration of Israel. This prose speech tells of Israel's destruction, first by the Assyrians and then by the Babylonians. While Babylon will be punished, Israel will be redeemed and restored to its land. Israel's and Judah's sins will be forgiven.

50:21-32. Yahweh fights against Babylon. This oracle describes Yahweh's assault against Babylon. "Double rebellion" (*Merathaim*) is a word play on the name of southern Babylonia, while "punishment" (*Pekod*) is a word play on an east Babylonian tribe named *Puqudu*. Two prose additions are inserted. Verse 28 speaks of Jewish refugees from Babylon coming home to Zion to declare Yahweh's vengeance, including his vengeance for his Temple. Verses 29-30, also in prose, tell the invading army to lay siege to the city and let none escape. Verses 31-32 present Yahweh's invective against Babylon, promising the arrogant city that it will fall. A self-exalted pride is the basis for Babylonia's judgment (see Ezek 28).

50:33-34. Yahweh will give rest to Israel and Judah. In this prose sermon, Yahweh promises to redeem the oppressed people of Israel and Judah.

50:35-38. A sword against the Babylonians. The sword will destroy the Babylonians.

50:39-40. A deserted city fit only for wild animals. Only wild animals shall inhabit Babylon, a city that never again will have a human population.

50:41-43. Invaders from the north country. In images similar to the "Foe from the North" in chaps. 4–10, Babylon the once mighty and feared northern foe is now terrified at the approach of its own foe from the North.

50:44-46. Yahweh will conquer Babylon. Yahweh promises the fall of Babylon and the appointment of a new shepherd of his choosing to rule over it.

51:1-4. The winnowing of Babylon. Yahweh will send a destructive wind to winnow Babylon like grain.

51:5-10. Israel and Judah are not forsaken. Israel and Judah have not been abandoned by Yahweh. The Jewish inhabitants of Babylon are warned to flee and escape the wrath that Yahweh is bringing.

51:11-19. Prepare for Yahweh's attack. Yahweh gives the command to the defenders of Babylon to prepare for the invasion (identified in the prose insertion as the Medes) to attack the city. Yahweh as the creator of the world and the one who commands the elements is contrasted with lifeless, worthless idols. Verses 15-19 are taken from 10:12-16. Media, located in modern northwest Iran, was a separate empire that helped overthrow the Assyrians at the end of the seventh century B.C.E. It became a Persian province in 549 B.C.E. and participated in the defeat of the Babylonians (see Isa 13:17).

51:20-23. Persia is Yahweh's hammer. These words appear to be addressed to Cyrus, described as the hammer used by Yahweh to smash nations (cf. Isa 41:2-3).

51:24. Yahweh's repayment of Babylon. Yahweh announces repayment against Babylon for their evil doings in Jerusalem.

51:25-26. Yahweh is against Babylon. Babylon, called a *destroying mountain*, will be levelled with no stone being reused for building other structures.

51:27-33. The nations war against Babylon. Nations are summoned to wage war against Babylon. Ararat (Urartu) refers to people inhabiting a region near Lake Van (southeast Turkey and northwest Iran); Minni (Mannaya) refers to people who lived in an area south of Lake Urmia in modern northern Iraq; and Ashkenaz likely refers to an Indo-European people who lived near modern Armenia, identified as the Scythians by Herodotus.

51:34-40. Jerusalem will be revenged. The inhabitants of Jerusalem who suffered so much at the hand of Nebuchadrezzar call for revenge. Yahweh responds that he will take vengeance on their behalf.

51:41-49. Babylon has fallen. Sheshach is a cipher for Babylon. The city has fallen, and the Jewish survivors are admonished to flee the destruction.

51:50-58. The sounds of Babylon's destruction. The Jewish exiles are to remember Jerusalem. They confess their guilt. Babylon will be destroyed. Even now the sounds of its destruction can be heard.

51:59-64. Jeremiah's prophecies against Babylon are taken to the exiles. This narrative is an etymology that seeks to explain the origins of the collection of oracles against Babylon. According to this story, Jeremiah wrote down these oracles and had Seraiah take them to Babylon. He is to read the scroll aloud, remind Yahweh of his promised destruction of Babylon, and then attach to it a stone weight and cast it into the Euphrates. This symbolic act is to be accompanied by the announcement that Babylon likewise shall sink. The date given is the fourth year of the reign of King Zedekiah (593 B.C.E.). Seraiah was Baruch's brother (see 32:12).

Historical Appendix, 52:1-34

Most of this chapter is taken from 2 Kgs 24:18–25:30. The chapter, coupled with 39:1-10, narrates the story of Zedekiah's rebellion against the Babylonians, the fall of Jerusalem, and the exile. Written by deuteronomic editors, this material does end on a note of hopeful anticipation resulting from Jehoiachin's release from a Babylonian prison (vv. 31-34).

52:1-3. The reign of Zedekiah. The introduction provides a succinct summary of Zedekiah's reign. His wickedness is said to be the basis for what happened to Jerusalem. This is the standard deuteronomic assessment of the reigns of most kings in Israel and Judah.

52:4-11. The fall of Jerusalem. These verses describe the siege and fall of Jerusalem along with the capture, torture, and exile of Zedekiah.

52:12-16. The burning of Jerusalem and the exile. Nebuzaradan, the captain of Nebuchadrezzar's guard, burns the city of Jerusalem and takes the captives into exile.

52:17-23. The spoils of the Temple. These verses list the booty stolen from the Temple.

52:24-27. The execution of high officials and priests. The chief priest, Seraiah (see 36:26), and the second priest, Zephaniah (see 21:1; 29:24-32), are executed at Riblah along with important military leaders, royal advisers, and leaders of the *people of the land.*

52:28-30. The lists of exiles for three deportations. The number of exiles from three deportations is given (597, 587, 582 B.C.E.).

52:31-34. King Jehoiachin released from prison. Evil-merodach (Amel-Marduk, 562–560 B.C.E.) releases Jehoiachin, the king of Judah exiled in 597 B.C.E. He was honored above other exiled kings, allowed to eat daily at the Babylonian king's table, and given a royal allowance. This release occurred in the thirty-seventh year of his captivity (560 B.C.E.). Amel-Marduk, the son and successor of Nebuchadrezzar, was overthrown by his brother-in-law, Neriglissar. The release of the king from prison must have given some hope to the Babylonian exiles about a future restoration.

The account of the change of fortunes for Jehoiachin, taken from the end of 2 Kings and thus the ending of the "Former Prophets," is a way by which the Deuteronomic editors of Jeremiah and the Deuteronomistic History (Joshua–2 Kings) affirm that God has not abandoned the exiles. Indeed, the editors hope that even kingship will be restored. In addition, Jehoiachin's release indicates that life even in exile can be good (see chap. 29).

Ezekiel

[MCB 673-708]

Joel F. Drinkard, Jr.

Introduction

The Book of Ezekiel stands in English Bibles (as in the Hebrew Bible) as the last of the Great Prophets, so called due to their size. It is the shortest of the three, and, in terms of the historical setting of the PROPHET whose name the book bears, the latest of the three.

The Person

Although the OT gives more biographical information on EZEKIEL than on any other prophet, there is still relatively little precise information, certainly not enough to piece together any full biography.

The name Ezekiel (יְחֶזְקֵאל) means "God (El) will strengthen" or "May God strengthen." The name has been interpreted as a note of hope to a people in exile.

Ezekiel's father was named Buzi, and apparently both were priests. Ezekiel's priestly role is evident throughout the book in his great concern with holiness, the defilement of the Temple, CLEAN/UNCLEAN, Torah, and in his many references to the legal codes, especially the Holiness Code.

Ezekiel was among the leaders of Judah deported to Babylonia in the first EXILE of 597 B.C.E. (Brownlee 1986 holds a different view; see the Setting, below). There he lived among a contingent of the exiles at an unknown site Tel Abib on the banks of the Chebar River, usually identified with a major irrigation canal that ran from Babylon past Nippur to Erech. He apparently lived out his life in Babylonia.

Ezekiel was married. He records the sickness and death of his wife while in Babylonia (24:15-18), but no reference is made to children.

One of the most intriguing, and most debated, issues concerning Ezekiel is his personality and the likelihood of physical and/or personality disorders. The strange behavior associated with Ezekiel (muteness, lying on one side and then on the other for 390 days, trembling as he takes food) are described in the book as his being overwhelmed by God's spirit as he began his ministry and as he experienced later visions. The interpretation most scholars today assume, and as will be followed here, is that these symptoms are to be related to the prophetic experience: they relate to the ecstatic state the prophet experiences in his calling and in his vision-messages. Therefore, no attempt to psychologize or diagnose will be made; instead the behaviors will be treated theologically.

The Setting

The book opens with a reference to *the thirtieth year* (1:1). Some scholars relate that to the thirtieth year of the Exile and suggest that was the date some edition of the Book of Ezekiel was completed. If the date refers to the Exile, it is the latest date in the book and would correspond approximately to 567 B.C.E. However, it seems better to take the reference to the thirtieth year as referring to the prophet's age when he had the call experience of chap. 1. Such a date would place Ezekiel's birth near 623 B.C.E.

Ezekiel's childhood and early teen years would have been under the reign of the reformer King JOSIAH, whose sweeping religious reforms began about the time of Ezekiel's birth. If his father was a priest, Ezekiel and his family must have been profoundly influenced by those reforms.

Ezekiel lived in a time of great political change. The Assyrian Empire was on the wane. Josiah's reforms were possible largely because of Assyrian weakness. Nineveh fell in 612 B.C.E. to a coalition of the Babylonians and others. Egypt now exerted more authority in Syria/Palestine. In 609 B.C.E. Pharaoh Necho of Egypt marched northward through Judah in support of a remnant of the Assyrian army attempting to form a state in the upper Euphrates valley. On that march, Necho was opposed by the Judean King Josiah, who was killed in battle at MEGIDDO. Interim King JEHOAHAZ was deposed by Necho three months later and a pro-Egyptian king, JEHOIAKIM, was placed on the throne.

Quite soon it became clear that Babylon was now the major political force throughout Mesopotamia. After the battle of CARCHEMISH in 605 B.C.E., Babylonian forces led by the crown prince, and soon-to-be-king, NEBUCHADREZZAR pursued Necho and his Egyptian forces back through Syria/Palestine to the border of Egypt. Judah now became a vassal of Babylon. Several of the small states of Syria/Palestine revolted against Babylon during the next six to eight years, resulting in Babylonian incursions into the region. Jehoiakim revolted against Babylon in 598 B.C.E.; he died or was assassinated late that year and was replaced by his son Jehoiachin. Jerusalem fell to Nebuchadrezzar early in 597 B.C.E. after a short siege; Jehoiachin, the queen mother, and many of the leading royal, military and administrative officials were taken captive to Babylonia. The Babylonian Chronicle places the number of exiles at 3,000. The OT adds 1,000 craftsmen and 7,000 soldiers. Heavy tribute was also exacted as part of the punishment. Ezekiel was among the captives.

As the Book of Ezekiel makes clear, this initial deportation did not end the intrigue in Judah, nor the suffering. ZEDEKIAH, the puppet-king placed on the throne by Nebuchadrezzar, also revolted against Babylon, expecting to receive Egyptian aid. The aid never materialized; retribution was swift and thorough. Judah was again invaded and besieged; the siege of Jerusalem lasted approximately eighteen months.

When it fell, Jerusalem was devastated and burned; the Temple was destroyed. The second deportation of 587 B.C.E. brought additional captives to Babylonia. Date formulas within the book place the call of Ezekiel in the fifth year of captivity, about 593 B.C.E. Most of these formulas refer to the years of Jehoiachin's captivity, suggesting that Ezekiel and the Babylonian exiles considered Jehoiachin still to be the legitimate ruler of Judah.

The last date formula in the book (assuming the thirtieth year refers to Ezekiel's age as suggested above) mentions the twenty-seventh year of exile, approximately 571. B.C.E. If this formula lies close to the end of Ezekiel's ministry, then that ministry spanned a period of at least twenty-two years. Also, if Ezekiel was thirty years old when the call experience took place, he would have been about twenty-five at the time of his exile, and about fifty-two at the time of the last dated message.

The book has no reference to the overthrow of the Babylonian Empire by the Persians in 539 B.C.E., nor any reference to the restoration of the exiles in 538 B.C.E. This suggests a relatively short time frame for the composition and initial editing of the book. It is, of course, possible and even likely that the editorial-redactional work continued over a longer period.

The geographical setting of the book is taken to be Babylonia. The principal location is an otherwise unknown site, Tel Abib, on the banks of the River Chebar. The river itself is usually identified with the *naru kabari*, "great river," mentioned in inscriptions from Nippur. That river was actually a major irrigation canal that ran from Babylon southward past Nippur and Erech and then rejoined the Euphrates. That location, along with the "plain" or "valley" associated with it, is the site of several of Ezekiel's visions. The great detail with which he recounts events and places in Judah, particularly Jerusalem, has suggested to some scholars that Ezekiel traveled back and forth to Judah, or that he had a prior prophetic ministry in Jerusalem, or that the entire ministry was set in Judah, and only redactionally placed in Babylon (see Brownlee 1986, xxiii–xxv). This commentary will follow the most commonly accepted view, that Ezekiel's prophetic ministry was located in Babylon and that he was taken there as an exile in 597 B.C.E.

The exiles themselves apparently were not living in extreme circumstances. There is no evidence of duress, of concentration camps or prisoner-of-war intern-ment. Apparently the exiles enjoyed freedom of movement and the possibility of practicing their occupations. They were free to build homes and plant gardens; they even had some communication with the Judean community back home. The exiles may have had an easier time than many of the ones left behind in war-torn and decimated Judah, especially after 587 B.C.E.

The Book of a Community

That the Book of Ezekiel, like other books of the OT, underwent editorial-redac-tional processes is clear. The third person introduction of 1:1-3, followed by a first person work, and the use of catchwords to collect originally diverse materials together, and the larger process of grouping together oracles of judgment against Jerusalem and Judah, oracles of judgment against foreign nations, and oracles of hope, all point to an editorial-redactional process. The recognition of such a process does not indicate responsibility for the process. The issue of who is responsible for this process, and when it was completed, is still unresolved after over a century of vigorous debate. Many scholars hold that Ezekiel himself, or a disciple, was responsible for most of the editorial work. Some, although a minority, maintain that Ezekiel was responsible for virtually none of the book. Without debating the merits, this commentary will follow the former position.

The book itself, after the extended call vision of chaps. 1:1–3:15, has a broad outline found in a number of the OT prophets: (1) oracles of judgment against Israel-Judah; (2) oracles of judgment against foreign nations; (3) oracles of hope and restoration. Similar patterns may be found, though not necessarily to the same degree, or in the same order, in Amos, Isaiah, and Jeremiah. It may be that these messages were the expected content of a prophetic ministry.

In Ezekiel these broad divisions form an outline. In addition, much of the attempt to date the material in the oracles (using Ezekiel's own date formulas where appropriate) relates the material as follows:

(1) Chapters 1–24, oracles of judgment against Judah and Jerusalem, are mostly dated before the fall of Jerusalem in 587 B.C.E. The judgment proclaimed is precisely the kind experienced in the invasions and exiles of 597 B.C.E. and 587 B.C.E. Having himself experienced the siege warfare of 597 and remembering the defeat and death of Josiah in 609 B.C.E., Ezekiel could well be expected to anticipate similar devastation and judgment on the people for their sins. And knowing first-hand the might of the Babylonians, he would naturally depict them as the instruments God would use again in that judgment.

(2) Chapters 25–32, the oracles against foreign nations, are mostly dated after 587 B.C.E. The context of the oracles against the nations presupposes that Jerusalem has already fallen. The judgment spoken against the nations is based largely on those nations' response to the fall of Judah and Jerusalem. Some took delight in Judah's plight; others took advantage of Judah's defeat to expand their borders; and still others offered no aid to Judah, or aided the Babylonians in the assault against Judah. Because of their response, they too will be judged.

(3) Chapters 33–48, the oracles of hope and restoration, are also dated after 587 B.C.E. They likewise presuppose that Judah and Jerusalem have fallen. However, these chapters maintain that judgment is not the final word God has, even for a rebellious people. If they will repent, God may restore both people and land. There is yet a future hope.

One should not be too strong in asserting the independence of the divisions of the Book of Ezekiel. Clear links serve to tie together the sections and the book as a whole. Indeed, it may be argued that the Book of Ezekiel displays more literary unity than any other of the great prophetic collections. Here are a few of these links:

the departure of the glory of chaps. 8–11 is paralleled by its return in chaps. 40–48, especially chap. 43. Furthermore, the glory in those sections picks up the references to the glory in the inaugural vision of chaps. 1–3. Even more broadly, the destruction of Jerusalem described in many of the oracles of chaps. 1–24 is paralleled by the restoration hope of chaps. 40–48. The sixth chapter speaks of devastation of the mountains of Judah because of idolatrous worship practices; chap. 36 describes the transformation of those same mountains in preparation for the restoration. The commission to be a watchman in 3:16-21 is paralleled by an oracle concerning watchmen in 33:1-9. Likewise the message on individual responsibility in chap. 18, with its cry that the individual who sins will be judged for his or her own sins, is paralleled by a call to individual repentance with the promise of forgiveness in 33:10-20. Thus the book exhibits many examples of literary unity or coherence.

The Book of Ezekiel has many of the literary elements found in other prophetic books. Especially prevalent are the visions, allegories, symbolic prophetic acts, and autobiographical material. Unlike the literature of most of the preexilic prophets, the material in Ezekiel is predominantly prose. Ezekiel has fewer of the short oracles; the book is noted for its extended visions and metaphors. Typical Ezekielian phrases include the prophetic proof formula *that you may know that I am the LORD* (e.g., 20:20), *O mortal* (e.g., 2:1; KJV, RSV, "son of man" = "human being"), *set your face* (e.g., 4:3), and *the glory of the LORD* (e.g., 1:28) as the symbol of the LORD's presence.

Even in his use of the genre of preexilic prophets, Ezekiel serves as a transition toward postexilic prophetism. The movement is away from oracles and more toward the allegories. His concern with priestly matters of holiness, cleanness, and purity becomes a major concern of the postexilic community. His extended visions include elements that seem to be precursors of apocalyptic.

Theology

Ezekiel's theology centers around a God who is intimately involved with the people. The prophet declares God's judgment on the people due to their sins, and that judgment is devastating—the total destruction of the nation and its religious institutions. But this God also offers restoration if the people will repent. And in that glorious restored community God will be ever-present with them (48:35; *Yahweh-shammah, The LORD is There*, is the name of the restored city).

According to Ezekiel, Israel's and Judah's history had been one filled with sin; the people were entirely rebellious. Not only was the society sinful, but especially was the people's cultic (religious) life—and this was especially abhorrent to God. Thus judgment was certain and thorough. The fall of the nation and the destruction of the Temple were the direct result of the people's rebelliousness. Nevertheless, judgment was not the last word to Israel-Judah. The prophet also issues a call to repentance. This call if heeded could not avert the judgment that was pronounced. But it could lead to a restoration. Repentance alone would not bring deliverance.

Just as judgment came from God, so also restoration must come from God. But the prophet announces that if the people truly repent, the LORD will graciously offer restoration just as surely as God had earlier brought judgment.

Another major theological concern of Ezekiel's is that of individual accountability or responsibility. Both nations and individuals fall under God's law. Just as surely as rebellious nations will be judged, so also will rebellious individuals be judged. And the judgment is based on that individual's actions. No person is to be held accountable for the actions of another, not for a parent's action nor for a child's action. One is accountable only for oneself. Likewise, repentance is an individual matter. The case law principle (if a person does this, then the result or judgment is this) is held to be applicable. And the Deuteronomic principle is the basis for the actions of God: If you obey, you will live long in the land; but if you disobey, you will be exiled and die outside the land.

Again it must be stated that the book closes on a note of restoration. The final word is one of future hope. As terrible as the judgment for the peoples' sins was, and as rebellious as they had been to deserve such judgment, restoration was still a possibility. And if they would indeed repent, the future would become reality. That was a promise.

For Further Study

In the *Mercer Dictionary of the Bible*: BABYLONIAN EMPIRE; EXILE; EZEKIEL; EZEKIEL, BOOK OF; JERUSALEM; NEBUCHADREZZAR; PROPHECY; PROPHET; ORACLE; SYMBOL; TEMPLE/TEMPLES; THEOPHANY; VISION; ZEDEKIAH.

In other sources: L. C. Allen, *Ezekiel 20–48*, WBC; W. H. Brownlee, *Ezekiel 1–19*, WBC; K. W. Carley, *Ezekiel among the Prophets*, SBT; G. A. Cooke, *A Critical and Exegetical Commentary on the Book of Ezekiel*, ICC; W. Eichrodt, *Ezekiel*, OTL; M. Greenberg, *Ezekiel 1–20*, AncB; R. M. Hall, *Ezekiel*, FOTL; J. D. Levenson, *Theology of the Program of Restoration of Ezekiel 40–48*, HSM; D. M. G. Stalker, *Ezekiel*, TBC; J. B. Taylor, *Ezekiel*, TOTC; B. Vawter and L. J. Hoppe, *A New Heart: Ezekiel*, ITC; J. W. Wevers, *Ezekiel*, NCB; R. R. Wilson, "Ezekiel," HBC, 652–94; W. Zimmerli, *Ezekiel*, Herm.

Commentary

An Outline

The Book of Ezekiel may be divided most simply into three sections following the extended call of 1:1–3:15. These divisions are: messages of judgment against Jerusalem and Judah (3:16–24:27); oracles against foreign nations (chaps. 25–32); and oracles of hope and consolation (chaps. 33–48).

The book begins with the prophet's call and commission. Many OT prophets had a call experience (cf. Amos 7, Isa 6, Jer 1), but none is reported so thoroughly and extensively as is Ezekiel's.

Ezekiel's Call and Commission, 1:1–3:15

Introduction, 1:1-3

This brief introduction gives vital information concerning Ezekiel: his father's name, Buzi, his vocation as priest, his situation as an exile in Babylonia near the River Chebar. The second and third verses are among the only third-person materials in the book; unlike most of the OT prophets, Ezekiel is written primarily in first person.

1:1. In the thirtieth year. As discussed in the introduction, this date formula is taken as Ezekiel's age at his call. The date formula in v. 2 relates the time to political events with which the reader would be familiar (the fifth year of King Jehoiachin's exile, 593 B.C.E.).

1:3. And the hand of the LORD was on him there. This is one of the phrases used frequently in Ezekiel to describe the experience with God, usually related to a vision or its aftermath.

The Chariot-Throne Vision, 1:4-28

The VISION begins with the description of a natural phenomenon, a thunderstorm with heavy lightning, before it moves to the supernatural realm. Throughout the vision are recurrent references to the sights and sounds of the thunderstorm. Three major images are combined in the vision: the thunderstorm, the chariot-throne attended by the living creatures, and the glory of the LORD. The vision progresses as that which is at a distance draws ever closer, disclosing more and more details. It reaches its climax with *the appearance of the likeness of the glory* (v. 28).

1:4. The storm wind out of the north. North was one of the locations mentioned as the LORD's abode (see Isa 14:13). Mount Zion/Jerusalem as God's abode is even said symbolically to be in the far north (Ps 48:2). So the storm is to be understood as coming from God; indeed God is present in the midst of this storm. The use of storm, cloud, lightning, and fire imagery is common in OT theophanies (e.g., Ps 29), and plays a major role as a symbol of God's presence and guidance in the wilderness by means of the pillar of cloud and the pillar of fire. Cloud and fire serve both to reveal and to conceal God. Both symbolize the divine presence, but surround and conceal the fullness of God, which no one could experience.

1:5-14. The four living creatures. The living creatures are clearly related to the cherubim that were over the ARK (1 Sam 4:4) and the seraphs of Isaiah's vision (Isa 6:2-6). Both are understood as attendants of the deity. The iconography of the cherubim was undoubtedly intended to depict those attendants with God enthroned above them and the ark. Ezek 10:20-22 specifically relates the living creatures to the cherubim on the ark of the covenant. Such part-human, part-animal, part-bird imagery is well known from MESOPOTAMIA. The gates of Mesopotamian cities and the throne rooms of palaces were often decorated with such beings, who were the attendants of the Mesopotamian deities also. The rabbis understood the four faces of the living creatures as representing the most exalted of all creation (humans), and the most exalted of the birds, domestic animals, and wild animals. The number four represents completeness or wholeness.

The burning coals and torches moving to and fro (v. 13) are reminiscent of Isaiah's call (Isa 6:6) and Abraham's THEOPHANY with the burning fire pot (Gen 15:17) respectively.

1:15-21. The wheeled chariot. Although the chariot-throne itself is not described, its wheels are. The image of the ark as a chariot-throne is shared by 1 Chr 28:18. Related images are those of the chariots and horses of the LORD (2 Kgs 11:17) and the LORD as a rider of the clouds or heavens or winds (Pss 68:4, 33; 104:3). The wheels are specifically related to the cherubim of the ark in Ezek 10:2-20.

1:22-25. The dome. Above the chariot-throne, Ezekiel sees a dome (uyqr), the same word as used in Gen 1 for the dome of heaven that separates the waters above from the waters below. Here the dome separates the throne of God from the realm where Ezekiel and the living creatures are. God's throne is above this dome or platform. Similarly a pavement separated God from Moses and the elders (Exod 24:10). The dome is transparent; Ezekiel can see into the realm above it.

Now Ezekiel also hears sounds; the noise of the living creatures' wings is *like the sound of mighty waters* (v. 24); and from above the dome he hears *a voice* (v. 25).

1:26-28. The appearance of the glory of the LORD. The climax of Ezekiel's vision is the description of *the glory of the LORD* (v. 28). First there is something like a throne with a human-like form seated upon it. Surrounding this human-like form was something like fire and the colors of the rainbow in its splendor. Ezekiel goes to great lengths to say that the vision is indescribable. Qualifiers are added to virtually every phrase in the vision. He does not say that God *had* a human form, only that he saw something *like* a human form— likewise he saw *something like . . . living creatures* (1:5) and *something like a wheel within a wheel* (1:16). Nor does he say that he saw God; instead he says, *This was the appearance of the likeness of the glory of the LORD* (1:28).

Ezekiel's response to this vision of God's glory was to fall on his face (cf. Gen 17:3; Exod 3:6). Then he heard the sound of someone speaking to him.

Commission to Go to a Rebellious People, 2:1-7

2:1. O mortal. Most often translated as SON OF MAN (KJV, RSV), בֶּן־אָדָם denotes one who is human in contrast to the divine speaker. The phrase occurs nearly ninety times in Ezekiel, almost always as a title for the prophet in the visions and messages he receives from God. It later became a messianic title, as it is in the NT, although even there it, along with another messianic title, SON OF GOD, may point to the human and divine aspects of the messiah respectively.

2:1-2. Stand up! Although Ezekiel had fallen on his face at *the appearance of the likeness of the glory* (1:28), he is now told to stand, and a spirit brings him to his feet. Whether from internal or external motivation (i.e., is it his spirit or God's?) he obeys.

2:3-7. The audience. The message to the prophet identifies the audience to whom he is to speak. In this call experience Ezekiel, unlike Jeremiah, is commissioned only to Israel and not to other nations. This limited commission is made even more definite in chap. 3 below.

Israel is called a *rebellious house* (v. 7), and this rebellion is dated from the time of the ancestors. Again somewhat in contrast to Hosea and Jeremiah, Ezekiel finds no period of obedience in Israel's history. All of them were *rebels, ancestors* (v. 3) and *descendants* (v. 4) to the present day (v. 3).

To this rebellious house, Ezekiel is commissioned with the prophetic message, *Thus says the Lord GOD* (v. 4). His message is clearly from God and directed to Israel. Ezekiel's task is to proclaim the message; it is not necessarily to bring change and repentance. Whether they hear or reject the word (vv. 5, 7), Ezekiel is to speak that word. As in the later sentinel passages (3:16-21; 33:1-20), Ezekiel's task is to sound the alarm of the Lord's message, and to do so as convincingly as possible. But the response is in the hearers' hands. Already the theme of individual accountability (cf. chap. 18) enters the message.

Another formula introduced in these verses is the prophetic recognition or proof saying *(they shall know that . . .* [v. 5]). By the words he speaks and the signs he does, the people will be aware that Ezekiel is indeed the LORD's prophet. Like Jeremiah, Ezekiel is told not to be afraid of those to whom he speaks.

The Scroll Containing the Message, 2:8–3:3

2:8-10. A taste of woe. The prophet is now told not to be like the rebellious people, but to be obedient, to consume what he sees. Again there is a shift in senses from sound back to sight, and even to taste (v. 8). Ezekiel sees an outstretched hand holding a scroll with writing on both sides. Written on the scroll are words of lamentation, mourning and woe, the initial message Ezekiel is to bring. Although some scholars would argue that Ezekiel's message was only one of judgment and that later disciples or editors added the message of hope, that is too much to read from this passage. Certainly in this first call experience his message is to be judgmental. But this awareness does not preclude other messages given later in his ministry.

3:1-3. God's sweet word. Obediently, Ezekiel takes and eats the scroll. He accepts by this action the prophetic commission and commits himself to proclaim God's message to Israel. The sweetness of the scroll (cf. Jer 15:16) should not be interpreted as any delight Ezekiel felt in delivering his judgmental message. Indeed, he is bitter and angry over that message (3:14). But the scroll is sweet because it is God's word.

Explanation of the Call and Ezekiel's Response, 3:4-15

3:4-11. The commission. Three aspects of the commission receive attention in these verses: the people Ezekiel will address, their response, and Ezekiel's empowerment for the people's negative response. Sound is now the dominant sense mode again.

3:4-6. Ezekiel's own people. These verses give renewed emphasis concerning the intended audience: Ezekiel's mission is to his own people. The task would be easier if he were sent to a foreign people. Certainly their difficult language would present a barrier, but at least they would listen!

3:7. Israel's rebelliousness. Israel has a stubborn and rebellious nature that has not changed. They will not listen to Ezekiel. The warning implied in 2:5-7 is made explicit. Just like so many of the prophets before him (Amos 7, Isa 6, Jer 1), Ezekiel is to proclaim the message, but should not expect a positive hearing.

3:8-9. Ezekiel empowered by God. If the people have hard heads and stubborn hearts, God has made Ezekiel's face and head harder than theirs; God has fortified or strengthened (חזק) Ezekiel, a play on his name (יחזקאל, "God will strengthen"). Similarly God strengthened Jeremiah (Jer 1:17-19) and his servant (Isa 50:7).

3:10-11. The commission repeated. After the assurance of empowerment, Ezekiel is reminded again of the task: speak to the exiles, *Thus says the Lord GOD.*

3:12-15. The close of the vision and Ezekiel's response. The vision closes with Ezekiel being lifted up and the LORD's glory also rising. Ezekiel is returned to his people, the exiles by the River Chebar. It is not that he had been physically removed from them, but in his prophetic vision he had been transported into God's presence. Now he is transported back to the realm of human existence.

Ezekiel is not happy with the task and the message he is to bring. He has *bitterness* (v. 14) and anger, but God's hand was on him strongly. A clear wordplay is present between Ezekiel's bitterness (מר) and the people's rebelliousness (מרי). Ezekiel is not rebellious, but he does not easily embrace his commission. Ezekiel expresses the same feelings as Jeremiah in several of his confessions (Jer 15:16-18; 20:7-9, 14-18). He returns to his regular life among the exiles, but is too *stunned* (v. 15, RSV "overwhelmed") by the message to speak for seven days. The Hebrew indicates another probable wordplay between different significances of שמם: the prophet is *stunned*, the people are to be *devastated, ravaged, desolate.* The latter usage is common to both Jeremiah and Ezekiel.

Messages of Judgment against Jerusalem and Judah, 3:16–24:27

Ezekiel's call experience leads directly into a series of messages against Jerusalem, Judah-Israel. These messages are partly spoken and partly symbolic actions enacting the judgment God is bringing against the people.

The Prophet as Sentinel, 3:16-21

A transition paragraph ties the call experience to the messages—the description of the prophet as a sentinel. A temporal clause, *at the end of seven days* (v. 16), connects this paragraph with the conclusion of the call experience. There Ezekiel was too stunned to speak for seven days. After that time the LORD again speaks to him.

The job of the sentinel is to stand watch and sound the alarm when danger appears. Ezekiel's role as prophet is described as that type of watchman for the nation. Here, however, the primary thrust of the passage is on the responsibility of the prophet to give warning. If the sentinel fails to warn, he will be held account-able for the judgment that befalls the nation—they must be warned in order to respond. But if he faithfully warns, then the people are accountable for their response, whether they heed the warning or not (cf. chaps. 18 [individual responsibility] and 33 [sentinel image again]).

The Muted Prophet, 3:22-27

Again the prophet feels the hand of the LORD upon him, taking him *out into the valley* (or "plain," v. 22). Again he encounters the glory of the LORD. Strangely, this sentinel prophet is now made mute (אלם, "bound, silenced") by God, so that he cannot warn the people (v. 26). He is told that he will be able to speak only when God opens his mouth and removes his muteness (v. 27). Also he will be *bound* (אסר, "tied, bound, imprisoned") with *cords* (v. 25); his mobility will be limited by some means, so that he cannot go freely among the people. This limitation of mobility may indicate a physical restriction placed on the prophet, or it may be symbolic of the lack of mobility that results from siege warfare.

Many commentators take these two "bindings" to refer to serious illness such as a stroke, but the binding may not have been an actual physical disability. Certainly the actions that follow in chaps. 4 and 5 are interpreted as having symbolic meaning, and probably actual cords were used visually to indicate the binding. The muteness is clearly connected with 24:25-27, which speaks of Ezekiel's silence being ended at the news of the fall of Jerusalem (see also 33:21-22). Such muteness may refer to silence in terms of public pronouncements, broken only when the prophet is given a specific word of the LORD. In effect, the people are left virtually without a prophet. The muteness begins with the beginning of the oracles of judgment; its removal is reported at the close of the oracles of judgment.

Four Symbolic Action Messages and an Interpretation, 4:1–5:17

Following directly upon the previous message, the prophet is given four symbolic actions to carry out (4:1–5:4). These four actions are followed by an interpretation (5:5-17) explaining the significance of the actions. No specific word is given that Ezekiel actually carried out the actions, but that is implied. For the most part, the actions are self-explanatory. No interpretation is required. However, the interpretation given makes the meaning more explicit for Jerusalem and the nation.

4:1-3. The first action: portraying siege warfare on a brick. Ezekiel is to take a large building brick, such as might be used in the construction of a house or city wall, and draw on it a depiction of Jerusalem surrounded by *siegeworks*. He himself is symbolically to press the siege against the city with an iron griddle or baking pan. The very stuff of city and household walls is used to depict their destruction in Jerusalem. The iron pan placed on the hot coals to cook its contents indicates the heat of the siege set against the people. Ezekiel sets his face against the city, but it is the LORD who presses the siege. Ezekiel represents God's actions; God is behind the siege, not the Babylonians. The purpose of the action is to serve as a sign (v. 3), a warning that takes on some of the essence of the judgment signified.

4:4-8. The second action: lying on one side and then the other. Ezekiel is to lie 390 days on his left side followed by forty days on his right side. These time periods are explained as representing the years of bearing the punishment of Israel and Judah respectively, a day for a year. Is the prophet suffering vicariously for his people? He certainly is symbolically bearing their guilt and punishment. However, if the prophet represents the LORD, as was the case in the previous paragraph, the message would be that God has been bearing the sin of the people for all this time.

The time periods have produced many interpretations, none fully satisfactory. The LXX has 190 days rather than MT 390. But that date still presents as many difficulties. The forty years of Judah's sin, guilt, and punishment could relate to the forty years of wandering in the wilderness for the people's sin at Sinai. Forty years could also represent a generation in general terms. Might the 390 years represent an approximate period from the establishment of the monarchy or the building of the Temple to the EXILE of 597 B.C.E. or 587 B.C.E.? Such a figure would fit well Ezekiel's understanding that the people had never been faithful, but continually rebellious and sinful.

As he lies first on the one side and then the other, Ezekiel is to continue facing the siege depiction on the brick and to prophesy against Jerusalem. He is to have his arm bared, representing the LORD's arm outstretched against the people. The imagery reverses the expectations of the people who thought the LORD would bare the divine arm against Israel's enemies. Now Israel is the enemy!

The cords mentioned earlier (3:25) are again mentioned. The prophet is to be bound in cords so that he cannot move from one side to the other until the symbolic demonstration is completed. One can easily visualize Ezekiel taking his position each day, entwined with cords, lying on one side, facing the brick depicting the siege, and having one arm bared, prophesying against Israel and Jerusalem as God gave a word, and silent the rest of the time.

4:9-17. The third action: siege famine portrayed. In keeping with the siege imagery of the previous two prophetic actions, Ezekiel is to prepare and eat a multigrain bread for food. Unlike the previous two actions where the prophet represents God and God's actions, here the prophet clearly depicts the people and what will happen to them. The combination of grains and the small quantity (usually figured at only about eight ozs. per day), indicate the famine-like conditions of siege and exile. Likewise the small quantity of water (taken to be just over a pint) indicates the rigors of siege. Normally bread was prepared of flour from a single kind of grain and was eaten with other vegetables. Here only bread is available.

When commanded to bake this bread in the sight of his fellow exiles using *human dung* for fuel (v. 12), Ezekiel protests. In the midst of siege, human dung might be the only fuel available, but the thought is too much for Ezekiel. He is a priest; use of human dung would defile him and the food. He compares eating bread baked in that manner with eating *carrion flesh*. So God relents, having made the point in the command itself; Ezekiel may use cow dung to bake his bread.

The final paragraph of the chapter (vv. 16-17) amplifies and repeats the main imagery of the action. The staff of bread, the food supply, of Jerusalem is going to be broken. The people will eat with anxiety and dread; they will drink with appallment (שִׁמָּמוֹן). Because of the famine they will be appalled (שָׁמֵם) at one another and they will waste away (qqm). The last word returns to Ezekiel's remark that he had never eaten carrion; now the people will virtually become carrion.

5:1-4. The fourth action: shaving the head and beard, and dividing the hair. Ezekiel is to shave his head and beard, often a sign of mourning, but also a sign of disgrace and punishment. In this case, the latter seems more likely. Ezekiel again represents the people themselves. What happens to him (the disgrace and punishment), and to his hair (being cut off and destroyed) is precisely the judgment to come upon the people. One third of the people will die in the siege (apparently of pestilence and famine) just as one third of the hair is burned. One third of the people will die by the sword just as one third of the hair is cut in pieces with a sword. The last third of the people will be scattered in exile as the last third of the hair is scattered by the wind. A few hairs are taken and bound up in the hem of the prophet's garment, but even some of these are burned in fire. These few remaining hairs represent the remnant that will be preserved. Like the previous actions, this one maintains the imagery of siege warfare and judgment to come on the people.

5:5-17. Interpretation of the prophetic actions. Two components make up the interpretation found in these verses: the reason for God's judgment and a description of that judgment.

5:5. This is Jerusalem. This phrase clearly identifies the city that is the subject of the four symbolic actions as Jerusalem. This had been stated at the beginning of the actions (4:1) and repeated throughout them; it is now mentioned again emphatically lest any hearer miss the subject of God's judgment. Jerusalem is described as being the center of the nations, an *omphalos* (= navel, center of the earth) metaphor. The Hebrew concept emphasizes God's election choice of Jerusalem, with the concomitant responsibility of the people to do God's bidding.

Unfortunately, Jerusalem has not fulfilled its responsibility. Instead it has *rebelled*, disobeying God's *ordinances* and *statutes* (v. 6). Indeed, it has become worse than any of the nations around it; they lacked the advantage of knowing God's laws and expectations, but Jerusalem knew them and refused to heed them. Instead, it followed the practices of the other nations. As a result, the LORD will bring *judgments* (v. 8) on the people.

5:9-12. Sins of the people. The specific sins of the people are called *abominations* (v. 9), most often a reference to proscribed religious or cultic acts such as child sacrifice, idolatry, witchcraft, and the like. God's intended action is so striking that God has never done anything like it before and will never do so again (v. 9).

The famine will be so severe during the judgment that cannibalism will occur; parents will eat their children and children, their parents (v. 10).

The nature of the people's sins is clarified somewhat in v. 11. The people have defiled the sanctuary with their *detestable things* (usually a reference to idolatry and idolatrous practices) and their *abominations* (v. 11). So repugnant are their actions to God that God swears by the divine life itself to have no pity on them. Verse 12 repeats the judgment of the fourth prophetic action: one third each will fall by pestilence or famine, by sword, or be scattered in exile.

5:13-17. God's anger. The LORD's anger will be furious against the people. The enormity of judgment matches the enormity of their sinfulness. But God's anger is not forever. After bringing judgment, God will be satisfied (v. 13, "ease oneself, be comforted, have compassion"). Whether this indicates that God's anger is satisfied, or that God takes compassion on his people, there is an indication of an end to the anger and judgment. Nevertheless, the emphasis in this passage is on the judgment rather than its completion. But when God has completed or spent the divine anger, the people *shall know* (v. 13) that the LORD is the one who has done it—another example of a prophetic proof statement. Specifically, they will know that the LORD in divine *jealousy* (or better, "zeal"), has spoken (דבר) and done this. The verb indicates both a spoken word and a deed carried out. With this understanding, one can immediately see that both God's spoken word and action deed are not only intertwined, but in many respects are one and the same. The spoken word becomes the deed.

At least five words are used to describe the devastation of the people and its results. They will become a *desolation* (v. 14), an object of mocking or a *mockery*, a *taunt*, a *warning*, and a *horror* (v. 15). Most of these words are identical with words JEREMIAH used to describe the devastation of the people. The words describe the results of military defeat and the disparagement of the conquered by the victors. Likewise, the people become an example, a warning to others not to rebel. The threefold judgments of famine, pestilence and sword are typical of siege warfare, and are also found in Jeremiah. The threefold statement *I the LORD have spoken* (vv. 13, 15, 17) serves to emphasize that this ORACLE is not from the prophet; it is God speaking. When this devastation comes, the people are to remember that it comes not from the Babylonians or any other political or military force; it comes from the LORD! Further, the repetition serves to highlight the word-deed aspect of the oracle: the spoken word is as good as done.

Oracles against Israel, 6:1–7:27

6:1-10. Against the mountainous high places. The oracle is directed specifically against *the mountains* and *hills* although *ravines* and *valleys* are also mentioned. Judgment is spoken against the high places in particular. These *high places* (v. 3) were cultic sites that were used in the worship of Canaanite and other pagan deities. The Deuteronomist speaks of those who worship "on every high hill and under every green tree" (see Jer 3:6) suggesting open air sites, some found in groves of trees. Other passages relate the worship of Asherah to trees and wooden poles planted like trees. Certainly the prophet is speaking against similar worship practices. This people was practicing a syncretistic religion that worshiped the LORD and pagan deities both. Such was an abomination to God. To be destroyed are all the accessories of worship: idols, altars, incense stands, and the HIGH PLACE itself. The people will be slain alongside the idols. The *high places* will be torn down, desecrated, and defiled by the presence of corpses and bones. The depiction is apparently that of people worshiping their pagan deities even as the invading army comes through. The army destroys the site and kills the people. The dead remain unburied. For a similar action by a reformer king, see the report of Josiah's deeds (2 Kgs 23:4-20).

Verses 8-10 return to the remnant themes. Some will be spared and scattered in exile. Those who are spared are to remember how God was crushed by their rebelliousness and idolatry. This recognition will cause them to loathe themselves for their actions and abominable practices.

Where the previous chapter depicted the shame or disgrace committed upon the exiles (5:1), this passage indicates the shame they feel because of their actions. It will also remind them that God did not warn them about coming disaster for nought. These verses also serve as a transition from the oracle against the mountains to the oracle against abominations.

6:11-14. Against the abominations of Israel. The prophet is commanded to clap his hands and stamp his foot, applauding God's action of judgment on the abominations of the people. It is not that Ezekiel (or God) delights in bringing judgment, but that the judgment is correct for the circumstance. A stubborn and rebellious people who have refused all correction, all warning, must now face God's anger.

The judgment itself is described as the threefold *sword, famine,* and *pestilence.* All will fall victim to God's judgment, those nearby and those far away alike. The destruction of the high places and slaughter of the worshipers relates this paragraph to 6:1-7. A full description of the location of these high places is given: *on every high hill, on all the mountain tops, under every green tree, and under every leafy oak* (v. 13). The totality of devastation covers the whole land. The phrase *from the wilderness to Riblah* (v. 14) compares with Amos 6:14, "from Lebo-hamath to the Wadi Arabah," as descriptive of the whole land (see also Ezek 47:13-20 for similar boundaries of the restored land). *Riblah* is also noteworthy for the fact that in 587 B.C.E. it was the location of Nebuchadrezzar's headquarters where ZEDEKIAH was brought after the fall of Jerusalem. There his sons were killed before his eyes, and he was blinded for his rebellion.

7:1-27. Poetic oracles. Unlike most of the book, this chapter is predominantly poetry; the poetry addresses imminent judgment. Terse cries punctuate the oracles, resembling the cries of alarm of a sentinel: *An end! The end has come* (vv. 1, 6); *Disaster after disaster! See, it comes* (v. 5); *Your doom has come/gone out* (vv. 7, 10); *The time has come* (vv. 7, 12); *the day is/draws near* (vv. 7, 12); *See, the day!*

See, it comes! (v. 10). The warnings have been sounded; now the battle is being joined.

7:1-4. An announcement of judgment. This oracle is addressed against *the land* (v. 2) relating it to chap. 6 and the oracle against the *mountains*. *The land* becomes the symbol of the people. In vv. 3 and 4, God shifts speech to address the people directly: *Now the end is upon you.* Judgment is brought against their *ways*, their practices, and their *abominations*. The judgment is simply called *the end*, although later paragraphs in the chapter clarify that military defeat in siege warfare is the means of this end. God warns that he will not spare nor pity the people. The result of this ultimate judgment will be that they *shall know that I am the LORD* (v. 4). The judgment will finally prove that God is God and that God vindicates the divine commands and promises.

7:5-9. A second announcement of judgment. This oracle builds on the previous one and increases the level of intensity. There is a repetition of terminology: *the end has come* (v. 6). But more is added now: *Disaster after disaster . . . comes* (v. 5). In a wordplay Ezekiel says the *end* (Jq) has *awakened* (Jyq) against the people. The cry is one of doom.

Ezekiel then introduces two of the cultic terms familiar to his hearers. He says *the time* has come and *the day* is near (v. 7). The people would naturally have thought the time referred to one of the sacred times, the holy times and seasons of their CALENDAR. Further, the day would refer to the day of the LORD's appearing, the Day of the LORD, when God would vindicate the people and defeat all their enemies. Both terms were common in the worship practices. But, as in Amos, Ezekiel states that the *time* and *day* will not be a day of celebration and shouting; it will be tumult and panic of battle. God is coming, but coming to attack rather than to defend the people of God.

Verses 8b-9 repeat almost verbatim vv. 3b-4. This repetition intensifies God's resolve. The mood of doom is made more pervasive. The prophetic proof formula is also repeated, with one addition: now the people will know that it is the LORD who strikes. They are to remember that the army of the Babylonians is not bringing disaster and doom upon them; the LORD is bringing it.

7:10-13. A third announcement of judgment. In the previous judgment oracle, reference was made to the time and the day. In increasing intensity, this paragraph focuses on those concepts. Now that day has arrived. And instead of a day of worship and celebration, a day of rejoicing and reveling, it will be a day of defeat and disaster. The blossoming rod (v. 10) would remind the hearer of Aaron's budding rod (Num 17: 5, 8), a sign to the murmuring Hebrews of God's presence and election of Aaron to be priest. But here the rod is one of *pride* (v. 10), *violence*, and *wickedness* (v. 11). It will indicate judgment and not election; the people of Israel are the rebels here. The vocabulary of this paragraph is very reminiscent of Amos, especially Amos 8 and 9 with references to buying and selling, mourning and celebrating, and none remaining. *It shall not be revoked* (v. 13), referring to the vision of judgment, is clearly similar to Amos's repeated formula: "For three transgressions . . . and for four, I will not revoke the punishment" (the phrase appears eight times in Amos 1-2). The last phrase, *they cannot maintain* (חזק, "strengthen") *their lives* (v. 13), is another play on Ezekiel's name. God strengthens (the Hebrew meaning of Ezekiel); but the people cannot strengthen their own lives by themselves.

7:14-19. The battle and its results. The alarm has sounded; the battle should have been joined—but no one has gone out to do battle. Why? Because God has already brought down divine wrath upon them. The phrase is virtually identical with the last phrase of v. 12, tying the two paragraphs together and building to a climax. The addition here is that the wrath is specified as *my* (i.e., God's) *wrath* (v. 14). The outcome of God's wrath is devastating: those outside the city die by the sword, and those inside die of pestilence and famine. The description of the people in vv. 17-18 could reflect the ravages of famine and pestilence, or it could indicate the terror at defeat and the mandated submission to an enemy. Silver and gold are flung into the streets, useless. Either the people recognize that their money cannot save them nor buy them food (there was no food to be bought because of the siege), or the invading army ransacks and pillages, tossing prized possessions into the streets as booty. No bribery can save the inhabitants now.

7:20-27. The Temple pillaged. Verses 20-24 describe the desecration of the Temple by the invading army. It is called a *beautiful ornament* and *treasured place*; it will be profaned and plundered, because there the people made and placed their *abominable images* and *detestable things*. The judgment has moved to the very center of Israel's existence. From the invasion of the land to the siege of Jerusalem, now to the desecration and destruction of the Temple, this chapter has brought every aspect of life under judgment.

They *seek peace* (v. 25), but there is none. The people probably are not seeking a military truce to surrender; they are seeking God's peace and comfort in the Temple—but there is none. Ezekiel takes up a proverbial saying, also cited by Jeremiah (Jer 18:18), that the people keep seeking vision from the prophet, instruction from the priest, and counsel from the elders. But it is all in vain; no response is forthcoming. God will deal with the people according to their own ways; the LORD will mete out to them the same kind of justice they have been practicing. The chapter ends with another proof formula: *And they shall know that I am the LORD* (v. 27).

The Temple Vision, 8:1–11:25

The Temple vision, like the chariot-throne vision of chaps. 1–3, is a unit. In this vision, Ezekiel is transported to the Temple in Jerusalem where he witnesses the abominable, idolatrous practices of the people. He also sees six executioners killing the inhabitants of the city. He then sees the departure of God's glory from that place paving the way for its destruction. But God is not destroyed; God is the one bringing the destruction. This destruction falls heavy on those who had considered themselves as God's favored ones and had thought of the exiles as those under special judgment. Instead, the exiles are described as the remnant who will restore Israel.

8:1-6. An abomination in Jerusalem. The date formula at the beginning of this paragraph sets the time frame a year and two months after the initial call experience. The elders of the people in exile with Ezekiel are gathered at his house when the LORD's hand is upon him and he is transported in a vision to Jerusalem to the northern gateway of the inner court of the Temple, *to the seat of the image of jealousy* (v. 3). The glory of the LORD was there, in the Temple, just as it had been in his vision in the valley.

The *image of jealousy* was an idol, probably of Asherah the Canaanite goddess, which had been set up in the temple courtyard. Such abominable worship practices by the people were driving God from the Temple, but even greater abominations were being practiced.

8:7-13. A second abomination. Then Ezekiel was told to dig through a hole in a wall, and there he saw seventy elders of the people worshiping all kinds of creeping and unclean animals in the dark. The worship of serpents was associated with the Asherah cult, as well as other Canaanite and Egyptian cults. The fact that this worship was taking place in the dark suggests an association with underworld deities. Perhaps the most appalling aspect of all was that the elders of Israel, the people's leaders, were participating in such abominable activities. And they are saying, *the LORD does not see us, the LORD has forsaken the land* (v. 12). When the leaders have so lost their faith, what will become of the people? But even greater abominations awaited Ezekiel.

8:14-15. A third abomination. Ezekiel is moved again, this time to the north gate of the Temple. There he sees women *weeping for Tammuz*. The cult of TAMMUZ, also known as Dumuzi and Adonis, was a Mesopotamian cult of a dying and rising god. Tammuz was a vegetation god who died each summer in the great heat and drought. His adherents would hold a midsummer festival of mourning for him. With the intervention of his consort Inanna/Ishtar, he is brought back to life with the fall and winter rains. The new vegetation of winter and spring indicates his rising. The practice of this Mesopotamian cult was also taking place within the Temple precincts. But still greater abominations were taking place.

8:16-18. A fourth abomination. Ezekiel is brought to the door of the Temple itself. There between the Temple and the altar were twenty-five men facing eastward, away from the Temple, bowing down in worship of the sun. Solar worship was common in the ancient Near East, whether as Shamash, Shipish, Marduk, or one of the Egyptian solar deities. More appalling than the worship of the particular deity is the location of this worship in front of the Temple. And the worshipers, perhaps priests because of the location, turn their backs to God rather than their faces—the worst offense of all.

Because of all their abominations, and especially because they have themselves desecrated the Temple, God will now act: the LORD *will act in wrath*; his *eye will not spare*, nor will he *have pity* (v. 18; cf. 5:11).

<u>9:1-11. Jerusalem's execution.</u> This chapter follows directly on chap. 8. The last line of that chapter is linked with a similar catchword phrase to this chapter. God will not listen to the people of Jerusalem even though *they cry in* his *hearing with a loud voice* (8:18). Now God *cried in* Ezekiel's *hearing with a loud voice* (9:1).

<u>9:1-2. Summoning the executioners.</u> Six executioners are summoned, each with his destroying weapon or war club in his hand. A seventh individual dressed in linen and carrying a writing case is in their midst. They stand beside the bronze altar, the altar of burnt offerings (1 Kgs 8:64).

<u>9:3-7. Sending the executioners out.</u> First the one in linen is sent out to place a mark on the foreheads of those who lament the abominations committed in the Temple. At least a remnant will be spared from the executioners. Then the other six are sent out to kill everyone not marked. No one is to be spared, not man nor woman nor child. The instructions given to the executioners are exactly what God has previously said of himself, *your eye shall not spare, and you shall show no pity* (v. 5). These executioners are reminiscent of the Passover at the Exodus when the LORD destroyed all the firstborn of Egypt; there all with a mark on their houses rather than their foreheads were spared (Exod 12). This execution begins at the sanctuary with the elders, apparently the same ones involved in sun worship.

<u>9:8-11. Ezekiel's intercession.</u> Ezekiel is left alone in the Temple, surrounded by the ones slain. He cries out to God, *Will you destroy all who remain of Israel?* (v. 8). Ezekiel may have a forehead harder than flint to deal with the rebellious people, but his heart is touched by this slaughter. God's response, however, gives little occasion for hope. God speaks of the great guilt, the bloodshed and perversity of the people. Again God responds that his eye will not spare, nor will he have pity. He will simply bring down their own deeds upon their heads. The judgment is clearly that of individual accountability. No direct mention is made of those spared. The last verse does remind readers of those spared, however: the individual dressed in linen returns and states that he has done just as God commanded.

<u>10:1-22. Departure of the glory.</u> Accompanying the slaughter of the people is the departure of the LORD's glory from the Temple prior to its destruction. The elders had said the LORD had forsaken the land (8:12; 9:9); now, in fact, the LORD was departing. The land would be godforsaken indeed. In this chapter the glory moves from over the ark of the covenant in the holy of holies (although the ark is never mentioned by name, but is clearly indicated throughout by references to *the cherubim*), to the threshold of the Temple, and then to the east gate of the Temple courtyard.

<u>10:1-8. Scattering coals.</u> The individual in linen is instructed to take *burning coals* from the altar under *the cherubim* and scatter them over the city. As he enters the Temple building, the theophanic cloud fills the inner court and the glory moves from over the cherubim to the threshold. One of the cherubim takes coals from the fire within the wheelwork of the chariot-throne and gives the coals to the individual in linen, and he goes out to scatter the coals.

10:9-17, 20-22. Cherubim and chariot-throne. In these two paragraphs the cherubim and the chariot-throne, which are clearly associated with the ark of the covenant in the Temple, are identified as the cherubim and chariot-throne of Ezekiel's inaugural vision by the River Chebar. The importance is two-fold. Not only are Ezekiel's two visions interrelated by the identity, but also the LORD, who was believed by many to reside only in the Jerusalem Temple, is shown to be with Ezekiel and the exiles in Babylonia as well. The glory of the LORD, that symbol of the LORD's presence, is not limited to the land of Israel.

10:18-19. From threshold to gate. Once again the cherubim and the glory of the LORD move. This time they move from the threshold of the Temple to the east gate. The tension mounts as it becomes evident that the glory of the LORD is departing from the Temple by stages: from the inner sanctuary to the threshold and then to the eastern gate. But the chapter closes before the departure is finalized.

11:1-25. Another view of the destruction. This chapter presents another view of the judgment God has brought on Jerusalem. Ezekiel is brought to the east gate of the Temple, the same location where, according to chap. 10, the glory of the LORD had paused.

11:1-4. Wicked counselors. Here Ezekiel sees a group of twenty-five men against whom he is to prophesy. The sin of these individuals is that they *devise iniquity* and *give wicked counsel* (v. 2). They claim to be ones under special protection of God: they are the select meat in the pot, and Jerusalem is the pot. The implication drawn later in the chapter is that the exiles must be considered by them to be the refuse who have been cast off.

11:5-12. The prophet speaks. God's spirit falls upon Ezekiel and he prophesies against the men. Those who have been slain are the select meat; these men will be removed from the pot. God will bring the sword on them, and give them into the hands of foreigners. Twice it is said that God will judge them at the border of Israel, a probable reference to Riblah of 6:14 where NEBUCHADREZZAR set up his camp during the final siege of Jerusalem.

11:13. The prophet intercedes. In his vision, Ezekiel sees one of the men die even as he prophesies. And similarly to 9:8, he intercedes for the people, *will you make a full end of the remnant of Israel?* The question suggests that the ones still in the land were considered to be the remnant, just as their comment about the meat and the pot implied.

11:14-21. Hope for the exiles. This paragraph interprets for Ezekiel the reality that the exiles were not in captivity because they were most guilty. Those remaining in the land assumed that the divine inheritance had been given to them. Now God tells Ezekiel that the exiles will be gathered and the land will be given to them. When the exiles return to the land there will be renewal. They will remove all the idolatrous images and practices from the worship (v. 18), and God will remove their stony heart and *give them a heart of flesh*. They will also have *one heart, and . . . a new spirit* (v. 19). As a result they will be obedient to God. This covenant renewal has God's promise, *they shall be my people, and I will be their God* (v. 20). However, should any follow after the former idolatrous practices, they will be held accountable. The promises are repeated in the later part of the book, the section of hope and restoration, in 36:24-27 and 37:21-28. The paragraph closes with the prophetic messenger formula, lest any think Ezekiel himself was responsible for the words.

11:22-25. The vision concluded. The cherubim then rise up and the glory of the LORD moves away from the Temple. It moves from the midst of the city to the mountain east of the city, where it stops. Here the vision is concluded and Ezekiel is brought back to the exiles in Babylonia. He then tells them of his vision.

Two Symbolic Action Messages and the Imminence of Judgment, 12:1-28

In a scene somewhat reminiscent of chaps. 4–5, Ezekiel is once more told to act out a message. His actions will depict symbolically the judgment God is speaking to the people of Jerusalem and Judah.

12:1-7. An exile's baggage. Ezekiel is commanded to gather together baggage as an exile would. Only a few necessary belongings could be taken, only what one could carry easily, for the way would be difficult, and there would be no one to help carry heavy burdens. As instructed, Ezekiel gathered his baggage by day. Then by night he dug through the wall and went out the hole, just as one fleeing from imminent invasion might try to escape. He also covered his face so that he would not see the land.

The message is two-fold. The oracles to this point have all indicated the imminent judgment on Jerusalem. But, not only were the people in Jerusalem a rebellious people; even those in exile with Ezekiel did not believe these oracles. They too were a rebellious people who had *eyes to see* and *ears to hear*, but did neither (v. 2). Therefore, this message is enacted for their benefit so that perhaps they will understand.

12:8-16. An interpretation. The next morning Ezekiel is told to explain his actions to his fellow exiles. The focus of the oracle is the king of Judah—here called *the prince in Jerusalem* (v. 10). He will try to flee captivity with an escape from Jerusalem. But he will be caught and brought to Babylon where he will die in captivity. All his supporters will be killed or dispersed. A few will survive to tell of their sins in the place where they are exiled.

12:17-20. Eating and drinking with trembling. The prophet is told to eat and drink with quaking, fear and trembling, for the people of Jerusalem will live in similar fear and dread. Again a judgment of devastation and desolation for Jerusalem is given.

12:21-28. Certainty of swift judgment. In response to a proverbial saying that prophetic visions and oracles were not being fulfilled in the present time, God instructs Ezekiel to tell the people that these visions and prophecies would take place very soon, in their days. Further, there would be no more flattering words of false prophets. God guarantees that he will both speak and fulfill the word, and that very soon.

A second oracle responds to another proverb, that visions and prophesies were for distant future days. Here again the warning (or assurance) is given that these words are for the present; they will not be delayed.

Oracles against False Prophecy and Idolatry, 13:1–14:23

These two chapters speak judgment against groups of leaders among the people, against male and female prophets who speak falsely, and against idolatrous elders. If the officials to whom the people turn for guidance are misleading, there is little hope for the people. But more to the point, these leaders are giving the people what they want, and telling them what they want to hear.

13:1-16. False prophecy. The charge against these false prophets is threefold: that they *prophesy out of their own imagination* (v. 2); *follow their own spirit* (v. 3) rather than God's spirit (cf. 3:12, 14, 24 and often); and *envision falsehood and lying divination* (v. 6). While the exact content of the false prophecies cannot be ascertained, it may well have been the *flattering divination* mentioned in 12:24. Such a message would be similar to Jeremiah's complaint against ones who prophesy "Peace, peace" when there is no peace (v. 10, cf., e.g., Jer 14:13, 7:1-15). Nor may one discover whether these *senseless prophets* (v. 3) were deliberately bringing false messages, or actually believed the content of their own messages to come from God. In either case, Ezekiel speaks God's judgment on the content: *they say "Says the LORD," when the LORD has not sent them* (v. 6). Further, these false prophets have not been building up the nation; their influence has been destructive in the long run. If their message was a pleasing message of reassurance, it gave the people a false assurance rather than calling them to repent and respond to the LORD's warning.

Because of their false messages, God has set himself against these false prophets; they will not endure in places of leadership. Ezekiel compares them and their message to whitewash painted on a wall in place of proper plaster. The whitewashed wall looks fine to the casual observer, and all is well in fair weather. But when the rains and storms come, the whitewash offers no protection to the mudbrick wall; it has not sealed the pores like plaster, so the wall collapses. So it will be with the messages of these false prophets. False assurance will be of no help in the day of judgment. The wall and those depending on the wall for protection will all fall in that day. The false prophets will fall as does the wall.

13:17-23. Women who prophesy falsely. Along with the condemnation of male false prophets, is a special word for the women who prophesy falsely. These are women who prophesy, but they are never specifically called prophets or prophetesses. Therefore these women are often designated as sorceresses or witches (Taylor 1969, 123). Nevertheless, they are designated similarly to the male prophets, *who prophesy out of their own imagination* (v. 17, cf. v. 2). The purpose of the *bands* for wrists and full length *veils* (v. 18) is not known. Usually some magical function is ascribed to these objects. Like the false prophets, these deceiving women discourage the righteous and encourage the wicked. They are accused, not only for their false practices, but also because they do not lead the wicked to turn from their ways. They are sentinels who have been false (3:16-21; 33:1-20). The outcome is clear: the magic will prove ineffective and the people will be delivered from such false practices. In addition the outcome will be another proof that God is the LORD.

14:1-11. Idolatrous elders. Ezekiel was visited by *certain elders of Israel* (v. 1), apparently seeking an oracle. These were among the elders in exile living near Ezekiel. Because of their idolatrous practices, no oracle is forthcoming from the LORD through Ezekiel. Instead, the LORD promises to answer (ענה) them directly (v. 4), a word used with double meaning in the prophets, either responding positively (Hos 2:21-22; Isa 49:8), or of bringing judgment (Hos 5:5, 7:10; Isa 3:9). The idolatrous acts are not specified, whether they are taken from Babylonian cultic practices, or practices of the sort Ezekiel was shown in Jerusalem (see chap. 8).

The call to all the people, including the elders, is to repent (שׁוב, "turn, return, repent"), to *turn away from . . . idols* and abominable practices (v. 6). This is the classic call of the prophets for repentance; the double use of the verb in two linguistic stems is common for emphasis. If anyone continues to practice idolatry and seeks an oracle from God, that person will be cut off, completely ostracized and accursed. Furthermore, the prophet who gives an oracle to such a person will receive the same judgment. Any true prophet would know that idolatrous practices were an abomination to God, and would know that God would not condone them. Therefore to offer an oracle is to become as guilty as the one practicing idolatry.

14:12-23. Even the righteous will save only themselves. The situation is so bad that even persons who were the epitome of righteousness would save only themselves. The emphasis is only on individual accountability. Each person will be held responsible for his or her own actions and judged on that basis. Unlike the intercession for Sodom and Gomorrah, where ABRAHAM bargained with God, such that even ten righteous ones would have sufficed to save the cities (Gen 18), here no surplus of righteousness in one individual can help another. Even more in contrast with both the story of NOAH and Sodom and Gomorrah, God states specifically that not even the families of righteous ones would be spared because of that individual's righteousness (vv. 16, 18, 20). The principle is that of individual accountability as prescribed more fully in chap. 18 below.

In case the oracle might have seemed too theoretical for the hearers, the point is made more explicit. God is ready to send against Jerusalem sword, wild animals, famine and pestilence. Hardly anyone will survive. Those who do survive will recount the sins of Jerusalem that have caused this judgment. Then the exiles will understand why Jerusalem had to be destroyed.

Four Allegories, 15:1–17:24

15:1-8. The allegory of the vine. The vine becomes an image of judgment for Ezekiel. In a manner similar to the parable of the vineyard in Isa 5, Ezekiel uses what was a popular positive metaphor concerning the people and turns it into judgment. The continued use of the vine metaphor may be seen from Jotham's fable (Judg 9) to Jesus' teachings (John 15). The vine was prized for its produce of grapes and wine (Num 13 in the spying of the land) and was a symbol of God's blessing. But Ezekiel reminds his readers that the wood of the vine has no practical use. Indeed he describes Jerusalem as a vine that has been burned once and is now charred and less than useless. Further, the vine will now be completely consumed. A burned, charred vine produces no fruit. This vine is burned from both ends, root and branch; it is good only as fuel, but since it is half-burned, it is scarcely even valuable as fuel.

16:1-63. The allegory of Jerusalem as a prostitute. This allegory has six scenes or paragraphs describing Jerusalem. Beginning with God's mercy extended to an exposed infant, Jerusalem's story is told. God rescued, provided for and gave his covenant to her. She was false to that covenant and thus judgment is certain. But beyond judgment, restoration is possible.

16:1-7. Jerusalem, an infant exposed at birth. Jerusalem's parentage is given; her mother was Hittite, her father Amorite. This mixed-breed baby, born in the land of Canaan, was abandoned at birth. She was unceremoniously thrown out and left to die, unclean, unwashed, naked. But the LORD came along, saw her, and gave her life. No descent from the gods is claimed for Jerusalem and Israel; they are the offspring of the land of Canaan. Both Amorites and Hittites are said to inhabit Canaan. From the very beginning, her existence was dependent on God's grace. But for the LORD, she would surely have died. She grew and developedinto a beautiful young woman; but was still naked, unprotected.

16:8-14. Jerusalem and the marriage covenant with God. When Jerusalem reached marriageable age, God entered into covenant relationship with her. The spreading of the cloak over Jerusalem (v. 8) was a sign of marriage pledge (Ruth 3) as well as providing cover for her nakedness and protection. Following the metaphor of the previous paragraph, God then washes, cleanses, anoints Jerusalem and provides her with the finest attire and jewelry. The result was that Jerusalem's fame and beauty both grew. But one is reminded that her fame and beauty come from the splendor or majesty that God had bestowed. Again the emphasis is on what God has made of Jerusalem; by herself, she would still be unclean, unwashed, and naked.

16:15-34. Jerusalem as a prostitute. In imagery well known from Hosea (e.g., Hos 2:9) and Jeremiah (e.g., Jer 2–3), Ezekiel describes Jerusalem's adulterous activities—playing the whore to shrines she made to pagan deities—giving to these false gods the gifts of food, clothing, oil and drink that the LORD had provided for her. She even offered her children in child sacrifice, an abomination Jeremiah also condemns (Jer 7; 19). But most of all she was unfaithful to the LORD and forgot all God's provision and sustenance for her.

The passion of Ezekiel's language is clear from the repeated appearance of the verb *play the whore* (זנה, seven occurrences in this paragraph) and the noun *whorings* (תזנות, eight occurrences in this paragraph) as well as the participle *adulterous* (נאף). In the legal codes adultery and prostitution were punishable by death (Lev 20:10; Deut 22:20-21). So also was playing the whore after other gods (Lev 20:1-6; Exod 34:15-16). Jerusalem stands convicted of a capital crime.

The people were guilty of liaisons with Egypt, Assyria and Chaldea (Babylon). In God's sight, political alliances showed the same lack of faith in the deity as did religious syncretism. To be involved in a political alliance with a foreign nation meant acknowledging the power of that nation's gods, and probable involvement with the religious cults of that nation. Clearly the *platforms* and *lofty places* mentioned in vv. 24, 31, 39 were related to foreign cults.

Ezekiel accuses Jerusalem of being worse than common whores. Whores receive payment or gifts for their prostitution. But Israel paid others rather than receiving payment for her prostitution.

16:35-43. Judgment on Jerusalem for her prostitution. Here Jerusalem is directly addressed as a whore. The sentence of one caught in prostitution is to be exacted against her—death. All her lovers, all those foreign nations whose deities she had worshiped and with whom she had entered into political alliances will turn on her and destroy her. She will be left naked and destitute, just as she was when God first found her.

16:44-58. Jerusalem like her sisters, Samaria and Sodom. Going back to the original allegory of Jerusalem having a Hittite mother and an Amorite father, Ezekiel now adds two sisters to the family. The *elder* sister (literally "big") is Samaria, the *younger* (literally "small") is Sodom. The major point of comparison is that both these cities and their *daughters* (i.e., villages) have been destroyed because of their wickedness. Sodom was a well-known byword for God's judgment on wickedness; here the wickedness is not caring for the poor and needy, and practicing abominations. Samaria, the capital of Israel, had been destroyed over a century prior to Ezekiel's time; it had been the subject of prophetic outcry for its wickedness (Amos and Hosea). Yet Ezekiel says that, by comparison with Jerusalem, those two cities were righteous. The implication is clear—Jerusalem will suffer the same fate as her two "sisters." Jerusalem's sin is so bad that were God to restore all three, Samaria and Sodom would be consoled that their sins were not as great as Jerusalem's. No longer would Sodom be a byword of wickedness; now Jerusalem would replace Sodom.

16:59-63. Threat and promise. This last paragraph of the chapter begins with a renewed word of judgment. God will deal with Jerusalem according to her deeds; she will be held accountable (cf. chap. 18). But then beyond the certain judgment comes a ray of hope demonstrating God's grace. Despite the fact that Jerusalem has broken covenant with him, God will remember the covenant (v. 8), and will re-establish with Jerusalem an *everlasting covenant* (v. 60; see also 36:22-32 and 37:24-38). Jerusalem, though forgiven, will remember her sins and be ashamed. Even though she was more wicked than Samaria or Sodom, those two cities will be placed under her dominion by God's grace. She will then know that she indeed exists only because of God's mercy and grace, certainly not due to her own merits.

17:1-21. Allegory of two eagles, cedar, and vine. Ezekiel is told to use the form of *riddle* or *allegory* (v. 1; the Heb. for *allegory* could also mean "proverb" or "parable") in speaking to Israel. Nevertheless, just as in some of the parables of Jesus (e.g., Matt 13; Mark 4), the allegory is followed by an explicit interpretation. This interpretation relates to a specific set of events in Judah's recent history as Ezekiel speaks. The *great eagle*, Nebuchadrezzar, came to the Lebanon (Jerusalem, perhaps specifically the palace, one portion of which was called "the House of the Forest of Lebanon" [1 Kgs 7:2]), and took *the topmost* shoot of the cedar (the king, Jehoiachin) to *a land of trade* (Babylon). In place of that topmost shoot, he planted a seed that became a vine with branches and foliage (Zedekiah, whom Nebuchadrezzar placed on the throne). Surely no hearer could miss the implication in vv. 1-6 that this vine was far inferior to the cedar.

The second *great eagle* is the Pharaoh of Egypt, Hophra. Zedekiah renounced vassalage to Babylon and turned to Egypt for assistance. Such a policy reflected the Judean court politics, which included both pro-Egypt and pro-Babylon factions. In the allegory, this shift of policy is described as the vine being transplanted. But the transplant will be unsuccessful, the vine will only be weakened so that an east wind (another reference to Babylon) will cause it to wither.

The explanation makes clear that Egypt will provide no aid. When the siege is set against Jerusalem, Egypt will not help; Jerusalem will fall. Zedekiah will not escape; he will be brought to Babylon in captivity.

17:22-24. Allegory of the sprig from the topmost cedar. The final allegory of this section presents another message of future hope. The same image of the cedar found in the previous allegory is present here. However, it is *the Lord GOD* himself, not a foreign ruler, who takes and plants a *sprig* from the topmost of the cedar. The sprig will be planted *on a high and lofty mountain, on the mountain height of Israel* (vv. 22-23), a clear reference to Jerusalem (cf. Isa 2:2-4, Mic 4:1-4). This restored ruler will prosper *and become a noble cedar* (v. 23). This image of a future ruler may be compared with Isa 11:1. The result envisioned in v. 24 indicates that this restoration will cause all nations (*trees*) to know that God is the LORD. Further, the restoration will result in a reversal, the high and mighty will be brought low while the lowly will be elevated (1 Sam 2:1-10, Luke 1:46-55); the green tree will dry up and the dry tree will blossom forth.

Individual Accountability, 18:1-32

Although this chapter begins with a *proverb* (v. 2, the same word translated as "allegory" in 17:2), it is not allegorical. The proverbial saying simply serves as the point of departure for a discourse on individual accountability.

18:1-3. A proverb rebutted. The proverb suggests that the younger generation suffers for the sins of the older generation. The proverb itself is also mentioned in Jeremiah (Jer 31:29-30). Both prophets speak of the termination of this proverb. One must acknowledge that in some instances this proverb seems to hold true. Lam 5:7 reflects the expression of the proverb. Many politicians today argue that our generation has mortgaged our children's future by amassing an enormous national debt. In addition, some interpreters of Scripture would point to "crack babies"—those born with drug addiction—and babies born HIV-positive as proof of the proverb. Nevertheless, the thrust of this discourse is to disprove the proverb. Each individual will be held accountable before God for his or her actions and only for his or her actions. Examples may on the surface seem to support the proverb, but ultimately they will not stand.

18:4. Each individual is accountable. The major premise is stated in v. 4: *all lives are mine . . . . it is only the person who sins that shall die*. God's justice here is consistent with the Deuteronomic paradigm: obedience results in blessing and life, disobedience results in curse and death.

18:5-18. Three cases. These verses present three cases set over three generations that illustrate the premise. The individual representing the first generation is completely righteous; that person will live. The acts of this person are noteworthy: he practices no idolatry, adultery, oppression, robbery, charges no interest on loans. Positively he gives to the needy, executes justice and obeys the statutes and ordinances of God.

Apart from the reference to idolatry, the specific actions mentioned are all from the realm of interpersonal relationships rather than from the realm of religious acts. No mention is made of the sacrificial system or tithing. What this individual does in relationship to other people is primary (cf. Mic 6:6-8).

The second case presents a son of the first individual. This man is the opposite of the father. He commits all the wicked acts his father avoided and does none of the righteous acts. The judgment is that he will surely die for his actions. The third case, a son of the second man, again presents a reversal. This man sees the sins of his father and does not do them. Instead he does righteously. He will live.

18:19-20. Summary and premise restated. Parents will not be held responsible for the sins of their children, nor will children be held accountable for the sins of their parents. Each person will be accountable for, and only for, his or her own sins.

18:21-24. Previous actions do not replace current actions. What about the person who changes? Do previous actions preclude any change in God's response to an individual? No. If a wicked person repents and turns from wickedness, that person will live. Further, if a righteous person turns to iniquity, that person will die. This paragraph offers hope to anyone who repents, but a warning against turning to wickedness.

18:25-29. Is the LORD's way unfair? Israel was accusing God of being unfair. God reverses the question back on Israel: Is it not rather that Israel's way is unfair? If one who has been righteous turns and becomes wicked, that person will die for his or her wicked acts. That is justice in action. If a wicked person repents and turns from the wickedness, that person will live. That is God's grace and mercy in action.

Nothing is unfair, unless one accuses God of being unfair by being merciful and forgiving.

18:30-32. A warning and a renewed call to repentance. The chapter closes with the statement of God's justice: God will judge every one in Israel according to each individual's ways. This warning is followed by a renewed call to repentance. God does not seek to condemn anyone. The call is to turn, to repent and to live. If one would repent, God would give *a new heart and a new spirit* (v. 31; see also 36:22-32). Such a renewal is itself a grace gift of God.

Although we generally refer to this entire chapter as a message concerning individual responsibility, and the major examples of the chapter do reflect accountability, we must note that the chapter is addressed to the whole people. The opening proverb (vv. 1-4) is a proverb *concerning the land of Israel* (v. 2). The final two paragraphs (vv. 25-32) also address the entire nation, *house of Israel* (vv. 25, 29, 30, 31). Ezekiel is making clear that larger entities than the individual are also held accountable for corporate sins. The whole *house of Israel* is accountable for its transgressions.

Two Laments, 19:1-14

This chapter is called a lament in the INCLUSIO (i.e., the use of the same term at the beginning and end of a literary unit) found in vv. 1 and 14. Furthermore, most of the lines of the poem are in the 3+2 *qinah* rhythm of the lament. The laments themselves are allegorical.

19:1-9. Lament of the lioness bereft of two cubs. The image of lion is associated with Judah (Gen 49:9-10), so the lioness therefore represents the nation Israel/Judah. This lioness raises up two cubs, each of which becomes a strong predator, and each of which is ultimately captured and taken captive, the one to Egypt and the other to Babylon. Usually these two cubs are associated with Jehoahaz and Jehoiachin who were taken captive to those lands. But neither of those kings ruled long (approx. three months each); nor was either a strong predator. It seems preferable to see these two cubs as strong rulers such as JOSIAH and JEHOIAKIM or as symbols for the royal throne representing no specific person. The ending of the first lament has the land without a lion's voice—without a ruler.

19:10-14. Lament for a burned vine. Ezekiel returns to the vine image (see chap. 17) as descriptive of the nation. The vine prospers; its strongest stem becomes a ruler towering high. But then the stem is plucked up and cast down; it withers and is burned. The fire consumes branches and fruit so that no strong stem remains. Again the nation is left without a ruler. This second lament probably depicts Zedekiah as the strong stem, although as above no person need necessarily be intended. In both instances the lament is less for the ruler who is removed than for the nation that remains. The lament is over the lack of a ruler; the land is left leaderless.

Past, Present, and Future, 20:1-44

This chapter opens with a date formula, *the seventh year, the fifth month*, and *the tenth day of the month* (v. 1). The date would place the oracle in 591 B.C.E., about eleven months later than the date set in chap. 8. Some of the elders in captivity had come to Ezekiel's house to receive an oracle. They receive an oracle, but not what they anticipate. Following a lengthy review of Israel's history (vv. 5-29), a brief application to the present situation is given (vv. 30-32), followed by an oracle speaking both judgment and hope (vv. 33-44).

20:1-4. Context for the oracle. Both the date and the context are set in these verses. The elders come to Ezekiel, seeking an oracle. The specific elements of their request are not mentioned. However, the LORD makes clear that the deity will not give an oracle based on their desires or expectations. The oracle presented reminds the elders of the *abominations of their ancestors* (v. 4). Note however that the oracle does not indicate that their present condition in exile is due to the sins of the ancestors; such would be antithetical to much of Ezekiel's teaching concerning individual accountability (see chap. 18).

20:5-29. Retelling Israel's history. Ezekiel retells Israel's history, mentioning four periods of its early history, each indicating the utter sinfulness of the nation. Not even in its earliest period was Israel faithful to the LORD. Unlike Hosea (Hos 2:15 [2:17 MT]) and Jeremiah (Jer 2:23) who point to Israel's early period in the wilderness as a period of faithfulness to the LORD, Ezekiel paints even that period as one of rebellion and sinfulness. Never was Israel pure and faithful. All through its history, only God's grace has sustained the people.

20:5-9. Israel's election. Israel's election by the LORD is set in Egypt. The only call upon the people was to cast off idolatry and serve only the LORD. But even there they were not faithful; they continued their idolatry. God considered bringing judgment on Israel in Egypt, but did not. Instead, God remained faithful to the divine promise and brought Israel out of Egypt.

20:10-17. God's statutes. In the wilderness, God gave Israel statutes and laws so that they might know how to live obediently. God gave them sabbath to be a sign of covenant between the nation and himself. Despite all this, the people continued to rebel against God, disobeying his laws and profaning his sabbaths. Although God did judge that generation, and did not permit them to enter the land, God did not totally destroy the nation. The children were spared.

20:18-26. Like parent, like child. The children themselves were commanded to follow God's ordinances and statutes and to keep his sabbaths. But, like their parents, they also rebelled against God. God considered destroying them in the wilderness, but again refrained. Yet God held out the possibility of eventual exile and dispersion in judgment for their sins.

The statutes that were *not good* and the ordinances by which Israel *could not live* (v. 25) are usually understood to refer to God's requirement that the firstborn males be presented to the deity (see Exod 22:29b-30 [MT 22:28b-29]). Apparently,

Ezekiel is saying that the people were being tested: would they actually engage in human sacrifice, or would they understand that God was calling for an act of dedication and devotion of what was dearest and most valuable to them?

20:27-29. Continuing in sin. Once in the promised land the younger generation continued their sinful ways. They began following the Canaanite worship practices, making offerings to the baals and other pagan deities.

20:30-32. Application to the present. The present generation is no different from the past ones. They are still practicing the same sins, and still rebelling against God. Therefore, God will not be consulted by them as they desire. Verse 32 points to one possible request the elders made, to be permitted to worship the LORD using stone and wood images. (Perhaps the request went something like this: "Our children see all the Babylonian children worshiping images of their gods Marduk and Nebo. Let us make similar images of the LORD so that our children will have something concrete to worship, and therefore will not begin worshiping those false gods.") Never will God permit such worship.

20:33-44. Judgment and restoration, threat and promise. God's response to this continued sinfulness is one of judgment. The full measure of judgment, which God so far has withheld, will now be brought to bear. God will bring his wrath against all opponents, those in the land and those in exile. All rebels will be purged away. Those who wish to serve idols may do so, but they will not be able to claim that they are worshiping God.

Further, God will restore the faithful to Israel and Zion. No longer will the profane worship there; Zion will be a place of obedience. The LORD will reign as king, and God's faithful will serve him there.

Fire and Sword, 20:45–21:32 (MT 21:1-37)

The motif of judgment found in the previous paragraph continues in this section. Here the judgment is unabated and no mention of restoration or hope is included (unless vv. 30-32 offer a prelude to hope).

20:45–21:7 (MT 21:1-12). Fire and sword against Israel. The image of a devouring fire as a symbol of destruction by warfare was well-known to the prophets. AMOS, ISAIAH and JEREMIAH used the same imagery (e.g., Amos 1:4, 7, 10; Isa 1:7, 5:24; Jer 3:4, 5:14-17). Ezekiel speaks judgment against the south-land from a fire kindled by the LORD. But the hearers do not understand; they say that Ezekiel is just *a maker of allegories* (20:49). Thus the second oracle is given to interpret the first. In the second message, the land is specified as Jerusalem and Israel. The image shifts from fire to the sword. No one could misunderstand the relationship between the sword and warfare as the means of God's retribution. The devastation of this judgment will fall on all equally, both on the *righteous and wicked* (v. 4). Ezekiel further is commanded to *moan* (v. 6) as he delivers this message. The moan is to be that of one who has just received news of terrible tragedy: the tragedy to come upon Jerusalem when it falls.

21:8-17 (MT 13-22). Song of the sword. This poetic oracle is probably based on a song of a sword known to the hearers. Some commentators suggest that a dance with a sword accompanied the song (Taylor 1969, 162). The image portrayed is striking and clearly evokes the picture of destruction whether an actual sword was used or not. The repeated phrases of the sword's being *sharpened* (vv. 9, 10, 11), *polished* (vv. 9, 11) *flashing* (vv. 10, 15), and *slaughter* (vv. 10, 15) add intensity to the scene. Because Israel has refused discipline (v. 10), the most severe sentence possible will now befall the people: the sword of warfare.

21:18-32 (MT 23-37). Sword of the king of Babylon. A further explanation of the judgment against the nation is given. Specifically, God will use the sword of the king of Babylon as his agent. Ezekiel is told to mark out two roads for the Babylonians to follow, one leading to Rabbah, the capital of the Ammonites, and the other leading to Jerusalem. The king casts lots to decide which to attack first, and the lot falls to Jerusalem. The oracle continues to say that Jerusalem may indeed fall first, but ultimately both will be taken.

Verses 24-27 state that Jerusalem's sins, and especially those of its ruler, its *prince* (v. 25), have brought this siege. *Turban*, *crown* (v. 26), and all symbols of power and prestige will be gone. The fortified city will become *a ruin* (v. 27). The threefold repetition of the word indicates the greatest intensity possible (cf. the threefold "holy, holy, holy, is the LORD of hosts" in Isa 6:3).

The one *whose right it* (i.e., Jerusalem) *is* (v. 27) could refer to Nebuchadrezzar, to whom God has given the city because of its wickedness, or to Jehoiachin, whom many of the exiles considered still to be the rightful ruler of Israel, or to a future messianic ruler. The text does not clarify the issue.

An oracle against the Ammonites follows in vv. 28-32. The oracle began (vv. 19-20) with the king of Babylon at the crossroads. He moved first against Jerusalem. Now he moves against the Ammonites also. The sword of warfare is to destroy the Ammonites as well as the Israelites. They should not assume they have been spared just because Nebuchadrezzar moved first against Israel.

Interpretations of vv. 30-32 vary. They could refer to the judgment against the Ammonites. But the words *Return it* (the sword) *to its sheath* (v. 30) are strange. Normally that would indicate an end of the warfare. Some commentators take this as a reference to judgment falling upon Babylon itself: that after God uses Babylon as his agent of judgment on Israel, God will turn the sword on Babylon also (so Stalker 1968, 183, and Allen 1990, 28; cf. Jer 25; Isa 10).

Judgment against the Bloody City, 22:1-31

22:1-16. Jerusalem the city of bloodshed. The sins of Jerusalem are related to bloodshed. The sacrificial system, where animals were slaughtered to make atonement for sins, has been abused. The people have continued their sacrifices, but to pagan gods and idols. Further, in their interpersonal relationships the leaders and citizens have abused those lacking protection, thus shedding innocent blood. A catalog of sins is listed in vv. 7-12: dishonoring parents, oppressing foreigners, orphans and widows, profaning sacred times and places; engaging in slander, adultery, and extortion; charging interest and practicing bribery. All these sins point to the ultimate sin: *you have forgotten me, says the Lord GOD* (v. 12). The judgment spoken for these sins is exile and dispersion (v. 15).

22:17-22. Smelting Israel. The image shifts to one of smelting ore to remove the dross or slag from the pure metal. Israel has become like pure metal mixed with dross. Worse yet, Ezekiel describes the nation as the dross. When melted in the smelting furnace, the slag floats to the top of the pure metal and is removed by the smelter. Similarly, God will refine the people to remove all impurities. But more slag is present here than pure metal. The remnant of pure metal will be small.

22:23-31. Like leaders, like people. All the people are guilty of similar sins: the *princes* (v. 25), the *priests* (v. 26), the *officials* (v. 27), the *prophets* (v. 28), and the *people* (v. 29). Priests and prophets have profaned God's teachings and sacred institutions; they have taught lies. Princes and officials have oppressed and destroyed people for gain. All the people have done similarly. God sought for one to stand in the breach like Moses (Ps 106:23; cf. Ezek 14:14), to intercede so that God might not destroy, but none was found. The whole people were utterly corrupt. Therefore God speaks absolute judgment on the people.

Allegory of the Two Sisters: Oholah and Oholibah, 23:1-49

23:1-4. The two sisters introduced. In this allegory, the two nations Israel and Judah are represented by their capitals SAMARIA and JERUSALEM. Oholah (אׇהֳלָה, "her tent[-shrine]") is Samaria, and Oholibah (אׇהֳלִיבָה, "my tent[-shrine] is in her") is Jerusalem. The names are usually interpreted as referring to the Northern Kingdom's illegitimate sanctuaries—she has her own tent shrine, but it is not the LORD's—in contrast to Judah's legitimate sanctuary—my (the LORD's) tent is in her. These two nations are depicted as sisters in Egypt, perhaps indicating something of their original separateness prior to the United Kingdom of DAVID and SOLOMON. More importantly, both are depicted as prostituting themselves while in Egypt. This is no depiction of a pure, innocent Israel in its early history. Even in earliest times they prostituted themselves to other lovers than the LORD (see 20:5-29).

23:5-10. The elder sister: Oholah, Samaria. That Samaria is called *the elder* (v. 4, lit. "the greater") need not speak of antiquity. The Northern Kingdom was certainly the larger, more populous, and, probably, more prosperous of the two. But Oholah sought other lovers than the LORD (cf. Hos 2). She went after political alliances with Assyria, and practiced the idolatry of the foreign nations. For these sins she was destroyed and became a byword.

23:11-21. The younger sister: Oholibah, Jerusalem. Surely one would expect that when Oholibah saw the judgment on her own elder sister she would learn and turn from her own sinfulness. Yet the very opposite was the case. Oholibah was even worse in her sins than her sister. Not only did she prostitute herself with political alliances and religious practices of the Assyrians; she also went after the Chaldeans, Babylonians, and Egyptians. Not content with one lover, Oholibah spurned one after another, turning to more adulteries. God's response was to *turn in disgust from her* (v. 18). The very strong sexual language of the passage was intended to incense hearers with the strongest disgust, precisely what God felt about the people's sins.

23:22-35. Consequences of Oholibah's actions. Just as the elder sister, Oholah, was destroyed for her sins, so also Oholibah would pay for her sins. The LORD, whom she had spurned, would rouse other spurned lovers to come against her: *the Babylonians, and all the Chaldeans, Pekod and Shoa and Koa* (probably tribal groups from the area north and east of Babylon and Assyria, so Allen 1990, 50, and Taylor 1969, 174), *and all the Assyrians* (v. 23). Although these nations would be the destroyers, it is the LORD who directs and brings them. God uses them as instruments of divine judgment, even letting them judge the nation *according to their ordinances* (v. 24). The result will be devastation, destruction, disgrace and death.

Using the metaphor of the cup also known to Jeremiah (Jer 25, 49), Ezekiel speaks of Jerusalem's drinking from the cup of her sister. The cup will bring *drunkenness and sorrow, horror and desolation* (v. 33). The final verse of the paragraph reiterates the cause of this terrible judgment and the resulting accountability: *because you have forgotten me* (i.e., the LORD) *and cast me behind your back, therefore bear the consequences* (v. 35).

23:36-49. Trial, sentence and execution of the two sisters. These verses depict a court scene where the two sisters, Oholah and Oholibah, are charged, brought to trial, convicted, sentenced and executed. The charges are stated: adultery (worship of other gods), sacrifice to other gods, child sacrifice, defiling the sanctuary, profaning sabbath (vv. 37-39). Their political alliances with foreign powers are described in terms of a prostitute serving a banquet for her lover (vv. 40-44). The judges declare the two defendants guilty as charged. The sentence is execution. They will be stoned, cut down with the sword, their children killed, and their houses burned (v. 47). Stoning was the legal sentence for adultery (Lev 20:2, 10). The remainder of the judgments clearly depict the results of warfare on the land. Samaria had been destroyed by warfare over a century earlier. Yet the two sisters are placed together in guilt and in punishment. Jerusalem was about to suffer the fate of her elder sister.

Fall of Jerusalem Announced, and the Death of Ezekiel's Wife, 24:1-27

24:1-2. The date. A new date formula is given: *the ninth year, the tenth month, the tenth day of the month* (v. 1). Ezekiel is told to record this date precisely, for this is the very day the king of Babylon had laid siege to Jerusalem (v. 2). This date is traditionally set as January 15, 588 B.C.E. The same date is mentioned in 2 Kgs 25:1 and Jer 52:4. Zech 8:19 may refer to the same date as a fast day for the postexilic community.

24:3-14. Allegory of the rusty pot. The allegory begins with the description of a pot filled with choice pieces of meat and set to boiling. Although the pot could represent a common household pot, it seems more likely that Ezekiel has in mind the pots used in the sanctuary for cooking the meat of sacrifices.

The pot is now identified as being the bloody city (see 22:2), and is a pot with rust inside it. Further, the pot is filled with blood. A rusty pot would be considered unclean or polluted. And meat with blood remaining in it was also unclean (Lev 17:10-14). Thus, whether the meat was for consumption or a sacrifice, clearly it was improperly prepared. Allowing the blood to remain in the meat for either use was an affront to God; the life was considered to be in the blood, so the blood was to be treated properly. Since the people have shed blood and done so openly, God will now bring judgment on them.

The pot becomes a symbol of God's judgment. God himself will heap up the logs, kindle the fire and cook the meat (v. 10). Further, God will heat the fire so hot that the copper of the pot will glow and the rust will be burned away (v. 11). Yet even this action does not remove all the rust (v. 13). So God's judgment will be unsparing and unrelenting (v. 14), a clear indication of the fall of Jerusalem in 587 B.C.E.

24:15-24. The death of Ezekiel's wife. God also told Ezekiel that his wife would die and that he was not to mourn her death. He could *sigh, but not aloud* (v. 17), and was to carry out none of the normal mourning rites. He reported this oracle to the people in the morning, and that night his wife died. When the people asked why Ezekiel was behaving in this manner, he interpreted his behavior as due to God's actions. God was about to destroy Israel's beloved: Jerusalem, the Temple and the people. Those in exile were not to mourn aloud the destruction or loss of family there. The command not to mourn aloud and publicly may be intended to affirm the justice of God's judgment. It may also be designed, in part, to avoid giving satisfaction to Israel's enemies. And indeed, the exiles may be intended to draw hope and consolation from this command. Exiles may yet return to the land of promise.

24:25-27. Muteness to be removed. The prophet was silenced in 3:25-27. He was told that he would speak only when the word of the LORD came upon him. Such silence probably referred only to public or prophetic proclamations. However, now he is told that when a survivor of the fall of Jerusalem brings news of its fall, he will no longer be mute. Once again he will be able to prophesy and intercede freely. Perhaps the removal of the muteness is intended to mark the transition in the prophecy from judgment to hope and restoration. This passage is related to 33:21-22, which also reports the removal of the muteness. The muteness was announced at the beginning of the oracles of judgment against Jerusalem/Judah; the report of its impending removal closes the oracles of judgment. The muteness of the prophet serves almost as an INCLUSIO for those oracles. The muteness is removed near the beginning of the messages of hope and restoration (see below, 33:21-22).

Oracles against the Nations, 25:1–32:32

This section serves as a transition from judgment to hope. The ultimate judgment against Jerusalem has been spoken. The final siege has been laid. Only the fall of the city itself remains. But God's justice reaches all peoples. The same justice that is meted out to Israel and Judah will also be meted out to the nations. This unit describes oracles of judgment on foreign nations. Further, the judgment meted out against foreign nations may be seen as the first step in the restoration of Israel. Among the charges against these nations is that they profited from or made light of the fall of Jerusalem/Judah. Such charges place the oracles in a context after 587 B.C.E. and may justify their incorporation at this juncture in the book. The number seven plays an important role in these oracles. Seven nations are judged in these oracles: the Ammonites, Moab, Edom, Philistia, Tyre, Sidon and Egypt. The seventh nation, Egypt, has seven separate oracles directed against it. And the seventh oracle mentions seven nations who have been destroyed and are in SHEOL.

Oracle against the Ammonites, 25:1-7

The Ammonites are condemned for expressing glee over the fall of Jerusalem: the sanctuary being profaned, the land made desolate, and the people going into exile. The judgment is that people from the east, tent dwellers and camel owners, will inhabit the land. The reference is to the displacement of the Ammonites by nomadic peoples from the desert to the east.

Oracle against Moab, 25:8-11

The Moabites said that Judah was like all other nations, not recognizing Israel as God's chosen. So Moab will suffer the same fate as the Ammonites; it will be occupied by tent dwellers from the eastern desert regions.

Oracle against Edom, 25:12-14

The Edomites are accused of *taking vengeance* (v. 12) against Judah, of taking part in the fall of Jerusalem, or perhaps invading and occupying part of Judah after the fall. Ps 137:7 and the Book of Obadiah reflect the bitterness the postexilic Israelites felt toward the Edomites. The judgment against the Edomites will come at the hand of Israel rather than another group.

Oracle against Philistia, 25:15-17

The Philistines are also accused of taking vengeance on Judah at its fall. The judgment against Philistia mentions no human agent: God himself will exact the sentence.

Oracles against Tyre, 26:1–28:19

Four separate but intertwined oracles make up the judgment against Tyre. Unlike the previous oracles in chap. 25, the material against Tyre begins with a date formula. It is set *in the eleventh year, on the first day of the month* (v. 1). No month is mentioned; however, many commentators suggest that it was the eleventh month (so Zimmerli 1983, 33; Stalker 1968, 209; and Taylor 1969, 190; each follows Albright 1932, 93). Such a date would place the oracles early in 586 B.C.E., shortly after the fall of Jerusalem, which Jer 52:12 places in the fifth month.

26:1-6. Tyre's glee and punishment. Much like the oracles against Ammon, Moab, Edom and Philistia, this brief oracle accuses Tyre of taking glee and seeking profit from the fall of Jerusalem. The judgment is that Tyre, that mighty island state, will be buffeted and destroyed by nations, as a raging stormy sea buffets and destroys an island.

26:7-14. Nebuchadrezzar will destroy Tyre. Building on the previous section, this paragraph identifies Nebuchadrezzar, the Babylonian king, as the one who will destroy Tyre. The siege, breaching of the walls, and plunder of the city are depicted. Tyre will be left like a *bare rock* (v. 14) never to be rebuilt. The image here is that of a barren rocky island standing uninhabited in the ocean. The same words (צחיח סלע) were used in 24:7-8 of the blood of Jerusalem's sacrifices, left exposed for all to see. So too will Tyre be exposed.

26:15-18. Mourning over Tyre. Other maritime powers and their rulers are depicted as mourning and lamenting the fall of Tyre. Tyre was such an important sea power at this time that its demise would have impact across the Mediterranean world. Especially would that impact be felt along the Syro-Palestinian coast since Tyre was the major seafaring power there.

26:19-21. Tyre brought down to Sheol. The destruction of Tyre is to be absolute and final. Tyre will be brought down to *the Pit* (v. 20), a synonym for Sheol, the abode of the dead. It will exist no longer, unlike Israel, which will at least have some survivors.

27:1-36. The great ship Tyre. In this allegory, Tyre, both an island-state and a great maritime power, is depicted as a ship.

27:1-11. The ship described in its perfection. The phrase *perfect in beauty* (vv. 3, 4, 11) forms an inclusio marking off this section. The ship is described as being built of the finest components. The craftsmen who built it were the most skilled available. The oarsmen, pilots, artisans, and warriors on the ship were also the best of their trades. This ship-state was the finest possible—it was unsinkable. One thinks immediately of the "unsinkable" *Titanic*.

27:12-25a. The merchandise on the ship. The double reference to Tarshish (vv. 12, 25a) forms an inclusio for this section. Within this paragraph is a catalog of the varied merchandise and items of trade the ship Tyre carried. Tyre was the main center of Phoenician trade during this period. It stood at a crossroads linking overland trade from Mesopotamia, Asia Minor, Syria-Palestine, and the Arabian peninsula with sea trade from Egypt, North Africa, Greece, Rome, Tarshish (=Spain?), and the Mediterranean islands. Goods from all parts of the Near Eastern world flowed through its port. This catalog of merchandise suggests the extent of the city's trade and influence. It is also an important inventory of economic activity characteristic of this general period.

27:25b-36. Sinking of the ship. This magnificent ship, filled with every kind of merchandise, set sail into the sea. A great east wind arose and wrecked the ship, causing it to sink. All was lost at sea: the ship, its merchandise, its crew and passengers. All the lands around are horrified at the collapse of the great ship, Tyre. The reference to the east wind undoubtedly refers to Nebuchadrezzar and his army coming from the east against Tyre. Again the fall of Tyre is depicted as leaving no survivors.

28:1-10. The pride of the king of Tyre. As in several oracles against Judah/Israel, this message is directed against the ruler of Tyre. The ruler considered himself a god (vv. 2, 6, 9), sitting on the throne of gods. This claim is not one of descent from the gods, but a statement of arrogance and pride. It is less directed toward a particular ruler than to the king as representative of the nation. Yet this claim will be shown unfounded; this *god* will be shown to be a mere mortal (vv. 2, 9).

Both the wisdom and the wealth of this ruler/state are acknowledged (vv. 3-5). But the pride engendered by this wealth and wisdom will bring forth destruction. Foreigners will come against this king/state and slay it. The ruler/state will go down to the Pit, to Sheol, and die. Even worse, Tyre will die a disgraceful, dishonorable death—the death of the uncircumcised (v. 10).

28:11-19. Lament over the king of Tyre. This lament over the king of Tyre uses imagery from the Eden tradition to show how great was the fall of Tyre. Like the original humans, Tyre "had it all." Tyre was in Eden (עֵדֶן, "delight, luxury"). He was perfect in wisdom and beauty. Every precious stone was his (each of those mentioned was found on the high priest's breastplate [Exod 28:17-20]). But like the first human couple, this ruler was brought down by pride (v. 17). He became corrupted by all his possessions; he sinned, and committed violence. Therefore, like that first human couple, the king of Tyre was cast down and driven out (v. 16); he was consumed with fire, and completely destroyed (vv. 18-19).

Oracle against Sidon, 28:20-23

Sidon was another of the Phoenician city-states, usually under the influence of the larger and stronger Tyre to its north. Although Sidon is not charged with any specific sins, it too will be judged and destroyed. The same warfare that destroys Tyre will destroy Sidon.

Restoration of Israel, 28:24-26

These few verses mark the first indication of restoration for Israel within the oracles against foreign nations. No longer will these nearest neighbors of Israel serve as a *thorn* and a *brier* (v. 24) to the people. God promises to gather the scattered of Israel safely and securely; they will build houses and plant vineyards in their land. Their safety and security are assured by God's judgment on the neighboring nations.

Oracles against Egypt, 29:1–32:32

Seven oracles make up the condemnation of Egypt. This material begins with a date formula, *the tenth year, the tenth month, the twelfth day of the month* (29:1), early in 587 B.C.E. if the traditional dates are accepted.

29:1-16. Brief oracles against Egypt. The first oracle is actually a pair of metaphors followed by a prediction of Egypt's fall.

29:1-6a. Pharaoh the dragon (crocodile). Pharaoh is described as a *great dragon* (v. 3). This metaphor could refer to the mythical sea monster or dragon as the NRSV understands or to the crocodiles that inhabit the waters of the Nile (Zimmerli 1983, 111–12; Vawter and Hoppe 1991, 137). The dragon image would bring to mind LEVIATHAN and chaos combat with God. The Egyptians themselves prayed that Pharaoh would be a crocodile to their enemies. Either is an apt image. Like the king of Tyre, Pharaoh is depicted as claiming deity: *My Nile is my own; I made it for myself* (v. 3). For such a claim, God threatens to destroy the dragon (crocodile) and all the fish of the channels. The fish refer either to the people of Egypt or its army. Egypt's death will be disgraceful—exposure without proper burial.

29:6b-9a. Egypt, a reed staff for Israel. Egypt was a land of reeds, especially well known for its papyrus reeds. But when Israel turned to Egypt for assistance after rebelling against Babylon, Egypt's assistance was as helpful as a reed staff. A staff was often used by shepherds to defend themselves from wild animals, or to help a sheep that had fallen into a hole. It was also used to steady and support oneself in uncertain terrain. Egypt proved to be a reed staff, a flimsy stalk that broke the first time one tried to lean on it. Because of this lack of support, God will judge Egypt.

29:9b-16. Mighty Egypt will become lowliest of nations. Reference is again made to Pharaoh's claim to have made the Nile. God threatens to make all Egypt desolate and waste for forty years. In a surprising development and unlike the other nations that are to be destroyed completely, Egypt is to be restored somewhat after a period of forty years. Forty years may indicate a full generation; it was the period of wilderness wandering for the Hebrews, during which time the entire generation from Egypt died. After the forty years of exile, Egypt will be returned to its land, but will be the lowliest of nations, never again to rule or exalt itself. This sentence is related directly to Egypt's lack of aid to Judah when Judah turned to it.

29:17-21. Egypt given to Nebuchadrezzar instead of Tyre. This brief oracle has the latest date formula found in the book, *the twenty-seventh year, the first month, the first day of the month* (v. 17). The date would be 571 B.C.E. The oracle substitutes Egypt as booty for Nebuchadrezzar in place of Tyre. Ezekiel had prophesied the fall of Tyre to Nebuchadrezzar (26:7). And Nebuchadrezzar had brought armies against Tyre and had besieged the city. But after thirteen years of siege Nebuchadrezzar was still unable to capture it; apparently a negotiated settlement took place under the terms of which Tyre acknowledged Babylonian supremacy but maintained self-rule. Since the Babylonians did not thus get the spoils of Tyre, they are now

198 MERCER COMMENTARY ON THE BIBLE: PROPHETS

given Egypt to despoil instead. Also, this event will vindicate Ezekiel and his oracles to the people of Israel, since the previous oracle had not been fulfilled.

30:1-19. The Day of the LORD against Egypt. The emphasis of this entire oracle is on the Day of the LORD concept. Very similar to the way in which the Day of the Lord was depicted against Israel earlier (7:10-12), it is now described against Egypt. The popular expectation of the Day of the LORD was that it would be a day of Israel's vindication and God's judgment on its enemies. That is precisely the way the Day of the LORD is described in this pericope. While Israel's vindication is not mentioned, its enemies, Egypt, and *the nations* (v. 3) are all destroyed by the LORD.

30:1-5. Alas for the day. The oracle begins with a cry of despair. Ezekiel here raises the cry of the citizens of Egypt. Just as Israel had lamented with despair over God's judgment, so now does Egypt.

30:6-9. Egypt and its allies will all fall. The destruction and devastation that befalls Egypt will also fall upon all its allies. The allies will be destroyed by the sword and lie desolate and waste. God's judgment will reach as far south as Ethiopia.

30:10-12. Nebuchadrezzar to be the agent of destruction. Again Ezekiel's prophecy is specific in indicating that Nebuchadrezzar will be the human agent the LORD uses to bring down Egypt. The result will be devastation.

30:13-19. All Egypt to be destroyed. This section gives a catalog of the principal cities of Egypt, all of which are to be destroyed. The list includes political and religious centers of Upper and Lower Egypt. All Egypt will come to know the LORD.

30:20-26. Breaking the arm of Pharaoh. This oracle is dated to *the eleventh year, the first month, the seventh day* (v. 20), sometime in 587 B.C.E. The oracle speaks of the arm (זרוע, often "might, power") of Pharaoh being broken and not healing. Most likely, this oracle refers to the abortive movement of Egyptian forces against Nebuchadrezzar in 588 B.C.E. in response to a request by Zedekiah (Jer 37). The result was a brief respite from siege for Jerusalem. However, after minor engagements, the Egyptian army retreated back to Egypt. That retreat is described here as the broken arm. The oracle further says that both Pharaoh's arms will be broken; Pharaoh and Egypt will fall, and the Egyptians will be exiled.

31:1-18. Allegory of the cedar, fall of Assyria and Pharaoh. The date formula, *the eleventh year . . . the third month . . . the first day of the month* (v. 1), places this oracle in 588 B.C.E. just a couple of months later than the previous oracle.

31:1-9. Assyria like a cedar of Lebanon. Egypt is asked with what it would compare its greatness. The Assyrians? Assyria is described as a great cedar of Lebanon, tall, full of branches, and filled with birds' nests. Earlier in chap. 17, the king of Judah was described as a cedar of Lebanon. This tree, Assyria, was like the trees of Eden in beauty (cf. 28:11-14). But all the hearers knew what must follow: Assyria had been destroyed more than two decades previously. The greatest empire known to that part of the world had ceased to exist.

31:10-17. The cedar cut down, cast to Sheol. That tall, magnificent and proud cedar was cut down. Foreigners felled it. Where the mighty cedar once stood now only broken branches and a trunk remain. The mighty nation was sent down to Sheol with all its allies.

31:18. Pharaoh's fate is the same. In a single verse application is made to Pharaoh. He can expect no better treatment than Assyria. Egypt also will be brought down to Sheol, and will lie with the unclean foreigners. Perhaps the linkage of Egypt with Assyria recalls that Pharaoh Necho was allied with the remnants of the Assyrians when he marched through Judah and killed King Josiah in 609 B.C.E.

32:1-16. Lament for the dragon (crocodile). This oracle is dated to *the twelfth year . . . the twelfth month . . . the first day of the month* (v. 1), March 585 B.C.E. Much of it is in the *qinah* or lamentation rhythm. Pharaoh considers himself to be a lion, king of beasts. In reality he is a dragon (crocodile) who will be captured, killed, and thrown out into the open countryside for wild animals and birds to feast upon. The land will be filled with Egypt's blood; even the skies will be darkened as from a great sandstorm. The destruction will come at the hand of the Babylonians. Livestock and people alike will be killed and only desolation will remain.

32:17-32. Egypt in Sheol with the foreign nations. The date formula places this oracle prior to the previous one by about eleven months. Nevertheless, the content clearly makes this oracle the climax to the oracles against Egypt, and to the oracles against foreign nations as a whole. The *qinah* lament meter continues in the first half of this oracle. Egypt is mourned as it goes down to Sheol. It dwells there with the other foreign nations that have been destroyed. A total of seven nations are listed as being in Sheol: Egypt, Assyria, Elam, Meshech, Tubal, Edom, and Sidon. Great powers and lesser groups—all suffer the same fate; all are judged by God for their actions and all are destroyed.

The one surprising element in the oracles against foreign nations is the omission of Babylon among the nations. In many of the oracles Babylon serves as the instrument of God's judgment. Perhaps for political reasons Ezekiel omitted Babylon since he was living among the exiles there, or perhaps there was the hope that Babylon would also be the agent to bring about Israel's restoration. In any case Babylon escapes the strong denunciation of the other nations. It should be mentioned that the Book of Jeremiah includes oracles against Babylon. There the oracles against Babylon are placed at the very end of the oracles against the nations (see Jer 50–51).

Messages of Hope and Restoration, 33:1–48:35

The third and final major section of the Book of Ezekiel represents a shift in the content of his messages after the fall of Jerusalem. The judgment that had been proclaimed on Israel/Judah for its sins is an accomplished fact. The foreign nations have received similar messages of judgment based on their actions. But God is not finished with the elect people. The judgment on Israel, while necessary, is not final.

If the remnant who remain, those in exile and those in the land, will repent and turn back to God, there still is hope. Had God not said that their God took no delight in the death of sinners? Had the LORD not said that God would rather the wicked turn from their sins so they might be delivered and live?

One might expect such a message of hope to be received gladly. However, apparently that was not the case. Just as the people had refused to heed the warning the prophet had previously given, now they have lost all hope and refuse to hear his words of hope. As we know, there *were* faithful exiles and faithful Israelites in Judah; Ezekiel describes a general refusal to heed the prophet's call to repentance.

The Prophet as Sentinel Revisited, 33:1-20

This opening oracle of the messages of hope has many parallels with 3:16-21. It serves both as a transition to the messages of hope and a link to the oracles of judgment. The message of individual accountability is stressed in the passage. The prophet as sentinel is accountable for bringing the message God gives him, both words of warning and words of consolation. The warning of the prophet need not be seen only as a prelude to judgment; the warnings also included a call to repentance with a promise of life for those who repented. The repetition of that message should offer hope to the hearers. God takes no pleasure in the death of the wicked; the LORD would much prefer that the wicked turn from their sin and live. But God will be just. The wicked will die; the righteous will live. If one who has been righteous turns to wickedness, that one will die. If one who has been wicked repents and returns to God, that one will live. That simple formula is how God's justice operates, whether on a personal or a communal or national level.

Report of Fall of Jerusalem; Muteness Removed, 33:21-22

The Book of Ezekiel opened with the call experience of the prophet, followed by an oracle of the prophet as sentinel. The prophet was then made mute, except when he spoke words of judgment against Jerusalem/Judah. In the previous paragraph, the prophet as sentinel has been revisited. Now follows the report of the fall of Jerusalem (see 24:26-27) and the removal of the prophet's muteness. The stark words of the survivor, *The city has fallen* (v. 21), mark the end of judgment. The fall of the city now allows the proclamation of restoration. So long as the city remained uncaptured, messages of restoration would hold little meaning. But once the city has fallen and lies in ruins, the message of restoration offers hope for the future.

Oracle concerning Those Remaining in the Land, 33:23-29

Those who survived yet another exile and remained in the land, the ones Jeremiah calls the poorest people of the land, vinedressers and tillers of the soil (Jer 52:16), were assuming they were the inheritors of the land. Because they remained, they must be the righteous remnant. Ezekiel proclaims that they are guilty of the same sins as those who have been exiled or killed. They too will be destroyed and the land will be left a desolation and a waste.

The Entertainer, 33:30-33

A prophet's lot was never an easy one. Ezekiel was now receiving a measure of respect as a prophet of God. He had proclaimed the fall of Jerusalem and Jerusalem had fallen. Yet this brief oracle addressed to Ezekiel makes clear that the people, or at least many of them, had not truly understood his message nor obeyed it. They heard the words, but they did not repent and act on those words. They were still concerned only about their own individual well-being. Now that he was proclaiming a message of hope and restoration, they gladly received his words. But to them the prophet was just an entertainer, *a singer of love songs*, with *a beautiful voice*, and who *plays well on an instrument* (v. 32). How tragic that they hear, but do not act on those words, for the restoration was based on accountability and repentance. But every generation has more who *hear* than who *do*. When finally the restoration becomes reality as did the fall, then the people will know a prophet has been in their midst!

The Shepherds, the Ideal Shepherd, and the Sheep, 34:1-31

34:1-6. Israel's shepherd-rulers. The prophets used the metaphor of shepherd for the rulers of the nation (see Jer 23, 1 Kgs 22:17). The image depicts the care, protection and leadership expected of the rulers. As in Jeremiah, Ezekiel decries the violence of these shepherd-rulers. They have fed on the sheep rather than caring for them. Because the sheep have in reality had no shepherd, they have become scattered.

34:7-10. The LORD against the shepherds. Because the shepherds have abandoned their responsibility, because they have not protected the flock nor cared for it, the LORD himself will intervene. God will rescue the sheep from their false shepherds. The vivid image of rescuing the sheep from the mouth of the shepherds shows the shepherds as they actually are: ravening animals who feed on the flock.

34:11-16. The LORD as shepherd. Now the LORD himself will become the shepherd-ruler of the people. Using imagery well known from Psalms (especially Pss 23; 95:7; 100:3) Ezekiel describes God's actions. God will rescue and gather the scattered sheep, will feed them, making them lie down in rich pastures, and will especially minister to the injured and weak.

34:17-22. God judges between the sheep. Even among the sheep, there are strong and weak. The stronger were bulling their way over the weaker, taking the best of the pasture, and trampling down the rest, getting to the water hole first and fouling it before the weaker could drink. God will intervene on behalf of the weaker ones. The LORD will give all the people equal justice, the weak and the strong, the powerful and those without advocate.

34:23-24. One shepherd. When God has rescued and restored the flock, *one shepherd* (v. 23) will lead them. The fact that one shepherd is specified indicates Ezekiel's vision of a single restored nation, Israel, rather than a divided monarchy.

This shepherd is identified as *my servant David* (v. 23); he will be a king of the Davidic line. He will be a servant ruler, one who does God's bidding. The covenant will be restored for *the LORD will be their God* (v. 24). The Davidic ruler is not called king, but *prince* (v. 24). He will not "lord it over the people." Further, he will be *prince among them*, that is, he will be one with them rather than over them (see also Jer 31:21).

34:25-31. Covenant of peace. This restoration will result in a covenant of peace. Under this covenant all will live securely and peacefully. Wild animals will be banished. No longer will Israel be enslaved or plundered. Their existence will be one of idyllic bliss and blessing. The Lord will be their God; the people will be God's people and the sheep of God's pasture.

Desolation of Edom, 35:1-15

The desolation of Edom (*Mount Seir*) is the focus of this chapter. The word root שׁמם, "to make desolate" or "desolation," occurs ten times in the chapter. Edom had been briefly mentioned in an earlier oracle (25:12-14), but is here treated in more detail. The preference for the term *Mount Seir* in this oracle may parallel the references to *the mountains of Israel* in this chapter and in the next.

Following the introduction of the oracle in vv. 1-2, the substance of the judgment is presented in poetic form in vv. 3-4. The fifth verse presents the charge against Edom introduced by *because* (יען). Verse 6 moves to the judgment introduced by *therefore* (לכן). The ultimate result is given in v. 9, *Then you shall know that I am the LORD*.

Exactly the same pattern occurs in vv. 10-15: v. 10 presents the charge again, introduced by *because*; v. 11 presents the judgment introduced by *therefore*; and v. 15 closes with the result *Then they shall know that I am the LORD*.

The two sets of charges and judgment are parallel. Edom is charged with invading Judah at the time of the fall of Judah and Jerusalem to Babylon; Edom does so in order to expand its borders, *cherish[ing] an ancient enmity* (v. 5). The enmity may refer to that between Esau and Jacob (Gen 28:41), or to more recent strife as mentioned in Amos 1:11-12. The invading of Judah's territory by Edom is mentioned in Obad 10-14.

The *two nations* (v. 10) refers to Israel and Judah. Perhaps it was feared that Edom's incursions into the Negev, the southern portion of Judah, would extend also into the territory of the Northern Kingdom as well. Continued Edomite presence in the Negev is shown by the region's name in later Hellenistic and Roman times: Idumea.

The judgment spoken in the poetic oracle, and in the prose expansions of the oracle as well, is desolation. Mount Seir, and all Edom, will become desolate. As Judah was made desolate, so shall Edom.

Restoration of the Mountains of Israel, 36:1-15

This oracle concerning the restoration of the mountains of Israel has two major points of reference previously in Ezekiel: the desolation of *Mount Seir* in the previous chapter, and the desolation of the same mountains of Israel in chap. 6. This chapter serves as a counterpoint to each of those two oracles. Chapter 6 spoke of a desolation that would come upon the mountains of Israel, and that desolation came with the fall of Judah and Jerusalem in 587 B.C.E. However, that destruction was not the end of the story. This chapter proclaims the restoration of those mountains. Similarly, Edom, which had enlarged and enriched itself when Judah fell, is to be made desolate while Israel is to be restored. In each point-counterpoint pair there is desolation and restoration.

The same structural elements that were found in chap. 35 also occur here: *because* (יַעַן, vv. 2, 3, 6, 13), *therefore* (לָכֵן, vv. 3, 4, 5, 6, 7, 14), and *Then you shall know that I am the LORD* (v. 12). However, in this oracle the elements do not list charges and judgment. Instead, the elements list the afflictions the land has already suffered and offer a word of comfort and consolation.

This message is the undoing of judgment on the mountains of Israel. Now the judgment will fall on the other nations (vv. 5, 7), and especially Edom (v. 5). But for the mountains of Israel, there will come restoration, renewed agriculture (v. 9), rebuilding and repopulation (v. 10) by humans and by domestic animals (v. 11). They will *increase and be fruitful* (v. 11), a clear reference to God's command in creation (Gen 1:22, 28). In this restoration, God *will do more good* to the mountains *than ever before* (v. 11). The land will become fruitful like Eden. With the restoration, the land will be populated by the LORD's people, Israel, as their inheritance (v. 12).

Restoration of the People of Israel, 36:16-38

Not only are the mountains of Israel to be restored; so also are the people. But the restoration of the people is not just a return of the same sinful people to the land. The people are to be transformed as certainly as the mountains, from a desolate waste of a people into a new, fruitful people.

Ezekiel does not mince words in describing the peoples' sins. They have been exiled, but they fully deserved it. They had defiled the land with their sins, and accordingly they were exiled from it (vv. 16-19). Even in exile they continued to profane the LORD's name (vv. 20-21).

When God restores the people, it will not be for their sake, but for the sake of God's holy name (vv. 22-24, 32). The result of this restoration will not be to glorify the people of Israel, but to glorify God's holy name and to cause the nations to know that God is the LORD (v. 23).

The people themselves will be transformed and restored. The transformation is an inner one brought about by God, who will cleanse all their uncleanness (v. 25) and give the people *a new heart*, and *a new spirit* (v. 26; cf. Ps 51:10 [51:12 MT] and Jer 31:31-34). The new heart will not be like the old stony one, stubborn and unmoving, but will be *a heart of flesh* (v. 26), warm and soft and obedient (v. 27). The new spirit will be God's spirit (v. 27) within them.

When the people are transformed, they will recognize their former sinful ways and despise themselves for those practices (v. 31). That the transformation had not yet taken place for Ezekiel's hearers is evident from the injunction in v. 32: *Be ashamed and dismayed for your ways.*

Once this inner transformation occurs, the people will again live in the land of promise and the covenant relationship will be restored: *you shall be my people, and I will be your God* (v. 28). The land is also transformed in that it will become fruitful and never again blighted with famine (vv. 29-30). Likewise, along with restored agriculture will come the rebuilding of towns and desolate places (vv. 33-36). And the population will increase like the flocks that formerly filled the lands (vv. 37-38). Passers-by will say that the land, once desolate, has become like the garden of Eden (v. 35).

The Valley of Dry Bones, 37:1-14

Ezekiel is taken by the hand and *spirit of the LORD* out to a valley filled with dry bones. No location is indicated. The valley may be a visionary one. If the scene is not visionary but a real one, then the valley was apparently the site of a major catastrophe, such as a calamitous battle. So great was the disaster that the bodies of the dead were left unburied, a horrible fate to any Hebrew. Further, touching such bones would mean being unclean for seven days (Num 19:16-18). As a priest, Ezekiel was not to come near any corpse except for the body of some member of his immediate family. Here he is put in the midst of innumerable dead. There is no doubt that these people were dead. All flesh had decayed; the bones were very dry, bleached white.

Ezekiel is asked: *Mortal, can these bones live?* (v. 3). The question seems absurd. These bones are the very epitome of death and desolation; these are no "warm bodies"; these are dried, bleached bones left behind even by the scavenging animals. Though they are very numerous, there is no life in them. Ezekiel's response, *O LORD God, you know* (v. 3), probably means "LORD, you surely know there is no life in them." Ezekiel has more to learn!

Ezekiel is then commanded to prophesy to these dead, dry bones, that breath come into them and that they live (vv. 4-5). Ezekiel prophesies as commanded: the bones form into their skeletons, and then sinew and flesh and skin appear on them (vv. 7-8). Ezekiel prophesies again to them and breath comes into them and they come alive (vv. 9-10).

The climax of the episode explains what the bones represent. Israel in exile was describing itself as being like bones dried up, dead, without hope, completely cut off (v. 12). But to a hopeless people, God has a message of hope: "I am going to bring you back from the dead." This people, this nation would live again and would return to its land. A God who can restore life to dry bones can also gather people from nations where they have been scattered and restore them to their land.

The Two Sticks: A Symbolic Action, 37:15-28

Ezekiel is told to take two sticks, one representing *Judah*, and the other representing *Joseph*—also called *Ephraim*—and to *join them* (v. 17; Heb., "bring near") as one in his hand. This action clearly symbolizes the reunification of the former Northern and Southern Kingdoms. The restoration envisioned by Ezekiel is not limited to survivors of 597 B.C.E and 587 B.C.E. from the fall of Jerusalem and Judah. In addition, the survivors of the earlier fall of the Northern Kingdom, or their descendants, will also be brought into this restored nation. In the restored nation there will be one kingdom, never again to be divided, and one king. Further, this restored nation will be cleansed from its idolatries and apostasies (v. 23) and the covenant will be restored: *they shall be my people and I will be their God* (v. 23).

The one king will be a Davidic ruler who will shepherd them; and all will be obedient to God. The land will be theirs forever. The covenant will be *a covenant of peace* and *an everlasting covenant* (v. 26). God will place the divine sanctuary, God's dwelling place, the place of God's very presence, in their midst forever. To ones in exile, many of whom had been eyewitnesses to the destruction of the Temple, this is a powerful message of hope, a message that will be elaborated in chaps. 40–48. In the restored land there will be one nation, one people, one ruler, one covenant, and one God over all who will dwell in the midst of the people.

The Gog Oracles, 38:1–39:29

These oracles break into the flow of the text that would otherwise move from the hopeful message of restoration in chap. 37 to the vision of the restored land and community in chaps. 40–48. They serve to reinforce God's resolve to restore Israel in its place permanently. God could and did use a foe from the north such as Assyria or Babylonia to bring judgment on the people for their sins. But could it happen again? What about some great military power in the future? Could such a power thwart God's promise of restoration? What would become of the eternal covenant of peace (see 37:26)? These oracles address such a possibility. The oracles fit in this context to reinforce the hope expressed in chap. 37, affirming that such desolation as the nation had suffered will never happen again.

38:1-13. Gog, his armies, and the plan. The identity of *Gog of the land of Magog, chief prince of Meshech and Tubal* (v. 2) is unknown. Some commentators relate him to a seventh century ruler of Lydia in Asia Minor known to the Greeks as Gyges, and to the Assyrians as Gugu (see Allen 1990, 204). Others suggest that the oracle was intended against Babylon, but is deliberately put in cryptic style since Ezekiel was himself an exile in Babylonia (Wells 1990, 284). Perhaps the identity of Gog was as mysterious to the original hearers as it is to us today (see Vawter and Hoppe 1991, 175). Clearly, the identity and homeland of Gog are not primary in the oracles; what is important is his power and the real threat his armies pose for a restored Israel. As with Assyria and Babylonia, God is the one who leads these armies out. But unlike other armies who wreak God's judgment on Israel, these armies will themselves be destroyed in a show of God's power. This destruction is foreshadowed in the description of the call of Gog and his armies: *I will turn you around and put hooks into your jaws; and I will lead you out* (v. 4). Gog is treated just like the dragon (crocodile) Egypt (29:4) and will suffer the same fate—death.

But before the destruction of Gog is described, we see him throwing all his might against God's land and God's people. Only by this action will it be known that God will keep the divine covenant of peace with Israel. So the armies are gathered. From every direction they advance against the mountains of Israel, the restored nation. Amos depicts a similar assembly of Philistines and Egyptians against the mountains of Samaria (Amos 3:9-11). The plan is to fall upon this peaceful people, this people of unwalled villages without gates or bars (v. 11) to plunder, despoil, and lay waste (vv. 12-13). The contrast between the people of Israel, who dwell in peace and security, and this advancing, powerful army is striking. Why do the people not act to defend themselves? Because the LORD dwells in their midst and their trust is in God, not in weapons or walls for defense.

38:14-23. The battle and its outcome. The stage is set for the battle. The invading hordes are ready; the land lies defenseless before them. Then a critical question is raised by the LORD:

Are you he of whom I spoke in former days by my servants the prophets of Israel, who in those days prophesied for years that I would bring you against them? (v. 17).

Many commentators follow LXX and Vulgate and take this as a statement rather than a question: "You are he of whom I spoke" (so Zimmerli 1983, 288, 312; Allen 1990, 198, 201, 206). But if one retains the question, as in MT, the passage reinforces God's promise of an eternal covenant of peace. *No*, this Gog is *not* the one about whom the earlier prophets spoke (see v. 17). For the earlier prophets had spoken of one who was God's instrument of judgment on the people for their sins. That judgment has come. This scene follows restoration and forgiveness when the eternal covenant of peace has already been restored. The LORD has brought up Gog, not to judge Israel, but to judge Gog and to let all nations know that the LORD is God and that God has a covenant with the restored people.

The results are devastating—against Gog. The LORD's presence produces great shaking and quaking and upheaval in the land, as in an earthquake. Then God brings all the dreadful plagues against Gog: sword, pestilence, bloodshed, rain, hailstones, fire and sulfur (vv. 21-22). The result will be that the nations will know God is the LORD (v. 23).

39:1-20. Death and burial of Gog and his army. This chapter begins with words almost identical to those that open chap. 38. This repetition is one of many parallels between the two chapters. Both speak God's judgment against Gog. When God brings Gog against the mountains of Israel, Gog and all his forces will fall (vv. 4-5);

they will be given as prey to the carnivorous birds and wild animals (v. 4). Magog, Gog's land, will be burned (v. 6). God will not permit the divine name to be profaned by any opponent (vv. 7-8).

So numerous will be the weapons left by the destroyed army that the people of Israel will use them as firewood for seven years (vv. 9-10). Now, instead of being despoiled and plundered by the weapons, Israel will despoil and plunder the weapons Gog's army brought with it.

Gog and all his forces will be buried there in Israel, in a valley to be called the *Valley of Travelers* (עברים, "ones passing through" or "ones passing away, perishing") or the *Valley of Hamon-gog* (i.e., the Horde of Gog [v. 11]). All those fallen will be buried to cleanse the land; so many must be buried that the burial will take seven months (vv. 12-16).

In a parallel description of the end of Gog and his forces, one that picks up on the imagery of v. 4, all birds of prey and wild animals are assembled for a great feast (v. 17). They feast on the flesh and blood of the fallen forces of the invading army (v. 18). This gory banquet is the sacrificial feast the LORD is preparing on the mountains of Israel. That which Gog and his forces planned for the people of Israel, a slaughter, is what becomes of them. It is God's vindication on enemies, on any who would attack God's restored people and land.

39:21-29. Recapitulation and hope. When Israel was exiled, it was because of its sins against God. When Gog and his forces are destroyed, it will be due to their presumption in attacking God's people. But just as God can bring exile and judgment, so also can God in mercy bring restoration. God's promise to Israel is that they can hope in that mercy. They need never fear any human armies of Gog or any other despot. God will gather all the exiles of Israel, leaving none behind; God will bring them into their own land where they will live securely with none to make them afraid. Such is the hope for Israel's future, if they will but trust God.

The New Temple, 40:1–42:20

The nine chapters from 40 to 48 are a unit that describes the new Temple in the restored land, new worship regulations, and a new allotment of the land. The unit begins with a visionary experience similar to that reported in chaps. 8–11 where the prophet is taken to Jerusalem and into the Temple. In many regards this whole unit becomes the reversal of the judgment of chaps. 8–11. In those earlier chapters Ezekiel was shown many abominable practices that led to the departure of God's glory and the giving up of the city for destruction. In chaps. 40–48 there is the description of a new Temple, followed by the return of God's glory, new cultic practices that are according to God's commands, and the permanent blessing God's indwelling presence affords. These chapters from Ezekiel influenced the author of the TEMPLE SCROLL, the largest of the manuscripts found at Qumran.

40:1-4. An introduction. The account begins with a date formula, the tenth day of the first month of the twenty-fifth year of exile, approximately April 573 B.C.E. This date is also the fourteenth year after the destruction of Jerusalem. Ezekiel is brought in a vision to Jerusalem and is presented with a new Temple structure. He is to measure and report this structure to the exiles.

40:5-47. The outer and inner courts of the Temple. Ezekiel enters the outer court of the Temple through the eastern gate. There are three gates to the outer court, one each on the north, south and east. The outer wall forms a square; there is no gate on the western side because the Temple building adjoins the wall. The gates are identical in size and have side rooms or chambers in them. In addition, there are chambers along the length of the north, east and south walls of the outer court. Another wall separates the outer court from the inner court. Three gateways lead from the outer to the inner court.

The Temple and its courtyards have an east-west orientation. The east gate is the primary entrance into the outer and inner courtyards. The entrance to the Temple building itself is on the east.

Special mention is made of the area where the sacrificial animals are slaughtered and prepared for offering; this act takes place in a chamber in the vestibule of the north gateway that leads into the inner court (vv. 38-43). Mention is also made of two groups of priests and their chambers. Those simply called the priests have charge of the Temple and have chambers on the north side of the inner court (v. 45); they will later be called simply the Levites. The Zadokite priests have charge of the altar and have chambers on the south side of the inner court nearer the altar (v. 46). These Zadokite priests only *may come near to the LORD to minister to him* (v. 46). Thus a hierarchy of priests is indicated.

40:48–41:4. The vestibule, nave and inner sanctuary. Considering all the detail of measurement for the courtyards, the Temple building itself is described in very cursory fashion. Like the Solomonic Temple, this one has three primary parts: the vestibule or porch, the nave, and the inner sanctuary, here called *the most holy place* (v. 4). It is interesting to note that Ezekiel is brought into the nave, which priests could enter, but only his visionary guide enters and measures the most holy place. This understanding of holiness and restricted boundaries is like that of Lev 17 where only the high priest may enter the most holy place, and then only on the Day of Atonement after proper preparation.

41:5-26. Further description of the Temple and adjacent buildings. The exterior of the Temple was three stories high and had chambers on both sides. The whole Temple structure was on a raised platform above the inner court. There was also a Temple yard surrounding the Temple and on the west side a building whose function is not described. The nave and vestibule were decorated with paneling having cherubim and palm trees on them. There was also a table resembling a wooden altar in the nave in front of the most holy place (vv. 21-22).

42:1-14. The priests' chambers. The priests' chambers lay along the north and south wall of the inner court. They filled much of the area of the inner court immediately north and south of the Temple building itself. Here the Zadokite priests were to eat the most holy offerings. Also in these chambers the most holy offerings were to be deposited, and here the priests were to leave the clothing they wore into the nave before they went into the outer court. That clothing was too holy to wear when they went into an area open to the people in general (see below, 44:15-31).

42:15-20. Final measurements, purpose of enclosure wall. The outer measurements of the Temple enclosure wall are made: the enclosure is 500 cubits square. The purpose of the enclosure wall is made clear: it separates the common from the holy. Only that which is holy may enter the Temple courts. Greater holiness is necessary to enter the inner precincts, and only the priests may enter the vestibule and nave of the Temple. The most holy place was the dwelling place of the LORD himself. Without discussing each measurement individually, one can note that each move inward from outside the Temple enclosure ultimately to the most holy place involves moving into increasingly smaller spaces and increasingly elevated spaces. The inner court is smaller than the outer court; it is also raised above the outer court. Likewise the Temple building sits on a raised platform. Even the altar in the inner court sits on a raised platform. In the case of the Temple building, the entryways become increasingly smaller as one moves from the vestibule to the nave and to the most holy place. The elevation, the smaller space, and the increasingly limited access all were indicators of increasing sacredness.

Return of the Glory of the LORD, 43:1-12

Following the completion of the measurements of the Temple, Ezekiel is brought to the east gate of the Temple compound. There he sees the glory of the LORD returning from the east. Ezekiel makes clear that the vision he sees is the same glory that he saw by the River Chebar in his call experience and the same as the departing and destroying vision he had seen in chaps. 8–11. The LORD's glory enters the Temple courtyard through the eastern gate, and as Ezekiel himself is brought to the inner courtyard, the LORD's glory fills the Temple building.

Ezekiel hears the LORD's voice proclaiming that this place, the Temple, is God's throne and footstool from which God will dwell with the people of God forever (v. 7). The people are to abandon their idolatry (v. 9) and their burial practices of burying persons, especially the kings, too close to the sacred precincts (vv. 7-9). Such practices were defiling God's name.

Then Ezekiel is commanded to relate all the Temple plan to the people. They are to repent of their iniquities. Then they are to follow all the plan and ordinances of the Temple. The return of the LORD's glory completes the reversal of God's judgment given in chaps. 8–11. The return of the glory is the return of blessing and life. The same God who judged the people for their sins now offers restoration and blessing to a transformed and repentant people. This future hope is still based on repentance, but it is a glorious hope if they will only repent. The restoration is not merely a return to the former condition; it is a return to a new Temple, new worship practices, and an eternal presence.

Consecration of the Altar, 43:13-27

Once the glory of the LORD has returned, the Temple can be consecrated and the practices of worship can begin. Ezekiel begins with the altar of burnt offerings, the focal point of atonement and worship. The altar is first described and its dimensions given (vv. 13-17). Only the Zadokite priests are permitted to offer sacrifices on the altar (v. 19); they are to consecrate the altar by offering the appropriate sin offerings and burnt offerings for the altar for a period of seven days. On the first day a bull for a sin offering is sacrificed. Some of its blood is put on the horns of the altar, the corners of the ledges, and along the rim. The sacrificed animal is burned outside the sacred precinct (vv. 18-21). On the second through the seventh days a goat, a bull, and a ram are offered as burnt offerings (vv. 22-26). At the end of the seven days, the altar will be purified and consecrated, and the people may bring their burnt offerings and offerings of well-being; then God will accept the people and their offerings (v. 27).

East Gate of Temple Closed Permanently, 44:1-3

Ezekiel is taken back to the eastern gate of the sanctuary—referring to the entire Temple enclosure, not just the Temple building—and finds that the gate is shut. The LORD says that it is to remain shut. The reason is twofold: since the LORD entered this gate it has great holiness attached to it and no one else is holy enough to pass through the gate; and, secondly, in a symbolic sense, the closed gate indicates that the LORD will remain permanently within the sanctuary. In this passage the glory of the LORD is identified with the LORD himself, for previously it was the LORD's glorythat was said to have entered the Temple by the eastern gate (43:1-4).

Although no one may enter or leave by the eastern gate, the prince is permitted to eat a meal in the LORD's presence within the chambers or vestibule of the gate (v. 3). But he is to enter the gate area from the outer court and leave the same way.

Ordinances concerning the Priests, 44:4-31

44:4-9. Exclusion of foreigners from sanctuary. No foreigners (i.e, non-Jews, uncircumcised) are to be admitted to the sanctuary in this new Temple. The only reference to foreigners being admitted to the Solomonic Temple is the Carite guards mentioned in 2 Kgs 11 who, as palace guards, also had duties around the sacred precinct. This exclusivism seems to contrast other restoration ideals that envision the nations as flowing up to the mountain/house of the LORD (Isa 2:2; Mic 4:1,2); even Ezekiel would allot foreigners living in the land a portion of the land (47:22-23). This exclusivism is noted in the Herodian Temple by the historian Josephus who mentions a sign written in Greek and Latin forbidding foreigners entry into the inner courts under threat of death. The apostle Paul was accused of bringing an uncircumcised gentile into the Temple (see Acts 21:27-29).

44:10-14. Responsibilities of the Levites. The Levites' duties as mentioned in 40:45 are expanded here. Because the Levites went after idolatry at some time, they are not to come into the most sacred precincts nor handle the sacred offerings. They are to have charge of the Temple; they are to stand before the people and minister to them; they are to slaughter the burnt offering and sacrifices of the people. But the Levites are not to offer the sacred portions nor minister before the LORD, nor enter the most sacred precincts. The idolatry of which they are accused may have been the worship in the rural shrines and sanctuaries prior to Josiah's reform, which centralized all worship at the Temple in Jerusalem (2 Kgs 23:8-9). Clearly, Ezekiel has the Levites in a lesser role than the Zadokite priests, although he still recognizes them as having a legitimate role in the Temple.

44:15-31. Responsibilities of the Zadokite priests. In this section, only the Zadokites are considered as true priests. They are the ones who come into God's presence and minister at the table and handle the most sacred offerings on the altar. This is because they did not go astray as the people of Israel did, nor did they commit the idolatry of the Levites. They are to wear special clothes made entirely of linen while they are within the inner court and Temple. They are to change clothes before they go into the outer court among the people because of the holiness of the clothes worn in the inner court. Holy things have been set apart for God; such holiness could be dangerous to the common person who had not made proper preparation to handle that which was set apart.

Other regulations for the priests included directions concerning cutting the hair, abstinence from wine when entering the inner court, and marriage. The priests were not to marry a widow or divorced woman (unless the widow had been married to a priest). They were to marry only ones who were full Israelites.

They were responsible for teaching the people the difference between the holy and the common, the clean and the unclean. Some of the regulations involved teaching the people by example. The priests were also to serve as judges, deciding cases on the basis of God's justice. They were responsible for the proper observation of festivals, holy days, and sabbaths. The priests were not to defile themselves by going near or touching a dead person; only for their immediate family were they to so defile themselves. Then they had to undergo ritual purification before they could function as priest again.

The priests were to have no inheritance of the land: the LORD himself was their inheritance. They were to have the grain offerings, the sin offerings, the guilt offerings, all devoted things (things consecrated to God that could not be redeemed), the first or best of the first fruits, and even the first of the dough. These offerings were to supply their needs and to replace an inheritance of land. Finally, the priests were prohibited from eating any meat of an animal that died of natural causes or was killed by other animals.

Property for Sanctuary, Priests, Levites, City, and Prince, 45:1-9

In the restored land, there is to be a redistribution of the tribal inheritance. Each tribe will receive an equal inheritance (see below, 47:13–48:29). Surrounding the sanctuary itself will be portions of land reserved for the homes of the priests and

the Levites. This entire tract is a holy district. The sanctuary itself, the most holy
land, is to be flanked on all sides by the priests' land. Next comes the Levites' land.
The city of Jerusalem has a tract adjacent to the holy district. The portion allotted
to the prince extends the width of the holy district and the city's district; in length
it runs from the western to the eastern border of the land. The purpose of this allotment to the prince is to limit his holdings. No longer will he be able to dispossess
people of their inheritance and enlarge his own holdings. The purpose of enumer-
ating these allotments at this point is to show how the land, like the Temple
grounds, is set in varying degrees of holiness, from the common land of the tribal
allotments to the most holy portion where the sanctuary sits (cf. chaps. 40–42
above).

Weights and Measures, 45:10-12

Along with a redistribution of the land was to come a standardization of
WEIGHTS AND MEASURES. Furthermore, the people are exhorted to use honest
weights and measures in their transactions. Practices in daily life, in trade and
commerce, were as important to God as worship practices.

Offerings and Festivals, 45:13–46:15

A new schedule of offerings is indicated in this section. Of the wheat and
barley, one-sixtieth is to be given; of the oil, one one-hundredth; and of the sheep,
one two-hundredth. No mention is made of other products. These offerings are for
grain offerings, burnt offerings and offerings of well-being to make atonement for
the people. All the people, from the prince down, were responsible for bringing
these offerings of their produce. The prince had special responsibility to provide
certain sacrifices at the festivals and sabbaths. He also provides leadership at certain
of the festivals, by his sacrifices representing the whole people. Whether these
sacrifices provided by the prince came from taxation of the people or from his own
holdings is not indicated.

Three festivals are mentioned in this calendar of festivals, though they do not
directly parallel the other priestly calendars. New Year's Day is here a Spring
Festival along with Passover, unlike the more familiar Fall New Year's Day. The
New Year's Day ritual is intended as a purification for the sanctuary. This
purification is followed on the seventh day (or if the LXX is followed, on the first
day of the seventh month) by an additional purification ritual. By these rituals, the
Temple was preserved from any uncleanness caused by those who had unwittingly
sinned and thus polluted the Temple.

Even the movements of the people are prescribed in this section (46:9-10). The
prince may enter into the vestibule of the inner court for certain sacrifices and
festivals; the people may only come to the gateway of the inner court. This indicates
that the prince had a measure of holiness beyond that of the people—he could come
more closely into the LORD's presence. In general, the descriptions of the offerings
and festivals are intended to suggest the orderliness of the worship. Prescribed

sacrifices and festivals were to be observed at fixed times, and certain movement in and out of the Temple areas was permitted at fixed times. Everything was to be done in a proper and orderly fashion.

The Prince's Property, 46:16-18

A further reference is made to the prince's holdings (see 45:7-9). Here the regulations deal with inheritance rather than the extent of the holdings. Three principles are set out in these regulations. (1) The prince may bequeath to his children portions of land for their permanent inheritance. (2) The prince may grant tracts of his property to his officials; however, this property will revert to the prince at the *year of liberty* (v. 17), either at the end of seven years when slaves were freed, or at the year of jubilee, the fiftieth year. This regulation prevents later generations of the royal family from being impoverished by a lack of land holdings. (3) The prince is not to dispossess any of the people of their inheritance or build up his holdings, or provide additional holdings for his children.

Two Cooking Areas, 46:19-24

The preparation, cooking and baking of the holy offerings, those reserved for the priests' use, was to take place in a section of the inner court west of the priests' quarters. In this manner the holiness of the offerings could be preserved. Presumably these offerings were also to be consumed within the inner court. In the corners of the outer court were four additional food preparation areas. Here the Levites were to prepare the sacrifices of the people. This food was consumed as a communal meal by the worshipers and their families and the Levites. These sacrifices were not considered as filled with holiness, and therefore did not represent the same danger of transmitting that holiness to the people.

River of Water from the Temple, 47:1-12

Ezekiel is brought back to the entrance into the Temple. Here he is shown water flowing out from under the threshold of the Temple and just south of the altar. The water flowed eastward and under the eastern wall of the Temple enclosure, south of the eastern gate. The volume of water increases as Ezekiel is led eastward. One thousand cubits away from the Temple (about 1,500 ft.) it is ankle deep; after another 1,000 cubits it is knee deep; yet another 1,000 cubits and it is waist deep; a final 1,000 cubits is measured and the water is so deep that Ezekiel cannot cross it; one would have to swim across it.

This great river flows eastward down to the Dead Sea. Its waters will change the Dead Sea into fresh water filled with all kinds of fish and water life. As in 37:1-14, that which is dead will be restored to full life. In chap. 37 it is dead bones that live again, symbolic of a hopeless people; here it is a barren wilderness and a dead sea that are restored. People and land are both restored by God's blessing. The banks of this river will be filled with every kind of tree. The leaves will not wilt or fall from these trees, and they will bear fresh fruit every month. The fruit will be for food and the leaves for healing.

The image is one of paradise. Eden's four rivers are replaced with one flowing from God's sanctuary. There are trees here, just as there were in Eden. The paradisal blessing of this river seems comparable to that of the Tree of Life in the garden of Eden. Ps 46:4 apparently refers to the same tradition of a river flowing out of the Temple, as do the postexilic prophecies of Zechariah (14:8) and Joel (3:18 [MT 4:18]) and the NT Book of Revelation (22:1).

Boundaries of the Land and Tribal Allotments, 47:13–48:29

The borders of the restored land are given, beginning at the north and then moving east, south, and west. The northern borders cannot be identified with certainty. Most scholars consider the borders to be comparable to those of classical Canaan, modern Palestine and southern Syria. The northern border is often placed in the vicinity of, or just north of, Tyre (see Allen 1990, 280–81) and runs eastward from the Mediterranean Sea to the territory of Damascus. The east border runs between Hauran (roughly comparable to Bashan) and Damascus, and then follows the Jordan River to the south end of the Dead Sea. The border then runs southwest to Meribath-Kadesh (Kadesh Barnea) and then northwest to the Wadi of Egypt, south of Philistia. The Mediterranean Sea forms the western border.

The tribal allotments are to be equal in size (47:14), each one a roughly rectangular strip from the Mediterranean Sea to the Jordan River (or border of Hauran north of the Sea of Galilee). There were to be twelve allotments, ten tribes each receiving one allotment, Levi receiving no property allotment, but receiving the offerings for maintaining the Temple, and the Joseph half-tribes of Ephraim and Manasseh each receiving a full allotment. Even those foreigners who reside in the land are to receive an inheritance. They are to be treated like citizens in terms of land allotments; they receive the same portion as any Israelite family in the tribal territory in which they live.

The tribal locations do not fully match those of Joshua (Josh 13–19). Dan is still the northernmost (as it was following the migration recorded in Judg 18). Benjamin and Judah still are closest to Jerusalem, though in reverse order. Emphasis is placed on the equal size of the tribal allotments rather than location.

Gates of the City and its Name, 48:30-35

The city itself will be square; it will have twelve gates, three on a side. Each of the gates will be named for one of the twelve tribes. The city will have a new name from that time forward. It will be called *Yahweh-shammah, The LORD is There* (v. 35). The new name represents the promise of God's eternal presence within the city as surely as the closed eastern gate (44:1-2) depicts God's eternal presence within the sanctuary.

Works Cited

Albright, W. F. 1932. "The Seal of Eliakim and the Latest Preexilic History of Judah, with Some Observations on Ezekiel." *JBL* 51:77–106.

Allen, Leslie C. 1990. *Ezekiel 20–48*. WBC.

Brownlee, William H. 1986. *Ezekiel 1–19*. WBC.

Stalker, D. M. G. 1968. *Ezekiel*. TBC.

Taylor, John B. 1969. *Ezekiel*. TOTC.

Vawter, Bruce, and Leslie J. Hoppe. 1991. *A New Heart: A Commentary on the Book of Ezekiel*. ITC.

Wells, Roy D., Jr. 1990. "Ezekiel, Book of." MDB 283–84.

Zimmerli, Walther. 1979, 1983. *Ezekiel 1, 2*. Herm.

Daniel

Mitchell G. Reddish

Introduction

The Book of Daniel is one of the most enigmatic books in the Bible. Filled with visions, strange beasts, and angels, Daniel has often seemed to be an esoteric writing that has little relevance for the modern world. Understood in its historical and literary contexts, however, the book contains a powerful message of hope, encouragement, and faithfulness. Through the centuries Daniel has continued to inspire and challenge its readers with its emphasis on the sovereignty of God and the ultimate vindication of the righteous. The book has also produced some memorable images: the statue with feet of clay, the three men in the fiery furnace, the handwriting on the wall, Daniel in the lions' den, and the four beasts from the sea. Furthermore, its ideas of the SON OF MAN and individual resurrection have had a profound impact on JUDAISM and even more so on Christianity.

Literary Form

The LXX and the Vulgate place Daniel among the Prophets; the MT, however, considers it a part of the Writings. Modern critical scholars understand the book not as prophetic literature but as the only complete example in the Hebrew Bible of an apocalypse, a specific genre of literature that became popular in Judaism from the second century B.C.E. to the first century C.E.

The first six chapters contain stories of Daniel and his three friends in Babylon during the EXILE. These stories set the narrative context for the visions in the latter half of the book. According to form-critical studies, these stories are classified as court legends or court tales, whose purpose was not to provide historical information but to exhort and edify their readers.

The most apocalyptic section of Daniel is the last half, chaps. 7–12, which contains four eschatological visions received by Daniel and explained to him by angels. These visions correspond to the type of apocalypses classified as historical apocalypses because they contain summaries of historical events cast in the form of predictions of future happenings. The use of such *ex eventu* "prophecies" is a literary technique of many apocalyptic writers. The writer claims to be a famous person from the past who predicts major events yet to come. By presenting the past as future, the writer gains credibility and authority. If what is prophesied has proven true so far, then the reader likely assumes that events in the future will also occur as predicted.

Structure and Unity

The Book of Daniel divides easily into two major sections. Chapters 1–6, written in third person, contain six folk tales about DANIEL and his three friends in Babylonian Exile. Chapters 7–12, written in first person, contain Daniel's four apocalyptic visions and their interpretations. The two halves of the book are interlocked, however, in several ways.

First, the internal chronologies of the two sections overlap. The first six chapters refer to events in the reigns of Nebuchadnezzar (NEBUCHADREZZAR), BEL-SHAZZAR, and DARIUS the Mede. The visions of the last six chapters begin not after the supposed time of Darius but during the reign of Belshazzar and continue through the periods of Darius and CYRUS of Persia. (See "Date and Occasion," below, regarding difficulties with these chronologies.)

Second, the variation in languages in which Daniel was originally written helps tie the work together. Like the chronologies, the language shifts do not coincide with the break between chaps. 6 and 7. Chapters 1–2:4a and chaps. 8–12 are written in Hebrew; the center section (2:4b–7:28) is written in Aramaic.

Third, the contents of the chapters bind the work together. In a general way, the purpose of the tales and of the visions is the same: to encourage faithfulness to God in times of difficulty and to offer assurance of God's sovereignty.

Date and Occasion

The book presents itself as originating during the Babylonian Exile of the sixth century B.C.E., written by a pious Jew named Daniel who was among the Jewish people deported to Babylon. As early as the second century C.E., however, critics noted problems with this view. A major difficulty concerns historical problems or inaccuracies in the book, one of which is found in the opening verse of the book. The text describes the siege of Jerusalem as occurring during *the third year of the reign of Jehoiakim*, which would be 606 B.C.E. The first siege by Nebuchadnezzar, however, did not occur until 597. The author later describes Belshazzar as the son and successor to the throne of Nebuchadnezzar (5:2). Belshazzar was in reality the son of NABONIDUS, a later king, and was never officially the king but ruled only as viceroy during his father's absences. Even more problematic is the author's reference to *Darius the Mede* (5:31) as the successor to the neo-Babylonian kingdom. Babylon was captured by Cyrus of Persia, not Darius. Furthermore, Darius was Persian, not Median, and succeeded Cyrus rather than preceded him.

Much of the historical information presented in the visions, often in veiled form, is accurate and detailed. The focus of these reports is the reign of Antiochus IV Epiphanes, ruler of Syria 175–164 B.C.E., and persecutor of the Jews in Palestine.

The historical information becomes inaccurate again when describing the circumstances of the death of Antiochus. The combination of inaccurate information about the exilic period and detailed descriptions of events leading to and occurring during the reign of Antiochus points to a date of composition for Daniel during the second century B.C.E. The author is aware of the persecution by Antiochus and the desecration of the Jerusalem Temple (167 B.C.E.) but is unaware of the death of Antiochus or the rededication of the Temple by the MACCABEES (164 B.C.E.). The work can then be dated more closely between 165 and 164 B.C.E.

The purpose of the book was to give encouragement and hope to the Jews in Palestine during the second century B.C.E. The tales in chaps. 1–6 are older materials that were reworked and used by the author of Daniel. They betray no knowledge of Antiochus or his persecution. Persian and Hellenistic influences in the tales point to the third century B.C.E. as a likely date for their composition. These tales set the narrative context for the apocalyptic visions, provide information on the legendary figure Daniel, and serve as example stories and didactic material for the readers of Daniel.

Authorship

The identity of the author is unknown. As with almost all Jewish apocalypses, the Book of Daniel is pseudonymous. The purported author Daniel was a legendary figure known for his wisdom and righteousness (Ezek 14:14, 20; 28:3), perhaps derived from the fourteenth century B.C.E. Ugaritic legend of Dnil, a wise judge. Since Daniel was apparently not as well known as other persons to whom pseudonymous works were attributed, the author of the book precedes Daniel's apocalyptic visions with tales that demonstrate Daniel's wisdom and righteousness. Interest in the folk hero Daniel continued beyond the stories contained in the Hebrew Bible, as evidenced by the stories of SUSANNA and BEL AND THE DRAGON (contained in the Greek texts but not the MT of Daniel) and by references to Daniel in some of the manuscripts of the DEAD SEA SCROLLS.

The actual author of the book probably was a Jew of the second century who was apparently one of the *wise*, or *maskilim*, mentioned in 11:33-35 and 12:3. The *maskilim* were committed to righteousness and loyalty to God. They were revered by the masses as pious examples and teachers. These descriptions also fit the Hasidim, a pious sect in Palestine who rejected the Hellenizing measures of Antiochus and were strict in their faithfulness to Jewish law and customs. If the term *maskilim* is another designation for the Hasidim, as some scholars have argued, then the author of Daniel held to a more pacifist stance than did many of the Hasidim.

The author of Daniel certainly calls for resistance to the ways of Antiochus, but not for violent resistance. The Hasidim, on the other hand, joined forces with the Maccabees in the early years of the armed conflict with Antiochus (see 1 Macc 2:42-48). The author of Daniel views such efforts as only *a little help* (11:34) against the monstrous evil of Antiochus. Human efforts will fail. The only solution to the dilemma facing author and readers lay in supernatural intervention, the ending of the present world order, and the establishment of God's eternal kingdom. The task of God's people was to remain faithful, as Daniel and his three friends had done. As God had delivered them, so God would also deliver the faithful of every age, if not in this life, then in the age to come (12:1).

Language

The bilingual aspect of the Book of Daniel is puzzling. Why is the material in 2:4b–7:28 written in Aramaic and the material in 1:1–2:4a and 8:1–12:13 written in Hebrew? No completely satisfactory solution has been proposed. Most scholars agree that the tales in chaps. 2–6 were originally written in Aramaic. Some have argued that the entire work was originally written in Aramaic and then portions were later translated into Hebrew, possibly for religious or patriotic reasons.

Another plausible explanation for the bilingualism is as follows: (1) Chaps. 1–6 were originally written in Aramaic during the third century. (2) In the second century, chaps. 7–12 were written. Chap. 7 was written in Aramaic to tie the tales and visions together; chaps. 8–12 were written in Hebrew due to the author's nationalistic pride or desire to use "sacred" language. (3) When the tales and the visions were joined, 1:1–2:4a was translated into Hebrew in order to form a literary inclusion with the end of the book (4a is a natural break because the Chaldeans' speech would have been in Aramaic). (Collins, 1984b, 29-32.)

For Further Study

In the *Mercer Dictionary of the Bible*: APOCALYPTIC LITERATURE; BABYLONIAN EMPIRE; BEL AND THEDRAGON; CYRUS; DANIEL; DANIEL, BOOK OF; EXILE;HELLENISTIC WORLD; MACCABEES; MENE, MENE,TEKEL, PARSIN; NEBUCHADREZZAR; NUMBERS/NUMEROLOGY; PERSIAN EMPIRE; VISION.

In other sources: J. J. Collins, *The Apocalyptic Imagination*; *Daniel, First Maccabees, Second Maccabees*; and *Daniel, with an Introduction to Apocalyptic Literature*, FOTL; J. E. Goldingay, *Daniel*, WBC; L. F. Hartman and A. A. Di Lella, *The Book of Daniel*, AncB; A. Lacocque, *The Book of Daniel* and *Daniel in His Time*; N. W. Porteous, *Daniel*, OTL; W. S. Towner, *Daniel*, Interp.

Commentary

An Outline

I. Tales from the Exile 1:1–6:28
  A. Daniel and His Three Friends, 1:1-21
  B. Nebuchadnezzar's First Dream, 2:1-49
  C. Three Men in the Fiery Furnace, 3:1-30
  D. Nebuchadnezzar's Second Dream
    and Madness, 4:1-37
  E. Belshazzar's Arrogance

    and Punishment, 5:1-31
  F. Daniel in the Lion's Den, 6:1-28
II. Visions of the Future, 7:1–12:13
  A. The Four Beasts from the Sea, 7:1-28
  B. The Ram and the Male Goat, 8:1-27
  C. The Seventy Weeks of Years, 9:1-27
  D. The Last Days, 10:1–12:13

Tales from the Exile 1:1–6:28

Daniel and His Three Friends, 1:1-21

1:1-7. The setting. The opening verses set the supposed historical context for the book and introduce the main characters. Nebuchadnezzar, king of Babylon 605–562 B.C.E., has captured Jerusalem and deported many of its leading citizens. The statement that the siege of Jerusalem occurred *in the third year of the reign of King Jehoiakim* (v. 1) is inaccurate. This and other historical inaccuracies in the book are insignificant, however. The author's intent is to place Daniel and his friends in the king's court during the Exile.

Chapter 1 was possibly created as an introduction to the entire book, or more likely as an introduction to the other tales. (The benevolent attitude toward the foreign kings argues for a date of composition prior to the time of Antiochus.) Only in this introductory story do Daniel and his three friends appear together. (There is one exception in chap. 2. The role of the three youths in that story, however, is minor and probably secondary to the original tale.) The mention of the Temple vessels that were taken from Jerusalem prepares for the story in chap. 5. Daniel's ability to interpret dreams and visions sets the stage for his role in the subsequent tales.

1:8-17. Refusing royal rations. How the king's *food and wine* would defile Daniel and his three friends is not explained. Perhaps the story is intended to reflect the keeping of the food laws of the Torah, a practice that grew in importance during the time of Antiochus. Perhaps the young men feared that the food had been offered to idols. Or perhaps to accept the king's delicacies was to capitulate too much to the gentile culture. For whatever reason, Daniel and his friends refuse to compromise their beliefs while in the court of the gentile king. Instead, they propose a trial period during which they are fed only *vegetables . . . and water* (v. 12). The success of the test vindicates not only them but also their faith in God.

1:18-21. Health and more. Along with robust health, God grants Daniel and his friends knowledge and wisdom. Particularly significant for the remainder of the episodes is the statement that Daniel is given *insight into all visions and dreams* (1:17). The superiority of the four young men is recognized by Nebuchadnezzar, who grants them a position in his court. Here and elsewhere in the tales, strong similarities between the JOSEPH stories in Genesis and the Daniel stories are evident: young men in a foreign court, emphasis on wisdom and dream interpretation, change of names, and elevation to an important position in the court.

The larger issue addressed in this tale, aside from dietary scruples, is the question, "Can a person remain true to his or her faith in a hostile or secular environment?" That question was a serious one for Jews living in the Diaspora. For the earliest readers of Daniel, confronted with the physical threats of Antiochus and the religious encroachments of Hellenization, the question was of utmost importance. Through the example of Daniel and his friends the author illustrates that faithfulness to the laws of God is possible even in a difficult setting.

Nebuchadnezzar's First Dream, 2:1-49

2:1-11. A troubled king. The setting of the second tale is supposedly during *the second year* of Nebuchadnezzar. According to 1:5, 18, however, Daniel and his friends have already been in the royal court for at least three years. This inconsistency supports the contention that these were originally separate tales.

Bothered by a troubling dream, the king calls for his court sages to explain it to him. The exaggerated nature of the king's challenge heightens the drama of the tale. Not only must the sages interpret the dream, they must also reveal the dream itself. The key to the tale is in v. 11, when the king's wise men reply that no one except the gods can reveal such secrets to the king. Since the gods of the sages do not reveal the dream and its interpretation to the sages, then their gods must be weak and ineffective.

2:12-30. The king's rage. Furious over the failure of the wise men, the king orders them killed. Daniel intervenes in the situation and offers to interpret the dream for the king. Daniel's prayer of thanksgiving to God, as well as his statement to the king, emphasizes that the source of the wisdom displayed by Daniel is *the God of heaven* (v. 18) and not Daniel himself. Reminiscent of the Joseph episode in Gen 41, the message of the story is that the God of Daniel is superior to the gods of the court sages.

2:31-45. The dream made clear. The king's dream draws on imagery familiar in the ancient world. Greek and Persian writers portrayed the generations of humanity or the reigns of kings as various metals. In his interpretation Daniel identifies only the first kingdom—the gold signifies the neo-Babylonian kingdom of Nebuchadnezzar. The other three kingdoms are the Median, Persian, and Greek. In actuality, a Median kingdom did not exist as a major Near Eastern power between the time of the neo-Babylonian and Persian powers, as the author of the tales indicated (cf. 5:31–6:1).

Verse 43 interprets the mixture of iron and clay as signifying intermarriage, likely a reference to the intermarriages between the Seleucids and the Ptolemies (possibly a later addition to the tale).

The final kingdom, the stone cut by no human hands that becomes a great mountain, is the eternal kingdom established by God. Although this kingdom is an earthly kingdom, the text is ambiguous about its further identity. Jewish readers would certainly have understood this symbol as a reference to Israel.

2:46-49. Promotions. In response to Daniel's feat, the king "worships" him and promotes him and his three friends. Nebuchadnezzar's exclamation summarizes the message of this tale: *Truly, your God is God of gods and Lord of kings and a revealer of mysteries* (v. 47).

Three Men in the Fiery Furnace, 3:1-30

3:1-7. The king's demands. Daniel is absent from this tale. The protagonists are his three companions. The late date of this story is evidenced by the Persian titles of the officials and the Greek names of some of the musical instruments. Huge statues of gods or rulers were not uncommon in the ancient world. The text is ambiguous concerning the likeness of the colossal golden statue of this tale (approx. ninety ft. high). Apparently the image was that of either Nebuchadnezzar or, more likely, a Babylonian god (presumably Bel-Marduk).

3:8-18. Faithful refusal. As court officials, *Shadrach, Meshach, and Abednego* (v. 12) were conspicuous in their refusal to obey the king's command that everyone worship the golden statue. Their reply to the king is a classic statement of uncompromising religious faith. They believed that God would save them from this threat. Even if God does not rescue them, however, they will not abandon their trust in God. These words would have been especially meaningful during the persecution by Antiochus when many faithful Jews were *not* delivered from torture and death (cf. 2 Macc 6–7).

3:19-30. Punishment and salvation. The dramatic effect of the tale is heightened by the command to heat the furnace *seven times more than was customary* (v. 19). The furnace, or kiln, was a large structure with an opening at the top and one at ground level.

(The Greek texts of Daniel add, after v. 23, a passage known as the Prayer of Azariah and the Song of the Three Young Men. "Azariah" is the Hebrew name of Abednego. This addition contains Azariah's prayer for deliverance, a brief report on the young men while in the furnace, and their song of thanksgiving to God for deliverance. These additions to the Greek text are also treated in this commentary.)

After the men are thrown into the furnace, Nebuchadnezzar is astonished. Looking through the ground-level door, he sees four men, not three in the furnace. The fourth individual, described as having *the appearance of a god* (v. 25), is an *angel* (v. 28), a sign of divine intervention. God has not abandoned Shadrach, Meshach, and Abednego but is with them in their fiery ordeal. Their rescue is described in exaggerated terms: *the hair of their heads was not singed, their tunics were not harmed, and not even the smell of fire came from them* (v. 27). Amazed by the power of the God of the Jews, Nebuchadnezzar decrees that no one is to speak against this God. The question that the king raised earlier, *Who is the god that will deliver you out of my hands?* (v. 15), he now answers himself.

Few biblical stories have been as popular as this tale of Shadrach, Meshach, and Abednego. It is a story about the God of Israel who is more powerful than Nebuchadnezzar or any of his gods. It is a story of religious persecution and divine deliverance. More important, it is a story of a religious faith that does not surrender, a faith that endures even in the face of martyrdom.

Nebuchadnezzar's Second Dream and Madness, 4:1-37

4:1-8. Another dream. The fourth tale is cast in the form of a written decree, an epistle, from Nebuchadnezzar. The events of the tale explain why the king is offering praise to the God of Israel. Nebuchadnezzar had had a strange and frightening dream. As was the case earlier, his court sages were unable to interpret the dream. Once again Daniel provides the interpretation.

4:9-18. A contest. In the case of the first dream (chap. 2), the king refused to disclose its contents. He asked that his sages reveal to him both the dream and its interpretation. This aspect of the story intensified the contest between Daniel and the court sages. With the second dream, the element of competition between Daniel and the king's wise men is present, but is a minor part of the tale. The king readily divulges the contents of the dream. In this fourth tale, the interpretation of the dream is the major concern.

In his dream the king saw a massive tree that reached to heaven and provided shade, nesting, and food for all the animals of the earth. This tree is the mythological cosmic tree, located in the center of the earth. References to it can be found in myths of several ancient cultures. Ezekiel adapts the myth to describe the arrogance and downfall of Egypt (chap. 31). In this dream the tree represents the king.

The king's dream continues with the appearance of a *holy watcher* (v. 13), an angel. This term for a heavenly being is used extensively in certain pseudepigraphal works, such as *1 Enoch, Jubilees*, and the *Testaments of the Twelve Patriarchs*. The watcher orders the great tree to be cut down. The imagery undergoes a strange shift in v. 16. Instead of a tree, the fallen ruler is described as a human and his mind is now changed into the mind of an animal. This situation must last for *seven times* (v. 16), perhaps meaning seven years.

4:19-27. An interpretation. Daniel tells the king that the mighty tree represents Nebuchadnezzar and his great kingdom. As the tree in the vision was cut down, so the king shall lose his kingdom. He shall become like a wild animal, living in the open and eating grass for food. The affliction foretold by Daniel is a form of insanity known as zoanthropy in which a person believes he or she is an animal and acts accordingly. This ailment would befall Nebuchadnezzar because of his pride and arrogance. Once he has repented, he shall regain his kingdom. Daniel offers the king a way to avoid the disaster of his dream: he should act *with righteousness, . . . with mercy to the oppressed* (v. 27).

4:28-37. Advice ignored. Daniel's advice is ignored, however, and the judgment of the dream is fulfilled. The event that brings about the punishment is the king's boasting. Nebuchadnezzar fails to recognize that his reign and his accomplishments are transitory; true power and majesty belong to God. After the allotted time, Nebuchadnezzar comes to his senses, recognizes the sovereignty of God, and offers praises to God. The king then receives again his sanity and his kingdom from God. The purpose of this tale is to assert that the God of Israel is the sovereign of the universe, the one who *is able to bring low those who walk in pride* (v. 37).

This story is apparently an adaptation of a tradition about Nabonidus, the last king of Babylon. Ancient inscriptions report that Nabonidus left Babylon for ten years and stayed in the city of Tema. A fragmentary manuscript discovered at Qumran, known as the *Prayer of Nabonidus*, presents in first-person form Nabonidus's description of his seclusion at Tema for seven years. While there he is afflicted with an evil ulcer, from which he is finally delivered by a Jewish exorcist who is one of the exiles. After his healing, Nabonidus confesses that he had been guilty of idolatry. The similarities to the tale in Daniel are obvious. Both the Daniel tale and the *Prayer of Nabonidus* are likely variations on popular traditions about Nabonidus.

Belshazzar's Arrogance and Punishment, 5:1-31

5:1-12. Handwriting on the wall. In the fifth tale, Nebuchadnezzar is no longer the king. Instead, Belshazzar, said to be his son, is king. (The historical problem with this statement has already been mentioned above: see "Date and Occasion.") The setting is a great festival in which Belshazzar becomes intoxicated. In an act of arrogance and sacrilege, Belshazzar orders that the Temple vessels that had been brought from Jerusalem when the city was destroyed be brought to him. Belshazzar and his guests drink from the vessels and offer libations to their gods from them.

The sacrilege of Belshazzar leads to the famous scene in which Belshazzar literally "sees the handwriting on the wall." The fingers of a hand mysteriously appear and begin writing a message on the wall. Visibly shaken, Belshazzar calls for his court sages and offers a reward to anyone who can read the message on the wall or interpret it for the king. As in the earlier tales, the king's wise men are helpless.

The queen (v. 10) is apparently the queen mother, since she dares to approach the king uninvited, a practice that was forbidden to the king's wives. She informs Belshazzar that there is a person in the kingdom *endowed with a spirit of the holy gods* (v. 11) who can interpret the message for him.

5:13-31. Words of judgment. Belshazzar, who is unfamiliar with Daniel and his ability, offers Daniel a high reward (the third-highest position in the kingdom) if he can solve the riddle that has so terrified the king. Daniel boldly delivers a scathing denunciation of Belshazzar by comparing him to Nebuchadnezzar.

In a retelling of the events of chap. 4, Daniel describes how the mighty Nebuchadnezzar was brought low because of his arrogance and then regained his sanity and his kingdom because he came to realize that God is sovereign over the universe. Belshazzar, however, has not learned this lesson, even though he knew the experience of Nebuchadnezzar. Arrogance and idolatry, instead of humility and worship of God, characterize Belshazzar. Daniel's words are a ringing indictment: *You have praised the gods of silver and gold, of bronze, iron, wood, and stone, which do not see or hear or know; but the God in whose power is your very breath, and to whom belong all your ways, you have not honored* (v. 23).

Daniel then reads and interprets the Aramaic words written on the wall: *MENE, MENE, TEKEL, and PARSIN* (v. 25). The words are words of judgment against Belshazzar. The original meaning of these words is unclear. Most scholars agree the words are nouns, referring to weights or coins (the mina, the shekel, and the half-mina; the mina was equal to about sixty shekels). This saying was perhaps a popular wordplay describing certain kings or kingdoms and their relative worth.

Whatever the saying's original meaning, Daniel gives it a new interpretation built upon puns of the Aramaic words. The three words are treated as verbs meaning *numbered, weighed,* and *divided.* Applied to Belshazzar, the cryptic message foretells the impending loss of Belshazzar's kingdom to the Medes and Persians.

According to the tale, the prediction of Daniel comes true that very night when Belshazzar is killed and Darius the Mede takes over the neo-Babylonian empire. Although Cyrus of Persia was the actual conqueror of Babylon and history knows of no "Darius the Mede," the story in Daniel perhaps contains echoes of historical traditions. The Greek historians Herodotus (*Hist* 1.191) and Xenophon (*Cyr* 7.5) say that the capture of Babylon occurred while a feast was being held. Furthermore, Xenophon adds that the capture occurred at night. Also, Persia did later have a king named Darius—three, in fact.

Like the other tales in Daniel, this story of Belshazzar is a fictionalized account. But its status as fiction does not lessen the importance of its message. It is a graphic portrayal of the folly of human arrogance, pride, and insolence. God is ruler of the universe, not kings, or queens, or presidents, or generals. All worldly powers are ultimately subservient to the God who controls history. For Jews in the Diaspora, and especially for Jews suffering under Antiochus, that message would have been a powerful encouragement to faithfulness.

Daniel in the Lion's Den, 6:1-28

6:1-9. A familiar story. One of the best-known tales from the book, the story of Daniel in the lion's den, is set during the fictional reign of Darius the Mede, supposed successor to Belshazzar. The plot and intention of this story have much in common with the story of the three young men in the fiery furnace (chap. 3).

Daniel is given an important position in the Persian kingdom. He is appointed one of three presidents who oversee the 120 satrapies, or provinces, in the kingdom. (The later Darius I was responsible for organizing the Persian kingdom into satrapies. Ancient sources disagree concerning the number of these satrapies.) Each satrapy was administered for the king by an individual called a satrap. Daniel's abilities are recognized by the king who plans to appoint Daniel as chief over the other presidents and the satraps. Jealous of Daniel, they seek a way to thwart his success.

Daniel is such a righteous man and honorable servant of the king that his enemies must conspire to use his religious beliefs against him. The plotters convince the king to sign an irrevocable decree forbidding anyone to pray to any god or human for thirty days, except to the king. The men know that Daniel, the faithful Jew, will not be able to keep this new decree. The idea that a law of the Medes and the Persians could not be altered or revoked, while found also in Esther (1:19, 8:8), is poorly supported in other ancient sources.

6:10-18. Piety brings trouble. Because he is a pious individual, Daniel ignores the decree and continues his habit of privately praying *three times a day* (v. 10) to God. The practice of praying toward Jerusalem is mentioned already in 1 Kgs 8:44, 48. Daniel does not flaunt his faith nor does he court martyrdom. He simply perseveres quietly because he knows that the decrees of humanity do not negate the claims of God.

The story presents Darius as an unwilling participant in the scheme. He does not want to throw Daniel to the lions, but the irrevocable *law of the Medes and Persians* (v. 12) forces his hand. Darius is powerless to save Daniel, but he recognizes that Daniel's God may be able to deliver him. Accordingly, he offers a prayer on Daniel's behalf. Daniel is thrown to the lions, the den is sealed, and the king returns to his palace where he spends a sleepless night in worry over Daniel.

6:19-24. Saved from harm. At dawn the king rushes to the lions' den and cries out to Daniel, asking if his God had been able to save him. As was the case with Daniel's friends in the furnace, Daniel is unharmed. Because Daniel was blameless before God and the king and because he had trusted in God (vv. 22-23), God had sent an angel to close the mouths of the lions so they could not harm him. In retaliation for the unsuccessful plot against Daniel, the king orders that the men who had schemed against Daniel, along with their wives and children, be thrown to the lions. This gruesome justice (even vengeance) is in keeping with several passages in the Hebrew Bible (Deut 19:16-21; Num 16:25-33; Esth 7:10; 9:13-14).

6:25-28. Praise for the God of Israel. The last of the folk tales about Daniel ends on a jubilant note: a gentile king praises the God of Israel. Darius, like Nebuchadnezzar in chap. 3, issues a proclamation to all peoples in which he recognizes the sovereignty and power of this God who has miraculously delivered the faithful.

The six tales in Daniel served several purposes: (1) They were example stories, demonstrating how Jews in the Diaspora were to live. (2) They were calls to faithful endurance, urging the Jewish people not to give up on their faith. (3) They were also stories of encouragement, reminding the Jews that God and not Nebuchadnezzar or Belshazzar was in control of history. When read during the time of Antiochus Epiphanes, the stories continued to function in these ways, but with a greater intensity, for the situation had become more desperate for the Jewish people. (4) Finally, as a part of the larger work of Daniel, the tales also serve to set the narrative framework for the visions of Daniel, found in chaps. 7–12.

Visions of the Future, 7:1–12:13

The second half of Daniel is much different from the first half. The second half contains no court tales of contests, intrigues, or miraculous deliverances. As opposed to the first half in which Daniel is described in the third person, the second half is written as a first-person account from Daniel. Daniel is now not the interpreter of dreams, but the recipient. In place of human interpreters, Daniel's visions require angelic interpreters.

Daniel's three friends do not appear in the second half. Furthermore, a different worldview pervades the second half. Gentile rulers are no longer simply misguided, arrogant, or foolish; they do not regret their wrongful acts and offer praise to the God of Israel. Instead, gentile rulers are evil monsters, agents of chaos and destruction. The world has become a place of terror where justice and divine retribution no longer occur. The faithful are not encouraged to live exemplary lives in hopes that a beneficent gentile ruler will value and reward them. Hope lies in the future, when God will intervene to bring about the defeat of evil.

The Four Beasts from the Sea, 7:1-28

7:1-8. Vision at night. Daniel's first VISION occurs one night during the reign of Belshazzar. (These visions do not follow the tales in chronological order, but begin a new chronology that overlaps the former.) Daniel sees *four great beasts* arising from *the sea* (v. 2), an ancient mythological symbol for chaos, the untamed portion of creation that is opposed to the order and control of God. These beasts, like the various metals in the statue of chap. 2, represent four kings or kingdoms. In keeping with the vision in chap. 2, these four kingdoms would be the neo-Babylonian, the Median, the Persian, and the Greek. (The author's choice of *a lion* [v. 4], *a bear* [v. 5], *a leopard* [v. 6], and a *fourth beast . . . different from all the beasts that preceded it* [v. 7] may be based on Hos 13:7-8.) The *little* horn (v. 8) on the fourth beast is Antiochus Epiphanes, the persecutor of the Jews (175–164 B.C.E.), who attained his power by driving out several other claimants to the throne. The *mouth speaking arrogantly* (v. 8) is an appropriate description for one who issued decrees outlawing the practice of Judaism (cf. 1 Macc 1:54-61; 2 Macc 6:1-11). The *ten horns* (v. 7) that precede the little horn represent Hellenistic rulers, although scholars disagree concerning the identification of the ten.

To understand the beasts as referring to the four kingdoms is correct, but not adequate. These beasts are horrifying creatures, unlike any actual animal. Arising out of the primeval chaos, they are agents of evil. They represent a power that is larger than life. By using this imagery, the author is asserting that the struggle in which he and his readers are engaged is no mundane skirmish. They are involved in a cosmic struggle that is as old as creation itself—order versus chaos, God versus the forces of evil. Such an understanding elevates and gives new meaning to their sufferings and to the struggles in which they are involved.

7:9-14. The vision changes. The setting is now not the earth, but the heavenly throne room. Daniel sees God, *the Ancient One* (v. 13; Aramaic: "one like an ancient of days"), seated on a throne that is like a chariot with wheels of fire (cf. Ezek 1 and 10). The white clothing and white hair symbolize God's purity and glory. The white hair indicates also God's longevity. Flowing out from the chariot are streams of fire (cf. *1 Enoch* 14:19).

The scene is one of judgment, with God and the heavenly court in session. The heavenly books are opened and the judgment begins. Ancient Near Eastern traditions (including biblical traditions) refer to at least three types of heavenly books: those that contain all the deeds of each person by which people are judged, those that are a register of the heavenly inhabitants (the "book of life"), and those that contain the future course of world events. The first type seems to fit the present context.

The fourth beast, containing the arrogant little horn, is destroyed by fire. The other three beasts, whose evil does not equal that of the fourth, lose their power but have their lives prolonged for a brief period.

Daniel then sees the arrival of a new figure, *one like a human being* (v. 13), who comes with the clouds. The Aramaic phrase translates literally as "one like a SON OF MAN." God gives to this human-like figure everlasting and universal dominion. Who is this "son of man" figure? The answer to that question is one of the largest enigmas of the entire book. Some interpreters have seen him as the messiah. He does function as God's chosen and is granted sovereignty of this new kingdom, but he is never called God's anointed (messiah) and is not described as a Davidic ruler, the traditional messianic view. Is he an angel? His *coming with the clouds of heaven* seems to support that identification. Additional support for this identification comes from the later uses of *one . . . having the appearance of a man*, *man*, or *one in human form* (lit., "having the likeness of the sons of men") to describe angelic figures (see 8:15; 9:21; 10:16, 18). Since Michael is the angel who is described as the protector of Israel (12:1), the identification of this figure with Michael is most plausible.

This solution to the problem is only partially satisfactory, however. Later in this chapter the recipient of this new kingdom is not the son of man figure, but *the holy ones of the Most High* (vv. 18, 22) or *the people of the holy ones of the Most High* (v. 27). Who are these "holy ones" and what is their relationship with the son of man figure? In the Hebrew Bible "holy ones" is usually a designation for angels, but the term can also be applied to humans. In chap. 4 of Daniel, the *holy ones* (4:17) are certainly angels. That is probably their identification here as well.

In the present vision the connection between these holy ones and the faithful Jews who are persecuted under Antiochus is obvious (see v. 21). What is the key for understanding this confusing vision in which the human-like figure, the holy ones, and the faithful Jews seem to be identical, yet separate?

The worldview of Daniel presupposes that events in the heavenly world have their counterparts on earth. The struggle between Antiochus and the faithful is a cosmic struggle in which the angels are engaged also. This idea is more clearly present in chap. 10–12. John J. Collins cites a text from Qumran in which a similar idea is found. The passage from the WAR SCROLL says that God "will raise up the kingdom of Michael in the midst of the gods, and the realm of Israel in the midst of all flesh" (1QM 17:7-8; Collins 1984a, 84). When the text in Daniel states that Michael, the *one like a human being* (v. 13), the guardian angel of Israel, receives the kingdom it is saying that the faithful people of God receive the kingdom.

7:15-28. An interpretation. Puzzled and terrified by what he has seen, Daniel approaches one of the angels and asks for an interpretation of the vision. Verses 19-22 recount the major elements of the vision, after which the angel interprets the vision for Daniel. As in the vision, the focus of the interpretation is on the fourth kingdom, specifically the "little horn" of the fourth kingdom.

Verse 25 lists the atrocities of Antiochus: blasphemy, violence, and changing religious regulations and observances (cf. 2 Macc 6:1-11). Although Antiochus will be initially successful, his reign of terror will last only a short while, *for a time, two times, and half a time*, that is, three and a half years. (The duration of Antiochus' persecution was very close to this prediction, roughly 167–164 B.C.E. The statement, however, is likely only a figurative expression for a short period of time.) Then Antiochus will come under divine judgment and will be destroyed. God will then establish a new kingdom, an everlasting kingdom, which will be ruled by the faithful.

This vision offered hope to an oppressed people. To all appearances, Antiochus seemed in control of Israel's history. His persecution seemed endless. The vision asserts otherwise, however. It claims that Antiochus's day of reckoning will come, and soon. The faithful must endure a short while longer, but ultimately God will render judgment against Antiochus and all other tyrants. Then God's faithful will share in a new kingdom.

The Ram and the Male Goat, 8:1-27

8:1-14. Another vision. The second vision begins by locating Daniel in Susa, the winter residence of the Persian kings. Like Ezekiel when he received his first vision, Daniel is standing by a river when this vision appears to him. He sees a powerful ram with two horns who overpowers all the other beasts and has complete dominion. A challenger appears from the west in the form of a male goat with a single horn between its eyes. The male goat defeats the ram, but eventually its great horn is broken. In place of this horn, four prominent horns appear.

As the interpretation by the angel in the last half of the chapter makes clear, the ram with the two horns is a symbol for the Medo-Persian Empire. The male goat is the Greek kingdom begun by Alexander the Great, the great horn that is broken. At Alexander's death in 323 B.C.E. his kingdom was divided among his generals. The four prominent kingdoms that resulted from this breakup were Macedonia and Greece, Asia Minor, Syria and the Mesopotamian region, and Egypt. The ram and male goat were chosen to symbolize these powers because of their astrological associations in the ancient world. The ram was the zodiac sign (Aries) for Persia; the goat was the sign (Capricorn) for Syria, the kingdom over which the Seleucids (the family of Antiochus Epiphanes) would rule.

Verses 9-14 describe the emergence of Antiochus, the little horn. *The beautiful land* (v. 9) is a reference to Palestine, which had come under Seleucid control in 198 B.C.E., and against which Antiochus initiated stringent measures. His arrogance is so great that he reaches even to the heavens and casts down *some of the host and some of the stars* (v. 10) and tramples them.

The activity of Antiochus is not a minor, unimportant event. It is an assault on heaven itself. In the ancient world stars were often viewed as being supernatural beings. Antiochus's struggle is also seen as an attack on God. The act of Antiochus that is singled out in this passage is his desecration of the Jerusalem Temple, God's sanctuary. In December 167 Antiochus established inside the Temple an altar for the worship of Zeus Olympus. Sacrifices and offerings to the God of Israel ceased; in their place were offerings to Zeus. This event is the *transgression that makes desolate* that the angel of v. 13 asks about. In response to the question of how long this desecration will last, another angel replies that its duration will be 2,300 evenings and mornings (1,150 days), a figure similar to, though slightly less than, the three and a half years of 7:25.

8:15-27. An interpretation. As with the vision in chap. 7, Daniel does not understand this vision and asks for an interpretation. *A human voice* (v. 16, a heavenly being speaking human language) calls for the angel *Gabriel* to interpret the vision to Daniel. Daniel's bewilderment is understandable, for this vision concerns *the time of the end* (v. 17).

Through his interpretation, Gabriel assures Daniel that the arrogant little horn will be defeated, but *not by human hands* (v. 25). The Book of Daniel does not call for violent resistance to Antiochus. Such matters can be resolved only by divine intervention. The command to *seal up the vision* (v. 26) is a common motif in APOCALYPTIC LITERATURE. The message of the vision is not for Daniel's time, but for the future (the time of Antiochus). This technique serves to explain why this revelation, supposedly received during the time of Daniel in the sixth century, was not known until the second century. The message had been "sealed up" for the appropriate time.

The Seventy Weeks of Years, 9:1-27

9:1-19. Interpreting Jeremiah. Set in the fictitious reign of Darius the Mede, chap. 9 deals not with a vision (although the angel in 9:23 speaks of a *vision*) but with the interpretation (and novel application) of a biblical passage mediated to Daniel by an angel.

Daniel is perplexed by statements in Jeremiah (25:11, 12; 29:10) that the Jewish Exile will last seventy years. (In actuality, exiles began returning from Babylonia after about fifty years.) Having Daniel raise the issue of the seventy years is only a means of introducing the text from Jeremiah so it can be reapplied to the time of Antiochus.

Daniel prays to God, confessing the sins of the Jewish people and asking for mercy. The prayer reflects standard Deuteronomistic theology: Jerusalem deserves what has happened to it because of the sinfulness of the Jewish people. Daniel does not deny the people's guilt, but instead entreats God to show mercy on Jerusalem. This prayer is possibly a traditional prayer that the author of Daniel has incorporated here.

9:20-27. Angelic assistance. *Gabriel* (v. 21), the angel who appeared to Daniel in chap. 8, comes once again to provide an interpretation of the text to Daniel. The seventy years are in actuality seventy weeks of years, or 490 years. This application of the text from Jeremiah is probably inspired by the idea of the year of jubilee, described in Lev 25. The jubilee year followed a period of seven "weeks of years" (Lev 25:8), or forty-nine years. The emphasis of the jubilee year was "liberty throughout the land" (Lev 25:10). In the angel's periodization of history, the first seven weeks (forty-nine years) covers the period of the exile, ending with the coming of an anointed prince (either Zerubbabel or Joshua; cf. Zech 4:14). The exact referent of *the time when the word went out* (v. 25) is uncertain. Perhaps it applies to the time of Jeremiah's prophecies about the exile and restoration of the Jewish nation.

Following the first seven weeks is a period of sixty-two weeks of years that culminate in the destruction of Jerusalem and its Temple by *the prince*, obviously Antiochus. This begins the last week in the scheme. The anointed one who is cut off (v. 26) is a reference to the removal in 175 of Onias III as high priest or to his murder in 171 B.C.E. Neither Jerusalem nor the Temple was actually destroyed, but many *desolations* (v. 26) did occur, including the *abomination that desolates* (v. 27), the offering of sacrifices to Zeus in the Temple.

Nevertheless, as fearful as the reign of Antiochus is, it shall not last forever. The angel decrees that this despot shall rule only for one week (seven years). At that time, God will bring an end to "the desolator."

The author and the author's readers were living in the last half of the last week of history, according to the timetable presented here. The message of this chapter is that Antiochus's time is limited. Through this reapplication of Jeremiah's prediction, the author encourages all readers to endure in their faith. Antiochus's end is decreed. The time is set. They must remain faithful and wait.

The Last Days, 10:1–12:13

10:1–11:1. Conflict in heaven and on earth. This final section of the book is the longest. It is set in the reign of *Cyrus of Persia* (10:1), who supposedly follows Darius the Mede.

Daniel is mourning and fasting, perhaps in preparation for receiving a vision, since fasting is often associated with revelation. Daniel sees a figure, described in terms reminiscent of Ezekiel's description of God in his first vision (Ezek 1:26-28). Although not identified, this figure is probably Gabriel, who had appeared to Daniel in the two previous chapters.

Gabriel tells Daniel that God had heard his words when he first sought understanding (the beginning of the fast, three weeks prior; see 10:2). The angel had been deterred in coming to Daniel, however, due to conflict in heaven with the patron angel of Persia. He was able to come now only because the angel Michael had come to his assistance. Soon he must return and continue the struggle against the angel of Persia; he expects to be opposed also by the patron angel of Greece.

As seen already in chaps. 7 and 8, talk of heavenly conflict is a way of describing earthly conflict. When foreign nations fight against Israel, their gods (or, as here, patron angels) are understood as fighting against the LORD, the God of Israel. Chapter 11 describes in detail the earthly effects of this cosmic conflict, which are inscribed already in the heavenly *book of truth* (v. 21).

11:2-39. A review. This section is a thinly veiled review of history in the form of *ex eventu* prophecy. Anyone well-versed in the history of the Mediterranean world during the Hellenistic period can easily discern the historical referents. Verses 3-4 describe Alexander the Great and the breakup of his kingdom. The kings of the south described in the following verses are the Ptolemies. The kings of the north are the Seleucids. The major figures depicted in these verses are

Ptolemy I Lagi—*king of the south* (v. 5)
Seleucus I Nicator—*one of his officers* (v. 5)
Antiochus II Theos (a Seleucid) married to Bernice, daughter of Ptolemy II Philadelphus (v. 6)
Ptolemy III Euergetes—*a branch* (vv. 7-9)
Seleucus II Callinicus—*king of the north* (vv. 7-9)
Seleucus III Ceraunus—one of the sons (v. 10)
Antiochus III—one of the sons and *king of the north* (vv. 10-19)
Ptolemy IV Philopator—*king of the south* (vv. 11-12)
Ptolemy V Epiphanes—*king of the south* married to Cleopatra, daughter of Antiochus III (vv. 14-17)
Seleucus IV Philopator—the one who *shall arise* (v. 20)
Antiochus IV Epiphanes—the *contemptible person* (vv. 21-39)
Onias III, high priest—the *prince of the covenant* (v. 22)
Ptolemy VI—*king of the south* (vv. 25-27)
the Romans—*ships of Kittim* (v. 30)

The primary concern of this section is Antiochus Epiphanes, with whom the majority of the material deals. Verses 30-35 recount his campaign against Judaism, his desecration of the Jerusalem Temple, and his persecution of the faithful Jews.

The wise among the people (v. 33) is likely the group to which the author of Daniel belongs. The *little help* (v. 34) possibly refers to the Maccabees, who led an armed revolt against the forces of Antiochus. Although the Maccabees were ultimately successful, the author of Daniel (who is apparently writing prior to the success of the Maccabees) does not see them as the solution to the crisis. In the author's understanding, deliverance will come only by God's hands and at *the time appointed* (v. 35). Human efforts against Antiochus are futile, because *he shall prosper until the period of wrath is completed, for what is determined shall be done* (v. 36).

11:40-45. Events to come. The description of Antiochus shifts in v. 40 from a rather detailed, accurate review of history to erroneous predictions of events yet to occur. This shift is a clear indication that the author of Daniel actually wrote after the events of v. 39 but before the events of vv. 40-45. The events described in vv. 40-45 did not occur (another war with Ptolemy VI, the capture of Libya, Egypt, and Ethiopia by Antiochus, and the death of Antiochus along the coastal route during one of his military campaigns).

12:1-4. Close of the age. These verses bring to an end the revelation that began in chap. 10. They describe the consummation of the present age and the rewards and punishments that follow. After the death of Antiochus, Michael, the guardian prince of Israel, will bring the present age to an end. Although a time of great distress and trouble will precede the end, the faithful Jews, those whose names are inscribed in the heavenly book of life, will be delivered.

The author gives few details about the events of the end. He does introduce, however, an important idea into biblical eschatology: the concept of resurrection. Verse 2 is the only undisputed text in the Hebrew Bible that mentions individual resurrection. The resurrection envisioned by the author of this passage is apparently a limited resurrection. *Many . . . shall awake,* some for reward of everlasting life, some for punishment. Those who are resurrected for reward include *the wise,* who have led *many to righteousness* (v. 3) through their teachings and their examples. They will *shine like the stars forever and ever* (v. 3), apparently meaning they will join the hosts of angels.

For Daniel to divulge the message that he has received would be premature, because the revelation is intended for the end times. For this reason the angel tells Daniel to *keep the words secret and the book sealed* (v. 4; cf. 8:26).

12:5-13. How long? The final verses of the book are intended to answer the question, *How long shall it be until the end* (v. 6) will come? Two angelic figures appear at the river where Daniel and Gabriel are. One asks Gabriel (*the man clothed in linen* [v. 7]), *How long?* Gabriel's answer (three and a half years) is in agreement with the prediction in 7:25. Once more the importance of secrecy is urged upon Daniel. Verses 11 and 12, which give different answers, are problematic. They are possibly later additions to the text. After the three and a half years of 7:25 and 12:7 (as well as the 1,150 days of 8:14) had passed and the end had not yet arrived, a pious Jew added the prediction of 1,290 days. Shortly thereafter, an even later prediction of 1,335 days was added.

The Book of Daniel ends with a promise to Daniel that he will share in the resurrection that awaits God's faithful at the end of time. As the differing figures attest, the value of the visions in Daniel lies not in the accuracy of their timetables. Rather, their enduring message is that the God of Israel is the God of history. Ultimately the kingdom of God shall prevail over all earthly tyrants and political powers.

Works Cited

Collins, John J. 1984a. *The Apocalyptic Imagination.* 1984b. *Daniel, with an Introduction to Apocalyptic Literature.* FOTL.

Hosea [MCB 721-34]

Jeffrey S. Rogers

Introduction

Hosea is frequently designated "the prophet of love." Indeed, no book in the Bible depicts God's love for God's people more winsomely. But it is also the case that the language and imagery that this book uses to express God's relations with the people of God's affection are often as violent as they are tender, and as oppressive as they are profound.

The violence, especially that directed toward women and children, is patently offensive to anyone who is sensitive to the real physical, psychological, and social consequences of such acts. The threat of public humiliation and death for a wife and mother (Hos 2:3-10 [MT 2:5-12]), a prayer calling for miscarriage (9:14), and a proclamation that the divine will is to be fulfilled when *their little ones shall be dashed in pieces, and their pregnant women ripped open* (13:16) are hardly words one would expect from a "prophet of love."

The greatest challenge in interpreting this small book is to do justice to it without doing ourselves and others injustice, and vice versa. But its explicit violence and overt sexuality, its depiction of treachery in domestic politics and duplicity in foreign policy, and its experience with self-centered and self-serving religion contribute to making Hosea read as one of the most contemporary of all the books in the canon. It gives offense to many modern readers precisely because it is too much a mirror on our own present in addition to being a window on ancient Israel's history.

Historical Setting

The Book of Hosea can be assigned with confidence to roughly 750–725 B.C.E., in the Northern Kingdom of ISRAEL. Some portions of the book point to the stable, prosperous years at the close of the reign of JEROBOAM II (786–746 B.C.E.). For instance, Hos 10:1 speaks of a nation experiencing increased agricultural production (and religious building projects as a result), and 12:8 is familiar with the considerable commercial successes of this period.

Other passages reflect the stormy domestic and international developments that overtook the Northern Kingdom soon after Jeroboam II's death. Hosea 1:4 anticipates the demise of the dynasty of JEHU, and Hos 8:4 depicts the political machinations surrounding the assassinations of four Israelite kings between 746 B.C.E. and 732 B.C.E.

Several passages (e.g., 5:8-14; 7:8-17) reflect the turbulent years of the so-called Syro-Ephraimite conflict (736–732 B.C.E.) in which Israel and JUDAH became bitter enemies over the northern kingdom's anti-Assyrian political and military maneuvering. The end of Israel's existence is portrayed in 13:15-16 which portends the inevitable and brutal Assyrian onslaught. There are no passages in the book that depict the fall of SAMARIA in 722/1 B.C.E. as an accomplished fact.

A few brief portions of the book probably derive from a later period, as copyists in Judah attempted to ensure that the timely message of this thoroughly northern document would not be lost on southern audiences. However, it is a mistake to assume, as some commentators have, that an Israelite prophet who frequently criticized developments in Israel's relations with Assyria and Egypt would seldom or never have spoken of Judah in his oracles.

Religious Setting

This PROPHET is clearly engaged in a struggle for the heart of the nation. As typically portrayed, Hosea represents authentic, moral Israelite religion ("Yahwism") embattled against the expanding powers of foreign, immoral Canaanite religion ("Baalism"). This typical portrayal rests on several faulty assumptions.

First, "Israelite" and "Canaanite" are not mutually exclusive terms in the history of religion. Ancient Israelite religion is essentially "a subset of Canaanite religion" (Coogan, 1987, 115). Evidence of obvious similarities in texts and materials testify to "Israel's *continuity* with her religious world" (Miller 1985, 207–208; emphasis added). The typical portrayal misrepresents the complexity of the interrelation of "Israelite" and "Canaanite" religion.

Second, there was considerable diversity within ancient Israel's religion. The remarkable inscriptions from KUNTILLET 'AJRÛD that refer to "Yahweh and his Asherah" and to "Yahweh of Samaria" and "Yahweh of Tenan" are simply the most striking of many indications of the multiformity of Israelite religion. Even Hosea acknowledged that the "Baalism" that he condemned was ancestral among the Israelites, that is, it began with the ancestors prior to entry into the promised land (Hos 9:11; cf. Josh 24:14). The typical portrayal's assumption of a homogeneous religious "orthodoxy" in Israel is contrary to the biblical and archaeological evidence.

Third, despite the prevalent sexual imagery in Hosea, it is not at all certain that "sexual orgies" (Hos 4:18) were central and pervasive in Canaanite (and Israelite) religious practice. In particular, the assumption of widespread "cultic prostitution" has little direct evidence to support it. To take the sexual imagery of prophetic polemics as a reliable description of Canaanite religion is to mistake a caricature for a portrait. Thus, the typical portrayal of Canaanite religion as an immoral "fertility religion" is a misleading oversimplification of a rich and complex religious system.

The central issue in the Book of Hosea, then, is not a conflict between "Canaanite" and "Israelite" belief and practice, but a struggle between ancient and competing *Israelite* traditions of belief and practice within a larger Canaanite framework. Furthermore, the prevalent cultic and sexual allusions in this book are employed by the prophet in the service of a comprehensive indictment that addresses much wider domestic and international issues in which Israel's very existence is at stake.

Message

The Book of Hosea offers no reactionary "back-to-Moses" program. It is striking that although Hosea knows and uses traditions associated with exodus, wilderness, and Decalogue, Moses is referred to only once, and then as an anonymous *prophet* (Hos 12:3). Hosea champions a sophisticated and profound conservatism in addressing the ills of a nation torn by competing interests and conflicting ideologies.

Domestic affairs—political, social, and religious— are in disarray (4:2; 7:3-7; 10:3, 13; 12:8). Foreign policy is flighty and fickle (7:8-11; 8:8-10; 12:1). Clearly, the violent attempts at "final solutions" in the previous century—Jezebel's pogrom against prophets of Yahweh (1 Kings 18:13), Elijah's wholesale slaughter of prophets of Baal (1 Kgs 18:40), and Jehu's massacre of worshipers of BAAL (2 Kgs 10:18-28)—brought neither peace nor integrity to the Northern Kingdom.

The proclamation of Hosea presents a creative, indeed, an inspired alternative to narrow-minded and reactionary factionalism that inevitably hastens the demise of the very thing it tries desperately to preserve. Hosea puts forward a remarkable synthesis that preserves competing ancient traditions of belief and practice by charting a mediating course between thoroughgoing Baalism and rabidly exclusivistic Yahwism. He combines the Baalistic categories of divine marriage, dying and rising, and the revelatory capacity of nature with Yahwism's historic traditions and covenantal principles.

Hosea draws on these competing traditions to proclaim that the essential character and activity of God are not revealed in deterministic processes (in nature or history) or in tribalistic exclusivism but in God's passionate relationship with persons and the world such that God does not fail to judge obstinateness, faithlessness, and injustice and yet heals disloyalty, loves without constraint, and turns from anger. Furthermore, according to Hosea, this God expects the same character and activity from all who would say, "I do," to the divine invitation to relationship.

Perhaps the best way to hear the full range of the message of this remarkable little book is to begin reading the text (and commentary) at Hos 4:1. After becoming thoroughly familiar with chaps. 4–14, the reader can then appreciate the most famous part of the book, chaps. 1–3, for what it is: an overture that highlights (very) few themes and motifs in a major dramatic work.

For Further Study

In the *Mercer Dictionary of the Bible*: ADULTRY IN THE OT; BAAL; FAMILY; HARLOT; HOSEA; HOSEA, BOOK OF; ISRAEL; JEROBOAM II; MARRIAGE IN THE OT; NAMES; ORACLE; PROPHET.

In other sources: P. Bird, "'To Play the Harlot': An Inquiry into an OT Metaphor," in *Gender and Difference in Ancient Israel*, ed. P. L. Day, 75–94; J. Blenkinsopp, *A History of Prophecy in Israel*; F. M. Cross, *Canaanite Myth and Hebrew Epic*; P. D. Miller et al., eds., *Ancient Israelite Religion*; J. Rogers, "Women in the Hands of an Abusive God?" in *Interpreting Hosea for Preaching and Teaching*; C. L. Seow, "Hosea, Book of," *AncBD*; G. A. Yee, "Hosea," *TWBC*.

Commentary

An Outline

Editorial Superscription, 1:1
I. Overture: Yahweh's Wife—Israel, 1:2–3:5
  A. Hosea's Family as Signs, 1:2–2:1
    [MT 1:2–2:3]
  B. Yahweh's Marriage Dissolved
    and Restored, 2:2-23 [MT 2:4-25]
  C. Recapitulation, 3:1-5
II. Main Section: Impending Desolation, 4:1–9:17
  A. Indictment, 4:1–5:7

  B. First Alarm, 5:8–7:16
  C. Second Alarm, 8:1–9:17
III. Conclusion: Retrospect and Prospect,
    10:1–14:9 [MT 10:1–14:10]
  A. From Egypt to Exile and Back, 10:1–11:11
  B. Ephraim's Bitter Offense, 11:12–13:14
    [MT 12:1–13:14]
  C. Death and Rebirth of Israel, 13:1–14:9
    [MT 13:1–14:10]

Editorial Superscription, 1:1

The relation of this verse to the book as a whole is problematic because it gives priority to southern kings and makes no reference to northern kings after JEROBOAM II. In its present form, it is certainly a product of Judean editing.

Overture: Yahweh's Wife—Israel, 1:2–3:5

The metaphor of marriage and family, applied to the deity, is a conception typical of Canaanite religion: the deity (e.g., BAAL) has a consort (in Baal's case, Anat or sometimes Astarte or Asherah), and their relationship is essential to fertility, productivity and prosperity in the world.

According to the overture of the Book of Hosea, Yahweh also has a partner, indeed a wife, Israel; and the well-being of the world is dependent on their relationship (see, negatively, 2:3, 9, 12 and 4:2; positively, 2:18, 21-22). When Hosea presents Yahweh as the male partner in a marriage and then ascribes to the deity marital vows of a distinctively covenantal character (see 2:19-20), the prophet has produced a remarkable synthesis of Baalistic and Yahwistic traditions.

Hosea's Family as Signs, 1:2–2:1 [MT 1:2–2:3]

1:2-9. Signs of judgment. Four commands of Yahweh and the interpretation of each (vv. 2, 4, 6, 9) depict Hosea's spouse and three children as dramatic signs of God's dissatisfaction with God's people.

Hosea's marriage to Gomer, representing the relationship of Yahweh to Israel, has been the subject of considerable debate, as has the nature of Gomer's *whoredom* (v. 2), representing Israel's *forsaking the LORD*. Chapter 2 associates Gomer's promiscuity with misunderstanding agricultural produce as gifts of the Canaanite deity BAAL (2:5, 8, 12-3), but Hosea employs the imagery of promiscuity and adultery to express Israel's inconstancy in many different areas of the nation's life (e.g., domestic affairs, 7:3-4; foreign policy, 8:9). The image of the wayward wife never appears outside the overture.

The children's names symbolize Yahweh's intention toward Israel and Israel's condition in relation to Yahweh. The place-name *Jezreel* (v. 4) is employed to announce the end of the dynasty of JEHU (of which Jeroboam II's son ZECHARIAH was the last member) which began with a bloodbath when Jehu overthrew the dynasty of King Omri in the preceding century. A daughter named "Not-pitied" (v. 6, mrg.) and a son named "Not-my-people" (v. 9, mrg.) are signs of Israel's estrangement from God.

It is remarkable that Hosea would speak negatively of the radically anti-baalist Jehu (v. 4) whose purge of worshipers of Baal in 2 Kgs 12:18-28 was praised in 2 Kgs 12:30—unless, of course, radical anti-Baalism was not consistent with Hosea's vision of what was necessary for Israel to be healed of its inconstancy.

1:10–2:1. Signs of salvation. In this loosely connected section, the children's symbolic names are transposed into signs of salvation and are related to one of the great themes of Israel's salvation history: the repeated promises to the ancestors of innumerable progeny and the possession of the land (Gen 13:14-17; 17:4-8; 26:2-5; 28:13-14; 35:11-12). "Not-my-people" becomes innumerable *Children of the living God* (v. 10), *My-people* again (2:1). *Jezreel* becomes a sign of the political reunification of Israel and Judah and their possession of the land (v. 11). "Not-pitied" is once again "Pitied" (2:1). Judgment has not been avoided; but as is the case throughout this book, judgment is not God's final word or act.

Yahweh's Marriage Dissolved and Restored 2:2-23

2:2-5 Dissolution. On grounds of infidelity, God's relationship with Israel is effectively dissolved in v. 2: *she is not my wife, and I am not her husband.* This statement is an obvious play on the reversal of the formula, "I will take you as my people, and I will be your God" (Exod 6:7), which appears in Hos 1:9: *you are not my people and I am not your God.* The children are also rejected, on account of their mother's infidelity (v. 5). The spouse is threatened with public humiliation (2:10) and death (v. 3) for seeking sustenance from other providers (*lovers*, v. 5).

The imagery of domination and degradation of a woman in this chapter—and the next—is neither redemptive nor prophetic in the modern world, and the portrayal of God as a husband who metes out physical punishment (even to death) on a wife is among numerous offensive images for the deity contained in this book (e.g., God is like *maggots* and *rottenness*, 5:12; a slayer of children, 9:12, 16; a *wild animal* ripping open, devouring, and mangling, 13:8). The prophet's attention-getting image of God as a cuckolded and enraged male is no more constitutive of the divine nature than is the imagery of maggots, rottenness, and so on.

2:6-13 Punishment. The punishment threatened in 2:3 is detailed in vv. 6-13. Confinement and futility (vv. 6-7), agricultural failure (vv. 9, 12), exposure (vv. 9-10; see Sanderson 1992, 219–20), the removal of *mirth* (v. 11), and devouring animals (v. 12) are the deity's response to Israel's waywardness. This catalogue of punishments has striking parallels among traditional maledictions and treaty curses (see Deut 28; Lev 26; Hillers 1964). Although this passage focuses on Baalism as Israel's failure, similar indictments for misplaced trust recur in political and economic contexts (5:13; 10:13-14; 12:8-9), as does the sequence of debasement and death (5:9, 11-12; 7:11-13; 13:15-16).

2:14-23 Restoration. The tone of the chapter changes dramatically in v. 14. The language is quite suggestive, as the Hebrew verb translated *allure* appears also in Exod 22:16: "When a man *seduces* a virgin who is not engaged to be married, and lies with her" (emphasis added). Seductive, tender speech (v. 14) will result in willing responsiveness on Israel's part (v. 15). As in chap. 1, reconciliation follows judgment (see Rogers 1993).

The courtship of vv. 14-15 ends in v. 16, where the relationship previously dissolved is reconstituted by Yahweh whom Israel will call "my marriage partner" (*My husband*) instead of "my master" (*My Baal*). Although Yahweh rejects being called *Baal*, the Baalistic marital imagery remains intact. In the verses that follow, the Yahwistic category of *covenant* (v. 18) defines the marriage relationship.

Yahweh's threefold commitment to Israel, *I will take you as my wife* (vv. 19-20), evokes a legal conclusion of a marriage contract (Mays 1969, 50) in obvious contrast to the beginning of the chapter (2:2). The substance of Yahweh's commitment is portrayed in terminology associated with covenant: *righteousness, justice, steadfast love, mercy*, and *faithfulness*. Remarkably, Yahweh promises to Israel precisely what Israel had failed to deliver to Yahweh.

A double entendre closes this section in v. 20: *and you shall know the LORD.* The metaphorical progression is obvious: courtship (vv. 14-15), betrothal (vv. 19-20), and consummation (v. 20; on *know* in the OT as a euphemism for sexual intercourse, see TDOT 5:464). "Knowing the LORD" expresses above all comprehensive fidelity to covenantal principles and behaviors, but both senses of the double entendre are central to the prophet's message.

The essence of fidelity to the covenant is an intimate and passionate relationship with the God who invites, even seduces, people into willing and faithful partnership.

The children are also restored to their former status, as is clear in the transformation of their names from signs of alienation to signs of renewed relation (vv. 21-23).

Recapitulation 3:1-5

Considerable effort has been expended on attempts to explain the relation of these verses to chap. 1, but the closer thematic connection is to chap. 2 (Wolff 1974, 59). Hosea (representing God) pursues a promiscuous spouse (representing the people, v. 1) who will experience deprivation but will eventually return (vv. 3-5).

The statement in v. 1, *the LORD loves the people of Israel, though they turn to other gods*, is sometimes taken as the thematic center of the entire book. However, the rhetorical discontinuity in this verse is that the LORD *loves the people*, but *the people love raisin cakes*. These baked goods are associated elsewhere with pagan worship (Isa 16:7; Jer 7:18), but David distributed the same delicacy as part of the celebration of the arrival of the ark of Yahweh in Jerusalem (2 Sam 6:19). The cakes themselves were not a problem. But the misplaced love for them instead of for Yahweh and the turning to other gods are both symptomatic of a common religious disorder: an obsession with the external and material benefits of religion rather than devotion to the relationships, principles, and behaviors that are its source and substance.

Main Section: Impending Desolation, 4:1–9:17

Indictment, 4:1–5:7

In 4:1–5:7 a number of smaller units are organized into a scathing indictment of all *the inhabitants of the land* (4:1): people (4:1, 6, 8-9, 12, 14), priest (4:4, 9; 5:1), prophet (4:5), and ruling officials and royal court (5:1). The section is framed by a primary and comprehensive failing: there is *no knowledge of God in the land* (4:1); *they do not know the LORD* (5:4).

The indictment closes with the announcement of the withdrawal of the divine presence (5:6), a catastrophic development, in light of Moses' response to Yahweh at Sinai:

> If your presence will not go, do not carry us up from here. For how shall
> it be known that I have found favor in your sight, I and your people, unless
> you go with us? In this way, we shall be distinct, I and your people, from
> every people on the face of the earth.   (Exod 33:15-16)

It is Yahweh's presence that constitutes Israel's well-being and identity as a people, but now *he has withdrawn from them* (5:6).

4:1-3. Yahweh's case against Israel. The opening salvo in this segment is a typical prophetic call to the *people* to *Hear the word of the LORD* (v. 1a; cf. Amos 7:16; Isa 1:10; Jer 2:4). This form of speech identifies the prophet as a spokesperson (or "messenger") of Yahweh, and it introduces not only this section but the entire collection at least through the end of the climactic chap. 9 (see commentary on 9:10-17). The proceedings are reminiscent of a courtroom scene with an indictment (v. 1b), an accusation (v. 2), and a sentence (v. 3).

The accusation includes nine elements. The first three, *no faithfulness or loyalty, and no knowledge of God* (v. 1), constitute a comprehensive complaint against Israel for failing to live all aspects of its life according to covenantal principles and behaviors. As the remainder of the book makes abundantly clear, there can be no authentic relationship with Yahweh that is not also a relationship with neighbor, at home and abroad.

But Israel's foreign policy plays one potential ally off against another: *they call to Egypt* at the same time that they *go to Assyria* (7:11; see 12:1); *they bargain with the nations* (8:10). Above all, *falsehood and violence* characterize their international affairs (12:1). On the domestic front, they make contracts they do not fulfill, *so litigation springs up like poisonous weeds* (10:4). Unscrupulous business practices (e.g., the use of *false balances*) are exacerbated by self-righteous exoneration (12:7-8). Governmental officials delight in *wickedness* and *treachery* (7:3). According to the first three elements of the accusation, Israel has no integrity in any of its dealings.

The next five elements (v. 2a) correspond to specific prohibitions in the Decalogue, which is presented in Exod 20:1-17 (and Deut 5:6-21) as the stipulations of a covenant with Yahweh. The five cited here all address acts involving interpersonal relationships. *Swearing* is a violation of the injunction against "wrongful use of the name of the LORD your God" (Exod 20:7) in treaties, contracts, oaths, etc. (cf. Hos 10:4). *Lying* violates the prohibition against false statements against one's neighbor (Exod 20:16; cf. Hos 10:13; 11:12).

The ninth and final element is best paraphrased, "capital crimes abound." *Bloodshed* here is employed in the sense of "bloodguilt" (Wolff 1974, 18; see NRSV's *crimes* in 12:15 and "bloodguilt" in Exod 22:1 for the same Heb. word).

According to v. 3, the consequences of Israel's violation of the terms of its relationship with Yahweh are catastrophic, not only for Israel but also for the entire created order. In the Book of Hosea, then, right relationship with God is not principally a private and personal religious affair; it is inevitably a matter of the greatest social, political, economic, and even ecological consequence.

4:4–5:2. Failure of Israel's leadership. The shortcomings of the people are cited (4:6, 8, 12, 14), but ultimately it is Israel's leaders who are responsible for the people's well-being. *Priest* (4:4; 5:1), *prophet* (4:5), ruling officials (*house of Israel*, 5:1; see Micah 3:1, 9), and royal court (*house of the king*, 5:1) are designated as responsible parties in Israel's failure. They have been to the people *a snare, a net,* and *a pit dug deep* (5:1-2) and will by no means escape judgment. The operant principle is illustrated in 4:13b-14: God will not punish dependents in the family (*daughters* and *daughters-in-law*) while the heads of the family (*the men*) are themselves irresponsible.

Cultic language abounds, including references to sacrifices (4:8, 13, 14, 19), divination (4:12), incense (NRSV, *offerings*, 4:13), cultic centers (*tops of the mountains*, *hills*, and woodland shrines, 4:13; *Gilgal* and Bethel—derogatorily referred to as "house of wickedness" instead of "house of God", 4:15; *Mizpah* and *Tabor*, 5:1), and *idols* (4:17). Sexual language is pervasive (promiscuity, 4:10-15; *adultery*, 4:13-14; prostitution, 4:14; *sexual orgies* and *lewdness*, 4:18). Whatever literal basis the latter language may have, it is above all a polemical metaphor in Hosea. The former—that is, the corruption of worship—is but one example of the failure of people and leadership alike.

5:3-7. Withdrawal of divine presence. The indictment closes with a recapitulation of motifs and themes appearing previously in this section (lack of knowledge, promiscuity, stumbling, sacrifices and divination, children). The climax of the section arrives in v. 6 with the announcement of the withdrawal of Yahweh's presence from Israel: *they will not find him; he has withdrawn from them*. It is set up by the antitheses of Yahweh's knowing Israel (v. 3) but Israel's not knowing Yahweh (v. 4) and Israel's way not being hidden from Yahweh (v. 3) but Yahweh's being hidden from Israel (v. 6). Just as Israel has *forsaken* Yahweh (4:10, 12), Yahweh has now forsaken Israel.

First Alarm, 5:8–7:16

Beginning with an alarm (5:8) on account of the impending desolation of Ephraim (5:9, 11), this section is framed by depictions of Yahweh as the bringer of destruction and death (5:12-14; 7:12-14) and by Ephraim's ineffectual cries for help (5:15–6:6; 7:14). At the center is an accusatory litany on the *corruption of Ephraim* (7:1), especially its leadership (*priests*, 6:9; *king*, 7:3; and *officials*, 7:3, 5, 16). Both domestic (6:7–7:7) and foreign affairs (5:13; 7:8-11, 16) are featured as areas in which Ephraim has failed to exhibit the covenantal behaviors of *steadfast love* ("unfailing loyalty to one's commitments" or "faithfulness in action," Sakenfeld 1985) and *knowledge of God* (6:6; see commentary on 2:20). This section is a pointed illustration of both the rationale for and the consequences of Yahweh's withdrawal from Israel, which was the climax of the preceding section.

5:8-15. Desolation and death. After the alarm (v. 8) and declaration of Ephraim's desolation (vv. 9-11), Yahweh is portrayed in deathly imagery (*like maggots* and *rottenness* in a *wound*, vv. 12-13; *like a lion* that tears its prey and carries it off, v. 14). Israel's demise is imminent and inevitable.

In contrast to the previous section, which featured cultic affairs as the arena of Ephraim's inconstancy, this one focuses on politics. Ephraim has sought healing and a cure for its problems by turning to *Assyria* and appealing *to the great king* (v. 13), a common title for the monarch in Assyrian documents. Verse 15 closes this part of the larger section by reaffirming Yahweh's withdrawal from Israel; but it also indicates that Yahweh's absence will last only *until they acknowledge their guilt and seek my face.*

6:1-3. Plea to be raised up. Introduced at the end of 5:15 (*they will beg my favor*), the impassioned prayer of vv. 1-3 begins with Israel's summons to itself to *return to the LORD* (v. 1). To return implies turning away from sin and turning to Yahweh, in other words, authentic repentance. The prayer acknowledges that what the people have suffered is the judgment of Yahweh (*it is he who has torn; he has struck down*), and it expresses confidence in Yahweh's mercy and grace after wrath (*he will heal us; he will bind us up*).

The second verse of the prayer confesses that Yahweh will give us life (NRSV, *revive us*) and *raise us up* so that *we may live* in his presence (NRSV, *before him*). Israel trusts that its return to Yahweh will result in a return of Yahweh to Israel. Because Israel has turned to *know the LORD* (v. 3) and thereby rectified its principal shortcoming according to the indictment of 4:1-5:7, Yahweh will surely once again "appear" among Israel: *he will come to us.*

The imagery of v. 3 (*as sure as the dawn; like the spring rains*) is both beautiful and essentially Baalistic. The sequence of death (5:12-15) followed by new life (v. 2) associated with the spring rains and the reappearance of the deity is a decidedly Baalistic complex.

6:4-6. Yahweh's response. The prayer of 6:1-3 is ineffectual. Yahweh's immediate response in vv. 4-6 is even more impassioned than the plea: *What shall I do with you . . . ? What shall I do with you . . . ?* Your love is like a morning cloud, like the dew that goes early away. The people want Yahweh to be as the life-giving spring rains to them, but they are to Yahweh as a cloud in the morning that promises rain but does not deliver. They are as dew that dries up.

There is no indication that the prayer is rejected because it is couched in Baalistic categories (dying, rising, reappearing, and raining). In fact, the response takes up the rain imagery and employs it with reference to the people. The crux of the response is that the people's professed repentance is just one more example of their inconstancy. According to Yahweh's response, a statement of repentance is not necessarily any more indicative of *steadfast love* and *knowledge of God* than *sacrifice, burnt offerings* (v. 6).

What, then, can Israel do to satisfy Yahweh's demand for *steadfast love* and *knowledge of God*? A direct and explicit answer to that question is given in a later dying and rising sequence in chaps. 13–14. For now, the focus remains on documenting the *corruption of Ephraim* (7:1).

6:7–7:10. The corruption of Ephraim. Three independent units catalogue Ephraim's failures. The first (6:7-10) concerns domestic affairs. The focus is on cultic (or at least priestly) abuses. The second (6:11–7:7) also addresses the domestic scene, though the focus shifts from priests to *the king* (7:3, 5, 7) and *officials* (7:3, 5) who revel in the *wickedness* and *treachery* that surround them (7:3).

Of particular interest is the assertion that Yahweh would, in fact, turn to *restore the fortunes* of the people and to *heal Israel* (6:11b; 7:1; cf. 5:13), but the *corruption of Ephraim* and the *wicked deeds of Samaria* are too great.

The third and shortest unit (7:8-10) takes up the issue of international relations, which are featured in the next segment. The final verse of the unit reaffirms the negative assessment of Israel's plea in 6:1-3: *they do not return to the LORD their God, or seek him, for all of this* (7:10).

7:11-16. Destruction to them. In keeping with the opening segment of this section (5:8-15), destruction and death are the result of Ephraim's failures, both political (vv. 11, 16) and cultic (v. 14).

Because of their flightiness in international affairs, Yahweh will cast a net over them and *bring them down like birds*. The dramatic center of this segment is v. 13 in which appears the first of only two woe-oracles in the book. *Destruction* is decreed (cf. 5:9). In keeping with 6:11-7:1, Yahweh *would redeem them*, but their duplicity alienates them from their only real source of salvation (v. 13).

The cries and ritual acts of repentance that Yahweh sees (e.g., 6:1-3) are motivated by material concerns (*for grain and wine*, v. 14). Despite the deity's past acts of nurture and provision, *they plot evil* against Yahweh (v. 15). The blow of judgment specified at the end falls principally on the leadership whose duplicity has no doubt come to light in Egypt or Assyria (see v. 11): *their officials shall fall by the sword* (v. 16). This limited blow stands in stark contrast to the conclusion of the next section.

Second Alarm, 8:1–9:17

As did the last section, this one begins with an alarm and Israel's ineffectual cry to God (8:1-2) and ends with destruction and death (9:10-17). The parts of this section are intricately related (e.g., *my God* at the beginning in 8:2; at the end in 9:17; and in the climactic unit in 9:8). Political and cultic sins (8:4-14) are followed by their respective consequences (9:1-4), all of which pales by comparison with the rejection of the prophet(9:5-9) and the corresponding rejection of Ephraim(9:10-17).

8:1-14. Political and cultic sins. The initial alarm and cry (v. 2b) in the first unit are fragmentary and desperate (contrast 5:8 and 6:1-3). The truncated alarm does not even include a verb: "to your lips a trumpet!" The abrupt plea, *My God, we—Israel—know you!* (v. 2) contributes to a picture of Israel in full retreat before its enemies (v. 3b). The expression *house of the LORD* frames the first two segments of the larger section (v. 1; 9:15) and appears only here in the book. It refers to *the land of the LORD* (9:3) rather than to a temple (see Wolff 1974, 137).

According to the next unit (vv. 4-6) Israel's politics (v. 4a) and worship (vv. 4b-6) are both anathema to Yahweh. The reference to *kings* and *princes* set up without Yahweh's approval (v. 4) asserts Yahweh's right to sovereignty over political affairs.

The *calf of Samaria* (v. 6), is problematic, since the official temple of Baal in SAMARIA (built by AHAB, 1 Kgs 16:32) was destroyed by JEHU in the previous century and furthermore did not contain such an image, according to the evidence of 2 Kgs 10:26-27. According to Hos 10:5, the calf before which the people of Samaria worshiped was at BETHEL (Wolff 1974, 140). Bethel was a "royal sanctuary" (Amos 7:13), one of two containing bull images set up by JEROBOAM I as a northern alternative to the Temple in Jerusalem (1 Kgs 12:26-29).

Calf imagery had an ancient and storied (and not always negative) past in Israelite religion (see CALF, GOLDEN). The calves themselves were not worshiped as a deity (despite the polemical intimations of Hos 10:5 and 13:2). Rather, they served the same purpose as the ARK of Yahweh and the winged cherubim of the Jerusalem Temple, which were pedestals above which the invisible presence of God was enthroned and thus were pre-eminent symbols of the divine presence. The rejection of the calf symbolizes the rejection of Bethel and its cult as a sacred site that mediated the presence of Yahweh to the people (cf. Hos 4:15; 10:5, 15).

The focus in the third unit (vv. 7-10) is international affairs. Imagery drawn from nature and agriculture (v. 7) makes clear that Israel's duplicitous foreign policy will result in futility. Rather than being Yahweh's "treasured possession out of all the peoples" (Exod 19:5; cf. Deut 7:6), Israel is *among the nations as a useless vessel* (v. 8). The image of alien *lovers* with whom Ephraim *has bargained* expresses the nation's political inconstancy. The appeal to ASSYRIA (v. 9) will result in the *burden* of foreign domination (v. 10).

The fourth unit (vv. 11-14) highlights the cult once again. The accusation here might or might not involve worshiping other gods. Either way, the prophet sees the problem as a cultic innovation departing from the *instructions* (or "laws") that Yahweh provided (v. 12). Expanding sacrificial activity would have resulted in considerable economic benefit, especially for priests and for those who had the resources to make many *choice sacrifices*, since priest and worshiper shared the *flesh*. Again, the prophet attacks an appetite for material benefits of religious activity rather than a genuine devotion to God (cf. the love for *raisin cakes* in 3:1).

A related failing is in view at the close of this unit (v. 14) where Israel and Judah are condemned for having *forgotten* their *Maker* when they attempt to provide for themselves luxury (*palaces*) and security (*fortified cities*).

9:1-4. Political and cultic consequences. An introduction (v. 1) addresses Israel in the second-person singular with a prohibition of celebration (v. 1a) followed by a blanket accusation (v. 1b) in the language of promiscuity typical of Hosea. The *threshing floors* are a logical location of Israel's "prostitution," since these open, public places served as sites for cultic activity (e.g., 2 Sam 24:18-25) and even for international coalitioning (1 Kgs 22:10), among other activities.

With a shift to third-person plural and the theme of futility the focus moves to political and economic consequences of Israel's sin. Loss of the produce of the land (v. 2) escalates into loss of the land itself in v. 3 (Yahweh's land, not Israel's; cf.

house of the LORD, 8:1 and 9:4). The political catastrophe is also a religious disaster, since expulsion from the house of the LORD means alienation from Yahweh's presence and the reversal of the first element in God's great salvation-history promise to Israel's ancestors (see commentary on 1:10-11).

The *unclean food* (v. 3) of exile results in the complete collapse of the cult (v. 4a). The people's alienation from Yahweh is now complete, not only because eating unclean food makes people defiled (v. 4) before Yahweh but also because their drink offerings and sacrifices (v. 4) were always to be taken from the very best stock that the people had for themselves. Reduced to eating unclean food, they have nothing to offer which can please Yahweh.

9:5-9. Rejection of the prophetic word. Alternating between second- and third-person discourse, these rather unassuming verses are not only the catalyst for the vituperative close of this section (9:10-17); they are also the dramatic climax of the book.

This segment opens with a bitterly ironic question: *What will you do?* One would expect the *day of the appointed festival, the day of the festival of the LORD* (v. 5), to be a day of celebration of God's gracious acts on Israel's behalf.

A joyful autumnal harvest festival was probably the setting for the original proclamation (see Wolff 1974, 153), a context that would significantly heighten the offense to the audience that such words as these would give. Israel has nothing for which to rejoice (9:1), because the *days of punishment* and *recompense have come* (v. 7). The futility motif returns in v. 6 with an intensification of the reversal of the promise of the land: even those who *escape destruction* will die in *Egypt*.

Then, for the first time in the book we hear clearly and in the audience's own words how the proclamation of Hosea was received: he was condemned as *a fool* and *mad* (v. 7). The aphoristic reply—great sin makes for great animosity—reflects the people's anger back on themselves, but the ominous import of the next two verses cannot be underestimated. The prophet has been true to his task as a *sentinel* who keeps watch and announces the approach of good and bad alike (thus the alarms of 5:8; 8:1). But his service has been met with threats to his person (*a fowler's snare is on all his ways*) and open *hostility* to his message (v. 8).

The invocation of GIBEAH associated with "profound corruption" recalls the brutal and horrifying events of Judg 19–20, about which it was said, "Such a thing has not happened or been seen since the day that the Israelites came up from the land of Egypt until this day" (Judg 19:30). By its explicit rejection of the prophetic proclamation, Hosea's audience has irredeemably compounded its guilt.

The climax of the book is here, because the Israel whom Hosea addressed has not only disregarded Yahweh's instructions or law (8:1, 12; cf. 4:6), but it has also now rejected the corrective and *redemptive word of the LORD* (4:1) that Yahweh has put "in the mouth of the prophet" (Deut 18:18). Of the one "who does not heed the words that the prophet shall speak in my name," says Yahweh, "I myself will hold accountable" (Deut 18:19). Indeed, *he will remember their iniquity, he will punish their sins* (v. 9). It is one thing to err in one's ways; it is another thing entirely to reject with open hostility the salvation available through correction. Israel has now done both.

9:10-17. Rejection of Ephraim. And so the Book of Hosea reaches its thematic nadir in a brutal and horrifying segment of its own. Now added to the loss of the land and the cult (9:3-4) is the loss of fertility and the slaughter of children, marking the reversal of the second element in the great promise to the ancestors (see commentary on 1:10-11). Associated with the loss of fertility is the loss of divine presence (vv. 11-12; see commentary on 5:6).

The first of two units (vv. 10-14) opens with a brief historical precis (v. 10). Until the reference to *the days of Gibeah* in the preceding unit (9:9), Hos 4–11 focused exclusively on "current events"—present shortcomings of the people and their leaders. In v. 10, however, the book begins to take up a retrospective approach in which present ills and judgments are intertwined with failures of the past. With the loss of promise assured, Israel's salvation-history begins to "pass before its eyes" as a history of ignominy.

Despite the potential for good fruit that Yahweh saw in them (v. 10a), the people became *detestable* even before they entered the land of promise (v. 10b; see Num 25:1-18). Recollection of past failure is juxtaposed with present judgment (vv. 11-14) highlighting the loss of fertility (v. 11b) and the utter futility of it should it occur (vv. 12a, 13b, 16b).

The association of the loss of fecundity and fertility with the absence of the deity (the departure of *glory* in v. 11a; cf. the departure of the presence of Yahweh in 1 Sam 4:21-22; Ezek 10:18-19; 11:22-23) is a typically Canaanite motif. Here, the flight of *Ephraim's glory* refers with bitter irony to the loss of divine presence when the preeminent symbol of it at Bethel, the golden calf, is removed by the Assyrians (cf. 10:5-6; see commentary on 8:6).

The second of the two woe-oracles in the book plays on Israel's misconception by pointing out the departure that really will be devastating: *Woe to them indeed when I depart from them!* (v. 12). The two woes are a matching pair that reflect the character of the respective sections of the book in which they occur. The first pronounces woe for Israel's departure from Yahweh (7:13), and the second pronounces woe for Yahweh's departure from Israel.

The vicious prayer of the prophet at the end of this unit, with its repeated *give them!* (v. 14) requesting miscarriage and *dry breasts* in Israel, is indicative of Hosea's personal and emotional response to the opposition and threats of his audience evident in 9:7-8 (cf. Jer 11:20b; 12:3b; 15:15a; 17:18; 18:21-23; 20:12b).

The second unit (vv. 15-17) begins with an extremely brief reference to GILGAL (v. 15; the Heb. text says only "all their evil at Gilgal"). The sequence Peor-Gilgal in vv. 10, 15 can hardly be accidental. The apostasy at Peor occurred "While Israel was staying at Shittim" (Num 25:1), the last camp in the trans-Jordan. Gilgal was Israel's first camp in the promised land (Josh 5:19). Hosea 9:15 is probably best understood when translated: "All their evil was (i.e., remained with them) at Gilgal; even there I hated them." Exile from the land—being driven *out of my house* (v. 15; see commentary on 8:1)—is thus artfully juxtaposed with the traditions of the entry into it. According to Hosea, Israel did not begin with a "clean slate" in the promised land. They *became detestable* at Peor (v. 9) and have only become more so ever since.

The recapitulation of the reversal of the promises of progeny (v. 16) and land (v. 17) lends an ultimate finality to the close of the unit and the larger section. In fact, there is an even more comprehensive closure here that reinforces the climactic rejection of Hosea's proclamation (9:5-9). The prophetic summons with which the indictment began, *Hear (šimĕ'û) the word of the LORD, O people of Israel* (4:1), was in the end ineffectual: *they have not listened* (v. 17, *lō'šāmĕ û*). Those who were addressed as *the inhabitants of the land* (4:1) now *shall become wanderers among the nations* (v. 17).

Conclusion: Retrospect and Prospect, 10:1–14:9 [MT 10:1–14:10]

From Egypt to Exile and Back, 10:1–11:11

After the dramatic climax of the book in the preceding section, the denouement begins in this section with a brief sketch of Israel's past and present that portrays the coming judgment as a necessary and inevitable response to a people who *are bent on turning away* (11:7).

But because of the passionate nature of Yahweh's character and of Yahweh's love for Israel, wrath and judgment are not Israel's only prospect. After a remarkable soliloquy revealing the depth and power of the emotional struggle within the deity's own self (11:8-9), for the first time in chaps. 4–14 comes the clear indication that destruction is not God's only intention for Israel (11:10-11).

10:1-15. End of cult and king. The loss of the land entails the loss the two principal institutions that connected the people to Yahweh in monarchical Israel: the cult and the king. The first unit (vv. 1-8) begins by reflecting on the destruction of the most prominent features of Israel's religious building programs (*altars* and sacred *pillars*, vv. 1-2). Those who contributed to them no doubt considered these expansion programs to be grand expressions of their devotion to God, but Yahweh saw them as one more indication of self-centeredness and sinfulness (v. 2; cf. 4:7-9; 8:11).

The absence of a king does not appear particularly disconcerting to the people (v. 3; a human king or the "divine king"—Yahweh—may be in view here), but they will *mourn* when the *calf* from the sanctuary at Bethel (v. 5, *Beth-aven*; see commentary on 4:15) is *carried to Assyria* as part of the spoils of the conquest of Israel (vv. 5-6).

The unit closes with the people bereft of king and cult (vv. 7-8) and crying out for their own destruction as the only relief available to them (v. 8).

The second unit (vv. 9-15) is less reflective and more accusatory. It begins by invoking the sin of Gibeah (see commentary on 9:9) which resulted in a devastating internecine war with eleven tribes of Israel aligned against Benjamin to punish it. This time, however, it is Yahweh who *will come against the wayward people to punish them* (v. 10). The instrument of Yahweh's wrath will be *nations . . . gathered against them*. The middle verses in this unit employ similar agricultural imagery to make three very different points. In v. 11 the coming change in Ephraim's life is expressed as the difference between the relatively easy existence of a *heifer that loved to thresh* (Wolff 1974, 185 points to the frisking heifer of Jer 50:11 and the provision for feeding in Deut 25:4) and the laborious work to *break the ground*.

In v. 12 the admonitions to *sow . . . righteousness* and *reap steadfast love* are attached to an exhortation to *seek the LORD*, the first time in the Book of Hosea that such an explicit call to covenantal behavior occurs. As previously (6:3), the hoped-for coming of the deity is associated with the arrival of "spring rains" (Andersen and Freedman 1980, 568), a typically Canaanite complex.

The prophet is calling the people to do the antithesis of what they have been doing: they have *plowed wickedness* and *reaped injustice* (v. 13a). Furthermore, their self-centered religion has been accompanied by a self-reliant militarism that will contribute to their downfall (vv. 13b-14). The final verse invokes the demise of *Bethel* and the *king* together (v. 15) and thus recapitulates the two central concerns of the unit.

11:1-7. From Egypt to exile. This segment presents the briefest synopsis of the span of Israel's history with Yahweh as presented in the book to this point: *called out of Egypt* (vv. 1-2) and condemned to *return* there (v. 5). In the most poignant imagery in the entire book, Israel is depicted in the first unit (vv. 1-4) as a child *loved* (v. 1) and nurtured (vv. 3-4) by God, despite the child's waywardness. Thus, God's love for Israel never was dependent on Israel's right behavior (v. 2) or conscious recognition of God's saving (v. 3) and sustaining activity (v. 4). God's love is the sole basis for Israel's relationship with God.

Israel's *return to the land of Egypt* (and/or exile to Assyria) comes not because Israel transgressed, but because *they have refused to return to me* (v. 5) when the error of their ways was called to their attention by the prophet (see commentary on 9:7-9; cf. Deut 18:19). The text of v. 7b is extremely difficult and highly disputed; but NRSV's rendering, *To the Most High they call, but he does not raise them up at all* is a vast improvement over RSV and KJV. As rendered, this verse recapitulates Yahweh's refusal to respond favorably to the people's cries recounted in 6:1-3 and 8:2.

11:8-11. And back. This segment suggests for the first time in chaps. 4–11 that judgment is not God's final word (cf. 1:10–2:1; 2:14-23; 3:5).

The passionate soliloquy of God in vv. 8-9 depicting an agonizing struggle in the deity's own *heart* (v. 9) is the most sophisticated theological achievement in the book. On the one hand, it employs the anthropomorphic image of a God whose *heart recoils within* and whose *compassion grows warm and tender* (v. 8). At the same time it declares that God is *no mortal* at all (11:9); and thus it affirms that any depiction of God in human terms, however revelatory, is ultimately insufficient as a depiction of holiness itself *(the Holy One)*. This striking unit simultaneously confirms and subverts both the language of the prophetic proclamation and the entire enterprise of Christian theology.

Because the *Holy One* "acts" (a metaphor with essentially anthropomorphic underpinnings) in a manner consistent solely with the nature of holiness itself (i.e., independently of the actions of others; see Wolff 1974, 202), it is God's determination to *return them to their homes* after the execution of judgment (v. 11). Thus, in 10:11-12 imagery that was previously employed to express the destructive intent of the deity—*the LORD, who roars like a lion* (cf. 5:14; 13:7-8) and the people like *birds* (cf. 7:11-12)—is now transposed into salvation imagery. The closing formula, *says the LORD* (or "saying of Yahweh"; v. 11), appears only here in chaps. 4–11 and not only marks the end of a unit but also authorizes this new and remarkable word in the book.

Ephraim's Bitter Offense, 11:12–13:14 [MT 12:1–13:14]

This relatively brief section appears at first glance to have no particular connection to what precedes it. However, it develops the theme of the rejection of prophetic proclamation which is the *bitter offense* (12:14) of Ephraim.

11:12–12:9. The roots of rejection. Although the speaker who is surrounded by *lies* and *deceit* (v. 12) is conventionally understood to be Yahweh (see Andersen and Freedman 1980, 600–601), Wolff has argued quite cogently that it is the prophet (1974, 208–209). Elsewhere in Hosea, *lies* appears as terminology for a wrong against other people (see commentary on 4:2; cf. 7:3—NRSV, *treachery*; 10:13). The otherwise sudden and incongruous introduction of *the prophets* to whom Yahweh spoke in 12:10, 13 makes perfect sense if the "me" of v. 12 is Hosea rather than Yahweh. The slander and the *hostility* faced by the prophet (9:7b-8), here called *lies* and *deceit*, are characteristic of Ephraim in all its dealings *(they multiply falsehood and violence*, 12:1), even with the superpowers Assyria and Egypt.

Two units revealing Israel's character explain "the betrayal of the word of Yahweh spoken through his prophet" (Wolff 1974, 209). The first (12:2-6) reaches back to the eponymous ancestor, Jacob. The intended punishment of *Jacob* (i.e., Israel *according to his ways* and *according to his deeds* (12:2) with which this unit begins forms an INCLUSIO with the impending return to wilderness-wandering at the end of the second unit (12:9b).

Jacob (=Israel) has been a supplanter from the first (12:3). From the beginning he has attempted to wrest all he could from God (and anyone else with whom he dealt; see 12:12) by force of might or wit. He has always trusted in his own *manhood* or "strength" (the word is translated *wealth* in the next unit, 12:8).

The faithful alternative, expressed in the first explicit prophetic call to *return* in the entire book, is to *hold fast to love and justice, and wait continually for your God* (12:6). The first two terms emphasize integrity in social relations. *Love* here is unfailing loyalty to all one's commitments (NRSV typically uses "steadfast love" for this Heb. term); *justice* is action that puts the well-being of neighbor and community on the same plane as that of self. The concluding exhortation to live in expectant anticipation of God's blessing and deliverance stands in marked contrast to Jacob in 12:3-4 (and Israel throughout the book). Inconstancy, self-centeredness, and a proclivity for attempting to seize the reins of control from God is a character flaw in Jacob-Israel from the outset, according to the prophet's testimony.

The second unit (12:7-9) employs the imagery of commerce. In addition to the deceitful business practice of using *false balances* (fraudulent weights and measures; see Lev 19:35-36; Prov 11:1; 20:23), there is an obvious play on words, as well, since the term *trader* here is "Canaan" (12:7). *Ephraim* (12:8) so thoroughly *mixes himself with the peoples* (6:8) that he is indistinguishable in character from those around him.

As did the ancestor Jacob, Ephraim revels in his *wealth* (or "strength"; see 12:3, *manhood*) which he pronounces to be honest *gain* because *no offense has been found in him* (12:8). There is clear dramatic irony here, since the reader knows what Ephraim appears not to know in his self-righteous claim concerning his practices: the offense has indeed *been found* by Yahweh. In translation an artful juxtaposition appears in Ephraim's self-adulatory *I am rich* (12:8) and Yahweh's auto-kerygmatic (but!) *I am the LORD your God* (12:9) which introduces the judgment in which Ephraim will lose all that he has gained.

In addition to the theme of rebellious self-reliance, there are several allusive ties in this unit to the rejection of prophetic proclamation. The *false balances* (12:7a) are, literally, balances of *deceit*, the same term which was used synonymously with *lies* in 11:12 expressing the response to the prophet's message. The associated terminology of oppression (12:7b), though typically employed in economic and social contexts (see Amos 4:1; Jer 7:6; 22:3), also appears quite suggestively in Amos 3:9 in a context in which rejection of Yahweh's prophets (and the concomitant judgment) is at the fore (Amos 2:11-16; 3:1-8).

The final phrase invoking the *appointed festival* (12:9b) reprises the opening of the climactic unit in which the rejection of Hosea's proclamation is taken up (9:5-9), and the tent-dwelling recapitulates the rejection of Ephraim for not having *listened* to God speaking through the prophet: *they shall become wanderers* (9:17).

12:10-14. Bitter offense. As Israel's rejection of the prophet has been shown to be consistent with its historic pattern of behavior, so too Yahweh's working through prophets is seen to be of considerable antiquity. The variety of prophetic activity is considerable: they hear, as Yahweh "speaks" to them; they see *visions* that Yahweh gives them; they are agents of *destruction* that Yahweh brings (v. 10); they are instruments of deliverance that Yahweh works; and they are ministers of Yahweh's protection or oversight of Israel (implicit in the passive verb *was guarded* is a concluding phrase, "by Yahweh" v. 13).

Israel, in the meantime, has paid no attention to prophets, so involved has it been in its self-interest at cultic centers such as in Gilead and at Gilgal, which will not escape *destruction* (v. 11).

Moses is obviously the prophet by whom *the LORD brought Israel up from Egypt* (v. 13a). The synonymously parallel reference in v. 13b may also be to MO-SES (Wolff 1974, 216), or it may be to a second eminent prophet (Andersen and Freedman 1980, 621). If so, the most likely candidate is SAMUEL. Jeremiah identifies the pair by name in the context of a condemnation of Judah: "Though Moses and Samuel stood before me, yet my heart would not turn toward this people. Send them out of my sight, and let them go!" (15:1).

The *bitter offense* of *Ephraim* (v. 14), then, is the rejection of the prophet through whom Yahweh would deliver and protect Israel (v. 13) but through whom now Yahweh will *pay him back* for *his crimes* and *his insults* (v. 14; cf. *bring destruction*, v. 10). The term translated *bitter offense* involves a play on the root of the previously repeated *deceit* (see 11:12; 12:7) and thus ties the beginning, middle, and end of the section together.

Death and Rebirth of Israel, 13:1–14:9 [MT 13:1–14:10]

At the close of the collection comes a promise of healing, love, and fruitfulness (14:4-8) after the brutal and horrifying destruction that Israel will experience (13:7-16). After having rejected previous pleas (see 6:1-3; 8:2), Yahweh will in the end respond favorably to a plea (14:2-3) that the prophet instructs the people to take to Yahweh. Thus, rebirth comes with accepting the prophetic instruction.

Remarkably, the imagery of new life with Yahweh is drawn exclusively from the language of fertility and fecundity—in other words, from the rich matrix of the Canaanite religious thought-world.

13:1-3. Ephraim's death. The introductory segment raises up Ephraim's *guilt through Baal* and the death that results (v. 1). Past *guilt* (v. 1), present *sinning* (v. 2), and future futility (v. 3) encapsulate Hosea's perspective on the history of Israel's relationship with Yahweh.

13:4-16. The blast from the LORD. The first unit (vv. 4-8) of this violent and troubling section begins with Yahweh's own interpretation of Israel's salvation history. *God* and *savior* to Israel *ever since the land of Egypt* (v. 4) and provider *in the wilderness*, Yahweh has watched as the people became *satisfied, and their heart was proud; therefore they forgot me* (v. 6). Here the people's physical and material satiation and their arrogant self-centeredness are presented as the cause of their loss of knowledge of God. That this all-important concept is at issue here is clearer in the Hebrew text with its juxtaposition of *you know no God but me* in v. 4 with "I knew (NRSV, *fed*; see mrg.) you" *in the wilderness* in v. 5 (cf. 5:3-4). The unit closes with stunning and terrifying animal imagery depicting Yahweh's coming in judgment that will inevitably result in Israel's death (vv. 7-8).

The next four brief units (vv. 9-11, 12-13, 14, 15-16) elaborate on this death. The blunt *I will destroy you, O Israel* of v. 9 colors all that follows down to the final *Compassion is hidden from my eyes* in v. 14. There is no political solution this time; *king* and *rulers* can offer no hope of salvation (vv. 10-11).

The *iniquity* and *sin* which is *bound up* and *kept in store* is more than pictur-esque speech (so Mays 1969, 180). Andersen and Freedman propose the secreting of idols for safekeeping (1980, 637–38). However, it is quite suggestive that in re-sponse to the rejection of his proclamation concerning the Syro-Ephraimite conflict, Hosea's southern contemporary Isaiah ordered that his prediction be "bound up" and "sealed" until such time that it had come to pass, whereupon it could be opened and he vindicated as a "true" prophet of Yahweh (Isa 8:16; Roberts 1992, 214).

So, too, with Hosea's prediction of deportation from the land (9:3-6), which was met with slander and *hostility* (9:7-8). It has been recorded, sealed, and stored until the time that Yahweh *will remember their iniquity* and *will punish their sins* (9:9; note the same word pair as in v. 12). Then the prophet who was attacked as a *fool* and *mad* (9:9) will be exonerated (a life-and-death matter for a prophet; see Deut 18:20-22).

The *childbirth* imagery of the next verse, with its emphasis on knowing *the proper time*, further illustrates Ephraim's rejection of the prophetic word, as one of the essential tasks of the prophet throughout the ancient Near East was to reveal the "times" (see Roberts 1988, 212). Ephraim, however, is *unwise* and has failed to *present himself* when the opportunity for life was offered by Yahweh through the corrective proclamation of the prophet.

The first two rhetorical questions of v. 14 are reminiscent of the internal struggle of Yahweh in 11:8 in which God's *compassion* for Israel won out over *fierce anger* (vv. 8-9). Here, however, Yahweh calls out impatiently for *Death* to bring on its *plagues* and for *Sheol* to deliver its *destruction*. This time, *Compassion is hidden* from Yahweh's eyes (v. 14; cf. v. 9).

Although for a time Ephraim may flourish, *a blast from the LORD* is coming (v. 15). In 16 the *sword*, previously wielded against duplicitous envoys (*officials*, 7:16) and then raging in surrounding *cities* (11:6), now comes to the heart of the Northern Kingdom, *Samaria*. The historical correlate of the thematic nadir of the collection (9:10-17) is reached here with the anticipated slaughter of innocents in the destruction of Samaria.

14:1-9. Return and rebirth. For only the second time in the book, the explicit prophetic call to *return* appears in vv. 1-2a (cf. 12:6). But far more important than the call itself is the model prayer that follows it (vv. 2b-3) as the "words to take with you," i.e., as the appropriate verbal expression of authentic repentance.

The model prayer begins with an acknowledgment of sin in the request that *guilt* be taken away. The entreaty that Yahweh *accept that which is good* does not refer to the words being offered here. This often repeated interpretation reflects an antisacrificial bias foreign to Hosea. The good here is an acceptable sacrifice or offering (see the priestly discrimination between "good" and "bad" for votary offerings in Num 27:10, 14, 33) without which no Israelite was to appear before Yahweh (Exod 23:15; 34:20).

Hosea's animosity toward the cult as practiced in his day should not be misinterpreted as a call for life without tangible offerings to Yahweh. The prophet himself cited just such an existence as one of the horrors of exile (9:4).

The third element, *the fruit of our lips*, refers to the vows of renunciation that follow. But here, too, words are not all that is involved: it includes the fulfillment in action of what the words have promised. Words (like sacrifices) have been offered before and were rejected as insufficient (see 6:1-3; 8:2).

Authentic repentance requires the renunciation of self-sufficiency and self-centeredness. Israel's attempt to manufacture security through political coalitioning (with Assyria), militarism (*riding upon horses*), and cultic innovation (*work of our hands*) was a denial of the sovereignty and sufficiency of God. The final element (*the orphan*) reinforces the necessary shift from self-centeredness to concern for the vulnerable. It also brings the book full circle, as the verb translated *finds mercy* is from the same Hebrew root as the name of Hosea's daughter, *Lo-ruhamah*, "Not pitied" (1:6), who is renamed *Ruhamah*, "Pitied" (2:1).

In contrast to the previous occasions of Israel's appeal, Yahweh responds immediately with a promise to *heal* and to *love them* without constraint (v. 4). Renewed relationship with Yahweh comes when Israel finally accepts prophetic instruction. However, even on the other side of judgment and repentance, Israel's character is no different—*disloyalty* remains. Yahweh has chosen to do what Israel could not do for itself—effect healing—not because Israel now deserves it, but because Yahweh's *anger has turned from them.*

In rich botanical imagery (with a particular emphasis on the fruitfulness of Lebanon; vv. 5, 6, 7), vv. 5-8 employs language and imagery common in love songs (see Wolff 1974, 234–38) to characterize new life with Yahweh. Sumptuous sensory images abound (sight, smell, taste) to communicate safety, security, and well-being. There is salvation here, but no hint of "salvation history." In fact, the Israel earlier condemned for its penchant for enjoying the *shade* of trees (4:13) is now offered the "shade" (NRSV *shadow*, v. 7; the Heb. term is identical) of Yahweh, who is depicted as an *evergreen* tree (v. 8).

Remarkably, the God who repeatedly reminded Israel, *I am the LORD your God from the land of Egypt* (12:9; 13:4; cf. 11:1; 12:13), says in the end, *I am like an evergreen cypress* (v. 8). For this great prophet, then, Yahweh the God of Israel remains every bit as authentically revealed in the nature and agriculture of Canaan as in the historical traditions of Israel.

The last verse in the book employs the language of wisdom literature, an international idiom in the ancient Near East. In contrast to the superscription (1:1), which directs the reader's attention to the specific historical context of the preaching of Hosea, this postscript points to the universal applicability of the message of the book.

Works Cited

Andersen, F. L., and D. N. Freedman. 1980. *Hosea.* AncB.

Coogan, M. D. 1987. "Canaanite Origins and Lineage: Reflections on the Religion of Ancient Israel," *Ancient Israelite Religion,* 115–24.

Hillers, D. R. 1964. *Treaty-Curses and the Old Testament Prophets.*

Mays, J. L. 1969. *Hosea.* OTL.

Miller, P. D. 1985. "Israelite Religion," *The Hebrew Bible and Its Modern Interpreters,* ed. D. A. Knight and G. M. Tucker, 201–37.

Rogers, J. S. 1993. "Women in the Hands of an Abusive God? The Trouble with Hosea 2." *Interpreting Hosea for Preaching and Teaching,* ed. C. P. Staton, Jr., 21–30.

Sakenfeld, K. D. 1985. *Faithfulness in Action.*

Sanderson, J. E. 1992. "Nahum," *The Women's Bible Commentary,* ed. C. A. Newsome and S. H. Ringe, 217–21.

Wolff, H. W. 1974. *Hosea.* Herm.

Joel

Margaret Dee Bratcher

Introduction

The Book of Joel, the second in the collection of twelve prophetic books known as the Book of the Twelve, announces the coming of the Day of Yahweh, the Day of the LORD, as a day of judgment and salvation for JUDAH and JERUSALEM in the wake of a devastating infestation of locusts. This proclamation is the most extensive depiction of the Day of Yahweh in the OT.

In its interpretation of the natural disaster brought on by the locusts, the Book of Joel contributes a distinctive understanding of the acts of Yahweh within history and nature. In addition, its employment of other biblical writings provides a remarkable example of the continued transmission and application of the language of Israel's faith into new settings and time periods.

Date and Place in the Canon

A common feature of the prophetic literature is a superscription placed at the beginning of each book. These superscriptions usually identify briefly the prophet whose message follows and provide other pertinent information, such as the people to whom the message is directed, the time period in which it is given, and perhaps even the substance of the message itself. Usually the prophetic books also contain concrete references to events and people that help to date them.

The Book of Joel, however, lacks any chronological reference in its superscription as well as any specific references to events or people. In the absence of such indications of time period, OT scholars up to the beginning of the nineteenth century usually maintained that Joel was a preexilic PROPHET because of the book's place in the CANON between the eighth-century prophets HOSEA and AMOS.

The dating of Joel in recent OT scholarship depends more on allusions in the text that suggest a time period and on certain features of style and content rather than the book's place in the canon. For example, Joel assumes the postexilic rebuilding of the Temple in 515 B.C.E. and the walls of Jerusalem in 445 B.C.E. (see 1:9, 14, 16; 2:7, 9, 17; 3:18). The depiction of Judah as a well-organized religious community under the leadership of the priesthood and elders suggests a date after the reforms of EZRA and NEHEMIAH (see 1:2, 9, 13-14; 2:14, 16-17, 19), and references to Judah's neighbors seem to describe the geopolitical scene in the late Persian period, before the conquest of ALEXANDER (see 3:4, 6, 17, 19).

Moreover, Hebrew terms and expressions are used in Joel that appear elsewhere only in later OT books (see Wolff 1977, 10–11; Thompson 1956, 731–32 for a detailed list). The book shows a dependence on the thought of other prophets, including notably the late prophets OBADIAH (v. 17; see Joel 2:32) and MALACHI (3:2; 4:5; see Joel 2:11, 31).

These examples suggest that Joel must be dated sometime after the reforms of Ezra and Nehemiah and before the Hellenistic conquest of Judah, most likely the first half of the fourth century B.C.E. or the end of the fifth century B.C.E.

The related issue of the arrangement of the Book of the Twelve in the canon is a difficult question to resolve, but several factors appear to have influenced the arrangement of the books. For example, when a book's superscription contains information that locates it in a particular time period, the book is placed in approximate chronological order. For example, Hosea, Amos, JONAH, and MICAH are all identified with persons or events in the eighth century B.C.E.

As a result of the arguments above about the date of Joel, the rationale for the position of Joel in the canon now seems to be the connection between its themes and those of other books, rather than the date of its message. That is, the language of Joel 2:31 and 3:16, 18, 19 concerning the Day of Yahweh closely resembles the beginning of Amos. Most likely, then, Joel was placed before Amos as an introduction to Amos's proclamation of the coming of the Day of Yahweh against Judah and its neighbors. The arrangement of the Greek collection of the Twelve supports this proposal, since it appears to be more interested in chronology than the Hebrew and places Joel later in its collection (see Wolff 1977, 3–5 for a fuller discussion of these issues).

The Structure and Unity of Joel

The three chapters in the Book of Joel (1) lament the coming of a locust plague, (2) announce the Day of Yahweh as a comprehensive disaster for Judah and Jerusalem, and (3) promise a future salvation. A major issue in the study of the book is how these chapters relate to each other and whether they indicate any compositional unity.

Joel 2:17-18 is usually considered the midpoint of the book, for there the tone of the book turns from judgment and destruction for Judah to the proclamation of salvation for Yahweh's people. The book is also usually judged to be a unified work by a single author, with perhaps some minor materials added by a later editor, indicated by the continuity of themes and language throughout the book (see Wolff 1977 and Childs 1979 for discussion of the arguments).

Joel 2:27-28, however, has also been understood as the midpoint in the book, a turn from history to eschatology. That is, prior to this point the message of Joel has been directed at the agricultural crisis caused by the locusts, interpreting it as the Day of Yahweh in judgment on Judah and as a sign of the coming, eschatological Day of Yahweh. After 2:27 the focus of Joel is entirely on the coming eschatological battle between Yahweh and his enemies, which will result in Israel's ultimate vindication and Yahweh's exaltation, and references to the locusts and the present distress of Judah disappear (a view first stated by Bernhard Duhm in 1911).

Recent efforts to understand and articulate the structure and unity of Joel suggest that chap. 3 represents additional oracles added to a lament about a locust invasion and Yahweh's response to that lament in 1:5–2:27, but that these materials have been edited in such a way as to give internal coherence to the entire book (Hiebert 1992, 874).

The primary discussion of the coherence of the book comes from Hans Walter Wolff, who points out that the materials after the midpoint in 2:17-18 correspond inversely to those that precede it. That is, 1:14-20, a lament over destroyed harvest and pastures in the aftermath of the locusts, is reversed by the promise of abundance in 2:21-27. The announcement of coming judgment against Jerusalem and Judah in 2:1-11 is reversed in 3:1-3, 9-17 by their vindication over their enemies. The call to repentance in 2:12-17 is reversed by the promise of the pouring out of the spirit in 2:28-32 (Wolff 1977, 7).

Theme and Style

The primary theme of Joel is the coming of the Day of the LORD, the Day of Yahweh. Although the term itself, "Day of the LORD," appears in the OT only sixteen times (five times in Joel alone), the earliest instance of which is Amos 5:18, 20, the concept is found in at least twenty other contexts and is very ancient. It denotes a decisive event of Yahweh's activity, understood first in Israel's thinking as Yahweh's giving victory to Israel over its enemies, but understood later as Yahweh's own judgment upon Israel. The language that describes the Day of Yahweh derives most likely from the traditions of holy war and from descriptions of THEO-PHANY, God's appearance to the people in their acts of worship or in times of danger. For example, descriptions of the Day of Yahweh typically depict Yahweh's leading his army into battle against his enemies to overturn them; they also frequently portray the response of creation, heaven and earth, at the coming of Yahweh.

The Book of Joel reflects the last stage in Israel's understanding of the Day of the LORD: it is a day of both judgment and salvation for ISRAEL. In Joel, the day comes in the natural disasters of locust plague and drought that devastate the land and call the people to return to Yahweh (1:15; 2:1, 11). The day comes in the cosmic eschatological battle between Yahweh and his enemies that results in Israel's final deliverance (2:31; 3:14).

The book continues to describe the Day of Yahweh in the language of HOLY WAR and theophany and repeatedly draws on earlier traditions through its quotation and paraphrase of those materials. For example, the description of the locusts as an invading army both calls to mind the Exodus plague of locusts and prepares for their identification with the Day of Yahweh. The book thereby exhibits a fine depth of shading in its portrayal of the Day of Yahweh. At once a present devastating infestation of locusts evokes the locust plague of the Exodus and portends the coming final battle between Yahweh and the hordes of his enemies. The crisis in nature is understood as an omen for the Day of Yahweh, both ancient acts of Yahweh and future ones.

This concern for the past, present, and future acts of Yahweh is an explicit part of the purpose of Joel: the events described within the book, without parallel in Israel's experience (1:2; 2:2), become a lesson for the generations of Israel to come (1:3), so that they may know that their LORD is God, *and there is no other* (2:27). Yahweh transforms judgment into salvation; the people of Yahweh are returned to their God, and Yahweh alone is acknowledged and exalted as the one true God.

For Further Study

In the *Mercer Dictionary of the Bible*: ESCHATOLOGY IN THE OT; JOEL, BOOK OF; JUDGMENT, DAY OF; ORACLE; PROPHET; VISION.

In other sources: B. S. Childs. *Introduction to the OT as Scripture.*; J. Limburg. *Hosea–Micah*. Interp; H. W. Wolff. *Joel and Amos*. Herm.

Commentary

An Outline

I. Superscription, 1:1
II. The Locust Plague, 1:2-4
III. A Call to Lamentation, 1:5–2:17
    A. Affected Groups, 1:5-14
    B. Lamenting the People's Distress, 1:15-20
    C. The Day of the LORD, 2:1-11
    D. Call to Repentance, 2:12-17

IV. Promises of Salvation, 2:18–3:21
    [MT 2:18–4:21]
    A. Devastation Reversed, 2:18-27
    B. The Spirit Poured Out, 2:28-29
    [MT 2:28–3:2]
    C. Further Oracles of Salvation, 2:30–3:21 [MT 3:3–4:21]

Superscription, 1:1

The superscription of the Book of Joel is similar to the beginnings of the prophetic books HOSEA, MICAH, ZEPHANIAH, and JONAH in describing the book as *the word of the LORD that came to* the PROPHET. The assertion is a claim that the message of the book derives from Yahweh, not the prophet himself. These are Yahweh's words for his people.

The name Joel means "Yahweh is God" and is attested in the OT most frequently in writings from the postexilic period (for example, the Chronicler's History). The name of Joel's father, *Pethuel*, is otherwise unattested in the OT, and its meaning is uncertain.

The Locust Plague, 1:2-4

Verses 2-3 call the people of JUDAH and JERUSALEM to attention and emphatically assert the purpose of the book: an extraordinary crisis has befallen the people, and they are to tell its story for generations to come. The exhortation to make this present event known to the future introduces a fundamental idea in Joel: events may teach lessons not only to those who experience them but also to those who live in their aftermath.

The phrase *hear . . . give ear* is a typical call to receive instruction. The address to the *elders* and *inhabitants of the land* (v. 2) is an address to the community of Yahweh's people in Judah and Jerusalem and their leaders.

A rhetorical question highlights the singular circumstances of this crisis: *Has such a thing happened?* The people are to compare this crisis with their own experiences of trouble and with the experiences of earlier generations; implicit within the question is the answer that nothing compares with this crisis. The crisis, then, is so extraordinary that it holds greater meaning for Israel than some chance occurrence of trouble. This event will be instructive for generations long to come.

One generation is to hand the story on to the next in an unbroken line of tradition. Of the numerous references to the next generations in the OT, the most emphatic is the one found here, to the fourth generation, the generation of great grandchildren. To live to see great grandchildren effectively marks the longest length of a person's life in the OT. The prophet thus commends the retelling of these events into the farthest reaches of the future one may envision.

Verse 4 makes clear what kind of crisis has come upon the people: a swarm of locusts has thoroughly devastated the land. The repeated statement that the remains left by one swarm of locusts is eaten by the next dramatizes the complete destruction of the land. The locusts have left nothing. The terminology for the locusts, *cutting . . . swarming . . . hopping . . . destroying,* is usually understood as descriptive of the developmental stages in the lifespan of the common desert locust, although some interpreters understand it as a description of successive waves of invasions (see Thompson 1956, 737; Wolff 1977, 27–28; Hiebert 1992, 876).

A Call to Lamentation, 1:5–2:17

This section of the book is a lament in response to the locust plague. References throughout the section to the drying up of the harvest suggest the presence of drought conditions in addition to the locust infestation. The section may be subdivided into 1:5-14, a call to lament in the aftermath of the locusts; 1:15-20, the lament of the community and prophet; 2:1-11, a description of the Day of the LORD, understood as foreshadowed in the plague; and 2:12-17, another call to the people for prayer and fasting.

Affected Groups, 1:5-14

These verses call the people to cry their lament to Yahweh in time of distress. The unit consists of four calls to lament, in vv. 5-7, 8-10, 11-12, and 13-14, addressed to the groups most affected by the crisis. The basic pattern of each call is an introductory line of address consisting of imperatives, in which the second imperative is *wail*, and vocatives of address. A statement of the reason for the lament and description of the situation of distress follow. Verses 8-10 differ from this structure, perhaps due to faulty transmission of the text. The rearrangement of the stanza, with v. 9b preceding v. 8, suggests the original order.

1:5-7. Drunkards and wine-drinkers. The *drunkards* and *wine-drinkers* (v. 5) are wakened to the crisis of the complete destruction of the vineyards. The locusts are likened to an invading nation, *powerful and innumerable* (v. 6), a depiction that prefigures the description of the army of *the day of the LORD* in 2:1-11. Their force, which strips clean vine and branch, is compared to *the fangs of a lioness* (v. 6), a common OT image for fierce, destructive power. The use of the first person, *my vines* and *my branches* (v. 7), evokes the direct language of the prophets in speaking for Yahweh and reminds the audience of whose interests are ultimately involved: Yahweh is the owner of these vineyards.

1:8-10. Grain and drink offerings lost. The second call to lament is for the loss of the grain offering and drink offering. In the devastation of the fields, the grain, wine, and oil that provide the grain and drink offerings are lost. Such a loss calls forth the mourning of the priests, the ministers of the altar, whose responsibility it is to offer sacrifices, for the crisis threatens the very worship of Yahweh. Moreover, the recitation of the series *grain . . . wine . . . oil* recalls the classic harvest of the land in OT tradition, where the land is recognized as the gift of Yahweh and the harvest as the sign of his blessing. The loss of these, then, signifies the loss of Yahweh's blessing and the coming of his judgment, evoking the mourning of the land itself. The comparison of lamenting like a virgin in sackcloth (an onomatopoeic word from the Heb. *saq*) for the husband of her youth refers to dressing in garments of mourning like a young woman whose bridegroom has been killed. It is the announcement that all the joy and hope of the future are cut off.

1:11-12. The disgrace of farmers and vine-dressers. Those who work the land, *farmers* and *vine-dressers*, face the ruin of their harvest. The call to lament in v. 11, *be dismayed* or *be ashamed*, probably refers to the disgrace of the farmers at the loss of Yahweh's favor, indicated by the devastation of the harvest. The joy of the people at the gift of Yahweh's blessing is dried up and becomes shame.

1:13-14. Instructions to the priests. The final call to lament instructs the priests to dress themselves in sackcloth, lament, and call a fast for the community. These activities are the community's responses in worship to the catastrophe that they have experienced.

Lamenting the People's Distress, 1:15-20

This unit laments the people's distress and announces the coming of the Day of Yahweh (v. 15). The swath of destruction cut through the land by the locust invasion makes clear that the Day of Yahweh is near and that it comes as destruction from Yahweh. Word play between *destruction* (*shōd*) and *the Almighty* (*Shaddai*) helps to evoke the terror of the approaching judgment of the LORD.

Verses 16-18 confirm the proclamation about the significance of the community's crisis. The rhetorical questions in v. 16 provide the ground for the announcement of the Day of Yahweh. The loss of the harvest and the threat to the sacrifices of the Temple service signal its coming, and illustrations of the ruined condition of the land follow in vv. 17 and 18. Seed has shriveled in the soil and granaries have fallen to ruins because they have stood empty. The grazing animals, large and small, suffer from lack of pasture. The effects of both locusts and drought are suggested in these verses.

Verses 19-20 express the prophet's lament, *to you, O LORD, I cry*, and report the animals' lament for the loss of pasture.

The Day of the LORD, 2:1-11

This section describes the approaching Day of Yahweh, which has been introduced in 1:15. The unit begins with a cry of alarm raised to warn of the threat of armed attack. A description of the approaching army, the army of Yahweh, follows in three paragraphs: vv. 3-5, 6-9, and 10-11. The vivid imagery used here to describe the army of the Day of Yahweh is consistent with both the descriptions of the locusts of chap. 1, whose invasion has served as a sign of the coming day, and the customary depictions of the Day of Yahweh found in holy war traditions. The prophet Joel thereby points away from the present crisis to its real meaning, the coming of Yahweh in judgment.

2:1-2. A cry of alarm. The unit begins with the call to *blow the trumpet* and *sound the alarm*. The purpose of the alarm is to warn Jerusalem (*Zion . . . my holy mountain*) of the approaching threat of the Day of Yahweh. The trumpet is the *shophar*, or ram's horn, used in Israel in several contexts: to signal danger at an approaching army, to sound a battle cry, as well as to call the community to religious ceremonies. The *shophar* also appears in texts that describe the presence and activity of Yahweh himself, such as the coming of Yahweh as judge in Ps 98:6-9 and the coming of the Day of Yahweh in Zeph 1:14-16.

The description of the Day of the LORD as *a day of darkness and gloom, a day of clouds and thick darkness* (v. 2), derives from Amos 5:18, 20, the earliest reference to the term "the day of Yahweh" (a description followed by Zeph 1:15; see Deut 4:11, 5:22-23 and Ps 97:2 for similar phenomena accompanying Yahweh's presence or coming, but not specifically the Day of Yahweh).

Verse 2b makes explicit what the Day of Yahweh means: the coming of a *great and powerful army* (Heb. *'am rab we'āsûm*, "great and powerful people"). The phrase recalls both 1:6, the description of the locusts as *a nation . . . powerful and innumerable*, and also the army of the Day of the LORD in Isa 13:4, an important passage on the Day of Yahweh (*'am rab*; NRSV "great multitude"). That *their like has never been from of old, nor will be again after them in ages to come* represents the unique instance of this force over the farthest extent of time, from memory past to the future ahead. The description intensifies the distinctiveness of the locust invasion in 1:2 and also evokes the description of the locust plague in the Exodus tradition (Exod 10:14-15). Those forces, so distinctive then, will be overshadowed by comparison with the coming Day of Yahweh.

The translation *like blackness spread upon the mountains* (v. 2b) is without textual witness, but is suggested by the references to the darkness of the day in v. 2a and the blackening of the land caused by the Exodus locusts in Exod 10:14. The MT vocalization reads "like dawn spread upon the mountains" (so NIV, KJV), which may refer to the shining of light upon the locust wings (Wolff 1977, 43).

2:3. Devastation. Verse 3 describes the effect of this army: the complete, fiery devastation of the land. The reference to *fire . . . in front of them and behind them a flame* may echo Pss 97:3 and 50:3 in their portrayal of the coming of Yahweh as a devouring fire. The contrast between the land as like the garden of Eden before their coming and as a wilderness afterward is not only a poetic description of the contrast between verdant growth before and charred stubble afterward, but also a reversal of the prophetic image of salvation describing the end of the Exile, when Yahweh would turn the land from wilderness into a new Eden (Ezek 36:35; Isa 51:3). It serves, therefore, as a stark proclamation of judgment upon Jerusalem and Judah.

2:4-9. A charging army. In vv. 4-5, the army is pictured as a cavalry of horses and chariots charging upon the mountains (see Judg 6:5, 7:12; Jer 46:23, 51:27; Nah 3:16-17; Job 39:20; Rev 9:7 for similar metaphors). The scene conveys both their devastating power and number (*powerful army drawn up for battle*) and the tumultuous noise with which they invade (*as with the rumbling of chariots* and *like the crackling of a flame of fire devouring the stubble*).

In vv. 6-9 the army is compared with infantry advancing on a city, overrunning its defenses and unstoppable. The paragraph begins with a reminder of the tragedy wrought by such an onslaught—*peoples are in anguish, all faces grow pale*. The remaining phrases in the stanza emphasize the power of the attacking forces and explain why there is such terror and suffering. The army invades the city, advancing in line and overpowering all the city's defenses as they scale the walls and enter people's homes. No place is safe from violation.

2:10-11. Cosmic results. The prophet reaches the climactic description concerning the attack in vv. 10-11: Even *the earth quakes* and *the heavens tremble* before this host, and *the sun and the moon are darkened*, for Yahweh is *at the head of his army*. The shaking of the cosmos is a motif found in THEOPHANY accounts in the OT (Judg 5:4; Pss 18:8, 68:9, 77:19) and in connection with the coming of the

Day of Yahweh (Isa 13:13; Ezek 38:19-20). The approach of the army is experienced throughout creation precisely *because* Yahweh is at its head. Moreover, the note of alarm sounded with the trembling of the people in v. 1 at the approach of an army is intensified here with the trembling of the heavens at the approach of Yahweh himself and the impossibility of escape. The uttering of Yahweh's voice is a familiar prophetic expression for the unleashing of Yahweh's judgment (see Amos 1:2).

An INCLUSIO formed by the repetition in v. 11 of *the day of the LORD* from 2:1 ends the paragraph. The repetition reinforces how very imminent is Yahweh's coming and how terrible is the predicament of his people. Who can endure it?

Call to Repentance, 2:12-17

This unit is a call to repentance, divided into two sections. Verses 12-14 assert the need for sincere, inward repentance and probe the possibility of Yahweh's relenting. Verses 15-17 provide direction for the expression of repentance in the rituals of worship.

2:12-14. Return to the LORD. Two calls for the people to return to Yahweh appear here, one prescribing what the people must do and the other reminding them of the source of their hope, Yahweh's compassionate nature and actions.

The people are called to return, or repent (Heb. *shūv*), in the traditional prophetic understanding of repentance, as an entire reordering of priorities (see Amos 4:6-11; Hos 3:5; 14:2; Jer 3:10; 24:7). The call to return with one's heart, which is in Hebrew the center of the will, is a call to turn toward Yahweh exercising the very center of the self's power to choose its way, establish its priorities, and fix its loyalties. *Fasting, with weeping, and with mourning* (v. 12) are accompanying signs of repentance. *Rend your hearts and not your clothing* (v. 13) is a play on the ritual act of mourning—the tearing of one's garments before putting on sackcloth. The prophet thus enjoins a sincere, inward experience of sorrow, repentance, and recommitment to Yahweh.

The reason for hope in Yahweh's relenting from judgment is found in v. 13: *the LORD . . . is gracious and merciful, slow to anger, and abounding in steadfast love.* The prophet repeats a traditional confession of faith that describes the gracious, compassionate character of Yahweh (see Exod 34:6-7; Neh 9:17, 31; Ps 86:15 et al.). The phrase *relents from punishing* (v. 13) applies the confession to the community's crisis; the hope for Israel is that a compassionate Yahweh will turn from his punishment. Rather than the scorched earth described in 2:3, then, Yahweh would *leave a blessing behind him* (v. 14); that is, the land would be revitalized so that the *grain offering* and *drink offering* may be brought forth from it and given to Yahweh.

2:15-17. Call to worship. The call to *blow the trumpet* (v. 15) repeats the call of 2:1, but whereas then it sounded an alarm because of a threat, now it calls the people to repentant worship in response to that threat. The command to *sanctify a fast, call a solemn assembly* indicates what religious rites are to be performed in response to the call to repentance. Three groups within the community are summoned specifically: the old, the young, and the newly married. These are ones who were frequently excused from participation in the services, but just as the coming of the Day of Yahweh will allow no one to escape, so this call to repentance must involve everyone in the community, without exception.

Verse 17 instructs the priests to ask Yahweh to spare his people; the reason is an appeal to Yahweh's own righteousness and majesty. Common in the prophets (see e.g., Ezek 20), this appeal links the fortunes of Israel with the nation's understanding of the sovereignty of Yahweh: for Yahweh to preserve Israel is to show his sovereignty to the nations. Their welfare reflects back upon the nations' estimation of Yahweh.

Promises of Salvation, 2:18–3:21 [MT 2:18–4:21]

This section contains Yahweh's response to the people's prayer, addressing both the present crisis and also the larger threat of the Day of Yahweh. The message of comfort and hope promised by Yahweh's response in 2:18-27 is further extended by short oracles of salvation in 2:28-29 (MT 3:1-2) and 2:30-32 (MT 3:3-5). A longer oracle against the nations in 3:1-21 (MT 4:1-21) concludes the section.

Devastation Reversed, 2:18-27

2:18. An introduction. The acts that follow are because Yahweh *became jealous for his land and had pity on his people.* Yahweh's jealousy is his "saving zeal," as in Ezek 39:25, Zech 1:14, 8:2; and Zeph 1:18. The Day of Yahweh becomes a Day of Yahweh's compassionate, zealous salvation for his land and people.

2:19-20. A promise. These verses promise the turning of lamentation into harvest joy and the removal of danger, for Yahweh will replenish the *grain, wine, and oil*" (cf. 1:10, 16) and destroy the threatening army. The army is at once the locust horde and the army of the Day of Yahweh; in addition, the description *northern army* alludes to the enemy brought by Yahweh according to the proclamation of earlier prophets (see Jer 1:14-15; 4:6; 6:1, 22; Ezek 38:6, 15; 39:2).

2:21-27. The LORD's deliverance. These verses expand the assurance of Yahweh's deliverance in the present agricultural crisis, reversing point by point the lament of 1:16-20 with the promise of full granaries, pastures, and rain. Land, people, and animals had once mourned, but now they are called to rejoice at Yahweh's salvation. Verse 27, the climax in this proclamation of salvation, speaks to the larger theological issue of Israel's relationship to Yahweh: Israel will acknowledge and experience the presence of Yahweh in its midst and his exaltation as the one true God.

The Spirit Poured Out, 2:28-29 [MT 2:28–3:2]

Once the present, imminent crises have been deflected, vv. 28-29 announce the pouring out of Yahweh's spirit. In the past, the Spirit had been given only to certain people, commissioned with special tasks: judges, kings, and above all in Joel's day, the prophets. The pouring out of Yahweh's Spirit here, however, depicts the entire nation as a community of inspired prophets. *Prophesy*, *dreams*, and *visions* are parallel terms for prophetic inspiration. The references to young and old, male and female, and slave and free in v. 29 encompass the entire community. These human divisions and distinctions are rendered void by the coming of the Spirit, for all will share the presence of Yahweh. *All flesh*, all weak mortality, therefore, will be transformed by the ultimate saving action, the very presence of Yahweh poured out upon all of the people.

Further Oracles of Salvation, 2:30–3:21 [MT 3:3–4:21]

The Book of Joel concludes with a pair of oracles. The first oracle (2:30-32 [MT 3:3-5]) is an announcement of salvation for the people of Yahweh. The second oracle (3:1-21 [MT 4:1-12]) is an extended pronouncement directed toward *all the nations* (3:2).

2:30-32. The day of salvation. This oracle proclaims the coming Day of Yahweh as a day of salvation for Yahweh's people. *Blood and fire and columns of smoke* are signs, or portents, on earth that precede the coming day; they refer to the devastating effects of warfare. The darkening of the sun and reddening of the moon portend the coming day in the heavens. The promise of salvation is for *everyone who calls upon the name of the LORD*, that is, those who worship Yahweh; and the promise of escape is for all those threatened with no escape from the judgment of 2:3, 11—if they turn to Yahweh in faithful worship.

3:1-21. An oracle against the nations. The Book of Joel closes with a lengthy proclamation directed against Judah's enemies and exalting the power and actions of Yahweh in Judah's behalf. The oracle has four subunits: vv. 1-3, 4-8, 9-17, and 18-21.

Verses 1-3 make clear that the day of salvation for Judah and Jerusalem means Yahweh's judgment on the nations. The *valley of Jehoshaphat*, the place of judgment, appears only here in the OT. It is a symbolic name, meaning "Yahweh judges," and expresses a play on words with the reference to judgment which follows it (Heb. *shāphat*, "to judge"). The provocation for this judgment is the EXILE, the dispersion of Judah. Although the Exile occurred years ago, Israel still struggles to reestablish itself in the land, and the agony and humiliation that Israel experienced have not faded with the passing of time. The bitterness of Jerusalem's destruction and of the exile are grimly captured in the image of the selling of Israel's children to hire prostitutes and to purchase drink.

Verses 4-8 are an oracle against foreign nations, a frequent element in the prophetic literature. The oracle is against *Philistia* and the Phoenician cities of *Tyre and Sidon* (v. 4). For their crimes against Judah, plundering wealth and selling people into slavery (see Amos 1:6, 9; Ezek 27:13), they will experience a similar fate, the selling of their own sons and daughters. Such correspondence between a crime and its punishment is frequent in the OT, especially in Deuteronomy and the prophets. The pattern affirms the justice inherent in Yahweh's actions and relates it to the outworkings of human choices to do evil. *The Sabeans* (v. 8) are the people of Sheba in southern Arabia.

A call to arms and a description of the final judgment are found in vv. 9-17. The call for the nations to prepare for war and to present themselves at Yahweh's judgment opens the section (vv. 9-12). The impact of the call is dramatized in the inversion of the promise of salvation found in Isa 2:4 and Mic 4:3: tools of peace are to be converted into weapons of war.

The description of Yahweh's judgment follows in vv. 13-15. It is likened to a harvest: *put in the sickle . . . go in, tread. The harvest is ripe,* the *winepress is full,* and the *vats overflow* offer parallel imagery for the excessive wickedness of the nations. The phrase *valley of decision* in place of the valley of Jehoshaphat points specifically to the verdict, the final judgment awaiting the nations. The paragraph closes with an echo of 2:10, affirming the cosmic ramifications of the events.

Verses 16-17 appear as a coda to the announced judgment, moving attention to the fundamental meaning of these events. Verse 16 quotes Amos 1:2, announcing the sending forth of Yahweh's judgment like a lion's roar. The impact is felt in the shaking of the cosmos, but its outcome is the security of Yahweh's people in Jerusalem, for Yahweh dwells with them there. The promises of v. 17, that Israel will *know* that Yahweh dwells with them and will protect them, recall the assurances of 2:27; these promises address the ultimate concerns of Yahweh's people.

Finally, vv. 18-21 convey a similar promise. In that day, the land will produce abundantly and the watercourses flow plentifully. The reference to the fountain flowing from the Temple is akin to the stream in Ezek 47:1-12 (see also Zech 14:8): it signals the marvelous abundance of the land as a result of Yahweh's dwelling there. Yahweh's presence in the Temple, in the land, and among the people gives them life and security and results in the destruction of their enemies.

Works Cited

Childs, Brevard S. 1979. *Introduction to the Old Testament as Scripture.*
Hiebert, Theodore. 1992. "Book of Joel." AncBD.
Thompson, John A. 1956. "Joel. Introduction and Exegesis." IB.
Wolff, Hans Walter. 1977. *Joel and Amos.* Herm.

Amos
John C. Shelley

Introduction

In the Hebrew Bible, Amos is the third member of the Book of the Twelve, a collection sometimes bearing the misleading title "the minor prophets." Except for its relative brevity there is nothing "minor" about Amos. This little book has generated a major corpus of secondary literature and has exerted extraordinary influence in shaping modern notions of human rights and social justice. Many will recall the stirring oratory of Martin Luther King, Jr., challenging the forces of segregation with Amos's powerful rhetoric: *But let justice roll down like waters, and righteousness like an everflowing stream* (5:24).

Author

Except for a brief quotation (of 8:10a) in Tob 2:6 and a passing reference in 2 Esdr 1:39, AMOS is not mentioned in the Bible outside the book that bears his name. He is widely viewed as the first of the classical or "writing" prophets, but he himself refuses the appellation of *prophet* (7:14). He is identified only as one found *among the shepherds of Tekoa* (1:1) and as *a herdsman, and a dresser of sycamore trees* (7:14). This identification has led to the popular image of Amos as a poor, uneducated common laborer commissioned by God to challenge the rich and powerful. Yet it is difficult to believe that a simple, untutored shepherd could have penned such dramatic poetry and prose or that such a person could even have commanded an audience in BETHEL. It seems likely that Amos was a person of some standing, more like a cattle rancher than a common shepherd. In fact, the terms translated *shepherd* and *herdsman* in the NRSV are not the usual Hebrew terms for shepherd, and in 2 Kgs 3:4 the latter is rendered "sheep breeder." In addition to his remarkable passion for justice, Amos was blessed with a keen intellect, a thorough familiarity with literary genres and techniques, an astute knowledge of national and international politics, and a poet's genius for creating pictures with words.

Setting

Amos prophesied during the reign of JEROBOAM II (786–746 B.C.E.). Given scant attention by the Deuteronomist (2 Kgs 14:23-29), Jeroboam's reign of forty-one years was marked by economic and territorial expansion, military resurgence, and religious revival. The leading economic indicators pointed to stability, growth, and prosperity, traditional "signs" of God's favor. The sanctuaries at Bethel and other shrines were thronged with worshipers. For Amos, however, things were not what they seemed. The booming economy was fueled by exploitation of the poor, and its actual beneficiaries were few—the king, the royal court, government bureaucrats, wealthy land owners. Israel was becoming two distinct societies, an ever-widening gap separating rich and poor.

The premonarchical traditions that protected the poor, the widows, and the orphans, and that governed the use and transfer of land were being eroded. The lavish lifestyles of the few depended upon wine and olives for export, inciting the wealthy to acquire more and more land. But that demanded a disregard for the tradition of the *nahala*, the affirmation that tribal lands belonged to YHWH and therefore could not be sold in perpetuity (Lev 25:23). Jezebel's ploy to gain control of Naboth's vineyard a century earlier (1 Kgs 21:1-29) had become common stuff in Amos's time.

The situation addressed by Amos is similar to that found today in many third world countries: The richest arable land is owned by a few wealthy families and used to grow export crops (coffee, tea, bananas, etc.), while the poor are left to subsist on the remaining scraps. As landholdings accumulated in the hands of a few, the poor became more and more vulnerable to exploitation, often finding their children sold into slavery to pay family debts (2 Kgs 4:1-7). Israel had finally discovered the "ways of the king" (1 Sam 8:10-18).

Interpretation of Amos

The modern interpreter of Amos is confronted with several problems. For one, there is little doubt that Amos has been subject to editing in both the pre- and post-exilic periods, although the extent of such interpolation and its specific occurrences in Amos are widely debated. One should not assume, however, that editorial changes and additions are necessarily contaminants that must be excised to get back to the pure message of Amos. For one thing, historical judgments distinguishing Amos from his editors are risky business and can never be made with certainty. But more importantly, such changes and additions, which may indeed be in some tension with what Amos said, are neither arbitrary nor narrowly orthodox. Rather, as a good wine enhances the flavor of a good meal, such interpolations often bring to light meanings hidden to a purely historical approach. The interpreter, therefore, must be prepared to move back and forth between at least two fronts: the message of the historical Amos and the message of the book as it stands. Generally speaking, the former task emphasizes the historical-critical method, while the latter depends more heavily on literary approaches. Both are necessary to see and enjoy the full richness of Amos.

Two additional problems facing the interpreter of Amos are closely related. The first lies in the fact that Amos contains an unusual number of unique words and grammatical constructions (the technical term for such constructions is *hapax legomena*), that is, words and constructions not found elsewhere in the Bible or in the literature of the ancient Near East. One must use imagination to envision the possibilities Amos may have had in mind.

The second problem involves Amos's poetic genius. Amos is not a theologian or philosopher who constructs a carefully reasoned argument. He is an artist who paints pictures with words. To understand Amos it is imperative to grasp the image or picture and then construct meaning by the process of analogy.

For Further Study

In the *Mercer Dictionary of the Bible*: AMOS; AMOS, BOOK OF; BAAL; BETHEL; CHRONOLOGY; GILGAL; ISRAEL; ORACLE; POETRY; PROPHET; RELIGIONS OF THE AN-CIENT NEAR EAST; SAMARIA; VISION.

In other sources: P. Hanson, *The People Called*; H. Marks, "The Twelve Prophets," in *The Literary Guide to the Bible*, ed. R. Alter and F. Kermode; J. L. Mays, *Amos*, OTL; S. Paul, *Amos*, Herm; S. N. Rosenbaum, *Amos of Israel*; J. D. Smart, "Amos," IDB; J. D. W. Watts, *Vision and Prophecy in Amos*; H. W. Wolff, *Joel and Amos*, Herm.

Commentary

An Outline

I. Superscription and Epigraph, 1:1-2
   A. Superscription, 1:1
   B. Epigraph, 1:2
II. A Sermon against the Nations, 1:3–2:16
   A. The Crimes of Israel's Neighboring Enemies, 1:3–2:3
   B. Judah's Idolatry, 2:4-5
   C. Israel's Social Injustice, 2:6-16
III. Israel's Sinfulness and God's Punishment, 3:1–6:14
   A. Election to Punishment, 3:1-15

   B. Excessive Luxury, Sinful Piety, Unheeded Warnings, 4:1-13
   C. Requiem for a Fallen Maiden, 5:1-17
   D. Delusions of Grandeur, 5:18–6:14
IV. Prophetic Vision: Judgment, Irony, and a New Beginning 7:1–9:15
   A. Three Visions: Locusts, Fire, a Plumb line, 7:1-9
   B. A Confrontation of Authorities, 7:10-17
   C. Visions of the End, 8:1–9:6
   D. No Immunity for Israel, 9:7-10
   E. A New Beginning, 9:11-15

Superscription and Epigraph, 1:1-2

Superscription, 1:1

The superscription is the most complete of any of the prophetic books, giving Amos's occupation, hometown, and historical era (see "Introduction"). The reference to the *words* that Amos *saw* indicates the visionary character of prophetic experience (cf. 7:1-9; 8:1-3; 9:1-4). The *earthquake* must have been one of unusual magnitude, for it was recalled centuries later by Zechariah (14:4-5). That the earthquake is mentioned here probably means it was seen as partial fulfillment of Amos's prophecies (e.g., 9:1).

Epigraph, 1:2

Although often ascribed to a later Judean editor, this verse functions both as an epigraph to the entire book and as a prologue to the Sermon against the Nations (1:3–2:16). The theme of the passage is thoroughly fitting for a Judean called to prophesy in the northern kingdom of Israel. The word of YHWH, which comes to Amos in Jerusalem, reaches to Carmel and beyond. The "roaring lion" as a metaphor for the voice of God appears again in 3:8 and is common enough in the Bible and the literature of the ancient Near East. The "roar" signals judgment, as the voice of God withers the pastures and dries up the lush and fertile slopes of Mount Carmel. The epigraph sets the tone for what follows.

A Sermon against the Nations, 1:3–2:16

Oracles against foreign nations were standard fare for the court prophets of ancient Israel. Such oracles typically functioned as political propaganda, arousing support for the king's wars and diverting attention from domestic ills. Here Amos adapts this prophetic form for his own purposes, engaging the attention of his hearers with attacks on Israel's enemies (1:3–2:5) and then startling and probably rankling them with an abrupt shift to the crimes of Israel (2:6-16).

Some scholars have questioned, on formal and historical grounds, the authenticity of the oracles against Tyre, Edom, and Judah. Literary considerations, however, support the authenticity of all eight oracles. In the ancient world the number seven was the typological symbol for completeness and finality. Amos's audience, therefore, likely expected the climax, and the conclusion, of the sermon to come with the seventh member of the series, the attack on Judah (2:4-5). The hearers were then totally unprepared when Amos suddenly launched a prophecy against Israel. Amos uses a similar technique in 3:3-8; elsewhere also he betrays a decided penchant for sequences of seven (e.g., 2:6-8, 14-16; 4:6-12; 5:8-9; 9:1-4) and for unexpected conclusions (e.g., 3:1-2; 5:18-20, 21-24; 8:1-3).

The oracles follow a similar pattern, each beginning with *Thus says the* LORD, a phrase that accentuates the Hebrew understanding of prophet (*nabi*) as a messenger of YHWH. This is immediately followed by a graduated number saying: *For three transgressions . . . and for four, I will not revoke the punishment.* Such sayings are common in the literature of the Bible and the ancient Near East and typically are used in two ways: (1) to indicate an indefinite or approximate number or (2) if followed by a list of specific items (e.g., transgressions), to single out for emphasis the member that corresponds to the second number in the saying (in the present case, *four*). But Amos's use is not typical. He does not follow each saying with a specified list of crimes, nor does he seem to mean an indefinite or approximate number. Given that *three*, like the number seven, was a typological number for wholeness in the ancient world, it is likely that the combination of *three* and *four* suggests both completeness and finality. A complete and final transgression, therefore, would mean the most heinous of crimes, "the most vile, abominable, and despicable of all, thereby causing God to intervene directly and execute punishment" (Paul 1991, 29). Those are in fact the very things Amos singles out for attention.

Transgression (REB; NJB, "crime") in this context suggests revolt, the refusal to acknowledge authority. These heinous crimes against humanity are understood as a revolt against God. Here Amos, perhaps for the first time in Hebrew history, renders explicit the MONOTHEISM of the Sinai Covenant. YHWH, the God of Judah and Israel, is also the sovereign of all nations.

The Crimes of Israel's Neighboring Enemies, 1:3–2:3

The first seven oracles, slightly more than half the sermon, are directed against the seven nations that shared Israel's borders. The first three—Aram (Syria), Philistia, and Phoenicia—are indicated metonymically by their major cities: *Damascus* (1:3), *Gaza* (1:6), and *Tyre* (1:9), respectively. Israel enjoyed little in common with these three, but did share strong ethnic ties with Edom (Gen 36:1-43), with Ammon and Moab (Gen 19:30-38), and especially Judah, with whom it also shared the covenantal traditions of Yahwism. Yet, except for brief alliances, none had been a model neighbor. Relationships fractured by a long history of violence simmered in suspicion and mistrust. No doubt Amos's hearers in BETHEL shivered with nationalistic fervor and self-righteous glee as he announced the terrible consuming fire that God had decreed as punishment for the unspeakable crimes against humanity perpetrated by Israel's enemies.

The transgressions cited in the first six oracles are vicious crimes: brutalizing inhabitants and the land with a scorched earth policy (1:3), developing and maintaining a slave trade with Edom (1:6, 9), pursuing one's brother without respite (1:11), ripping open the wombs of pregnant women in Gilead in search of more land (1:13), burning the bones of a neighboring king to acquire lime for use in building construction (2:1). There seems little doubt that Amos is referring to actual historical events, but these are now lost to us. It may be significant that the crime charged to Moab (2:1-3) involves neither Israel nor Judah. Amos leaves no doubt that a crime against Edom is just as despicable as a crime committed against Israel or Judah.

In all cases the punishment is a consuming fire. In Amos 7:4 fire is a metaphor for scorching heat and drought, but here it is a harbinger of war and total destruction. In 1:4-5, for example, in describing the punishment of Damascus, Amos paints a vivid picture of battle in the ancient Near East: enemy forces set fire to the city; they break the bars of the gate and rush in upon the defenseless population; they block the escape routes, even for the king, and slaughter those who are trapped; they take the survivors into exile. Details vary in the succeeding oracles but the result is the same: devastation, exile, death.

Judah's Idolatry, 2:4-5

The ORACLE against Judah begins like the others, a tacit signal that even God's chosen are not exempt from judgment. The charges are nonspecific but clearly relate to violations of the COVENANT, *the law of the LORD*. The emphasis is probably on IDOLATRY since *led astray* almost always refers to the worship of false gods. Yet, as the message of Amos unfolds, it becomes clear that faithfulness to the covenant is not simply a matter of renouncing pagan deities and offering sacrifices only to YHWH. The true worship of YHWH is unconditionally fused with justice and righteousness in personal relationships and in the social sphere (e.g., 5:21-24).

Israel's Social Injustice, 2:6-16

As with Judah the covenant does not grant Israel immunity from prosecution but becomes the actual basis for judgment. Precisely because Israel is God's chosen, the standards will be more strict and the community will be punished for all its iniquities (3:2).

2:6-8. Crimes of Israel. Instead of one transgression, Amos lists seven, the sum of all the others combined. Yet the crimes of Israel are of a different order. They are not the atrocities perpetrated against the enemy in the heat of a military campaign, nor are they simple idolatry. Scholars disagree about specific nuances of interpretation, but there is little disagreement about the central charge: Israel is guilty of oppressing and exploiting the poor and vulnerable among its own people.

The crimes are allusions to the Book of the Covenant (Exod 20:22–23:33). *They sell the righteous for silver* (v. 6) may refer to bribes paid to judges to rule against an innocent party, but more likely it refers to the poor being forced into slavery for debts they cannot pay. In either case, it is suggested that the legal system is being subverted in violation of Exod 23:6. *They sell . . . the needy for a pair of sandals* (v. 6) suggests that debts are called in and mortgages foreclosed even for the most paltry sums, again resulting in bonded slavery for the debtor and perhaps a claim against the debtor's land. *They who trample the head of the poor into the dust of the earth, and push the afflicted out of the way* (v. 7) point to gross violations of basic rights.

Father and son go in to the same girl (v. 7) is often understood as referring to sacred prostitution connected with the worship of BAAL and other fertility gods. But given the other crimes that Amos mentions, it seems more likely that the phrase refers to father and son taking advantage of a slave or indentured servant (Exod 21:7-11).

So that my holy name is profaned (v. 7) may refer to the immediately preceding crime, but it is likely a reference to all the crimes mentioned thus far. It is not just sexual misconduct that profanes the name of God but the exploitation of the poor and vulnerable.

The two crimes listed in v. 8 give a picture of people worshiping in their sanctuaries with garments taken in pledge (in violation of Exod 22:25-27) and wine purchased with fines imposed. The worshipers profane YHWH's name because they see no incongruity between their worship and their immoral treatment of their fellow human beings.

2:9-11. Care of YHWH. The focus shifts from what Israel has done to what YHWH has done for Israel. Amos reminds his hearers of the conquest of the Amorites (v. 9), the escape from Egypt and the wandering in the wilderness that preceded the conquest (v. 10), the gift of prophets and nazirites (v. 11). This summary of YHWH's great deeds may well carry an allusion to the preface of the TEN COMMANDMENTS (Exod 20:1), setting Israel's obligations within the context of YHWH's gracious initiative in delivering Israel from bondage in Egypt.

2:12. No respect. Israel has failed to respect the NAZIRITE vows and has refused to heed the message of the prophets (2:12). Therefore, like its neighbors, Israel will be punished.

2:13-16. Judgment. YHWH makes war on Israel. The metaphor of an overloaded cart that makes ruts in the soft earth perhaps suggests that Israel will be ground into the earth just as it has done to the poor (2:7). In vv. 14-16 a picture of terror is drawn such that even the swift and powerful armies of Israel cannot stand up against YHWH (just as the Amorites could not). The archers, the foot soldiers, the cavalry—even *those who are stout of heart* (REB, NJB, "the bravest of warriors")—will flee in terror.

Israel's Sinfulness and God's Punishment, 3:1–6:14

This second major section of Amos does not have the literary unity of chaps. 1–2, although there is unmistakable thematic coherence. Many commentators find three collections of oracles here, each beginning with *Hear this word* (3:1, 4:1, 5:1).

Election to Punishment, 3:1-15

3:1-2. Election. The chapter and verse divisions are both a blessing and a curse. They give order to the text and provide a most helpful standard of reference, but they often obscure important literary connections within the text. For example, should vv. 1-2 be seen only as the beginning of a new section? Or might it also function as a concluding coda for the Sermon against the Nations, an exclamation point sealing the case against Israel?

In any case Amos here invokes the theme of ELECTION (e.g., Exod 19:3-6) but with jarring irony reverses the traditional logic. Election is not for salvation but for punishment. *Known* is to be understood relationally, not cognitively. There is obvious tension between v. 2a and the universalism reflected in 9:7, and one cannot be certain whether Amos is here affirming that Israel is indeed God's chosen or whether he is satirizing the view of election held by his contemporaries. In either case, Israel does not have moral license to mistreat the poor.

3:3-8. A familiar pattern. These six verses are a carefully crafted unit following the same 7/8 structure of the Sermon against the Nations. It begins with a sequence that builds to an apparent climax with the seventh member, which is then transcended by the surprise introduction of an eighth member. Amos snatches the attention of his audience with a series of rhetorical questions dealing with obvious instances of cause and effect, something like "Is the Pope Catholic?" or "Is the sky blue?" Most problematic is v. 3: the NRSV (*Do two walk together unless they have made an appointment?*) suggests too much precalculation or preplanning. The REB is better: "Do two people travel together unless they have so agreed?"

Amos's choice of images—a lion hunting prey, a bird caught in a snare, disaster befalling a city—carry veiled allusions to the judgment that is to come upon Israel. The sixth and seventh members of the sequence (v. 6) shift the frame of reference to the human world, and in v. 6b the name of YHWH is introduced for the first time. The audience is captured and Amos presses his point: given the fact that God does call prophets and reveals the divine secrets to them (cf. 2:11), then who can refuse to prophesy when God has so commanded? This is, clearly, Amos's defense of his calling, possibly in response to criticism and charges that he not be taken seriously (7:10-12). But it is also a defense of all other prophets whose voices have gone unheeded (2:12b). If the world is indeed structured by precise sequences of cause and effect, then how can one deny the prophets a hearing?

3:9-11. Questioning protection. Note the recurring use of *strongholds*, the walled cities or fortresses that shielded the rich and powerful. The setting is in court as Amos summons the strongholds of *Ashdod* (a Philistine city) and Egypt to bear witness to the *tumults* and *oppression* in SAMARIA. The real addressee, of course, is the accused, the aristocracy of Israel whose strongholds have been built and maintained by *violence and robbery*. The sentence, to be carried out by an anonymous adversary, reflects the justice of *lex talionis* (Exod 21:23-25): Israel's own strongholds shall be plundered. As is the case in several oracles of Amos, there is clever wordplay in the Hebrew that is lost in English.

3:12. Judgment. Although likely reflecting a separate oracle, v. 12 serves in the present context to expand the judgment against Israel announced in 3:11. The image of a shepherd snatching *two legs, or a piece of an ear* from the mouth of a lion probably alludes to Exod 22:13: shepherds were not held responsible for a sheep mangled by wild beasts if they could produce acceptable evidence. The salvaging of *two legs* and/or *a piece of an ear* does not suggest that a remnant will be saved (cf. 5:15); it testifies to total destruction. The precise image intended in the last part of the verse is uncertain; but given the parallel with the shepherd, the NRSV certainly captures the essential meaning with *corner of a couch and part of a bed.*

3:13-15. Destruction. This oracle, which further details the destruction of Samaria announced in 3:11, includes the first mention of BETHEL. Literally the "house of the god El," Bethel had long been a sacred place and became increasingly important during the period of the divided kingdom. It seems strange to *punish the altars of Bethel*, but the meaning probably relates to the use of the altar for sanctuary or asylum (Exod 21:12-14; 1 Kgs 1:50-53; 2:28-34). In other words, the altar will provide no refuge. Probably the meaning is even broader, for altar is a metonym for religious ritual (cf. 5:4-5). The recurring references to *house* in v. 15 suggest excessive luxury—two residences, lavishly decorated, etc. These shall come to an end.

Excessive Luxury, Sinful Piety, Unheeded Warnings, 4:1-13

4:1-3. The folly of coveteousness. Bashan was a territory east of Galilee noted for its agricultural riches (cf. Deut 32:14; Ps 22:12; Ezek 39:18). *Cows of Bashan* is a striking metaphor, therefore, for excessive luxury. Although an interesting case has been made for a fertility cult whose deity is symbolized by a bull of Bashan (see Rosenbaum 1990, 57), the phrase probably refers to the rich women of Samaria. The women *oppress the poor* and *crush the needy*, not directly, but through their insatiable appetite for luxury and leisure. Their sin is not simply collaboration with injustice but an unchecked covetousness that both initiates and maintains the war against the poor. The image is certainly chauvinistic, but it does point to the connection between covetousness (Exod 20:17) and injustice. Covetousness is decidedly not restricted to the women alone.

The punishment is announced in v. 2a in the form of an oath. *The time is surely coming* probably has something of an eschatological bearing, suggesting radical disjunction between this age and the next. The key terms in v. 2b (NRSV, *hooks* and *fishhooks*; REB, "shields" and "fish-baskets") are difficult to decipher. The most literal meanings are "shields" and "pots," respectively, but both terms can also mean "thorns" and, by extension, "hooks." If Amos is continuing the metaphor of cattle, the reference may be to harpoon-like devices that double as cattle prods or perhaps as hooks used to drag a carcass (Mays 1969, 72–73). If he is switching metaphors, Amos probably means the wire baskets and pots used both to catch and transport fish (Paul 1991, 130–35).

Another lexical difficulty arises in v. 3. The first clause is relatively clear, suggesting numerous breaches in the city wall through which the inhabitants can be carried straight out, with no need for detours. The difficulty is with *Harmon*, an unknown term. It is obviously a place, but does it designate a geographical area or a specific location? Is it a place of death or a place of exile? Should it be emended to read "Hermon" (i.e., Mount Hermon) which is located in Bashan? The REB rendering "dunghill" is an interesting guess.

4:4-5. A parody. In a bitter parody of Israelite worship Amos attacks religion that has become a tool of self-interest and the occasion for evading God's commandments. BETHEL and GILGAL were sanctuaries with long and venerable histories, and Amos assumes the posture of a cultic official welcoming the pilgrims to the shrine. But again Amos surprises, and certainly infuriates, his hearers with a jarring conclusion: *Come to Bethel—and transgress; to Gilgal—and multiply transgression!* *Transgression* is the same term used repeatedly in the opening Sermon against the Nations (1:3–2:16). The point is not subtle: the worship of God has itself become rebellion. The rituals of offering, established to atone for human sin and thereby restore the relationship between God and human beings, have themselves become occasions for sin. Amos anticipates the tireless warnings of Reinhold Niebuhr that it is precisely in their worship that human beings are most powerfully assailed by temptation.

It is difficult to identify precisely the sacrifices and offerings that Amos mentions, but there are noticeable similarities with Lev 7:11-18 and Deut 12:6. More important is his use of second person pronouns—*your sacrifices*, *your tithes*, *for so you love to do*—which suggest that worship has become a means of addressing Israel's own agenda instead of attending to God's desires and demands. In violation of the third commandment (Exod 20:7), religion has been co-opted for selfish ends. As Amaziah protests to Amos (7:13), Bethel has become *the king's sanctuary, a temple of the kingdom*; but to Amos that means that it is no longer YHWH's.

It is possible to read this and similar passages (e.g., 5:21-24) as Amos's total repudiation of the cult, a reduction of religion to ethics like that of the philosopher Immanuel Kant. It is more likely, however, that Amos did not attack the cult per se but a theology that failed to acknowledge the connection between those worship practices and YHWH's demands for justice and righteousness. Both the Hebrew Bible and the NT are adamant that faithfulness to God cannot be separated from responsibility to one's neighbor.

4:6-13. Reversal. In an ironic reversal of tradition, Amos reminds his hearers of seven calamities that God has visited upon Israel. The irony is especially apparent when seen in connection both with YHWH's gracious acts of deliverance (highlighted in 2:9-12), and the description of rebellious piety described in vv. 4-5. It was expected that faithfulness to the covenant would bring good and prosperous times and that disobedience would bring misfortune. The calamities, therefore, should have been a warning that things were not right, but the warnings went unheeded. Now, like the Pharaoh whose heart was hardened, Israel has no more opportunity to repent.

In describing the seven calamities Amos again draws upon his genius for image making. Famine is described as *cleanness of teeth* (v. 6). The effects of drought are portrayed in the figure of a dehydrated person staggering from town to town in search of water (v. 8). Military disaster is captured in the stench of rotting flesh (human and animal) that burns the nostrils (v. 10b). The earthquake and the resulting conflagration recall the destruction of Sodom and Gomorrah (v. 11). The other calamities are less vivid but no less destructive: *blight and mildew* (v. 9a), locusts (v. 9b), and *pestilence* (v. 10a). The sequence is punctuated five times by an unsettling refrain: *yet you did not return to me, says the LORD* (vv. 6, 8, 9, 10, 11).

In v. 12 Amos shifts from past to future. This is another example of a sequence apparently climaxing with the seventh member (the earthquake reminiscent of Sodom and Gomorrah in v. 11), only to be followed by an eighth. The eighth calamity is not described, except that it involves a face to face meeting with God. Seven warnings were enough. God will now meet Israel face to face. The lack of description is probably deliberate, for the unknown is always more terrifying than what is known.

The doxology in v. 13 is the first of three in Amos (see also 5:8-9; 9:5-6), all of which may derive from the same hymn. There is no reason to challenge the broad consensus that these are later additions to the book, but it is quite remarkable how well the first and third doxologies fit the context. The THEOPHANY described here (v. 13) is a suitable epilogue to the final warning of v. 12: *Prepare to meet your God, O Israel!* Israel must prepare to meet YHWH, the God of hosts, who creates the mountains and who is manifest in the wind and clouds of a morning thunderstorm. The clouds darken the sky and hide the mountain peaks.

Requiem for a Fallen Maiden, 5:1-17

The first seventeen verses of chap. 5 appear at first glance to be a random collection of oracles. However, recent studies (e.g., Paul 1991, 157–81) have shown convincingly that this passage is a composite collection of oracles arranged precisely in a CHIASM, a repetition in reverse order. Assuming that the doxology of 5:8-9 is an interpolation, the passage can be diagrammed as follows.

A 5:1-3, Requiem for a fallen Israel
  B 5:4-6, Seek YHWH and live
    C 5:7, 10-13, An evil time
  B′ 5:14-15, Seek good and not evil
A′ 5:16-17, Requiem for a fallen Israel

5:1-3. Requiem for a fallen Israel. The word of the prophet in v. 2 is a carefully constructed elegy in the meter of Israel's funeral dirges. Written in present perfect tense, it is a dramatic and electrifying presentation of what is yet future. Israel's funeral is pictured as that of a young maiden, still a virgin, who is raped, beaten, and left to die by an invading army. The tragedy occurs on her own land, where help would be expected, perhaps even by YHWH (see 1 Sam 2:8; Hos 6:2; Amos 9:11), but there is *no one to raise her up*. The image of military disaster continues with the word of the *Lord GOD* in v. 3: casualties will total ninety percent of those who march out to fight. Like Ebenezer Scrooge encountering his own tombstone, Amos's audience must have been terrified to hear their own obituary (Mays 1969, 84). For Amos himself it must have been a moment of unbearable sorrow (cf. 6:6).

5:4-6. Seek YHWH and live. There is still hope that disaster may be averted. But everything hinges on Israel's response to YHWH's invitation. The NRSV rendering of *seek me* (v. 4) seems misleading here since what is meant is something like "make your way to me" (REB) or "turn to me." The invitation must have been baffling to Amos's hearers, especially when coupled with the negative imperatives regarding *Bethel, Gilgal*, and *Beer-sheba*. No doubt they thought they *were* turning to YHWH by offering sacrifices at these prominent sanctuaries. The invitation is repeated in v. 6 and followed by the judgment for disobedience, the fire that signals the devastation of war.

This passage continues Amos's assault upon the cult. Just as YHWH is not to be found in ritual (4:4-5), neither is the deity found in "holy places." Amos thus reiterates a biblical theme that culminates in Stephen's speech in Acts: "Yet the Most High does not dwell in houses made with human hands" (Acts 7:48). Amos does not indicate here just where YHWH is to be found, but the answer comes in 5:14-15: YHWH is to be found in doing good and establishing justice.

5:8-9. Doxology. This, the second of the doxologies (cf. 4:13; 9:5-6), quite obviously interrupts the flow between 5:7 and 5:10 (the REB is surely correct in linking 5:7 directly with 5:10-13). Internally, the doxology has problems of its own. For example, the closing line of v. 8, *the LORD* (YHWH) *is his name*, fits much better at the end of v. 9. The meaning is relatively clear, however, praising YHWH both as lord of nature (v. 8) and as lord of the nations (v. 9). As the one who controls the stars and the sun as well as the rains, YHWH is the sovereign of time. As an interpolation, the doxology may have been inserted here to suggest reasons why YHWH is not found in the sanctuaries (5:4-5). As the Creator of the world and the sovereign of time and the nations, YHWH cannot be confined to "holy places."

5:7, 10-13. An evil time. This passage marks the middle term in the chiasm. Coming on the heels of 5:6, it details evidence that Israel has not turned to YHWH. The passage as a whole assumes a setting in Israel's courts of justice, the proceedings of which took place *in the gate* (v. 10; 5:15). The courts were established to administer justice (e.g., Exod 23:1-9), but Amos charges that they have been corrupted, with the assistance of the "judges" themselves, to serve the interests of the rich and powerful.

The terms JUSTICE and RIGHTEOUSNESS (v. 7) also appear together in 5:24 and 6:12. The terms are closely related but not identical. *Righteousness* is the broader term; it describes the will of YHWH, especially as that will ought to be manifest in the relationships of a given community or society. *Justice* has a narrower legal focus, the process by which righteousness is restored to the community.

Israel is guilty both of unrighteousness and injustice. The poor have been brutally mistreated, trampled upon with heavy taxes (v. 11). They turn to the courts seeking justice; but they are hated for filing charges and telling the truth (v. 10), and they are bullied and ignored by the courts (v. 12). Note the irony of the punishment in v. 11 (having built houses and planted vineyards with money extorted from the poor, they will enjoy neither) and the despair of v. 13.

5:14-15. Seek good and not evil. The chiastic parallel to 5:4-6, this passage answers the question as to where YHWH is to be found. To *seek the LORD and live* (5:6) means *to seek good and not evil* (v. 14). YHWH, and therefore life, is not to be found in the holy places or in the formality of worship, but in turning and devoting oneself wholly to what is *good*. The closing phrase of v. 14, *just as you have said*, indicates that Amos is quoting from his hearers who have insisted all along that "YHWH is with us." Seek good and YHWH *will be with you* (v. 14). But Israel must change its ways, establishing justice instead of tearing it down. The reticence of v. 15b, *it may be*, declares that God's graciousness cannot be presumed upon; God cannot be manipulated for selfish ends.

<u>5:16-17. Requiem for a fallen Israel.</u> These verses return to the elegy with which the unit began. The wailing includes every aspect of society: the city dwellers, the farmers, the professional mourners (*those skilled in lamentation*). Even the vineyards, normally a place of celebration, are invaded with scenes of mourning (v. 17). *I will pass through the midst of you* may allude to the death angel of Exod 12:12, 23.

Delusions of Grandeur, 5:18–6:14

<u>5:18-20. A powerful image.</u> The *day of the LORD* makes its earliest appearance in biblical literature in the words of Amos, but there can be little doubt that it already functioned as a powerful image in the popular ideology of Israel. Scholars are divided on the precise origins of the concept, but the meaning is clear. The *day of the LORD* referred to that future time when God would intervene decisively on Israel's behalf and destroy her enemies. For Israel, the reign of JEROBOAM II was filled with signs of God's favor and hence pointed to God's continuing presence in Israel. Amos attacks this popular notion with two rhetorical questions (vv. 18, 20) that envelop a vivid description of catastrophe from which there is no final escape (v. 19; cf. 2:13-16).

<u>5:21-24. Questioning the popular.</u> Returning to the theme of 4:4-5, Amos contradicts the popular view of religious ceremony, leaving no doubt that ritual is not YHWH's concern. The *solemn assemblies* (v. 21) are the lavish ceremonies that marked holiday festivals and sought help in times of trouble. *I will not accept them* means, literally, "I will not smell them." Thus the cumulative image of vv. 22-23 is God's holding the nose, shutting the eyes, and closing the ears to Israel's ceremonies. The reason is that God is concerned about *justice* and *righteousness* (v. 24). The image of an *everflowing stream* is especially powerful in a country crisscrossed with so many wadis, the dry riverbeds that carry water only during a storm.

<u>5:25-27. Another question.</u> This passage, which many scholars regard as a later addition, is more intricately connected to 5:21-24 than first appearances suggest. The rhetorical question is intended to show that during Israel's wilderness experience YHWH was known through justice and righteousness and not through the ritual of sacrifice (cf. Jer 7:22-23). It seems that Amos looks back to the wilderness wanderings as the golden age of Israel, while the Israelites look with nostalgia to the time of DAVID and SOLOMON. *Sakkuth* and *Kaiwan* designate Mesopotamian deities, whose effigies are taken up as part of a solemn procession. The bitter irony is that the procession of worshipers and their idols is driven into exile by none other than YHWH, the God of hosts. *Beyond Damascus* (v. 27) is understood by many as a veiled reference to ASSYRIA, but Paul (1991, 198) sees this as a second irony, namely, that exile will take Israel even farther than its military conquests.

<u>6:1-7. Affliction for the comfortable.</u> In graphic terms, Amos describes the lavish self-indulgence and cockiness of Israel's leaders. *Notables* (v. 1; REB, "men of mark") is possibly a self-designation used by those who thought of themselves as the "first families" in *the first of the nations* (v. 1). *Calneh, Hamath,* and *Gath*

were wealthy commercial centers that once boasted of their invincibility before going down to defeat. The rhetorical questions of vv. 2-3 thus serve to warn the notables of their delusion of grandeur. The *evil day* (v. 3) is probably identical to the *day of the LORD* (5:18). The point of v. 3 seems to be that deliberate disregard for the approaching day of judgment is causally linked to the violent exploitation of the poor.

The feast depicted in vv. 4-6a may be a description of a *marzeah*, a religious and social fraternity of the wealthy. In any case the picture is one of obscene extravagance: the guests recline on expensive furniture; they enjoy the choicest cuts of meat while being serenaded with music; they gulp their wine from widemouthed bowls and garnish themselves with the finest perfumes. In the social sphere such self-indulgence eventually leads to apathy, the inability to grieve and show compassion to those who suffer. The oracle ends on a note of irony: the *notables of the first of the nations* (v. 1) will be *the first to go into exile* (v. 7).

6:8-11. Judgment. YHWH's oath suggests the irrevocability of the judgment to come. YHWH's anger is directed at the *pride of Jacob* (v. 8), Israel's cocky arrogance, and quite possibly a nationalistic slogan used by the Israelites themselves (cf. Ps 47:4). In 6:9-10 the scene shifts to a specific household, although the precise circumstances are not clear. Perhaps Amos intends a devastating plague from which there is no escape. Those responsible for disposing of the bodies (REB, "a relative and an embalmer") fear even to mention the name of YHWH, lest they too suffer the same fate. The *great house* and the *little house* (v. 11) are a composite symbol for Israel.

6:12-14. Disastrous consequences. The rhetorical questions of v. 12a indicate the disastrous consequences that occur when the natural order is violated. One would be a fool to run one's horse over the rocks or attempt to plow the sea (or perhaps the rocks) with oxen. Yet the perversion of justice and righteousness is just as foolish (v. 12b). *Lo-debar* and *Karnaim* were towns conquered by Jeroboam II in an earlier campaign (see 2 Kgs 14:25). Amos's sarcasm is evident in the literal meaning of *Lo-debar*: (REB, "nothing"). The boast of v. 13b is likely a quotation from the Israelites themselves. Hence the irony of v. 14 in which YHWH, *the God of hosts*, speaks of the deity's own military plans.

Prophetic Vision: Judgment, Irony, and a New Beginning, 7:1–9:15

The third major section of Amos features five visions (7:1-3, 4-6, 7-9; 8:1-3; 9:1-4), but it also includes a narrative account of Amos's confrontation with Amaziah (7:10-17), additional oracles of judgment (8:4-14; 9:7-10), a doxology (9:5-6), and a prophecy of hope (9:11-15). The five visions are probably the most intensely studied, and the most passionately debated, sections of the book.

Visions were commonly understood in the ancient world as a means of divine communication and hence the source of a prophet's message. Partly because of the prominence of VISION in the call of Isaiah (Isa 6:1-13), it has often been assumed that the five visions of Amos relate specifically to his call and thus precede the other oracles in the book. But there is nothing thematic about the visions that warrants this conclusion. Furthermore, the visions portray Amos as already having assumed the mantle of a prophet (Paul 1991, 222–25). The five visions bear striking similarities, but it is the subtle differences that provide the key to their interpretation.

Three Visions: Locusts, Fire, and a Plumb line, 7:1-9

7:1-3. Locusts. Amos has no difficulty understanding the first two visions, the *locusts* and the *shower of fire* (7:4). The *time of the latter growth* (v. 1) refers to the period in the spring just after the vegetable crops have sprouted. The grain crops are planted earlier (cf. the "winter wheat" crops in the United States), and although showing signs of maturity by spring, they are not ready for harvest. Thus the *locusts* attack at a particularly vulnerable time, destroying both the grain and the vegetable crops. The meaning of *the king's mowings* is not certain but likely refers to a share of the harvest demanded by the king.

Amos assumes the mantle of the prophet in interceding for Israel. *He is so small* (v. 2) refers simply to Israel's vulnerability, its inability to survive such a catastrophe. Making no appeal to the covenant and relying entirely upon God's mercy, Amos asks for a complete pardon. God does not grant the pardon but does offer a temporary reprieve (Paul 1991, 229), patiently extending the deadline for repentance.

7:4-6. Fire. The *shower of fire* is a scorching heat wave with cosmic consequences. In Hebrew cosmology the *great deep* is the cosmic aquifier that supplies all springs and rivers. When it dries up, everything becomes desert. Again Amos intercedes, but this time the petition is not to pardon but only to *cease* (v. 5).

7:7-9. Plumb line. Visions three and four are puzzling for Amos, rendering him speechless. Instead of a scene of destruction he "sees" ordinary objects (v. 7, *plumb line*; 8:1, *summer fruit*), which he can identify but the meaning of which he is unable to decipher. He is in a sense stripped of his role as intercessor and is given a message to proclaim to the people. The *plumb line* is a metaphor for the COVENANT, the standard by which Israel (*my people Israel*) was created. But now as God takes the measure of Israel's moral rectitude, the people are found to be grossly aslant. Hence the prophecy of judgment. The *high places of Isaac* (v. 9) is a pejorative reference to the various sanctuaries of Israel and Judah (see 2 Kgs 17:7-18), intimating the worship of idols.

A Confrontation of Authorities, 7:10-17

The encounter between Amos and Amaziah is in essence a confrontation between YHWH and JEROBOAM II. The issue is one of authority. Whom does Israel serve? YHWH or Jeroboam? Bethel has become *the king's sanctuary . . . a temple of the kingdom* (v. 13). It bows to the king's authority and thus serves the interests of the state. Having been squeezed out of the sanctuary, YHWH must now assert divine authority from outside. God does so through Amos, a reluctant outsider.

7:10-13. Amaziah speaks. Amaziah has no doubt about whom he serves. He reports Amos as a dangerous conspirator who must be silenced lest his words incite rebellion. He seems not to consider that Amos might indeed be a true prophet of YHWH. As reported, the message to Jeroboam includes only those themes that relate directly to the king, suggesting that Amaziah has deliberately concealed Amos's prophecies against the high places and sanctuaries, since these are his own concern.

Amaziah's words to Amos are not in themselves mocking or disrespectful and may even indicate an eagerness to be rid of Amos without further confrontation. A *seer* (Heb. *roeh*) is practically synonymous with "prophet" (Heb. *nabi*), although more directly related to visionary experience. The *king's sanctuary* (v. 13) refers to the fact that shortly after the division of the kingdom, Bethel had been designated an official sanctuary of the northern kingdom. The move was intended to break the ties to the sanctuary in Jerusalem that remained in Judah. The tragedy is that the king's authority has replaced the authority of YHWH. YHWH is forced to speak from the outside.

7:14-15. Amos responds. Amos's opening response to Amaziah is one of the most perplexing statements in the book. It is clear that Amos was not a *prophet's son* (v. 14), that is, a member of a prophetic guild. But what does Amos mean when he insists that he is not a *prophet* (Heb. *nabi*)? One reading, followed by the REB, sees this statement in the past tense: "I was no prophet, nor was I a prophet's son." The point is that he was not a prophet until he was called by God to prophesy to Israel (v. 15). A second reading understands *prophet* here to refer to one of the professional cultic prophets. These professionals were paid by the royal court and were expected to serve the interests of the king. The point of this second reading is that Amos speaks as an outsider and not as one of the professionals retained by the king. In either case, especially in view of 2:12, Amos surely identified with that line of prophets like Elijah who spoke from outside the cult and the royal court.

7:16-17. Judgment on Amaziah. This is the only oracle in the entire book directed to an individual. Since Amaziah has sought to stifle the prophecy of Amos (cf. 2:12), the punishment will be especially severe. The reference to an *unclean land* (v. 17) is surely ironic, since it means the forfeiture of Amaziah's vocation. The one who has tried to silence Amos will himself be silenced.

Visions of the End, 8:1–9:6

8:1-3. Summer fruit. The fourth vision is very similar to the third, but now the judgment is extended to the nation as a whole. *Summer fruit* refers to fresh tree-ripened fruit, probably figs, harvested in late summer and normally a sign of celebration. But in a dramatic play on words the image of *summer fruit* (Heb. *qayitz*) is transmuted into a symbol for Israel's imminent *end* (Heb. *qētz*). The cause of the catastrophe is unspecified, but the results are graphically depicted in v. 3. The command to *be silent* recalls 6:10 and may indicate a fear that speaking will invoke further disaster.

8:4-8. Concern for the poor. This oracle is directed at the merchants who exploit the poor and needy with deceitful business practices and even traffic in the slave trade. Israel observed a lunar calendar and attached special significance to the monthly observance of the festival of the *new moon*. The festival was observed with sumptuous feasts and accompanied by sacrifices (cf. 1 Sam 20:5). As with sabbath observance, the festival of the new moon demanded the suspension of all business dealings. The merchants, eager to resume their dishonest wheeling and dealing, protest these "blue laws" even as they piously observe the festivals (v. 5a).

The *ephah* was a dry measure that corresponded to something like our modern bushel. The *shekel* here is not a unit of currency, but a unit of weight used to determine the amount of payment (usually in silver). The images in v. 6a recall the selling of debtors into slavery in 2:6, only here the focus is on those who buy the slaves.

YHWH's judgment is pronounced in vv. 7-8 in the form of an irrevocable oath. *Their deeds* refer to the deceitful and inhumane practices of the merchants just mentioned (vv. 5-6). The remarkable rise and fall of the NILE River, an annual occurrence now known to be caused by the tilt of the earth's axis, was widely considered an ancient wonder. Here it depicts the upheavals of a horrendous earthquake.

8:9-10. Day of judgment. *That day*, the day of judgment, is here compared to a solar eclipse at high noon. In the ancient world, eclipses, solar and lunar, were almost universally regarded as portents of disaster. Even for sophisticated moderns a solar eclipse sends chills down the spine. The darkness recalls Amos's earlier words about *the day of the LORD* (5:18-20). Again the precise nature of the calamity is not spelled out, but it will bring a reversal of the festive air that pervades the current life of the rich and powerful. Donning sackcloth and shaving the head were traditional expressions of mourning. The pain of that *bitter day* can only be likened to the death of an only child.

8:11-14. The absence of YHWH. The two preceding oracles portray disaster in terms of the destructive presence of God. Here the disaster is just the opposite, *a famine . . . of hearing the words of the LORD*, the complete absence of YHWH. YHWH has been present to Israel, but not in the way Israel thought. YHWH was not in the worship at Bethel and Gilgal but in the words of the prophet. Failing to heed the prophet, Israel is left on its own without divine guidance. The futile search for divine guidance is pictured in v. 12 using verbs that suggest a staggering and unsteady gait. *From sea to sea* probably means "from the Mediterranean to the Dead Sea." *From north to east* seems a bit strange and one would expect something like "from north to south." The omission of any reference to the south may be deliberate, suggesting obliquely that the famine will not extend to Judah.

While vv. 13-14 was originally a separate oracle, it adds to the sense of futility expressed in vv. 11-12. In YHWH's absence the people turn to other gods; but these gods, like mirages in the desert, cannot slake the thirst for YHWH's word and presence. It was a widespread custom in the ancient world to invoke the deity to guarantee one's credibility.

There are serious difficulties regarding the exact identity of the gods in v. 14, but the essential point is not hard to see: The indictment falls upon those who swear by—and in effect, worship—the gods of Bethel, Dan, and Beer-sheba. Bethel, of course, was the principal sanctuary of Samaria, and Dan and Beer-sheba defined the northern and southern boundaries of the early tribal league and the united monarchy (Judg 20:1; 1 Sam 3:20; 1 Kgs 4:25). Hence the specific mention of these three sanctuaries is a symbolic way of designating all sanctuaries of Israel and Judah. According to an early tradition, the name *Beer-sheba* was related to the swearing of an oath (Gen 21:25-31).

9:1-4. Earthquake. The fifth vision is the most despairing of all. Amos glimpses YHWH standing by the altar (cf. Isa 6:1-5), probably the altar at Bethel during a festival when the sanctuary is crowded with worshipers. It is not clear to whom the order is given to *strike the capitals* (the prophet? the heavenly hosts?), but the image is an earthquake that topples the massive stone columns of the sanctuary and virtually annihilates the assembled worshipers. The message is another variation on a theme: there is no salvation in the cult at Bethel. YHWH's presence there is not a saving presence.

The remainder of the vision (vv. 1b-4) reiterates another theme of Amos: God's omnipresence renders impossible the escape of those who survive the initial assault. God is sovereign throughout the cosmos, from the depths of Sheol to the highest reaches of heaven. In a dramatic reversal of images Amos pictures God's hand snatching the people from Sheol, only this time for destruction. God's sovereignty also extends throughout the earth, from the dense forests on the top of Mount Carmel to the bottom of the sea and into all alien lands. Even deportation to a foreign land is no means of escape. The *eyes* of God (v. 4b) typically suggest God's favor; here they suggest a destructive gaze.

9:5-6. Hymn of praise. In context, on the heels of 9:1-4, this hymn of praise extolling the power of the Creator becomes in effect a hymn of judgment, affirming the power of YHWH to carry out the punishment. At God's mere touch the earth "heaves" (REB) and quivers like a liquid, rising and falling like the Nile (cf. 8:8). The picture of the cosmos in v. 6 is strikingly similar to that of Gen 1, a firmament or vault setting the boundaries of the earth.

No Immunity for Israel, 9:7-10

9:7. God's Sovereignty. Two rhetorical questions push the theme of God's universal sovereignty in a radical direction. The first question compares Israel to the Ethiopians, the biblical Cushites who lived at the periphery of the known world. The suggestion is that no nation has special claim upon God's favor. The second question compares Israel to its closest neighbors, declaring that both the Philistines and

Arameans were also beneficiaries of an exodus experience. Thus Israel's tradition of exodus is no guarantee of immunity from judgment.

9:8. Sinful kingdom. Interpretative difficulties abound in v. 8. Is *the sinful kingdom* a generic reference—that is, does it refer to any nation that sins? Or does it refer specifically to Israel, who is so obviously singled out in the book? If the former, the exception clause of v. 8c would seem to reintroduce Israel's special status in that it is the recipient of God's mercy in a way other nations are not. Understandably, many commentators have come to view v. 8c as a later addition. If, however, the reference is specifically to Israel as *the sinful kingdom*, the intended contrast is between *kingdom* and *the house of Jacob*, that is, between Israel as a political entity (e.g., a nation) and Israel as a people. In this case, it is the nation that will be destroyed, but a remnant may survive, even if in exile.

9:9-10. Judgment. The latter interpretation seems supported by the image of sifting in v. 9. It is not clear just what kind of *sieve* is intended, but the focus is on the separation of the wheat and the chaff, an analogy for the separation of the righteous from the sinners. The judgment seems to be specifically on the sinners, those who are so arrogant or cocky as to claim, *"Evil shall not overtake or meet us"* (v. 10). The quotation is almost certainly a statement that Amos has heard from his opponents.

A New Beginning, 9:11-15

The two oracles in vv. 11-15 give the Book of Amos a stunning and startling conclusion. The unqualified and unconditional announcement that God will restore *the booth of David that is fallen* (v. 11) seems a radical departure from the terrible judgments and qualified hopes of the previous oracles. Yet, while it is quite likely that these verses were penned by an unknown postexilic author, they devise a fitting conclusion to the book, reminding the reader that God does not punish simply for the sake of punishment. "The prophet's chastisement is meant to serve as a transitional stage to a period of future restoration, at least for the surviving remnant" (Paul 1991, 289). Judgment is not the whole of the prophetic word, nor is it the final word.

9:11-12. Restoration. Elsewhere in Amos (8:3, 9, 13) *that day* signals impending judgment; here it proclaims a time of restoration. The *booth of David* (v. 11) is an unusual construction that has elicited several different interpretations. The specific images in v. 11b suggest the restoration of a walled city, leading many commentators to see this as a reference to the fall of Jerusalem in 587/6. Other scholars see it referring to the division of the kingdom after the death of Solomon and/or to the bleak and precarious state of affairs that existed throughout much of the era of the divided kingdom. In either case the restoration is conceived in terms of a return to the era of David. *All the nations who are called by my name* (v. 12) is likely a reference to the neighboring states that were conquered and ruled by David. These are the same nations charged with heinous crimes in 1:3–2:3. They are included in the restoration as well as Israel and Judah.

9:13-15. Salvation. The announcement of unconditional salvation continues. In contrast to the drought and famine of earlier oracles, v. 13 pictures a time of optimal agricultural conditions and abundant harvest. Normally, the growing season was from November to May, which meant a wait of six months between the harvest and the next planting. But now conditions will be such that planting will begin before the harvest is gathered, and the grape harvest will be so abundant that treading will not be completed until the new seed is sown. The image of mountains dripping with wine both recalls the earlier vision of a "land flowing with milk and honey" (Exod 3:17) and symbolizes for some early Christians the coming of the messianic age (John 2:1-11).

The promises of restoration in v. 14 signal the undoing of the curses in 5:11. Similarly, the promise of v. 15 reverses the judgment of exile that figures so prominently in the book. Like a tree carefully planted and cared for, Israel will never again be uprooted. The land, the original gift of Yahweh, will be unconditionally returned (Wolff 1977, 354).

Works Cited

Mays, James L. 1969. *Amos. A Commentary.* OTL.
Paul, Shalom M. 1991. *Amos. A Commentary on the Book of Amos.* Herm.
Wolff, Hans Walter. 1977. *Joel and Amos. A Commentary on the Books of the Prophets Joel and Amos.*

Obadiah [MCB 757-61]

Cecil P. Staton, Jr.

Introduction

Only twenty-one verses in length, the Book of Obadiah is the shortest book in the OT. This interesting but often overlooked book is a collection of brief prophetic utterances that hurl both words of judgment toward Edom, Israel's enemy (and relative—see Gen 25:19-34; 27:1–28:9) to the southeast (vv. 1-14, 15b), and words of hope toward ISRAEL (vv. 15a, 16-21).

Frequently criticized for a retributive spirit and a narrow nationalism, Obadiah suffers from a neglect few portions of scripture can rival. To its credit the book offers the student of scripture a unique glimpse into a period of Israel's history about which we know all too little. Although Obadiah is not likely to attain the status of a much-loved biblical text, when viewed against the backdrop of its original setting an appreciation for Obadiah may be recovered.

The Book of Obadiah served as a "word from God" for a particularly difficult moment in Israel's history—a word with surprising contemporary relevance. Obadiah declares the terrible consequences for those who participate in cruel and inhuman oppression of neighbors or stand idly by while others do so (vv. 1-14, 15b). Moreover the prophet offers the promise of a future in YHWH's kingdom for those who suffer under the enormous burden of oppression (vv. 15a, 16-21).

The Prophet

Almost nothing is known of the person Obadiah, whose name means "servant of Yahweh" (a name shared by twelve different individuals in the OT). What little can be learned of Obadiah and his ministry must be deduced from the few details revealed in the collection of prophetic utterances that bear his name.

Date

Much of the limited scholarly attention given to Obadiah has focused on two central issues: the literary unity of the book and its setting in Israel's history (see Childs 1979, 412–13).

Whereas the first section of the book (vv. 1-14, 15b) generally employs the second-person-singular form of speech, the second part (vv. 15a, 16-21) utilizes the second-person plural. On this basis it is generally accepted that vv. 15a and 15b were reversed at some point during the transmission of the text. Although some interpreters discern signs of a complicated and lengthy process of literary development (see Wolff 1986, 21, 37f.), in its present form the text reflects a careful organization around both subject (Edom and Israel) and message (judgment and hope). Those interested in pursuing the literary unity or history of exegesis are referred to the larger commentaries, especially Wolff.

Fortunately several significant clues in the text of Obadiah offer assistance to the interpreter searching for both a plausible date and a life setting for the prophet's work.

Evidence pointing to a possible date for Obadiah's ministry is found in vv. 11-14. The pronouncement against Edom recalls *the day* (nine times) when foreigners entered the gates of Jerusalem and deported the people of Judah. The Edomites, though relatives and neighbors of the Jews, gloatingly looked on during this disaster and ultimately participated in looting Judah's resources. They further contributed to Judah's downfall by betraying the survivors of the catastrophe to their enemy (vv. 11-14). These verses can refer only to the events surrounding the destruction of JERUSALEM during the Babylonian conquest of 587/6 B.C.E.

The question of date may also be enhanced by the fact that Obad 1b-5 closely parallels Jer 49:9, 12-15 (in the Hebrew Bible three-fourths of the words are exactly parallel). Did the prophetic tradition *concerning Edom* (v. 1b) originate with Obadiah, or Jeremiah, or did both rely upon a common prophetic tradition?

Jeremiah's ministry dates from 627 to sometime after 587/6 when he probably died in Egypt. The material in the Book of Jeremiah therefore was collected and edited initially in the years following the destruction of Jerusalem, or during the early exilic period. A review of Obadiah's use of the material (see Wolff 1986, 38–42) suggests that the prophet is adopting a traditional prophetic announcement of judgment which he expounds upon and applies to a new situation. In the aftermath of the destruction of Jerusalem in 587/6 B.C.E., Obadiah announces both a word of judgment for Israel's old enemy, the Edomites, and a word of hope for the survivors who now face an uncertain future.

Possible Life Setting

Zechariah 7:3-6 and 8:18-23 suggest that sometime after 587/6 annual services were held to commemorate the fall of Jerusalem and the destruction of the Temple. The form of Obadiah itself—a word of judgment for Israel's enemies followed by a word of hope for Israel—offers the possibility of an example of the kind of preaching that was heard in these services of lamentation.

Edom is addressed first (vv. 1-14, 15b). Its betrayal of family and neighbor is described poetically and an indictment is offered. Obadiah announces Yahweh's sentence: *As you have done, it shall be done to you; your deeds shall return on your own head* (v. 15b). Edom will learn firsthand the tribulation experienced by Israel.

The second section addresses Israel. All the nations shall taste the cup of Yahweh's wrath from which Israel has already drunk. A similar fate awaits all who seek to thwart God and God's people. The prophet announces the good news that the Edoms of this world will not be ultimately successful. The future of God's people is with Yahweh who will reign over all: *the kingdom shall be the LORD's* (v. 21).

The role of the prophetic individual who stands behind this brief collection is in many ways that of the modern-day preacher. Obadiah takes a text and applies it to his own setting and time. Obadiah reveals a minister reaching back into the prophetic traditions of his people in order to bring an important message to his hearers. Perhaps Obadiah functioned as a cult prophet in the aftermath of the destruction of Jerusalem (Wolff 1986, 19). He served as Yahweh's spokesperson at a particularly difficult moment when the dejected people of God needed the assurance that their enemies would reap the consequences of their tragic actions and that Yahweh was still in control of their future.

It is also likely that Obadiah's words continued to be used in the postexilic age when the Jews returned to their ancestral homeland. For those who later faced new problems and challenges that threatened their future, Edom became symbolic of all powers that seek to thwart God's purposes and God's people. Obadiah's assurance that Yahweh would ultimately reign over all would have become words of enormous hope and strength for later generations of Jews who faced the difficult postexilic period.

For Further Study

In the *Mercer Dictionary of the Bible*: BABYLONIAN EMPIRE; EDOM/EDOM-ITES/IDUMAEA; ESAU; EXILE; JACOB; JEREMIAH; JEREMIAH, BOOK OF; JERUSALEM; JUDAH, KINGDOM OF; JUSTICE/JUDGMENT; OBADIAH; OBADIAH, BOOK OF; PROPHET; VISION.

In other sources: B. S. Childs, "Obadiah," in *Introduction to the O.T. as Scripture*; J. Limburg, *Hosea–Micah*, Interp; H. W. Wolff, *Obadiah and Jonah*, Herm.

Commentary

An Outline

I. Superscription, 1a
II. The Consequences of Betrayal and Pride, 1b-14, 15b
  A. The Humbling of Edom, 1b-10
  B. The Indictment against Edom, 11-14

  C. The Obvious Conclusion, 15b
III. The Day of Yahweh is Near, 15a, 16-21
  A. Hope for Mount Zion
    and the House of Jacob, 15a, 16-21a
  B. The Obvious Conclusion, 21b

Superscription, 1a

Verse 1a, the briefest of OT prophetic superscriptions, identifies the oracles that follow as *the vision of Obadiah* (cf. Isa 1:1; Nah 1:1). The word *vision* is a derivative of the Hebrew word *hazah*, "to see," from which the word *hozeh*, "seer," also originates (see 1 Sam 9:9). In its oldest usage "vision" probably refers to the divine communication received during the ecstatic state of the prophet while under divine inspiration (translated "prophetic frenzy" in the NRSV; cf. 1 Sam 19:18-24). In time the word "vision" became a technical term for prophetic communication and here identifies what follows as prophetic utterances.

The Consequences of Betrayal and Pride, 1b-14, 15b

The Humbling of Edom, 1b-10

Verse 1b identifies the subject of Obadiah's vision. What follows is a word from *the Lord GOD concerning Edom*. A knowledge of Edom's relationship with Israel is crucial for understanding Obadiah. Edom is addressed in vv. 1-15. Verses 16-21 are addressed to Judah. Even here, however, the dominant subject is the ultimate triumph over Edom.

The territory of ancient Edom, located southwest of Israel, extended for some 100 mi. between the River Zered and the Gulf of Aqaba. The OT portrays a long history of enmity between Israel and Edom. The Edomites began settling this territory as early as 1300 B.C.E., or just before the arrival of Israelite tribes in Palestine. Notable biblical references to this ongoing hostility include the struggle of the twins in Rebekah's womb (JACOB and ESAU), which became symbolic of the struggle between Israel and Edom (Gen 25:19-34); the Israelite confrontation with the king of Edom during the Exodus (Deut 2:1-8; cf. Num 21:4); the Edomite conflict with King Saul (1 Sam 14:47); and David's eventual conquest and subjugation of the Edomites (2 Sam 8:13-14; see Kelm, 232–33 for a more complete review of the biblical witness).

Nothing was remembered with more enmity, however, than Edom's conduct at the time of the fall of Jerusalem in 587/6 B.C.E. Obadiah's severe words concerning Edom are reflected in similar texts from other sixth- and fifth-century writers (cf. Ps 137:7; Isa 34:5-7; 63:1-6; Lam 4:21-22; Ezek 25:12-14; 35:1-15; Mal 1:2-4). Nowhere is this recalled more vividly, however, than in the brief Book of Obadiah.

1b-4. Pride goeth before the fall. Obadiah chooses as the launching point for his sermon a text pregnant with meaning for his people. He borrows a text from the prophetic tradition that announces the humbling of Edom (cf. Jer 49:9, 14-16). The text begins with a familiar call to arms: *Rise up! Let us rise against it for battle* (v. 1b). The nations are coming together to bring low the one nation that lives *in the clefts of the rocks* and *in the heights* (v. 3; on the habitations of the Edomites see Kelm 1990, 232–33 and Fry 1990, 679). With fateful pride Edom asked, *Who will bring me down to the ground?* (v. 3). Obadiah wastes no time in announcing Yahweh's judgment for such an arrogant people. Edom's proud heart has deceived him: *I will bring you down, says the LORD* (v. 4).

5-10. The pillager is now the pillaged. In these verses the prophet speaks of future events as if they had already occurred, a common form of prophetic speech sometimes called the "prophetic future" tense. The prophet envisages a future when *Esau* (v. 6, Jacob's twin and father of the Edomites) is pillaged in the same manner as Edom pillaged Jacob. Moreover, unlike those robbers who take only what they desire, Edom's plunderers will take it all: *How you have been destroyed!* (v. 5). Edom will find no refuge with its allies (v. 7). Its legendary wisdom and the renowned strength of its warriors will not be enough to stand against the ravages of this enemy (vv. 8-9). Why? It is all *for the slaughter and violence done to your brother Jacob* (v. 10).

The Indictment against Edom, 11-14

The most detailed description of Edom's conduct at the time of Jerusalem's fall in 587/6 B.C.E. appears in vv. 11-14. *On that day*, indelibly written upon the collective memory of Israel, Edom committed the most horrendous of atrocities. The first act mentioned is perhaps the worst. Initially Edom *stood aside* (v. 11). Edom became a bystander to a horrible act of injustice. It watched as *strangers* (i.e., Babylon) entered Jerusalem's gates and carried off its resources (v. 11). The guilt of the one who stands idly by while such injustices occur before one's very eyes is clear: *you too were like one of them* (v. 11). By its actions or lack of them Edom became just as guilty as those perpetrating the crime.

Unfortunately it did not stop there. Afterwards Edom *gloated*, even *rejoiced*, over Judah's misfortune (v. 12). Edom shoved it in Judah's face—poured salt into their wounds. Edom entered the gates of Jerusalem and gloated over Judah's disaster on the day of their calamity. It gets worse! Apparently Edom joined in the looting of Jerusalem's resources and even cut off those attempting to flee and delivered them to their captors (vv. 13-14). What could Edom expect in return for its betrayal of family and neighbor in the day of their greatest need?

The Obvious Conclusion, 15b

There is but one conclusion to this sad description of the ultimate betrayal. Obadiah declares, *As you have done, it shall be done to you; your deeds shall return on your own head.* The Christian is reminded here of Jesus' words on the night of his betrayal, "for all who take the sword will perish by the sword" (Matt 26:52), or the words of Paul, "for you reap whatever you sow" (Gal 6:7). Perhaps more significant for the one who stands idly by while harm comes to another are Jesus' words from Matt 25:40, 45: "just as you did it to one of the least of these who are members of my family, you did it to me . . . just as you did not do it to one of the least of these, you did not do it to me."

The Day of Yahweh is Near, 15a, 16-21

Hope for Mount Zion and the House of Jacob, 15a, 16-21a

Beginning with vv. 15a, 16-21 the *you* is no longer Edom (second person sing.), but now Israel during the exile—and the Jews of the postexilic age—and, still later, other people of faith longing for a word of hope while languishing under enormous oppression (second person pl.).

This section is linked to the first in significant ways. Although the prophet's words are now addressed to a different audience, Edom is still the major focus. Israel now receives the news that there *is* a future for the house of Jacob; all the nations hostile to Yahweh and his people and especially Edom (Esau) will be subjugated.

The two sections are also tied together by the use of the word *day*. In the first section *the day* that Edom *stood aside* (v. 11) was contrasted with *the day* of Edom's demise (v. 8). In fact *day* appears nine times in vv. 11-14 alone. This must now be contrasted with *the day of the* LORD, which will be a day of judgment for all the nations (v. 15a; cf. Joel 2).

As Israel has *drunk* the cup of Yahweh's punishment in the events of 587/6 B.C.E., so now the nations must also drink, even *gulp down* their penalty (v. 16; cf. Ps 75:8; Isa 51:22-23; Jer 51:7; see Limburg 1988, 133–34). Yet some will escape, and gather on Mount Zion, the holy residence of Yahweh's presence. The house of Jacob shall become the possessor rather than the dispossessed (v. 17).

From *all the nations* (v. 15) the focus of v. 18 returns specifically to Edom. Esau is now but stubble to be consumed by the fires of the people of God. The authority for this action is nothing less than the word of Yahweh, *for the* LORD *has spoken*.

Verses 19-20 describe the full extent of the new territorial possessions of the formerly *dispossessed* (v. 17). Israel will inhabit its former territory as well as that of its enemies Edom and PHOENICIA. Borders will be extended in the north as far as ZAREPHATH and in the south into *the Negeb* (v. 19; see Hopkins 1990 for details on geography). One final jab at Edom occurs in 21a. Proud *Mount Esau* will now be ruled from *Mount Zion*, geographically a far less notable mountain. Theologically, however, there is no higher place than this. Israel will once again dominate Edom—politically and theologically.

The Obvious Conclusion, 21b

Following a survey of the rugged terrain of the little Book of Obadiah the student of scripture may be inclined to join the chorus of criticism advanced by those who find here a retributive spirit and a narrow nationalism. One may very well conclude that Obadiah deserves the neglect it receives.

Yet when viewed against the backdrop of its original setting a greater appreciation for Obadiah is possible. On the surface the modern reader is inclined to find what Wolff describes as "pure, primitive hate." Wolff is surely correct, however, when he writes:

> But anyone who is prepared to enter imaginatively into the historical hour in which these sayings were written discovers a wretched people in a ruined city, in dire need of comfort. It is only if we try to picture the ser-

vice of mourning in the rubble of Jerusalem after the days of catastrophe in 587 that we can begin to understand the proclamation of the prophetic spokesman. (Wolff 1986, 22)

The fact is that the Book of Obadiah is included in the canon of scripture embraced by people of faith, both Jews and Christians. Surely this is because history is filled with many stories of "Edoms" and "Israels" in both national and interpersonal relationships. Obadiah's message was a "word from God" for a particularly difficult moment in the history of the people of God, yet a moment that has recurred more than once since these words were spoken.

Obadiah declares the terrible consequences for those who participate in cruel and inhuman oppression of neighbors or stand idly by while others do (vv. 1-14, 15b). Moreover the prophet offers the promise of a future in Yahweh's kingdom for those who suffer under the enormous burden of oppression (vv. 15a, 16-21). This prophet joins the chorus of the larger biblical witness in announcing the good news all sufferers long to hear, *the kingdom shall be the LORD's* (v. 21).

Works Cited

Childs, Brevard S. 1979. "Obadiah," in *Introduction to the Old Testament as Scripture.*

Fry, Virgil. 1990. "Petra," MDB.

Hopkins, David D. 1990. "Palestine, Geography of," MDB.

Kelm, George L. 1989. "Edom/Edomites/Idumaea," MDB.

Limburg, James. 1988. *Hosea–Micah*, Interp.

Wolff, Hans Walter. 1986. *Obadiah and Jonah, A Commentary.* Herm.

Jonah

Kenneth M. Craig, Jr.

Introduction

No one doubts that Jonah, the fifth in a collection of twelve short prophetic books, is unique. The author focuses on the actions of the prophet rather than on his prophecy. Jonah's proclamation to Nineveh in 3:4 consists of only five words in the Hebrew. Outside the book, JONAH is mentioned only in 2 Kgs 14:25, a verse that refers to the prophet's home town of Gath-hepher, a city of modest size identified with Khirbet Ez-Zurra three miles northeast of Nazareth. In the Book of Jonah, the PROPHET is commissioned to set out for Nineveh, the capital of the ancient Assyrian empire. From an Israelite perspective, ASSYRIA was synonymous with oppression and domination.

Authorship

The book never identifies its author. Like SAMUEL and other famous characters of the Hebrew Bible, Jonah never claims to have written the book that bears his name. Arguments for and against the eighth century prophet as author are discussed in *MDB* (see JONAH, BOOK OF). The wide range of possible dates (see below) cautions against assigning a specific author and time of composition.

Date

The date of the Book of Jonah is difficult to determine. The time of the prophet mentioned in 2 Kings (ca. 780 B.C.E.) is not necessarily the time of composition. It may be that the story makes more sense before the fall of Nineveh (612 B.C.E.), but a date after this time is also possible since Nineveh could have been subject to judgment after 612. The reference to *the king of Nineveh* (instead of to "the king of Assyria") in 3:6 clouds the issue since Assyrian records never use the title. If the last two chapters allude to Jer 18 and Joel 2, a postexilic date is likely. References to Persian customs such as domestic animals participating in mourning ceremonies (3:8), and the mention of *the king and his nobles* together (3:7) may suggest a date during the Persian period (550–330 B.C.E.). The use of nonbiblical sea motifs ("great fish," "being swallowed," "vomited up") makes a date in the early Hellenistic period (330–200 B.C.E.) possible. According to Sir 49:10 the Book of Jonah (included in the reference to "Twelve Prophets") was known by 200 B.C.E. This range of dates and the lack of compelling evidence for any one period lead to the general observation that the book was written sometime between 750 and 250 B.C.E.

Literary Form and Primary Themes

Virtually every imaginable genre or genre-like label has been applied to the book including didactic tale, short story, satire, sermon, fable, myth, folk tale, allegory, parable, midrash, legend, *erzählte Dogmatik* ("narrated dogmatics"), and sensational didactic historical narrative (Trible 1963, 126–77; Craig 1989, 24–33). The appearance of so many labels for the Book of Jonah suggests that George Landes is correct in calling attention to the literary category of *mashal*. This type of writing does not refer to a specific literary form but rather to the way multiple forms are shaped to serve a specific didactic purpose (Landes 1978, 137–58). The writer is not a systematic theologian, but the story does touch on a number of important theological themes. These themes include: justice, mercy, repentance, creation, the encompassing nature of God's love, and the free nature of God's compassion. An additional theme may be described as the relationship between Creator and creature. In the scene outside Nineveh, the LORD asks the prophet: *Is it right for you to be angry about the bush?* (4:9). This rebuke is reminiscent of the LORD's response to Job from the whirlwind in Job 38–41.

For Further Study

In the Mercer Dictionary of the Bible: ASSYRIA; JONAH; JONAH, BOOK OF; POETRY; PROPHET.

In other sources: J. S. Ackerman, "Jonah," *The Literary Guide to the Bible*, ed. R. Alter and F. Kermode; L. Allen, *The Books of Joel, Obadiah, Jonah, and Micah*, NICOT; K. M. Craig, Jr., *A Poetics of Jonah*; G. M. Landes, "Jonah: A Mashal?," in *Israelite Wisdom: Theological and Literary Essays in Honor of Samuel Terrien*, and "The Kerygma of the Book of Jonah: The Contextual Interpretation of the Jonah Psalm," *Int* 21 (1967): 3–31; J. H. Sasson, *Jonah*, AncB; D. Stuart, *Hosea–Jonah*, WBC; P. L. Trible, "Studies in the Book of Jonah," Ph.D. diss., Columbia University, 1963; H. W. Wolff, *Obadiah and Jonah*, Herm.

Commentary

An Outline

I. Jonah's Call, Disobedience, and Adventures, 1:1-16
   A. Jonah Resists the Commission, 1:1-3
   B. The Storm at Sea, 1:4-5
   C. Jonah Is Singled Out, 1:6-16
II. The LORD Rescues Jonah, 1:17–2:10 [MT 2:1-11]
   A. The Fish Swallows Jonah, 1:17–2:2a [MT 2:1-3a]

   B. Jonah Prays, 2:2b-9 (MT 2:3b-10)
   C. Return to Dry Land, 2:10 [MT 2:11]
III. Jonah in Nineveh, 3:1-10
   A. A Re-Commission, 3:1-3a
   B. Proclamation and Repentance, 3:3b-10
IV. Conversation between Jonah and the LORD, 4:1-11
   A. Jonah's Complaint, 4:1-3
   B. The LORD's Response, 4:4-11

Jonah's Call, Disobedience, and Adventures, 1:1-16

Jonah Resists the Commission, 1:1-3

The brief introduction alludes to 2 Kgs 14:25 where "Jonah son of Amittai," is also mentioned. The divine commission in v. 2 is presented with familiar words also reminiscent of language from Kings: "Arise, go to Zarephath" (1 Kgs 17:9, RSV). Prophets were not ordinarily summoned to travel long distances to deliver a message. They usually spoke against foreign nations (Ezek 27–32; Isa 13,15–19; Jer 46–51; Amos 1–2:3; Obad; Nah 1–3), but rarely traveled to them. The content of the message is not told to the reader until chap. 3. Jonah, like MOSES, ISAIAH, and JEREMIAH before him, is reluctant. Unlike other prophets, however, Jonah protests with his feet instead of with words. In a blatant act of disobedience, he heads for Tarshish, a city usually identified with southwest Spain. The focus on action in v. 3 (*set out, flee, went down, found, paid, went, go*) indicates the extreme measures to which Jonah goes in order to resist the LORD's call. The introduction sets the fast-paced tempo for this story.

The Storm at Sea, 1:4-5

Jonah soon learns of the LORD's power. The emphasis in v. 4 is on a chain reaction set in motion by the LORD. The LORD causes a wind, which causes a storm, which causes the ship to virtually break up. The passage also introduces key words (*throwing, hurling, the sea,* and *fear*) that will be developed in the remainder of the chapter. In v. 5 the author contrasts the sailors who cry out to their gods and hurl the cargo overboard with Jonah who falls asleep.

Jonah Is Singled Out, 1:6-16

The captain of the sailors comes to Jonah, wakes him up, and instructs him to *get up* and *call* (v. 6). These commanding words are the same two words that the LORD spoke to Jonah in 1:2. In an effort to find the cause of their problems, the sailors then cast lots that determine Jonah's guilt. Thus far in the story (1:1-8a), Jonah's speech has not been quoted by the narrator. This portrayal of a laconic prophet is reinforced when we notice that Jonah responds in the first chapter only when he is asked questions (1:8, 11). As soon as the lots determine Jonah's guilt, the sailors bombard him with a series of questions (v. 8). Since nationality and religion were inextricably tied together in the ancient Near East, the sailors ask about his nationality in an attempt to discover which god is responsible for this disaster. Jonah responds by telling them that he is *a Hebrew* who worships *the LORD, the God of heaven, who made the sea and the dry land* (v. 9). This statement is charged with irony. If he fears God who made the sea and dry land, what does he hope to accomplish by fleeing? After the men consider their options, Jonah responds by advising them to pick him up and throw him into the sea. One notices an acceleration in the action and emotions in the first chapter: *the mariners were afraid* (1:5); *the men were even more afraid* (v. 10); *then the men feared the LORD even more* (v. 16). The crescendo effect is also accomplished in the description of the storm at sea: *such a mighty storm came upon the sea* (1:4); *the sea was growing more and more tempestuous* (v. 11); *the sea grew more and more stormy against them* (v. 13). Surprisingly, Jonah's disobedience produces some significant results. In v. 14 the sailors cry out and address the LORD by invoking God's intimate name, and in v. 16 they offer a sacrifice and make vows.

The LORD Rescues Jonah, 1:17–2:10 (MT 2:1-11)

The Fish Swallows Jonah, 1:17–2:2a (MT 2:1-3a)

The LORD continues to assume a commanding role by providing a fish that swallows Jonah. While some interpreters emphasize the fish as punishment motif, it may also be properly understood as a shelter for the drowning prophet. The author reports that Jonah *prayed to the LORD his God* (2:1 [MT 2:2]). Praying or crying out to God emerges as a central issue in this story (1:5; 1:6b; 1:14; 2:2-9 [MT 2:3-10]; 3:8; 4:2-3). Once again, in the opening verses of this chapter, we focus on the action between the two principal characters, Jonah and the LORD. The great fish, which will later be echoed in Matt 12:40, refers to any large fish.

Jonah Prays, 2:2b-9 (MT 2:3b-10)

Jonah finally calls out to the LORD, as the captain and sailors had begged him to before (1:6; 1:14). Four standard elements of the Thanksgiving Psalm type are found in Jonah's poetic prayer: reports of answered prayer, personal crisis, divine rescue, and a vow of praise. Numerous parallels exist between Jonah's prayer from the belly of the fish and prayers from the Psalter. In fact, the prayer that Jonah offers consists almost entirely of phrases from Psalms. The distinguishing feature of the Jonah psalm is that it is spoken by one person in a specific context. With these words, the author establishes that Jonah is in fact *a Hebrew* who worships *the LORD . . . who made the sea and the dry land* (1:9). This pastiche also highlights the prophet's frenzied mental state. The psalm is connected by recurring words and motifs. For many years it was regarded as an extraneous or arbitrary addition, but a number of clues suggests that it is intimately connected to the surrounding prose narrative. For example, Jonah's two verbal formulations of prayer (vv. 2-9 [MT 2:3-10] and 4:2-3) share three key words: (a) חַסְדָּם, *their true loyalty* (v. 8 [MT 2:9]); *steadfast love* (4:2); (b) חַיָּי, *my life* (v. 6 [MT 2:7]); *to live* (4:3); (c) נַפְשִׁי, *me* (v. 5 [MT 2:6]); *my life* (4:3) (Allen 1976, 198–99). The prayer uttered from the belly of the fish also displays thematic similarities to the action and words of the previous chapter. In the opening scene, Jonah's descent began when he went down to Joppa. Jonah also went down into the ship (1:3) and continued to descend into its recesses (1:5). Even the sailors' activity reinforces this movement. They cast lots that "fall" to Jonah (1:7) and then finally throw him overboard (1:15). This descent motif continues in the first half of the psalm, and is reversed beginning in v. 6b [MT 2:7b] when Jonah recounts that the LORD brought him up *from the Pit*. The prophet's concluding remarks at the end of the prayer in v. 9 [MT 2:10] may remind the reader of the sailors' action at the end of the previous scene (1:16).

Return to Dry Land, 2:10 (MT 2:11)

The fish responds to the LORD's command and *spews Jonah out upon the dry land*. The specific location of Jonah's place on land is not mentioned. With Jonah out of the water, the story returns to prose. The prophet's plan to flee from the LORD was unsuccessful. The first half of the story concludes.

Jonah in Nineveh, 3:1-10

A Re-Commission, 3:1-3a

This brief passage serves resumptive and transitional functions. The commission is repeated word for word (3:2a=1:2a) in the Hebrew. The parallel between the two scenes ends, however, when we learn that this time Jonah sets out for Nineveh *according to the word of the LORD* (v. 3a). Like the wind, sea, and fish before him, Jonah now bends to the will of the LORD. A sense of mystery surrounds the proclamation itself. What is it? Will the city be punished, destroyed, or spared?

Proclamation and Repentance, 3:3b-10

When this scene begins, Jonah is (finally) in Nineveh. His message to the Ninevites, *Forty days more, and Nineveh shall be overthrown!* (v. 4), is somewhat open-ended. Do his words suggest that the Ninevites have reason to hope that they may be spared if they repent? No conditions are attached to the proclamation, and the prophet says nothing about what could or should be done. The message to the Ninevites contains the only words that the prophet will speak in the third chapter. In the midst of foreigners, Jonah is, once again, laconic.

After the proclamation, the author focuses on the events in Nineveh. Jonah fades to the background. The prophet's words stir the Ninevites, and the overall effect of the proclamation is reported in v. 5. The people *believed God . . . proclaimed a fast, and . . . put on sackcloth*. These elements of threat and/or disaster followed by acts of penitence and eventual divine intervention (vv. 4b-10) are part of a pattern found in several portions of the Hebrew Bible (1 Sam 7:3-14; 2 Sam 24; Ezra 8:21-23; Esth 3:7–4:17; Joel 1:1–2:27). The Hebrew word for *fast* (צום) implies abstention from food as well as accompanying mourning and repentance. The focus on religious activity is made from three angles: the response of the people, the king's reaction, followed by the king's official decree (which virtually mirrors the response that the people had already made). The encompassing nature of the decree includes even animals who, along with humans, are to be covered with sackcloth (v. 8). Such actions by the foreigners have a good effect once again for *God changed his mind . . . and he did not do it* (v. 10; cf. 1:16; Joel 2:12-14 and Jer 18:7-10).

Conversation between Jonah and the LORD, 4:1-11

Jonah's Complaint, 4:1-3

The first verses of chap. 4 signal a drastic turn of events. As the LORD's anger ceases, Jonah's begins. Once again, Jonah prays. He begins by focusing on himself

What I said while I was still in my own country . . . I fled . . . for I knew (v. 2a, emphasis added) and concludes by describing God in traditional language in v. 2b (cf. Exod 34:6; Num 14:18; Pss 86:15; 103:8; 145:8; Nah 1:3; Neh 9:17). Jonah's prayer in v. 2 contrasts with his earlier praise and thanksgiving (2:9 [MT 2:10]). The words of this second prayer also reveal that the author has kept information from the readers or listeners until this opportune moment. At this late stage, Jonah says, *Is this not what I said . . . at the beginning* (v. 2)? The request that his life be taken from him in v. 3 is reminiscent of Elijah's prayer in 1 Kgs 19:4.

The LORD's Response, 4:4-11

The LORD quickly challenges Jonah's right to be angry by asking an incisive rhetorical question in v. 4. Verse 5 may be viewed as a flashback, or it may reflect Jonah's expectation that something might yet happen in the city of Nineveh. Just as Jonah in the initial part of the story did not respond to the LORD with words, he, once again, displays a defiant attitude with actions (v. 5).

Beginning in v. 6, the LORD launches a game by sending a shade plant that causes Jonah to become *very happy*. God then appoints *a worm* and prepares *a sultry east wind* (vv. 7-8). Jonah asks a second time that his life be taken from him (v. 8). When God's rhetorical question comes to Jonah once again (v. 9), the first clause is repeated verbatim and then an additional phrase is added (*Is it right for you to be angry about the bush?*). The prophet's anger has surfaced because of the shade that was lost over his head. Jonah insists in the strongest possible words that the bush is important to him. He loves it. He is "extremely happy" about it (v. 6), and when it withers, he is furious (v. 9). The prophet is so mad that the thought of death seems better than the idea of living without the plant! This game is intended as an object lesson to teach Jonah something about the inconsistency of his own position compared with God's. The LORD's final words to the prophet (vv. 10-11) focus on the word "concern." Jonah is concerned about the plant because he lost the shade it provided. The LORD is concerned about the people and animals of Nineveh. Jonah and the audience are left with the profound rhetorical question at the end of the book. Despite the many harrowing experiences, no human or animal loses its life in the story. The prophet's emotions that had previously been emphasized starting with the first verse in chap. 4 (rage, disappointment, extraordinary happiness, frustration) are now summarily contrasted with the compassion that the LORD feels for all of creation.

Works Cited

Allen, L. 1976. *The Books of Joel, Obadiah, Jonah, and Micah*. NICOT.
Craig, K. M. 1989. "The Poetics of the Book of Jonah: Toward an Understanding of Narrative Strategy," Ph.D. diss., Southern Baptist Theological Seminary.
Landes, G. M. 1978. "Jonah: A Mashal?" in *Israelite Wisdom: Theological and Literary Essays in Honor of Samuel Terrien*.
Trible, P. L. 1963. "Studies in the Book of Jonah," Ph.D. diss., Columbia University.

Micah

Jerome F. D. Creach

Introduction

The Book of Micah is a collection of prophetic sayings reportedly spoken by Micah, an eighth-century PROPHET from *Moresheth* (1:1). The content of the book is similar to that of other prophetic works of the same period. Both AMOS and Micah emphasize social justice (Mic 2:1-2, 8-9; 3:9-10; 6:11-12; Amos 2:6-8; 4:1; 5:10-12; 8:4-6). Micah and ISAIAH have one common passage (Mic 4:1-3 = Isa 2:2-4) and numerous other thematically similar texts (Mic 1:8~Isa 20:3; Mic 2:6~Isa 30:9-10; Mic 3:1-3~Isa 5:20; Mic 5:4~Isa 40:11). These analogous passages are the reason Micah is sometimes described as "Amos *redivivus*" or "Isaiah in miniature."

Despite its many shared ideas, Micah stands alone with at least two distinctive features that prevent the work from being read as merely a condensed derivative of these larger contemporary collections. First, Micah is the only prophetic work from the eighth century to include a prediction of the fall of JERUSALEM (3:9-12). This inflammatory speech against Judah's capital was so shocking that JEREMIAH was arrested for proclaiming an similar message nearly 100 years later (Jer 26:1-9). In the ensuing trial Jeremiah was successfully defended because of an appeal to the earlier prediction of Micah (Jer 26:16-19). Second, the book foretells the birth of an Israelite ruler, reminiscent of DAVID, who hails from BETHLEHEM (5:2). The NT identifies this regent as Jesus (see Matt 2:6; also see the debate in John 7:40-43 that contains the same understanding, although ironically spoken in ignorance by Jesus' opponents). Thus, the Book of Micah makes a unique contribution to the prophetic tradition of ancient Israel and provides the early Christian church with a central claim concerning the birth of Jesus, confessed to be the MESSIAH. The Christian claims notwithstanding, Micah deserves to be examined on its own merit and for its distinctive contribution to Israelite prophecy and OT thought in general.

The Prophet

Apart from the brief biographical sketch of Micah in 1:1, the only information known about the prophet's social status or prophetic vocation is that implied in the prophetic utterances of the man. The prophet Micah (the name means "who is like YHWH?") is identified by his town of origin, *Moresheth* (1:1). This name probably refers to Moresheth-Gath, a settlement about twenty-four mi. southwest of Jerusalem. The prophet's provincial identification implies that Micah was not part of the ruling class of Jerusalem. Indeed, he distances himself from the corrupt practices of the professional prophets, priests, and rulers of the capital city (see Mic 3:5-8). This explains why Micah was described in relation to a locality rather than by reference to his father (cf. Hos 1:1; Isa 1:1) or by his sense of a "call" to be a prophet (cf. Amos 1:1; Jer 1:1; Ezek 1:1) (Wolff 1990, 6–7). Micah spoke as an outsider, uttering a cry for "justice" (מִשְׁפָּט) for those oppressed in Judah by the Jerusalem elite (Mic 2:1-2).

Micah proclaimed YHWH's message *in the days of Kings Jotham, Ahaz, and Hezekiah of Judah* (1:1), that is, between 750 and 687 B.C.E. During this turbulent period in Israel's history ASSYRIA established control over Syria-Palestine. After repeated rebellions against the Assyrian yoke, the Northern Kingdom and its capital, SAMARIA, were finally decimated in 722 by the powerful Assyrian army. The Assyrian threat forced the Southern Kingdom into a state of vassalage, but Judah survived as an independent political entity. Micah makes reference to these events (1:6-9), with the apparent implication that Assyria is YHWH's instrument of judgment on Israel and Judah, although he never mentions Assyria directly, as Isaiah did (10:5).

Scholars generally limit material original to Micah to chaps. 1–3, excluding 1:1, 2:12-13, and brief editorial additions. Some other passages, however, may be debated because they seem to correlate with an eighth century context (e.g., 5:2-6 [MT 5:1-5]). Still other passages appear anachronistic (e.g., 7:11-13) because they assume an exilic setting in which the people hope for the restoration of Zion. The authentic words of Micah tell that the prophet protested against the unjust seizure of land by wealthy citizens (2:2) and the mercenary motives of prophets, priests, and judges (3:1-3, 5-6a, 9-11). Micah identified himself as one *filled with power, with the spirit of the LORD, and with justice and might, to declare to Jacob his transgression and to Israel his sin* (3:8). In other words, Micah saw himself as one called to uncover the wrongful acts of the nation's leaders. As punishment for their deeds, the capitals of Israel (Samaria) and Judah (Jerusalem) would be destroyed.

The Form of the Book of Micah

The Book of Micah is not merely a group of disjointed oracles haphazardly ordered in the work's final form. In fact, the book's organization assists in the interpretation of individual units. Micah contains two fairly distinct sections: 1:2–5:15 and 6:1–7:20 with 1:1 as an introduction. Both divisions open with the imperative *Hear* (שִׁמְעוּ), which introduces a juridical setting. In 1:2–5:15 the audience is the *earth, and all that is in it* (1:2). In this universal context the prophet declares that YHWH will come in THEOPHANY to wreak destruction upon the earth because of the transgressions of Israel and Judah (1:3-7).

Chapters 2–3 indicate the reason for the devastation as the failure of the nation's leaders. The pivotal point in this first section then comes with the prediction that Jerusalem will be razed (3:9-12). In stark contrast, chaps. 4–5 present hope for restoration. However, chaps. 1–3 and 4–5 are connected by the emphasis on Zion, its destruction (3:12) and subsequent rebirth (4:1-4). The phrases, *the mountain of the house* (3:12) and *the mountain of the LORD's house* (4:1) provide an unmistakable link between the two sections.

As a unit, chaps. 1–5 contrast the failed human leadership in Israel (3:1-7) with the righteous rule of YHWH (4:7b). After YHWH metes out punishment to his people (1:6-16; 3:12), he will re-establish them under the domain of a powerful shepherd king from Bethlehem (5:2-6 [MT 5:1-5]). Israel will be characterized by perfect trust in YHWH (5:7-9). Then the nation will be protected from all its foes (5:10-15).

Chapters 6–7 mirror the development of chaps. 1–5. Micah 6:1-2 introduces a *controversy* (רִיב) between the LORD and his people. These two chapters emphasize God's covenant faithfulness on the one hand (6:4-5) and the wicked perversion of justice by his people on the other hand (6:10-12). The climactic point is evident, however, in 7:1-7 when the personified city of Jerusalem confesses the sins of its leaders and declares trust in YHWH alone (v. 7). YHWH is called to *shepherd [the] people* (7:14).

The book closes with the assurance that YHWH will pardon Israel for its sins (7:18-20). Thus, like chaps. 1–5, chaps. 6–7 highlight YHWH's governance of Israel after the nation has been punished for its transgressions. Both sections of the book reverberate with the themes of justice (or lack thereof) and God's kingship. Under the sovereignty of YHWH the oppressed of the land are able to dwell secure (4:4) and those who suffered from the unfaithfulness of Israel's rulers are revivified (4:6-7; 7:11-12).

The Formation of the Book of Micah

The question of the book's formation, or redactional history, is very difficult and any conclusions will be hypothetical. However, three general stages of growth seem evident. First, the book began with a core of oracles that originated with the prophet Micah in the eighth century B.C.E. These sayings can be located only in chaps. 1–3 with certainty. Second, editors added brief statements approximately one century later in order to reapply Micah's words to the time of the reforms of King JOSIAH and the Babylonian crisis (e.g., 5:10-15 [MT 5:9-14]). Finally, in the exilic and postexilic periods, sections were added to round out the bleak picture of destruction with a more complete word of hope for the revitalization of Zion and of the people who lived there (e.g., 4:6-7).

For Further Study

In the *Mercer Dictionary of the Bible*: ASSYRIA; CHRONOLOGY; ISAIAH; ISAIAH, BOOK OF; JEREMIAH; JEREMIAH, BOOK OF; JERUSALEM; MICAH; MICAH, BOOK OF; ORACLE; PROPHET.

In other sources: D. G. Hagstrom, *The Coherence of the Book of Micah: A Literary Analysis*; D. R. Hillers, *Micah*, Herm; K. Koch, *The Prophets*, 1:573–74; J. L. Mays, "Justice: Perspectives from the Prophetic Tradition," *Int* 37/1 (1983): 5–17, and *Micah*, OTL; H. W. Wolff, *Micah*.

Commentary

An Outline

Superscription, 1:1

I. YHWH's Court Case against All the Earth, 1:2–5:15 (MT 1:2–5:14)
  A. Punishment of Two Capital Cities, 1:2-16
  B. Crimes and Punishment of Israel's Leaders, 2:1–3:12
  C. Superiority of Reconstructed Zion, 4:1–5:6 (MT 4:1–5:5)
  D. The Faithful Remnant, 5:7-15 (MT 5:6-14)

II. YHWH's Controversy with His People, 6:1–7:20
  A. Requirements of Covenant Loyalty, 6:1-8
  B. Jerusalem's Sins and YHWH's Intolerance, 6:9-16
  C. Despair over Ubiquitous Evil, 7:1-6
  D. Confession and Assurance of Pardon, 7:7-20

Superscription, 1:1

The opening verse of the Book of Micah has a form much like the introduction to other prophetic books (e.g., Isa 1:1; 2:1; Jer 1:1-3; Hos 1:1; Joel 1:1; Amos 1:1). The fact that Micah's work is dated with a list of Southern kings indicates that the prophet spoke primarily to Judah (the reference to *Samaria* is probably influenced by the emphasis on the Northern capital in 1:5-7).

YHWH's Court Case against All the Earth, 1:2–5:15 (MT 1:2–5:14)

Punishment of Two Capital Cities, 1:2-16

1:2-7. Announcement of controversy and judgment. This passage is set in the heavenly council where YHWH reigns as judge. The imperative, *listen, O earth* (v. 2), indicates that YHWH is concerned with establishing justice in the whole cosmos. However, the focus quickly moves to the iniquities of a single nation, ISRAEL. Because of the transgressions of Samaria and the idolatry of Jerusalem, God is about to come *out of his place* (v. 3, indicating the Temple), in an awesome theophany that will shake the foundations of the earth.

1:8-9. Lament of the prophet. As a sign of mourning, the prophet will *go barefoot and naked* (v. 8) to presage the shameful condition of capture and deportation (cf. Isa 20:3). Verse 9 probably refers to the Assyrian presence in Judah in the late eighth century B.C.E.

1:10-16. Roll-call of cities facing destruction. This is one of the most difficult passages in the book to comprehend. Most scholars think the town names are part of a word play. For example, in v. 10 the word, *dust* (עָפָר) is clearly a play on the place name, *Beth-leaphrah* (בֵית לְעַפְרָה). However, since such a pun does not exist in every case, scholars must amend the MT to make the theory work. The most certain proposal for the passage is that the cities listed were in danger of Assyrian invasion, or perhaps had already been decimated by SENNACHERIB (701

B.C.E.), when the ORACLE was spoken. The mention of baldness (v. 16) refers to a rite of mourning that was practiced on the occasion of military defeat.

Crimes and Punishment of Israel's Leaders, 2:1–3:12

2:1-5. Seizure of land and its consequences. This first specific indictment addresses wealthy landowners who, probably through foreclosure on loans, obtain the property of less powerful individuals. Such action is repugnant for two reasons. First, those implicated seized the estates of others because they coveted them (v. 2), in violation of the tenth commandment (Exod 20:17a, b). Second, in ancient Israel ownership of land determined identity and the benefits of citizenship. Thus, the loss of property stripped an individual of dignity and social standing. During the eighth century B.C.E. an ever-widening gap between rich and poor highlighted the results of this practice. For such greed and disobedience, these land owners will lose the *fields* (vv. 2, 4) they took. Verse 4 probably refers to a postexilic redistribution of land from which these profiteers would be excluded.

2:6-11. False preaching and false prosperity. This unit reveals much about the reception of Micah's proclamation. Like Amos (7:12-13), Micah is told, *do not preach* (v. 6). The ensuing message of doom angered Judah's authorities because it was an affront to their theology and social position. They could not conceive of their nation's being destroyed, nor could they accept the charge that their activity was unacceptable to YHWH. However, Micah identified these opponents with the perpetrators of injustice in 2:1-5. They were capitalists (to employ a modern term) who dispossessed women and children in order to build their own estates (Mays 1983, 9). The victims are defended and described as the *peaceful, . . . those who pass by trustingly*, and those who do not consider war (v. 8). These terms portray people who are innocent, rely upon YHWH, and have no power to oppress others. Micah's opponents, on the other hand, are not upright (v. 7).

2:12-13. Gathering and deportation. Most scholars read this passage as a hopeful promise of return from dispersion (like 4:6-7). However, it is difficult to accept such an idea when the unit sits in the midst of overt declarations of punishment. One solution is to read these verses as an oracle of doom. The ambiguity of v. 13 makes such a reading viable. Indeed, breaking through a gate probably should be understood as a negative action. Thus, the fact that YHWH breaches the entrance to the sheepfold (a metaphor for city) may mean that YHWH will lead an invading army to take Judah away into exile (Mays 1976, 73–76).

3:1-4. The abuse of power and the LORD's reaction. The imperative, *listen* (v. 1), harks back to the court setting at the beginning of the book (1:2). Here, however, the command is addressed to the defendants, not the witnesses in the case. *Heads of Jacob and rulers of the house of Israel* (v. 1) are synonymous expressions that Micah uses to describe the Jerusalem officials responsible for establishing justice (see 3:9). The prophet argues they are committed to their own avaricious desire for gain more than to the founding of an equitable society. The graphic image of cannibalism communicates the offensive nature of their feeding off the people entrusted to their care (cf. Hos 4:8).

3:5-8. Prostitution of the prophetic office. Continuing the catalogue of sins of Israel's leaders, Micah's attention shifts to the prophets, the ones responsible for relaying the word of YHWH to the people. The official prophets of Jerusalem prophesy solely for monetary reward. They speak favorably for those who pay for their services; they *declare war* (v. 5) on those who refuse, that is, they show hostility (see 2:8). Therefore, the LORD will remove all revelation from these false seers. In contrast to their unfaithfulness, Micah declares his message to be truly the word of YHWH, untainted by bribes and physical rewards (v. 8).

3:9-12. Summary indictment of leaders. In this decisive passage of the first section of the book, the expression *hear this* (v. 9) signals a concluding oracle of judgment (see 1:2; 3:1). The imperative is a sweeping address to all of Israel's leaders: rulers, chiefs, priests, and prophets. All of the groups are charged again with perverting their professions, bringing injustice upon God's people. To assure themselves, they declare, *Surely the Lord is with us* (v. 11), as if to anticipate Micah's prediction of destruction for Jerusalem. Their belief in Zion's impregnability is understandable. Jerusalem was thought to be a place of supreme beauty (Ps 48:2 [MT 48:3]), a city founded by YHWH (Ps 87:1-3 [MT 87:1-2]), a place YHWH protected as a warrior king (Pss 46, 48). Yet, the corruption of Israel's ruling classes would bring YHWH's wrath; a conquering army would devastate the capital (v. 12). Undoubtedly Micah thought of Assyria as the conqueror; thus, this prediction did not come to pass. However, a later tradition (Jer 26:16-19) indicates that the city was spared because of the repentance of HEZEKIAH. The prediction later materialized in 587 B.C.E. when the Babylonians defeated and destroyed the city.

Superiority of Reconstructed Zion, 4:1–5:6 (MT 4:1–5:5)

4:1-5. Zion as a center of world government and peace. This unit is the beginning of a larger section emphasizing the restoration of Zion (4:2, 7, 8, 10, 11, 13). The placement of this passage after 3:9-12 apparently is intended to show the failure of Israel's rulers, and consequently the downfall of the city they established with bloodshed. Micah 4:1-5 indicates that the city will prosper in a time to come, dominated by YHWH's just rule. As Mays states, "the promise of peace is founded on a prior promise that the reign of YHWH shall become the center of order for all peoples" (Mays 1976, 93). Indeed, *in days to come* (v. 1) when Zion is governed by YHWH's *instruction* (v. 2, תּוֹרָה), this city shall be the place where all nations will find peace and security. Such a glorious vision is hard to image within history as we know it. Yet the text indicates no knowledge of a period outside the temporal historical realm. Many interpreters concede, however, that 4:1-5 can only occur when the limits of the present time are transcended.

4:6-7. Renewed life under YHWH's kingship. The opening words, *in that day* (v. 6), connect this unit to 4:1-5. Logically, this section follows the more general prediction of Zion's recovery, adding the specific promise that the people of Israel will return from dispersion. The promise is not for renewed political strength in the traditional sense. Rather, the sole characteristic of these people is that they live under the kingship of YHWH.

4:8. The new Zion, a royal capital. Here the prophet portrays Zion as a secure dwelling for the *flock* of YHWH. The term *tower* (מִגְדַּל), refers to part of the defensive structure of a city wall. Also, *hill* (עֹפֶל) is associated with a place of lookout (see Isa 32:14). This city, which houses the remnant, the prophet proclaims, shall regain royal power and standing. The nature of the renewed kingdom, however, is unclear.

4:9–5:6 [MT 4:9–5:5]. The birth pangs of Zion. This conclusion of the *Zion* section (4:1–5:6 [MT 4:1–5:5]) features three units united by the introductory *now*. Each of these sayings describes a present, threatening situation followed by a promise of rescue by YHWH. The first set of verses (vv. 9-10) likens Zion's troubles to the travail of a woman whose labor pains (a metaphor for the Babylonian exile) will soon end. The second unit (vv. 11-13) gives a kind of theology of military and political world events, similar to Isaiah (e.g., Isa 19:16-17). Specifically, Micah assures the people of Zion that YHWH has a plan for the eventual destruction of the nations that currently are destroying their land. The final *now* saying (5:1-6 [MT 4:14–5:5]) promises a ruler, following the model of David, who will lead Israel to peace. The statement, *when she who is in labor has brought forth* (5:3 [MT 5:2]) is probably another metaphor for the groaning of exile (see 4:9-10). After the return from Babylon, the "new David" (the fruit of the exile?) will defend Israel from *Assyria* (v. 6), perhaps a generic symbol for any foe from the north (cf. Ezra 6:22). The third person singular verb in MT, *rescue* (v. 6, הִצִּיל), probably refers to the action of the ruler from Bethlehem.

The Faithful Remnant, 5:7-15 (MT 5:6-14)

5:7-9 [MT 5:6-8]. Dependence upon YHWH. The comparison of Israel to *dew* and *showers* is a promise that the remnant will be characterized by its dependence on YHWH (v. 7). Because they *wait* for YHWH (that is, "trust in" or "depend on"), the Israelites will be empowered to dominate the surrounding nations (vv. 8-9).

5:10-15 [MT 5:9-14]). Purification of Israel's relationship to YHWH. The final saying of the first section of the book describes an eschatological event in which YHWH will remove all objects that garner Israel's trust and devotion. YHWH insisted that his people not rely upon military might (e.g., Ps 44:6). Also, Israel was prohibited from setting up any image of the deity (Exod 20:4).

YHWH's Controversy with His People, 6:1–7:20

Requirements of Covenant Loyalty, 6:1-8

Like Mic 1:2, the opening of the book's second section introduces a court case between YHWH and his people with the imperative, *hear* (v. 1). In this section the prophet broaches the problem of covenant faithfulness. YHWH addresses the rebellious Israelites (v. 3) with a reminder of several key events in their foundational story (vv. 4-5). The effect is a heightened sense of YHWH's steadfastness to the covenant agreement with Israel. Following this summary, a representative of the people proposes increasingly drastic ritual acts meant to assuage their guilt and reestablish proper relationship with God (vv. 6-7). The list begins with common burnt offerings but extends to the more unusual act of child sacrifice. This catalogue of ritual acts prepares for the prophetic voice of v. 8, *what does the Lord require of you but to do justice, and to love kindness, and to walk humbly with your God?* Herein lies the key to covenant faithfulness (cf. Ps 50; Amos 5:24; Hos 2:19-20; 6:6; Isa 7:9; 30:15). The call for justice connects well with Micah's criticism of Israel's leaders (see 3:9-11).

Jerusalem's Sins and YHWH's Intolerance, 6:9-16

YHWH again (see 6:1) opens a controversy, this time against *the city* of Jerusalem (v. 9). The capital's inhabitants are guilty of dishonest business practices, a failure to *do justice* (6:8), and following the example of the dynasty of King OMRI in IDOLATRY (2 Kgs 10:18; 21:3). Therefore, YHWH declares, the city will be destroyed. This prediction is roughly parallel to 3:9-12 in the first major section of the book.

Despair over Ubiquitous Evil, 7:1-6

The speaker of 7:1-6 may be the city of Jerusalem personified. Like chaps. 2–3 this unit exposes the profligate leaders of Judah (vv. 3-4). Unfaithfulness runs so deep that not even the closest friend, relative, or spouse can be trusted.

Confession and Assurance of Pardon, 7:7-20

The Book of Micah ends with a liturgical piece that sums up many of the major themes of the whole work. Verse 7 responds to the widespread unrighteousness in the land (7:1-6) with a resolve to *wait for the God of my salvation* (v. 7). In form the verse is similar to so-called "psalms of confidence" (cf. Ps 52:8-9 [MT 52:10-11]); thematically, the line is related to Micah's description of the righteous remnant in 5:7. Verses 8-10 treat the threat to Zion or to God's people posed by enemies, a major concern of the book (1:15-16; 3:12; 4:10, 11-13; 5:5-6). The speaker recognizes the sins of the nation (v. 9) and their consequences; however, he or she also looks forward to a time when YHWH's wrath will abate and Israel's enemies will be punished (cf. 4:5–5:6 [MT 4:5–5:5]). This hope takes on more specificity in vv. 11-13. Here the address to Jerusalem looks forward to NEHEMIAH's rebuilding of the city (445–433 B.C.E.). Continuing the concern for vindication among the nations, vv. 14-17 call on YHWH to *shepherd* the people while putting the nations to shame. The shepherd image in the ancient Near East is a royal metaphor; thus, these verses request YHWH to lead Israel as king (cf. 4:7). Finally, the book closes with an assurance of pardon from YHWH (7:18-20). Thus, Micah opened with a portrait of YHWH's anger being displayed in theophany and now concludes with the assertion that he *will cast all our sins into the depths of the sea* (v. 19).

Works Cited

Mays, James L. 1983. "Justice: Perspectives from the Prophetic Tradition," *Int* 37/1:5–17. 1976. *Micah*. OTL.

Nahum
William P. Steeger

Introduction

Midway into the last half of the seventh century B.C.E., the PROPHET Nahum raised his hymns of Yahweh's greatness and thundered his taunts over Nineveh's fall. ASSYRIA's cruelty and power had swept through the ancient Near East oblivious of the legacy of God's love and call to repentance left by the prophet JONAH a century and a half before (see 2 Kgs 14:25). His messages, often couched in outstanding POETRY, proclaimed doom to Assyria's capital, hope to struggling Judah, and promised restoration to outcast ISRAEL. Nahum's intricate weaving of the threads of Yahweh's love amidst the awesome tapestry of his wrath, provided assurance to the faithful that Yahweh is sovereign of history.

Nahum's prophecy is the seventh in the "Book of the Twelve," or minor prophets, coming just before HABAKKUK. Although following Jonah in the LXX, Nahum comes after MICAH in the MT. The ministry of Nahum probably is much broader than the handful of poetic oracles preserved in this book might suggest. Although the heart of his message focuses on the sure destruction of Nineveh and the justice of Yahweh that will not let sin go unpunished, Nahum knows of the coming restoration of all Israel, the follies of IDOLATRY and immorality, and the importance of social responsibility. He is not simply a partisan prophet blasting a world super power. Nahum's message encompasses the very character of Yahweh. God's justice and judgment are applied in a universal fairness. No nation is exempt from God's standards of righteousness. Like the prophets before him (cf. Amos 1–2), Nahum proclaims Yahweh's judgment and vindication upon foreign powers.

Authorship

This prophecy presents the message of Nahum, mentioned only here in 1:1 (the Nahum listed in Luke 3:25 most certainly refers to another individual by the same name in the ancestry of Jesus). Although the name is found in nonbiblical sources, little is known about this prophet. Nahum means "comforted," or "consoled," and is possibly a shortened version of the common biblical name NEHEMIAH. He is called the Elkoshite, although the exact location of *Elkosh* is unknown. Some have suggested a location on the TIGRIS (modern Elkush), or in GALILEE (ancient CAPERNAUM, i.e., "village of Nahum," a frequent proposal), or one of three sites in JUDAH. Current scholarship favors one of the southern locations, since by the time of the composition of Nahum the northern Kingdom was already in exile. However, the specific mention of *the LORD is restoring the majesty of Jacob, as well as the majesty of Israel* (2:2) lends credence to a possible Galilean site. Nahum's general familiarity with Nineveh conforms to the common knowledge of his day and does not require the manufacture of theories that place his family in exile in Assyria prior to his proposed return to Judah.

Date

Although no exact date is given in the superscription, internal evidence provides a framework within the mid-seventh century B.C.E. Mention of the fall of the Egyptian city of *Thebes* (663 B.C.E.) in 3:8 and the anticipation of the destruction of Nineveh (612 B.C.E.) provide terminal points of reference. Those suggesting a date after the fall of Nineveh usually understand the prophecy as a cultic liturgy. For the most part, contemporary scholarship has not accepted this view. The prophet's constant assurance of Nineveh's coming destruction, in order to calm the fears of an oppressed Judah, seems highly unlikely after the fall of Nineveh. Nahum's discussion of the prowess and strength of Assyria mandates a time prior to the death of Assyria's greatest king, ASSHURBANAPAL (668–627 B.C.E.). Assyria declined rapidly following his death. Silence regarding the growing menace of Babylon (rebelling against Assyria around 625 B.C.E.) further strengthens this dating. During the reign of MANASSEH (667/6–673 B.C.E.) Judah felt the heaviest Assyrian hand. Under JO-SIAH's rule (640–609 B.C.E.) Judah experienced some relief from Assyrian oppression. The resurgence of Thebes in the last quarter of the seventh-century would make the illustration of 3:8 weak and meaningless if the prophecy is dated to that period. A date in the third quarter of the seventh-century seems most likely.

Literary Form

The superscription (1:1) calls the prophecy an *oracle* (lit. "burden," as in KJV). Although not always associated with judgment, as here in Nahum, the ORACLE form is well known in prophetic writing. Nahum uses an abundance of literary devices and forms. The rhetorical question is common throughout his prophecy. Rich metaphors and similes, drawn from nature and history, appear in each dramatic poem and punctuate all the prose. The opening hymn of praise flows quickly into a courtroom scene where alternating decrees of judgment and acquittal are pronounced upon Nineveh and Judah. The second chapter invites the reader to smell the smoke and see the flames in the vivid descriptions of battle and the terrifying pictures of a city under siege. Irony brackets the limping meter of lament in the dramatic funeral dirge that sweeps the prophecy to a dynamic conclusion in chap. 3.

Most scholarly attention has focused on the puzzling form of the opening hymn. The presence and extent of a purported alphabetic acrostic is the issue. Such acrostic poems are well known in scripture (cf. Pss 111; 112; 119; Lam 1; 2; 3; 4). Since the last century, many suggested that 1:2-8 forms such an acrostic, although only about half of the full alphabet is recognizable. Elaborate reconstruction of the text is necessary to identify a complete alphabetic acrostic (all without manuscript evidence) and efforts to present the first half of the alphabet (*aleph* through *kaph*) require textual emendations in at least four of the eleven lines of this poem (some critics continue the acrostic through *mem*; see below.) While many contemporary scholars argue for an acrostic structure, the fact remains that the poem as presented in the MT is completely comprehensible and the possible acrostic form was not suspected until late in the last century. The function, form, and extent of such an acrostic fragment will be debated for years to come.

For Further Study

In the *Mercer Dictionary of the Bible*: ASSYRIA; JONAH, BOOK OF; LORD OF HOSTS; NAHUM; NAHUM, BOOK OF; ORACLE; POETRY; PROPHET.

In other sources: D. W. Baker, *Nahum, Habakkuk, Zephaniah*, TOTC; E. R. Daglish, "Nahum," BBC; R. D. Patterson, *Nahum, Habakkuk, Zephaniah*, WEC; J. J. M. Roberts, *Nahum, Habakkuk, and Zephaniah*, OTL; R. L. Smith, *Micah–Malachi*, WBC.

Commentary

AnOutline

Superscription, 1:1
I. A Hymn to the Sovereign Lord, 1:2-15
   [MT 1:2–2:1]
   A. Lord of Wrath and Love: General, 1:2-8
   B. Lord of Wrath and Love:
      Specific, 1:9-15 [MT 1:9–2:1]
II. An Oracle of Nineveh's Fall Assured,
   2:1-13 [MT 2:2-14]
   A. A Call to Arms, 2:1-2 [MT 2:2-3]
   B. Nineveh's Siege Described, 2:3-5 [MT 2:4-6]

C. Nineveh's People Displaced, 2:6-9
   [MT 2:7-10]
D. Nineveh's Greatness Destroyed,
   2:10-13 [MT 2:11-14]
III. A Taunt Song on Nineveh's Fall Secured,
   3:1-19
   A. Nineveh: City of Bloodshed, 3:1-7
   B. Nineveh: Like All the Nations, 3:8-15
   C. Nineveh: Mortally Wounded, 3:16-19

Superscription, 1:1

The superscription explains the formal nature of Nahum's message as an *oracle* (lit. "burden" as in KJV) and is a common expression for God's revelation to the prophets. The term calls attention to the serious nature of the message and often describes a note of impending judgment (note, e.g., the play upon the word "oracle" in Jer 23:33-38.) The word *book* does not preclude an oral delivery of these sermons but does call attention to the written form they soon assumed. The term *vision* also is frequent in prophetic literature (Hab 1:1; Amos 1:1; Mic 1:1; Obad 1:1) and emphasizes the dynamic impact of God's message upon the prophet. Nahum's vivid language paints graphic pictures of Nineveh's fall, giving full meaning to the visual theme developed throughout the book. For the meaning of *Nahum of Elkosh* see the introduction above.

A Hymn to the Sovereign Lord, 1:2-15 [MT 1:2–2:1]

Lord of Wrath and Love: General, 1:2-8

This majestic poem describes Yahweh in alternating pictures of wrath and love. Like the two sides of a coin, both are needed to describe divine nature. Some modern scholarship finds portions of an alphabetic acrostic in vv. 2-8 (others include v. 9, see below). The poem does not mention Nineveh by name, causing some commentators to suggest that Nahum has selected a previously prepared poem for the introduction of his book. Details, however, in the actual wording of the hymn (see v. 8) may focus on the doomed city. Adopting an acrostic structure for this hymn necessitates a forced and fragmented use of the present text. The awesome sovereignty of Yahweh unfolds as follows:

א: *A jealous and avenging God is the* LORD (v. 2);
ב: *His way is in the whirlwind and storm* (v. 3b);
ג: *He rebukes the sea and makes it dry* (v. 4);
(ד is missing);
ה: *The mountains quake before him, and the hills melt*; (v. 5a);
ו: *the earth heaves before him* (v. 5b);
ז: *Who can stand before his indignation?* (v. 6a);
ח: *His wrath is poured out like fire* (v. 6b);
ט: *The* LORD *is good* (v. 7a);
י: *he protects those who take refuge in him* (v. 7b);
כ: *He will make a full end of his adversaries* (v. 8).

Making v. 9 a part of the acrostic requires reversing the present order of the lines. The vision of Yahweh's majesty as evidenced in nature is a familiar theme (cf. Pss 18; 29; Hab 3) and often associated with the salvation history passages of the OT.

1:2. God of vengeance. The opening lines of the poem declare Yahweh's jealous and avenging nature. Alliteration in the Hebrew text and the stair-step repetition of key related words (*jealous, avenging, vengeance*) heighten the forcefulness of the message. Calling attention to *jealous* emphasizes God's serious dealings with sin. The terms *vengeance* and *avenging* reflect a Hebrew verbal root that is basic to biblical theology, appearing seventy times in the OT. Divine vengeance is set in the context of God's MERCY and must be understood in light of JUSTICE and HOLINESS. Both the OT and the NT balance God's wrath against sin with divine mercy and redemption from sin. Wrath is necessary for mercy to be meaningful. Vengeance is under God's control alone (Lev 19:18; Deut 32:35-41). The day of the Lord's vengeance is an important theme in other prophets (Isa 38:8; 61:2; 63:1-6). This hymn shows the balance in God's nature by noting that *The* LORD *is slow to anger* (1:3), and *The*

LORD *is good, a stronghold in a day of trouble; he protects those who take refuge in him* (1:7).

1:3-6. God of patience and power. The majestic power of God is evidenced in nature (vv. 3b-6). References in v. 4 to God's drying the sea and the rivers point to the mighty acts of God in Israel's redemptive history (cf. Pss 18:7-19; 106:9; 114; Isa 50:2; Hab 3:8). *Bashan, Carmel,* and *Lebanon* (v. 4) were known as exceptionally fertile territories. Many see these references and those to *the mountains* (v. 5) as challenges to Canaanite mythology. Yahweh, not BAAL or any foreign god, controls the forces of nature and moves them toward divine ends. From this vivid picture of *whirlwind, storm,* earthquake, and drought (vv. 3-5), Nahum assures Judah that Yahweh is sovereign over nature and history.

1:7-8. God of goodness and justice. Following the penetrating questions of 1:6, the surety of God's coming wrath is pronounced. Yet in the midst of this vision of vengeance, God reaches out to embrace and protect the people *who take refuge in him* (v. 7). The goodness of God is one of the most common OT themes. This great promise has brought hope and comfort to countless of God's people living in a violent and oppressive world. The arrangement of the words of the text is debated but the meaning of the passage is clear. The awful fate of the enemy is contrasted to the protection and refuge afforded *those who take refuge in him.* Nahum's hymn echoes the themes of Ps 46. God's justice is certain. No evil can outrun divine vengeance. The slowness of God's anger (v. 3) is no indication of the speed and certainty of holy wrath (v. 8). Some commentators see in the opening line of v. 8 a reference to the actual fall of Nineveh, which was accompanied by a flooding of the Tigris.

Lord of Wrath and Love: Specific, 1:9-15 [MT 1:9–2:1]

The hymn now turns from the general proclamation of God's wrath and love to the specific verdict given in a formal legal suit. The prophet alternates pronouncements of judgment and salvation upon Assyria and Judah, respectively.

1:9-11. Judgment against Nineveh. Nineveh's foolish plots against the LORD will bring certain destruction. There will be no recovery from this fall. Indeed, following Nineveh's fall in 612 B.C.E., a small remnant, under the leadership of Asshur-uballit II, fled to HARAN and established a capital. There they were finally overrun in 609 B.C.E. Assyria was gone from the pages of history. Nahum questions Nineveh directly (v. 9): *Why do you plot against the LORD?* Some include this verse in the proposed acrostic (see introduction above). The total destruction pictured in v. 10 is clear, although the passage is difficult and provides a variety of scholarly opinion. Many evil kings have gone out from Nineveh over the years (the *you* of v. 11 should be understood collectively).

1:12-13. Comfort to Judah. Beginning with the familiar prophetic cry of authority, Nahum proclaims comfort to Judah in the destruction of Assyria (v. 12a) and the promise of relief from his judgment (v. 12b). Like the prophet ISAIAH,

Nahum understands the oppression of Judah by Assyria as God's judgment upon the people (Isa 10:5). The promises of relief and release are certain (v. 13).

1:14. Judgment against Nineveh. Once again the prophet addresses Nineveh directly, proclaiming their sure and permanent defeat (see above 1:9-11). In the mindset of the ancient Near East, the power of a nation's gods determined the power of a nation. Yahweh declares the gods and nation of Assyria defeated and worthless.

1:15 [MT 2:1]. Call to rejoicing. The familiar ring of this messianic cry of good news (cf. Isa 52:7) is a fitting conclusion to Nahum's hymn in praise of God's majesty. News of the destruction of Nineveh and the collapse of the Assyrian Empire will be welcome words of *peace* to Judah. Nahum uses such a time of rejoicing to admonish God's people to religious faithfulness (*fulfill your vows*) and offer assurance of Nineveh's permanent defeat.

An Oracle of Nineveh's Fall Assured, 2:1-13 [MT 2:2-14]

The poems that conclude the Book of Nahum are vivid descriptions of battle and detailed explanations of defeat. Although some claim that the name of God is not mentioned in the poems, *the LORD* is clearly in view in Israel's restoration (v. 2:2) and the *LORD of hosts* (v. 13; 3:5) is the subject of the frequent use of the first person pronoun that follows. The English translation and MT are one verse out of line throughout chap. 2 (see above on 1:15). The vivid description of battle does not necessitate a date after 612 B.C.E. since battle scenes were a part of Judah's national experience.

A Call to Arms, 2:1-2 [MT 2:2-3]

This passage forms a transition to the battle scene that follows. As in the preceding verses, Nahum first addresses Assyria and then Judah. In biting satire he charges Nineveh to prepare for battle. The *shatterer* (v. 1; lit. "attacker," or "scatterer") has come and no preparation can stay the flood of Yahweh's wrath even if they *collect all [their] strength*. Although Medes, Babylonians, and Scythians compose the besieging army, it is Yahweh, the LORD OF HOSTS, who has come up against Nineveh. Just as God's actions assure the defeat of Assyria (v. 1), they also secure the restoration of Israel (v. 2). A reunited Israel is in view. Judah has been the focus of the preceding verses of comfort and hope, but here the scattered Northern Kingdom (with its many *ruined . . . branches* is the subject. The vine is a well known OT picture of Israel (cf. Isa 5:1-7). The restoration of a united Israel is a frequent prophetic theme (cf. Ezek 37:15-23; Amos 9:11; Zech 10:6-12).

Nineveh's Siege Described, 2:3-5 [MT 2:4-6]

The three stanzas of this poem of Nineveh's defeat (vv. 3-5; 6-9; 10-13) form one of the classic descriptions of battle. Each phrase succinctly captures the full flavor of the city's siege. The *red* (v. 3) may refer to the splendor of the uniform of the Medes (as reported by Xenophon) and the colorful array of the Babylonian army (cf. Ezek 23:14-15). The bright metal fittings of the racing chariots flash in the sunlight. The NRSV reads *the chargers prance* (v. 3), but there is no need to emend the text. The Hebrew "the cypresses are made to quiver" can easily be understood as spears or other instruments of war made from wood. As the battle intensifies the chariots race through the streets of Nineveh (v. 4) and officers stumble through the confusion as they seek to man the weakening wall (v. 5). The term *mantelet* (Heb. "protector") probably refers to the temporary covering of shields raised by the besieging soldiers at the foot of the city wall.

Nineveh's People Displaced, 2:6-9 [MT 2:7-10]

In one profoundly simple verse the fall of the great city is etched permanently into world history (v. 6). Descriptions of the dislocation of people and the plundering of property consume the remainder of the stanza. The *river gates* (v. 6) may be a figurative expression for the invading armies. The suggestion that the fall of Nineveh was aided by the flooding Tigris overflowing the adjoining canals and crumbling the city's defenses, causing the palace to tremble (lit. "melt"), is tempting. The nonbiblical supporting evidence (the Babylonian Chronicle) is deficient at this point. As Assyria has treated its captives, so its cruelty returns upon its own head. The population is enslaved and deported (v. 7). The phrase *it is decreed* (v. 7) is an attempt to translate an uncertain Hebrew expression (*huzzab*). Some suggest that the term is a symbolic name for the city, or is related to a deity (in which case the last phrase may refer to the deity's female slaves being taken captive). The city is clearly identified in the midst of this poem as Nineveh. The mighty army of Assyria (here compared to *a pool* of water no longer held back by secure banks) is routed. Even the command to *Halt!* (v. 8) can not cause its fleeing soldiers to return and protect the city's treasures from the spoilers. Centuries of looting and tribute-taking made Nineveh a wealthy storehouse of the ancient Near East. *There is no end of treasure! An abundance of every precious thing!* (v. 9).

Nineveh's Greatness Destroyed, 2:10-13 [MT 2:11-14]

As the previous stanza began with a profoundly simple statement of Nineveh's fall, so this stanza begins with a simple word play. David Baker observes, "The progressive stages of intensifying dereliction are indicated by three Hebrew words, each adding one syllable to the preceding word, i.e., *buqa, mebuqa, mebullaqa*" (1988, 35). This stanza is known as the taunt proper. Following the initial cry of devastation, the stunned survivors stand trembling as the looted city crumbles around them (v. 10). A lions' den is the closing metaphor of this taunt and *What became of the lions' den . . . ?* (v. 11) is the startling reality of Nineveh's plight. Centuries of plunder and bringing home the spoil have proved fruitless. The Assyrian lion is defeated and devastated. The taunt is brought to a formal conclusion with the powerful pronouncement of Yahweh, *See, I am against you, says the Lord of hosts* (v. 13). Although some see this passage as transitional, it is climactic. God calls attention the divine nature (lit. "behold me"). The focus is *the LORD of hosts*. With this declaration, Nahum pulls the varying threads of his poem to a grand conclusion and unites the picture of the battle's fury with the metaphor of the lions' den.

A Taunt Song on Nineveh's Fall Secured, 3:1-19

This final poem (possibly a collection of poems) represents the finest of Israel's battle songs. The short crisp phrases press home each vivid picture. The speed of conquest and the depth of sin are graphically portrayed. Nahum explains the reasons for Nineveh's fall. As it lived by the sword so it will die by the sword (cf. Matt 26:52b). This taunt song follows the classic prophetic form of a woe oracle found frequently in the OT (cf. Isa 5:8-15; 10:1-4; Hab 2:6-20; Zeph 3:1-8).

The NRSV is not consistent in translating the Heb. הוֹי. The Hebrew word for "woe" is אוֹי; הוֹי is rightly translated by several terms, chiefly "Ah!," "Alas!," etc. The first word of v. 1 translated *Ah!* is the same as those found in Hab 2:6, 9, 12, 15, and 19 translated "Alas," and is a key to the proper recognition and understanding of this literary form.

Nineveh: City of Bloodshed, 3:1-7

The term *Ah!* or "woe" is a powerful expression of pending doom found in formal laments for the dead. The lament (*qina*) meter is used here, adding to the heightened tension and gloom. *Bloodshed, deceit, booty,* and *plunder* (v. 1) beautifully describe the foundations of Assyrian society. Built upon the spoils of conquest and fed by the fuel of tribute and plunder, Nineveh is aptly described. The rapid staccato expressions of vv. 3-4 paint pictures of battle reminiscent of the poem above (2:3-10 [MT 2:4-11]). From the initial charge (as the *crack of the whip* is heard) to the agony of defeat (as the *piles of dead, heaps of corpses, dead bodies without end* are stumbled over), Nahum's poem outlines the conquest. Reasons for Nineveh's fall are enumerated in a metaphor of a greedy harlot who *enslaves nations through her debaucheries* (v. 4). The harlot metaphor is well known in prophetic literature of both testaments (cf. Isa 1:21; 23:16; Ezek 16; 23; Hos 5:4; Rev 17–18).

The stanza races to a climax in v. 5, where *the LORD of hosts* declares: *I am against you*. The humiliation pronounced upon Nineveh is reminiscent of other prophetic judgments (cf. Isa 47:3; Jer 13:22; Ezek 16:37-39; Hos 2:3, 9; Amos 4:2-3; Mic 1:11). Made a spectacle to the nations, Nineveh will be pelted with *filth* and treated *with contempt* (v. 6). There will be no one to mourn its passing or comfort the grieving exiles. Once again the city is mentioned by name (v. 7, as in 2:8).

Nineveh: Like All the Nations, 3:8-15

Nineveh is no less vulnerable than the surrounding nations. In a biting reminder, Nahum recalls the fall of mighty *Thebes* (Heb. *No-amon*). This ancient city spread majestically on both sides of the NILE and boasted grand temples, courts, and imperial luxury. The impressive temple ruins of Luxor and Karnak are ample testimony to the greatness and grandeur of Thebes. Protected by the Nile and its canals, strengthened by alliances with Ethiopia, Put and Libya, Thebes still was not secure. Shall Nineveh fare better? Certainly not! In another of Nahum's rhetorical questions, Assyria is humiliated again (vv. 8-9). The same afflictions Assyria hurled upon Thebes would return to haunt Nineveh: exile, captivity, infanticide, slavery, and chains (v. 10). The vivid list reads like Assyria's own conquering cruelties. Just as Thebes fell to the onslaught of ASSHURBANAPAL in 663 B.C.E. (see introduction), so also Nineveh was doomed.

As the battle rages, Nineveh's mighty defenders will appear *drunken* and run into *hiding* (v. 11), but no refuge will be found (the only refuge is in *the LORD*, 1:7). The ring of fortresses surrounding the city will be useless. Like a fig tree laden with ripe fruit, a mere shaking will bring them all down into the mouth of the enemy (v. 12). The demoralized troops are like *women in your midst* and the battered defenses stand as open gates to the invading armies (v. 13). In harsh satire Nahum calls once again for the majestic city to prepare for war (v. 14; cf. 2:1). The irony is evident. *Draw water for the siege*, he cries, but the flooding waters of the Tigris aided Nineveh's demise. *Strengthen your forts*, he urges, but the surrounding fortresses fell like ripened figs. *Trample the clay, tread the mortar, take hold of the brick mold!* he pleads, but the defenses are already breached (v. 14). The *fire* and *sword* are coming. Like a plague of locusts settling on a field of green and leaving it brown and barren, nothing will remain of Nineveh. Nahum makes one final call to arms: *Multiply yourselves like the locust* (v. 15). Not even superior numbers can avert Assyria's coming disaster.

Nineveh: Mortally Wounded, 3:16-19

Nahum's final stanza ridicules the fickle Assyrian merchants, the self-serving military, the opportunist scribes, the slumbering rulers, the complacent nobility, and the destitute masses. The *merchants* had grown more numerous than *the stars of the heavens* and are known in some detail from the trade records of the ancient Near East. These businessmen are fair-weather friends, swarming on Nineveh like locusts to enjoy the treasures sparkling in the summer sun. However, they soon shed their skin and fly away to greener pastures (v. 16). The military (*guards*) and *scribes* are like grasshoppers and locusts who huddle together for common warmth on a cold day but quickly fly away when the sun comes up (v. 17). The scribes may have served a special function associated with Assyrian military recruitment practices.

Nahum addresses the king of Assyria directly in his final condemning charge. The term *shepherds* often serves as a metaphor for leaders in the OT (cf. Jer 17:16; Ezek 34; Zech 10:2-3). The Assyrian king is advised that his leaders and *nobles* are sleeping on the job, oblivious of the precarious condition of the sheep (citizens) *scattered on the mountains* (v. 18). The *people* are deserted: without economic support, protection, leadership, or example. Assyria's wound is fatal! There is no cure for its hurt. Instead of expected sympathy, comfort, or mourning, comes only the clapping of hands and rejoicing at Nineveh's helpless estate. The empire's *endless cruelty* showed mercy to none (v. 19). In return, Nineveh's passing will be a time of celebration.

Within a generation Assyria was gone from the pages of history. Nahum's prophecy was complete. For Judah the moment is not a time of gloating but a time of recognizing God's vindication of evil. Sin is punished. With the closing phrases comes a reminder for Judah to heed a similar warning. Scarcely half a century beyond Nahum's taunt, Judah too would hear the sobering message of God through Ezekiel: "prophesy against the shepherds of Israel" (Ezek 34:2ff.). God's justice is sure. Each nation and individual is measured against no earthly standard but called to conform to God's righteousness alone and to find *refuge in him* (1:7).

Work Cited

Baker, David W. 1988. *Nahum, Habakkuk, Zephaniah: An Introduction and Commentary.*

Habakkuk
William P. Steeger

Introduction

Habakkuk's prophecy stands unique among the prophetic books called the Minor Prophets or the Book of the Twelve and is as relevant today as it was in the crisis period of the late sixth century B.C.E. Where other prophets focused on the LORD's word to ISRAEL, HABAKKUK carried the burden of the oppressed of his people to the LORD. The autobiographical style provides a fresh and forceful approach. The PROPHET delivered his burden to the people of Judah in an unusual format. He shared the doubts and questionings of his heart and reported the response these met from the LORD. This theodicy, i.e., a questioning of God's justice and actions, begins with Habakkuk's prayers. The prophet decried the injustice rampant in Judah and questioned God's apparent lack of concern for the innocent. After Habakkuk's three queries, God challenges this limited view of history and divine sovereignty. He declares that the wicked will meet an appropriate end but the righteous live by trusting in God's control of history and waiting for the completion of his ultimate purposes. The prophet evaluates the LORD's ORACLE that *the righteous live by their faith* (2:4), and concludes with a vision of Yahweh's sovereign majesty as he marches to deliver his people throughout history.

Authorship

Few scholars still challenge the traditional authorship of Habakkuk, although little is known of the prophet apart from this book. Conjecture regarding the meaning of his name ranges from an Assyrian word for a plant to Luther's suggestion of "embrace" (based on 2 Kgs 4:16). The liturgical references surrounding the concluding hymn of the prophecy (3:1, 19) suggest that Habakkuk served in the Temple or was from a priestly family. The apocryphal book BEL AND THE DRAGON reports his ministry to DANIEL.

Date

The exact date of the prophecy depends upon internal critical judgments: (1) the problem of structure and unity of the book, (2) the canonical form of the prophecy, (3) various social and political issues, (4) and textual evidence (including the DEAD

SEA SCROLLS). Suggestions for dating this prophecy range from the eighth through the second century B.C.E. Contemporary scholarship favors the late sixth century B.C.E. Some writers prefer a date during the wicked reign of MANASSEH (686–643 B.C.E.), or during the reign of JOSIAH (prior to the reforms of 621 B.C.E.). The evidence best supports a time during the reign of JEHOIAKIM (609–598 B.C.E.) and can be sharpened even further.

The Egyptian army defeated Judah and killed King Josiah (609 B.C.E.). After three months, Pharaoh Necho dethroned Jehoahaz (Josiah's son and successor) and exiled him to Egypt, placing a subservient Jehoiakim on Judah's throne. The neo-Babylonians (Chaldeans) were an expanding threat in the collapsing ruins of the Assyrian Empire and defeated Egypt at Carchemish (605 B.C.E.). In 1:5-6 *the Chaldeans* are mentioned as if the invasion was still in the future and the astonishment mentioned in v. 5 requires a date prior to 605 B.C.E. The reference in 3:2 to *in our own time revive it* (or "let him live") and in 3:13 to *to save your anointed*, may indicate Habakkuk's call for the return of JEHOAHAZ from Egyptian exile (or the placing of a new Davidic king on the throne). This dictates a date closer to 609 B.C.E.

Literary Form

Modern scholarship affirms the unity of the book but suggests a variety of settings and possible backgrounds. The dialogue form of the prophecy graphically portrays the prophet as an intermediary. He was not performing a cultic rite, but engaged in dynamic dialogue with God. This resembles more the debate and actions of court life, or elders at the city gate, than the formality of the Temple cult. Habakkuk adopted the "prophetic I" and presented the revelation he received in autobiographical form. The various sections of his prophecy move from this dramatic dialogue to oracle, taunt-song (woe oracle), prayer, hymn of praise, and vow of commitment.

For Further Study

In the *Mercer Dictionary of the Bible*: HABAKKUK; HABAKKUK, BOOK OF; NEBUCHADREZZAR; ORACLE; POETRY; PROPHET; VISION.

In other sources: D. W. Baker, *Nahum, Habakkuk, Zephaniah*, TOTC; D. D. Garland, "Habakkuk," BBC; D. M. Lloyd-Jones, *From Fear to Faith*; R. D. Patterson, *Nahum, Habakkuk, Zephaniah*, WEC; J. J. M. Roberts, *Nahum, Habakkuk, and Zephaniah*, OTL.

Commentary

An Outline

Dialogue with God, 1:1–2:5

Superscription, 1:1

The opening verse calls Habakkuk's entire prophecy an *oracle* (lit. "burden," as in KJV), a common expression for God's revelation to the prophets, emphasizing the deep concern placed upon their hearts. The verb *saw* is rarely used with *oracle* (see Isa 13:1; however the element of VISION and references to "seeing" the word of the LORD are frequent in prophetic literature; cf. Nah 1:1; Amos 1:1; Mic 1:1; Obad 1) and emphasizes the dynamic impact of God's message upon the prophet. This visual theme is developed throughout the prophecy: *Why do you make me see wrongdoing and look at trouble?* (1:3); *Write the vision, make it plain on tablets, so that a runner may read it* (2:2); and most distinctively in the powerful theophanic vision of the LORD's march through history in the prayer-hymn of 3:3-15.

Prayer and Response, 1:2–2:5

1:2-4. Habakkuk's lament. The prophet's first prayer arises from his encounter with the corruption and injustice prevalent during the reign of JEHOIAKIM. Many identify *the wicked* in v. 4 with *the Chaldeans* introduced in 1:6. However, such an interpretation contradicts the surprise element of the response in 1:5-11.

The complaint raised is similar to the liturgical laments in many of the psalms and the theme of much of Jeremiah's preaching dating to the same period. Habakkuk has cried to the LORD repeatedly and now questions why God has ignored his prayers and failed to respond to the needs of the innocent. The word *save* (v. 2) is a cry for a redeemer. This is a key theme in Habakkuk and linked to the *anointed* mentioned in 3:13 (see also the introduction). Why does God tarry? Why does the promised redeemer not come and deal with the *violence* and *wrongdoing*?

The words used to describe the *violence, strife,* and *contention* Habakkuk saw are strong expressions, reflecting the utter degradation of the times (cf. 2 Kgs 23:34–24:7; 2 Chr 36:4-8). The people of JUDAH suffered under the heavy hand of Jehoiakim as he struggled to exact taxes sufficient to meet the demands of the Egyptian tribute and his own extravagant life style (see Jer 22:13-19). The revival and reform program of JOSIAH collapsed. The corruption, perversity, and utter wickedness experienced during the reign of MANASSEH (2 Kgs 21:1-18; 2 Chr 33:1-

20) returned. The imposition of Egyptian (and later Babylonian) religious influences added to the complexities and problems caused by the revival of Canaanite Baalism. The greed and exploitation of this perverse age prostituted the justice and judgment characteristic of God's holiness (the model for Judah's legal structure).

1:5-11. The LORD's reply. The LORD responds to Habakkuk's questions of his justice and concern in the most unexpected way in this powerful oracle. As if to say "you haven't seen anything yet," the LORD challenges the prophet to gaze beyond the limits of the confines of Judah (and beyond the limits of his own imagination) and be astonished at what the LORD is doing in the nations near and far (v. 5).

The groundwork for the message of faith (2:4) is laid. The Chaldean threat seemed unbelievable, for they would not become a menacing world power until after the defeat of the Egyptians (605 B.C.E.). The sovereign creator of the universe is not limited to the regions of Judah to accomplish divine purposes. God has roused *the Chaldeans* (v. 6) and is using them as instruments of judgment. The person of faith lives in the understanding that the LORD controls history. Even *that fierce and impetuous nation* (v. 6, i.e., *the Chaldeans*) falls under God's scepter.

Graphic metaphors punctuate the description of *the Chaldeans*. This dreaded and fearsome nation is a tool in the hand of the sovereign LORD, used to bring judgment upon many nations and the wicked of Habakkuk's Judah. Three strophes explain their preparation (vv. 5-6), their power (vv. 7-8), and their purpose (vv. 9-11). Each verse sweeps over the hearer pounding home a message of fear and dread. *The Chaldeans* are a law unto themselves (v. 7) whose cavalry, like *leopards* and *wolves*, comes swooping into history to devour its prey like swift eagles (v. 8). This passage races toward a climax as the army, like a mighty desert sand storm (v. 9), scoffs at kings and builds earthen ramparts to breach the fortresses where cowering rulers await defeat (v. 10). Their goal is to glory in their might and make their own strength (military machine) their god (v. 11).

1:12-17. Habakkuk's lament. The abruptness and boldness of his first prayer met an unexpected answer. Habakkuk now uses a more flattering technique of challenging God's justice. How could a holy and righteous God allow the wicked to encompass the righteous? How could he use such an idolatrous force as the Chaldeans to discipline and punish? These questions form the heart of Habakkuk's cry. The first three verses of this lament (12-14) focus on the LORD, while the last three (vv. 15-17) depict the Chaldean enemy.

The lament opens with two questions (v. 12). The first flows from God's eternity and the second from the expected salvation and preservation of the people. The NRSV departs from the MT (following an ancient Jewish scribal correction) in translating *You shall not die* instead of "We shall not die" (see NRSV mg.). The better reading is "Shall we not die?" This phrase is a question introduced by the interrogative particle serving both queries. The OT frequently applies the names and metaphors for God used here. The questions of v. 13 emphasize Habakkuk's dissatisfaction with God's earlier response. The people of the world are like *fish of the sea* (v. 14) and the Chaldeans have developed a war machine with nets, seines, and fishing gear capable of vast destruction. Will the Chaldean army devastate the world unchecked?

2:1. Habakkuk's wait. The prophet expected a response from God. The silence was deafening. Perhaps the community demanded an explanation from Habakkuk. The MT reads "I will answer" (not the *he will answer* of the NRSV) suggesting such a challenge. Habakkuk stationed himself at his watchpost awaiting what God would say *to* him (lit. "in"), seeking the equipping and opportunity to serve as God's spokesman. The concept of the "watchman prophet" is well known (Isa 21:8; Jer 6:17; Ezek 3:17; 33:2-3). The stationing of Habakkuk on the *rampart* suggests a city under siege. (Some suggest a tower in an open field or vineyard, others even the Temple, but the Hebrew word is used to describe a fortified town.) As God's messenger to a desperate age, the besieged prophet needed a fresh word from the LORD for life's most perplexing questions.

2:2-5. The LORD's reply. The long awaited response finally comes. Verses 2-4 provide initial instructions for the preserving of the oracle. Habakkuk must *write the vision* clearly *on tablets* (v. 2) so anyone running past may read it. God's revelation may be long in arriving but it will surely come. Some suggest the vision in question was already given in 1:5-11. However the location of the oracle and the threefold reference in the NT (Rom 1:17; Gal 3:11; Heb 10:38-39) surely affirm vv. 4-5 as the vision to be written. These verses contrast the wicked and the righteous. The former are proud, wealthy, and arrogant. Their greed is never satiated. The righteous live by their faith (v. 4).

The Hebrew noun is better translated "faithfulness" and conveys the idea of a stance of faith that is "secure," "firm," or "steady" (Exod 17:12 provides a beautiful illustration of this identical word: "Moses' hands were steady"). Persons of faith flesh out their faithfulness in deeds of righteousness (cf. Isa 1:17; Mic 6:8; Jas 1:27), thereby demonstrating that they have a firm and steady trust in God's judgment and actions. The NT's use of v. 4 continued this line of thinking. Persons of faith look at life through a long view of history. One cannot see the world properly from the bottom of a well. Persons of faith look at God's mighty acts of salvation through the vast stretches of time and cling steadily to the LORD. They know that God has acted faithfully in the past and can be trusted to deliver his people once again. Individuals may walk through dark valleys and nations pass through periods of grave despair, but God comes in salvation to those who live by faith and patiently wait for his deliverance.

Questions from Life, 2:6-20

In these five three-verse taunt songs the classic prophetic form of "woe oracle" (each indicated in the NRSV by *alas*, vv. 6, 9, 12, 15, 19) is used (cf. Isa 5:8-25; 10:1-14; Nah 3:1-7; Zeph 3:1-8). This passage also belongs to a class of prophecies known as "oracles against foreign nations." God speaks these oracles, although

Habakkuk may be placing the cry of woe in the mouth of the nations oppressed by Babylon. The prophet is also recalling the exploitation of his own people at the hands of local tyrants (the abuses common in numerous ages). Many of these stanzas reflect atrocities perpetrated during the reign of Jehoiakim and form a protest and cry for radical social change. Judah needs a redeemer. The prophecy rushes toward the cry for such a deliverer and the theophany of chap. 3, where the record of precisely such deliverance is recounted in praise.

2:6-8. Woe to exploiters and plunderers. The object of the taunt and *mocking riddles* (v. 6) is translated *such people* and *them* in NRSV (lit. "him"). The immediate reference is to the *proud* (2:4) but may be broadened to include the Babylonians and the wicked of Judah discussed in the previous chapter. God proclaims that all exploiters shall be repaid like the plundering Babylonians who will suffer a similar fate at the hands of their victims. The references to *goods taken in pledge* and *your own creditors* (vv. 6, 7; cf. Amos 2:8) refers to the injustice within Judah (cf. 1:3-4). Babylon is amassing a great debt at the expense of *human bloodshed, and violence to the earth, to cities and all who live in them* (v. 8). That debt will be repaid in kind.

2:9-11. Woe to self-seekers. These verses denounce the splendors of ancient Babylon and promise that kingdoms built on ill-gotten gain must fall. The details of this stanza reflect a similar taunt song in Jer 22:13-19, where that prophet castigated Jehoiakim for building a lofty palace during a time of grave international crisis. Perhaps Habakkuk is speaking to the same situation. The righteous were abused and pressed into service without wages and the people exploited by taxation and conscription to meet the avarice of a tyrant. Habakkuk's song shares the same pain and echoes again the cry of despair in 1:3-4.

2:12-14. Woe to false kings. God denounces abusive and wicked kings, whether NEBUCHADREZZAR is enhancing the grandeur of Babylon or Jehoiakim beautifying the city of Jerusalem. Habakkuk's barb in v. 13 resembles Jeremiah's attack on Nebuchadrezzar in Jer 51:58. God's kingdom is coming. Like a mighty river of justice flowing from his throne, the glory of the LORD will sweep away the hatred and debris of scurrilous kingdoms and bring the justice and righteousness of the knowledge of the LORD. In v. 14, Habakkuk echoes the refrain of Isa 11:9.

2:15-17. Woe to oppressors. Habakkuk contrasts *the glory of the LORD* (2:14) with the glory turned into shame of abusive tyrants (twice in v. 16). Nebuchadrezzar and Jehoiakim may both be in view, for the *violence done to Lebanon* (v. 17) may refer equally well to Jehoiakim's excessive building material demands and to Nebuchadrezzar's raids. These oppressors are likened to exploitative neighbors who intoxicate others to abuse them. The expression *stagger* (v. 16) in the received Hebrew text is "be uncircumcised," referring to the debauching acts of pagan surroundings. This may favor the Judean setting rather than the Babylonian. The *cup in the LORD's right hand* (v. 16) is a familiar biblical reference to God's firm and decisive judgment (Ps 75:8; Isa 51:17; Jer 25:15-17; 49:12; 51:7; Ezek 23:31-34).

2:18-20. Woe to idolaters. The final stanza of woe attacks the foolishness of idolatry, whether the proud statues of Babylon and its mighty war machine (cf. 1:16) or the reintroduction of Canaanite worship under Jehoiakim. The conclusion (v. 20) serves a dual purpose of contrasting idolatry with the LORD's sovereignty (similar to the function of 2:14) and forms a powerful climax to the entire taunt song. This is an excellent backdrop for the majesty of the LORD's theophany in chap. 3. The prophet does have a response to those demanding answers from him (cf. 2:1). The LORD is sovereign (*in his holy temple*, v. 20); let there be *silence*! A vividly clear answer meets Habakkuk's questions of God's justice: Be still! The LORD is in control!

Solutions for the Faithful, 3:1-19

Superscription, 3:1

While Habakkuk's prayer is written in a formal liturgical style (reflected in the technical expressions included in the introduction and conclusion, 3:1, 19b), an intensely personal tone is evident throughout the hymn (cf. 3:2, 16-19a). Some scholars rejected the poem (3:2-19a) as an integral part of Habakkuk's prophecy. The discovery of the Qumran commentary (*pesher*), without comments on this section, seemed to confirm the suspicion. Further evaluation has reversed that conclusion and most scholars now support the unity of Habakkuk. Superscriptions to Pss 146–148 in the LXX indicate that other prophets (HAGGAI and ZECHARIAH) recorded prayers also. The term "prayer" occurs as the title for the entire collection of Davidic psalms concluding in 72:20 and is also found in the titles of Pss 17; 86; 90; 102; 142. *Shigionoth* is a technical term for an emotional or enthusiastic song. Further liturgical elements are evident in the use of *selah* (vv. 3, 9, 13) and the final reference to *choirmaster* and *stringed instruments* (v. 19).

Prayer of Faith, 3:2-19a

3:2. Confession and cry for mercy. Habakkuk's emotional prayer anticipates the great hymn of praise that follows. *I stand in awe* (lit. "afraid") is the formal attitude of worship in the OT. This is reverence and awe that leads to a life of obedience and service. *Revive it* may also be translated "let him live," a possible cry for restoration of the rightful king (see v. 13 *save your anointed*) or a cry for the redeemer to come and perform God's work of salvation and deliverance in Habakkuk's tragic age. This portion of the prayer concludes with a plea for mercy and sets the stage for the majestic theophany of vv. 3-15, a rehearsal of the LORD's many past deeds of mercy.

3:3-15. Hymn of praise for God's presence in history. This majestic hymn recounts the story of "salvation history" and the LORD's deliverance in ages past. The poetry is difficult and often reminiscent of similar ancient songs (cf. Deut 33; Judg 5). It is one of the greatest poems in a long line of passages that form a nearly creedal recitation of the LORD's love, mercy, and deliverance (cf. Deut 6:20-25;

26:1-11; Josh 24:2-13; Judg 6:8-10; 1 Sam 12: 6-12; Pss 68:7-14; 74:12-17; 78:12-72; 104; 105; 106; 114; 136; Isa 43:15-18; 48:20-22; 51:9-11; Jer 2:6-8; 23:7-8; 32:17-24; etc.). Many of these passages end in personal testimony or strong affirmations of faith in God as Redeemer. Flowing through biblical narrative in many forms, these majestic songs burst into narrative portions, form small or large sections of psalms, punctuate the messages of prophets, and become the structure for dramatic passages (sermons, poems, and narrative) in the NT (Acts 7:2-50; 13:17-25; Eph 1:3-14; Heb 11) where Jesus is presented as the ultimate anointed one to bring the promised deliverance.

God challenged Habakkuk to live by faith (2:4). The prophet's recitation of the mighty acts of the LORD in this poem reminds him of God's faithfulness to his people and bolsters that faith for the coming Babylonian crisis. Habakkuk ransacks history, filling his poem with fleeting references to numerous historical events in Israel's journey to the promised land. The poem becomes metaphorical of the prophet's personal pilgrimage from perplexing and handicapping fear to power and victorious faith in the LORD of history.

Some scholars suggest two poems (vv. 3-7/8 and 7/8-15). The first describes the LORD's triumphal march in front of his people as he leads them out of the wilderness into the promised land. The second poem extols the deliverance from Egypt. The possible reference to creation and the jumping from one moment in history to another suggest that the prophet, overwhelmed at the LORD's majesty, is recalling many of the lessons from the past at once. The poem is singular, a unit of vast diversity.

The THEOPHANY begins in *Teman* and *Paran* (v. 3), the southern trans-Jordanian regions through which Israel passed on their trek to Canaan (cf. Deut 33:1-2; Judg 5:4). God is described in great splendor with rays of his glory emanating from him like those of the sun. His march shakes the earth and scatters the mountains (cf. Ps 114; Nah 1:2-8). The mention of *Cushan* and *Midian* (v. 7) may refer to portions of the Exodus experience or events in the days of Gideon (Judg 6–8).

The moon stood still (v. 11) probably refers to Joshua's battle at the valley of Aijalon, where another ancient poem records that "the sun stood still, and the moon stopped" (Josh 10:12-14). Verse 8 focuses on the crossing of the sea (Exod 14) and the Jordan River (Josh 3–4).

Interpretation suggestions for the *anointed* in v. 13 range from Moses, David, a later Davidic king, and the Messiah, to the nation Israel. Certainly an individual is in view. A Davidic king or the Messiah seems most appropriate. The emphasis throughout this hymn is on deliverance.

3:16-19a. Commitment and vow of trust. Exhausted from wrestling with God and overcome by the vision of God's mighty acts of salvation in history, Habakkuk's weak knees and quivering lips now give way to a calm assurance that sweeps over his limp body (v. 16). The person of faith can stand in the day of trouble. Let the Babylonians come! Let them destroy houses, fields, and flocks. The righteous person will find strength in the LORD, not the artificial props of any materialistic society (v. 17-19a). The theophanic vision has brought a long view of history to the prophet. He can now look beyond immediate calamity to see the ultimate victory of the sovereign LORD of history. The difficult questions and nearly blasphemous accusations of 1:2-4 have melted into the peaceful assurance of the person of faith. Habakkuk's own experience (*my salvation* v. 18) stands as a powerful testimony to the truth of the central oracle of 2:4.

Postscription, 3:19b

Liturgical instructions bring the prophecy to a conclusion. Some argue that the traditional titles found in the Book of Psalms may not be headings for the psalms that follow but colophons for the psalms that precede such references. This passage supports such suggestions. The reference to *my stringed instruments* may suggest the prophet's formal connection to the Temple.

Zephaniah

John Joseph Owens

Introduction

The Book of Zephaniah is the ninth segment of the book known as "The Twelve" (Prophets). It forms a link between Habakkuk (a liturgy attacking the religious syncretism of the times) and Haggai (a champion of the reform of the worship of the LORD). Modern interpreters have so isolated the individual units of "The Twelve" that they have deprived students of signs of the unity of this great book of prophecy.

The three final sections of "The Twelve," for example, begin in the same way: "An Oracle (of) the word of the LORD" (Zech 9:1; 12:1; Mal 1:1). This phrase suggests that what follows, or perhaps what precedes, marks a distinct literary unity. Readers should be alert to the signs erected for them by the original writer and editors.

Author, Date, and Setting

ZEPHANIAH (650–625 B.C.E.) was a contemporary of HABAKKUK. The name "Zephaniah" means "Yahweh has treasured (hidden)." The three letters of the name, Z, P, and N, are also the three consonants in the Hebrew word "north." This may be coincidental or it may be a clever punning device of the author: giving the prophet a name that underscores the influence of the Northern Kingdom (ISRAEL) over JUDAH in that day.

The Assyrians from the north has exerted superiority over Palestine for a long period. They had captured SAMARIA (North Israel) in 722 B.C.E. They laid siege to Jerusalem (Judah) ca. 701 B.C.E. and captured forty-six of the fortified cities of Judah. Kings MANASSEH (687–642 B.C.E.) and AMON (642–640 B.C.E.) of Judah were practically vassals of the Assyrian superpower.

The opening verse of the book gives an unusual four-generation heritage, instead of a one- or two-generation heritage. The fourth generation name is HEZEKIAH. It is not possible to be certain of the identity of this Hezekiah, but the name strongly suggests that Zephaniah was of royal heritage. King Hezekiah of Judah (727–698 B.C.E.) ruled in the time of Isaiah. Isaiah was an influential prophet during Hezekiah's rule. Zephaniah reasserted the teaching of Isaiah after more than seventy years of extreme Assyrian influence upon Judah. Just as AMOS, HOSEA, ISAIAH, and

MICAH had been raised up during the time of the dissolution of the Kingdom of Israel, so God raised up NAHUM, Habakkuk, JEREMIAH, and Zephaniah in the final century of the state of Judah.

The ministry of Zephaniah is set *during the reign of Josiah* (639–608 B.C.E.). Zephaniah 1:2-6 describe an impending destruction, probably to be associated with the Scythian invasion of Palestine, ca. 627 B.C.E. Other interpreters refer this devastation to the coming breakup of the Assyrian empire, ca. 612 B.C.E.

The prophet's style is direct, forceful, and vigorous. His figures of speech are concrete and clear. The literary style is the *qinah* meter, a mournful, melancholy, or plaintive poem, often used as a funeral song or a lament for the dead. The *qinah* meter is a five-beat line of POETRY, generally divided as 3 + 2 or 2 + 3 accented syllables. The opening message of the book well fits this literary style. Like the opening oracle of the Book of Isaiah, the Book of Zephaniah opens with the assertion that Israel is so sinful that complete annihilation is well deserved.

For Further Study

In the *Mercer Dictionary of the Bible:* CHRONOLOGY; ORACLE; POETRY; PROPHET; ZEPHANIAH; ZEPHANIAH, BOOK OF; VISION.

In other sources: T. P. Wahl, "Zephaniah," *The New Jerome Biblical Commentary,* 255–58; "Zephaniah, Book of," *Nelson's Illustrated Bible Dictionary,* 1121–22.

Commentary

An Outline

I. Superscription, 1:1
II. God's Cosmic Judgment, 1:2-6
III. The Day of the LORD, 1:7–3:13
    A. Against Judah, 1:7-13
    B. Against the Whole Earth, 1:14-18

C. God's Offer of Hope, 2:1-15
D. Against Jerusalem, 3:1-7
E. Hope for All Nations, 3:8
F. Hope and the Day of the LORD, 3:9-13
IV. God's Restoration of Zion, 3:14-20

Superscription, 1:1

As noted above, the four-generation genealogy given for Zephaniah, tracing his lineage back to Hezekiah, may be intended to place the prophet within the royal house of Judah, descendants of King DAVID. As in the case of Isaiah, Zephaniah's royal family connections do not prevent him from speaking out against Judah's leaders and against the corrupt capital city.

God's Cosmic Judgment, 1:2-6

In 722 B.C.E. the Assyrian army came from the north and destroyed the Northern Kingdom (Isa 10:5-6). The Southern Kingdom became very self-righteous. Their interpretation of the world scene was that their neighbors deserved God's condemnation. In contrast, since they had the temple, they were God's *only* people;

they were secure. Instead of being warned by the prophet, they were guilty of perpetual backsliding (Jer 8:5). The prophet had a difficult task of changing a people, a nation, its leaders, and its individual members.

Yahweh *will sweep away everything* (v. 2). This would also include the self-righteous remnant of God's people. The people of Judah deserved condemnation because they had so enraged the LORD as to cause the threat of world-wide destruction. Judah's misinterpretation of God's action is part of the reason for the universal threat.

Judah and the world are interrelated, *I will sweep away everything* (v. 2). This includes beast, birds, and sea animals (v. 3) as well as humanity throughout the world. Pursuant to the abolition of Israel in 722 B.C.E. by the Assyrian horde, Judah had mental fantasies about their exaltation, importance, and uniqueness within God's plans. Yahweh's oracle moves from the cosmic vista to the self-exalted citizens of Judah. The reason for such universal destruction is outlined in vv. 4-6. Isaiah had expressed his disgust at those who claimed to be God's exclusive people: "They have forsaken the Lord, they have spurned the Holy One of Israel" (Isa 1:4). He condemns their syncretism: *all who dress themselves in foreign attire* (v. 8). Even though Yahweh was their Lord, Zephaniah points out that there were idolatrous priests who followed BAAL (a Canaanite deity), those who prostrate themselves to the hosts of heaven (an Assyrian god), and those who swear by Milcom (god of the Ammonites).

The Day of the LORD, 1:7–3:13

The central idea in the Book of Zephaniah is the "Day of Yahweh."

Against Judah, 1:7-13

The day of Yahweh was for them a day of exclusive exaltation, rather than a day of mourning and repentance for their sins.

1:7-9. They copy Assyria. The LORD dashes their hopes by accusing them of seeking to appease the foreigners and the foreign gods. The officials and the king's family appeared in Assyrian habits.

Also Judah was guilty of leaping *over the thresholds* (v. 9). This is a rare expression. It could be a reference to their making unusual entry for the purpose of robbing the poor. It may have reference to the manner in which the priests entered the place of worship to avoid contamination by proximity to the various gods. The prophet points out the violence and unjust dealings of the officials and royal family.

1:10-11. No business dealings. *The Fish Gate, . . . the Second Quarter, . . . the hills*, and *the Mortar* will be different by virtue of the loud moans. This moaning was brought on by the elimination of the traders and merchants.

1:12-13. Power confused. It is strangely common that mortals who attain a position of authority or power assume that they bring power to the position. In reality the position offers, even to the second-rate person, any authority available. Persons of inferior ability have a tendency to be complacent.

Zephaniah agrees with Mal 2:17 in portraying the human community as suggesting that God does not act in human affairs. All of Judah shall be shown that God is a definite part of their lives, whether they cooperate with him or not. No element can be hidden from God's light.

Against the Whole Earth, 1:14-19

Even though Judah's view of the Day of Yahweh was of a day of exaltation, Zephaniah enlarges the people's vision.

1:14-16. The great day is imminent and coming quickly. It is close enough to be seen and heard. This brings bitterness and anguish, not praise and compliment.

1:17-18. The great day is upon all the earth. The cause of all this terror is that persons *have sinned against the* LORD. The writer includes *the whole earth*.

Even when the Day of Yahweh is portrayed as terror, there is hope. For God is a redeeming God. This does not invalidate, but rather confirms, God as one who is interested in and involved with the entire created order.

God's Offer of Hope, 2:1-15

2:1-4. The imperative for Judah. Just as the prophet had pled with Judah to *be silent* (1:7), he urges this *shameless nation* to *seek the Lord . . . righteousness . . .* [and] *humility*. These are commands. The people's only hope was to eradicate their shame and become the *humble of the land*. Then perhaps they could escape the fury of the judgment. Even the long-time settlers of their land (the prophet mentions four of the five main Philistine strongholds) will be decimated.

2:5-15. Woe to the nations. The extent of God's wrath is shown in 2:5-3:8.

2:5-11. The nations with whom they were involved are singled out by name and description. If they seek the LORD, Judah could still win victory over the PHILIS-TINES, ASHKELON, MOAB, and AMMON. The promise to which Judah clung so tenaciously, *restore their fortunes* (v. 7), is extended to these nations. Just as the threat is for the whole world, so also is the promise.

2:12-15. The remote nations. God's hands reach to the far south, Cush or ETHIOPIA. But he will extend his power to the north (*zaphon*) and destroy ASSYRIA. This was spoken before 612 B.C.E., when Nineveh was destroyed. Nineveh had ruled from 747–612 B.C.E., exalting notions of its worldwide authority and power. Prosperity would be turned into derision.

Against Jerusalem, 3:1-7

Verses 1-2 identify the aim of the message. Woe to the *soiled, defiled, oppressing city* refers to Jerusalem. The officials, judges, prophets, and priests are the ones who were doing the opposite of what their trust dictated. They had assumed that they were the source of their nations's pride. But they were the cause of the nations's downfall.

Nations had been brought low (v. 6) in the hope that Judah would take warning.

Hope for All Nations, 3:8

Once more hope is explained: *wait for me*. God will gather all nations and judge them. The reality of sin dictates that *all the earth will be consumed* unless the imperatives are followed, that is, *be silent* (1:7), and *gather together* (2:1).

Hope and the Day of the LORD, 3:9-13

Then and *on that day* are the imperative connectors. Based on the power and presence of God, hope can be reality. All the world will be given a purified way of expression to the end that all of them may worship the LORD. This does not downgrade Judah. There will always be a remnant who are characterized by humility (v. 12). These are they who seek refuge in God.

God's Restoration of Zion, 3:14-20

The changed congregation shall seek refuge in God's name. The remnant of Israel are the ones referred to as *daughter Zion*. They will have the stigma removed. *On that day* reminds us that the evil has been removed, the thoughts are purified, condemnation is no longer. God is very active within their world. Within the day of the LORD, there is purification. The prophet's point is that those who are silent (submissive) to the LORD, who wait for him, who rejoice in him will be preserved. These will have the presence of the warrior Yahweh, the grounds for their joy and singing. In the day of the LORD, God will punish the guilty, change the negative to positive, unify all humankind (instead of isolating or dividing).

The prophet concludes his prophecy with the sixth century promise to *restore their fortunes* (v. 20). This is the promise for many nations, including Judah (and Israel). This promise is found repeatedly in Jeremiah, one of Zephaniah's contemporaries: 29:14, 30:3, 31:23. 32:44, 33:7, 26. These passages and Ezek 39:25 involve Judah (including Israel). Jeremiah 46:26 and Ezek 29:14 give a promise to EGYPT. Ezekiel 16:53 even makes a promise to SODOM and SAMARIA. Jeremiah 48:47 includes Moab, Jer 49:6 includes Ammon, and Jer 49:39 includes Elam with the same Hebrew terms as used in the promises to Judah (including Israel). This term appears in only eight other places (three in the Prophets and once each in Deuteronomy, Psalms, Job, and Lamentations). Whereas Judah had misinterpreted the promises to apply all the good things to itself and all the bad things to its enemies, the Day of the Lord will be to punish sin in all nations (including Judah), to bring out the humility and lowliness of all nations to turn these repentant ones to God, to give grounds for joy and exultation, and to reward with restoration and glory all those who think his way and call on his name.

Haggai [MCB 789-92]

Jon L. Berquist

Introduction

This lesser known PROPHET delivered a message in a time of crisis, during August through December of 520 B.C.E., while Jerusalem, which was now a small colony within the vast PERSIAN EMPIRE, was experiencing great turmoil and uncertainty. HAGGAI was politically astute, and his utterances conveyed a theological interpretation of contemporary events in Jerusalem.

Prophecy under the Persian Empire

The Persian Empire had allowed the return of exiled populations, including the Jews, as early as 539 B.C.E., but most of the Jews chose not to return. Instead, they stayed in Babylonia, the homeland of their parents and grandparents. The return from EXILE was a slow process of immigration over decades. Near Jerusalem, a Jewish culture had maintained itself after the devastation of the land in 587 B.C.E., and these natives resented and resisted the influx of immigrants from Babylonia (see Neh 5:1-13).

The Persian Empire showed little concern with its western border, including Jerusalem, until Persia's third emperor, DARIUS, took the throne in early 521 B.C.E. Darius intended to capture Egypt. At the time of Haggai's prophecies, Darius's army was approaching Jerusalem on its way to conquer Egypt. This army lived off the land through which it passed, presenting an economic drain on the surrounding territories. In preparation, the Persian Empire built administrative facilities at state expense along the path. Jerusalem was one of the sites slated for an administrative complex, which became Jerusalem's Second Temple. Built during 520–515 B.C.E., this temple served the political administrative needs of the Persian Empire and its local colonial government (cf. Neh 13:6-9), as well as the religious needs of the Jerusalemites. Haggai's prophecies encouraged the construction of this temple and persuaded the people not to fear the approaching army.

The Setting of the Book of Haggai

Haggai's prophecies reflect the early phases of temple construction, in which he argued against various reasons for delay in building. This collection of oracles might have originally reminded the people of the necessity of temple construction. Once these oracles were placed within an editorial framework of precise dates, the character of the book changed. The book in its current form may have functioned as a historical reminiscence of the support of prophet, priest, governor, and people for the temple construction. Perhaps such a compilation would have been part of the liturgy at the dedication of the new temple in 515 B.C.E., although such a notion must remain speculative.

For Further Study

In the *Mercer Dictionary of the Bible*: DARIUS; EXILE; HAGGAI; HAGGAI, BOOK OF; ORACLE; PERSIAN EMPIRE; PROPHET; ZERUBBABEL.

In other sources: R. J. Coggins, *Haggai, Zechariah, Malachi*; P. D. Hanson, *Dawn of Apocalyptic*; C. L. Meyers and E. M. Meyers, *Haggai, Zechariah 1–8*, AncB; D. L. Petersen, *Haggai and Zechariah 1–8*, OTL; D. L. Smith, *Religion of the Landless*; H. W. Wolff, *Haggai*; E. M. Yamauchi, *Persia and the Bible*.

Commentary

An Outline

I. The Call to Build the Second Temple, 1:1-15	II. Promises for the Second Temple, 2:1-23
A. Introduction, 1:1	A. Wealth and Glory, 2:1-9
B. Current Failings, 1:2-6	B. The Communicability of Holiness, 2:10-14
C. Protection against Disaster, 1:7-11	C. Blessing instead of Lack, 2:15-19
D. God's Presence with the Builders, 1:12-15	D. Zerubbabel's Protection, 2:20-23

The Call to Build the Second Temple, 1:1-15

Introduction, 1:1

The introduction refers to the second year of the reign of DARIUS, the third ruler of the PERSIAN EMPIRE. This date formula also indicates the book's orientation. These prophecies connect the life of the religious community around Jerusalem to the larger world, especially the world of Persian imperial politics. In addition to Haggai and the emperor, Darius, two others play significant roles in these prophecies: Joshua the high priest (see Zech 3:1-10 and EZRA 3:1-13) and ZERUB-BABEL the governor (see Zech 4:1-14 and Ezra 4:1-5). Thus Haggai's concerns are at the intersection of religion and politics within Jerusalem.

Current Failings, 1:2-6

Haggai's first prophetic statement moves directly to the root of the people's problem, and only then describes its economic symptoms. Haggai offers a theological perspective on the people's experiences. Because the people have failed to build a temple for God, they suffer deprivation.

1:2-4. Time to build. The people of Jerusalem have refrained from constructing a temple, claiming that the time was not yet right. Haggai disagrees; God charges the people with living too well. This provides the first clue into the audience's economic condition. These Jerusalemites have not been suffering economically in the past.

1:5-6. Economic disaster. Through Haggai, God directs these people to "set their hearts upon their paths" (the import of *concern . . . in* v. 5; see also 1:7; 2:15, 18 [twice])—that is, to decide future activity based on consideration of current events. Haggai argues for a decision in favor of temple construction because of the current economy. The frustrating futility of agriculture in v. 6 refers to the inability to keep what the people produce. Taxation seems to be the material problem, possibly reflecting an imperial tax upon the populace of Jerusalem to feed the Persian army as it marched to Egypt. Haggai understands temple construction as the proper response to this economic crisis. If the Persian army was the chief temporal concern, then adherence to a Persian policy of temple construction would allow for future prosperity. Haggai interprets the source of the difficulties as God, who also will solve the problems once the people build a proper temple.

Protection against Disaster, 1:7-11

Once again, God calls the people to decisive action. They should immediately begin the work of temple construction. The prophet repeats that construction is the solution to economic deprivation (v. 9). Here the text states clearly that the reason for the current lack is God's displeasure at the lack of a temple.

God's Presence with the Builders, 1:12-15

Haggai is one of the few prophets in the Hebrew Bible who meets immediate success and receives credit in the scriptural records.

1:12. Statement of success. *Zerubbabel* the governor and *Joshua . . . the high priest*, plus all the people of Jerusalem, obeyed God and Haggai and started construction, after appropriate worship.

1:13-15. Statement of God's presence. Construction began twenty-three days after Haggai's first message. The temple project is much more than human politics; it is the working of God's spirit (cf. Zech 4:6).

Promises for the Second Temple, 2:1-23

Wealth and Glory, 2:1-9

Haggai's prophetic activity resumed about a month after the beginning of temple construction (v. 1). The project was underway, but the prophet knew that there would be opportunities to delay, and so he offered words of persistent encouragement.

2:1-3. The diminished Temple. This message comes to all the people, but the leaders Zerubbabel and Joshua receive special mention. The new construction hardly compares with the grandeur of the old temple, which had been built with Solomon's wealth and which had expanded with three and a half centuries of use. However, the size and the stature of the new temple are not the point; its *existence* is the essential issue.

2:4-5. Be strong. The two leaders receive personalized messages: *Take courage.* The strength leads to a second command: *work*! God repeats the assurance of the spirit's presence (cf. 1:13-14). Since the EXODUS from Egypt, God has agreed to bring the people into Jerusalem and center them around a temple. This is not an innovation, forced upon the Jerusalemites from outside by their imperial masters; the construction of the temple has been part of God's plan since forming the people into a nation. Thus, there should be no fear.

2:6-7. Shaking the earth. God will soon shake all creation. The term *shake* refers to an earthquake, but is probably not literal; the term can connote other natural or human-made calamities. The noisy marching of the huge Persian army could well suggest an earthquake. This approaching threat would provide ample cause for alarm and fear. The prophet encouraged the people to remain steadfast in their project. The coming forces will only work for the benefit of the new temple and thus also for the people who participate in its construction. Through Persia's approach, God will fill the temple with glory.

2:8-9. Glory and peace. God owns *the silver* and *the gold*, and presumably God will choose to place the silver and gold of other nations in the temple itself. In this way, the glory of the second Temple will be greater than that of the first Temple. Glory and wealth go hand in hand. God then offers a further promise: the new temple will encompass peace. Peace also exists within this military and economic framework. The army comes not as aggressor, but as a harmless, stabilizing force. *Peace* refers to more than the avoidance of war, though that is certainly at issue here; *peace* indicates a time of security and *prosperity* for all persons, and the passing of the Persian army will bring this condition to all the people of Jerusalem.

The Communicability of Holiness, 2:10-14

The construction of the temple at Persian behest and the presence of these foreigners in large numbers created several religious problems. At stake was the purity of the temple. Only a ritual cleanliness gave the temple the ability to atone for the people. Would the Persian involvement render the temple unclean, and thus useless for Jerusalem's faithful? Would the Persians be able to use this temple for their own benefit, to win God's favor for themselves?

2:10-11. Introduction. This ORACLE occurred exactly three months after the beginning of construction (1:15). Like the previous unit (2:1-9), it came at a time when temple construction was in jeopardy. Haggai offered divine words to encourage that the construction proceed without interruption. In this case, Haggai conducted the prophecy in a question-and-answer format with the priests, who strongly encouraged the construction of a temple.

2:12. The first question. If a priest carries something holy, and then touches something that is not holy, does the holiness transfer from the holy object to the other? The answer is *No*. Holiness does not spread. If the priests offer unclean sacrifices or touch the offerings of pagans, such as the Persians, there can be no benefit gained for these foreigners. The holiness of the temple itself does not make everything offered therein holy; one must still offer right sacrifices. There is no indication that the holy object, or the priest or the temple itself, becomes unclean through this contact. Instead, neither holiness nor uncleanness is communicable. Impurity cannot endanger the holy, and the impure receive no benefit from their contact with the holy. The Jews are safe from the Persians, and the Persians shall receive no benefit.

2:13-14. The second question. The next question concerns persons who have become impure through the touching of a corpse. This may well refer to the Persian soldiers. Because these persons are unclean, their offerings are unclean. Once more, there is no indication that the other holy objects, the priests, or the temple itself become unclean through this contact. Haggai and the priests formulated a theology of holiness that protected the Jews against the Persians while still maintaining the possibility of operating a pure temple in the midst of a foreign occupation. Haggai then provided a summary: everything that this nation touches is defiled. This is not a condemnation of Jewish worship; Haggai uses the term *nation* in reference to Persia or other world powers. Haggai's interest in the religious effects of occupation is consistent with the themes found throughout the book.

Blessing instead of Lack, 2:15-19

Haggai's next-to-last oracle returns to the need for decisive action in building the temple in order to solve the economic problems. Obedience to God, as expressed in the construction of the temple desired by the Persian Empire, will bring an end to the suffering of the people.

2:15-17. Severe lack. Before the temple construction began, there was economic hardship. Again, the difficulty was the overtaxation of Jerusalem to finance the passing Persian army. Anyone who wished to draw from the stores of food and wine could take only a fraction of what was there; the rest was reserved for the soldiers. Haggai interprets this as God's reaction against the people for their refusal to build previously.

2:18-19. Blessing. This climax to the oracle repeats the earlier date, three months after the beginning of construction (2:10). The time to build is *now*, on this very day. Haggai encouraged construction by showing the people that they possess the resources for their future. There was still grain in the storage silos, and some of the trees were still yielding. Haggai assures the people that these goods will remain, and that now—since construction has begun—God will bless them. The signs of blessing were not manna from heaven, but the tools with which to build in partnership with God. God's blessing to the people would come as a response to their faithfulness.

Zerubbabel's Protection, 2:20-23

Haggai's last oracle turns from the religious and economic issues of the previous unit to military concerns. The approaching Persian army brings fear into the hearts of Jerusalemites. Thus, the prophet assures them of safety, if they follow the dictates of their governor, Zerubbabel.

2:20-22. Turning aside chariots. This final oracle occurs on the same day as the previous ones (2:10-19). The shift is both a switch of audience from the people as a whole to their leader, *Zerubbabel*, and a movement of topic from internal to external political realities. God's message is that the heavens and earth soon will shake, repeating a message of hope and expectation (2:6-7). Here, the oracle continues and gains specificity:

> I am causing the heavens and the earth to quake.
>   I will turn aside the throne of the kingdoms,
>   and I will exterminate the strength
>   of the kingdoms of the nations.
>   I will turn aside the chariotry and its riders,
>   and the horses and their riders will go down,
>   each by the sword of the other.   (vv. 21b-22, author trans.)

When the earth shakes from the army's near passage, God promises that the Persian forces will not attack Jerusalem, but will turn away from that city and go down to Egypt. This was the intention of the Persian Empire, and it presumably had been announced, at least to the Persian governor, Zerubbabel. The army's intended target was Egypt, not Jerusalem, even though the last army of that size so close to Jerusalem had brought it destruction and exile in 587 B.C.E. Haggai expects that these two huge armies, from Persia and Egypt, would clash mightily and destroy each other in Egypt, leaving Jerusalem to enjoy an era of peace without any external pressure. Such was not the case; Egypt surrendered to Persia immediately and crowned the Persian Emperor Darius as the Egyptian Pharaoh. Haggai's prophecy remains, however, because its promise of safety to Jerusalem was fulfilled.

2:23. God's choice of Zerubbabel. God declares a special choice of *Zerubbabel*, who becomes the privileged leader on the day that the Persian army passes around Jerusalem. Zerubbabel becomes *like* God's *signet ring*, an indication that God will use Zerubbabel for God's own tasks. The previous use of the "signet ring" image was negative, when Judah's king, JEHOIACHIN, was compared to a signet ring cast off from God's finger (Jer 22:24). Now, Zerubbabel was God's chosen one to fulfill the role left vacant by the true kings. Zerubbabel protects Jerusalem from Persian harm, and God protects Zerubbabel as a chosen leader.

Zechariah [MCB 793-98]

Jon L. Berquist

Introduction

Zechariah's prophecies are remarkable in their variety. ZECHARIAH walks through visions accompanied by an ANGEL who interprets the viewed symbolism. The PROPHET utters oracles of a restored and peaceful community. The harsh visions near the end of the book are close to the APOCALYPTIC LITERATURE found among noncanonical works.

Authorship

The variety of the book is so striking that most scholars perceive multiple authors. Chapters 1–8 are the work of a prophet of the late sixth century, whose name is given as *Zechariah son of Berechiah* (1:1, 7). Despite the differences in form between the visions and the oracles in these eight chapters, the thematic connections among this material are very strong, and there is no reason to assume alternative authorship for parts of these chapters. However, the material changes sharply with chaps. 9–14, which seem to be a group of oracles from one or more visionaries in a time much later than Zechariah.

Historical Setting of Zechariah ben-Berechiah

The Book of Zechariah dates Zechariah son of Berechiah's prophecies to 520–518 B.C.E., mostly after the prophecies of his contemporary, HAGGAI. Certainly, there are strong connections in the historical situation between these two prophets. Both were concerned with the construction of the Temple, which the PERSIAN EMPIRE had funded and which, according to the two prophets, God supported. Both prophets were very sensitive to the religious issues of constructing a new society that included the natives in the Jerusalem area and the immigrants from Babylonia whose families were returning after seven decades of EXILE. Both assured the people that the approaching army under the command of DARIUS, emperor of Persia, did not intend to destroy JERUSALEM, but to pass nearby on its way to conquer EGYPT.

Despite these thematic similarities between Haggai and Zechariah, Zech 1–8 forms a very different expression of these concerns than Haggai 1–2. Zechariah experienced God through visions and reported what he saw, along with some interpretive comments provided by an accompanying angel. These visions occurred while the Persian Empire's army was marching through the surrounding territory. In chaps. 1 and 6, Zechariah assured the community that the army offered no threat, because God controlled international events. Zechariah 1 and 7 frame the book's concern that safety requires obedience to the prophetic word and to Jerusalem's leadership. Zechariah 8 offers an idyllic portrait of life in the wake of Persia's army.

Historical Setting of the Later Additions

The later additions (chaps. 9–14) are very difficult to date. Although there are connections among the various oracles, there is little evidence that these oracles derive from the same person or even from the same period. The material probably dates from the fifth and/or fourth centuries B.C.E., composed by persons familiar with the themes and perspectives of Zech 1–8. There may be a separation between chaps. 9–11 and chaps. 12–14. Certainly, the outlook becomes increasingly negative closer to the end of the book.

The writers of these later additions experienced life in a fundamentally different way than Zechariah did. Whereas the prophet lived in a time of hope even in the face of danger, these later writers doubted their own present and future. They were very much concerned with the problems among the leadership, including governmental corruption. Zechariah lived in a time of international peace (as long as the people maintained loyalty to Persia), but the later writers felt profound insecurity. They envisioned the need for God's violent intervention to save them from destruction. This may reflect a time in the later Persian Empire, when the empire's attention turned away from the Palestine area, allowing social fragmentation. Under the mounting pressures of these times, these writers added their own fears and their yearnings for power and revenge.

For Further Study

In the *Mercer Dictionary of the Bible*: APOCALYPTIC LITERATURE; EXILE; PERSIAN EMPIRE; PROPHET; ORACLE; VISION; ZECHARIAH; ZECHARIAH, BOOK OF.

In other sources: R. J. Coggins, *Haggai, Zechariah, Malachi*; C. L. Meyers and E. M. Meyers, *Haggai, Zechariah 1–8*, AncB; D. L. Petersen, *Haggai and Zechariah 1–8*, OTL; D. L. Petersen, "Zechariah," HBC 747–52; E. M. Yamauchi, *Persia and the Bible*.

Commentary

An Outline

Visions and Oracles of Zechariah, 1:1–8:23

Introduction, 1:1-6

The thematic introduction to the prophecies of Zechariah begins with a date formula placing the prophecy in October or November 520 B.C.E., toward the end of Darius's second year as Persian emperor. Zechariah begins his prophecy just before Haggai's last recorded ORACLE. According to Ezra 5:1 and 6:14, HAGGAI and ZECHARIAH worked together.

The introduction provides a summary statement with DEUTERONOMISTIC overtones, interpreting the EXILE as a result of the people's violation of God's law. Zechariah states that the people repented (v. 6), recognizing that they had deserved God's punishment.

Horses and Horns, 1:7-21 [MT 1:7–2:4]

Many of Zechariah's prophecies appear in the form of VISION reports. Often, an angel accompanies Zechariah to explain the symbolic visions. Zechariah 1:7 dates the first visions to the middle of February, 519 B.C.E., during the Jerusalem Temple construction.

1:7-17. First vision of the horses. Zechariah sees four horses who report to God that they have investigated all the world. At this time, the Persian army was marching toward Jerusalem, but the prophet proclaims that there is no cause for alarm here; all is at peace.

God intends to return to Jerusalem, after an absence of seventy years during the exile. God's absence from Jerusalem reflects the notion that God required a temple; thus, the Temple construction project is at the forefront of Zechariah's prophecy. When the construction is finished and God once more inhabits Jerusalem, then there will be prosperity.

1:18-21. Vision of the four horns. Zechariah sees horns, which symbolize the nations and armies (principally, Babylonia) that destroyed Jerusalem in 587 B.C.E. The ANGEL explains that craftspersons have arrived to scare off the horns and to prevent destruction. These craftspersons build the Temple; their presence shows the loyalty to God's desire and to the Persian Empire that will keep Jerusalem safe.

Jerusalem, 2:1-13 [MT 2:5-17]

This section of Zechariah focuses on Jerusalem's future. God's chosen city will once more be the center of life, especially the life of faith. The city will remain undefended, except by God's own power in Jerusalem's center. The exiled Jews will all return.

2:1-5. A city without walls. Zechariah watches the measuring of the city under construction. The angel declares that the new city will have no walls. The angel claims that the population will be too large to be contained; this indefensibility accords with Persian policy that colonies not fortify themselves. God promises to be *a wall of fire* around the city, offering it all needed protection without constructing physical barriers. Again, Persian policy and divine command coalesce.

2:6-13. Call to come to Jerusalem. Those Jews *from . . . the north*, that is, from Babylonia, are invited to immigrate to Jerusalem. When they arrive at the Temple's completion, God will live in the people's midst, and Jerusalem will be protected and blessed.

Joshua and Zerubbabel, 3:1–4:14

In the next two chapters Zechariah turns attention to leadership in Jerusalem. Both *the high priest* (3:1) and the governor deal directly with the Temple, and the holders of each office were Persian-born Jews. Both would have been charged with enforcing Persian policy in Jerusalem. Zechariah supports a sharing of powers between these two officials, although he deals with each in distinct ways. Many scholars have envisioned a dyarchy that collapses into a rule by the high priest after the removal of Zerubbabel, but there is insufficient evidence for such a view.

3:1-10. Joshua, the high priest. Zechariah observes Joshua, the high priest, standing in the presence of God and Satan. Satan opposes Joshua, but God supports the priest, forgives his sins, and provides him with new, expensive garments. An angel repeats God's promise to give Joshua control of the Temple, since God intends to bring a day of purity and prosperity to the land through Joshua (v. 9). This vision provides unflagging support to Joshua, equating submission to this Persian-appointed priest's authority with God's plan and identifying any political opposition to Joshua with the work of the Accuser, Satan.

4:1-14. The Temple and Zerubbabel. In this vision, Zechariah examines the Temple furnishings that symbolize God's protection of Jerusalem's inhabitants. In large part, this protection comes through the governor, Zerubbabel, whose work is described in an oddly inserted section (vv. 6-10a). Zerubbabel began the Temple construction, and God firmly supports his completion of the project (v. 9). In this vision's hyperbole, Zerubbabel levels mountains and brings the people to rejoicing. The Temple construction proceeds *not by might nor by power, but by [God's] spirit* (v. 6). The military might of Persia and its economic power are not the real reasons for the Temple; they are only God's agents. This section concludes with the statement that there are two—presumably Joshua (chap. 3) and Zerubbabel (chap. 4)—who serve God in a special way.

Destroying Wickedness, 5:1-11

The power of the completed Temple to destroy evil is an important theme for Zechariah. The prophet senses the disasters that had befallen the people through the exile and recognizes the extent of impurity that must be eradicated. Thus, Zechariah envisions the removal of iniquity itself from Jerusalem.

5:1-4. The flying scroll. Zechariah sees a scroll flying throughout the land, searching out thieves and liars. Wherever the scroll finds such a sinner, it enters the house and destroys it with fire. Perhaps this indicates an attempt to purge those who were withholding from the Temple project.

5:5-11. Wickedness in a basket. Zechariah now gazes upon a large basket, which contains the iniquity of Jerusalem. This wickedness is sent through the air to Babylonia, where a house or temple will be built for it. This is a powerful image of deliverance, as God removes the source of sin from the people. It may critique pagan Babylonian religions, claiming that such practices are so contrary to the true worship of God that they would construct shrines to sin itself. There may also be more concrete political overtones, perhaps pointing toward a policy of deportation for those who opposed Temple construction and who thus were, in Zechariah's eyes, wicked.

Safety and Government, 6:1-15

Zechariah's political concerns reappear in both the international and the local arenas. The prophet sees horses once more that represent God's involvement in international affairs, and then God oversees the crowning of Joshua for his role in Temple construction.

6:1-8. Second vision of the horses. This vision is not identical to that of 1:7-17, but shares many of the same details and certainly the same concerns. These horses have matching chariots, and they examine the four corners of the earth on God's behalf. They report that there is safety to the north. Once more, Zechariah reaffirms that the Persian army presents no danger.

6:9-15. Joshua's crown. This passage oddly envisions the crowning and enthronement of a priest, rather than a king. This oddity, along with the text's mention of *two* crowns, has caused many scholars to wonder if an earlier version of this story included Zerubbabel, but the branch symbolism has already been connected to Joshua, and both of these leaders have legitimate roles in the Temple construction. There is no reason to read a rejection of Zerubbabel into this emphasis on Joshua. Both are God's agents in Temple construction; Zechariah refers to the harmony between temple and throne (6:13). A unified leadership structure that extends into Persia is envisioned and valued for its effectiveness in bringing prosperity and respect to the colony.

Fasting Laws and Visions of Community, 7:1–8:23

These final two chapters of Zechariah's prophecies are dated to December, 518 B.C.E. Temple construction continues, but there is international stability. The Persian army has passed by Jerusalem; God has ensured the city's safety as promised through the prophets. Zechariah's concerns now turn to thoughts of how the members of the community can live together in a lasting peace.

7:1-14. Fasting laws. Zechariah intervenes in a priestly discussion about the fasts of the fifth and seventh months. Zechariah attacks the people, charging that their fasting was never a truly religious act (vv. 4-7). Instead, God calls the people to social justice as the true religion. Because the people failed to listen to the earlier prophets' message, they suffered the EXILE. The fasts mourning that exile would be useless unless the people first addressed the problems behind it, through a new commitment to social justice. Zechariah answered the fasting question in 8:18-23.

8:1-17. Visions of community. In this section, the prophet reports seven sayings of God. God first acknowledges intensity of emotion for Zion (v. 2), and then states plans to return to Jerusalem, bringing truth and holiness (v. 3). The city will be a place of idyllic peace, where the eldest and the youngest share the streets together (vv. 4-5). In the central statement, God declares how amazing all of this seems—even to God (v. 6). The fifth saying promises the immigration of Jews from throughout the world to live in Jerusalem in right relationship with God (vv. 7-8). God then encourages the Temple construction and promises blessings of fertility upon completion (vv. 9-13; cf. Hag 2:1-5, 15-19). The final statement supplies a vital summary of Israel's traditional morality: speak truth, give true justice, do not plan evil, do not love lies. This simple and powerful moral code forms the basis for God's good community of faith (vv. 14-17).

8:18-23. Fasts of joy. Zechariah now answers the questions about fasting (7:1-14). All fasts should become times of celebration, not mourning. Then, people from throughout the world will flock to Jerusalem because of God's obvious presence. Because of the ideals of community presented in 8:1-17, the city has become an attractive place to the nations, who see God's goodness made manifest in the daily life of God's own people.

God's Protection for Judah, 9:1–11:17

At this point, the nature of the prophetic material changes. No longer are there visions and oracles from the peace of 520–518 B.C.E. Instead, these three chapters reflect a time of fear and promise that God will protect Jerusalem from severe threats.

God the Watchful Defender, 9:1-8

This first oracle promises God's protection through the divine destruction of Israel's neighbors. Now that God is keeping watch, there will be no destruction for Jerusalem.

Zion's Joyous Salvation, 9:9-17

This vision of striking beauty depicts God's joyful salvation of Jerusalem. Jerusalem receives its king, *riding on a donkey* (v. 9), and then God takes away all implements of war from Israel and extends a peaceful rule throughout the world. God will free Israel's prisoners and restore Israel's losses. But struggle is not over; Zion will attack Greece. This prophecy derives from a later time, when Greece had begun to overshadow Persia's influence in the region. Still, Israel maintained its loyalty to Persia and envisioned a struggle against the pagan Greeks. God will lead the battle, fighting on Israel's behalf, and will rescue the Israelites.

Anger against the Shepherds, 10:1-5

The prophet rails against poor leadership. It is the LORD, not any other god, who brings rain in its season; thus those who seek truth from idols and diviners mislead themselves. With these kinds of leaders, the people are like sheep without a shepherd. God promises to destroy those shepherds and leaders who have failed their task.

Strength for Judah, 10:6-12

God will provide strength for Judah. Survivors will return from throughout the world, and there will be overpopulation. Despite the crowding, everyone will have enough to eat, and the boundaries of the land will expand. Assyria and Egypt will give up their captives, and the evil nations will be destroyed.

Destruction for Lebanon, 11:1-3

Fire will destroy the strength of Lebanon and the northern stretches of the JORDAN. This oracle directs attention to the problematic shepherds, whom God also destroys.

Two Shepherds, 11:4-17

As a sign-act, the prophet shepherds the flock that has been marked for slaughter. This flock's shepherds have concerned themselves only with profit and wealth. When the prophet takes over the shepherding, using staffs called Grace and Union (*Favor* and *Unity* in NRSV), three of these evil shepherds are forced from office. The prophet tires of caring for the sheep and destroys the staffs, symbolizing God's rejection of the people despite God's own promises. The owners of the flock pay the prophet *thirty shekels of silver* (v. 12), which are then flung into the potter's field. This sign act, taken by the gospels as a symbol of Judas (Matt 27:3-10, which inaccurately cites Jeremiah), demonstrates the desire of the wealthy to pay off God for the abandonment of the oppressed. However, God raises up another worthless, evil shepherd to oppress the people; God then curses this shepherd. This confusing allegory tells of Israel's history, throughout which leaders oppressed the people, despite God's desires to heal them.

Apocalyptic Visions of Destruction, 12:1–14:21

In the final three chapters of the Book of Zechariah, the text becomes more apocalyptic. The severity of the visions and the deep despair of the people are undeniable. Salvation for Jerusalem will be achieved only at the fearsome price of destruction for the rest of the world.

Judah the Destroyer, 12:1-9

In this ORACLE, Jerusalem comes under siege by many strong nations, but God remains watchful over Judah. Because of their faith, God enables the leaders of Jerusalem to destroy the besieging nations. God's strengthening of the people will be so great that even the poorest will be as rich as DAVID, and David's house will be like God.

Weeping for God, 12:10-14

In that day of deliverance, the inhabitants of Jerusalem will realize their sin and will pray to God for forgiveness. All will recognize that they have injured God through their disobedience, and they will weep because of this sin. Their crying will be like that at JOSIAH's death at the battle of MEGIDDO, that horrific battle that became a symbol of utterly demoralizing defeat (2 Kgs 23:29-30; cf. Rev 16:16, where God reverses that defeat). The penitent weeping will be shared by representatives of Jerusalem's political, prophetic, and priestly groups.

Purification, 13:1-6

In response to the weeping, God prepares a fountain that will remove sin for all the inhabitants of Jerusalem. The purification will bring an end to two types of religious practices that this visionary abhors: idolatry and prophecy. All idols will cease from the land, and the remaining prophets will deny their prior work. This passage derives from a Jerusalem faction that disparaged the possibility of receiving true words from God through prophecy.

Destruction for the Sheep, 13:7-9

In a passage reminiscent of the remnant thought of earlier prophets (Isa 10:20-23; Ezek 5), this visionary declares that God will bring destruction among the people. Firstly, God will destroy the shepherd. Then, two-thirds of the people will perish. God will refine and purify the remaining third, so that in the end they will respond to God, and claim intimate connection between God and themselves.

The Future Day of Battle, 14:1-21

The book's concluding vision presents a cataclysmic vision of God's rescue. God brings the nations to destroy Jerusalem, and they succeed in exiling half the population. Then God appears to defend the chosen city. The *Mount of Olives* (v. 4) splits into a huge valley to allow escape; on that day, nature ceases its normal processes (vv. 6-8). Jerusalem remains eternally safe, but the surrounding countryside is devastated. The nations that had fought Jerusalem suffer from horrible plagues, along with their livestock. All the survivors of the nations are forced to join in the worship of God, who destroyed them, lest they face drought. Canaanites, Israel's ancient enemies, will suffer complete genocide.

This stark vision demonstrates the depths of despair that these Jerusalemites experience. The desire for revenge overwhelms them, and they celebrate a God who brings destruction. Even worship becomes sullied through its compulsory nature; God threatens other nations to join in false celebration. The older visions of the nations flocking to Jerusalem in joy and desire to know God (8:20-23) are reversed; the nations worship their destroyer out of fear. Surely this reflects a time in Jerusalem's life when their own sense of disaster had brought bitterness.

Malachi
Jon L. Berquist

Introduction

Malachi is the last book in the canon of the Protestant OT. Although Malachi is probably not the last written of the Prophets, it reflects one of the last recorded impulses of Israelite prophecy, centuries after the better-known prophets. Malachi deals with the vital question of cooperation between priests and laity as together they serve God in the context of the early Second Temple period.

Authorship

This book has been traditionally attributed to a PROPHET named MALACHI, but "Malachi" means "my messenger." It is quite likely Malachi was not a person's name, but a title taken by this prophetic messenger of God. The book lacks a prophetic call narrative, genealogical information, biographical data, and any unambiguous note of the prophet's social location, affirming a sense of anonymity. The prophet's name and past are not important. This prophet could be anyone, and speaks not to kings and rulers but to common people, calling them to repentance and to the fullness of faith.

Historical Setting

The Book of Malachi is extraordinarily difficult to date. There are no references to specific rulers or persons. Early in this century, several scholars argued for a late date for the book, perhaps as late as the Maccabean period, but these arguments have been generally rejected. Other dates have ranged as early as 605 B.C.E. Typically, scholars dated the book by its references to intermarriage and divorce (2:10-16). Since EZRA and NEHEMIAH also mention these social problems, it is tempting to date Malachi near them, in the second half of the fifth century B.C.E. However, Malachi's marriage and divorce passage is a metaphorical discussion of the worship of other gods, and so there is no clear connection to Ezra and Nehemiah.

Malachi discusses a decrease in the seriousness accorded to the temple offerings. This may correspond to certain political realignments in the first half of the fifth century B.C.E., during the time of the PERSIAN EMPIRE. Under the reign of the emperor DARIUS, the Persian Empire built the Second Temple in Jerusalem (see commentary on HAGGAI and ZECHARIAH). Xerxes replaced Darius as emperor in 486 B.C.E., and Xerxes redirected funding away from provincial temples. The decrease in imperial funding for local temples may have created the specific crisis that faced Malachi: the people of Jerusalem needed to raise more funds to pay for their own temple worship. Some people did not want to pay for full worship, but thought that God would still accept less costly worship. Malachi argues that God would accept only the best worship, faithful to the oldest traditions. The prophet then encouraged priests and laity to rise to the challenge together.

Form

Malachi uses a distinctive form in its prophecy. The book's six main units are organized into sets of questions and answers. Typically, the unit begins with a categorical statement by God, followed by a reactive rhetorical question by the people. This allows God, through the prophet, to expound upon the issue at hand. At times, the question-answer format is repeated within a unit (1:6-7; 2:7-8). These six units are framed by an introductory phrase (1:1) and by two endings (4:4-6), all of which are probably later additions.

For Further Study

In the *Mercer Dictionary of the Bible*: EXILE; MALACHI; MALACHI, BOOK OF; ORACLE; PERSIAN EMPIRE; PROPHET; WORSHIP IN THE OT.

In other sources: J. L. Berquist, "The Social Setting of Malachi," *BTB* 19 (1989); R. J. Coggins, *Haggai, Zechariah, Malachi*; B. Glazier-McDonald, *Malachi: The Divine Messenger*, SBLDS; J. M. O'Brien, *Priests and Levites in Malachi*, SBLDS.

Commentary

An Outline

I. Introduction, 1:1
II. God's Love for Jacob, 1:2-5
III. Problems with the Sacrifices, 1:6–2:9
  A. Unacceptable Offerings, 1:6-14
  B. Covenant for the Priests, 2:1-9
IV. A Marriage Metaphor, 2:10-16
  A. The Rejection of God, 2:10-12
  B. Godly Offspring, 2:13-16
V. A Day of Judgment, 2:17–3:5
  A. Wearying God, 2:17
  B. God's Messenger, 3:1-4

  C. Justice, 3:5
VI. Tithes and Offerings, 3:6-12
  A. Call to Repentance, 3:6-7
  B. Tithes, Offerings, and Blessings, 3:8-12
VII. Those who Fear the LORD, 3:13–4:3
  A. A Time for Repentance, 3:13-18
  B. A Day of Judgment, 4:1-3
VIII. Conclusion, 4:4-6
  A. Moses, 4:4
  B. Elijah, 4:5-6

Introduction, 1:1

The brief introduction identifies the book as an ORACLE, similar to the introductory statements in Zech 9:1 and 12:1. "Malachi" may be a title, meaning "[God's] messenger." No temporal information is given. *Israel* in this postexilic time refers not to a nation, but to a people.

God's Love for Jacob, 1:2-5

The first unit begins with a categorical statement of God's love for Israel. Immediately, the people ask God for proof. God compares Israel with its enemy, Edom, the descendants of Esau (Gen 36). Although Israel's ancestor, Jacob, was Esau's brother, the peoples derived from these siblings have met different ends. Because God loved Israel and hated Edom, Edom is doomed to permanent devastation; all their attempts at rebuilding will fail. But Israel has God's blessings for reconstruction. If Israel rebuilds itself, God will respond.

This states clearly the essential theme of Malachi. The prophet calls the people to rebuild themselves and their society, with the assurance that God will support their actions and will not frustrate their work. There is no indication that God will rebuild Israel, but that Israel has the ability—and the call—to rebuild itself.

Problems with the Sacrifices, 1:6–2:9

Unacceptable Offerings, 1:6-14

After the unconditionally positive statement in 1:2-5, the shift to indictment in vv. 6-14 seems severe. Nevertheless, it shares the same intention: God's people can rebuild themselves into a community of proper worship. Malachi argues against those who would block true worship.

1:6-8. The priests' defilement. The priests have not given God the due respect, because they have sacrificed unacceptable animals. Malachi affirms the ancient priestly codes that the priests should know: crippled and diseased animals should not be offered to God (Lev 22:17-25). Malachi presses the point further: the priests would not dare to deliver such defective animals to the governor (probably for payment in taxes, although possibly for some state-sponsored religious ceremony). They should give God at least the same level of respect.

1:9-11. A worldwide God. In angry rhetorical flourish, the prophet expounds on the scope of God's concerns. God has plans larger than Jerusalem. In this striking departure from ancient priestly traditions of the temple as the *only* place of God's presence, the prophet reflects the reality of the postexilic period, in which the worship of God was spreading throughout the Persian Empire. This also portrays Malachi's bias toward the laity, who can worship in places other than the Jerusalem temple.

1:12-14. A curse. The prophet closes the first half of this unit with a condemnation of the laity. God curses those who have the resources to bring unblemished animals but who hoard their wealth. There is never condemnation for the poor who lack the ability to give pure animals, here or elsewhere in the Hebrew Bible (Lev 5:7-13; 14:21-22; 27:8). Malachi sees both priests and laity as responsible for the quality of worship in the temple.

Covenant for the Priests, 2:1-9

The subject returns to the priests in this unit's second half. The priests have offered inadequate sacrifices (1:7-8); now the prophet calls them to live by their own highest standards. The challenge criticizes the priests in light of priestly tradition.

2:1-3. Curses. The priests risk curses because of their activity, turning their attempts to bring blessing to the people into cursing, if they refuse to listen to the prophetic warnings. The curses here are conditional; there are still opportunities for avoiding them.

2:4-9. The covenant with Levi. Despite the priests' failings, they can return to the covenant of LEVI. This covenant is otherwise unknown in the Hebrew Bible, but there is a clear reference to Moses' blessing of Levi (Deut 33:8-11), in which three elements appear: rejection of partiality (Deut 33:9; cf. Mal 2:9), teaching the Torah of God to all (Deut 33:10a; cf. Mal 2:6-7), and correct worship (Deut 33:10b-11a; cf. Mal 1:7-8). The priests must establish the right relationship with the laity, through impartiality, effective teaching, and proper worship. Even though the priests have stumbled from the ideal and caused others to stumble, the priests can still be faithful.

A Marriage Metaphor, 2:10-16

The Rejection of God, 2:10-12

Malachi's third unit emphasizes the need for unified faithfulness among all the followers of God. Many interpretations of 2:10-16 have attempted literal treatments of the marriage images, but the text itself does not support such use of the metaphors. Literal interpretations force themselves into the inconsistency of desiring the end of wrong marriages (v. 11) and also rejecting divorce (2:15-16), which Israel's governors favored in subsequent years (Ezra 9–10; Neh 13:23-28). This inconsistency demonstrates Malachi's intention to use the marriage language symbolically to describe the relationship between the people and God, reflecting the same prophetic concerns as the rest of the book.

Although all the people share common parentage in God, divisions have shattered proper relationships among God's people (v. 10b). In addition to these damaging divisions, some of the people have used the temple to worship other deities (v. 11). Malachi's solution is simple but drastic: excommunication for those who reject the worship of God (v. 12).

Godly Offspring, 2:13-16

The marriage metaphor shifts in Mal 2:13-14, which describes God as the deserted wife of one's youth. Even though the people approach God in tears, God the spurned spouse is hesitant and wary. God desires a productive relationship, like that between spouses (v. 15). This requires a relationship that precludes attraction to other deities. The separation that God condemns (v. 16) is not human divorce but separation from God.

A Day of Judgment, 2:17–3:5

Wearying God, 2:17

Through their complaints, the people have tired God. They have asserted that God rewards the evil and that God's justice is absent. Both are such fundamental misunderstandings of God's activity that they deny the possibilities for relationship between God and humans. Belief in God's presence and morality is essential to the faithful life.

God's Messenger, 3:1-4

God promises future decisive action that will remove the misconceptions of those who have wearied God. First, a messenger will appear, and then God will arrive in the temple. God's presence within the temple will purify the people, including the Levites; God will again accept sacrifices. Malachi understands this as a return to a much earlier condition.

Justice, 3:5

God proves the divine justice by listing those guilty ones who will suffer judgment. This list, like many others throughout the Hebrew Bible, focuses on the protection for society's weakest. God's judgment also convicts those who practice the kind of unreality that wearies God, especially those who practice magic and who lie in court.

Tithes and Offerings, 3:6-12

Call to Repentance, 3:6-7

Malachi's fifth unit begins with a call to repentance. In light of the future divine action discussed in the previous unit, the people should return to God. God affirms the divine constancy, by which the people have not been destroyed, despite their intransigence. The people ask what kind of return God desires.

Tithes, Offerings, and Blessings, 3:8-12

God responds that the people should return by ceasing to rob God. They should reinstate the full practices of tithes and offerings. These two terms appear together only here. The tithe is the temple tax paid to the Levites, their only source of income (Num 18:20-30); the offering, a general term, usually refers to sacrifices presented in worship. This command would mandate full payment of wages to the temple staff, as well as the presentation of right sacrifices for worship. Again, laity and priests appear in partnership, with the laity responsible for funding right worship.

Once priests and laity cooperate, God's faithfulness will be made manifest. The blessings of heaven will overflow, but they will not remove the need for human activity. This is not a *quid pro quo* in which God's blessings rain down upon the people as fecund rewards for right action. Instead, the people work together with God. Partnership is the ideal. God will prevent the insects from devouring the produce (v. 11), but the people are still responsible for planting and harvesting. Human effort meets divine effort, and together the produce reaches the table in such abundance that the nations call the people blessed (v. 12).

Those who Fear the LORD, 3:13–4:3

A Time for Repentance, 3:13-18

Malachi's final unit repeats the call for REPENTANCE. At the beginning, Malachi returns attention to the people's negative statements about God, but then the possibilities for healing and the consequences of rejection become clear.

3:13-15. Charges against God. The people have charged God with injustice. Certainly, the wicked do not receive their due in the short term, but these accusations distort the reality of God (cf. 2:17). These statements caused discouragement; the people no longer find any benefit in serving God. Perhaps the temple worship is the primary service envisioned here, but certainly the issue is larger.

3:16-18. A scroll of remembrance. A narrative note interrupts the prophetic dialogue. The faithful discuss together, and the LORD responds to these who fear the LORD, honor God's name, and serve the LORD. A scroll records the meeting, and God declares that these faithful ones will be God's treasured possession, to be spared on the day of God's action (v. 17). At that point, the argument shifts once more. Earlier, Malachi depicted a rejected group (3:5); in vv. 16-17, a group that God accepts completely. For Malachi these form the righteous and the wicked, but neither is the audience for Malachi's speaking. Both the righteous and wicked appear only in third-person statements, but Malachi tells a separate audience that, in the day when God acts, "if you return, you will see the difference between the righteous one and the wicked one, between the one who serves God and the one who does not serve God" (v. 18, author trans.).

The audience consists of those who are not completely right but who are also not completely wrong. This middle group receives the call to repentance. They have not rejected God through their lack of belief, but they have not fully accepted God's intentions for the world. Malachi calls them forward to a day when the distinctions between the righteous and the wicked, in the present so vague, will be perfectly clear; this vision of future decisive action encourages present repentance.

A Day of Judgment, 4:1-3

Malachi's vision of God's future action includes a day of utter destruction for all the wicked. The faithful will receive healing through brilliant righteousness, in which God's intended order will be restored (v. 2). They will leap like calves released from stalls of captivity, and in this freedom they will trample the wicked, completing the destruction begun in the wicked's rejection of God.

Conclusion, 4:4-6

Moses, 4:4

Two endings were added to the book later, perhaps as a summary to the entire Book of the Twelve. The first ending is a call to obey the law of MOSES. Certainly, amid later concerns about possible conflicts between the Law and the Prophets, such a verse concluded the Prophets with the affirmation that there was no inconsistency between these parts of the canon.

Elijah, 4:5-6

The second ending has become important in later religious traditions. In JUDA- ISM, this forms the basis for the expectation of Elijah's return at Passover, at which a vacant chair is set at the table in anticipation. Within Christian tradition, the expectation of ELIJAH as a forerunner appears in the interpretations of JOHN THE BAPTIST (Luke 1:17; cf. John 1:21).

Mercer Commentary on the Bible.
Volume 4. *The Prophets.*

Mercer University Press, Macon, Georgia 31210-3960.
Isbn 0-86554-509-X. Catalog and warehouse pick number: MUP/P136.
Text, interior, and cover designs, composition, and layout by Edd Rowell.
Cover illustration (*The Vision of Ezekiel*) by Raphael (see p. ii, above).
Camera-ready pages composed on a Gateway 2000
    via dos WordPerfect 5.1 and WordPerfect for Windows 5.1/5.2
        and printed on a LaserMaster 1000.
Text fonts: TimesNewRomanPS 10/12; ATECH Hebrew and Greek.
Display font: TimesNewRomanPS bf and bi,
    plus University Roman titles (covers and title page).
Printed and bound by McNaughton & Gunn Inc., Saline MI 48176,
    via offset lithography on 50# Natural Offset and perfectbound into 10-pt.
        c1s stock, with 4-color-process illustration and lay-flat lamination.
[September 1996]
